Martindale's unclaimed money, lands and estates manual : devoted to the interests of all who are in search of unclaimed money, lands or estates, next of kin, heirs at law, legatees, etc. - Primary Source Edition

Martindale, James B. (James Boyd), 1836-1904

Nabu Public Domain Reprints:

You are holding a reproduction of an original work published before 1923 that is in the public domain in the United States of America, and possibly other countries. You may freely copy and distribute this work as no entity (individual or corporate) has a copyright on the body of the work. This book may contain prior copyright references, and library stamps (as most of these works were scanned from library copies). These have been scanned and retained as part of the historical artifact.

This book may have occasional imperfections such as missing or blurred pages, poor pictures, errant marks, etc. that were either part of the original artifact, or were introduced by the scanning process. We believe this work is culturally important, and despite the imperfections, have elected to bring it back into print as part of our continuing commitment to the preservation of printed works worldwide. We appreciate your understanding of the imperfections in the preservation process, and hope you enjoy this valuable book.

MARTINDALE'S
UNCLAIMED MONEY, LANDS AND ESTATES
MANUAL.

DEVOTED TO THE INTERESTS OF ALL WHO ARE IN SEARCH OF UNCLAIMED MONEY, LANDS OR ESTATES—NEXT OF KIN—HEIRS AT LAW—LEGATEES, Etc. Etc. Etc.

—BY—

J. B. MARTINDALE,

ATTORNEY AND COUNSELOR AT LAW.

[Author of "Martindale's United States Law Directory," "The Commercial and Legal Guide," and late Editor of "The American Law Magazine"]

PRICE, $2.00.

CHICAGO:
J. B. MARTINDALE.

B 108621

Entered according to Act of Congress, in the year 1884, by J. B. MARTINDALE, in the office of the Librarian of Congress, at Washington D. C

PRESS OF
OTTAWAY PRINTING CO.,
CHICAGO.

CONTENTS.

	PAGE.
PROEM	3
UNCLAIMED MONEY, LANDS AND ESTATES BUREAU	8

CHAPTER I.
ENGLISH LAW OF LIMITATIONS 9

CHAPTER II.
LIMITATION LAWS—UNITED STATES 14

CHAPTER III.
PUBLIC LAND LAWS OF THE UNITED STATES 21

CHAPTER IV.
CURIOSITIES OF NEXT OF KIN 25

CHAPTER V.
DORMANT FUNDS IN CHANCERY 31

CHAPTER VI.
ENGLISH ESTATES REVERTING TO THE CROWN 40

CHAPTER VII.
CLAIMANTS 48

CHAPTER VIII.
TRINITY CHURCH HISTORY—ANETJE JANS ESTATE 52

CHAPTER IX.
Estates in Chancery.

ESTATE OF JOHN TURNER	61
THE MANGINI-BROWN ESTATE	62
CATHARINE CHAPMAN ESTATE	64
RICHARD THOMAS ESTATE	65
R. GOODMAN'S TRUST	66
PATTERSON ESTATE	67

CHAPTER X.
LOST AT SEA 69

CHAPTER XI.
HEIRS AT LAW vs. CHARITIES 74

CHAPTER XII.
BANK OF ENGLAND—UNCLAIMED DIVIDENDS 78

CHAPTER XIII.
BANKRUPTCY—UNCLAIMED DIVIDENDS 84

CONTENTS—Continued.

CHAPTER XIV.
Misers 88

CHAPTER XV.
Wills 92

CHAPTER XVI
Lapsed Legacies 105

CHAPTER XVII
Missing Relatives 108

CHAPTER XVIII.
Unexpected Assets 112

CHAPTER XIX.
Treasure Trove 118

CHAPTER XX
Escheats 120
CONCLUSION 124
Special List No 1 125
"   "   "   2 129
"   "   "   3 133
"   "   "   4 136
"   "   "   5 151
"   "   "   6 152
"   "   "   7 159
"   "   "   8 164
"   "   "   9 170
"   "   "   10 172
"   "   "   11 177
"   "   "   12 181
"   "   "   13 185
"   "   "   14 189
"   "   "   15 190
"   "   "   16 193
"   "   "   17 200
Table of Distribution of Intestates' Estates 206

ERRATUM.

"Estates in Chancery," (Chap. 9), should have been credited to *De Barnardy's Next of Kin Gazette.* By a typographical error the credit was omitted.

PROEM.

We make no apology for engaging in the business set forth on our title-page, but wish briefly to outline the policy pursued and to be pursued. But for the abuse by adventurers and swindlers of a business in itself as legitimate as that of the lawyer, the banker, or the broker, we would not consider even this explanation necessary. We may never be able to rid the business of its present odium, but we do pledge ourselves to do all in our power to that end, and shall never shrink from the task of publicly exposing frauds by which over-sanguine claimants are swindled out of their money, whenever such cases are brought to our notice. We shall endeavor to raise no false hopes, but when convinced that a claim is hopeless, will, as far as possible, prevent such claimant from expending money on it. We have, and can always have, plenty of legitimate business, and want nothing to do with imagined estates or visionary claimants. So much has been said and done respecting large estates supposed to exist in the old country, that it becomes our duty, right in the outset to say that which may have the effect of dispelling many a blissful dream; but the dreamer may have his reward, if he will, by the saving of his money. We do not dispute the fact that large sums of money do exist in almost every European country awaiting rightful claimants, many of whom are residents of America; but, although in the aggregate they amount to millions, yet they consist for the most part of a multitude of small estates. Those amounting to millions, or hundreds of millions, are very "few and far between." There is a tradition in a vast number, we might say in most of the old families, that they are entitled to a large estate in England, France, Germany, or some other European country; and as such traditions descend from father to son, the expected value always increases till it often reaches a sum too large for a common mind to grasp. Numerous associations have at different times been formed for the purpose of prosecuting these fictitious claims. One or two ingenious persons proceed to set the ball rolling by sensational articles in the newspapers, or by circulars, calling all persons of a certain name to apply to them respecting a large derelict estate in the Old World. The statements are made with circumstantial details, having every appearance of truth, and, although seemingly harmless, are often the cause of great disappointment, trouble and expense. A list of names of the expectant heirs is prepared, a liberal estimate of expenses is formed for a trip to the old country, and the amount required is divided *pro rata* amongst all the claimants, who are then called upon to contribute their respective shares. It is understood in such case that they will be entitled to participate in the estate in proportion to the money subscribed, and so we get a joint-stock company. The scrip of such an adventure has been known to sell as high as two per cent of the supposed value of the estate. It requires but one or two to lead the way, and, like a flock of sheep, they all follow blindly, regardless of the most patent facts. Many cannot trace their pedigrees a generation back. They do not even know who has left the fortune sought to be recovered. A simple and vague statement that one "Hyde," "Lawrence," "Jennings," or others died in England a century ago suffices. Such trifles as a Will or the Statute of Limitations do not trouble them. The supposition that a person of their surname was at one time possessed of wealth is sufficient to create all these subscribers to fortune "heirs to vast estates." They are unaware how little the mere similarity of name is worth in genealogical researches. Once possessed of the idea, it becomes their pet child, and their fancies range over a vast domain of possibilities which may place them in affluence. The demon of speculation becomes as strong in them as in any dealer in "options" on the Chicago Board of Trade. They are nearly always poor or ignorant people, who are dazzled by the prospect of becoming suddenly rich, and are lured on until the exhaustion of their means puts an end to the investigation. But the dream remains as vivid as ever; the delusion is clung to with even greater tenacity; and all that remains for them to do is to complain of their wrongs, of the injustice of the law, or the fraud of some unknown trustee. The legend will, perhaps, be handed down to their children, who in their turn may seek possession of these imaginary millions. What is the result of these "associations," which, it may here be remarked, are by no means of recent date, some having been formed nearly half a century since? The agent (generally the promoter) deputed to discover the broad acres, on arrival in the old country, spends most of his time at the Probate Registry, endeavoring to connect a Testator, or an Intestate, with a member of the Association; and, when the locality is known, he has recourse to the Parish Registers. Finally, he seeks the assistance of a lawyer, who in most instances dissuades him from proceeding further with the vague information in his possession. After a prolonged and useless stay, he returns to the States, and a "Report" is then printed, containing copies of wills, a few extracts from Parish Registers, and sometimes a copy of a crest. This is sent to each member of the syndicate. Notice of a second meeting is given, and, if sufficient funds are raised, another visit is made to Europe, and so the matter goes merrily on until the funds are exhausted. In some instances the agent reports that he has been unable to find the estate; or that, owing to the lapse of time, it cannot be recovered; or, mayhap, it is in the possession of the rightful owner. In one case, no less than three of the expectant heirs and two lawyers went to London, to endeavor to recover a small square in the East End. In another, an agent for some twenty years past has derived a living from the pseudo-claimants to a Townley estate which has long since been claimed and properly disposed of. A third has actually crossed the Atlantic no less than seventeen times. Not one of these associations has ever succeeded in recovering the estate, or, we would say, of even finding any vacant recoverable estate, whether real or personal; but, as an unsupported assertion is easily made, a locality is chosen by the agent bearing the name of the association, and is declared to be the estate sought for. It is to no one's interest to go to the expense of proving a negative, and so the assertion remains, if not unchallenged, at least not disproved by evidence. Thus the "Hyde," "Knight," "Harland," and "Hungerford" estates are said to consist respectively of "Hyde Park," "Knightsbridge," "Harland Square," and "Hungerford Market and Bridge." If titles to real estate were to be upset upon such slender foundations as the mere coincidence of a name, owners of property would have to consider in title deeds the name of the street in which their houses are situated. We should advise all persons who believe themselves entitled to property to be very cautious how they expend their money in verifying their suppositions. Large estates are few in number, and any one wishing to know whether there is any foundation for a report that an estate is unclaimed, can readily do so by applying to some responsible person engaged in that line of business. If any such estates exist, they are invariably known, and are usually placed in due course of Administration by the Chancery Courts. Many persons are undoubtedly entitled to money which can still be recovered, although such claim may have been in abeyance for upwards of a century. We do not advise persons to go to the other extreme, and take no interest in the subject, because they fancy that, owing to the impecunious position of their family, they cannot be entitled to a fortune. Although correct so far as "fortune" is concerned, they may yet recover an amount to compensate them fully for their trouble, as these moneys generally find their way into the pockets of those who least expect it.

In the following pages lists are given of persons who (if living, or, if dead, whose heirs) are entitled to money, and in most instances the persons mentioned are entitled to sums well worth recovering. In some cases investigation has not been made to ascertain what is really due, and in some cases the amount may prove too small to justify undertaking its recovery. It may be, in some instances, the money has recently been, or is now, in the course of recovery by the persons entitled to it; yet they are all worth looking into, inasmuch as the fees charged for a preliminary examination are usually small.

Advertisements for Heirs-at-Law, Next of Kin, Owners of Unclaimed Money, etc., which have appeared in the newspapers of the United States, Canada, Great Britain, France, and Germany since the year 1600 have been carefully preserved, classified and numbered, and the names of persons wanted numbering over 100,000 are in the possession of this BUREAU.*

The following specimens of these advertisements are here inserted, simply to show their character in general.

"BARBARA ANDERSON '(deceased.) If William Anderson, formerly of Elgin, North Britain, a relative of the above, and who is supposed to have gone abroad many years since, or, if dead, his widow or children, will communicate with Messrs. ——— — ———, Solicitors, he, she or they may hear of something to their advantage."

"ELIZABETH MORRIS.—The heirs or next of kin of Mrs Elizabeth Morris, who lately died in the State of Pennsylvania, and who was formerly the wife of Oliver Morris (comedian), are requested to make themselves known to Messrs. ——— The said Elizabeth Morris left England for America between 1770 and 1775, and paid a visit to England about the year 1802."

"JOHN DARBY AND OLIVER JACKSON, Esqs.—The addresses of these gentlemen are required, in order that legacies of $5,000 each may be paid them. Address ———."

"ANN EATON.—If the relatives or next of kin of Ann Eaton, late of Ormskirk, County of Lancaster, Spinster, deceased, will

---

*For rate of fees for information respecting these advertisements, see eighth page of this Manual

apply to Messrs. ———— —— ————, Solicitors, they will hear of something to their advantage. *   *   *   *   (Note.—This person died intestate, and her effects went to the Crown, who would recoup, the same on Next of Kin substantiating their claim.)"

"THOMAS NICHOLSON, formerly of Chapel End, Walthamstow, in the County of Essex, (shoemaker,) about the year 1830 left England for Upper Canada; returned to England on a short visit about ten years ago, but sailed again for Canada. If living, he is about sixty-two years of age. If he or his heirs will apply to ———— — ————, Solicitors, they may receive a large sum of money."

This Manual will be thoroughly revised and published every year, and Supplements issued between times, as frequently as may be required; so that names for insertion may be sent in at any time. We trust we shall have the hearty co-operation of all our correspondents, as no charge is made for insertion of advertisements, and the benefits are to be mutual.

In the preparation of this Manual we have had access to similar works published in Europe, to the authors of which we feel under obligations, and take this public method of acknowledging the same. Amongst those from whose works we have drawn valuable data, we wish to name Robert Gun, Esq., Messrs. De Barnardy Brothers, and Edward Preston, Esq., all of London, England.

THE UNCLAIMED MONEY, LANDS AND ESTATES
BUREAU.

The name of this Bureau is indicative of its nature, object and aims. It was begun in 1875, and has been in successful operation ever since. Having a complete chain of connections with similar Bureaus in Europe, and having access to information relative to unclaimed estates there, that have been accumulating for over one hundred and fifty years, and concerns property of many millions of dollars, the rightful heirs to much of which now reside in America, and having correspondents in every county in the United States, we are enabled to collect and disperse information which speedily leads to the finding of rightful heirs and the recovery of long unclaimed estates.

Advertisements for Heirs at Law, Next of Kin, Owners of Unclaimed Money, etc., which have appeared in the newspapers of the United States, Canada, Great Britain, France and Germany since the year 1600, have been carefully preserved, classified and numbered, and the names of persons wanted numbering over 100,000, are in the possession of this Bureau. Information will be given as to whether or not any particular name appears in these lists, on receipt of a fee of $2.00. An abstract of the advertisement in which any name has appeared will be given on receipt of a fee of $5.00. This fee will be deducted from the fee for a full copy of such advertisement, should it be afterward desired. The fee for full copy of any advertisement is $10.00. Five or ten dollars expended in this way is often of more real value to a claimant than five hundred or a thousand dollars spent in sending an agent to Europe. These advertisements do not cover *all* the claims that may arise

The fee for searching the records for a will is $10.00, where the date of the testator's death can be given within two years. If this cannot be done, the fee is $3.00 additional for each additional year, and, at this rate, the search may be extended over a period of two hundred years if desired.

The Bank of England keeps what is called "Unclaimed Dividend Books." They are now seven in number, and date back to the year 1780, and represent the money deposited in that bank, and for various reasons never called for since the beginning of the last century. They contain the names of over 120,000 depositors, with description as to profession and place of residence of each. These books can be personally inspected and any name searched for by our London Associate, for the same fee as above set forth for searching for a will.

There are thousands of tracts of land, especially in the Western States and Territories, the owners of which are non-residents and unknown, or dead, and their heirs ignorant of the ownership. Tax titles are maturing to much of it, and "land pirates" have possession of a large amount under forged or "bogus" titles. We hunt up these lands, and with such facts as we can get concerning the owners, and by means of extensive advertising can generally find the real owner or his heirs and place them in rightful possession No charge is made for advertising names, but we are to share in the profits of the case should the party advertised for be found. We urge our attorneys and clients to send in such names as they desire advertised, with all facts pertaining to them.

Every letter of inquiry to this Bureau must be accompanied by a fee of $1.00 to insure an answer.

Address all communications to—

J. B. MARTINDALE, General Manager,

142 LaSalle Street, CHICAGO.

CHAPTER I.

ENGLISH LAW OF LIMITATIONS.

AS the recovery of real estate is altogether barred if an action is not brought within a specified time, we have thought it advisable to give briefly the present existing law of England on the subject of Limitation of actions, as it effects real estate.

It is not necessary however for present purposes to discuss or do any thing more than briefly allude to the various ancient Statutes of Limitation, which date from the year 1540, and most of which, if not all, have been repealed either actually or by implication. No case can now arise under them, and they are of interest to the antiquary rather than to the lawyer. Of existing interest there are two groups of facts and phases of Law to be considered. First, the Law as it stood previously to the 1st of January, 1879; and second, the Law as it now stands. The old Act, as will be seen, has now no force or operation whatever as to such parts of it as are repealed by the new one. In enacting these and other limitation measures, the Legislature has acted on the principle that, where any person should fortuitously find himself in possession of realty to which some other person is rightfully entitled, such other person should, in the interest of the public, be placed under some restrictions as to the limit of time for his claim to be properly asserted. To divest any one of what he has had for many years, and has made provision for enjoying in perpetuity, would probably cause more harm in the end than to permit an ignorant or negligent claimant to agitate, and carry out long dormant schemes for an indefinite period.

To dispose first of claims by the Crown. By 9 Geo. III., cap. 16 (passed in 1769), and its amending Statutes, such claims and rights in any lands are now, and have since that date, been barred after the lapse of sixty years. Next, with regard to all other persons Under the Law as it stood previous to the 1st of January, 1879, the Statute 3 & 4 Will IV, cap. 27 (passed in 1832), absolutely prevented any one from bringing an action for the recovery of land, except within twenty years next after the time at which the right to bring such an action first accrued to him, or to any ancestor or other person through whom his claim might be founded or arise. This Act contained the very reasonable proviso that with respect to Estates in reversion or remainder, or other future Estates, the right before alluded to should be deemed to have first accrued at the time when any such Estate became an Estate in possession. That is to say, a person entitled to succeed to the possession of an Estate on the death of another person who held it for life, was allowed twenty years to prosecute his claim from the date of the death of the life possessor, on whose death he would become entitled, and not before, to, himself enjoy an unfettered interest in the property. However, under Section 14 of that Act, a written acknowledgment of the title of the person entitled, given to him or his agent, and signed by the person in possession, extended the time of claim to twenty years from the date of such acknowledgment. With respect to disabilities, the Act provided, that if, when the right to bring such an action first accrued, the person entitled should be under disability to sue, by reason of infancy, coverture (if a woman), lunacy, or absence beyond the seas, ten years were allowed from the time when the person entitled should have ceased to be under such disability, or should have died, notwithstanding that the period of twenty years before mentioned should have then expired, but with the definite proviso that the whole period do not, including the time of disability, exceed forty years. As an example, we may take a case of a right first accruing in 1840. The land would have been forfeited twenty years after, or in 1860. Supposing the person entitled had been under a disability, such as absence beyond seas, when his right first accrued (1840), a further period of ten years was granted, provided the whole time did not exceed forty years, from the date of his having ceased to be beyond seas, i. e., had he returned in 1855 his right would have disappeared ten years after that date, or in 1865, but had he returned in 1875 it would have been forfeited under that Law in 1880, and not 1885, when the whole period would have exceeded forty years. As a matter of fact, however, the right to recover would actually have been lost on the 1st of January, 1879, when the new Act hereinafter alluded to became Law. Moreover, no further time was allowed on account of the disability of any other person than the one to whom the right of action first accrued. By that Act, also, a mortgagee in possession was assured of a quiet possessory title at the expiration of twenty years next after he entered or gave a written acknowledgment such as that before alluded to, of the mortgagor's title or right to redeem An illustration of the Law on this point, as it relates to mortgagees, may be of use Let us suppose that A. has mortgaged his freehold property to B. for a certain sum, at a fixed rate of interest. The interest is not paid, and B., instead of exercising the power of sale he no doubt possesses under the mortgage deed, enters into possession, and pays himself his interest out of the rents of the property As soon as he has been in possession twenty years under the Law then in force (or twelve years now), the right of A to redeem and get his property back again becomes absolutely barred in the absence of the undertaking or acknowledgment before alluded to. As to an Advowson—which, it may be remarked, is a perpetual right of presentation to an ecclesiastical benefice—no action could be brought to enforce a right of presentation after the happening of three successive incumbencies, or sixty years (whichever should last happen), or 100 years in all, in case three remarkably long-lived ecclesiastics should happen to have been in possession for the whole century. Twenty years, too, was the limit for the recovery of money secured by mortgage, rents-service, or rents-charge and tithes; or by judgment, or otherwise charged on land and legacies, in the absence of the statutory acknowledgment to which we have already alluded. In every case where any person who could have brought an action or suit for the recovery of the interests alluded to failed to do so, his right was altogether extinguished. For all practical purposes this is an epitome of the Law as it stood prior to the 1st of January, 1879. The Real Property Limitation Act of 1874, which took effect from the 1st of January, 1879, made very important changes in the Law. Such changes, however, may be readily grasped by those who have carefully perused the following remarks, as, with one small exception, they are merely an alteration of figures in certain cases. The period of twelve years is substituted for twenty, as the limit of time for bringing an action for the recovery of land, or all corporeal hereditaments, and most tithes and rent or other periodical payments charged on land, from any person under the circumstances mentioned in the former Act and before alluded to. A good number of possessors with no title to their holdings other than the fact that they were in possession of them, must have blessed the passing of an Act that secured them the property after they had been only twelve years in occupation of it. Thus any one who had taken unto himself a property in the year 1867, was assured, under the new Statute, in the quiet enjoyment of it, by the corresponding day of the year 1879, instead of 1887, as would have been the case, if the Act had not relieved him. The disability clause is also reduced to twelve years, with six years' grace, from death, or ceasing of disability, whichever shall first happen, provided that the whole period does not exceed thirty years. It may be here conveniently remarked that "absence beyond seas" ceases altogether to be a disability under the new Act—a fact of some importance to foreigners. These are the brief, but important alterations the Law made by the Statute of 1879 which has been rather more than five years in operation.

There are certain other Statutes and many cases affecting the limitation of time for recovery of incorporeal hereditaments, such as way and water leaves and other rights, which, as they are hardly likely to be of any particular interest to our readers, we do not propose to discuss.

Generally it may be stated, that in no case has a Claimant any chance of ousting a possessor, unless he has the amplest proofs that those in possession—who may be there by an agent, if not personally—are there in consequence of concealed fraud, or as Trustees for such Claimant. It is seldom, if ever, that these very difficult facts have been proven to the satisfaction of a Court of Law. The foregoing remarks do not, however, apply to personal property, i. e., cash, or securities for cash in Government Stocks, the Court of Chancery, and in most public Companies, as such investments are held by the Companies as Trustees for their Shareholders, or Stockholders as the case may be, and can always be recovered, together with the accrued dividends. Legacies bequeathed by Testators, and which remain unclaimed, are in the same position as the Stocks before mentioned, as also are shares under intestacies.

All realty must be conveyed by a deed signed and sealed by the seller, which is delivered to the buyer as evidence of his title; but it is a matter of considerable difficulty when a person dies intestate, or makes no allusion in his Will as to his realty, to ascertain when and how it has been disposed of; for it is only by application to those immediately concerned, that the actual ownership of land can be discovered, unless, however, it is situated in the following two counties or one district, in which disposition of land and similar property, whether by Deed or Will, must be registered.

These counties and this district are provided with Registry Offices (established in the years mentioned), viz., Middlesex in 1708, West Riding of York in 1704, East Riding of New York in 1707 (including the town and county of Kingston-upon-Hull), North Riding of York in 1737. The great district of the Fens known as the Bedford Level, which was reclaimed some time since, has a special Act, vesting certain powers in the freeholder, and among others, that of requiring a registration similar to what is already in force in the counties, etc , above mentioned

The foregoing remarks comprise all the instances in which registration is compulsory for perfecting a title. In 1862 an Act was passed, entitled the "Land Registry Act" (25 and 26 Vict., cap. 53), making provision for an *optional* official investigation, by a Commissioner or Registrar appointed by the Government, of any title an owner might desire to have brought under the provisions of |the Act. On a title being found to be good, a certificate was delivered to the owner, which formed his evidence that he was duly and properly in possession. However, after two or three decisions of the Judges, that the evidence on which the certificate was obtained was open to resifting at any time, the Statute became unworkable; so much so, indeed, that Lord St Leonard, perhaps the most skillful conveyancer who has ever sat on the Woolsack, stated that the Act in question made a title "absolutely indefeasible except in the event of any flaw being found in it," a piece of sarcasm which completely finished its career as a practical reform.

In 1875 the "Land Titles and Transfer Act" repealed the foregoing Statute, and established an optional Land Registry for England and Wales (commencing 1st January, 1876), on a basis somewhat extended beyond the limits of its predecessor. A Registrar of Titles and an Assistant Registrar have been appointed, with a large staff of clerks, both professional and otherwise These gentlemen act very much in the same way as if they were concerned for purchasers of property, the titles of which owners bring before them. A series of General Rules and Orders regulate the practice, and a strict investigation is made. If the title be found good, a certificate of "absolute title" is delivered. If the owner has a possessory title only, a certificate stating such to be the case is furnished him. No case has yet arisen in which a certificate of either of these kinds has been taken exception to. The Act contains a variety of clauses as to registration of mortgages and leases of land subject to its provisions which, being of a technical nature, it is unnecessary for us to note here. The principal facts are as stated. As a reform and a general benefit, however, it has wholly failed, and almost as signally so as its predecessor. Lawyers, for obvious reasons, do not advise the adoption of its provisions, and owners are shy of it because it does them no immediate good, and takes heavy fees out of their pockets without any immediate benefit Those with good titles do not want them made better, and such as have bad ones do not want it to be known that they are so. A man who contemplates mortgaging his land—and two-thirds of the land in England and Wales is mortgaged in some manner—does not wish to place himself in such a position that the fact may become known. This is a practical detail the framers of the Act overlooked altogether Not one title in a thousand is registered under its clauses, which are, be it remembered, merely optional. The Statute is at present, of chief, if not of only, advantage to the officials who draw large salaries for administering it; but it is to be hoped that an alteration will take place in the Legislation so as to render the registration of mortgages, and conveyances of land, compulsory, as in France where it has worked smoothly for many years past. Such an alteration would save much useless litigation and great expense, besides conferring on the possessor an absolute and perfect title. A person may also dispose of his personal Estate by deed of gift, for which there are no Registry Offices. It is by no means rare to find an aged man giving both realty and personalty to his issue or to a stranger to avoid paying the Government duties on his decease. In many instances, therefore, as has been shown, it is next to impossible to discover the actual ownership of property, whether real or personal, without knowledge obtained from parties able to disclose it. If therefore, any person believes himself entitled to property so disposed of, he would have to commence proceedings against the person in possession, who, after giving him notice that he has a perfect title, would produce the deed properly verified to the Court; and, if it is in due and proper form, the person bringing the action would be condemned to pay all the costs of it, as the burden of proof in this as in all other cases, rests with the person seeking relief.—*De Barnardy's Unclaimed Money Register.*

CHAPTER II.

LIMITATION LAWS---UNITED STATES.

THE following brief synopsis of the Statutes of Limitation of the several States is not sufficiently full to be of practical use to attorneys, but will serve to give a general idea of the law to those who may be interested:

ALABAMA—Suits on judgments of courts of any State or Territory, or of the United States, twenty years. Suits on sealed contracts, and for bonds or any interest therein, ten years. Suits for trespass, trover or detinue, on simple contracts, stated or liquidated accounts, and for use and occupation of land, six years. Suits on unliquidated accounts, three years.

ARIZONA—Open account or contract not in writing, two years; contract in writing, four years; real actions, adverse possession, five years.

ARKANSAS—Open accounts, three years; promissory notes and written instruments, five years; judgments and decrees, ten years; for recovery of real estate, seven years.

CALIFORNIA—For a demand or obligation, in writing or not, created out of the State, two years; open account or verbal contract, two years; written contract or obligation executed in the State, four years; real actions, or on judgments or decrees of any court, five years.

CONNECTICUT—Actions upon instruments under seal, and promissory notes not negotiable, must be brought within seventeen years after the right of action accrues. Upon negotiable notes, book accounts, debt and simple contract, within six years.

COLORADO—Actions on contracts, upon judgments of Court not of record for writ, for waste and trespass, for taking personal property, must be begun within six years; most other actions within three years.

DAKOTA—On judgments or sealed instruments, twenty years; on contract, obligation or liability expressed or implied, except as above; liability created by statute other than penalty or forfeiture for trespass on real property; taking, detaining or injuring goods or chattels; for the specific recovery of personal property, criminal conversation, or other injury to the person, or rights of another not arising on contract, and for relief on grounds of fraud, six years; action against Sheriff, Coroner or Constable, except in case of escape, on statute for a penalty or forfeiture, three years; action for libel, slander, assault, battery, or false imprisonment, upon a statute for a forfeiture or penalty to the people of the territory, two years; action against Sheriff or other officer for escape of prisoners, one year.

DELAWARE—The following causes of action are barred after three years: Trespass, replevin, detinue, account, debt not on an instrument signed by the party, assumpsit and case. [Promissory notes, bills of exchange and writings, obligatory after six years. Married women, infants, and persons *non compos mentis*, may sue within three years after the disability is removed; and absent debtors may be sued within three years after their return; and if a debtor remove after the cause of action has accrued, the time of his absence is not computed.

DISTRICT OF COLUMBIA—Actions of account or simple contract, note or book account, detinue, replevin and trespass must be brought within three years; on specialties, within twelve years, subject to usual qualifications and exceptions. Part payment or new promise operates as a revivor of the debt.

GEORGIA—Suits must be brought as follows, after right of action accrues: On foreign judgments, five years; for enforcements of rights accruing to individuals under statutes, acts of incorporations, or by operation of law, twenty years; upon promissory notes, bills of exchange, and other simple contracts in writing, six years; upon open accounts, four years; upon instruments under seal, twenty years. Domestic judgments become dormant in seven years from the time of their rendition, or when execution has been issued, and seven years have expired from the time of their redition, or when execution has been issued, and seven years have expired from the time of the last entry upon such execution, made by an officer authorized to execute and return the same. Such judgments may be revived by *fieri facias*, or be sued on, within three years from the time they become dormant.

ILLINOIS—Personal actions, on unwritten contracts, express or implied, five years; actions on bonds, notes, etc., ten years; judgments lien on real property for seven years, if execution is issued within one year; may be revived by *sci. fa.*; or action of debt may be brought thereon at any time within twenty years.

INDIANA—Open accounts and contracts not in writing, six years; actions not limited by statute, fifteen years; written contracts, other than those for the payment of money, judgments of Courts of Record and real actions, twenty years. On a mutual current account, the time runs from the date of the last item on either side; contracts for the payment of money, ten years.

IOWA—Actions for injuries to person or reputation, or to recover a statutory penalty, must be brought within two years; to enforce a mechanic's lien, two years; on unwritten contracts, five years: on written contracts, ten years; on judgments of Courts of Record, twenty years; to recover real estate, ten years. The time during which defendant is a non-resident of the State of Iowa, not computed, but a suit that has been fully barred by the laws of another State, prior to the defendant coming to, or being found in this State, cannot be maintained, except where the cause of action arose in this State. Revivor:—Admission of debt or new promise to pay, which must be in writing.

KANSAS—To recover real property sold on execution, five years after record of deed; to recover real property, sold by executors, etc., five years; real property sold for taxes, two years from date of recording tax deed; other actions for recovery of real property, fifteen years; forcible entry and detainer, two years; persons under legal disability, when cause of action accrues, may bring action two years after disabilty is removed; contract not in writing, or liability created by statute, except a forfeiture or penalty, three years; trespass on real property; taking or injuring personal property, or recovery of personal property; injury to rights of another, not on contract, relief on the ground of fraud, two years; other actions, except *quasi* criminal, five years.

KENTUCKY—Promissory notes (not placed on the footing of bills of exchange), are barred after fifteen years as to principals, and after seven years as to sureties; merchants' accounts against merchants are barred after five years; merchants' accounts against other patrons are barred after two years next succeeding the first day of January after the account is made. Actions on bills of exchange, promissory notes, placed on the footing of bills of exchange, checks, drafts and orders, and endorsements thereof, are barred after five years, after cause of action arose. A new promise to pay the debt before it is entirely barred, takes away the benefit of the statute of limitation up to the date of the promise.

LOUISIANA—Open accounts, three years; notes and bills, five years; acknowledgments or closed accounts, judgments, personal obligations and mortgages, ten years. Judgments can be revived every ten years and thus perpetuated. When prescription has once accrued, a waiver must be in writing to be effective.

MAINE—Debt contracts and liabilities, express or implied, not under seal, six years; special action on the case, two years; all other actions, twenty years.

MARYLAND—Notes and accounts are barred after three years. Sealed instruments and judgments after twelve years.

MASSACHUSETTS—Contracts or liabilities not under seal, express or implied, six years; real actions upon an attested note, and personal actions on contracts not otherwise limited, twenty years.

MICHIGAN—The following actions are required to be brought within six years next after the cause of action shall accrue: First, all actions of debt, founded upon any contract or liability not under seal, except such as are brought upon the judgment or decree of some Court of Record of the United States, or of this or some other of the United States; second, all actions upon judgments rendered in Courts not of record; third, actions for rent; fourth, all actions of assumpsit, or upon the case founded upon any contract, express or implied; fifth, all actions for waste; also actions of replevin, trover and other actions for taking, detaining or injuring goods, also all other actions on the case, except those for slander or libel, which must be brought within two years after the action accrues; all actions for a trespass on lands, an assault or for false imprisonment, two years; actions against Sheriffs for the acts of deputies, three years; in actions brought to recover the balance due upon a mutual and open account current to the cause of action, shall be deemed to have accrued at the time of the last item proved in such account; actions on judgments and decrees of Courts of Record, and on contracts not otherwise limited, must be brought within two years

Part payment or promise in writing will revive a debt, barred by the statute of limitations.

MINNESOTA—Actions concerning real property, twenty years; to foreclose mortgage by advertisement, fifteen years; by action, ten years; on judgments and decrees, ten years; contracts, express or implied, six years; revival must be in writing, or by part payment. If cause accrued and is barred in another State, it can be sustained here only in favor of a citizen who has held it from beginning. If defendant is absent when cause accrues statute does not begin to run till his return, and when he departs after it accrues, period of absence is deducted.

MISSISSIPPI—Real actions, ten years; mortgages, ten years after possession taken; mortgage debt is barred when action upon writing secured is barred; remedy in equity is barred when that at law shall be barred; land, ten years adverse possession, saving to infants and lunatics the right to sue within ten years after removal of disability; actions for which no other period is prescribed, six years after cause of action accrues; open and stated accounts, not acknowledged in writing, and unwritten contracts, three years; penalties and forfeitures under penal statutes, one year; domestic judgments and decrees, seven years; foreign judgments, seven years; but if judgment debtor is a resident of this State, three years; executor or administrator, four years after qualification. Infants and lunatics may sue within prescribed time after disability is removed; statute does not run against absentees from the State during period of absence, nor against any concealed fraud. Lien of judgments, seven years. Actions barred in State where debt accrued, and where defendant resided, are barred here.

MISSOURI—Two years.—Actions in ejectment and all actions on written contracts or instruments. Five years.—All actions on contracts not in writing, actions upon open accounts, actions for trespass on real estate, actions for damages to the person, and actions for damages for injury to personal property or for the possession thereof. Three years.—Actions against Sheriffs and other officers on official bonds. Two years.—Actions for libel, slander, assault, battery, false imprisonment or *crim con.* It is doubtful whether or not judgments are barred in ten years. At all events, they will be presumed to be paid in twenty, and perhaps, in ten years.

MONTANA—Upon contract or account not in writing, three years; contracts, obligations, etc., in writing; judgments and decrees of Courts, or acknowledgment in writing, six years. No limitation against banks, trust or loan companies, or Savings Banks. Upon mutual or current accounts, date from last item. Party out of Territory or injunction suspends statute.

Part payment, principal and interest, on bills, notes or instrument of writing, or a written promise or written acknowledgment of contract or account not in writing, will revive a barred right.

NEBRASKA—Within five years an action upon a specialty, agreement, contract, promise in writing or foreign judgment. Within four years, an action upon a contract not in writing, expressed or implied, an action upon a liability created by statute other than a forfeiture or penalty; also for an injury to the rights of the plaintiff not arising on contract. All actions or causes of action barred by the laws of any other State shall be deemed barred under the laws of this State.

NEVADA—Within six years:—An action upon a judgment or decree or liability founded upon an instrument in writing. Within four years:—An action on an open account, or upon a contract not founded upon an instrument in writing.

NEW HAMPSHIRE—Notes and accounts, six years from last promise; notes secured by mortgage, real actions and judgments, twenty years; against estate of deceased person, three years, and demand within two years of appointment of administrator of estate settled as insolvent claim, must be presented to Commissioner within six months. Debts outlawed in other States are revived for six years by debtor moving here.

NEW JERSEY—Debt not founded on specialty and all actions of account, six years; upon sealed instruments, sixteen years; judgments and real actions, twenty years

NEW MEXICO—Actions upon judgments are limited, to be brought within fifteen years; on notes and all other contracts in writing, within six years; on open accounts, four years, for conversion or injuries to property, and for relief against fraud, four years; for injuries to the person or reputation, two years The usual exception is provided in favor of persons under legal disability and allows one year after the termination of the disability. The statute was approved January 23d, 1880. Causes of action existing at the date of the appearance of this act must be sued on within two years. The representatives of a person having a cause of action, who dies within a year from the expiration of the period of limitation, have one year after death to commence suit

A cause of action founded on contract, express or implied, is revived by an admission that the debt is unpaid, or a promise to pay; such admission or new promise to be in writing.

NEW YORK—Contracts, express or implied, except those under seal, and upon judgments of a court not of record, six years; upon judgments of Courts of Record and sealed instruments, twenty years, actions to recover damages for a personal injury resulting from negligence, three years; for libel, slander, assault, battery, or false imprisonment, two years.

Acknowledgment by part payment or in writing, will revive a barred right.

NORTH CAROLINA—The statute of limitations was suspended from May 20th, 1861, to January 1st, 1870, on causes of action arising on contract prior to 1868. Actions on judgment of a Court of Record on sealed instruments for the foreclosure of a mortgage, and for the redemption of a mortgage, where the mortgagee has been in possession, must be commenced in ten years; actions on a Justice's judgment, seven years; actions on the bond of any public officer or executor, etc., must be commenced in six years, actions on any contract or liability, except as above, shall be commenced in three years.

Debts barred by the statute of limitations can only be revived by a promise in writing, signed by the party to be charged.

OHIO—One year.—Libel, slander, assault, battery, malicious prosecutions, false imprisonment and statutory penalties and forfeitures. Four years.—Trespass to real property, action pertaining to personal property, and for injuries to plaintiff's rights, not otherwise limited. Six years:—Contracts not in writing, express or implied, and liabilities created by statute other than forfeitures or penalties. Fifteen years:—Written instruments. Twenty-one years:—Recovery of real estate. Action upon official bonds or undertakings, given in pursuance of statute, ten years after right of action accrues

Part payment, or written promise or acknowledgment, will revive.

OREGON—Within ten years all actions for the recovery of real estate, upon sealed instruments and judgments or decrees. Within six years, all contracts not under seal, express or implied, written or verbally, for waste or trespass upon real property, and for taking, detaining or injuring personal property, or for the recovery thereof. Within three years, all actions against Sheriffs, Constables or Coroners upon a liability incurred while in office, except for escape, which is one year. Within two years, all actions for a penalty or forfeiture to the State; also, for libel, slander, false imprisonment, *crim. con.*, assault and battery, etc. To recover, a liability against which the statute has run, part payment, or a writing, signed by the party to be charged, is necessary.

PENNSYLVANIA—Book accounts, debts, notes, and contracts not under seal, six years; contracts under seal, twenty-one years. Adverse uninterrupted possession of real estate for twenty-one years, gives title as against every one except the Commonwealth, infants, persons not *sui juris*, or beyond the seas

RHODE ISLAND—For trespass, four years; tort, other than trespass, or on simple contracts, six years; on specialties, twenty years.

SOUTH CAROLINA—Upon a judgment or decree of any Court, or upon a sealed instrument, other than sealed notes and personal bonds for the payment of money only, twenty years; for recovery of property, ten years; upon contracts not under seal, sealed notes and personal bonds for the payment of money only, liability by statute other than a penalty or forfeiture, trespass on real property, and for recovery of personal property and upon open accounts, six years; action for balance due on open account current accrues from the date of the last item proved on either side.

TENNESSEE—On bonds, notes, bills of exchange, accounts and contracts, six years. Against sureties of guardians, administrators and public officers for non-feasances, etc., six years. Against such officers, personally, on their bonds, ten years. On judgments of Courts of Record and other cases not expressly provided for, ten years. Against personal representative of descendant, seven years from his death, notwithstanding any existing disability. Against personal representative after qualification, by resident within two and a half years, by non-resident, if cause accrued in life-time of deceased, three and a half years, otherwise from time cause of action accrued. Statute does not apply in commercial transactions, where accounts, mutual and reciprocal, are current; and where persons not merchants have mutual accounts time is computed from date of last item, unless amount is liquidated and balance struck.. After right of action accrues debt can be revived by express promise to pay

TEXAS—To personal actions, one year is allowed to bring suit; contracts in writing, four years; open accounts, except between merchant and merchant, their factors or agents, two years.

UTAH—Open accounts and contracts not in writing, two years; contracts or obligations founded on writing, four years; judgments, five years; recovery of lands, seven years.

VERMONT—Action against Sheriff for neglect of deputy against sureties in guardian's bond, four years; debts on contracts not under seal, debt for arrears of rent, account, assumpsit or case founded on contract; trespass on lands, replevin and other actions for taking or detaining, or injuring goods against towns or town clerks, for neglect of duty of clerk, six years; debt or *scire facias*, on judgment debt, on specialty covenant (except of seizure in deeds of land), covenant of warranty after final decision against title, eight years; action on promissory notes witnessed, fourteen years; action on covenant of seizing to recover lands or the possession thereof, fifteen years.

VIRGINIA—Upon bonds of officers, ten years; on sealed instruments in general, twenty years; on awards and unsealed written contracts, five years; on extra contracts, five years, unless for store account, which is two years.

WASHINGTON—The following actions must be commenced within three years from the time the cause of action accrues An action upon a contract or liability, not in writing or for taking, detaining or injuring personal property; an action for relief upon the ground of fraud The following actions must be commenced within six years from the time the cause of action accrues, viz . Upon a contract in writing, or liability, express or implied, arising out of a written agreement; for the rents and profits of real estate; upon a judgment of any Court. An action for the recovery of real estate must be commenced within ten years.

WEST VIRGINIA—Ejectment, ten years; on contract under seal, given prior to April 1, 1869, twenty years, and since, ten years; on promissory notes given prior to April 1, 1869, five years, since then, ten years, accounts, five years, except store accounts, three years; accounts between merchant and merchant, five years There are certain statutory savings in favor of persons under disability, and also where defendant has obstructed prosecution of right When contract is made in another State, the statute of such other State controls, except that a judgment had in another State is barred in ten years.

WISCONSIN—On all contracts not under seal, six years; on sealed instruments, twenty years

WYOMING—Contract, agreement or promise in writing, five years; not in writing, four years. Debts contracted prior to residence in the Territory, are barred after two years' *bona fide* residence here

CANADA

NEW BRUNSWICK—On contracts not under seal, six years; contracts under seal or judgments, twenty years; actions for assault, battery, wounding, imprisonment or for words, two years

NOVA SCOTIA—Actions of assumpsit, trespass, *quare clasum fregit, detinue*, trover, replevin, debt grounded upon any lending or contract, without specialty, or for rent account, or upon the case, must be brought with six years next after the cause of action Mortgages, judgments and legacies are deemed satisfied at the end of twenty years, if no payment is made or acknowledgment in writing in the meantime

ONTARIO—Simple contracts, six years, contracts under seal, twenty years, judgment, six years, but may be revived. Actions to recover land, ten years · distress for rent, six years; to recover wild lands granted by the Crown, but never in the possession of the grantor, twenty years; revivor by part payment or written acknowledgment.

CHAPTER III.

PUBLIC LAND LAWS OF THE UNITED STATES.

The Agricultural Lands are divided into two classes, one at $1.25 per acre, designated as minimum, lying outside of railroad limits; the other at $2.50 per acre as double minimum, lying within railroad limits. Titles are acquired by purchase at public sale, or by "ordinary private entry," and in virtue of the pre-emption, homestead, timber culture and other laws. Purchases at public sale are made when lands are "offered" at public auction to the highest bidder by proclamation of the President, or by order of the General Land Office. Lands so offered and not sold, and not since reserved or withdrawn from the market, can be secured by "private entry" or location.

But none of the lands in Northern Dakota have been " offered " at public sale, all having been reserved for homesteads, pre-emption and tree claims on account of their agricultural value, and because this system is more in accordance with the interests of the masses, and not for speculators, as under the public sale system. Sioux half-breed scrip can be used to purchase any surveyed land, but very little of this scrip is now outstanding. Soldiers additional homestead entries can also be purchased and laid upon any vacant surveyed land, thus acquiring title without residence thereon.

HOMESTEADS.

Any person who is the head of a family who has arrived at the age of twenty-one years, and is a citizen of the United States or has filed his declaration of intention to become such, is entitled to enter one-quarter section or less quantity of unappropriated land under the homestead laws. The applicant must make an affidavit that he is over the age of twenty-one or is the head of a family, and that he is a citizen of the United States or has declared his intention to become such, and that the entry is made for his exclusive use and benefit and for actual settlement and cultivation, and must pay the legal fee and that part of the commissions required to be paid when entry is made, as follows·

When within railroad limits, for 160 acres, fee $10, commission, $8; for eighty acres, fee $5, commission, $4. Outside of railroad limits, fee $10, commission $4, and in proportion for eighty acres. When these requirements are complied with the Receiver issues his receipt in duplicate and the matter is entered upon the records of the office. After faithful observance of the law in regard to actual settlement and cultivation for the continuous term of five years, at the expiration of that term or within two years thereafter, final proof must be made, and, if satisfactory to the land officers, that part of the commissions remaining unpaid (the same in amount so paid on entry) must be paid. The Register then issues his certificate and makes proper returns to the general land office. as the basis of a patent.

Any settler desiring to make final proof must first file with the Register a written notice of his intention, describing the land and giving the names of four witnesses by whom the facts as to settlement, continuous residence, cultivation, etc., are to be established. This notice must be accompanied by a deposit of money sufficient to pay the cost of publishing the notice which the Register is required to publish for thirty days (five times) in a newspaper designated by him, or arrange with the publisher of the paper therefor. Notice is also posted in the land office for the same period.

Final proof cannot be made until the expiration of five years from date of entry, and must be made within two years thereafter. In making final proof the homestead settler may appear in person at the district land office with his witnesses and there make the affidavit and proof required, or he may, if by reason of bodily infirmity or distance, it is inconvenient for him to appear at the land office with his witnesses, appear before the judge of a court of record of the county and state or district and territory in which the land is situated, and there make final proof. When a homestead settler dies before he can prove up, the widow, or in case of her death, her heirs may continue settlement and obtain title upon requisite proof at the proper time. In case of death of both parents, leaving infant children, the homestead may be sold for cash for the benefit of the children, and the purchaser will receive the title.

The sale of a homestead claim to another party before completion of title is not recognized. In making final proof the settler must swear that no part of the land has been alienated except for church, cemetery or school purposes, or right of way of railroad.

Homestead claims may be relinquished, but in such case the land reverts to the government. If a settler does not wish to remain five years on his tract, he may pay for it as under pre-emption law, in cash or warrants, at any time after six months of actual residence. This proof must be made before the district officers. Homesteaders are allowed six months after entry to commence improvements and establish residence.

The law allows but one homestead privilege to any one person.

Every person who served not less than ninety days in the army or navy of the United States during "the recent rebellion," who was honorably discharged and who has remained loyal to the government, may enter a homestead, and the time of his service shall be deducted from the period of five years, provided that the party shall reside upon and cultivate his homestead at least one year after he commences improvements. The widow of a soldier, or, if she be dead or has married again, the minor heirs (if any) may, through their guardian, make a homestead entry, and if the soldier died in the service, the whole term of his enlistment will be credited upon the term of required residence. Soldiers and sailors as above may file a homestead declaratory statement for a 160 acres of land through an agent, after which they have six months to file their homestead. This latter entry must be made in person. Thus a soldier who desires to secure a claim may do so by sending a power of attorney and certified copy of his discharge to some responsible party who can file for him up on the land selected. Lands acquired under the homestead laws are not liable for any debt contracted prior to the issuing of the patent therefor.

PRE-EMPTIONS.

Heads of families, widows or single persons (male or female) over the age of twenty-one years, citizens of the United States or who have declared their intention to become such under the naturalization laws, may enter upon any "offered" or "unoffered" lands or any unsurveyed lands to which the Indian title is extinguished, and purchase not exceeding 160 acres under pre-emption laws. After making settlement, if on "offered" land the applicant must file his declaratory statement with the district land office within thirty days, for which a fee of $2.00 is required, and within one year from date of settlement make final proof of his actual residence on and cultivation of the tract, and pay therefore at $1.25 per acre if outside of railroad limits, or $2.50 per acre if within these limits, and he may pay in cash or by military bounty, land warrants, agricultural college, private claim or supreme court scrip.

When the tract has been surveyed and is not "offered" land, the claimant must file his or her declaratory statement, and make proof and payment within thirty-three months from date of settlement. Settlement is the first thing to be done under the pre-emption laws.

When settlements are made on unsurveyed lands, settlers are required to file their declaratory statements within three months after date of the receipt at the district land office, of the approved plat of the township embracing their claims, and make proof and payment within thirty months from the expiration of said three months, payments the same as in case of offered land.

Pre-emptors may submit proof of residence and improvements at any time after six months of actual residence. He must show by his own testimony and by two credible witnesses such actual residence and cultivation—a habitable dwelling and other improvements, to the satisfaction of the land officers that the spirit of the law has been complied with.

At any time before the expiration of the time allowed for proof and payment, the settler may, by making proper application at the land office and payment of the required fee, convert his claim into a homestead, and the time he has resided upon the land is credited on homestead residence if he desires. No person who abandons his residence on his own land to reside on public land in the same state or territory, or who owns 320 acres of land, is entitled to the benefits of the pre-emption laws. It is held, however, that this does not apply to a house and lot in town. Claims cannot be transferred until title is perfected. The second filing of a declaratory statement by any pre-emptor, when the first filing was legal in all respects, is prohibited. Before proof and payment on pre-emption claim, written notice must be given by the claimants to the register, who must post a notice in his office and cause the same to be published in a newspaper nearest the land for at least thirty days as in case of homesteads.

TREE CLAIMS.

Under the timber culture laws not more than 160 acres on any one section, entirely devoid of timber can be entered, and no person can make more than one entry thereunder.

The qualifications of applicants are the same as under the pre-emption and homestead laws. The land office charges are, for 160 acres or more than eighty acres, $14 when entry is made and $4 at final proof. For 80 acres or less, $9 at entry and $4 for final proof. The applicant must make affidavit that the land specified in his application is exclusively prairie, or other land devoid of timber, that his filing and entry is for the cultivation of timber for his exclusive use and benefit; that the application is made in good faith and not for the purpose of speculation, or directly or indirectly for the use or benefit of any other person or persons, that he intends to hold and cultivate the land and comply with the laws, and that he has not previously made an entry under the timber culture law.

The party making an entry of a quarter section is required to break or plow five acres covered thereby during the first year, and five acres in addition during the second year. The five acres broken or plowed during the first year he is required to cultivate by raising a crop, or otherwise, during the second year, and to plant in timber, seeds or cuttings during the fourth year. For entries of less than 160 acres the amount of land to be cultivated must be *pro rata*. Provision is made for extension of time in case drought or grasshoppers destroy trees. These trees he must cultivate and protect, and if, at the expiration of eight years from date of entry, or at any time within five years thereafter, the entrant, or, if he be dead, his heirs, shall prove by two credible witnesses, the planting, cultivating and protecting the timber for not less than eight years, and that there were at the end of eight years at least 675 living, thrifty trees on each of the ten acres required to be planted, he, or they will be entitled to a patent. It should be added, that in making final proof it must be shown "not less than twenty-seven hundred trees were planted to each acre" Fruit trees are not considered timber in regard to cultivation of an entry under this act.

It is not necessary that the ten acres should be in a compact body.

Failure to comply with any of the requirements of the law, at any time after one year from date of entry, renders such entry liable to contest. And upon due proof of such failure the entry will be cancelled. No land under this law will, in any event, become liable to the satisfaction of any debt or debts, contracted prior to the issuing of the final certificate therefor.

CHAPTER IV

CURIOSITIES OF NEXT OF KIN.

WHILE compiling his index to Next of Kin advertisements, it occurred to Mr. Edward Preston that a summary of such advertisements might not only be amusing, but might chance to convey unexpected good news to some who should read it. For the same reason, and to give an idea of the character of such advertisements in general, we insert it in this MANUAL as it appeared in the *London Times*, with the comments of that paper upon it. When we consider that this summary is for only one year's advertisements in that one paper alone (the year 1876), we can form some idea of the magnitude of such advertising in the different newspapers of the whole civilized world, running through a hundred years or more:

"Some twenty-six persons are shown to have died without relatives, as the Treasury Solicitor advertised for the Next of Kin (if any) to make out their relationship. The amount of money thus reverting to the Crown is rarely made public, but it has 'oozed out' in the notable case of Mrs. Helen Blake, of Kensington, that the sum was not less than £140,000 personalty. In other cases large rewards were offered for marriage, baptismal, and burial certificates. A gentleman in distressed circumstances sought the representatives of a firm who carried on business in Calcutta in 1816. A reward was offered for information of a lady who, when a girl, was taken from Canada to Australia. Next of Kin were sought for numerous persons who had left England and settled in the Colonies, the United States, or India. Unclaimed dividends of the Agriculturist Cattle Insurance Company awaited claimants. Good fortune awaited the family of a certain cab driver.

A reverend gentleman, son of a Lincolnshire draper, was wanted for something to his advantage; and a gentleman who left England in 1854, was wanted to claim a certain residuary estate. Johann Bauer, born in 1820, and last heard of at Sydney, was "considered to be dead," without having left any Heir-at-Law, or by will, disposed of certain property; it was therefore forfeited to the Next of Kin. A son was anxious for his mother's address; two persons, living in London in 1831, or their descendants, were entitled to share in certain moneys. It would be to the advantage of a traveling herbalist to write to his wife; and a miner in the North of England would find it to his advantage to make himself known. Numerous notices were issued by the Bank of England with reference to retransfers of Unclaimed Stock or Dividends, from the Commissioners, for the Reduction of the National Debt, and a reward of £250 was offered for a clue to a marriage settlement by the relatives of a Testator, who, on his death-bed, could only utter the words "Lincoln's-Inn Fields."

The descendants of two persons of the name of Braat, born 1778 and 1782, were wanted "for their own interests"; a very old friend from abroad longed to meet J. B., of B——, a person who went to sea many years ago, and had not since been heard of, was entitled to funds; and another who went to sea in 1859, was wanted for something "greatly" to his advantage —such notices as these are not uncommon. A niece was anxious to hear from her uncle, "the friends she has left in England are all dead, she is now holding a good situation, and she only wants to hear from her uncle." H B was anxious to communicate with the individual who called on him "respecting property in Chancery"—there are many callers of this sort— and the relatives of a gentleman who went to New Zealand in 1862, desired much to know his whereabouts. E. C., late of Ipswich, "whose father was a miller, aged 28,"—so states the advertisement—was wanted for something greatly to her advantage; and a Hull pauper inherited £30,000 left him by a Scotch nobleman.

The descendants of one family were entitled to £12,000; those of another who, in 1798, were living in Bloomsbury, were anxiously sought; and tidings of a person reported to have been drowned in 1830, in the Merrimac River, would be liberally paid for. The Next of Kin of the Secretary of the late Earl Exmouth, were unknown; and the Heirs of a person who emigrated to America as long ago as 1683, were wanted to claim $2,000,000. A father affectionately enquired for his daughter, who ran away from home. "She will learn with regret"—so ran the sad notice— "that her mother died recently"; a son who left his home in 1850, was informed that something "very greatly to his advantage" awaited him—this advertisement was repeated many times in various newspapers. Something good was notified for a person who went to New Jersey in 1823—if dead, his Next of Kin were entitled; Winifred——, not having heard from her husband for twelve years, would be glad of any information within three months; and a gentleman having left two legacies to charitable institutions, which appear to have had no existence, claimants were sought.

Claimants to lands in Canada, and the relatives of two brothers who were drowned at Montreal, were also the subject of Next of Kin notifications. Inquiry was made as to the investments or property of one person, and an "expectant legatee" was willing to pay handsomely for a clue to some funds supposed to have been deposited in a Bank; a laborer was entitled to a legacy; and divers charitable institutions (including the Temporary Home for Lost or Starving Dogs), were invited to claim a share of a benevolent Testator's residuary estate. —— was requested to "write to Nephi Elsmore, Salt Lake City, Utah—it will be to his advantage"—some romance undoubtedly underlied this notice. Two sisters were informed of the sudden death of their brother at Melbourne, and the Heirs of Ninian F——, who was "a hind at Widdrington, in 1760," were unknown. The representatives of a certain merchant, who carried on business in the City of London, in 1820, were wanted for "something beneficial"; like notices are very frequent, as Unexpected Assets often accrue. A son was anxious to hear from his "mother, sister, or brother"; and Dinah ——, sought for something to her great advantage. The relatives of a captain, who died suddenly, were requested to communicate with the clergyman of the parish, and the "Next of Kin of the author of 'Sam Slick' will hear of something peculiarly interesting to them on applying to ——." Several domestic servants were entitled to legacies, a sister would hear of something to her advantage if she would make herself known to her brother; a gunner who deserted Her Majesty's service in 1862, or, if dead, his Next of Kin, were interested in an Irish Probate case, the Heirs-at-Law of several persons of unsound mind, were inquired for under the Lunacy Regulation Act, and a lady who seems to have enjoyed the luxury of being married four times, was entitled to a legacy left by her sister; the Heirs of a Spanish lady, an aged spinster of eighty-two, were inquired for by a Spanish Court—"all those who think they have a right to the inheritance are invited to apply", this Advertisement opens up a wide field for claimants. The representatives of another lady who died in 1809, at the venerable age of ninety-four, were inquired for by the High Court of Justice.

The following is rare:—"A Prussian gentleman named ——, is supposed to have fallen overboard or leapt into the sea, while on board a vessel bound for Mexico; being an expert swimmer, he may have been picked up by a passing vessel; if alive, he is implored to make known his whereabouts." Such an announcement as this naturally gives rise to a world of conjecture, and relatives are perhaps even now ignorant as to whether the unfortunate Prussian is dead or alive.

Solicitors were anxious to know if a certain lady "made a will of a more recent date than the one found at her death," and the Heirs of a Mr. Jones, Superintendent of a Lunatic Asylum, in 1826, were now for the first time inquired for. A niece was entreated to communicate with her uncle; and the representatives of the creditors of a person who died over forty years ago, are interested in a "windfall." A tailor would hear of something to his advantage, on applying at his old shop, and a son was informed of the death of his father at Charing Cross Hospital. An afflicted father was in search of his long-lost-sight-of-son; and tidings would be most thankfully received by the mother of a Queensland emigrant—last heard of eleven years ago.

The following contains a highly satisfactory announcement to a gentleman of the Jewish persuasion:—"Should this meet the eye of C. M. Moses, by applying to —— he will find a legacy from his aunt." A Swiss paper had the following:—"T Metzger (Heirs). All persons believing themselves to be heirs of the above, formerly Governor of Breda and Lieutenant-General of the Dutch Cavalry, are requested to communicate with ——, who is in possession of all documents necessary for the recovery of the inheritance." J Mitchell, who disappeared from Oxford some years ago, was wanted to claim a legacy, and Elizabeth M ——, who left England in 1850 for New Zealand, was wanted for a like purpose.

Colonial newspaper notices are remarkable for their pithiness. The following is from the *Sydney Morning Herald*—"Henry Ormerod.—Wanted, information; last heard of near Sydney; father dead. Write Mrs. Ormerod." Something advantageous awaited a hair-dresser, late of Romney, Hants, and a son, resident in Australia, informed his father, brother, cousin, or any of his friends, that they could communicate with him at ——. The Next of Kin of several soldiers of our Indian Army were wanted to claim various sums of money and effects. One of these soldiers had managed to save the sum of £308 19s. 11d. The unknown nephews and nieces were wanted of a gentleman who died at Lisbon; a person, last heard of in Queensland, was entitled to the residuary estate of his brother; two sons were wanted to claim an estate left them by their father, and the father of a child, left under the guardianship of a nurse, was informed that "his daughter died suddenly, to the great grief of the nurse."

A person who left Wales in 1857 was entitled to one-third of two farms; a surplus awaited division among the owners of slaughter-houses shambles, etc, in the neighborhood of old Newgate Market, and Mary Ann R—— was informed that "she will receive £800, left her by her father's friends," if she would only make herself known. A "Sailor Boy," who left his home early on ——, would hear of something to his advantage "by writing to Friend ——." Preparatory to receiving property due to him under his grandfather's will, F. J. S. was earnestly requested to communicate with his friends at once.

The Next of Kin of a spinster, who died at Bath in 1795, were only now sought; and the address of a father and son wanted by Solicitors in the following curious notice :—"—— Stacey, aged between 9 and 10; last heard of in care of his father; believed to be tramping about the country with him." Janet Taylor, who left Stirlingshire about forty years ago, is interested in a Scotch Succession case; and certain shareholders of the Star and Garter Hotel Company were wanted to claim a good dividend.

The Heirs of persons in all stations of life are occasionally sought through the medium of what is known as a Next of Kin Advertisement. The description of L. S is a "sausage-skin dresser"—an unsavory calling, but, doubtless, a profitable one, as the Heirs were inquired for J. T., who left England some years ago, is entitled to a share of his father's estate, "if he claims the same within two years"

A gentleman for some years missing was requested to communicate with Solicitors "who hold money belonging to him, for which they desire to account," and the heirs of a J. B. Baron were stated to be entitled to no less than £800,000

Unexpected assets of a very large amount awaited the representatives of the creditors of a gentleman who died in 1740, and the Next of Kin of persons who held shares in the West New Jersey Society as long ago as 1692-3 were entitled to funds, a student was implored to communicate with his parents; and to J B the joyful intelligence is conveyed "that he has been adjudicated bankrupt, and may return home without fear of molestation." A counsel's clerk is requested to "call at address given him by the lady whom he courageously rescued from drowning, in order to be thanked for his gallant conduct in risking his life on that occasion" Fortunes have occasionally been left for gallant conduct of a similar nature.

Similar summaries to the foregoing for the years 1877-1882 have appeared in the following, among other newspapers, namely, *Standard, Morning Post, Daily News, Broad Arrow,* and *Law Journal.* Space will not permit the reproduction of all these summaries, but the following are the more noticeable of the Kindred notices for 1882.

A lady who left England as long ago as 1826, or her children (if any), are wanted to share a legacy of £3,500; and a veterinary surgeon of Russell Square, in 1830, is interested in a pedigree case pending in Chancery. A gentleman who went to New Zealand would like to hear from any relative or friend now living; "it is thirty-three years since he heard from home, so full accounts of family, *cartes de visite,* etc., would be gladly received." J. G., of Mexico in 1832, and D G, at one time of Ohio are entitled to shares in an estate, the descendants of R B., who left England in 1810, are sought, and a large reward is offered for proof of the death of S A., at one time a barmaid.

The creditors of a late noble lord are informed that a sum of £4,000 is now divisible among them; by the death of his aunt, a sailor is entitled to freeholds; and a soldier who deserted from the Uhlan Guard, at Berlin, is among the missing ones wanted. J. D., of Bermuda in 1845, is believed to have been lost at sea; and J. W. H., "of the Rocky Mountains," is interested in his father's estate; L H. is wanted to administer the estate of her late husband, a Canadian farmer; while J. M., missing for many years, is presumed to be dead, and his wife is applying for letters of administration to his estate in Ireland. There were many similar applications to the Court of Session, under the Presumption of Life Limitation (Scotland) Act, by Next of Kin anxious to possess themselves of the estates of their missing relatives.

News is sought of a baronet, last heard of in Sydney, believed to have gone to Fiji; also of F W. C., who is supposed to have gone to Canada A. H., born in Burmah in 1853, married in 1869, went to sea in 1870, is among the lucky ones wanted for something to their advantage; and J. O'C., an apprentice on board a merchant vessel, last heard of in 1865 from a sailors' home, is asked to claim his estate, otherwise his sister will take the initiative.

E. P. died in Paris in 1871, and his Next of Kin are wanted to claim £591 Consols, with accumulated interest. H. K. N., first of Natal, then of the Australian gold-diggings, last heard of in New Zealand, is desired to make his whereabouts known; and Bridget R., who left Ireland for England thirty years ago, is entitled to share the estate of a brother who died in Australia.

A commission has been issued to take evidence as to the Heirs in England of E. R., who died suddenly in Bombay, and the nephews and nieces sought of W. T, who died in Portugal; A. M., last heard of in New York, is wanted for his own benefit; and W. T, once of Queensland, is a residuary legatee; Rudolph K., formerly of Western Australia, and afterwards of Colombo, is anxiously inquired for; also the Next of Kin of Sir M. B. C., at one time of Jamaica, and afterwards of Scotland

A man known as "Charcoal Dick," who left the Ballarat diggings for England, is informed that £4,000 or £5,000 lies in the Geelong Bank, and between 200 and 300 ounces of gold-dust in the Gold Treasury; and a reward is offered for proof of the death of J. E. S., who left Oxford twenty-five years ago. This individual seems to have had a chequered career. He is described as of "roving habits, tall, fine-built, but with club-foot, by trade a trunk-maker; believed to have exhibited a stuffed calf with two heads and seven legs; sometimes did a little business in booths in the art of self-defense."

If W. C. S. does not come forward and prove that he was in this country at a given date, he will forfeit a share of his mother's estate, and the landlord of J. W. threatens to take possession of a house greatly injured by J. W.'s prolonged absence.

In 1682, a lady of title devised certain lands; the heirs or assigns of such devises are now sought; also the Heir-male of T. R., of Oxford, in 1685. Merchants, shippers, consignees, captains, seamen, and others who may have sustained losses by the Confederate cruisers, are inquired for in connection with the Geneva Award. The Q. C. who is executor of a will bequeathing property of A. J S., is desired to make himself known; and T. R, aged seventy, is entitled to a final dividend.

About £5,000 is divisible in respect of certain tithe renewal funds;

the creditors of one J. S are entitled to £700; whilst another J. S. (a retired Sergeant-Major E. I. C. S.), is wanted for something to his benefit.

Persons having private property or papers belonging to J. L Y. (late of the Hussars), are sought, and the guardians of Mary E. D. M. (aged three years), are wanted, respecting matters of "great pecuniary importance." Fred J B , a midshipman, of Brisbane, in 1866, and R. C , late engineer on a ship plying on the Shanghai River, are both wanted for something to their advantage, also the son of a clergyman last heard of in New Zealand. The representatives of R. C. (excise officer), who left this country for the United States thirty years ago, are wanted; and a notice headed "Bequest" inquires for W. G., formerly of Belfast and lately of New York.

Valuable property has been left to G. C.; and W. H., last heard of at the Diamond Fields, South Africa, is a missing Legatee. Information is desired as to the property of a deceased Major, also a clue to several large sums due to the estate of C. R. H. Sylvius L. or his representatives are interested in the estate of an Indian Judge who died in 1820; A. L. (nee F. de Celigny), or her Heirs are wanted; and Judy, Michael and Pat Donohoe sought by the Irish Court of Probate.

J. McL. had an account with some banker unknown to his Next of Kin, and a clue is desired thereto. J. W. K F. M., last heard of at Surrey Hills, Sidney, W. H. of Hobart Town, and the representatives of R. P., who died in 1848, are all sought in connection with property at Limehouse.

J. M , who left England in the *Lalla Rookh* in 1848, informs his relatives that they can hear of him at Pretoria, the Heirs of M. M., who in 1844 owned lands in Ceylon, are wanted; and J. E. J. W , last heard of at Orange Free State, is entitled to a share of his aunt's estate. A Bombay firm desire to know if a certain lieutenant is alive, as they hold a policy on his life; while S. D., formerly of Perth, in consequence of the death of his brother is wanted for something greatly to his advantage.

One result of the unfortunate "Palmer Expedition" is that persons having property of the deceased in their hands are inquired for; while in the case of the estate of Mr Walter Powell, M. P. (lost at sea in a balloon), probate has been granted, death being assumed.

In addition to these multifarious notices many claimants were sought by the Bank of England authorities as to unclaimed Stocks and Dividends; the Treasury Solicitor advertised for Next of Kin in some forty "Crown windfall" cases, and the Crown Agents for the Colonies gave London *Gazette* publicity to a long list of Cape Intestates, the **Unknown Heirs** being entitled to about £20,000.

CHAPTER V.

DORMANT FUNDS IN CHANCERY.

BEFORE quoting statistics as to these Funds, it may be useful to give a little historical information (gathered from a Blue Book on Chancery Funds), as to the origin of the Accountant-General's Office, and as to the amount of funds belonging to the Suitors.

In the olden time the Masters in Chancery had the custody of all moneys and effects deposited in Court in the suits referred to them, and the Usher took charge of any property brought into Court in suits which had not been referred to one of the Masters. The Masters and the Usher were responsible for all moneys and other property received by them, and were bound to distribute the property so entrusted to them by Orders of the Court. In the meantime they employed the money in their hands for their own benefit. This practice continued until the bursting of the South Sea Bubble, when it was found that several of the Masters were defaulters The defalcation amounted to over £100,000; it was made good by increased fees on the Suitors, and stringent precautions were taken to prevent a recurrence of such a scandal. Each Master was directed by an Order of the Lord Chancellor of 1724 to procure and send to the Bank of England a chest with one lock, and hasps for two padlocks; the key of the lock to be kept by the Master, the key of one of the padlocks by one of the six Clerks in Chancery, and the key of the other by the Governor or Cashier of the Bank Each Master was ordered to deposit in his chest all moneys and securities in his hands belonging to the suitors, and the chests were then to be locked up and left in the custody of the Bank, and to be so kept that the Masters might have easy access thereto, under Orders of the Court. This plan did not work well, for it was found that by the rules of the Bank of England the vault where the chests were kept could not be opened unless two of the Directors were present with their keys; and it was soon found that great trouble, difficulty and expense would be occasioned to the Suitors by requiring the attendance of no less than five officials whenever any of the chests had to be opened to deliver out effects and to receive the interest due In 1725 therefore, a General Order was made directing that all money and effects should be taken from the Masters' chests and given into the custody of the Bank. Duplicate accounts were to be kept at the Bank and at the Chancery Report Office, and any dealing with the Suitor's money was to be certified to the Report Office. Another General Order extended the plan to moneys and effects in the custody of the Usher of the Court.

In 1726 the first Accountant-General of the Court of Chancery was appointed, and all funds in the custody of the Masters or Ushers were transferred to his charge. An act of Parliament passed in 1725, gives power to appoint an Accountant-General, and contains elaborate provisions with reference to the custody and safety of the Suitors' Funds. The following section evidently points to the misappropriations above referred to:

"To the end that all misapplications or wastings of the subject's money by any officer of the High Court of Chancery may be entirely prevented for the future. Be it therefore further enacted that the Accountant-General shall not meddle with the actual receipt of any of the money or effects of the Suitors, but shall only keep the account with the Bank and the said Accountant-General, observing the rules hereby presented, or hereafter to be presented to him by the said Court, shall not be answerable for any money or effects which he shall not actually receive; and the Bank of England shall be answerable for all the moneys and effects of the Suitors which are or shall be actually received by them."

Having thus glanced at the origin of the office of Accountant-General to the Court of Chancery, a word or two as to the funds dealt with by the Court may not be out of place here. From the Annual Budget of the Paymaster-General it appears that the receipts for the year ending 31st August, 1880, added to the securities then in Court, made up a grand total of £95,504,487 9s. 5d. After deducting payments during the year there remained in hand £75,108,835 5s. 1d, exclusive of foreign currencies of the value of about £400,000. These enormous sums were mainly thus invested.

Consolidated 3 per cent. Annuities, £47,542,458 9s. 9d.; cash, £5,234,015 15s. 4d.; reduced 3 per cent. Annuities, £5,855,591 16s. 10d.; new 3 per cent. Annuities, £8,470,314 6s. 9d. The residue was made up of India Stock, Exchequer Bills, Metropolitan Consolidated Stocks, and Stocks of most of the leading Railway, Dock and other Companies.

After being informed of these extraordinary investments, no one will be surprised to hear that very considerable sums of Unclaimed Money have, from time to time, accumulated; in fact, the Royal Courts of Justice have been built almost entirely with the surplus interest of the Suitors' money. By an Act passed in 1865 power is given to apply £1,000,000 from funds standing in the books of the Bank of England to an account entitled:

"Account of securities purchased with surplus interest arising from securities carried to the account of moneys placed out for the benefit and better security of the Suitors of the Court of Chancery."

It would seem, therefore, that these unclaimed funds have been utilized to lighten the burden of taxation, it being impossible to divide the surplus interest among the Suitors.

The Dormant Funds have frequently been the subject of investigation. From a Return presented to Parliament in 1829, it appears that the total amount of Stock on which the dividends had not been received for twenty years and upwards previous to that date (1829), was £127,904; for fifteen years, £22,288; for ten years, £70,498; and for five years, £201,558. The total amount of Suitors' Stock then in Court was £38,597,322.

In 1853 the Suitors' Further Relief Act was passed. By it the Lord Chancellor was empowered to cause an investigation to be made into the several accounts standing in the name of the Accountant-General to the credit of any cause or matter, the dividends of which had not been dealt with for fifteen years or upwards, and if, and when, he should be of opinion that it was not probable that any claim would be made for the same, to make Orders for the appropriation of the future dividends or such part of such dividends as he should be of opinion might safely and properly be so appropriated, for the benefit of the Suitors, and for the carrying the same over to an account, to be entitled "The Suitors' Unclaimed Dividend Account" and for the carrying over, from time to time, such part of the cash standing to the last mentioned account, as he might think fit, to the credit of "The Suitors' Fee Fund Account." Directions were also given for a similar investigation to be made at the expiration of every five years.

The first investigation under the provisions of the foregoing Act was made in 1854. By a Return made to the House of Commons in July, 1854, it appears that the number of accounts undealt with for fifteen years previously to 1st May, 1854, was 566, and the total amount of such Stock £256,175 2s. 8d., the total amount of Suitors' Stock then in Court being £46,000,000. In 1855, a list containing the titles of such accounts, but not stating the amounts, was printed and exhibited in the Chancery Offices, with the following highly satisfactory result: "Many persons came forward and preferred their claims, and about one-half of the Stock supposed to be unclaimed was transferred out of Court to successful claimants." A fact for skeptical people to ponder over, and very encouraging news for claimants.

In 1860 and 1866, similar lists were published, but the total amount of funds then lying dormant does not appear therein. The investigations under the "Suitors' Further Relief Act" are of a limited character, and do not apply to many unclaimed funds invested by the Accountant-General under the provisions of the "Infant Legacy Act," the "Trustee Relief Act," and other Acts.

The first investigation into the amount of Suitors' Unclaimed Cash in Court was made in 1850, and a Return was presented to Parliament showing the result as follows:

Number of accounts 4,013; valuation (cash and stocks), £562,039. This Return does not include cash arising from interest or dividends on the Unclaimed Stock.

When Mr Lowe (now Lord Sherbrooke), was Chancellor of the Exchequer, Rev. W. St. J. Wheelhouse, M. P., at the request of an influential deputation, put himself into communication with Mr Lowe, with a view to having greater publicity given to the list of Unclaimed Funds in Chancery, but Mr. Lowe could not be prevailed upon to alter the arrangements then existing, namely,—exhibiting the list in the Chancery Offices. However, in 1872, the Court of Chancery Funds Act was passed, and by the Rules made thereunder a List of Dormant Funds in Chancery was ordered to be triennially published in the *London Gazette*. The first list under the new Act was looked for in 1873, but it did not see the light till March, 1877. It contained about 2,500 entries, some of them curious. Thus:—

"Joseph Barlow—Absent beyond seas; Bowden v. Bayley—The account of unpaid claimants entitled to £100 each; Bryan v. Collins—The accumulated account; Baxter v. Facherell—The schooling and apprenticing fund; Bleadon v. Haynes—The plough, furniture, stock, and effects account; Brooks v. Levey—The legatees' and annuitants' account; Sophia Deacle—Present address unknown; Bryant v. Story—Legacy bequeathed for the relief of widows and orphans of soldiers killed in war; in the matter of the proceeds of derelict property brought into the Port of Nassau, in New Providence, and sold for the benefit of the rightful owner when appearing, according to the Act 12 Anne, c. 18, s. 2; Drever v Maudsley—The one hundred years term account; Gurden v. Badcock—The creditors under the deed of 2nd September, 1791; Heyden v. Owen—The account of the seamen belonging to H M ships Decade and Argonaut; Milner v Gilbert—The foreign securities and shares account; Mason v. Gee-The descended estate; Prince v. Bourjot-The ten hogsheads account; Winter v. Kent—Fund to answer the unclaimed legacy given by the will of the testator, James Underhill; Wroughton v. Wroughton—The plate and picture account; Yates v. Rawlins—The account of Shareholders who did not come in to substantiate their claims; the account of the unclaimed legacy of Sebastian Nash de Brissac."

In addition to the foregoing the Bank of England is custodian of a number of boxes, etc., belonging to the Suitors. The following are the most noticeable items.

"A box containing small articles of jewelry; a paper marked, 'George Colman, Will'; a box marked, 'Diamond Necklace, Coronet and Earrings'; a box containing plate and other articles; a bag of clipped money, etc, (Jones v. Lloyd, August, 1726); two boxes containing plate, belonging to a person of unsound mind"

Complaints were made in the House of Commons of the delay in issuing the List, and reform in this respect was promised.

The second List was not issued until 23 June, 1881. It contains some 4,000 entries, each representing an unclaimed fund of £50 or upwards. No improvement in the form of the list was observable, and the following notice of motion was given in the House of Commons:

"MR. STANLEY LEIGHTON.—Dormant Funds in Chancery.—To call attention to the unsatisfactory form in which the list of causes, to the credit of which unclaimed money belonging to the suitors is standing, is issued, and to move,—That future lists be strictly alphabetically arranged, with cross-references to the sub-titles; together with the names and last known addresses of the persons originally entitled; the date of the last decree or order; and the amount unclaimed.

On March 10, 1882, an interesting debate arose on Mr. Leighton's motion, of which the following is a short summary:

Mr. Leighton observed that an abuse existed which might be readily and easily removed. The magnitude of the question was apparent when it was considered that many millions of money passed through the hands of the Paymaster in Chancery every year. Large sums of the suitors' money were borrowed to enable the Chancellor of the Exchequer to carry through his financial operations, and the New Palace of Justice had been mainly built with the surplus interest of the suitors' money. In 1881 Mr. Gladstone borrowed no less than £40,000,000 of the suitors' money for National Debt purposes Therefore the suitors had some claim to consideration. The letter and the spirit of Acts of Parliament were in favor of publicity, which, indeed, was called for by common honesty. In the olden time, the Suitors' funds had been misappropriated by high officials, who were heavily fined. In our own time, Orders have been passed to the effect that a list of dormant funds should be published every three years, and in alphabetical order It was not published every three years, and when published, it was not in alphabetical order. .... Names and addresses ought to be given. This was done in the lists issued by the India Office and the War Office; some of these lists were replete with suggestive details, and would serve as useful models for our Chancery officials. The result of publishing insufficient information was that encouragement was given to the levying of blackmail. If proper lists were published, claimants would not have to pay a fancy percentage for information. The usual answer to these complaints was that unfounded claims had to be guarded against; but it was equally the duty of other Government departments to protect themselves against unfounded claims, and they did it without making a secret of information that ought to be published. What would be thought of a member of this House if he found in the Library a pocket-book containing bank-notes, and said nothing about it for fear an unfounded claim should be made? In respect to these funds, the Government were trustees, with duties to the public; and they were bound to give all the information they could. The true owners were those who would be claimants if they had the knowledge of their rights. The knowledge was kept back by the Office, which held and utilized the money. A stereotyped official reply had hitherto been given; but what he wished to do was to sweep away the cobwebs of officialism, and to secure the publication of intelligible lists. (Hear, hear.)

Mr Findlanter seconded the motion. He highly approved of the form of index suggested . . . the present system tended to confuse searchers . . . . officials might say that the present lists were sufficient, but the public were not satisfied, and the interests of the public ought to be first considered in the matter. Grave scandals sometimes occurred in consequence of the non-publication of information. His attention had recently been called to a case before the Master of the Rolls, in Ireland, from which it appeared that a clerk in the Accountant-General's Office in Ireland, had communicated, it was supposed innocently, to a solicitor in Dublin, the fact that a derelict fund of £8,000 was remaining in Court. The consequence was that the solicitor, having looked at the file of proceedings, communicated with the parties interested, and made a bargain with them that, if he told them of that particular fund, he should get one-third of the £8,000. The Master of the Rolls strongly animadverted on the matter, expressing a hope that that would be the last occasion on which, either casually or by design, such a communication would be made, and also a hope that steps would be taken to compel publication of accounts of derelict funds. In Ireland they had no Act similar to that under which even those defective lists were published in England. . . . Measures, he thought, ought to be adopted, both in this country and in Ireland, to prevent the appropriation of these funds by the Government.

The ATTORNEY-GENERAL.—These Dormant Funds amounted to about a hundredth part only of the total Chancery funds, and consisted, for the most part, of very small amounts.* After a lapse of time they were not thought sufficiently important for persons to make out a claim because they were so small. The list was not made out in strictly alphabetical order; but an alteration in that respect might be made. . . . . If there was an obligation to publish the list every three years, it certainly ought to be fulfilled . . . The further information desired would involve great labor and trouble as to small amounts, which the Paymaster could not undertake . . . . . He was quite sure that in this country, however poor

---

* This is a mistake, each fund represents a sum of £50 or upwards, the very small amounts are not published at all

a man might be, he would be able to employ a solicitor. . . . . Those having practical acquaintance with the whole question, thought that sufficient information was already furnished, to enable persons who had a claim, to support it, while shutting out those who made a trade of the matter

Mr. Salt.—What was wanted was sufficient publicity without too much of it. . . . . It might be well that the lists should be published annually instead of triennially.

Mr. Donaldson Hudson.—The funds did not always consist of small amounts, as had been stated by the Attorney-General. He knew a case in which upwards of £10,000 had been paid into the Suitors' Fund, where it totally escaped notice for twenty years without earning any interest for those entitled to the money. (Hear.) When a private person applied, all information was refused; the employment of a solicitor was essential. It was rather hard that those who had only small sums in Chancery should be refused all information except they employed a solicitor. The result was that some of those interested never got their money. Unless the lists were properly published, these Dormant Funds would go on increasing.

Dr. Lyons suggested that instead of claimants having to employ a solicitor, a fee of 1s. should be charged each applicant, as at Somerset House. He would like to see a similar step taken with regard to unclaimed stock and dividends in the public funds. (Hear, hear.)

Mr. Gray regretted that the Attorney-General had not referred to the subject of cross-indexes. The adoption of such a system would, he thought, be of advantage to the parties interested. He could not understand how it was that the motion was opposed. For his own part, he believed that, if carried, it would be attended with beneficial results.

The motion was unfortunately defeated by a majority of 19, but the question is too important to the public to be allowed to slumber.

On March 9, 1883, Mr. Stanley Leighton renewed his motion, and the Attorney-General promised that future Lists should contain sufficient information for legitimate claimants; the amount standing to the credit of each suit would be given. The next List would be published soon after 30 September, 1883.

The debate was commented on in the leading newspapers, thus:—

Times.—The subject of Dormant Funds in Chancery is one which relates to a matter of the greatest importance to a vast number of persons. A hundredth part of the Suitors' Funds mean more than £751,000. Looking at the question from the Suitors' point of view, it must be admitted that each person would prefer reading over the list himself, and finding there the clue which would lead to the discovery he hopes to make . . . . the particulars exist which might enable much of this money to be successfully claimed. It would, no doubt, be a work of some labor to re-publish the present list with the addition of all the information suggested, but it might be done if some official were told off to compile from the records the necessary facts. We can see no difficulty in providing effectual remedies against the abuses contemplated by the Attorney-General.

Observer.—Mr. Leighton has done good service in calling public attention to the funds now lying dormant in Chancery, and it is to be hoped that things will not be allowed to remain as they are. At intervals lists of these unclaimed funds are indeed published, but they are lists which any man of business would be ashamed of.

Standard.—Owners for these funds could presumably be found if proper facilities were afforded for investigation. If the existing lists were modified in the sense proposed by Mr. Stanley Leighton, there is no doubt that a large proportion of these Dormant Funds would find their way into the pockets of their rightful owners.

The next list of Dormant Funds will be looked for with some curiosity The one on which the debate arose was out of print soon after it was issued. Its great value may be estimated by the fact that the legal papers reprinted it *in extenso*

A good precedent for the suggested improvement in form of the List is a notice issued "for general information," by order of the Secretary of State for India, in 1879. That notice was published in the leading newspapers, and contains a List of "Unclaimed Balances," amounting to upwards of £10,000, and it gives the following particulars :—(1) date when account opened ; (2) title of account; and (3) amount in Government securities and Cash awaiting claimants. It is, not, therefore, easy to understand why information voluntarily given by one Department of the State should be refused by another.—*Preston's Unclaimed Money.*

The following is from the *London Law Journal* of recent date, and will be found interesting in this connection:

"The publication by the Chancery Pay Office of the list of causes having balances to their credit, which have not been dealt with for fifteen years, is likely to produce much investigation, and to give rise to many expectations, some reasonable and others absurd. If the document penetrates across the Atlantic, as in all probability it will, some heart-stirring may be expected among our American cousins, some of whom are credited with extravagant notions as to the fortunes merely waiting to be claimed by them in England. In 1855 the first of the lists was published—not printed, we believe, but exhibited in the Chancery offices—and, according to the report of the Chancery Funds Commissioners, ' many persons came forward and preferred their claims, and about one-half the stock supposed to be unclaimed was transferred out of Court to successful claimants.' This result is encouraging to investigators of the list; but, of course, the gleaners of 1855, being the first comers, had by far the best opportunities. In 1872 the Chancery Funds Act was passed, and the rules made in 1874, under the authority of that Act, after providing (Rule 90) that 'the Chancery Paymaster may, in his discretion, on a request in writing, supply such information with respect to any transactions in the Chancery Pay Office as may from time to time be required in any particular case,' continue (Rule 91) as follows.

As soon as conveniently, may be after September 1, 1875, and after the same day in every succeeding third year, a list shall be prepared by the Chancery Paymaster, and filed in the Report Office, and a copy thereof shall be inserted in the London *Gazette*, and exhibited in the several offices of the Court, of the titles of the causes and matters in the books at the Chancery Pay Office (other than the causes or matters referred to in Rule 92), to the credit of which any securities or any money amounting to or exceeding £50 may be standing, which money, or the dividends on which securities, have not been dealt with by the Accountant-General, or by the Chancery Paymaster (otherwise than by the continuous investment or placing on deposit of dividends) during the fifteen years immediately preceding such September 1, and no information shall be given by the Chancery Paymaster respecting any money or securities to the credit of a cause or matter contained in any such list, until he has been furnished with a statement in writing by a Solicitor, requiring such information, of the name of the person on whose behalf he applies, and that, in such Solicitor's opinion, the applicant is beneficially interested in such money or securities.'

As soon as conveniently, might be after September 1, 1875, was found to be no earlier than March 1, 1877, when the second list was published. Some impression on the unclaimed funds must have been made after that list was issued; and, now the third list has arrived, it will, no doubt, be found less open to attack, but still not to be overlooked by the enterprising. The object of the rule was, doubtless, that there should be a list every three years, but this intention has not been observed. It was only after some correspondence in these columns, and other pressure, that the present list is now produced. It has been suggested that the amount standing to the credit of the cause should be published, as well as its name. Some of the amounts would probably make the mouth water, and perhaps the officials are wise in not offering too tempting a bait to the cupidity of persons who may not be over-scrupulous in backing their claims. No amount, it should be observed, is less than £50—a sum to which even the richest do not usually object. There is, therefore, quite sufficient inducement to any one who may think he has an interest in the cause, to make inquiries. The names of some 3,000 causes are open to be scanned by hopeful eyes. The fact that the amount of the prize is unknown may, perhaps, add zest to the pursuit. But the fact that the property of the Chancery Division of the High Court amounts to a sum nearer £100,000,000 than £50,000,000 sterling—a not unhandsome slice of which is unclaimed—shows that much is to be won. The bulk of the enormous sum in the hands of the Chancery Division is, of course, left there, even when dividends are unclaimed for fifteen years. The Court is the great administrator of property which executors, trustees, and others prefer not to take the responsibility of distributing for themselves; and trusts for accumulation, life interests, and other causes, account for much that is left untouched for many years. Still, there are sure to be some happy discoveries, resulting in the receipt of welcome sums. Acute and persevering investigators need not fear that enough will not be left out of their leavings to finish the New Law Courts, and we hope that many of them will be successful in rescuing comfortable sums from the maw of the Commissioners for the Reduction of the National Debt.

Not so practically important, but more interesting to the average reader, is the list of 'boxes and other miscellaneous effects' remaining in the Bank of England to the credit of the Chancery Division. Compared with the list of causes with balances unclaimed for fifteen years, the list of boxes is short, but it gives some details which might well be given in the longer list. Most of the causes are marked with the 'letter, year, and number' which now appears in the title of every cause, the most material part of which is the year in which the writ was issued. The year is, of course, a useful guide to the searcher, and in future issues of the list of causes with unclaimed balances, we hope that it will appear, as well as in the list of boxes. It may be assumed that the causes in this latter list, which contain no numbers and letters, were commenced before it became the practice so to identify causes—that is, before 1853. Only one of those not so identified contains any indication of the date of the cause. All the rest must, therefore, be treated as 'aged,' like the horses whose years are not given in one of Mr Tattersall's catalogues. One box is not identified even by the name of a cause, but is described simply as 'a box containing small articles of jewelry.' It will probably be long before the contents of this box adorns any place more becoming than the Bank cellars, but even its chance of revisiting the light is not hopeless. Not long since, we related in these columns a romantic story of a similar box, the contents of which had been long condemned to the same obscurity. The Bank servants, some years ago, laid hands upon it, and it fell to pieces when touched. It was found to contain a quantity of plate of the period of Charles II. There was also a bundle of love letters, of the time of the Restoration, which performed the prosaic office of disclosing the owner of the plate, which his representative duly received. There are several entries of 'plate, jewelry and trinkets,' heirlooms, no doubt, of value and interest; otherwise they would hardly be where they are; one of 'family relics,' and one of 'presentation plate.' Many of the contents are described vaguely as 'securities,' and some as 'promissory notes'—baits which will not tempt investigation so strongly as solid silver. One box is marked, '*His Majesty, the King of Spain, v. Valles and others;* securities,' but we have no clue to which king it was, or whether the securities are Spanish bonds. A little investigation would, probably, soon disclose the owner of most of this property. The Chancery Division does not, it must be confessed, take a very high view of its duties in reference to the property deposited with it. If a trustee, who found himself possessed of valuable property belonging to his beneficiaries, were to use no more diligence to discover their owner than does the Chancery Division, no judge would fail to pronounce him guilty of a grave breach of duty. The highest Court of Equity in the Kingdom contents itself with playing a sort of game of hunt the slipper with the public. If ownership is satisfactorily proved, the Court will disgorge, but not otherwise. With regard to unclaimed funds and other property of long standing, an official ought to be appointed to discover by all the means available, and by advertisement, whose they are. As it is, the public are left to trust to the ingenuity and penetration of themselves and their legal advisers."

CHAPTER VI.

ENGLISH ESTATES REVERTING TO THE CROWN.

IN the category of successful claims on the Government for the refunding of estates which had reverted to the Crown by reason of persons dying intestate and leaving no known Next of Kin, is a singular case decided by the late Vice-Chancellor Malins. The facts were these:—In December, 1871, Mrs. Maria Mangin Brown, then of Hertford Street, Mayfair, died intestate, leaving personal property of the value of more than £200,000, and with no Next of Kin; the Treasury Solicitor took possession of her estate on behalf of the Crown, and paid all expenses of administration, Advertisements were then issued in the following form:—

"NEXT OF KIN.—Brown —The Relations or Next of Kin of Maria Mankin Brown, late of Hertford Street, Mayfair, who died on the 21st December, 1871, are requested to apply to the Solicitor of the Treasury, Whitehall, London"

Fourteen persons came in under this Advertisement, but only four of them succeeded in establishing their claims. These lucky four were Italians, residing abroad at the time of Mrs. Mangin Brown's death. The matter came on by petition, praying for payment of £192,535, the balance of the above sum of £200,000, to the petitioner, Fillippo Tomasso Mattia Freccia, after providing for succession duty and costs. After some discussion between Counsel, the Vice-Chancellor made the order as prayed.

Part of the funds had been paid out of Court, in pursuance of the Vice-Chancellor's Order, when several new claimants appeared on the scene, and a stop-order was obtained on the remaining funds in Court. A Special Examiner was appointed, a vast amount of evidence taken before the Chief Clerk, as to the genuineness of the alleged relationship of the new claimants.

The case was carried to the House of Lords, and in June, 1880, their Lordships affirmed the Order of the Vice-Chancellor.

One or two curious things concerning the lady whose estate has been the subject of such expensive litigation deserve a passing notice. It seems that the denizens of London are indebted to this Mrs Brown for a very beautiful drinking fountain, placed in Park-lane, close to the house wherein she resided for upwards of forty years. This work of art is said to have cost £5,000. It is also stated that this lady had in contemplation the formation of swimming baths in various parts of London at a large outlay, and that when the Metropolitan Board of Works desired to take her house for the purpose of widening Hamilton place, she proposed to carry out, at her own cost, an alternative scheme, the estimate for which was £50,000, that the deeds were, it is stated, prepared, but the lady died before she could carry out her good intentions

Lest it should be thought that the Mangin Brown case is an isolated one, and that it is impossible for many people to die without known relatives, I may say that between thirty and forty such cases annually occur. Those for 1882 are as follows.—

Beresford, John P (Middlesex).
Briggs, Eliza (Somerset).
Brown, Thos. (York)
Butler, Mary Ann (Middlesex).
Cain (or Kane, Michael (Chester)
Chandler, Jno. (ship's cook) died at sea.
Crook, Maria (Middlesex).
Daly, John (Middlesex)
Davis (or Davies), (Hertford).
Doyle, Ann (Ireland).
Gray, John (Middlesex).
Halfpenny, Daniel (Middlesex).
Harris, Selina (Surrey).
Hughes, Elizabeth (Chester).
Jones, Martha (Hereford).
Lacon, Dr. Henry (died abroad)
Langley, Catherine R. (Middlesex).
Langley, Charles (Solicitor)

Ludlow, Jane Maria (Middlesex).
Madsen, Mathias (London).
Martin, Frances (Middlesex).
Mostyn, Robt Capt (Ireland).
Newman, Alex. (Suffolk).
Pigott, D F (died abroad).
Rowlls, Ruth (or Irwin)
Smith, George (Middlesex)
Stokes, John Allen (Surrey).
Sweeney, Maria (Chester)
Symons, Caroline (Devon).
Tart, William (Dover).
Taylor, Geo (Monmouth).
Varley, Samuel (Worcester).
Welsh, Edwd G.(Commercial Traveler).
Welton, John (Middlesex).
Williams, Geo. (Middlesex).

The Next of Kin of the above are doubtless inquired for with reference to effects more or less valuable Such notices are, moreover, exceedingly interesting to relatives, as they are the means of affording a clue to the fate of some missing one.

The following notes of curious cases, in which successful claims have been made on the Crown, will be encouraging to persons having claims of a like kind.—

THE ATTORNEY GENERAL *v.* KOHLER AND OTHERS.

In 1802 the following Advertisement appeared.—

"If the Relations or Next of Kin (if any) of George Frederick Kohler. late Brigadier-General in his Majesty's Artillery, who died in Egypt on 29th December, 1800, a Widower and Intestate, will apply at the King's Proctor's Office, Doctors' Commons, London, they will hear of something to their advantage"

In 1813 the then Solicitor to the Treasury obtained, as nominee of the Crown, a grant of Letters of Administration to the estate and effects of George Frederick Kohler, an officer of Artillery, who died in Syria in 1800, intestate, and whose property up to that time had not been administered.

In 1820 Christiane Bauer, of Cronberg, laborer, and Elizabeth his wife, filed a bill, claiming to be entitled to General Kohler's property, as his Next of Kin. The bill alleged that the intestate was the only son of George Kohler, who was born at Bingen, on the Rhine, and who left there very early in life and became a soldier in the Royal Artillery; he afterwards entered the service of the East India Company, where he died or was killed in battle, leaving the intestate his only child. The bill prayed for the usual discovery and accounts

The answer to the bill denied all knowledge of the relationship of the plaintiffs to the intestate, and stated that the Crown Solicitor had paid, over the money to the King's Proctor, on warrant under the Sign Manual Exceptions were taken to the answer, which were allowed. An amended answer was put in, stating that the nominee of the Crown entered into a bond to the King's Proctor in a penal sum, which bond recited the death of General Kohler intestate and without issue or any known relation, whereby His Majesty, in right of his Royal prerogative, became entitled to the personal estate and effects aforesaid. It was stated that the balance (£7,842, 8s. 4d) had been, in 1814, paid to the King's Proctor.

In 1830 the suit was revived. In 1831 a decree was made directing inquiry as to who were the Next of Kin thus:—

"Pursuant to a Decree of His Majesty's Court of Exchequer, the Next of Kin of George Frederick Kohler, otherwise Keylor, late a Brigadier-General in His Majesty's Regiment of Artillery service, who died at Jaffa, in Egypt, in December, 1800, intestate, who were living at the time of his decease, and the personal representatives of such of them as are since dead."

Between 1831 and 1851 various proceedings were taken. On 26 February, 1859 (twenty-eight years after the inquiry was directed), the Master made his Report, by which he found that Jacob Kohler, Johann Michael Kohler, and Gertrandt Schmidt (formerly Kohler), were the paternal uncles and aunt, and sole Next of Kin of the intestate living at the time of his death, and that Philip Kohler, H——s Kohler, and Johann M. Schmidt, were respectively their personal representatives. Exceptions were taken to this Report, but it was confirmed by the Vice-Chancellor Kindersley on 9 June, 1859. A supplemental bill was filed, accounts were directed, and an Order made for paying what should be found due with interest at four per cent In 1860 the Chief Clerk certified that the sum of £7,842 8s. 4d. was due for principal, and £14,429 12s. 6d for interest, and an Order was made to pay into Court the sums thus found due. It is almost needless to say the Crown appealed from this decision

In July, 1861, the case came on in the House of Lords, when their Lordships affirmed the Vice-Chancellor's decision.

The foregoing case is especially noteworthy as showing that Next of Kin may successfully claim funds from the Crown, although over sixty years may have elapsed between the date of the intestate's death and the recovery of the money. It would be difficult to find a more encouraging case for claimants.

RE DEWELL—EDGAR v. REYNOLDS.

This case is remarkable, not for the largeness of the sum at stake, but from the fact that the Crown had to pay interest for a period of thirty years, the Vice-Chancellor being of opinion that the Crown " had no right to have money, as it were, wrapped up in a napkin." The facts were these·—In 1826 Thomas Dewell died intestate. At the time of his death no Next of Kin were forthcoming, and the Crown Solicitor took out Letters of Administration. The following Advertisement was issued:—

"If the Relations or Next of Kin of Thomas Dewell,—formerly of Cowes, Isle of Wight, and late of Elliott place, near Gosport, in the County of Southampton, Gentleman, a Lieutenant in Her Majesty's Army, deceased, will apply to ————, they may hear of something to their advantage"

No Next of Kin appeared. The clear amount that came to the Crown was £2,064 7s. 1d., which, under the then existing law, the Crown Solicitor paid over in 1828 to the King's Proctor, for the King's use. In 1857 a suit was instituted, and further Advertisements for Next of Kin were issued. In 1858 certain persons were proven to be Next of Kin, and the Crown were willing to pay the balance aforesaid; the only question was, whether interest could be claimed from the time when there was a clear balance in the hands of the administrator,—that is, in 1827. After a learned argument, the Vice-Chancellor said:—" In this case the Sovereign has, on his own account, or on behalf of the public, had the use of the property, and the Sovereign or the public is responsible, and therefore it appears to me there is a liability to pay interest." His Honor then made an Order for repayment by the Crown of the sum of £2,064 7s. 1d., with interest from the year 1827 to 1858,—the date of the Order

Another remarkable "Crown windfall" case is that of Mrs. Helen Blake, who died in 1876, at Kensington, intestate, leaving personalty of the value of £130,000, and without any known relatives. The usual notice was issued, thus:—

"BLAKE —Heir-at-Law.—Next of Kin —The Heir-at-Law and the Next of Kin of Mrs Helen Blake, late of No 4, Earl's Terrace, Kensington, Widow, deceased, are requested to apply to the Solicitor of the Treasury."

No one reading this very bald notice would guess that £140,000 only awaited proper proofs of identity prior to being handed over to the lucky Next of Kin. The amount in dispute is not stated in the Advertisement, nor are the Next of Kin informed, in the usual phraseology of such notices, that "something to their advantage" awaits them. Unless Next of Kin Advertisements state concisely what the Next of Kin are wanted for, they have rather a discouraging tendency than otherwise, for instances are not unknown where a creditor of a deceased person has advertised for Next of Kin in order to get his account settled However, in this case it would seem that claims have been lodged, as an action is pending in the Chancery Division.

Many people believe it impossible to recover property from the Crown, but there is little difficulty if the claimant's title is a clear one. The following is the record of a case in which no less a sum than £57,000 in the Three per Cents was thus recovered:—

In 1842, Mr. John Turner, of Middlesex, died intestate, and very wealthy. His effects were taken charge of by the Treasury Solicitor, who issued the following notice:—

"NEXT OF KIN.—If the relations or Next of Kin of John Turner late of Huntley Street, in the parish of St. Bancras, in the County of Middlesex, Esq., who died on or about the 30th day of January, 1842, will apply to ———— they may hear of something to their advantage."

The Next of Kin did eventually find it very much to their advantage, but several years elapsed before the Advertisement was brought under their notice Meanwhile the Solicitor to the Treasury had taken out Letters of Administration and sold the sum of £57,000 Three per Cents standing in the name of the intestate, and paid the proceeds into the Treasury. Next of Kin eventually appeared, and two Chancery suits were instituted.

In 1849, the Next of Kin having established their claims, the cause came on for further directions, and a question was raised whether the Solicitor to the Treasury must pay interest on the £57,000 Three per Cents from the time of its transfer to the Treasury.

Counsel for the Next of Kin contended that the nominee of the Crown was in the same position as any other administrator, and must replace the fund with interest at four per cent.

Counsel for the Crown submitted that the case was a peculiar one; that by the neglect of the Next of Kin to come forward, and the obscurity and difficulty which the intestate himself had created by using a Christian name different from that by which he had, as the jury had found, been baptized, the administrator was perfectly justified in the course which he had taken, and as he had made no interest by the fund, ought not to pay any. The case was like that of Unclaimed Dividends which were taken by the Crown, and upon which no interest was paid, the Crown retaining the interest or using the money as compensation for taking care of it, as was done, in fact, by bankers. The plaintiffs were not entitled, either in respect of contract or otherwise, to interest.

The Vice-Chancellor, however, was of opinion that as the Crown's nominee had, without any necessity arising in the course of the administration of the estate, sold the Stock; and then without any judicial decision, authority, or investigation, paid it over to those whom he considered entitled, the persons really entitled to the fund ought not to suffer by the proceeding. The Solicitor to the Treasury was therefore ordered to replace the sum produced by the sale, with interest at four per cent.

It would be difficult to find a more encouraging decision than the foregoing for persons having claims on the Crown arising out of Intestates' estates.

The Upcroft Estate Case (personalty valued at £160,000) excited a good deal of interest. The facts are these:—In November, 1861, the following notice appeared in the *Times*:—

"SUDDEN DEATH.—The Deputy-Coroner for West Middlesex held an inquest on Wednesday night . . . touching the sudden death of a gentleman of fortune named John Montague Upcroft, sixty years of age, residing at 301, Marylebone-road Mr. Norton, the deceased gentleman's medical adviser, deposed that he was found dead in his bedroom on Saturday morning last. The cause of death was phthisis and polypus of the heart, and disease of the lungs. The deceased was a man of large property, being worth at least £120,000, and a large amount of money was found in the house. As no relatives had come forward to claim it, the witness had deemed it his duty to employ a solicitor to seal up and take charge of the deceased's property, and to take such other proceedings as the law directed. In conformity with the medical evidence, a verdict of 'Death from natural causes' was returned."

In December, 1861, the Next of Kin were advertised for apparently without success, as in the session of 1877, Mr. Colman, M. P., gave the following notice:—

"To call attention to the case of John Montague Upcroft, an illegitimate, who died on the 23rd November, 1861, intestate, and to move for a Return of any allowance made out of the estate, and of any other application for allowance which has been made and not acceded to by the Treasury."

This notice, however, dropped out of the Order Book, and it may be useful to cite precedents for the information asked for by Mr Colman. In 1832, Mr Harvey (then M P. for Colchester) moved for a Return as to Intestates' Estates as follows:—

"Return of the number of cases and of the names of the parties in which the Crown has administered to the estate and effects of persons who have died intestate, leaving no lawful issue, since the year 1824 to 1830, both inclusive, specifying (1) the nature and extent of the property so obtained and now in progress of recovery, (2) the appropriation thereof, (3) what proceedings have been taken in the Courts of Law or Equity in respect thereof; and (4) the costs attending each case, and by and to whom paid, so far as relates to the office of the Solicitor of the Treasury."

The return fills 47 pp., and from it we extract the following;—Number of estates reverting to the Crown during the period between 1824-1830, about 150; amount received (in round numbers), £210,000; appropriated £131,000; amount in progress of recovery over £25,000; costs, about £20,000.

It may be interesting to add particulars of some of the estates included in this Return, thus :—

"Intestate's name.—Bolton Mainwaring. Amount obtained £6,061 2s. In progress of recovery, Nil. Crown's share paid to the King's Proctor, £1,502 2s. 3d.; Grant to Anna Priscilla Warrington, £4,259 12s. 3d.; Costs, £299 7s. 6d. Intestates name.—Samuel Ducket and John Watson; Amount obtained—Nil.; In progress of recovery—£1,000 East India Stock, and about £6,000 arrears of dividend." This suggestive note is attached to the entry :—"The difficulty of identifying the deceased parties has hitherto stopped the progress, and nothing has yet been recovered. Intestate's name.—John Turner—(Seaman's wages). Amount obtained £51 2s 4d.; Debt paid £19 19s. 6d; Grant to W. Player £2 11s. 2d; Costs £28 11s. 8d. Intestate's name —Charles Sidney—(Share of Deccan Prize money). Amount obtained £50 10s. 9d.; Crown's share £3 1s 1d; Grant to Mr. Sicard £25 17s. 8d.; Costs £30 12s. Intestate's name — Rachel Frances Antona Lee. Amount obtained £24,910 11s. 10d; Crown's share £5,770 8s. 2d.; Grant to Lady Ann Dashwood Trehurst £16,346 7d.; Costs £1,706 14s. 6d."

Many more details might be extracted from this Return, but the above are probably enough to prove that very large sums yearly revert to the Crown by reason of persons dying without known relatives.

One of the most recent "Crown windfall" cases is that of the undisposed of residue of the estate of a Mr George Perton who died at Prestbury, Gloucestershire, in 1881. The personalty was valued at £260,000; but £200,000 (the residue after payment of munificent legacies) was undisposed of by the testator's will An inquiry as to the legitimacy of the testator was held before Mr Dowdeswell, Q C.; the testator was proved to be illegitimate, and the £200,000 went to the Crown.

Before leaving this subject we would draw attention to the Treasury Solicitor Act of 1876, under which these estates are dealt with The title of the Act is "to incorporate the Solicitor for the affairs of Her Majesty's Treasury, and make further provision respecting the grant of the administration of the estate of deceased persons for the use of Her Majesty" The principal sections are as follows :—

Section 2—Enables her Majesty, by Royal Warrant, to nominate the Treasury Solicitor to act on behalf of her Majesty in cases where estates have reverted to the Crown by persons dying intestate or otherwise.

Section 4—Relates to the disposal of money and property received from administration or forfeiture . . . . of Unclaimed Grants, and empowers the Treasury to make Rules with reference thereto, thus—(1) Such money and all money arising from securities . . . is to be carried to an account to be called "The Crown's Nominee Account" (2) All money standing to the credit of the said account not required for purposes thereof is to be paid into the account of Her Majesty's Exchequer. (3) Money, securities, or property granted by Her Majesty to any person, and not claimed within the period fixed by the rules aforesaid, the Treasury may direct to be sold, and the proceeds carried to the Crown's Nominee Account.

Then follows this important proviso: If any person satisfies the Treasury of his right under the said grant to the whole or any part of such unclaimed money, securities, or property, the Treasury may direct the sum paid to the Crown's Nominee Account in respect of the same or of the part to which such person shows himself to be entitled, to be paid to such person out of the Consolidated Fund, or the growing produce thereof.

It will thus be seen that personal estate can be recovered from the Crown at any time on proper proofs of title being adduced

The section proceeds. The accounts of the receipts and expenditure on the Crown's Nominee Account shall be deemed public accounts; and such abstract thereof as may be directed by Rules under this Act shall be annually laid before Parliament.

Although the accounts are to be deemed "public accounts," they are issued in such a form as to be of no value whatever to the public No particulars are given as to the number of estates dealt with; the names and addresses of the intestates; the amount of each estate; the number of cases in which claimants have appeared; the amount of the funds handed over to the Next of Kin, and so-forth. All these particulars could be given with very little trouble, and the Parliamentary Paper would then indeed be a valuable one to the public.

Since the passing of the Treasury Solicitor Act the receipts have been as follows: 1877, £127,876 19s 11d; 1878, £139,769 9s 3d; 1879, £140,879 3s. 5d.; 1880, £56,448 13s. 11d.

After payment of the Crown's share, grants to persons having claims on the bounty of the Crown, costs, etc., the balance in hand in 1881 was £177,374 5s. 10d.

Attention has been called in the House of Commons to the meagre nature of the information afforded by the "Crown's Nominee Account," and Sir Herbert Maxwell, last session, gave the following notice:

"SIR HERBERT MAXWELL—Intestates' Estates reverting to the Crown —Return showing the total amount received on behalf of the Crown since the passing of the Treasury Solicitor Act, 1876, with the names and addresses of the Intestates; also the names and addresses of the Intestates whose estates are in course of administration, with the amount of each estate."

This notice, unfortunately, dropped out of the Order Book, but I hope to see it renewed. There are many precedents showing the great value of publicity in similar cases.

The evidence of the late Queen's Proctor before the legal Departments Commission, as to how these estates are ordinarily dealt with, is very interesting The following is the essence of it, extracted from a letter in the *Daily News* on "Windfalls for Royalty." The Queen's Proctor said:

"I take out letters of administration, and get in all the money for the Government in connection with the estates and Intestate bastards and

ENGLISH ESTATES REVERTING TO THE CROWN.

bona vacantia. . . . I recommend the Lords of the Treasury as to the disposition of the balance of the effects. . . . The Solicitor of the Treasury is appointed administrator. . . . I am known all over the world, and I correspond with solicitors and the people interested. . . . I ascertain what the effects are either at the Bank of England or with various public bodies. . . . Mr. Stephenson gets in the effects. . . . Sometimes there are large and heavy pedigree cases . . In a heavy case a short time ago, I fancied it was rather a fraudulent case on the part of the party who set up the claim. I got the facts together and took Counsel's opinion. . . . I went on and won the case, and a large sum was recovered. . . I have a lot of administrations going in shortly and among them is one estate worth £35,000 Occasionally I have much heavier amounts even than that. . . All these estates are vested in the Crown; they belong to Her Majesty in right of Her Royal prerogative . . . When bastards die there are always plenty of people only too ready to seize hold of their property and get wills made. . . . In one case there was a commission to America . . . It was an estate worth £70,000, I think. . . In ordinary cases the procedure is this: I receive a letter that A. B. is dead; that he had such and such property; that he was a bastard, or has left none but illegitimate relations. I then ascertain the facts, and find out who the Next of Kin are, or the persons to whom the Crown should make grants, and I recommend accordingly I take out from forty to fifty administrations in a year. Some are large amounts—£120,000 and sums of that sort."—*Preston's Unclaimed Money*.

CHAPTER VII.

CLAIMANTS

THERE are not a few estates in England the presumptive owners whereof, though having apparently a good title thereto, may be ousted by the rightful Heir—supposed long since to have departed this life—re-appearing on the scene. There are likewise people who, possessing every just right to a very desirable estate, are still liable to litigation and worry by reason of impostors setting up claims having a *prima facie* appearance of genuineness.

The catalogue of spurious claimants is a long one; such claims have been set up not only in our own day and in our own country, but also in the olden time both here and abroad. Claimants have rarely any difficulty in finding people ready to believe, not only in the genuineness of their claims, but also (and this is the strangest part of the business), to find the money to assist in substantiating them. The Magna Charta Association is a notable case in point, one of the principal objects of that Association being " to secure the release and establish the rights of Sir Roger Tichborne,"—not a very lively outlook for the trustees of the Tichborne estates, who have already had to obtain a Special Act of Parliament in order to raise funds for opposing the claim of Arthur Orton, the cost of such opposition being nearly £100,000.

It is easy for really just claims to arise, this is clearly shown by the following paragraph, which apppeared in a leading provincial newspaper some years ago.

"AN ESTATE WITHOUT AN OWNER.—At a meeting of the Historic Society of Lancashire and Cheshire, held in the Grand Jury Room of St. George's Hall, Liverpool, on Thursday night, Mr. George Meyer, who presided, in referring to an interesting seal belonging to the family of Moels, stated that the last owner of the property at Moels had a son of very dissolute character, who, getting into debt, collected the rents of the estate, to meet his extravagances. His father, vowing that he would be revenged on his son, set out to find him; but whether he did so is not known, as to this day neither father nor son have been heard of, and the whole of the estate is now in the hands of the tenants, and would be claimable should an Heir be found."

We often hear of searches for missing Heirs-at-Law, but it is rarely indeed that we find recorded an instance affording such ample material for the novelist as the foregoing. An aggrieved father goes in search of his erring son, and neither father nor son are heard of again—that is sufficiently romantic, in all conscience!

Lovers of the curious may like to consult a work entitled "Celebrated Claimants." Many and marvelous are the claims there recorded, including the history of a spurious claim to be no less a personge than the Sultan of Turkey. A pretender to the throne of England died only recently.

The following is a curious case of an abortive claim to large estates in the North of England:

Many years ago a Mr. William Swan was found dead in his bed, at an obscure lodging in London. He was the only surviving male Heir of the late Mr. Alderman Swan, Mayor of Hull, who left estates of the value of £20,000 per annum, or thereabouts, and which the unfortunate Heir had been trying (in vain) for over twenty years to recover. The history of the Heir is no less remarkable than that of his father, who, when nine years of age (to disinherit him), was abducted from the house of his father (Richard Swan, Esq., of Benwell Hall, near Newcastle), and put on board the New Britannia brig; was wrecked on the rocks of Scilly with Sir Cloudesley Shovel's fleet, and was afterward taken prisoner by an Algerine vessel, and sold for a slave, but, after four years imprisonment, he was set at liberty by the redeeming Friars. After this he was again shipwrecked, was carried and sold for a slave to a planter in South Carolina, where he suffered almost every human woe. He returned to his native home in 1726, after an absence of about twenty years, and was identified by one Mrs Grofton, of Newcastle, his nurse, and Thomas Chance, who had been his father's footman. He directly laid claim to the estates of Alderman Swan, but having neither money, nor friends living, to assist him, all his efforts proved abortive. After this, he settled at an obscure village, North Dalton, near Hull, where he married one Jane Cole, by whom he had one son, the above unfortunate William Swan. He afterwards died of a broken heart at the above village, 1735.

After reading the foregoing romantic story, it is easy to believe in the truth of the old song which says—

> 'Tis a very good world that we live in,
> To lend, or to spend, or to give in,
> But to beg, or to borrow, or get a man's own,
> 'Tis the very worst world, Sirs, that ever was known.

From the great uncertainty of human affairs, it not unfrequently happens that estates belonging to one family change owners several times in a generation. In the course of these transitions, the rightful Heir is occasionally lost sight of, and when he does revisit his native place, he finds it almost impossible to substantiate his heirship.

Advertisements for claimants are passed over by most people as having only a transitory value, but many of such notices are, nevertheless, the means of affording not only a clue to a very desirable estate, but also a clue to the whereabouts of some long-lost relative, who has possibly returned from abroad after many years' absence the happy possessor of an ample fortune, which he is anxious his Next of Kin should share, could he only find them.

The following is an advertisement for the descendants of a person who died 120 years prior to the issue of this notice:—

"WILLIAM CHAPMAN, DECEASED.—William Chapman, late of New Shoreham, in the County of Sussex, Mariner, who departed this life about the year 1732, and formerly of Deptford, in the County of Kent, had by his wife four sons and three daughters; the names of the sons were William, John, Joseph, and Clement, and the names of the daughters, Elizabeth, Margaret, and Annie. Any persons who can trace their descent (however remote) from either of the said Chapmans, may hear of something greatly to their advantage, upon application to——

The following is a very curious Claimant Advertisement:—

"To SOLICITORS AND OTHERS.—Twenty-eight years ago.—Wanted, the claims of YOUNG TOM SMITH, the shoemaker's son, of London Wall, to be TAKEN UP. Supposed to be dead.—T. Smith."

Such notices as the foregoing are not uncommon, and they show pretty clearly that claimant cases are constantly cropping up.

What is known as the "Great Jennens Case" has given rise to many Claimants. The facts are remarkable, and may be shortly stated thus:—

The late William Jennins, of Acton-place, Suffolk, and of Grosvenor-square, Esq., by whom the estates were left, attained the great age of 97, and died in the year 1798.

King William the Third, was godfather to William Jennens, and amongst other valuable presents at his baptism a silver ewer from that Sovereign was conspicuous. William Jennins was at one time page to George the First, and during the long period of his life remained a bacholor, more given to penuriousness than hospitality, and his accumulations multiplied even beyond the power of computation. He received £3,000 a year from what was known as the Exchequer Tontine. He had property in almost every fund, and the following were some of the chief items:—

South Sea Stock	£100,000
Indian Stock	23,800
Consols, Three per Cents	60,000
Bank Stock	35,000
Four and Five per Cent. ditto	54,000
Reduced Annuities	50,000
Long ditto	2,000 per ann.
Cash at five different bankers	107,000
Accumulated interest on Stocks, Funds, etc., about	150,000
On Mortgage, about	200,000
Landed estate, say	8,000 per ann
London Assurance (dividend due)	3,400
New River Concern (dividend due)	5,000

His wealth was immense. The dividends on most of his Stocks had not been received since 1788, nor the interest on his mortgages for years. In his iron chest, the key of which was found hidden in a mortgage deed, there were bank notes of the year 1788 to the amount of £19,000, and several thousand new guineas. About £20,000 in money and bank notes were found at his town and country houses, and also a key to the chest containing his mother's plate and valuables deposited with Messrs Childs, the bankers. He is reported to have always kept £50,000 in his bankers' hands for any sudden emergency; he had not drawn a draft on the bank for the last fourteen years of his life. It was only a short time before his death that he employed a steward. He was very regular and exact in his accounts; he even noticed his household bills when they exceeded their usual weekly amount. His expenses were supposed to be about £3,000 per annum only, although his property at his death was of the estimated value of two millions sterling. A Will was found in his coat-pocket, *sealed* but not *signed*. This was owing—so runs the tale—to his having left his spectacles at home when he went to his solicitor for the purpose of executing the Will. It is stated that by this Will the whole of his immense wealth was intended to be wholly alienated from the channels into which it fell.

Truly, indeed, do "great events from little causes spring." In this case, the disposition of no less than two millions worth of property appears to have been diverted, owing to the intending testator having forgotten his spectacles. The Heir-at-Law of Mr William Jennens was

George Augustus William Curzon, infant son of the Honorable Assheton Curzon, M. P., to whom all the real estate reverted. The personalty devolved to his cousins.

From the date of William Jennens's death, in 1798, to the present time, claimants have periodically made claim to these estates

One of the latest claimants was a person known as "Martin the Sexton." His claim was heard by Vice-Chancellor Bacon, and dismissed. The Court of Appeal upheld the Vice-Chancellor

The case of a still later set of claimants to these vast estates came before the late Vice-Chancellor Malins, and was dismissed.

Intending claimants would do well to ponder the learned Vice-Chancellor's judgment. His lordship said. "If such a claim could be allowed after a period of eighty-two years, no one would be safe in the possession of his property. He could see no ground whatever for alleging concealed fraud"

The Sir Andrew Chadwick Estate case has also given rise to numerous claimants. Sir Andrew died at Westminster in 1768, very wealthy. One remarkable fact in connection with this case is the getting up recently at Rochdale of an "Association of Claimants," 400 in number, claiming descent from Sir Andrew—all very anxious to obtain a share of his property, said to be now worth £7,000,000.

The case *Chadwick* v. *Chadwick* and Others, in which the plaintiff claims to be the Heir-at-Law of Sir Andrew, was lately before the Queen's Bench Division on a question of discovery. The trial of the cause has not yet been decided.

A few years since there appeared in the *New York World* a very interesting article headed *Phantom Estates*, giving "the chances of the Jennens's and others as interpreted by themselves." It shows that Americans in this, as in many other matters, like big figures:—

The following table shows the various Estates, their value, and the number of heirs among whom they will be divided.

	Heirs.	Estate.
Anneke, Jans	1,000	$317,000,000
Baker	87	250,000,000
Carpenter	—	200,000,000
Chadwick	5	37,000,000
Edwards	160	90,000,000
Hyde, N. S	200	12,500,000
Hyde, Ann	150	360,000,000
Hyde, Bklyn	1	5,000,000
Jennings	1,835	400,000,000
Kern	—	200,000,000
Leake	—	100,000,000
Mackey	1	10,000,000
Merritt	80	10,000,000
Shepherd	15	175,000,000
Trotter	200	200,000,000
Townley	—	1,800,000,000
Lawrence-Townley	50	500,000,000
Van Horn	20	4,000,000
Webber	60	50,000,000
Weiss	4	20,000,000

Grand total—20 estates, 3,868 heirs, value of estates, $4,740,500,000.

In one of these cases (the *Hyde Case*) several thousand dollars were spent in a vain endeavor to find the location of the property or money.—*Preston's Unclaimed Money*.

CHAPTER VIII.

TRINITY CHURCH HISTORY---ANETJE JANS ESTATE.

IN 1636, Roelof Jansen, who had been Assistant Superintendent of Farms at Rennselaerwick, obtained from the Dutch Director-General and Governor, Wouter Van Twiller, a grant of thirty-one morgend, or sixty-two acres, of land on Manhattan Island, a little to the north of Fort Amsterdam. On the city map to-day, the grant would cover a section beginning south of Warren Street, extending on Broadway to Duane, and thence northwesterly a mile and a half, to Christopher Street, forming an unequal triangle, with its base on North River. Soon after the grant, Jansen (or Jans) died, leaving a wife and four children. In 1638, the widow, Anetje Jans, married Dominie Everardus Bogardus, and her farm became the "Dominie's Bouwerie." Possibly, if Van Twiller could have foreseen this transfer, he would not have made the grant to Jans. The new Governor and the new dominie were fellow passengers to Manhattan in 1633, in the ship "Southberg," but after their arrival they did not harmonize. The Governor resented the dominie's interference in public affairs. Bogardus, in his pulpit, called Van Twiller "a child of Satan," which so incensed him that he never again darkened the dominie's door. In 1647, Bogardus sailed for home with William Kieft, who had been Governor since 1638, and now was superseded by Peter Stuyvesant. The ship was wrecked on the coast of Wales, and Bogardus, Kieft, and seventy-eight other passengers were lost. In 1664, by the English occupation, New Amsterdam became New York, and Colonel Richard Nicolls was Governor. The Jans grant had been confirmed to his heirs soon after the death of Bogardus; but in 1671 the heirs sold the property to Colonel Francis Lovelace, who succeeded Nicolls as Governor in 1668. At this sale one of the heirs failed to be present, but Lovelace considered his title good enough, and he bought the Bouwerie for his private property, not for the Crown. On July 29, 1673, while Lovelace was away on a pleasure tour, five Dutch ships sailed up the bay, anchored off the Battery, and cannonaded the city. Captain Colve, with six hundred men, landed, and the fort soon surrendered. When Lovelace returned, he was permitted to sail for England, where he was severely reprimanded for cowardice and treachery. The peace between England and the States-General, 1674, restored New York, and one of the first acts of the new Governor, Sir Edmund Andros, was to confiscate the estate of Lovelace to the Duke of York. The Jans-Bogardus Bouwerie was thus incorporated into what was called the Duke's farm, the King's farm (when the Duke of York became James II., and also under William and Mary), and the Queen's farm under Anne, in whose reign it was transferred to Trinity Church.

THE JANS HEIRS

Thus the Jans claim was wiped out; indeed, it hardly ever was heard of till about thirty years ago, and Dr. Berrian, in his "Historical Sketch of Trinity Church," published in 1847, does not even mention it. But since then, uneasy heirs, or supposed heirs, the descendants of the daughters of Anetje Jans Bogardus, the Kiersteds and all their kin, the Van Brughs and the sisters and the cousins and the aunts, and thousands more, are periodically stirred up by lawyers here and there, throughout the country, from Maine to Texas. Now and then a suit is suggested, with the representation that there are millions in it; but no scheme of Mulberry Sellers is more Utopian or hopeless. The State Courts repeatedly have re-affirmed the valid, subsisting, and absolute title of Trinity Church to all its property, and the claims of the Jans heirs are disposed of in "Sanford's Chancery Reports," vol. iv., p 633, as follows:

"The law on these claims is well settled, and it must be sustained in favor of religious corporations as well as private individuals. Indeed, it would be monstrous, if, after a possession such as has been proven in this case for nearly a century and one-half, open, notorious, and within sight of the temple of justice, the successive claimants, save one, being men of full age, and the courts open to them all the time (except for seven years of the war of the revolution), the title to lands were to be litigated successfully upon a claim which has been suspended for five generations. Few titles in the country would be secure under such an administration of the law; and its adoption would lead to scenes of fraud, corruption, foul injustice, and legal rapine, far worse in their consequences upon the peace, good order, and happiness of society than external war or domestic insurrection."

As for the story, sometime current, that Trinity corporation was willing to compromise such claims, it never has offered, and never will offer, one dollar for that purpose.

THE BEGINNING OF THE PARISH.

This prelude explains and disposes of the Anetje Jans claims in connection with the property of the corporation, and now properly begins the history of Trinity Church, especially in respect of its wealth, how its means were acquired, and how they have been and are dispensed, which we think will be interesting to the public at large, and especially to those who have at any time entertained a hope that they would some time become possessed of a large interest in it, as heirs of Anetje Jans.

Immediately after the Dutch surrender of the colony, the English Church service was first celebrated in New York, September 14, 1664, by the chaplain of the English forces, the Dutch permitting the use of their church after their own morning service, and for some years the two congregations used the same chapel, which was in the fort near the Battery. In 1678-80, the Rev. Charles Wooley, a graduate of Emanuel College, Cambridge, in 1677, was chaplain to the English garrison, and a journal of the time says: "We went at noon to hear the English minister, whose services took place after the Dutch church was out. There were not above twenty-five or thirty people in the church," which was a good congregation, for the entire population of the city was then only 2,500. In 1696-7, a church was built where Trinity now stands, and in 1697, the fifth year of the reign of William and Mary, by an act of the Assembly, approved and ratified by the Governor of the province, a royal grant was made of "a certain church and steeple lately built in the city of New York, together with a piece or parcel of ground adjoining thereunto, being in or near to a street without the north gate of the city, commonly called and known by the name of the "Broad Way." The name given to the church in the original charter was the same it bears to-day "The Parish of Trinity Church." The wardens and vestrymen appointed under this charter included Col. Caleb Heathcote, an ancestor of the late Bishop Delancey, and such names as Morris, Clarke, Read, Burroughs, Wilson, and Ludlow, familiar in this city now. The edifice was built by assessments and subscriptions mostly small, from £1 to £5; Gov Fletcher gave £25; Chidlay Brook, Esq., £30; and Col. Peter Schuyler subscribed £5, "to be paid in boards." In a subsequent separate subscription to build a steeple, in a total sum of £318, £5 12s. 3d was a "contribution from the Jews." In 1704, Sarah Knight, of Boston, kept a journal of her visit here, and she says of New York people: "They are generally of the Church of England and have a New England gentleman for their minister and a very fine church, set out with all customary requisites." This New England gentleman was the Rev. William Vesey, for whom Vesey Street was named. He was educated at Harvard, and was a dissenting preacher but was appointed rector "provided he should be admitted to holy orders," and he went to England and was ordained. His first service in Trinity was on March 13, 1698, and he was rector nearly fifty years, till his death, on July 11, 1746. At first his salary was £100, with £26 allowance for house rent, and afterwards the Easter Communion offerings and £24s from the weekly collections were allowed him. The clerk and sexton were paid from fees for christenings, marriages, funerals, and bell-ringings.

THE QUEEN'S FARM GRANT.

In 1705, in the reign of Queen Anne, a grant was made to the corporation to Trinity Church, by deed patent, signed by Lord Cornbury, then Governor of the province, of "the tract called the Queen's farm, lying on the west side of Manhattan Island," extending from what now is Vesey Street, northwardly along the river to Skinner Road, now Christopher Street. This tract included the confiscated Lovelace land, bought from the Jans-Bogardus heirs. It was literally a farm then and of no great value—the city, with less than 5,500 population, was wholly below Wall Street—and in its first year's ownership, the church let the entire farm to George Ryerse, for £35. In 1737 the church, originally a small square building, was enlarged to 148 in length by 72 feet breadth, with a steeple 175 feet high. "It stands," says a historian of the time, "very pleasantly upon the banks of Hudson's river, and has a large cemetery on each side, enclosed in the front by a painted, paled fence. Before it, a long walk is railed off from the Broadway, the pleasantest street of any in the town." It was a splendid church for its day. The tops of the pillars supporting the galleries were decked with the gilt busts of angels winged; two great glass branches were suspended from the ceiling; on the wall hung the arms of some of the principal benefactors, conspicuous among them Gov. Fletcher's. During the reigns of William and Mary, Queen Anne, and George I. were bestowed, by the bounty of the Crown, three full sets of Communion plate, inscribed with the initials of the donors and the royal arms. All the furniture of the altar, desk, and pulpit was of the richest and costliest kind; and John Clemm built the organ for £520, the vestry adding a gratuity of £40. But with all this show, and with a wealthy congregation, the corporation, rich in productive property, was comparatively poor, and for many years its wants were pressing. Among the early bequests are £50 from Abraham Depuyster, £500 from Thomas Duncan, £100 from Joseph Murray for the poor of the parish, and £50 from Paul Richards for the same purpose. From the year 1709 the church conducted and supported a charity school. From 1715 it had assistant ministers, the first of whom were catechists to the children, to the Indians, and especially to the negro slaves, numbers of whom were baptized and became communicants in the same church with their owners, who were the wealthiest and most prominent people in the city. For, of course, till the Revolution it was the Established Church, and for sixty years the corporation, the vestry, the pew owners, or patentees, as they were called, included members of his Majesty's Council, Mayors, Recorders, Aldermen, Attorneys-General, and other city and provincial magnates. At the same time the selection of wardens and vestrymen extended to all classes and callings, limited only by reference to the fitness, intelligence, and probity of those who were appointed.

RECTOR BARCLAY'S INDUCTION.

After the death of William Vesey, the Rev. Henry Barclay, father of Thomas Barclay, the first British Consul-General in the United States, and grandfather of Henry Barclay, British Consul in this city, was appointed rector, and was inducted into office October 22, 1746. An induction in those days required considerable red tape. First, letters from the vestry to the Lord Bishop of London, and to the Venerable Society for the Propagation of the Gospel in Foreign Parts, and next to his Excellency, the Hon. George Clinton, Esq., Captain-General and Governor-in-Chief in and over the Province of New York and territories thereon depending, in America, and Vice-Admiral of the same, and Vice-Admiral of the red squadron of his Majesty's fleet. To all this the Governor, signing himself simply G. Clinton, sent letters of admission and institution, and a mandate for the induction of "Henry Barclay, Clerk, able to be Rector of the Parish Church of Trinity Church, in the City of New York;" and rector he was for eighteen years, until he died, October 28, 1764. He gives its name to Barclay Street. And here it may be noted that Chambers, Desbrosses, Duane, Jay, Laight, Moore, Morris, Murray, some of them opened through church property, all were named for wardens and vestrymen of Trinity, and the derivation of Rector, Church, and so on, is obvious.

ST. GEORGE'S BUILT.

A few years after the induction of Mr. Barclay, the congregation had so increased that, although there were 2,000 sittings in the church, it was resolved to build a chapel. This was the beginning of St. George's. The church lands were still unproductive, but in July, 1749, the corporation bought from Henry Beekman six lots fronting on Nassau and Fair (Beekman) streets. These lots cost £645, and their estimated value in 1871 was $500,000. Trinity issued bonds for £2,000 to build the chapel. Some subscriptions came in The Archbishop of Canterbury sent £10; Sir Peter Warren (for whom, and not for General Warren, as some suppose, Warren Street was named) contributed £100. Sir Peter built for his town residence the house, 1 Broadway, which some authorities insist was built by Archibald Kennedy, some time Collector of this port, and afterward the Scotch Earl of Cassilis; but Warren built it in 1742, long before Kennedy lived in it. St. George's was opened July 1, 1752. It was a neat, stone-faced edifice, 92 feet long, 72 feet wide, with a steeple 175 feet high, and was furnished with " a fine large bell, which cost £88 3s. 2d. sterling." In 1811 St. George's separated from Trinity, but in 1812 Trinity endowed it with twenty-four lots on Greenwich, Barclay, Murray, Warren, Chambers, and Reade streets, then annually renting for $3,000 for twenty-one years, and $3,200 for a second term of twenty-one years. In 1813 the endowments were increased by eight lots on Reade, Murray, and Chambers streets, then renting for $1,020 annually, and Trinity bought from Cornelius J. Bogert, for $3,125, a lot to enlarge St. George's church-yard, besides paying $5,104 for an iron railing and some repairs in the church. In 1814 the church was burned, and Trinity rebuilt it at a cost of $31,000, besides buying, for $14,000, the adjacent estate of Thomas Burling. The gifts of Trinity to St. George's in money and lots, at their then value, amounted to nearly a quarter of a million In 1752 Trinity corporation gave to King's (Columbia) College the tract of land between Murray and Barclay streets, and extending from Church Street to the river. More than thirty years ago, this ground was very safely estimated to be worth " perhaps $400,000."

TRINITY MUSIC IN THE LAST CENTURY.

The Rev. Samuel Auchmuty, born in Boston, educated at Harvard College, and ordained in London, who had been assistant to Mr. Barclay and catechist to the blacks, succeeded to the rectorship of Trinity, September 1, 1764. The estate of the corporation had become more productive, but its income was still comparatively limited. Yet, in 1763, it was resolved to set apart the lots on Broadway and Partition (Fulton) Street for another chapel, and to borrow £15,750 to build St Paul's This beautiful building, the only church in the city now standing on its original site, and presenting substantially the same unchanged appearance it did more than a century ago, was opened for service October 30, 1766, and Dr. Auchmuty preached the dedication sermon, and the Governor, Sir Henry Moore, by permission of the vestry, introduced a band of music. Trinity, now famous for its choral service, paid much attention to its music long ago. The New York *Gazette*, January 15, 1761, notes that " on Sunday last, at Trinity Church, was performed an Anthem on the death of his late sacred Majesty" (George II, who died October 25, 1760, and the news was long in coming), composed by Mr Tuckey, organ part by Mr. Harrison, solo part by Mr. Tuckey, and chorus by the boys of the Charity School." In 1762 Trinity sold its old organ gave 700 guineas for a new one, and advanced the salary of the organist to £18 per quarter. The *Gazette* of September 23, 1762, announced that " Mr William Tuckey has obligated himself to teach a sufficient number of persons to perform the Te Deum, and he desires all persons, from lads of 10 years old, to be speedy in their application, and he will receive all qualified until there are fifty voices in the chorus." This was the beginning of boy choirs and choral service in the city. It is pleasant to note, too, in the *Gazette*, February 10, 1772, that a considerable sum of money was collected and charity sermons preached on the previous Sunday at Trinity, St. George's, and St. Paul's for the relief of the prisoners in the "Goal" of the city, "they being in want, not only of firing, but even of the common necessaries of life."

TRINITY IN THE REVOLUTION.

In 1774 New York was a prosperous place of some 22,000 population. In that year John Adams on his way to the Congress in Philadelphia, stopped here, and the simple-minded Bostonian, never before beyond the limits of New England, was much impressed, as his diary records, by "the opulence and splendor of the city." But troublous times soon came, and first to the Church of England clergymen who were loyalists. On April 14, 1776, Washington arrived in the city and took command of the American army, which, with his re-enforcements, numbered 10,235 men. Dr. Auchmuty was in New Jersey, and his assistant, the Rev. Charles Inglis, was notified that Washington would be at Trinity on Sunday, and "would be glad if the prayers for the King and royal family were omitted," but Inglis paid no regard to it. Not long after, while he was officiating, a company of 150 men entered the church, drums beating, fifes playing, and with loaded guns and fixed bayonets. The congregation was terrified, and several women fainted. It was feared that when Mr Inglis read the collects for the King and royal family he would be fired at, but he went on with the service as usual and was undisturbed. By the unanimous request of the members of the church he consented to preach on May 17, appointed by Congress as a day of fasting and prayer, but he made peace and repentance his subject and disclaimed having anything to do with "politics." At length it was thought expedient, by such of the vestry as remained in town, to shut up the churches. On September 15, the King's troops returned. Six days afterward a fire destroyed about one-fourth of the city, including Trinity Church, its rectory, its two charity schoolhouses, the whole costing £22,200, besides the loss to the corporation of £536 annual rent of 246 lots, on which the tenant's buildings were burnt. Poor Dr. Auchmuty forced his way back on foot and at night, through the lines, and raked the rubbish of the ruins, but found nothing valuable, except the church plate and his own. The registers of baptisms, marriages, and burials from the foundation of the parish were destroyed, and much family history was thus lost. Dr. Auchmuty preached his last sermon in St. Paul's, and two days afterward fell sick and died March 4, 1777. He was buried in the chancel of St. Paul's, and was succeeded as rector of Trinity parish March 20, by the Rev. Charles Inglis, who resigned November 1, 1783, just before the evacuation of the city by the British troops, and afterward became Bishop of Nova Scotia. He was a loyalist to the last, and one of the last loyalists in Trinity parish.

NINE RECTORS IN 182 YEARS.

The Legislature, April 17, 1784, passed "An act for making such alterations in the charter of the corporation of Trinity Church, so as to make it more conformable to the Constitution of the State." Robert R.

Livingston and James Duane were appointed wardens, and the vestry included Francis Lewis, one of the signers of the Declaration of Independence, Richard Morris, William Duer, Robert Troup, John Stevens, Anthony Lispenard, John Rutherford, and other historic names; and, April 22, "agreeable to the desire of the Whig Episcopalians," the Rv. Samuel Provoost was inducted rector. He was one of the nine in the first class graduated, in 1759, from King's (Columbia) College, which th n was a frame building in Trinity church-yard. He was consecrated Bishop of New York in 1787, and in 1789 was chosen chaplain to the United States Senate. On the day of Washington's inauguration he preached before the President and all the dignitaries in St. Paul's Chapel. The second Trinity Church building was erected on the site of the former one in 1788. Long afterward the inscribed tablet on the corner-stone was discovered in the church-yard, at some distance from the building, broken in two pieces, and in 1877 was set in the wall of the monument room of the church. Bishop Provoost was rector till he resigned December 22, 1800, and on that day the Rev. Benjamin Moore succeeded him. He was consecrated Bishop of New York in 1801, but continued rector of Trinity till he died, February 27, 1816. In 1803–7 St John's Chapel was built on the east side of Hudson Square, then a wild and marshy spot, with great ponds in the neighborhood—the resort of sportsmen in the summer and skaters in the winter. The chapel, which has undergone alteration and enlargement three times, originally cost nearly $173,000, and the organ, ordered just before the war of 1812 at an expense of $6,000, was captured by a British cruiser, and it cost $2,000 more to redeem it. John Henry Hobart who was graduated at Princeton, and who had been assistant minister since 1801, and assistant Bishop since May 29, 1811, was inducted March 11, 1816, and continued rector till his death September 12, 1830 His remains rest in the chancel. The Rev. William Berrian was rector from October 11, 1830, to his death, November 1, 1862. The present rector, the Rev Morgan Dix, D. D., was inducted November 11, 1862. Thus, in a period of 182 years, there have been but nine rectors of Trinity.

THE PRESENT CHURCH CONSECRATED.

In 1839 Trinity Church was pulled down, and the present splendid structure was begun by the architect, Mr Richard Upjohn. It was completed in seven years, at a cost, all told, including clock, chimes and organ, of $358,629.94—probably less than one-half the sum that would be required to build such a church now. It was consecrated on Ascension Day, May 21, 1846, by Bishop McCoskry of Michigan, and the procession, which included more than 150 Doctors of Divinity in surplices, started from Bunkers, which was then (it sounds queerly enough now), a fashionable hotel at 39 Broadway. Among the many old citizens present was John P. Groshon, who attended the opening of St Paul's in 1766, and, stranger still, in the audience was Mrs. Ann Livingston, who was at the consecration of the second edifice, and was baptized in the first. The reredos, erected in 1877 by Mr. John Jacob Astor and his brother, William, as a memorial to their father, cost them about $50,000, and at the same time the corporation expended some $40,000 in re-decorating the chancel, and building new robing rooms in the rear, Trinity Chapel, in Twenty-Fifth Street. built in 1851–56, cost $230,000 St. Chrysostom's Chapel, in Thirty-Ninth Street, built in 1869, cost for land $38,000 and buildings $60,000. St. Augustine's, in Houston Street, consecrated November 30, 1877, cost $260,000, and to build this fine church the corporation borrowed $200,000—its only debt to-day. St. Cornelius, on Governor's Island, which Trinity has supported since 1868, and supplied with a clergyman, who also acts as post chaplain, is included in the chapels of the corporation.

TRINITY'S GIFTS.

In the early history of the parish it was itself in need of assistance, but almost as soon as its property became productive it began to give it away. Since 1745 its gifts to other churches, in money, lots, communion plate, fonts, pulpits, carpets, bells, and everything that can enter into the construction and decoration of churches, are innumerable. At one time it gave £200 towards ground for a negro cemetery. In 1786 it granted three lots in Robinson Street (now Park place) for the use of the senior pastors of the Presbyterian congregations in the city. Besides the grants already noted, to Columbia College and St George's Church, it granted in 1795-98 to St. Mark's, built on land given by the Stuyvesants, besides some $20,000 in money, lots estimated thirty years ago to be worth $131,000; to Grace Church, in 1804-11, $120,000; Christ Church, $75,000; St. Thomas's, $32,300; St. Luke's, $55,800; All Saints', $31,500; Ascension, $15,500; St Philip's, $18,000; and to churches, colleges, and what not, all over the State and elsewhere, loans, gifts and grants, which, in 1847, were estimated at $2,000,000. The corporation was then cumbered with a debt of $440,000, and as most of its lots had been leased out at an early period on mere nominal rents, the annual revenue from ground rents, pew rents, and all other sources had never in any one year up to that time reached $58,000. The building of Trinity Chapel carried the debt of the corporation up to $668,000. In 1857 the deficits in revenue for ten years amounted to $273,597.35, and in the same time the corporation had contributed and given away outside of the parish $288,141 05. The deficits were met by the sale of real estate and the consequent consumption of the principal. Gen. John A Dix, a vestryman since 1849, and a warden and the comptroller of the corporation since 1876, was the first to suggest measures to put a stop to the general giving away of everything to everybody. In 1868 the sale of St John's Park to the Hudson River Railway Company, and about the same time the falling in of the Astor and Lispenard leases, enabled Trinity to wipe out its debt.

THE PARISH'S INCOME AND EXPENSES.

The property of the corporation, which common rumor makes cover pretty much the whole of lower New York, west of Broadway, and to be worth from seventy to one hundred millions, consists actually of 750 lots which, in 1877, yielded an income of $456,786 45, less than the legal interest on seven million dollars, and the whole property, except the ground occupied by seven churches, four schoolhouses, four cemeteries, a rectory, an infirmary, and a few vacant lots, was productive. In 1878 the income was a little less. The corporation is about to pull down a large building on the corner of King and Greenwich streets, and erect tenement houses on the site. For this purpose it will borrow money, as it now sells no lots, except in very rare instances, to accommodate adjacent owners who wish to enlarge their premises. Occasionally tenants have old houses which they neglect and let go to ruin, and these sometimes the corporation buys and puts in order to be rented.

Out of its revenue, say $450,000, the corporation pays city taxes, which, in 1877 were more than $100,500, besides considerable assessments. It wholly supports its seven churches, of which three are entirely free, two nearly free, and of the few pews rented in Trinity the highest brings but $85 a year. Besides its own churches, schools, infirmary, and sundry charities and societies, it supports wholly or in part eighteen more churches in the city, the principal of which are St. Luke's in Hudson Street, which is allowed $10,000 a year, and All Saints', at the corner of Henry and Scammel streets, which draws $6,000 a year. The total of such allowances outside of the parish amounted in 1877 to $47,660.19, and in 1878 to $44,971.22. Its infirmary costs $7,200, and beds at St. Luke's Hospital $2,000 a year. The corporation expends its entire revenue in purposes for which the trust from its foundation was designed, and does not hoard one dollar.

CHAPTER IX.

ESTATES IN CHANCERY.

ESTATE OF JOHN TURNER.

WE have had repeated inquiries respecting the above Estate, and as it is seldom the Treasury have occasion to administer to such a large amount of personalty, it may be of interest for many to know the history of the deceased, and of the litigation to which his intestacy gave rise.

In January, 1787, a Mr. John Turner, then a young man, entered as a junior clerk in the Ordnance Office in the Tower, at a salary of £70 a year. In April, 1787, he resigned that office and became clerk to the Sun Fire Office, where, in 1805 he rose to be chief clerk, and retired in 1825 on a pension of £200 a year. From 1807 to 1824 he lodged with Mrs. Derusier, at 120, Great Russell Street. In that year he removed to 13, Upper Thornhaugh Street (now Huntley Street), where he died on the 31st January, 1842, having, on the 21st March, 1841, been found a lunatic. He left a considerable fortune, estimated at the time from £80,000 to £100,000, the result of successful speculation, and more especially from the fortunate purchase of a lottery ticket.

After his death advertisements were inserted calling for his Next of Kin, but, none appearing, Mr. George Maule, Solicitor to the Treasury, obtained letters of Administration on behalf of the Crown, and the balance of the property, after payment of the debts and certain legacies left by an imperfect testamentary paper, was paid over to the Consolidated Fund. Some time after this payment, certain persons filed a Bill against Mr. Maule, claiming the property as the lawful Next of Kin.

They stated the Intestate to have been the son of John and Elizabeth Turner, married at Badwell Ash, near Burry, in 1755, that he was baptized 14th January, 1763, in the name of "Theophilus." He had three brothers and four sisters, two of whom survived him. When about sixteen years of age "Theophilus," then residing with his father, who was in the service of the Rev. Dr. Ord, at Farnham St. Martin's, left that place for some offense he had committed. It was proven that he was at school there.

No further trace of him is found, but the Plaintiff says he is identical with the "John Turner" who entered as a clerk in the Tower. The evidence showed that he had left his home, and his family understood Dr. Ord intended to bring him up to the sea; that he was called "Jack the Sailor," having been to sea for a short time, and the Claimant supposed that Dr. Ord had obtained for him the clerkship in the Tower. The Plaintiff produced also full evidence of statements made by Mr. John Turner, whilst a clerk in the Sun Fire Office, as to his early history, which showed that he was the "Theophilus" the son of Dr Ord's gardener. At his office he would say nothing as to his early life, but occasionally he fell in with persons of his own class with whom he would be more communicative. The evidence of two of the witnesses to whom Turner had told his history was to the effect that he (Turner), lived in Suffolk in his early years, and left it in dungeon with his relations there.

The Court of Chancery gave judgment in favor of the Plaintiff, and ordered Mr. Maule to pay into Court, before the 1st May, 1849, the sum of £52,173 2s. 11d., being the net balance of deceased's property. The gross amount realized from his estate was £60,430.

THE MANGINI-BROWN ESTATE.

It is not often that persons have wealth suddenly thrust upon them; and the five Italians who discovered themselves to be jointly entitled to more than £200,000 cannot be looked upon as otherwise than exceedingly fortunate persons. The money in question was the whole of the residuary estate of an aged lady named Maria Mangini Brown, who died in 1871 in Hertford Street, Mayfair, whose parentage and possessions we propose to shortly discuss. Mrs. Brown was the daughter of one Antonio Mangini, better known in England as Anthony Mangin, who filled various different positions in life, and subsequently towards the latter part of the last century found himself Agent and Consul-General in London of the Ligurian or Genoese Republic, one of those struggling states practically obliterated by the First Napolean. He was a commercial man who amassed much wealth; and married an Englishwoman who pre-deceased him. Mangini himself died in 1803, leaving the bulk of his property to his daughter Maria, who is supposed to have married one Aquila Brown, by whom she had a daughter who died before her and left descendants who, unluckily for themselves, are unable to produce any certificate or other evidence of a marriage between Brown and their grandmother. All Maria Mangini Brown's issue, therefor, being either extinct or shut out, it became necessary on her death, in 1871, to seek her Next of Kin from among Consul Mangini's descendants, she not having left any valid will. None of these being forthcoming, the Treasury administered to her estate and assumed possession of her accumulated wealth, subsequently paying it into the Court of Chancery. Here, then, was a wide field for claimants to come from. There was no reason to suppose Antonio Mangini illegitimate, and he must therefore have Next of Kin in existence somewhere. They came eventually, and were no less than thirteen in number, of whom one, a Mrs. Lane, actually got a Chancery decree made in her favor, ordering the payment to her alone of nearly the whole of the £200,000. Before, however, she could enjoy the fruits of her judgment, certain Italians named Freccia, proved themselves nearer of kin than Mrs. Lane to the defunct Consul, and got her judgment reversed in their favor. Two of these Freccias received their apportioned shares out of court, and retired to enjoy them to their native land; but before the remaining three received theirs, a Madame Sturla put in a claim on behalf of herself and four others, alleging that they in turn were armed with evidence which would prove that they could supplant the Freccias just as the Freccias had ousted the unfortunate Mrs. Lane. They did not deny that the Freccia family were Next of Kin to one Antonio Mangini who was born at St. Ilario, near Genoa, in 1735, but they asserted that Consul Mangini was quite another person of precisely the same name, who was born at Quarto, also near Genoa, in 1744, and from whom they were lineally descended. To support these different views of the case evidence was produced which took Vice-Chancellor Malins fourteen days to hear, and upwards of 2,000 pages of printed documents were filed by the different parties. The case lay in a nut-shell, but the kernel was difficult to extract. A strong point in the Freccia's favor as against the Sturlas was that on Consul Mangini's death in 1803 the ancestors of the former family asserted themselves to be his heirs, and instituted abortive Chancery proceedings for declaring Mrs. Brown illegitimate, and themselves entitled to her father's property. It was thought that the Quarto Manginis would have been the first to do this had they really been of kin; but it was never satisfactorily shown that their Counsel's contention—viz., that they never knew that any proceedings at all were going on—was a just one. The question then depended entirely on the identity of the Consul, as the chains of representation of the two families with their two namesake ancestors were unbroken. We have not space to go into the evidence, which was of the usual conflicting character. Among other proof the Sturla family relied to a great extent on a document relating to the Consul's appointment, discovered in the Genoese State Archives, which they alleged bore on their view of the case; but the Chief Clerk, to whom the matter was referred in the first instance, found that it had at some period been tampered with. This becoming known to the Italian Government they required the paper to be returned to them, so it was not available for the Vice-Chancellor's inspection. Ultimately, after as little delay as was compatible with the greatness of the case, the Vice-Chancellor decided that the assertion of Madam Sturla and her co-claimants as representatives of the Quarto Mangini family had failed, and that the Ligurian Consul having been the Antonio Mangini born at St. Ilario, the Freccias were entitled to the £200,000 left by his daughter. This judgment was delivered in his absence, and his reasons for it have yet to be made known. Be they what they may, however, the not-unsuspicious circumstance connected with the authenticity of Madam Sturla's documentary evidence, and the means, which it is admitted, were used to raise money to conduct her case, seems to point to the fact that had it been more just it would have been commenced sooner, and had she and her co-heirs been properly entitled they would not have needed a sort of joint-stock company, formed in Genoa, to raise funds for prosecuting it. The Vice-Chancellor dismissed the Sturlas' summons to vary his Chief Clerk's certificate, and also their action, with costs against them in each case. Whether the unsuccessful parties will appeal is not yet ascertained, and seems at least doubtful. Much stronger evidence will be needed to upset the case of their more fortunate opponents.

GAZETTE OF NOVEMBER, 1880.—It will be remembered that this celebrated case of unclaimed property which has now gone from the lowest to the highest of our Equity tribunals, was recently decided definitely by the House of Lords, against the appellants. A brief recapitulation of the facts of the case may be of interest. The deceased, Maria Mangini-Brown, an elderly widow lady, died at her residence, No. 28, Hertford Street, Mayfair, on 21st December, 1871, leaving about a quarter of a million sterling. All her descendants were either deceased or shut out, and as she made no valid testamentary disposition, the Crown took possession of her estate. Claimants were not long in coming forward, and ultimately the true Next of Kin of the deceased were found in the persons of a family named

Freccia. They obtained a decree in their favor, and a portion of the fund was paid out to two of the claimants. Very soon after this, however, certain other persons, among them a Mrs. Sturla, came forward, and asserted that they were the true Next of Kin of the intestate, whose father was not, as asserted by the Freccias, born at St. Ilario, near Genoa, in 1735, but another person, born at Quarto, not far from that town, in 1744. The question was one of identity, and although every authority before whom the case was brought, decided that the St Ilario Mangini was the real "Simon Pure," the disappointed Sturlas appealed from every decision until the case was decided against them by the highest judicial tribunal in the Realm

The case of Mrs Sturla and her co-heirs depended, as has been already stated, on a document purporting to have been obtained from the State Archives office in Genoa, and which had been tampered with at some period or other. They have not only failed in their attempt to prove themselves what they are not, but are also saddled with all the costs of the former decisions against them; they cannot even receive that condolence in their misfortune to which they would have been entitled had not questionable practices been resorted to in order to strengthen their claim.

CATHERINE CHAPMAN.—ESTATE.

The litigation to which the above intestacy has given rise, has been the subject of discussion in the county of Kent and elsewhere for some time past.

The intelligence that an heir was wanted to an estate of one Chapman, worth about £1,200 a year, is, of course, very interesting to all bearing that name; and the happy news did not long remain a privileged subject of gossip among the people of that county It was soon known over the country, and, as is usual in such cases, was quickly taken up by our American cousins, who, according as it suited their whims or fancies, added or subtracted particulars as to the family, taking care in all cases to increase considerably the original amount—in one instance to an incredible figure. The estate is situated between Ashford and Faversham, and the last possessors were two old ladies, Elizabeth and Catherine Chapman The former died in October, 1863, and bequeathed her moiety to the tenants, the other moiety was the property of Catherine Chapman, a lunatic, who died at Periton Court, Westwell, Kent, on 9th November, 1869, a spinster, and intestate, and was undisposed of. This is the subject of dispute Advertisements were inserted in 1863, by the Commissioners in Lunacy, calling for the heirs of Catherine Chapman, with a view of their being appointed committees of the lunatic. Inquiries and researches were made into the Chapman pedigree, but the result was such a multiplicity of Chapmans that, owing to the faulty way in which the old parish registers were kept, it was almost impossible to distinguish the different branches of the family. There were, in several instances, at the same time, more than one Chapman of the same Christian name in the same neighborhood, and of about the same age.

Col. Deedes, as lord of the manor, claimed the estate as an escheat in default of heirs; but, after two trials, the suit was decided against him, there being, indeed, no lack of heirs. The case came on in March last, before the Lord Chief Justice and a special jury, against the tenants of a farm in the parish of Great Chart, Kent, and forming part of the estate. Our space will not permit us to give particulars of the claimant's pedigree.

ESTATES IN CHANCERY.

Suffice it to say that the plaintiff in this instance claimed on the maternal line, as a descendant of the fifth generation of Susan Manooch, also married to a Chapman, the sister of Martha, wife of William Chapman, of Westwell, who died in 1748, and who was the great-grandfather of the intestate.

The defendants assert that the rightful heir is Thomas Elvey, a descendant of William Chapman, of Badlesmere, whom they state to be identical with the paternal ancestor of the intestate who died in 1748.

The difficulty was to determine who was the heir from the number of claimants, for, as Mr. Hawkins observed at a previous trial, there were about 450 relatives of John Chapman living about the neighborhood, where the Chapmans had been settled for centuries. The jury found in favor of the defendants, and another action must still be brought to determine who is entitled.

ESTATE OF RICHARD THOMAS.

Those who have had occasion to search the parochial registers in this country previous to the General Registration Act of 1837, cannot fail to have been struck by the extraordinary carelessness with which these records were kept. In some parishes the baptisms, marriages and burials were indiscriminately entered without any attempt at regularity, and in others in the form of a diary. In some instances even the facts have been altogether omitted to be entered, the certificate granted at the time remaining the only evidence. From many registers leaves have been destroyed and names cut out, and in some parishes whole volumes are wanting. It is but fair to state that in the towns they were naturally more carefully attended to.

Lay registration being unknown previous to 1837, it is frequently very difficult, if not impossible, to obtain certificates, and it is necessary then to have recourse to other means—family Bibles, wills, etc. We are in this respect, a striking contrast to our neighbors across the Channel, who have always attached the greatest importance to the preservation of these records. The way in which their registers are kept, and the full particulars they afford, render the compilation of any pedigree comparatively easy. A case came recently before Vice-Chancellor Sir Richard Malins which illustrates the impossibility of sometimes producing certificates and showing the secondary evidence which is admitted in such cases. A Mr. Richard Thomas died recently intestate as to the residue of his estate. An administration suit was instituted in the Chancery Division, and as is usual in such matters, a chief clerk was directed to inquire who were the testator's Next of Kin. He certified that there were twelve nephews and nieces of the testator who were entitled to share equally in the distribution of his residuary estate. Amongst these he included the five children of one Jonathan Mickleburgh, of Crediton, and Elizabeth, his wife, formerly Elizabeth Thomas, spinster, the sister of the testator. The other Next of Kin alleged that these five persons were illegitimate, their parents never having been married, and that, consequently, they were not entitled to share in distribution to the residuary estate of the testator. No actual evidence, either positive or negative was adduced in respect of this marriage. From the year 1804 down to the date of Mrs. Mickleburgh's death in 1835, the parties in question had lived together as man and wife, and were acknowledged and received as such by their friends and in society. Two old inhabitants of Crediton, stated that within their memory, Mr. and Mrs. Mickleburgh had always been considered by the inhabitants as man and wife. Moreover the testator himself believed his sister to have been properly married and left record of his belief by his will, in which a legacy is left to his niece, one of the daughters of his sister, Elizabeth Mickleburgh. The Vice-Chancellor observed that where two people had lived together for thirty years, during the whole of which time they were received in society as husband and wife, it would be very hard if their family were to be bastardized twenty-four years after the death of the survivor. In conclusion, his lordship said he should found his decision on the broad principle essential to the welfare of society, that where two persons have lived together for many years as husband and wife, have been universally received as such, and have had their children baptized in the usual manner, they should be considered as married. Accordingly, the Vice-Chancellor decided that the children of Jonathan and Elizabeth Mickleburgh are legitimate and entitled to rank as Next of Kin on the estate of the testator, Richard Thomas.

RE GOODMAN'S TRUSTS.

This appeal from a decision of the Master of the Rolls raises a very important question—whether the word children in the Statute for the distribution of Intestate Estates includes only children legitimate according to English law, or includes those who are legitimate according to the law of the country in which the parents are domiciled at the time of their birth, but illegitimate according to English law. The facts are briefly these. Miss Rachael Goodman, an English lady, died in London on the 15th March, 1878, intestate as to one-third of her estate. All her brothers and sisters had died in her life time, two only leaving issue who survived their aunt, viz.. Isaac Goodman, who left four children, and respecting whose rights as four of the Next of Kin there is no question, and Lyon Goodman who, according to English law, left but one legitimate child This Lyon Goodman lived in England with one Charlotte Smith, and by her had three illegitimate children who, being born in England, have raised no claim In 1820 he took up his abode in Amsterdam, and continued to reside in that city until 1826. Thither he was followed by Charlotte Smith and the three children. In 1821 a fourth child, named Hannah, was born to them. In the following year he married Charlotte Smith, and after the marriage he had by her another child, Mary. By the Dutch laws all children born before the marriage are legitimated by the marriage. Hannah Goodman, now Mrs Pieret, is to all intents and purposes legitimate in Holland, her native country, and the question in this matter arose, whether she is to be considered legitimate according to the law of England, and consequently entitled, as one of the Next of Kin, to a share in that portion of the estate as to which her late aunt died intestate. The Master of the Rolls held that the deceased, being a British subject domiciled in this country, her estate being administered according to English law, that such only can be considered as Next of Kin who are legitimate according to the laws of England, and not according to the laws of the country where the parents are domiciled at the time of the child's birth.

From this decision Mrs. Pieret appealed. The case was argued on the 4th of March, when their Lordships took time to consider their judgment, which was given at considerable length on the 13th inst. Lord Justice Lush was of opinion that the judgment of the Master of the Rolls was right, and ought to be affirmed, but Lords Justices Cotton and James being of a contrary opinion, the judgment was consequently reversed, in accordance with the views of the majority of the Court.

It is a recognized fact that the estate of a deceased person is distributed by the English Courts according to the laws of the country in which he is domiciled; and had Lyon Goodman, being domiciled in Holland, died intestate, his personal property in England would have been distributed according to Dutch law—that is, Mrs Pieret would have been considered as one of his lawful children. This fact was admitted on both sides; but the case before the Court was the administration of an estate according to English law. Lords Justices Cotton and James were of opinion that, in considering the legitimacy of a person born in a foreign country to rank as Next of Kin on an English estate, the law of England will so far depart from its own recognized rule, and consider as legitimate a person who is so in his native country, although illegitimate according to English law. Upon this point Lord Justice Lush differed from his colleagues. It would certainly appear an inconsistency that Mrs. Pieret should be considered in this said country as legitimate and entitled to succeed to her father's estate, and as illegitimate and debarred from all share in her aunt's estate; but English law affords many examples of such incongruities, the present decision being among the number, as, although Mrs Pieret is declared legitimate, and entitled to succeed to personalty as a collateral, she would be excluded from any share in real estate as illegitimate, according to the judgment of the House of Lords in "Birtwhistle v. Bardill." Our space is too limited to allow us to follow the arguments of the learned judges in this case; we can only briefly notice the facts. The judgments on both sides of the question are very forcible and evenly balanced; so much so that whichever side is considered first appears to be irrefutable by the force of its reasoning. Such could hardly be otherwise than the case, when we have such authorities as the Master of Rolls and Lord Justice Lush on the one side, and Lords Justices Cotton and James on the other. The case may yet be taken to a higher tribunal for final revision, and under the circumstances, as a matter of public interest, we may express the hope that such may be the case, although in the interest of the litigants, we should hope that it may rest where it is. The amount really involved by this question is not considerable (some £3,000, we believe), and we are afraid the recognized Next of Kin in the first instance will, even if successful on a further appeal, not reap much benefit from its decision.

ESTATE OF THE LATE MR. PATERSON, OF KILMARNOCK, N. B.

The administration of this estate was made the subject of debate in the House or Commons, attention being called thereto by Colonel Alexander, the member for South Ayrshire, and the discussion that ensued is fully reported in the *Times* of 27th June, 1877. Mr. Paterson, of Jamaica, having acquired a large fortune, bequeathed one-half to his sister and her children and the other half to his illegitimate son, expressly stipulating that should his said son die without heirs, his share should not go to the testator's sister or heir at-law, but to a distant cousin of his own.

The illegitimate son came to Scotland, where he lived a secluded life, and spent but little of his large income. He appears to have been most eccentric, sought to conceal his property, and was not on friendly terms with his father's relatives. He died in January, 1874, intestate, leaving personal property amounting to about £40,000, and being a bastard, the Treasury took possession of his estate.

Colonel Alexander claims that his constituent Mr. Paterson, of Montgomery, be put in the same position as he would have occupied had the deceased, his cousin-german been legitimate.

Mr. W. H. Smith, on behalf of the Treasury, submits that the law gives the property to the State, leaving a discretionary power to the Treasury as to its distribution. Although in this case no will had been produced, there is no evidence that one does not exist, as in another case a will had turned up, and the principal was claimed together with 4 per cent interest after fifty years. Several parties claim an interest in this estate, the solicitors alleging that the intestate intended leaving them a sum of nearly £30,000 which had stood in their names for the last twenty years. The Bailies of Kilmarnock represent it would be carrying out the wishes of the deceased if the money were given for the public objects of that town The minister of the High Church at Kilmarnock, confirmed the statement that the deceased entertained an antipathy against his relations, and he inferred that the deceased probably intended to leave him a legacy. The law, however, gave the estate to the Crown, and the relations had already been provided for to the extent of one-half the original property.

It was stated in the course of the inquiry that the property of intestate bastards was formerly administered to in Scotland by the old Scotch Lords of the Treasury, then by the Barons of the Exchequer, and since 1833 by the Lords of the Treasury Prior to 1836, in Scotland a bastard was unable to make a will, even in favor of his own children, his estate being dealt with by the Crown. The following is the general principal by which the Treasury is guided in dealing with the estates of intestate bastards, as stated by the Secretary to the Treasury in answer to a question by Mr. Grieve, and reported in the *Times* of the 24th February:—"First of all the claims of any individual are dealt with. An inquiry is made whether there is any evidence, either by an informal will or otherwise of an intention to make provision for that individual. Then they consider further whether a strong claim exists on the part of individuals with regard to whom there is no such evidence. Then they proceed to consider what would have been the disposal of the property supposing the deceased had been legitimate, and they follow the principles laid down by the law for the distribution of property in the case of legitimate persons who die intestate"

The resolution of Colonel Alexander was negatived by 197 to 135, showing a majority of 62

We have read with much interest the remarks of the hon. members on behalf of the Treasury, and especially of the disinterested way in which it appears that their Lordships distribute the funds of estates in their charge. We fully admit the great responsibility incumbent upon them, but we submit that where their Lordships deal with millions of the public money, they might be more communicative in their replies respecting estates under their control (in most cases amounting only to a few hundred pounds), and not endeavor to preclude inquiries by short, evasive replies which frequently deter claimants from establishing their title, and often inspire the public with the idea that the British Government consider "Might as Right."

CHAPTER X.

LOST AT SEA.

THE history of the "Lutine" is remarkable, not merely for the amount of specie got from time to time out of the wreck, but from the fact that, although the wreck occurred in the year 1799, salving operations have been continued to the present time. The facts are as follows:—On October 9, 1799 the "Lutine" of 32 guns, sailed from Yarmouth Roads with several passengers, and an immense quantity of treasure, for the Texel. In the course of the day it came on to blow a heavy gale, which continued the whole night; the ship drove on the outer bank of the Fly Island passage, and was lost. The darkness of the night and violence of the gale precluded all possibility of giving her the least assistance. At daylight not a vestige of the vessel was to be seen; she had gone to pieces, and every soul, excepting two, had perished. The money she had on board is said to have amounted to £140,000.

Conflicting accounts of the foregoing disaster appeared in the newspapers, and there was considerable difference of opinion as to the value of the lost specie; the lowest estimate is that given above, the highest £3,000,000. The most vague and contradictory statements were promulgated as to the contents of the "Lutine"; some writers stated that the Crown Jewels of Holland formed part of her cargo; others that the money to pay the British troops (then in Holland) was on board; while others insisted that the treasure was consigned by English to Hamburg merchants; each and all of these statements contained a certain substratum of truth. It appeared that the treasure had been consigned to Hamburg by certain mercantile firms, having been first very heavily insured in various offices On receipt of a certificate of the loss of the vessel, the underwriters promptly paid the claims. Salvage operations were then commenced, and in about eighteen months £80,000, or thereabouts rewarded the efforts of the divers and others engaged in the enterprise. The Dutch Government, by reason of the wreck having occurred on their coast, took two-thirds of the specie found, the remaining one-third going to the finders. Some silver spoons and a sword were among the articles found.

In 1814 further attempts were made to get at the wreck, which had become deeply imbedded in the sand, but with very indifferent success; The results of seven years' toil (1814-1821) being the recovery of only a few pieces of silver. In 1822 a Company was formed for the purpose of prosecuting a further search for the lost treasure, the Dutch Government by agreement taking half the amount recovered, in consideration of a sum of money advanced to the Company. Several thousand pounds were spent in diving operations, but the result was absolutely *nil*. Next, *Lloyd's* appeared on the scene, and after much negotiation the Dutch Government agreed to hand over half of any further salvage recovered to *Lloyd's*. From 1822 to 1857 spasmodic efforts were made to fish up further specie, but the result was merely anxiety and vexation of spirit to those engaged in the venture. In 1857 a further agreement was entered into between the Dutch Government and *Lloyd's*, and from 1857 to 1861 (sixty years after the wreck took place) great good fortune attended the efforts of the searchers, about £25,000 being the amount of *Lloyd's* share; some interesting relics were also found, including part of the ship's rudder, and her bell. By the destruction of the Royal Exchange by fire, in 1838, the books and papers relating to *Lloyd's* were lost, and the original underwriters of the "Lutine" cannot now be traced.

In 1871 the Society of *Lloyd's* applied for a special act of Parliament, the preamble of that Act concisely recites the history of the negotiations between *Lloyd's* and the Dutch Government, and states that the Committee of *Lloyd's* had in hand a sum of about £25,000, resulting from the salving operations aforesaid

The following extracts from that Act will be interesting to claimants:
"Section 34 provides that the Society of *Lloyd's* may from time to time aid in or undertake in such manner as to them seems fit the discovery, recovery, protection, and restoration, or other disposal of property before or after the passing of the Act, wrecked, sunk, lost, or abandoned, or found, or recovered in or beneath the sea, or on the shore at home or abroad,"

"Section 35 provides that the Society may from time to time do or join in doing all such lawful things as they think expedient, with a view to further salving from the wreck of the "Lutine", and hold, receive, and apply for that purpose so much of the money to be received by means of salving therefrom . . . . and the net money produced thereby, and the said sum of, £25,000 shall be applied for the purposes connected with shipping or marine insurance, according to a scheme to be prepared by the Society and confirmed by Order in Council on the recommendation of the Board of Trade after or subject to such public notice to claimants of any part of the money aforesaid to come in, and such investigation of claims and such barring of claims not made or not proved, and such reservation of rights (if any) as the Board of Trade thinks fit."

Possibly in years to come a violent storm may arise, and the bed of sand now covering the wreck be again shifted, thus affording scope for further diving operations

A parallel case to that of the "Lutine" was that of the "Thetis", a British frigate, wrecked on the coast of Brazil in 1830, with £162,000 in bullion on board. The hull went to pieces, leaving the treasure upon the bottom in five or six fathoms water. The Admiral on the Brazil Station and the captains and crew of four sloops-of-war were engaged for eighteen months in recovering the treasure. The service was attended with great skill, labor, and danger, and four lives were lost. A good deal of litigation was the result, as disputes arose between the parties as to the amount of reward for the salvors. The Court of Admiralty awarded £17,000, the Privy Council £29,000, and £25,800 for expenses.

Some years ago a Company, styled "The Wreck Recovery and Salvage Company (Limited)," was launched under distinguished patronage, for carrying on the business of "Ship Raisers and Cargo Salvors" It had however but a brief existence

The following Advertisement contains materials for an interesting tale of the sea :—

"Robert Fleurian, otherwise Florio, who, in 1792, went as steward on board a brig, which sailed from Wapping bound for the West Indies or America, and was compelled soon after to put into the port of Liverpool for repairs, where she lay up for some time. During such time the said Robert Flurian wrote to his brother in London, saying he thought he should not wait for the vessel, but get another ship, since which time nothing has been heard of him, nor of the said vessel, but it is supposed she sailed from Liverpool and was lost at sea, and that the said Robert Florio perished . . . He would, if now living, be entitled to certain property under the will of his mother, or if he is dead, his wife or children would have an interest in such property."

Some five and twenty years ago a whole family were lost in the wreck of an emigrant vessel. The following facts, taken from a report of the case, show conclusively that loss of life at sea may give rise to family complications and years of litigation :—

John Tulley, by his Will, bequeathed all his real and personal Estate to trustees for the benefit of his only child, Mary Ann, till she attained 21, or marriage, then to pay her £500, then, for her separate use, during life; on her decease, to her children. Testator died in 1832. In June, 1834, Mary Ann Tulley married John Underwood. Three children were born unto them—a daughter and two sons. By Orders of the Court of Chancery, the trust estate on the death of John Tulley's first executors became vested in the appellant, William Wing, and the respondent, Richard Angrave.

On October 4, 1853, Mary Ann Underwood duly made her will, and disposed of the property she took under her father's will, thus :—"to my husband, John Underwood, his heirs, etc., subject to the estates and interests of my children therein, under the will of my late father; and in case my said husband should die in my lifetime, then I bequeath the said hereditaments, etc., to William Wing . . . ." Her husband and Wing were named executors. John Underwood, on the same 4th day of October, 1853, executed his will, and thereby devised and bequeathed all his real and personal estate to the appellant upon trust for his wife, Mary Ann Underwood, her heirs, etc., absolutely. Then came the following proviso :—"and in case my said wife shall die in my lifetime, then I direct that my said real and personal estate shall be held by my said trustee, upon trust, for my three children, to be equally divided among them; and, in case all of them shall die under the age of twenty-one . . . . then to the said William Wing, his heirs, etc., absolutely." Testator appointed his wife and said William Wing, executrix and executor.

On October 13, 1853, John Underwood and his wife, with their three children, embarked together in the "Dalhousie," an emigrant ship, bound for Australia, and on the 19th of the same month the ship was wrecked off Beachy Head, and the father, mother, and three children were all drowned at sea. Now the complications began. Wing proved the wills of both John Underwood and his wife, Mrs. Underwood, senior, in January, 1854, took out Letters of Administration to the goods of her granddaughter Catherine, who was seen alive after her parents had perished. She also filed a bill against Wing, praying for an account of the personal estate of John Underwood, and of the separate estate of his wife, and that her own right as administratrix of Catherine in the residue of the two personal estates might be ascertained and declared. The bill alleged that in the events which had happened no beneficial right in the personal property vested in Wing,

Evidence was taken on the subject of the deaths of Mr. and Mrs. Underwood and their children, and a medical man explained the process of drowning. In his opinion, assuming the four persons in question to have been in a continued state of submersion, death would take place in the case of all in two minutes at the outside. Two persons, both in health, being totally submerged at the same moment, asphyxia would ensue in the case of each at the same instant, as nearly as he could conceive. A person of seventy would live as long in such circumstances as a person of thirty, —assuming them both to be in health,—and a female as long as a male, and a weak man as long as a strong one. He could not, medically or physiologically, give any opinion whether Mr. or Mrs Underwood was the survivor. This evidence was corroborated by another medical man. A witness for the defendant was of the opinion that the father survived the wife and two boys. Two other medical men confirmed this opinion. It will, therefore, be seen that in this, as in some other cases, the doctors differed and the lawyers consequently doubted. In 1854 the suit of Underwood v. Wing was heard before the Master of the Rolls, who made a decree declaring the Tulleys entitled in equal shares to the residuary personal estate of the testator, John Tulley. This decree was appealed against, but was, in 1855, affirmed. Another bill was filed against Wing and the Tulleys, and a similar decree was made to that made in the former suit. On the appeal to the House of Lords, both the suits were treated as involving the same question, so far as Wing was concerned. Elaborate arguments were urged by learned Counsel on both sides, and numerous authorities cited, but the result was that the former decrees were confirmed. The foregoing case illustrates the glorious uncertainty of the law, and shows that in case of shipwreck, the possession of an estate may depend upon whether one member of a family survived the other by a few seconds only.

A similar case came before the Civil Tribunal of Marseilles, in 1882. Husband and wife perished in a boat accident, and on the answer to the question who was the survivor, £75,000 depended.

The following case will be especially interesting to readers of the seafaring class, as it gives the history of property bequeathed to two seamen who, unfortunately, were lost at sea, and consequently never inherited the same. The facts were these.—Richard Corbitt, who died in 1829, by his will, directed the residue of his property to be converted and divided amongst his three children and grandchild. Of these children, James and Charles were merchant seamen, the former being the master and the latter the second mate of a ship called the "Thames," which traded between England and the West Indies. They left Demerara for England on the 9th of December, 1828, and touched at Dominica, on the 24th of that month, after which they were never seen nor heard of. Upon these facts being proven, the Master came to the conclusion that the sons survived the father.

The Master's Report was disputed, and after learned arguments, Vice-Chancellor Knight Bruce said :—

"The small amount of the property, the time and money which have been already consumed in the investigation of this matter, as well as the possibility that the expression of a judicial opinion on the question of fact may the more readily enable any party dissatisfied with my judgment to obtain that of the Lord Chancellor—all these considerations induce me to give and to act upon the opinion, which the evidence before me impresses upon my mind. . . . . There is no doubt the two men died. The question is, whether they died in their father's lifetime . . . . It is not for me now to decide what rule of evidence ought to guide the Court in a case where there is no probability one way or the other—where, for instance, there is no question of health or danger; but where, on a particular day, a healthy man is seen exposed to no danger, and is never seen nor heard of again—that is not a case which it is now necessary to decide. . . . . I am of opinion that these men died in their father's lifetime."

This decision seems to have given satisfaction to the parties, as it was not appealed from. Some very intricate questions on the construction of the testator's will, however, arose when the cause came on for further consideration, and possibly a very large share of the estate was frittered away in costs.

The following are specimens of Advertisements arising from loss of life at sea.—

FIVE POUNDS REWARD.—Whereas Samuel Brooks, of Jesus College, Cambridge, did, on the evening of Monday, the 25th of August, 1851, with his boatmen named Chellews and Stevens (both inhabitants of St. Ives, in Cornwall), sale from Milford Haven in a small yacht called the "Jackdaw", and neither the said Samuel Brooks nor the said boatmen have since returned to their homes. The said Samuel Brooks was short in statue and 23 years of age. The night of the 25th of August, 1851, was very stormy, and the "Jackdaw" and its crew are supposed to have been lost at sea. Any person giving information . . . tending to prove that the said Samuel Brooks is living, or if he is dead, or to prove the finding of the "Jackdaw," or any part of that vessel, shall receive the above reward.

The following appeared just 100 years ago, and relates to the loss of a ship and every soul on board:—

If the Next of Kin or any Relations of William Foster, late part-owner and master of the merchant ship "Commerce," who, with his wife and every person on board, was lost in the said ship, on her passage from Jamaica to Bristol, in a violent gale of wind, in September, 1782, will apply to . . . . they will hear of something greatly to their advantage.

It would be easy to multiply instances of persons supposed to have been lost at sea having been advertised for in connection with Unclaimed Money, but the foregoing are probably sufficient for the purposes of this Chapter.

The approximate value of vessels of all nationalities with their cargoes lost during the year 1880, is said to have been no less than £68,327,000, including British property of the value of £47,495,000. These are startling figures. During the same year, unfortunately, about 4,000 lives were lost.—*Preston's Unclaimed Money.*

CHAPTER XI.

HEIRS-AT-LAW VS. CHARITIES.

A GOOD many people are "making haste to be rich," and in the hurry of business charitable intentions are forgotten. If good resolutions are made, the putting of them into execution is too often deferred to a more convenient season, which in many cases never arrives, for death steps in and puts an end to further procrastination; while, in other cases, intending testators endeavor to make up for past neglect by bequeathing magnificent sums to Charities, in the hope of perpetuating the renown of their good deeds, as well as of benefiting the Charities. The news of such bequests must always be disappointing to Heirs-at-Law and to Next of Kin. These bequests are made under the belief, doubtless, that "a man may do what he likes with his own." Such a belief may be a very comforting one, but it rests on no sure foundation, as will be seen by the following extract from what is known as the Mortmain Act, passed in the reign of King George II..

"Whereas, gifts or alienations of lands, tenements, or hereditaments in mortmain are prohibited or restrained by Magna Charta and divers other wholesome laws, as prejudicial to and against the common utility, nevertheless this publick mischief has of late greatly increased by many large and improvident alienations or dispositions made by languishing or dying persons, or by other persons, to uses called charitable uses, to take place after their deaths, to the disherison of their lawful Heirs. For remedy whereof be it enacted, That from and after the 24th day of June, 1736, no manors, lands, nor any sum or sums of money, goods, chattels, stocks in the publick funds, securities for money, or any other personal estate whatsoever, to be laid out or disposed of in the purchase of any lands shall be given, granted to or upon any person or persons for the benefit of any charitable uses whatsoever, unless such gift be made by deed in the presence of two or more credible witnesses, twelve kalendar months at least before the death of such donor and be inrolled in His Majesty's High Court of Chancery within six kalendar months next after the execution thereof."

It is pretty evident that the provisions of the Mortmain Act are not generally known; otherwise testators would be more careful when making their last Wills and testaments. It may be said that any one wishing to dispose of a large sum of money for charitable purposes would naturally consult a solicitor as to the best mode of procedure, but it is a well-known fact that many wealthy and eccentric individuals dislike this course; hence the reason of so many "Wills of their Own" being made and upset.

The Mortmain Act appears to have been passed for the benefit of Heirs-at-Law and Next of Kin, as instances are not unknown of relatives being entirely "cut off" by a whimsical testator giving, in a pet, his whole fortune to eleemosynary uses but testators of this class cannot be too careful in framing their Wills, as may be seen by the following cases:

A testator gave his real and personal estate for building or purchasing a chapel; if any surplus, the same to go towards support of the minister, and, if further surplus, to charitable purposes, as executor should think fit. This trust was held to be wholly void; the real estate went to the Heir, and the personalty to the Next of Kin.

In another case, a testator gave his residuary estate for the purpose of bringing up children in the Roman Catholic faith. Here the fund did not go as the testator intended, nor did it go to the Next of Kin, but to the Crown, to be disposed of for some other charitable use under the Royal Sign Manual.

A case decided by the Master of the Rolls, known as "Smith's Poor Kin Case," arising out of a charitable bequest made 250 years ago, has given rise to a good deal of discussion. The facts were these: In 1627 Alderman Smith bequeathed £1,000 to be invested in land of the value of £60 a year, the income to be distributed for the relief and ransom of captives taken by the Turkish pirates. Also a further sum of £1,000, to be invested in like manner, the income to be applied for the relief of the poorest of his kindred—such as were not able to work for their living, namely,—"sick, aged, and impotent persons, and such as could not maintain their own charge." In pursuance of this benevolent testator's wishes, an estate was bought at Kensington, and the income applied as directed by the terms of the Will. In course of time the value of the estate increased prodigiously, and so did the poor kindred; there were only four in 1700, but in 1877 they numbered no less than 700. The estate is now valued at upwards of £11,000 a year

In 1772, the trustees having long since ceased to apply one moiety of the income for the relief of captives taken by Turkish pirates, obtained an Act of Parliament enabling them to apply the whole income for the benefit of the Poor Kin of Smith. The Charity Commissioners made inquiry with a view to the preparation of a scheme for the better management of these funds, and found that in 1772 there were only fifteen poor kindred entitled to share therein. In 1807 there were twelve families claimants, and in 1830 there were fourteen families, numbering in the aggregate 100 adults, recipients of, or candidates for, a share of Alderman Smith's bounty. In 1868 the 412 "poor" kindred lived in 110 households in the United Kingdom, France, and the Colonies. The claimants on this Charity comprise persons who were apparently never intended to be benefited by the terms of the original bequest. For instance, a retired druggist, a retired surgeon, a wholesale grocer, a gentleman (occupation not given), a surgeon, and a music master—these claimants admit, for the purposes of apportionment, that the income of each exceeds £300 a year. One claimant asks for the payment of a governess for his children, and another (who is described as an actor, a refreshment house keeper, and a cupper) begs for assistance to go to the seaside; another (a reduced pensioner) has £440 a year. One annuitant is described as occasionally coming to receive her dole (£40) with black eyes, saying "she had fallen down." One of Alderman Smith's poor kin is represented as ragged and destitute, and had, by his own statement, "been dying of consumption for above twenty years;" another, who had once been a soldier, and afterwards a bootmaker, had been in prison for deserting his family, while another is described as a regular beggar, in whose family the charity had done much mischief.

Another claimant wrote to the trustees thus:

"GENTLEMEN: I take the liberty of writeing again to inform you that I was entitled to my allowance at Christmas, and I don't see why I should be kept seven months without it. It his my right, and I did not send to ask for it till I inherrited it. If you will not send it to me, I will come and see the Trustees about it, ... and I shall expect you to pay my expenses there and back I am almost distressed. I owe £8 for rent and £4 for clothes, and £3 10s for provisions, and I have not got one shilling towards paying either of the bills, and I think it is very hard you will not send me my allowance and it his my rights, and which I ought to have had it last Christmas"

The Charity Commissioners have been directed to frame a new Scheme, and to apply a portion of the income to general charitable use. Judging by letters in the *Times* from Alderman Smith's Next of Kin, the decision of the Master of the Rolls has caused great dismay in the camp of the Smiths; they claim the whole fund, and regard appropriation of any portion thereof to general charitable uses as "confiscation."

Cases of a similar kind are exceedingly numerous. The following illustrates how uncertainly the Mortmain Act works:—A gentleman devised a freehold estate to trustees in trust to sell it, and pay the proceeds, together with his residuary personal estate, to the trustees of the British Museum, to be by them employed for the benefit of that institution. The question was whether this devise was void under the Mortmain Act Counsel for the trustees of the Museum contended that the British Museum was not a charitable institution It was founded by the munificence of the State for the benefit of the public. Every gift for the use of the public is not necessarily a charity. The Museum is National property, and for that reason it was held in Thellusson v. Woodford that the devise to the King for the use of the Sinking Fund was good. Counsel for the Heir-at-Law contended that the British Museum was no more National property than a Hospital or College of Royal foundation, and that the devise was void as being within the Statute of Mortmain. The Vice-Chancellor decided in favor of the Heir-at-Law, observing "that it had long been settled that a gift of the price of land is, in effect, a gift of land under the Mortmain Act. In Mr. Thellusson's Will there was a residuary gift, in certain events, towards payment of the National Debt; but those events had not happened, nor probably never would happen; and no decision had been given as to the validity of that gift. In this Will there is no such gift to the Nation, but a gift to an institution established by the Legislature for the collection and preservation of objects of science and of art, partly supplied at the public expense, and partly from individual liberality." The Vice-Chancellor added :—"I consider that every gift for a public purpose, whether local or general, is within the Mortmain Act, although not a charitable use within the common and narrow sense of these words; and consequently, I must declare this devise void as to the real estate."

Having shown how easy it is for a charitable donor's intentions to be frustrated by legal technicalities, it may be convenient to give a note of one or two cases where charitable bequests have been held to be valid.

A bequest to the Chancellor of the Exchequer for the time being, to be appropriated to the benefit and advantage of Great Britain, was held to be valid as a charitable bequest, as far as regarded property of a personal nature, but not as regarded realty.

In another case, a testator by his will directed that a sum not exceeding £50 a year should be paid to a literary man, preference to be given to one not more than forty years of age. By a codicil he declared that his object was to give what little assistance he could to a worthy literary person who had not been very successful in his career, and, as far as possible, to enable him to assist in extending the knowledge of those subjects in the various branches of literature to which the testator had turned his attention.—"Held, that, provided the literary works of the testator were consistent with religion and morality, this was a charity to which the law of England would give effect." Many a poor author has probably had cause to rejoice that this benevolent testator's intentions were not frustrated.

The following amusing anecdote is from the *Pall Mall Gazette*. It may be safely termed "An Unintentional Benefaction," and will be read with regret by expectant legatees:

"A gentleman who had been dining, 'not wisely, but too well,' in the course of the evening drew a check for a large amount, and, having signed it, poked it, by means of a stick, into a box placed at the gates of a charitable institution to receive the donations of passers-by. When he regained his sobriety the next morning, he remembered with horror his liberality of the previous night, and addressed a moving appeal to the Managers of the institution in question to restore the amount of the check, which he found had been cashed before he had time to dress himself or drink one bottle of *soda-water*. As it was found that the unfortunate man had absolutely left himself penniless, the Managers, it is believed, kindly allowed him a small sum, to carry him on till the next quarter; but the shock was too much for him, and, after a few days of intense mental agony, he fell into a state of total abstinence, from which he never rallied"

Disputes between Heirs-at-Law and Charities are very common, and the cases above noticed are sufficient for the purpose of showing that Heirs-at-Law and Next of Kin not unfrequently take the benefit of a bequest intended for some Charity.—*Preston's Unclaimed Money*.

CHAPTER XII.

BANK OF ENGLAND---UNCLAIMED DIVIDENDS.*

AMONG things not generally known is the fact that there annually lapses to the Government a very large sum from Unclaimed Dividends, presumably by reason of the representatives of the original Stockholders not being known to the Bank of England authorities.

A recent Parliamentary Paper shows that on January 4, 1882, the Dividends due and not demanded amounted to £818,909 12s. 6d., of which sum there was advanced to the Government £756,739 0s. 9d. The sums thus advanced to the Government are applied pursuant to the provisions of certain Acts of Parliament towards the reduction of the National Debt.

Too much publicity cannot be given to the fact that these Unclaimed Dividends belong to the representatives of deceased Stockholders; they only await legitimate claimants proving their title as such representatives, prior to being re-transferred from the Commissioners for the reduction of the National Debt.

In 1870, an Act was passed with the short title of the National Debt Act, which consolidated, with amendments, certain enactments relating to the National Debt. The provisions with reference to Unclaimed Dividends are collected together in Part VIII. of the Act. They are so important to the public, and the terms thereof so little known, that it may be useful to state their effect fully

Section 51 provides that all Stock, no dividend whereon is claimed for ten years . . . . . shall be transferred in the books of the Bank of England . . . . . to the National Debt Commissioners.

Section 52 provides that, immediately after every such transfer, the following particulars shall be entered in a list to be kept by the Bank.—(1) The name in which the Stock stood immediately before the transfer; (2) The residence and description of the parties; (3) The amount transferred; and (4) The date of the transfer; such lists to be open for inspection at the usual hours of transfer; duplicates of each list to be kept at the office of the National Debt Commissioners.

Section 53 relates to the mode of transfer, which is to be deemed as effectual to all intents as if signed by the person in whose name the Stock then stands.

Section 54 deals with subsequent Dividends. It provides that where

*See page 8 for rate of fees for searching the Bank records for Unclaimed Deposits

Stock is transferred, all Dividends accruing thereon after the transfer shall be paid to the National Debt Commissioners, and shall be from time to time invested by them in the purchase of other like Stock, to be placed to their account of Unclaimed Dividends. All such Dividends, and the Stock arising from the public investment thereof, shall be held by those Commissioners, subject to the claims of the parties entitled thereto.

Section 55 relates to re-transfer and payment to persons showing title. It is in substance as follows:—Re-transfer may be made to any person showing his right thereto. In case the authorities are dissatisfied with the claimant's title, he may by petition, in a summary way, state and verify his claim to the Court of Chancery and the Court may make such Order thereon, touching the Stock, Dividends, and costs of application, as to the Court seems just.

Section 56 provides that three months' notice must be given before re-transfer or payment, where the Stock or Dividends claimed exceed £20.

Section 57 provides that Advertisements as to the re-transfer shall be inserted in one or more newspapers circulating in London and elsewhere. Where any such Advertisement is ordered by the Court of Chancery, it is to state the purport of the Order.

Section 58 provides that at any time before re-transfer of Stock or payment of dividend to a claimant, application may be made to the Court of Chancery to rescind or vary any Order made for re-transfer or payment thereof.

Section 59.—It may be desirable to give this Section *in extenso*, as it relates to cases where a second claimant appears:—

"Where any stock or dividends having been re-transferred or paid as aforesaid to a claimant by either Bank is or are afterwards claimed by another person, the Bank and their officers shall not be responsible for the same to such other claimant, but he may have recourse against the person to whom the re-transfer or payment was made."

Section 60. This contains a very important proviso as to second claimants.—

"Provided that if in any case a new claimant establishes his title to any Stock or Dividends re-transferred or paid to a former claimant, and is unable to obtain transfer or payment thereof from the former claimant, the Court of Chancery shall, on application by petition by the new claimant, verified as the Court requires, order the National Debt Commissioners to transfer to him any such sum in Stock, and to pay to him such sum in money or Dividend as the Court thinks just."

This is good news for persons who have been defrauded by reason of a fictitious claim having been made to Stock and Dividends justly their own. Such cases are unfortunately not without precedent.

Section 61 relates to payment of Unclaimed Dividends to the National Debt Commissioners.

Section 62 relates to Unclaimed Stock, consisting of Stock Certificates and Unclaimed Coupons. These are dealt with in a similar manner as nearly as may be to Unclaimed Stock and Dividends thereon.

Section 63 enables the Treasury to empower the Bank of England or of Ireland to investigate the circumstances of any Stock or Dividends remaining unclaimed, with a view to ascertain the owners thereof, and allow to them such compensation for their trouble and expenses as to the Treasury seems just.

Section 66 grants indemnity to the Banks of England and Ireland

and their officers in respect of such re-transfers as aforesaid; they are to be in no way responsible to any person having or claiming any interest in such Stocks and Dividends.

From a careful perusal of the foregoing provisions, it would appear that the Legislature has provided proper means for dealing with Unclaimed Dividends of the Bank of England,—*First*, by applying them towards the reduction of the National Debt, and *secondly*, for re-transfer from the Commissioners to persons entitled thereto on proper proofs of identity being produced to the authorities

I am often asked why Dividends continue to remain Unclaimed year after year, and my answer is, that in many cases (owing to the lapse of time and other reasons) it is very difficult to trace the legal personal representatives of the original Stockholders, and the State will, therefore, always have a large annual "windfall." Many years ago the Bank of England authorities published Lists containing the names and descriptions of Stockholders entitled to Unclaimed Dividends, and the public were largely benefited thereby; but it was stated that such publication offered facilities for fraud, hence their discontinuance. It seems rather hard that the majority of persons interested in these funds should suffer for the delinquencies of a few black sheep, and it is utterly impossible to believe that the Bank of England Solicitors (to whom, doubtless, any questionable claim would be referred) could be deceived in many cases.

The means adopted by the Bank authorities for endeavoring to find claimants in the present day are, I believe, of a very limited character; they address a communication to the parties supposed to be interested, acquainting them that their names appear on the Bank books, and that, if they will take measures to establish any claim they may have, all proper assistance will be afforded them. As I have stated above, it is almost impossible, in many cases, for the Bank authorities to trace the persons really interested, and the fact of large sums being annually applied towards the reduction of the National Debt, arising from Unclaimed Dividends, would seem to show that more publicity is necessary in the interests of Heirs-at-Law and Next of Kin. Many thousands of persons are more or less interested in these dividends, (the Stockholders number nearly 250,000), and the more accessible Lists like those above referred to are made, the more chance would there be of the grand total of Unclaimed Dividends being reduced.

A specimen of an Advertisement issued by the Bank of England with reference to Unclaimed Dividends is subjoined —

"BANK OF ENGLAND.—Unclaimed Dividends.—Applications having been made to the Governors of the Bank of England to direct the payment of Two Dividends on the sum of £10,500 Consolidated £3 per cent. annuities, heretofore standing in the name of . . . . deceased, and which Dividends were paid over to the Commissioners for the Reduction of the National Debt, in consequence of the first thereof having remained unclaimed since . . . . Notice is Hereby Given, that, on the expiration of three months from this date, the said Dividends will be paid to . . . . one of the Executors of . . . . deceased, who has claimed the same unless some other claimant shall sooner appear and make out his claim thereto"

A remarkable case came before the late Vice-Chancellor Malins, in which it appeared that a lady died at Marseilles at the great age of ninety-eight, who, though entitled to £56,000 in the Funds, and to more than £20,000 accumulated dividends, was constantly borrowing money from her relatives; from which fact, it may be inferred, that this large deposit had escaped the aged lady's memory.

The following are extracted from Lists of Unclaimed Dividends published by the Bank of England. The numbers after the dates denote the number of Dividends due when the Unclaimed Dividends were transferred to the Commissioners, for the Reduction of the National Debt.

NAME	ADDRESS.	DATE.	DIVIDEND.
Aquilar, Benjamin	Welbeck Street	1781	84
Ashby, Francis	Whitehall	1774	98
Alexander, Robert	Edinburgh	1771	103
Barnes, John		1778	89
Burdett, Mary	Cleveland Row	1772	101
Brown, Sarah	Parliament Street	1766	114
Collinson, Ann	Lombard Street	1763	119
Campbell, Elizabeth	Park Street	1760	125
Croce, James	Cheapside	1759	127

In addition to Unclaimed Dividends, the Bank of England, doubtless, has large sums in the shape of Unclaimed Deposits. It is also custodian of boxes deposited in its cellars for safe custody. It is a pity that these boxes are not overhauled after the lapse of a certain number of years, and their contents advertised. It has occasionally oozed out that many of these consignments are not only of rare intrinsic and historical value, but of great romantic interest. For instance, some years ago the servants of the Bank of England discovered in its vaults a chest, which, on being moved, literally fell to pieces. On examining the contents a quantity of massive plate, of the period of Charles II, was discovered, along with a bundle of old love-letters indited during the period of the Restoration. The Directors of the Bank caused search to be made in their books,—the representative of the original depositor of the box was discovered, and the plate and love-letters handed over.—*Preston's Unclaimed Money.*

The following clipped from a newspaper of Hartford, Connecticut, of date of December, 1883, shows that unclaimed dividends and deposits are not a thing peculiar to the Bank of England:

"Returns received by the State Controller to this date show that there are in the several savings-banks deposits unclaimed for twenty years aggregating $69,000, and it is estimated that further reports to be received will bring the aggregate up to nearly $100,000. There are 705 depositors, averaging $98 each, whose accounts have not been disturbed for the period named or longer, and whose whereabouts are unknown to the officials of the banks. In Connecticut this unclaimed property does not escheat to the State, and the bank managers have earnestly fought every proposition for thus disposing of it or looking to such publicity regarding the individual deposits as would tend to enlighten heirs or others. Newspaper publication of the list was defeated before the Legislature, and the original bill was so emasculated that, as passed, it calls only for an annual statement of the names of and amounts due depositors, to be filed with the State Controller. Such a list gives next to nothing in the way of information, and when filed in a public office and not published in any form it is useless.

The Legislature will be asked next month to change all this, and to require that the banks give the last known residence and all other information in their possession regarding depositors. One single bank—the Society for Savings—in this city holds $52,000 of unclaimed deposits due 570 depositors, one having $2,964 to his credit and four others over $1,000 each. The New Haven Bank has seventy-five depositors who have not disturbed their deposits for twenty years or more, and several other banks from four to thirty each. It is a somewhat remarkable fact that the banks in the seaport towns, which might be supposed to have a considerable number of depositors lost at sea, make a comparatively small showing as contrasted with banks on inland towns and cities. The smallest unclaimed deposit in any bank is 52 cents, due one Julia Ennis, who, twenty years ago or more, did not think it worth while to draw some odd pennies of her deposit. There is but one other missing depositor reported by that bank in Southport, and against Julia Ennis's 52 cents, he has $711.11 to his credit."

For the lovers of the curious we append the following singular co-incidence in relation to bank notes.

"On one occasion the Bank of England proved much too accommodating for its own interests. Somewhere about the year 1840 one of its own Directors, a man of wealth and of unimpeachable honor, bought an estate for £30,000, and for convenience sake obtained a note for that amount. On returning home, just as he was about to put it under lock and key, he was called out of the room, and placed the note on the mantelpiece. On coming back, a few minutes later, no note was to be seen. No one had entered the room in his absence, and, after an anxious search, he came to the conclusion that the precious bit of paper had fallen into the fire and been consumed. Hurrying off to Threadneedle Street he told his colleagues what had happened, and they gave him a second note upon his undertaking to restore the lost one if it should come again into his hands, and, in case of its being presented by anybody else, repay the amount to the bank.

Thirty years afterward, when he had long been dead and his estate distributed among his heirs, the supposed non-existent note turned up at the bank counter, where it was presented for payment. All explanation of the circumstances connected with it were lost upon the presentee—the note had come to him from abroad in the course of business, and it must be honored without delay. There being no help for it, he was paid the £30,000. Application was made to the representatives of the defunct Director to refund the money, but they promptly disclaimed their liability, and the bank perforce had to put up with the loss. The story goes that it was discovered (how or when we are not informed) that the builder employed to pull down the dead man's house, preparatory to rearing a new one on the site, had found the note in a crevice of the chimney, and kept it and his own counsel until he thought it was safe to reap the reward of his patience and unscrupulousness, and so became a rich man at a stroke.

The executors of Sir Robert Burdett found no less than £270,000 worth of bank notes scattered here and there about his house, some slipped into bundles of old papers, some between the leaves of books, without a memorandum anywhere to apprise them of the existence of such valuables, much less of their whereabouts. A little better advised were the executors of the gentleman who left behind him a scrap of paper marked "Seven hundred pounds in Till," although they failed to interpret its meaning until they had disposed of all the dead man's belongings. When one of them recollected that his library had contained a folio edition of Tillotson's Sermons, and wondered if "Till" had any reference to it. The books had been sold to a bookseller, who luckily had not found a customer for them, although he had sent them on approval to a gentleman at Cambridge, who had returned them as not answering his expectations. The executor bought the Tillotson back again, and going carefully through the volume, recovered notes to the amount of $2,500.

The watchman of a factory at New Haven, Conn., afforded the administrators of his estate no clew whatever as to the hiding-place of the savings, of which they believed him to have died possessed. Overhauling his clothes preparatory to selling them by auction, one of them threw an old overcoat aside, when a dirty piece of cloth dropped out of one of the pockets. On examination this was found to be wrapped around a large cartridge shell, within which lay notes of $1,800 value, which, but for a mere chance, might unexpectedly have enriched a purchaser of second-hand clothing.

Some sixty years since a Bank of England £5 note was paid into a Liverpool merchant's office in the ordinary course of business. On holding it up to the light to test its genuineness the Cashier saw some faint red marks upon it. Examining them closely, he traced some half-effaced words between the printed lines and upon the margin of the note, written apparently in blood. After a long and minute scrutiny he made out the words: "If this note should fall into the hands of John Dean, of Longhill, near Carlisle, he will learn hereby that his brother is languishing a prisoner in Algiers." The merchant immediately communicated with Mr. Dean, and he lost no time in bringing the matter before the Government. Inquiries were set on foot, and the unfortunate man discovered and ransomed. He had been a slave to the Dey of Algiers for eleven years when the message he had traced with a splinter of wood dipped in his own blood reached the Liverpool counting-house. Liberty, however, came too late; the privations and hardships of the galleys had sapped his strength, and, although he was brought home to England, it was but to die.

CHAPTER XIII.

BANKRUPTCY---UNCLAIMED DIVIDENDS.

BEFORE quoting statistics concerning Unclaimed Dividends in Bankruptcy, it may not be out of place here to give a few extracts from the Bankruptcy Laws of the olden time. One of the earlier statutes prescribes the following penalty for the fraudulent conveying away of goods:—"If, on indictment, a bankrupt shall be convicted, he or she so convicted shall be set in the pillory in some public place for the space of two hours, and one of his or her ears nailed to the pillory and cut off." Persons fraudulently claiming the estate of a bankrupt were thus dealt with:—

"If at any time before or after a person becomes a bankrupt, any persons do fraudulently, or by collusion, claim, demand, recover, possess, or detain any debts, duties, goods, chattels, lands, or tenements, by writing, trust or otherwise, which were or shall be due, belonging, or appertaining to any such offender, other than such as he or they can and do prove to be due by right and conscience . . . . every such person shall forfeit and lose double as much as he or they shall so claim." After the creditors were satisfied, forfeitures were disposed of thus:—"One moiety to the Commissioners of Bankrupts to be paid unto the Queen's Majesty, Her Heirs and Successors, and the other moiety thereof . . . employed and distributed to, and amongst the poor within the hospitals in every city, town, or county where any such bankrupt shall happen to be." The disposal of one moiety of these forfeitures amongst the poor in hospitals no one would be disposed to cavil at—why the other moiety should go to the Queen's Majesty is not so clear.

As recently as the year 1761, a person named Parrott was executed at Smithfield for fraudulently concealing the true state of his affairs from his creditors.

A few years later on (in 1772) a noted firm of bankers stopped payment The event is thus dilated on in the newspapers of the day.—

"It is almost impossible to describe the general consternation in the Metropolis at this instant. No event for 50 years past has been remembered to have given so fatal a blow both to trade and public credit, an universal bankruptcy was expected; the stoppage of almost every banking house in London was looked for; the whole city was in an uproar; many of the best families in tears . . . . caused by the rumor that one of the greatest bankers in London had stopped payment, which afterwards proved true. . . . The principal merchants assembled, and means were immediately concerted to revive trade and restore the national credit."

Considering the distress the failure of a large firm causes, who can wonder at the penalties being so severe, in days gone by, for fraudulent bankruptcy?

BANKRUPTCY—UNCLAIMED DIVIDENDS.

In the year 1876 an Act had to be obtained arising out of the winding-up of the Western Bank of Scotland. That bank stopped payment in 1857, with liabilities amounting to nearly nine millions, and after the lapse of twenty years the fund, in the shape of Unclaimed Dividends, etc., remaining to be dealt with was £10,368. In the Liquidators' balance-sheet it is curious to note the alarming difference between nominal and estimated assets, thus :—Credits and overdrawn accounts, etc , set down in the Company's books at £2,800,000, or thereabouts, are estimated to realize the insignificant sum of £439 18s. 3d

A still more gigantic liquidation than that of the Western Bank of Scotland was that of the City of Glasgow Bank, which failed in 1878, and caused wide-spread ruin and misery. The liabilities were about £14,400,000, with very small available assets. Two calls were made, one of £500, the other of £2,250, in respect of each £100 of stock. These enormous calls enabled the Liquidators to pay off the great bulk of the liabilities, and in 1882 an Act was passed transferring the remaining assets and liabilities to the "Assets Company" The balance-sheet showed that no less than £260,000 in the shape of interest could be claimed by creditors, and that no claims had been lodged in respect of £54,143 17s. 7d. The names of the persons entitled to these large sums have never been published.

Acts of Parliament with reference to Bankruptcy have from time to time been passed, but, judging from correspondence in the newspapers, they have failed to give entire satisfaction to the public. A Memorial presented to Earl Cairns, when Lord Chancellor, contains some striking details concerning Unclaimed Dividends in Bankruptcy, of which the following is a summary —

In 1864 the Chief Registrar of the Bankruptcy Court stated before a Select Committee of the House of Commons that there was a fund called the "Unclaimed Dividend Account," producing £45,000 a year; that under the Trust Deed Clauses of the Act of 1861, and also under certain sections of the Act of 1869, very large sums had been received by trustees, none of whom were liable to any official supervision, or even rendered, as far as could be discovered, any amount of Unclaimed Dividends or undivided surplus to any person whatever. The value of bankrupts' estates and of estates administered under trust deeds during the period between 1864 and 1876 was £68,817,221 10s.

The Memorial proceeds :—"It will be seen that under Bankrupts' estates more than 30 per cent of the assets remain undivided at the end of the year, and that nearly £22,000 per annum has been paid to the Consolidated Fund from Unclaimed Dividends. The estates under liquidations and compositions are more than four times the value of bankrupt estates, and must therefore yield at the least nearly £90,000 a year in Unclaimed Dividends; . . . . also unemployed balances of at least a million and a half. Innumerable cases have been brought under my notice in which creditors under petitions for liquidation, which have been filed for months, have neither been able to get any dividend nor any information whatever respecting their debtors' estate, until, wearied by unavailing efforts, they have retired in hopeless disgust."

The foregoing probably in some degree accounts for the enormous sums lying idle in the shape of Unclaimed Dividends.

In 1877 the Secretary to the Mercantile Law Amendment Society wrote a long letter to the *Times*, which was characterized by the leading journal as an important and interesting document. We extract from it the following:—

"The figures to which I am now about to refer are so important that I trust they will be carefully considered. I venture to think they deserve the special consideration of the Chancellor of the Exchequer. It appears from the Comptroller's Return that on 31st December last, there remained in the hands of trustees under Bankrupts' estates, undistributed assets amounting to £441,364 2s. 10d., and that in the Bank of England there was a sum of £10,784 18s. 5d., being Unclaimed Dividends remaining after the close of bankruptcies. . . . immense sums of money in these cases must remain in the hands of trustees in the form of Unclaimed Dividends. Why should the Unclaimed Dividends be kept by these adventurers? . . . . Between 1862 and 1871 the gross value of the estates dealt with under the Bankruptcy Acts, 1861 and 1869, amounted to the immense sum of £74,564,326. . . . . All Unclaimed Dividends and undivided surpluses have been kept by the trustees . . . It would be very difficult to estimate with accuracy the actual amount of Unclaimed Dividends now in the hands of trustees, but there can be no doubt that there is at least seven or eight millions of money."

Some persons may possibly desire to be enlightened as to the prospect of obtaining their share of the funds referred to. The following section from the Bankruptcy Act of 1869 shows that Unclaimed Dividends may be recovered at any time, on proper reasons being given for the delay in sending in claims:—

"116. Where any dividends remain unclaimed for five years, then and in every such case the same shall be deemed vested in the Crown, and shall be disposed of as the Commissioners of Her Majesty's Treasury direct: Provided that at any time after such vesting the Lord Chancellor or any Court authorized by him may by reason of the disability or absence beyond seas of the person entitled to the sum so vested, or for any other reason appearing to him sufficient, direct that the said sum shall be repaid out of money provided by parliament."

A perusal of the foregoing facts will probably be sufficient to show what an important unit in the fabulous sums of money awaiting claimants are Unclaimed Dividends in Bankruptcy.

There appeared in the *Times*, some years ago, a letter from "An Executor," complaining bitterly of the delay in distributing Dividends; in this case the published correspondence showed that £900 had quite escaped notice for upwards of ten years, and the editor of the City article of the *Times*, when commenting on the case, said:—"Were a Parliamentary Return of the residues of estates in the hands of trustees in Bankruptcy to be ordered, people would be startled at the totals it would reveal."

Various attempts have been made by successive Governments to amend the law of Bankruptcy. Most of the Bills have contained a clause providing for the transfer to the Crown of all Undistributed Assets and Unclaimed dividends (estimated by the Comptroller at about £5,000,000). Before such transfer takes place the names and addresses of the creditors entitled, with the amounts divisible, should be published in the leading newspapers, so that they or their representatives may have a fair chance of making good their claims. By omitting sums under £5 as not worth the expense of recovery, the cost of advertising would be defrayed.—*Preston's Unclaimed Money.*

We have had no opportunity of searching Records to ascertain even the approximate amount of Unclaimed Dividends in Bankruptcy in the Courts of the United States, but we know that in the aggregate the amount is very large. Not in large sums to any one creditor, but in a multitude of small ones. The creditor of any Bankrupt having even a suspicion that a dividend may be remaining unclaimed, to his credit, would do well to inform this BUREAU of the fact, and have an investigation, as it will cost but a trifle.

CHAPTER XIV

MISERS.

THERE is every reason to believe that the hoards of money and other valuables one so often reads of as having been discovered by workmen while engaged in pulling down old houses, have been secreted by Misers; the result is that, in many cases, property thus found is taken possession of by persons whom the Misers never intended to benefit—namely, their Heirs-at-Law and Next of Kin.

It is pretty certain that misers of both sexes existed ages ago, as they do in our own day, and the following notes concerning some notable examples of this class of monomaniacs may not be uninteresting. Of these who made it a rule of their lives to—"Gather gear by every wile," the case of M Osterwald, who died at Paris in 1791, is remarkble, as showing that the richest man in a city may also be the most miserable one He was the son of a poor minister, and began life as a clerk in a banking-house, at Hamburg, where he acquired a small sum, which he augmented by his speculations in business and his economical mode of living; he afterwards came to Paris, where he accumulated his enormous fortune. He was a bachelor—the expenses of a wife and children being incompatible with his frugal mode of living. He had for a servant, a poor wretch, whom he never permitted to enter his apartment; he had always promised that at his death he should be handsomely recompensed, and accordingly he left him a pittance of six months' wages and a suit of clothes, but, as he expressly stated, "not the most new." A few days before his death some of his acquaintances, who saw that he was reduced to the last extremity by want of nourishment, proposed to him to have some soup. "Yes, yes," he replied, "it is easy to talk of soup—but what is to become of the meat?" Thus died one who was reported to be the richest man in Paris, more from want of care and proper nourishment than from disease. He is stated to have left to relations, whom he had probably never seen, the sum of three millions sterling. Under his bolster were found eight hundred thousand livres in paper money.

A miser died in Paris in 1880, leaving property supposed to be worth about £60 Some time elapsed before the heir presented himself, but on his doing so, a search was made in the miser's apartment, and no less a sum than £32,000 was discovered in a cupboard

The cases of these French misers strikingly illustrate the truth of the following lines:—

> To heirs unknown descends the unguarded store,
> Or wanders heaven-directed to the poor

In a recent case,—that of William Rhodes, known as the Hounslow miser,—two charities benefited largely by the miser's hoards. He was worth nearly £80,000, all of which he left to the Royal Free Hospital and the lifeboat Institution. The miser's nephews and nieces tried to upset the will, but it was upheld, the two charities consenting to pay 1,000 guineas to the Next of Kin. It is said that this miser commenced his savings by picking up cigar-ends and other unconsidered trifles. His household effects fetched £5 17s.

A still more extraordinary case is that of an English lady, who died in 1766, in a lodging-house near the Broadway, in Deptford, at the age of 96. Her name was Mary Luhorne. For upwards of forty years she lived in Greenwich and Deptford in the most penurious manner, denying herself the common necessaries of life. She was known not to have had any fire or candle in her apartment for fourteen years prior to her death She frequently begged on the high roads when she went on business to the city. Notwithstanding her wretched way of life, after her death there were found securities in the Bank, South Sea, East India, and other Stocks to the amount of £40,000 and upwards, besides jewels and other precious stones, plate, china clothes of every kind of the richest sort, great quantities of the finest silks, linen, velvets, etc, unmade of very great value, besides a large sum of money. To whom all this treasure reverted does not appear; it is to be hoped the miser's Next of Kin came in for a share of it.

The neighborhood where Mary Luhorne died seems to be still famous for its misers. In 1877 there died at Woolwich a Mr John Clark, aged eighty-six. He is described as having been a man of education, but a very singular character; although reputed as immensely wealthy, he was very miserly in his habits, and lived to the last in a squalid hovel in the poorest part of Woolwich; the greater portion of his life was spent in the accumulation of books, of which he left a large store. It was reported that the front shutters of his house had not been opened for over thirty years; he never took a regular meal, nor did he know the taste of wines or spirits. Yet, notwithstanding that he lived in such a den and suffered such privations, he reached an octogenarian age, and died worth £40,000, or thereabouts. This bookworm, as well as miser, seems to have been a strange combination of avarice and liberality, for by his will he left no less than £6,000 to his doctor, also £5,000 to his housekeeper, besides many legacies to local charities, and to a number of the poor neighbors by whom he was surrounded Knowing well he could not take his wealth with him, he appears to have tried to make some reparation for a wasted life by disposing of his treasures with a liberal hand. What his Next of Kin said about the legacy of £6,000 to the doctor is not recorded Bequests of this nature are a prolific source of litigation.

An instance of miserly habits in the great and noble is to be found in the case of that renowned captain, the Duke of Marlborough, of whom it is chronicled that, when in the last stage of life and very infirm, he would walk from the public room in Bath to his lodgings, on a cold, dark night, to save sixpence in chair hire. He died worth £1,500,000.

It is recorded of a Sir James Lowther that, after changing a piece of silver in George's Coffee-house, and paying twopence for his dish of coffee, he was helped into his chariot (he was then very lame and infirm), and went home Some time after, he returned to the same coffee-house on purpose to acquaint the woman who kept it that she had given him a bad halfpenny, and demanded another in exchange for it. Sir James is stated to have then had about £40,000 per annum coming in, and was at a loss whom to appoint his heir.

Sir Thomas Colby, an official high in office, shortened his existence by his passion for this world's goods, as appears by the following anecdote:—" He rose in the middle of the night, when he was in a very profuse perspiration, and walked down stairs to look for the key of his cellar, which he had inadvertently left on a table in the parlor; he was apprehensive that his servants might seize the key and rob him of a bottle of port wine, instead of which he himself was seized with a chill, and died intestate, leaving over £200,000 in the funds, which was shared by five or six day-laborers, who were his Next of Kin." Marvelous good luck for his poor relations!

Sir William Smyth, of Bedfordshire, when nearly seventy years of age, was wholly deprived of sight; he was persuaded to be couched by a celebrated oculist, who, by agreement, was to have sixty guineas if he restored his patient to any degree of sight. The oculist succeeded in his operation, and Sir William was able to read and write without the use of spectacles, during the rest of his life; but as soon as Sir William perceived the good effects of the oculist's skill, instead of being overjoyed, as any other grateful person would have been, he began to lament the loss (as he called it) of his sixty guineas. His contrivance, therefore, now was how to cheat the oculist. He pretended that he had only a glimmering, and could see nothing perfectly. For that reason the bandage on his eyes was continued a month longer than the usual time. By this means he obliged the oculist to compound the bargain, and accept of twenty guineas.

A covetous man thinks no artifice too mean which he may legally practice to save his money. The miserly knight was an old bachelor, and at the time the oculist couched him is reported to have had a fair estate, a large sum of money in the Stocks and not less than £5,000 in his house! Dr King, in *Anecdotes of His Own Times*, makes the following observation when quoting Sir William Smyth's case:—"If you could bestow on a man of this disposition the wealth of both the Indies, he would not have enough, because by enough (if such a word is to be found in the vocabulary of avarice), he always means something more than he is possessed of."

The following is an instance (by no means an isolated one) of good fortune accruing to Next of Kin by a miser dying intestate:

At Northfleet there died, in 1772, a Mr. Page, dealer in limestones and gun-flints, by which occupation, and by a most penurious way of living, he had accumulated a fortune of some £12,000. He lived alone, in a large house, for several years, no one coming near him but an old woman in the village, who, once a day, went to make his bed. His death was occasioned by his running a knife into the palm of his hand while opening an oyster. The wound inflamed, and at length mortified. Though repeatedly requested to apply to a surgeon, he refused, saying, "All of that profession were rogues, and would make a job of his misfortune." From his having died without a will, his money went to a relative in very embarrassed circumstances. During the latter years of his life, the miser would never suffer this poor relative to come to his house, and never gave him the smallest assistance.

Some years since, a chiffonnier (or rag and refuse gatherer) died intestate in France, having literally "scraped" together 400,000 francs, the whole of which went to the Heir-at-Law.

In another case, the body of an old man named Partridge, a rag and bone collector, was discovered on a heap of filth in a room in one of the back streets of Exeter. The deceased was in the habit of prowling about the city, collecting bones and garbage, and he had been seen to eat morsels of food picked up by him in the streets. He lived alone, in a room which was filled with rags, filth, and vermin. He had complained of illness a few days before his death, and had, marvelous to relate, resorted to intoxicating liquors as an antidote, of which he drank freely. After his death, a savings-bank book was found, from which it appeared he had a large sum of money in the bank, and had also lent £15 to his landlady, besides various sums of money to other persons. His death was, without doubt, caused by self-neglect, dirty habits, and insufficiency of food. By his dying without a will, a nice little windfall reverted to his Next of Kin.

Some years ago, there died at Surrey Hills, Sydney, an old lady, named Soliff, who was a native of England, and lived alone. None of her neighbors ever knew her to leave her house . she was very penurious . . . . never lit a fire . . . . lived a life of rigid seclusion from choice, though she possessed a large income from house property . . . . In her last illness, one of her latest injunctions to those around her was to "look after a few pence on the mantel-piece." . . . . She left nothing whatever to her relations in Australia, but everything to her Next of Kin in England After her death, three bags of money were found, containing £1,100 in gold and silver . . . a deposit note for £6,000 . . . . deeds relating to house property, and about eighty dresses of rare colors and great beauty, also rare and costly furs. . . . . It is said her husband was transported for stealing a bag of flour . . . She followed him, and got him signed to her. . . . . The husband died many years ago.—*Preston's Unclaimed Money.*

CHAPTER XV.

WILLS.

IF a testament be made in writing and afterwards lost, two unexceptional witnesses who saw and read the document and remembered the contents thereof, may, on deposing to the tenour of the Will, afford sufficient proof of its having been executed; and in such cases probate is usually granted according to the deposition of the witnesses. It is quite clear, according to the text-books, that the contents or substance of a testamentary instrument may be established in this way, though the instrument itself cannot be produced, upon satisfactory proof being given that the instrument was duly made by the testator, and was not revoked by him. For example, by showing that the instrument existed after the testator's death, or that it was destroyed in his lifetime without his privity or consent. Thus, where a testator had delivered his Will to a friend to take charge of for him, and died some years afterwards, the Will was found torn to pieces by rats, and in part illegible; on proof of the substance of the Will by the joining of the torn pieces, and by the aid of the memory of the witnesses, probate was granted.

In a case where, after the death of the testator, his Will and Codicil were, it was alleged, wrongfully torn by his eldest son, the Court having, by means of some pieces which were saved and by oral evidence, arrived at the substance of the instruments, admitted their validity. But where allegations of this serious nature are made they must be supported by the clearest evidence

In another case, where a Codicil has been burned by order of the testator, but not in his presence, as required by the statute, probate was granted on a draft copy. This case shows the necessity of having a solicitor at one's elbow, not only when making our testamentary dispositions, but also when destroying them, so that the destruction may be done in a legalized way.

Where a Will is duly executed, but afterwards destroyed in the lifetime of the testator without his authority, it may be established on satisfactory proof being given of its contents, and of it having been so destroyed. The law is the same where a wife, having power to dispose of property by her Will, makes her Will and afterwards destroys it by the compulsion of her husband.

The law as to suppressing or destroying Wills is clearly shown by the following case: "A person after the death of a testator possessed himself of the Will, and suppressed or destroyed it. On these facts being proven to the satisfaction of the Court, letters of administration were granted with the Will annexed to the residuary legatee." A case of this kind was tried in Ireland some seventy-five years ago. The following is from the newspaper report of the trial.

"A most extraordinary case was tried at the last Maryborough Assizes. The facts were these: Robert Baldwin, in March, 1782, made his will, by which he devised the lands in question to the children of his youngest son Soon after, his faculties failed him; he became altogether childish, and died in April, 1784, aged 80 or thereabouts. The defendant, testator's eldest son, immediately gave out that his father had destroyed the will, and, no will being found, he entered into possession of the estate, and so matters remained for twenty-one years, the whole family, during all that time, believing that their father had died without a will. But, after twenty-one years, the delusion vanished, and the defendant's own children became the immediate instruments of justice to the children of his brother. In 1802 the defendant's wife died, and he soon afterwards, at the age of 78, married a very young woman, which caused some anxiety to his two sons, Robert and Edwin, whose poignant expressions of regret so exasperated their father that he, in his resentment, executed his will to disinherit his eldest son, Robert, and, in his fit of anger, showed it to his second son, Edwin, who instantly determined to get at it and destroy it, in order to preserve the property to his elder brother With this view he broke open his father's desk, where he found, not his father's will which he sought, but the will of his grandfather, which was then altogether forgotten by the family. He read it, and found that the estate of which his father would have disinherited his brother, lawfully belonged to his cousins, the children of his late uncle John. He immediately communicated the important discovery to his brother, and he to their uncle Jonathan, in consequence of which the will was, about the beginning of the year 1805, lodged in the Prerogative Court. When the defendant was apprised of the discovery of the will, he said it was very true—his father never did cancel h s will, but that he did it away by two deeds, by which he afterwards conveyed the property to him, the defendant, and that those deeds were both registered It appeared, indeed, that one such deed had been registered since the discovery of the will; and both deeds appearing foully suspicious, a bill was filed in the Court of Exchequer, the cousins desiring to have the opinion of a jury on these alleged deeds After a long trial, the jury found a verdict for the plaintiffs, with the full approval of the Judge. By this verdict the plaintiffs (five in number) were restored to an estate of £300 a year, of which for twenty-five years they had been deprived by their uncle."

Old uncles (especially wealthy ones) are invariably looked up to with the profoundest respect by their nieces and nephews, but in this instance the confiding nephews appear to have been the victims of misplaced confidence.

A very hard case, namely, an action of ejectment by an eldest son, as Heir-at-Law, against his own mother, was tried some twenty-five years ago Such action would never have been commenced but for the loss of a carefully-prepared Will.

In the case of the goods of Miss Helen Jane Gladstone, who died in Germany in 1880, letters of administration had been granted to her brothers, Sir Thomas Gladstone and the Right Hon. W E. Gladstone. After the issuing of the grant, certain bills of costs were found among some loose papers belonging to the deceased, from which it appeared that the lady had made a Will in 1852. Upon further search, the will was found. The letters of administration were accordingly revoked and the long-missing Will admitted to probate.

In another case, the Will of a gentleman who died in Ireland in 1880, was discovered secreted behind a grate in a small back room, many months after the Heir-at-Law had taken possession of the estate. The discovery of the Will altered the destination of £40,000; instead of the Heir-at-Law being entitled to the whole, the Will showed that the testator's nephews and nieces were to share equally.

Instances are not unknown of bodies having been exhumed for the purpose of searching for Lost Wills. A case of this sort occurred in 1876. The facts were these:—In 1870 a clergyman died near Bedford. After his death, rumors were afloat that a Will had been buried with him, which document, if found, would alter the devolution of his estate. The representatives of the deceased memorialized the Home Office, and the Home Secretary ordered the exhumation of the body. The proceedings were conducted with grave decorum. A bundle of papers was found under the body, tied with red tape, but these are said to have been only old love letters; no Will was found. The village was in a great state of excitement during the proceedings, as village gossips would have it that a party of body-snatchers had visited the church-yard.

Advertisements for lost Wills are, unfortunately, only too common, and large rewards are occasionally offered for such missing documents. In the case of the late Lord St. Leonards, the sum so offered was £500. The noble Lord had made a Will and several Codicils, but on his death the Will could nowhere be found. Costly litigation ensued, which resulted in probate being granted on a copy of the Will drawn up from memory by his Lordship's daughter. This decision was appealed against, but was upheld.

It should be universally known that the Wills of living persons may be deposited in a place of security at Somerset House, on payment of a small fee. The enactment on the subject is 20 & 21 Vict., c. 77, s. 91, and is as follows:—

"One or more safe and convenient depository or depositories shall be provided, under the control and directions of the Court of Probate, for all such Wills of living persons as shall be deposited therein for safe custody; and all persons may deposit their Wills in such depository upon payment of such fees and under such regulations as the Judge shall from time to time by any Order direct."

In giving judgment in the case of the Lost Will of Lord St. Leonards, Mr. Justice Hennen drew attention to this Act of Parliament, and regretted that the public had not availed themselves of it more extensively.

The following is a specimen of an Advertisement seeking a clue to a Lost Will —

"£100 Reward.—Will of Stephen Merris Mills, Esq., wanted. He died at 25, Charlotte Square, Edinburgh, on June 10, 1858. It is believed that the Will was placed in a small table in that house, and the table and other furniture of the house were sold by auction, by Mr. Dowell, on April 18th, 1865. The above reward will be paid if the Will be handed over to . . . ."

A little more care on the part of testators as to the safe custody of their Wills, would save endless trouble and litigation, not to mention sometimes life-long family quarrels.

Extraordinary Will cases have a peculiar fascination to many people who are not in the smallest degree interested in the result from a money point of view, but only take an interest therein as lovers of the curious. Whimsical Wills have been, and still are, a prolific source of business for lawyers, and Heirs-at-Law and Next of Kin are occasionally indirectly benefited by a whimsical testator's Will being upset. Probably a solicitor is rarely consulted by an intending whimsical testator, from a natural fear that a damper might be thrown on his designs. Whimsical bequests have sometimes served a very useful purpose, and instances are not unknown of such bequests having been made by lawyers themselves. The following is a case in point:

William J. Haskett, a lawyer, who died in New York City, left a Will containing this very curiously worded clause:—

"I am informed that there is a Society composed of young men connected with the public press, and, as in early life, I was connected with the papers, I have a keen recollection of the toils and troubles that bubbled then and ever will bubble for the toilers of the world in their pottage cauldron, and, as I desire to thicken with a little savory herb, their thin broth, in the shape of a legacy, I do hereby bequeath to the New York Press Club, of the City of New York, 1,000 dollars, payable on the death of Mrs. Haskett."

We have a Newspaper Press Fund in London, and any similar legacy to that above noted would doubtless be very acceptable.

There is probably no more profitable class of business to a lawyer than that arising out of the disputes about Wills, and the following extract from a French Advocate's Will, pithily expresses his opinion of his clients:—

"I give 100,000 francs to the local madhouse. I got this money out of those who pass their lives in litigation; in bequeathing it for the use of lunatics, I only make restitution."

It is recorded of a rich old farmer that in giving instructions for his Will, he directed a legacy of £100 to be given to his wife. Being informed that some distinction was usually made in case the widow married again, he doubled the sum; and when told that this was quite contrary to custom, he said, with heartfelt sympathy for his possible successor, "Aye, but him as gets her'll desarve it."

It is possible for a whimsical testator to be very just, and at the same time very caustic, as appears by the following extract from the Will of John Hylett Stow, proved in 1781:—

"I hereby direct my executors to lay out five guineas in the purchase of a picture of the Viper biting the benevolent hand of the person who saved him from perishing in the snow, if the same can be bought for the money; and that they do, in memory of me, present it to . . . . a King's Counsel, whereby he may have frequent opportunities of contemplating on it, and by a comparison between that and his own virtue be able to form a certain judgment which is best and most profitable,—a grateful remembrance of past friendship and almost parental regard, or ingratitude and insolence. This I direct to be presented to him in lieu of a legacy of £3,000 I had by a former will, now revoked and burnt, left him."

If the learned Counsel interested happened to be present at the reading of the Will, his feelings may be well imagined.

That it is most unwise to make one's own Will, disputed Probate cases abundantly prove. The following verse from an old number of *Blackwood's Magazine* is appropriate:—

Testators are good; but a feeling more tender
Springs up when I think of the feminine gender;

> The testatrix for me, who, like Telemaque's mother,
> Unweaves at one time what she wove at another
> She bequeaths, she repents, she recalls a donation,
> And she ends by revoking her own revokation;
> Still scribbling or scratching some new Codicil,—
> Oh! success to the woman who makes her own Will.

Undoubtedly "a crusty old bachelor" must have been the Parisian merchant, Monsieur Columbies, who, when he died, left £1,200 to a lady of Rouen, for having, twenty years before, refused to marry him, "through which," states the will, "I was enabled to live independently and happily as a bachelor."

It has been, and no doubt will continue to be, the ambition of some prosperous men to be the founder of a rich and great family, and it has sometimes happened that, without abandoning this idea, they have, by an ingenious device, contrived to disappoint their immediate relations. The Will of Sir John Pakington, proved many years ago may be instanced. J. S Russell, Esq., was his nephew; at the death of Sir John this nephew had a son about four years of age, and to the eldest son that might be born of this child, Sir John bequeathed his large landed estates, so that the income must have accumulated for nearly forty years before it could be enjoyed by the prospective legatee; in default of issue the estates were to go to the descendants of the second son of Sir W. B. Cook; and in case of second default, the property would go to a grandson of Mr. Knight, of Lee Castle. Sir John thus effectually debarred any of his Next of Kin living at his death from the enjoyment of his property.

An uncommon case of eccentricity on the part of an Englishman occurred some fifty years ago. His Will contained the following unique provisoes:—

"I bequeath to my monkey, my dear and amusing Jacko, the sum of £10 sterling per annum, to be employed for his sole and exclusive use and benefit; to my faithful dog, Shock, and my well beloved cat, Tib, a pension of £5 sterling, and I desire that, in case of the death of either of the three, the lapsed pension shall pass to the other two, between whom it is to be equally divided. On the death of all three, the sum appropriated to this purpose shall become the property of my daughter Gertrude, to whom I give this preference among my children, because of the large family she has, and the difficulty she finds in bringing them up."

We have all heard of cases of "waiting for dead men's shoes"; but it would probably be difficult to find a parallel case to that above noted—namely, a bequest to a daughter on the falling in of three lives,—those of a *monkey*, a *dog*, and a *cat*.

Another instance of a bequest for the support of domestic pets is the following —

"In 1875, Mrs Elizabeth Balls, of Streatham, Surrey, after liberal Legacies to hospitals and other charitable institutions, set apart the sum of £65 per annum for the support of her late husband's cab mare, and £5 per annum for the keep and care of a greyhound; the mare to be kept in a comfortable, warm, loose box, and not to be put to work either in or out of harness, and that her back should not be crossed by any member of her late husband's family, but that she should be ridden by a person of light weight, not above four days a week, and not more than one hour each day, at a walking pace."

Bequests to canine pets often lead to law suits. The history of a case of this kind, tried in 1798, was shortly this:—Mrs. Hannah White, by a paper purporting to be her last Will and testament, left to the mother of one of her servants £25 per annum in trust for the maintenance of five favorite cats, during the course of their natural lives; to St. George's and Middlesex Hospitals, £1,000 each; a few legacies to domestics, and the residue of her estate, which was very considerable, to the apothecary attending her person. This curious document was witnessed by an attorney and the clerk of the parish. The Court of Delegates, on the Will being disputed by disappointed relatives, heard Sir William Scott in support of the Cats and the Apothecary, and other Advocates for the Next of Kin. The following is the substance of the decree:—"That the bequest to the apothecary be struck out of the Will, as being no part of the real Will of the deceased, and that probate be granted to the Next of Kin; that the legacies of £25 per annum for the maintenance of the five cats, and the bequests to the hospitals aforesaid, together with the legacies to the servants, be confirmed, as being the Will of the deceased." It will thus be seen that the intentions of this whimsical testatrix were upset, and the Next of Kin benefited, but how long the cats were allowed to live is not recorded.

In 1800, Mrs Elizabeth Shaw, of Pontefract, by her Will bequeathed the bulk of her property, valued at £15,000, to her housemaid, Mary Watson. The Heir-at-Law disputed the validity of the Will, and endeavored to prove that the deceased was in a complete state of intoxication when she executed her Will. This allegation, however, was not sustained, and the fortunate housemaid gained the day. If Mary were intoxicated with delight at her good fortune, such a frame of mind can be easily understood under the circumstances, but it was too bad of the disappointed Heir-at-Law to try to prove this whimsical testatrix "drunk and incapable."

A curious, and I may add a peculiarly hard, case came before Vice-Chancellor Bacon in 1880. The facts were these:—"Miss Turner devised large real estates to her father for life, and then to her brother, on the following conditions:—" But if my brother shall marry during my life without my consent in writing, or if he shall already have married, or shall hereafter marry a domestic servant, or a person who has been a domestic servant," then such bequest to her brother to be void. The brother came into possession of the said estates, and died in 1878, leaving a widow and two children. The suit was instituted against the widow and children, on the ground that the testatrix's brother had forfeited his title to the legacy by marrying a domestic servant. It was contended, on behalf of the widow, that she had been a housekeeper, and not a domestic servant. The Vice-Chancellor, however, was of opinion that a housekeeper was a domestic servant, and thus the legacy was forfeited.

A bequest, made by a Frenchman, may truly be styled "A new way to pay old debts." Vaugelas, the famous French grammarian, was in receipt of several pensions, but so prodigal was he in his charities, that he not only always remained poor but was rarely out of debt, and finally acquired among his intimates the sobriquet of *Le Hibou*, from his compulsory assumption of the habits of the owl, and only venturing in to the streets at night. After disposing of the little he possessed to meet the claims of his creditors, he adds:—

" Still, as it may be found that even after the sale of my library and effects these funds will not suffice to pay my debts the only means I can think of to meet them is that my body should be sold to the surgeons on the best terms that can be obtained, and the product applied, as far as it will go, towards the liquidation of any sums it may be found I still owe; I have been of very little service to society while I lived, I shall be glad if I can thus become of any use after I am dead."

Whether the creditors accepted this well-intentioned bequest in part satisfaction of their claims is not recorded.

Some few years since, a lady bequeathed her body to the Hunterian Museum for dissection, "understanding the Museum to be in great want of pathological specimens." After dissection, her body to be burned.

In 1774 a Mr Whitehead, much admired for his many literary publications, bequeathed, among other whimsical legacies: "his heart, with £50, to Lord le Despenser."

There is very little doubt that the fear of being thought eccentric or singular, prevents a good many people from giving vent to their peculiarities during life. But this fear of public opinion altogether loses its influence in the matter of testamentary dispositions. When, in the presence of an expectant throng of bereaved relatives, the reading of the Will takes place, the testator is quite beyond either reproach or reply. This probably accounts for many a whimsical bequest, and when an expectant legatee finds in place of a legacy, only a few personal failings pointed out, he receives an unkind cut indeed.

Dr Dunlop, of Scotch origin, afterwards a Member of the United States Senate, left a very singular Will. It has often been commented on, owing to its extreme singularity, but its principal provisions are so amusing, that no apology is necessary for reproducing them. The doctor is described as having been a jovial and kindly man, and his Will certainly bears out this character. In it he says:—

"I leave the property of Gairbread, and all the property I may be possessed of, to my sisters,————and————; the former because she is married to a minister who—may God help him—she henpecks; the latter because she is married to nobody, nor is she likely to be, for she is an old maid and not market rife. . . . . I leave my silver tankard to the eldest son of old John, as the representative of the family. I would have left it to old John himself, but he would have melted it down to make temperance medals, and that would have been a sacrilege. However, I leave him my big horn snuff-box; he can only make temperance horn spoons out of that. . . . I leave my brother-in-law, Allan, my punch-bowl, as he is a big, gauchy man, and likely to do credit to it. . . . . I leave to Parson Chevassie my big silver snuff-box as a small token of gratitude to him for taking my sister Maggie, whom no man of taste would have taken. . . . . I leave to John Caddell, a silver tea-pot, to the end that he may drink tea therefrom to comfort him under the affliction of a slatternly wife. . . . . I leave my silver cup, with the sovereign in the bottom of it, to my sister ————, because she is an old maid, and pious, and therefore necessarily given to hoarding; and also my grandmother's snuff-box, as it looks decent to see an old maid taking snuff. . . . ."

It was well for this affectionate brother that he had gone heavenward before the gist of his testamentary benefactions were made known, otherwise he might have been "interviewed" by his scandalized sisters.

The following very whimsical bequest I take from a Scotch newspaper:—"Some years ago an English gentleman bequeathed to his two daughters their weight in £1 bank notes. A finer pair of paper weights has never yet been heard of, for the eldest daughter got £51,200, and the younger £57,344."

The Will of Dr. Johnson, the celebrated lexicographer, who died in 1784, is noteworthy; by it the bulk of his property was left to "his faithful black servant"

The Chevalier Francois de Rosaz, who died in 1876, and who is reported to have been very successful in prosecuting claims for persons interested in Unclaimed Money, left a very singular Will. His personal estate was sworn under £45,000. The testator seems to have believed that in a "multitude of counselors there is wisdom," for he appointed no less than seven executors. His Will contains this very extraordinary paragraph :—

"I beg and supplicate our Merciful Redeemer to receive every one of us in His Holy Paradise. I supplicate our very Holy Mother, the Virgin Mary, the very Holy Mother of God, and all the angels and archangels, and all the cherubim and seraphim, all the throne and denominations, all the dominions and virtuesses of the heavens, all the saints and the seven million martyrs of the prosecution against our very holy religion, and all the inhabitants of the heavens, to obtain pity, mercy, and pardon of God for all our beloved family"

The bulk of his property he bequeathed to his wife for life; on her death, certain French and Italian Funds were to be set aside as a provision for charities in France; the entire residue of his property was to be applied in founding a Catholic Asylum for thirty orphan girls, a Protestant Asylum for thirty orphan girls, and charities for the relief of the infirm and distressed. A Chancery suit arose on the construction to be put on this whimsical testator's bequests, and the Heir-at-Law of the Chevalier was inquired for.

Peculiarly-worded Wills have led to the waste of many a goodly patrimony. Heirs, executors, and beneficiaries seem to take intense delight in squabbling over a testator's intentions. Montaigne, the celebrated philosopher, is stated to have got over any difficulties in the way of carrying out his testamentary intentions by the happy expedient of calling all the persons named in his Will around his death-bed, and counting out to them severally the bequest he had made them. Many a whimsical testator might usefully follow Montaigne's example; but there is always a risk of the donor getting better, and finding himself penniless. I once heard of a case of this sort. A small farmer in Suffolk, being very ill, was advised by his affectionate relatives to distribute his money, and thus save legacy duty. He did so, but got well again. The relatives declined to re-coup these supposed death-bed gifts, and left the poor old farmer to seek parish relief. Cases of this kind, it is to be hoped, are very rare.

Rhyming Wills are scarce, but amusing. In a case decided in the Probate Court in 1875, the testator made a codicil to his Will, as follows:—

> I, having neither kith nor kin,
> Bequeath all I have named herein
> To Margaret, my dearest wife,
> To have and hold as hers for life,
> While in good health and sound in mind
> This codicil I've undersigned.

His wife and executors having predeceased him, probate was granted to the Crown Solicitor, there being no Next of Kin. The publicity given to the case may be the means of bringing to the knowledge of some distant relatives of this evidently well-intentioned testator the news that the Crown holds, in trust, funds for their benefit.

Another curious specimen of a Will in rhyme is that of a Mr. John Hedges. The original may be seen at Somerset House:—

The fifth day of May,	And of that, God knows there's no sign.
Being airy and gay,	I do therefore enjoin,
And to hyp not inclined,	And do strictly command,
But of vigorous mind,	Of which witness my hand,
And my body in health,	That nought I have got
I'll dispose of my wealth,	Be brought into hotch-pot;
And all I'm to leave,	And I give and devise,
On this side the grave,	As much as in me lies.
To some one or other,	To the son of my mother,
And I think to my brother,	My own dear brother,
Because I foresaw	To have and to hold
That my brethren-in-law,	All my silver and gold,
If I did not take care,	As the affectionate pledges,
Would come in for their share,	Of his brother—
Which I nowise intended,	
Till their manners are mended,	John Hedges.

The following is an instance of marvelous good fortune for a day laborer, arising out of the Will of an eccentric testator.—In 1772,— Edmunds, Esq., of Monmouth, bequeathed a fortune of upwards of £20,000 to one Mills, a day laborer, residing near Monmouth. Mr. Edmunds, who so handsomely provided for this man, would not speak to or see him while he lived

Again, in 1775, a Mr. Henry Furstone, of Alton, Hampshire, died worth about £7,000 in the funds, and having no relation, he left this large sum of money to "the first man of his name who shall produce a woman of the same name, to be paid them on the day of their marriage."

We have all heard of unmanageable sons and scapegrace nephews being cut off with a shilling, but the following case of a wife having the sum of only one shilling bequeathed to her is very sarcastic, and shows to what lengths a long-suffering Benedict may be driven. In 1772, John G——e, Esq., of Surrey, died, and his Will contains this clause:

"Whereas, it was my misfortune to be made very uneasy by . . my wife, for many years from our marriage, by her turbulent behaviour, for she was not content with despising my admonition, but she contrived every method to make me unhappy; she was so perverse to her nature that she would not be reclaimed, but seemed only to be born to be a plague to me; the strength of Samson, the knowledge of Homer, the prudence of Augustus, the cunning of Pyrrhus, the patience of Job, the subtlety of Hannibal, and the watchfulness of Hermogones, could not have been sufficient to subdue her; for no skill or force in the world would make her good; and as we had lived separate and apart from each other eight years, and she having perverted her son to leave and totally abandon me, therefore I give her one shilling only."

One of the most whimsical bequests is recorded in a probate case decided in 1879. The testator left £10 to the undertaker who buried his wife

A French lady, who died in 1882, desired by her Will that her heart might be placed in the tomb of her second husband, but her body in her first husband's tomb, in America.

Mr. John Innes, a well-to-do Lincolnshire farmer, was evidently of opinion that a son having "expectations" is far less energetic than one having none, for it is recorded that he, for many years, suffered his son to go to another farmer as a laborer, but by his Will he left his hard-working son the handsome fortune of £15,000.

In the well-known Thellusson Will case, it has been computed that, had the testator's intentions been carried out in their entirety, the sum of money to be divided amongst the Next of Kin at the end of the period fixed by the Will for the money to accumulate, would have amounted to £140,000,000, or thereabouts.

The following case is interesting, as showing how prodigiously money accumulates at compound interest:

"M. Ricard appointed by his Will that the sum of 500 livres should be divided into five portions. The first, at the end of a hundred years, amounting to 13,100 livres, to be laid out in prizes for dissertations proving the lawfulness of putting out money to interest. The second, at the end of two centuries, amounting to 1,700 000 livres, to be employed in establishing a perpetual fund for prizes in literature and arts, and for virtuous actions. The third, at the end of three centuries, amounting to more than 226 millions of livres, to be employed for establishing patriotic banks, and founding museums with ample establishments. The fourth, at the end of four centuries, amounting to 30,000 millions, to be employed in building a hundred towns in France, containing each 150,000 inhabitants. The fifth, at the end of five centuries, amounting to four millions of millions of livres, to be appropriated for the payment of the National Debt of Britain and France, for producing an annual revenue to be divided among all the Powers of Europe, for buying up useless offices, purchasing a royal domain, increasing the income of the clergy, and abolishing fees for masses, for maintaining all children born in France till they be three years of age, for improving waste lands and bestowing them on married peasants, for purchasing manors and exempting the vassals from all servitude, for founding houses of education, workhouses, houses of health, and asylums for females, for portioning young women, for conferring honorary rewards on merit; besides a large surplus to be appointed at the discretion of his executors."

In the list of Dormant Funds in Chancery there is an entry—"The one hundred years term account." Can it have reference to the following whimsical Will case, a note of which appeared in the Madrid newspapers:—"A Spaniard, Juan Delgado, died, leaving a Will endorsed to the effect that it should not be opened until one hundred years after his death. The hundred years having elapsed, it is not surprising to find that the depository of the Will, as also the location of the property, are anxiously inquired for,"—no doubt by expectant Next of Kin.

A very short Will was proved in 1881. The exact words are these:—"All that I possess in the world I leave to my wife." But a still shorter one is recorded thus:—"Everything to my brother Tom."—*Preston's Unclaimed Money.*

In the principal registry of Her Majesty's Court of Probate, at Somerset House, there are Wills of which "approbation" was "had and obtained" nearly 500 years ago. The first Will recorded is in the year 1383, and is in Latin, as most of the very early Wills are. The first Will written in English is that of Lady Alice West, widow of Sir Thomas West, and was proven on September 1, 1395. It begins thus:—"In dei nomine. Amen. On Thursday—that is to sey, the xv day of the moneth of Jul, in the yer of the incarnacion of our Lord Ihu Crist a thousand and thre hundred and fourscore and fiftene—I, Alice West, lady of Hynton Martel, in hool estat of my body and in good mynde beynge, make my testament in the maner as hit folweth hereafter. In the begynnyng, I bequethe my soule to God Almighty and to his moder, Seynt Marie, and to al the seyntis of heuene, and my body to be beryed in Crischerch, in the priorie of the chanones in Hamptschire, by the Newe Forest, wher as myne auncestors leggeth." The writing of a Will of 1395 is not to be read as easily as the writing of the present day, in consequence of the difficulties connected with the different shape of the letters, the variations in and the uncertainty of the spelling, the unfamiliar abbreviations, and the obsolete words; but from the laborious carefulness with which they were originally engrossed, the pains taken with the formation of each letter, putting to shame the slipshod writing of the present day, and the great care taken of them by the officials who have their custody, they are in a wonderful state of preservation, and far more perfect and legible than many wills and documents of a much later date. The very slowness with which they were written seems to have been the means of rendering them, so far as writing can be made so, permanent. The writing has in many places, where the ink has faded, been since touched up; and in some places, where the parchment is worn, the words are illegible; but, generally, the writing stands out sharp and distinct, although a little browned by age. The Wills of persons of position were, in spirit, much the same in the fourteenth century as they now are; there are pecuniary and specific legacies to relatives, legacies to old and present servants, legacies for charitable purposes, and particular directions about the funeral and place of burial. Dame Alice West's Will is too long to give at length; but some extracts, showing the articles which at that period were so valuable as to be specially bequeathed, the amounts of the legacies, and the persons to whom they were left, may prove interesting. The lady commences the disposition of her property as follows:—"Also I devyse to Thomas, my sone, a bed of tapicers work, with all the tapices of sute, red of colour, ypouthered with chapes and scochons in the corners of myn auncestres armes, with that I bequethe to the same Thomas the stoffe longyng therto—that is to seye, my beste fether-bed and a clu canevas and a materas and twey blankettys and a peyre schetes of reynes and sex of my best pilwes," which he will choose. "Also, I bequethe to the same Thomas, my sone, a peyre matyns book and a peir bedes, and a ryng with which I was yspoused to God, which were my lordes his faderes." Except among small farmers and shopkeepers in Wales, by whom it is a common custom to bequeath bedding to different members of the family, it is an unusual thing in the present day to dispose of it in this manner by Will; and the reason is that feather-beds, mattresses, pillows, blankets, and sheets are comparatively cheap, and the use of them not confined to the wealthy, but in Lady Alice's time they must have been articles of luxury, and a considerable item in the dower of a bride. There are several bequests of beds in the Will which point to this conclusion—in one, forty marcs are bequeathed to Beatrice Wareyn, "and a bed convenable for a gentelwoman;" in another, testatrix bequeaths "to Idkyne, my chambrer, £20, and a bed convenable for her estat." Testatrix next thinks of her daughter-in-law. "Also I bequethe to Johane my doughter, my sone is wyf, a masse book and alle the bokes that I have of latyn, englisch, and frensch out take the forsayd matyns book that is bequeth to Thomas my sone. Also I bequethe to the same Johane all my vestyments of my chapell and my tapites whit and red paled, and blu and red paled, with alle my grene tapites that longeth to my chapell forsayd, and with the frontels of the forsayd auter, and with all the rydells and trussing cofres and all other apparaile that longeth to my chapelle forsayd." We wonder what books she had, and particularly what English books: a list of them would be most interesting. She could not have had many, and we cannot suggest what they were. It must be remembered that this Will was made more than five years before the death of Chaucer, and nearly eighty years before the first book was printed in English, and books in English must consequently have been few indeed; their scarcity made them of great value, they were carefully treasured, and their future ownership specially provided for by Will. Something might be said as to the education of ladies of the highest class at that time. Here was a lady possessing books in English, Latin, and French, which it is presumable she could read. Latin, however, was the language of her religion; French was probably the tongue she was brought up in, and was the language of the Court; and English was the language of her dependents, so that, almost as a matter of necessity, every lady of rank must have been familiar with all three languages. There are several other legacies to testatrix's daughter-in-law, Johane. She gets, among other things, "a basyn of silver, with boses upon the brerdes," and "a chales," we suppose for use in her chapel; and "my chare, and that I have longyng thereto. Also a chariot with twey standardes heled with lether which that serveth for myn harneys." Then come gifts to other members of her family:—To "Sir Nichol Clifton, Knyght, and to Alianore, his wif, my doughter, and to Thomas Clifton, here son, £120, euenliche to be departed betwix ham thre; and if Thomas here sone forsayd deyeth, I wol that it torne to profet of his fader and his moder;" and to "my suster Dame Luce Fitzherberd, prior-isse of Sheftebury, £40." The three following legacies speak for themselves:—"Also I bequethe £40 to be departed among alle my servants, men and women of myn household, as well for their attendance on Thomas her sone as for her, and as wel to hem that I have eny thyng bequethe to in this testament as to hem that I have nothyng bequethe, and I wole that it be departed trewely to every man and woman after his degre." "Also I bequethe £40 to be departed among my pouere tenantes where I have lordshype—that is to seye, to hem that have most nede." "Also I bequethe to Richard Fforster, which is a blyndman that was somtyme servant with my forsed lord, 20 marcs." We should not expect to find any Will previously to the Reformation without a legacy to say masses. Lady West gives £18, 10s, "for to synge and seye 4,400 masses for my lord Sir Thomas West is soule, and for myne, and for alle cristene soules," and they are to be "done" within "fourteen night after her deces." If it is reckoned up, it will be found that masses then cost about a penny each. There is another bequest to Christ Church, where she was to be buried, "to bidde and to rede and synge for my lordes soule forsayd, and myn, and alle cristene soules, while the world schal laste." Testatrix gives many sums of 100 shillings to bodies of religious women and communities of brothers, among others to the religious women the "menouresses" living without Aldgate of London, the "freres prechoure" within Ludgate of London in Flet-street, the Augustine brothers within Bishopsgate, and the Hospital of Seynt Marie Maudeleyne above Wynchester, and sometimes is added, "to the priests belonging to the same," "to be departed among them by evene portions for to synge and rede divine service, and to preye for my forseyd lordes soule and myn, and for alle cristene soules, and for the estat of Thomas my sone and Johane his wif and her children," and some smaller sums to several recluses for the same object. Having given all the legacies she desires, the testatrix then disposes of the remainder of her property:—" An al the residue of my godes, after the dettys that I owe ben quyt, and after my testament is parfoned, I bequethe to the forsayd Thomas my sone;" and, after all these directions and legacies, the good lady finishes her Will by ordering the manner of her own interment; when she dies her body is to be carried "to the forsayd priorie of Chrischerch,, and with right litel cost," buried at the first masse, with a taper of six pounds of wax burning at her head, and another taper of six pounds of wax burning at her feet.

CHAPTER XVI.

LAPSED LEGACIES.

IN 1852 this advertisement appeared: "NOTICE.—If Mr. William Snowdon, Joiner, late of West Herrington, in the County of Durham, will apply to any of the parties mentioned below, he will hear of something to his advantage. . . ."

Mr. Snowdon, however, did not apply, and the result was a Chancery suit, asking the directions of the Court, as to the disposal of the funds accumulated by reason of this legatee's disappearance. A decree was made by Vice-Chancellor Stuart directing (among other things) inquiry as to whether the aforesaid William Snowdon was living or dead. In consequence of that decree, further advertisements were issued, but the missing legatee was not traced. The matter came on again before Vice-Chancellor Stuart, and the following is an extract from the Vice-Chancellor's judgment:

"The rule was well-established that if a person could be shown not to have been heard of since a given day, and seven years or more have elapsed, one might presume at the expiration of that time that he was dead. Of course he might reappear, and such cases had happened. The executors in this case caused advertisements to be inserted in the newspapers respecting William Snowdon without effect, but that was no evidence that he died before the testator. There was no sufficient evidence to presume that he died at any particular time during the seven years. He must, therefore, be taken to be dead, but to have outlived the testator. . . ."

The foregoing is a fair specimen of many a lapsed legacy case. Nothing is more common than for persons to leave their native land, and take no further thought of kith or kin left behind. Should the legatee above referred to ever reappear, he will doubtless be able to recover his estate from the persons now enjoying the same. Such incidents are not without precedent.

Many very remarkable causes relating to Lapsed Legacies have been decided by the Court of Chancery, but it would probably be difficult to find one more curious in its incidents than the following, which came before Vice-Chancellor Malins, and in which a sum of £24,834 11s. 6d. Consols was in dispute. The facts were as follows: In 1869 Mr Duncombe, an aged Solicitor, of New Inn, Strand, died intestate, possessed of very considerable wealth. He had three children, namely, Henry Stuart Duncombe, Charles William Duncombe, and Anna Johnson, a widow. Mr Duncombe was not on good terms with Henry Stuart, his eldest son. In 1868 that son, then sixty-six years of age, went to his father's office for pecuniary help, but the old man dismissed him with half-a-crown.

From that time till the institution of the suit the son had never been heard of. In 1870 advertisements were inserted as follows:

"TWENTY POUNDS REWARD.—To Registrars of Deaths and Parish Clerks, Tailors' Trade Societies, and Masters of Union and other Workhouses.—Wanted, information of a person named Henry Stuart Duncombe, a journeyman tailor, much in the habit of traveling in the country, and who, if living, would be 67 years of age. Was last seen in London in August, 1868. Any person who can give information as to his whereabouts, or who can supply a certificate of his death, will receive the above reward on applying to . . . ."

Probably few people reading the foregoing advertisement would be likely to guess that the journeyman tailor inquired for was the son of a Solicitor and Heir to £25,000; and even had Mr. Duncombe seen the advertisement, he would not have been tempted to reply thereto. The notice seems carefully worded to glean information as to his death. He is not even told that his father is dead, nor is he informed that on applying to So-and-so he will "hear of something to his advantage."

No reply came to the advertisement in any shape or form. Mrs. Johnson (formerly Duncombe), when she married, executed a settlement by which, if Henry Stuart Duncombe predeceased her, her interest in his share of Mr Duncombe's estate would be bound, otherwise not. She died, leaving one child only, a boy. A suit was instituted with respect to the aforesaid sum of £24,834 11s. 6d., which represented the missing son's share of his father's estate. The question was, whether the trustee's of Mrs. Johnson's settlement were entitled to the fund, or whether it was divisible among the Next of Kin of the missing legatee, assuming him to have been alive at the end of seven years from the time when he was last seen in London, but now dead, intestate, and unmarried.

The Vice Chancellor, in his judgment, characterized the case as a most remarkable one, and after recapitulating the facts, said that having regard to the authorities, he must presume—(1) That Henry Stuart Duncombe did survive his father; and (2) that he was now dead. There remained another question, when did he die? Mrs. Johnson, the sister was now dead. If her brother died in her lifetime, she would, as one of his Next of Kin, have an interest in his share of the property. She had executed a settlement, and had left one child. If, however, her brother survived her, then his share would not be bound by her settlement of her interest in it. The only conclusion at which the Vice-Chancellor could arrive on this part of the case was that Henry Stuart Duncombe was now certainly dead, intestate, and that his brother and nephew were his sole Next of Kin. They would, therefore, take his share of his father's property in equal moieties, and there must be a declaration accordingly. If (added the Vice-Chancellor) hereafter Henry Stuart Duncombe should be found to be living, he must resort to his brother and nephew for the repayment of the money. It was entirely his own fault that he had not made his existence known (if he did exist); for it was hardly likely that if he was still alive he had not seen some of the very numerous advertisements issued for him. The Vice-Chancellor said he himself thought that Henry Stuart Duncombe was "as dead as a door-nail." Summed up shortly, the decree was this: "That Henry Stuart Duncombe survived his father, and was alive at the end of seven years from the time he was last seen (August, 1868); that he was now dead, intestate, and that his sole Next of Kin, his brother and nephew, were now entitled to his share of Mr Duncombe's property."

Many an exciting novel has far less foundation on fact than the Henry Stuart Duncombe case. The missing Heir would be eighty years old if living now, and if he were to put in an appearance and claim this £25,000, after being dismissed from his father's presence with half-a-crown, his doing so would be the very acme of romance.

The following is the note of a case decided in 1874, by the Court of Session, Scotland, after fifteen years' fruitless search for a Missing Legatee:

This was an action of multiplepoinding and exoneration, instituted in 1859, at the instance of Mr. C. M Barstow, C.A., judicial factor on the estate of the late William Maltman, of the East India Company's Service, who died at Elie, in the county of Fife, in March, 1854, leaving heritable and personal property to the value of £10,000, or thereabouts He had several brothers and sisters, all of whom predeceased him, with the exception of Gavin Maltman, who went abroad about 1814. This Gavin Maltman, who was born in November, 1792, and who had in the course of his life wandered over a considerable portion of the West Indian Islands and North America, was last heard of at Shediac, New Brunswick, in July, 1854. Various reports of his death were sent to this country, and the Court on two occasions sent a Commission abroad to inquire into the truthfulness of these reports, but they turned out to be unfounded. The Court, in consideration of Gavin Maltman's great age, his long absence, and the fact that he had been extensively advertised for and inquired after . . . . ordained the Judicial Factor to divide the personal estate among the Next of Kin of Walter Maltman other than Gavin Maltman, the Next of Kin being cousins once removed, and to convey the heritable estate to the Heirs-at-Law . . on the ground that Gavin Maltman, if alive, had had ample opportunity of appearing and claiming the Succession.

The passing of the Presumption of Life Limitation (Scotland) Act, 1881, has given rise to many claims by persons desirous of possessing themselves of the estates of relatives long lost sight of. The most important provision of the Act is, that persons not heard of for seven years or upwards are assumed to be dead, and the Next of Kin may institute proceedings to "uplift and enjoy" their estates and property

There will doubtless be some cases of hardship arising, by reason of the missing Heirs-at-Law returning home after the seven years limit and finding their estates distributed among their affectionate relatives. Incidents of this kind are on record, but I have only space for the following remarkable case:—

"In 1761 a certain French astronomer was sent to India by the Parisian Academy of Sciences, to watch the Transit of Venus He arrived, unfortunately, too late; but he had the patience to remain eight years in that country till the Transit of 1769. Ill-luck, however, still pursued him, for the state of the atmosphere prevented him from witnessing the second Transit. He then returned to France, where he found his friends under the impression that he had been dead and buried for years. His heirs were already in possession of his property."

The foregoing jottings are sufficient for the purpose of drawing attention to the fact, that large sums of money not unfrequently lapse to Heirs-at-Law and Next of Kin, owing to the legatee not being traceable.—*Preston's Unclaimed Money.*

CHAPTER XVII.

MISSING RELATIVES.

THERE is an old saying, "Out of sight, out of mind," and in many cases it is doubtless only too true, but at Christmas and on festive occasions when families meet together, there is no toast more heartily drank than that of "The Absent Ones." Some of these missing ones may have been lost sight of for years, and of their whereabouts it has not been possible to glean the slightest intelligence, though every known channel likely to afford the much-wished-for news has been resorted to. Enormous sums are annually spent in searching after Missing Relatives and Friends; in many cases these searches are crowned with success, while in others every effort proves abortive.

Scores of people at present belonging to a circle below that of the "Upper Ten" have really fair grounds for expecting a change of fortune in the right direction some day, but they lack the necessary clue on which all their hopes turn. It has frequently happened that a long-forgotten relative has been brought to remembrance by the delightful surprise of a substantial legacy, the news being conveyed through the medium of a newspaper Advertisement. Of such an announcement the following is a specimen:—

"PARTICULAR NOTICE.—MISSING RELATIVES.—Frederick Foot and B Foot (sons of Matthew Foot, late of Enniskerry, in the county of Wicklow, Ireland, deceased), who left Ireland in the year 1859, for the United States of America, are requested to communicate without delay to . . . . . . Solicitor, who can inform them of something to their advantage Any information relating to the above parties will be thankfully received.

Advertisements of the following kind are also very numerous; they are invaluable as a means of tracing Missing Relatives:—

"MISSING RELATIVE —THOMAS ALLEN or his Representative, who went from London to Australia about 22 years ago, will hear of something to their advantage by applying to . . . . . ."

The following must have been especially gratifying to the testator's poor relatives; it is the only Advertisement of the kind I have come across:—

"Pursuant to a Decree of the High Court of Chancery, made in the cause of . . . . . such of the Poor Relations of FRANCIS HODGSON, late of Lane House, in the County of Lancaster, Gentleman (who died sometime in the month of February, 1785), to whom he did not, in and by his last Will and Testament, give any Legacy, are . . . . . to come in and prove their kindred and relationship . . "

Here is another curious Missing Relative Advertisement:—

"INFORMATION.—Any person who can give information as to the

Relatives of HENRY FERGUSON, who died in 1808, aged 94 years, a native of America, will receive a good compensation for the favor The said Henry Ferguson was found dead near the Tower, and £1,500 in Bank-Notes were discovered sewn in between his clothes; a bundle of Manuscript was found in his pocket, containing a learned "History of the Progress of the Arts and Sciences from the period of the Romans up to the year 1808," In his wretched hovel near the City a very valuable Library was also found. Apply at . . . . ."

The following extraordinary Advertisement appeared in 1826; there are doubtless numbers of people equally as anxious as the advertiser was as to an uncle's testamentary dispositions:—

"THE ADVERTISER WISHES TO FIND HIS UNCLE OUT.—He is the son of James and Susan Hill, of Meikleham, Surrey; Mr. Webb, of East Hisley,; George Armon, that keeps the Post-Office, High Wickham, Buckingham; Mary Disten, Church Street, Bethnal Green; William Hill, Tottenham, baker; Thomas Scott, butcher; Elizabeth Button, of Burnham, in Essex—those are all Relations. If any person can give any information of this person, or any of the above, SO THAT HE MAY KNOW IF THEY HAVE RECEIVED ANY BENEFIT FROM HIS UNCLE, and where his effects lay, it being one-and-twenty years since he heard of him; George Harmon said the effects laid at Burnham."

"Whoever will endeavor to get the property shall receive a fourth part of it, as the Advertiser is the only Male Heir to this property. Direct to . . . . ."

Many domestic complications result from husbands leaving their homes, as appears from the following case:—In 1850 Maria Dunster married John Milton, and in 1854, well-knowing that her husband was alive, she went through the marriage ceremony, by the name of Maria Dunster Chapple, with one Francis Edwards, since deceased. Mrs Milton often saw her lawful husband, who was a Corporal in the Devon Militia. In May, 1870, however, she went through the ceremony of marriage with another man named Henry Melhuish, who being, it was alleged, ignorant of his supposed wife being already married, by his Will, dated August, 1870, gave her all his real and personal estate, and appointed her sole executrix. Henry Melhuish died in 1871, and Mrs. Milton proved the Will, the personality being of the value of about £800, or thereabouts. After 1871 Mrs. Milton returned to her husband. A Chancery suit resulted, the brother of Henry Melhuish being the plaintiff, and he claimed the fund as sole Next of Kin of his deceased brother, alleging that Mrs. Milton had obtained the money by fraudulently assuming the title of his brother's wife. Mrs. Milton denied that while living with Mr Melhuish, or at the time of going through the ceremony of marriage with him, she had ever heard of her husband, and affirmed that she had not, in fact, heard of him for nineteen years, and believed him to be dead. Such being the facts—and it would be difficult to find a parallel case—the Vice-Chancellor said he was of opinion that Melhuish had no certain evidence at the time of the ceremony of marriage having been performed, as to Milton being alive or dead, and he married Mrs. Milton, otherwise Edwards, notwithstanding The Vice-Chancellor added · " It would not be safe to assume that the character of wife was the only motive for the bequest. Might not the testator have intended that she should have the property in the events that had happened ? . . . . Fraud not being established, the bill must be dismissed with costs."

Here we have a case of a long lost husband turning up after nineteen years' absence on the scent of a legacy, and actually enjoying, after so long a lapse of time, the fortune left by Melhuish.

Here is a curious notice by a colonist.—

"If my wife Jane Young, last heard of in Sidney, in 1878, does not return or communicate with me within three months from date, I intend to marry again,—(signed) THOMAS YOUNG.

Port Douglas. 4th August, 1882."

In 1882 Sir James Hannen had to adjudicate on the following peculiar case.—

"Counsel applied on behalf of Augustus Alexander de Niceville for letters of administration to the property of his father, Mr. Stanislaus de Niceville, who must reasonably be supposed to be dead, as he has not been heard of since 1831, and if he were now alive he would be 105 years of age. In his early days he held a commission in the French army, but he came to this country in 1826, and settled in Devonshire. On the breaking out of the French Revolution he and his wife went to France. His wife returned to Devonshire, but kept up a correspondence with her husband till February 1831, when she ceased to hear from him. Every inquiry was made to try and trace the husband, but without avail. Madam de Niceville died in 1875 without having applied for letters of administration. Affidavits were read in support of these facts, and the learned President granted the application."

Nothwithstanding lavish expenditure of time and money, efforts to trace Missing Relatives occasionally prove abortive. Of this class of cases, probably the most notable instance on record is that of the search for Sir John Franklin, in the result of which many Heirs-at-Law and Next of Kin must have been interested.

The main facts are these·—In 1845 the *Erebus* and *Terror* left our shores, the number of officers and men on board being 138. The last despatches were received from Baffin's Bay, July 12, 1845, when Sir John wrote most cheeringly of the prospects of the Expedition, and expressed a hope that his wife and daughter would not be over anxious if the Expedition should not return by the date fixed (July, 1848); the latest date on which the Expedition was actually seen, was July 26, 1845, the ships were then moored to an iceberg, waiting for an opportunity to cross over to Lancaster Sound. In August, 1850, traces of the Expedition's first winter quarters were found by Captain Austin. In 1849 the then Board of Admiralty offered a reward of £20,000 to "any ship or ships of any country, or to any exploring party whatever which should render efficient assistance to the missing ships or their crews, or to any portion of them,"—with what result is too well known

Numerous Parliamentary Returns have from time to time been published as to the cost of these searching expeditions, and in 1854 it was estimated that between 1848 and 1853 over £800,000 had been thus spent. From 1854 to 1874 Arctic expeditions have gone on their perilous voyages, and have returned with more or less barren results. It has been estimated that the total outlay on these magnificent enterprises cannot have been less than two million sterling! Lady Franklin seems, to the last, to have nobly clung to the hope that tidings of her long-lost husband would be found, for shortly before her death, in 1873, she caused the following Advertisement to be inserted in the *Times*:—

"TWO THOUSAND POUNDS REWARD offered by Lady Franklin to

any one who will take to her, previous to the 1st of January, 1875, the whole of the Journals or other Records which he may find of the Expedition of the *Erebus* and *Terror*, and which are believed to have been deposited near Point Victory on King William's land by the survivors of the expedition in 1848."

The Franklin case is remarkable, not only for the amount of money spent in endeavoring to find a clew to the crews of missing ships, but also as showing the indomitable pluck and energy of British seamen in following up a forlorn hope.

In 1881 a reward of £300 was offered by the Sidney Government for a clew to a party of five persons who disappeared from the Coast of Australia, 200 miles south of Sidney, on a geological survey expedition. The search for the missing expedition, however, has, thus far, proved as unsuccessful as in the Franklin case.

Advertisements for Missing Relatives are increasing year by year; it would, therefore, seem as if the public found this kind of publicity answer the desired end. It cannot be too generally known that a record is kept of all such Advertisements, as it often happens that many years elapse before they are brought under the notice of the interested parties, owing to absence beyond seas, and other causes.

I take the following romantic story from a recent number of the *Toronto Mail*, and with it I may appropriately close these jottings on Missing Relatives:—

"About twenty years ago a French lad was kidnapped from Montreal, and taken to sea. He followed sailing for some years, and eventually settled in Michigan, being employed by a Mining Company. A few years ago a party of emigrants arrived at the station, and being strangers, and ignorant of the English language, they made inquiries as to the French families residing there, and were directed to the house of the young Frenchman, who gave them lodgings for the night. In the course of the evening the fact was disclosed that the emigrants and their host were originally from the same portion of the Dominion. The host repeated the story of his kidnapping. The family of emigrants had lost a son years ago, who mysteriously disappeared, and had never since been heard of. The interest of both parties was aroused, and further questioning proved the fact that the host of the emigrant family was the long-lost son."—*Preston's Unclaimed Money.*

CHAPTER XVIII.

UNEXPECTED ASSETS.

IT not unfrequently happens that accounts classed as "bad debts" in the books of many of the trading firms most unexpectedly bring in assets to the intense gratification of the creditors. One of the earliest examples of this kind of good fortune is contained in the following Advertisement extracted from the *London Gazette* of 1666.—

"Whereas, Jeremiah Snow, late of Lombard-street, Goldsmith, now living in Broad Street, did owe divers persons, Anno 1652, £8,300; who at his desire did accept of £6,225 in full, and gave him discharges absolute (which was occasioned by the failing of two French Merchants, who were at that time indebted to him £3,400, but never paid him a fifth part, as by the testimonials remaining with the Public Notary it may appear), since which time it has pleased God to bless his endeavours with some small estate: He, therefore, in gratitude and justice, invites them to receive the full remainder of their principal money, excepting such as by his oath he shall affirm to have paid in part or in full.

"And he declares this publication is not for vain glory (Retribution in this kind being indispensable) nor to get more credit, but because his friends have adjudged it conveniently necessary that his Vindication might be as publick as then was the Scandal."

Many a long-suffering creditor would doubtless be highly delighted to read a similar announcement to the above in the pages of some newspaper of the present day, and a perusal of this chapter will show that Unexpected Assets do often accrue for the benefit of creditors, or their representatives, long after all hope of twenty shillings in the pound has vanished.

In the autobiography of Benjamin Franklin a very remarkable case of the kind is given. Speaking of Mr. Denham, a Quaker friend of his, Franklin says:—

"I must record one trait of this good man's character. He had formerly been in business at Bristol, but failed, in debt to a number of people, compounded, and went to America. There, by close application to business, as a merchant, he acquired a plentiful fortune in a few years. Returning to England in the ship with me, he invited his old creditors to an entertainment, at which he thanked them for the easy composition they had favoured him with, and, when they expected nothing but the treat, every man, at his first remove, found under his plate an order on a banker for the full amount of the unpaid remainder, with interest."

This good Quaker's example is worthy of imitation, and many a bankrupt who has gone through the convenient process of whitewashing, and prospered again, might take the hint with the prospect of a wonderfully relieved conscience.

Here is another specimen of what may be called an Unexpected Asset Advertisement:—

A fund is available for the following parties (or their representatives), who, in 1825, resided as mentioned below, on application to . . . . & Co., Solicitors . . . . Dublin, or . . . . Solicitors . . . . London:—

Everington & Co., Ludgate Hill.
Thomas Hamilton, St. Pancras Street.
Vanilton & Carson, Prince's Street.
Jane Clarke, Regent Street.
Sarah Shirley, Salisbury Square.
John Thomas, Dover Street.

Watson & Co., Gutter Lane.
Wm. Frazier, Norfolk Street, Strand.
Thos. Caldwell, New Bridge Street, Blackfriars.
J. & W. Hayward, Oxford Street, all in the City of London.

The foregoing notice appeared thirty years after the persons named resided at the addresses given so that in all probability something worth looking after had unexpectedly accrued for them or their representatives.

Another case of the same class as the above is the following:—

"Lord Alvanley's Creditors. The following Debenture Creditor's of the late Lord Alvanley have omitted to receive their final dividends, namely:—

[Here follows a long List of Creditors.]

The sums payable may be obtained by the parties legally entitled by applying to . . . . Solicitors

The case of Ashley v. Ashley, decided, in 1876, by the Court of Appeal in Chancery, may be safely described as a remarkable Unexpected Asset case. The facts were these·—In 1748, a decree was made for the administration of the personal estate of a testator then recently deceased, the decree directing that his personal estate should be applied in payment of his debts, funeral expenses, and legacies In 1785, the cause came on to be heard on further directions and the Master having certified that the personal estate was insufficient to pay the debts, it was ordered that the testator's real estate should be sold, and the proceeds brought into Court This having been done, and certain specialty creditors who were entitled to prior charges having been paid, the Master, in June, 1792, made another Report, and in July, 1792, an Order was made that the cash therein mentioned should (after payment of cost and certain specialty debts) be divided among the simple contract creditors in proportion to the amounts due to them, and it was referred to the Master to make the apportionment. The Master made a further Report, stating the sums which were to be paid, and the majority of the creditors took out of Court the sums thus apportioned, but some of these sums were never applied for and were left unclaimed in Court for a great number of years. In the year 1867, attention was directed to these unclaimed sums, and about the same time·—more than one hundred and twenty years after the testator's death—a considerable sum of money unexpectedly accrued to the estate. The Heir-at-Law of the testator petitioned the Court, and an inquiry was directed to ascertain the persons who were entitled to the money in Court, both to the unclaimed sums and the newly accrued fund. Advertisements were issued, but only some of the creditors who had originally proved came forward. As to some of the apportioned sums which had remained in the Court unclaimed, no representatives of the persons to whom those sums had been originally apportioned came forward. The persons who did re-assert their claims asked also interest from August, from 1792, upon the unpaid balances of their debts, and contended that they were entitled to be paid out of the moneys in Court, the full amount of their debts with interest, and that those of the creditors who had not come forward again were to be treated as having abandoned their claims altogether. The Heir-at-Law and the Next of Kin of the testator also asserted their claims. The Court, however, held that the apportioned sums which had been left unclaimed were the property of the persons to whom they had originally been ordered to be paid, or their representatives, and that, in the absence of an Act of Parliament, there was no jurisdiction to order them to be paid out to any one else. Those sums must, therefore, remain in Court till some one came forward and showed a title to them. The newly accrued fund must, under the circumstances, be apportioned among all the persons who were originally found to be creditors. The Court also held that,—" the creditors whose debts carried interest were entitled to interest on the unpaid balances of their debts from August, 1792, with this exception, that those creditors who had left their money in Court could have no interest on the money so left. In this respect they must bear the consequences of their own neglect"

The foregoing case proves that it is not only possible for assets to accrue unexpectedly to an estate, but that even after the lapse of so long a period as from 1748 to 1876 the representatives of creditors can claim to share such funds.

In turning over old family papers, it is no uncommon thing for one to come across accounts of many year's standing, part payment only of which has been received, owing to the debtors having got into difficulties which necessitated either the creditors taking a composition of a few shillings in the pound, or losing the whole. These old accounts have long since been forgotten, the original creditors having died, and nothing more is done in the matter until the representatives of the deceased creditors receive a notification from the Court of Chancery or the Court of Bankruptcy that a sum of money awaits distribution in the shape of Unexpected Assets. It occasionally happens that very large sums are thus distributed, as will be seen by the following Advertisement relating to the affairs of a firm of Bankers who executed a Trust Deed in 1803, and whose creditors or their representatives were inquired for over sixty years after the execution of the said Trust Deed, namely, in 1864:—

"In Chancery—Whereas, in or about the month of July, 1803, a Deed of Trust was executed by Messrs. . . bankers, for the benefit of such of the creditors of the partnership firm as should execute the said deed. And whereas, in pursuance of certain decrees or orders . . . . various creditors came in and proved their debts. And, whereas, various of the said creditors it is believed are dead, and it is not known who are now their legal personal representatives or the parties entitled to such debts Now, pursuant to an Order . . . . the several persons and firms named in the schedule hereto named being creditors of the said firm at the date of the said Deed of Trust of 1803, and who duly executed such deed, and came in before the Master and proved their debts, or the legal personal representatives of any such creditors, and all other persons claiming to be entitled to such debts are by their Solicitors . . . . to come in and establish their right to such debts."

The Schedule contains the names and addresses of the original creditors (about 500) who signed the deed. The following were some of the largest creditors—the total amount due to creditors or their representatives was nearly £150,000.—

Names of Creditors.	Residence (where known).	Amount of Debt.		
		£	s.	d
Thomas Dudley, Esq., deceased, representatives of	Shutend, near Dudley	10,138	0	10
Sir Jno Kennaway, Bart., deceased, representatives of	Escott, near Exeter	10,265	7	5
Roger Pocklington & Wm. Dickinson, late bankers, (co-partners). assignees of	Retford Bank	18,912	15	11

On the transfer of the East Indian Railway to the Government, in the year 1880, the "Surplus Assets" of the Company amounted to about £110,000, arising from unclaimed dividends, interest on investments thereof, etc. No list of the persons entitled to these Unexpected Assets was published, as in the Thames Tunnel Company case before referred to (page 108) The fund was distributed thus. £34,160 to the late Chairman of the Company in commutation of his annuity; £15,000 to the then Chairman for extraordinary services; a portion thereof to the proprietors, and a further portion towards charitable objects.

In 1882, the representatives of the creditors of a gentleman who died in Suffolk as long ago as 1827 were inquired for. The amount to be distributed was nearly £1,200.

Advertisements for Creditors or their Representatives are often overlooked by the persons interested, owing to the Advertisement not appearing among Next of Kin notices. The following was inserted in a long string of Trustee Relief Act Advertisements, but it contains remarkable good news concerning Unexpected Assets.—

"JOSEPH LOMAS, Deceased.—Whereas, Joseph Lomas, late of . was . . . in the year 1821 . . . . carrying on the business of a cheese factor in partnership with . . . . And whereas, in or about the same year the said partners arranged with the creditors . . . .by paying a composition upon the amount of the debts due from them. And whereas, the said Joseph Lomas died . . . having by his will made certain provisions with respect to the payment of the balance of the debts so compounded for as aforesaid. Notice is hereby given, that all persons claiming to have been creditors of the said partnership at the date of the said composition or the legal personal representatives of such of them as may be dead, are hereby required to send particulars of their debts to . . . "

Two very remarkable cases of Unexpected Assets were chronicled in the year 1882. In one case the creditors of Mr C Newton,—the largest dry goods merchant in Sydney, a well-known exporter,—unexpectedly received the balance of their debts (5s. in the pound) Mr. Newton some twelve years before had been compelled to ask his creditors for time. This payment of 5s. in the pound is said to have absorbed £40,000. In recognition of Mr Newton's commercial honesty, his creditors presented him with a steam launch for fishing purposes; they also presented Mrs. Newton with a diamond bracelet and a diamond ring.

In the other case the creditors of a Mr. Archbald Winterbottom (who failed some fifteen years ago for £50,000, and paid a composition of 10s. in the pound) received the balance in full. It is said that this honorable transaction caused great excitement on the Bradford Exchange.

The following is an extract from an Advertisement which appeared in 1876, it proves that the representatives of creditors are sometimes inquired for nearly 150 years after a testator's decease:

"WHEREAS, certain sums of STOCK and CASH, of the value of £12,000 or thereabouts, are now standing to the credit of an old suit in Chancery . . . . which sums are alleged to be payable to the CREDITORS of CHARLES PITFIELD, formerly of Middlesex, who died in 1740, whose names are set out in the Report of Master Lane, bearing date August 9, 1792 . . . . And whereas certain of the said Creditors did not receive the amounts directed to be paid to them, and the said sums of STOCK and CASH have in part arisen from the investment and accumulation of such amount, and have in other part arisen from portions of the residuary personal estate of the said Charles Pitfield, which have been received since the date of the said Order. Now, therefore, all persons claiming to be legally or beneficially entitled to or interested in the said funds . . . . are to send notice of their claims to . . . . Solicitors.

[Here follows List of Creditors with amount of debt in each case.]—*Preston's Unclaimed Money.*

A romantic instance of restitution appeared in *Chamber's Edinburgh Journal* some fifty years ago. The narrative is headed, "Curious how things come about sometimes," and the following is a summary of it:—

There once resided within easy distance of a large town in the west of Scotland, a Mr. James Warrington, an extensive jeweler and watchmaker. His family consisted of himself, his wife, two sons, and two daughters. The name of the eldest son was Edward who was engaged to a young lady named Langdale, and their marriage was only delayed until the completion of certain business transactions. Matters, then, stood in this position with the family, when Warrington returned one morning from the shop in great agitation and excitement. "Jess," he said, addressing his wife, "we are ruined—utterly ruined. The shop has been broken into, and at least five thousand pounds' worth of plate and watches carried off I have been with the police through all the most blackguard haunts of the city, but can discover no trace of either the thieves or the goods. The police say there is great doubt of any of the property ever being recovered."

At the time this misfortune happened young Warrington was from home, and the intimation he had of it was from a newspaper paragraph, headed, "Extensive robbery of silver plate and watches." He hurried home; found the family in great distress, and to his further grief discovered that the extent of the robbery had not been exaggerated For many weeks the Warringtons indulged in the hopes that some clue would be found to the robbery. These hopes were never realized; the robbery had been, as the police said, clean and cleverly done. No trace of the perpetrators, or any part of the property, was ever discovered In the meantime, Mr Warrington had paid all his creditors and literally left himself almost without a sixpence. He might have urged the robbery as a plea for bankruptcy; but he was too upright and too conscientious a man to even think of such a course, so he paid his debts to the uttermost farthing. The ruin which had overtaken the Warringtons postponed the proposed union between Edward and Miss Langdale, and Mr. Warrington struggled on for a few years in a small way of business, his son Edward assisting him, but they could not make a living out of it In these circumstances both father and son eagerly embraced the offer of a relative to advance sufficient cash for the payment of their passage out to New South Wales, and also £200 or so to enable them to start in the grazing line there.

For several years after the Warringtons went to New South Wales they combated bravely with the difficulties most emigrants of limited means meet with, but fortune was still unkind, and after the lapse of ten years they found themselves again on the brink of ruin. During all this time Edward and Miss Langdale kept up a correspondence, until on one eventful evening Miss Langdale was alarmed by the sudden and totally unexpected re-appearance of Edward Warrington with the joyous intelligence that he and all the family had returned in excellent health and spirits, and with plenty of "gold in store." This happy termination to long years of anxiety, was thus brought about:—A person named Rapsley located himself on a farm next to the one the Warringtons had taken. He was a sheep farmer, and had by successful speculations in wool and grain, acquired a great deal of money. He evinced great interest in the Warringtons, and seemed to take special note of any facts relating to the robbery which had been the cause of all their misfortunes. It oozed out that Rapsley was an emancipated convict, and the Warringtons consequently gave him the cold shoulder, but he would not take the hint that his society was not wanted. At last this very undesirable neighbor requested a private interview with Mr. Warrington, which was granted. From the interview Mr. Warrington returned in a very excited state. It turned out that Rapsley was the identical person who had committed the memorable robbery, and that he was anxious to refund every farthing with interest. This he did by drafts on a Sydney bank for £7,500 On being thus strangely and unexpectedly put in possession of so large a sum, the Warringtons decided to return to their native land. This determination having been communicated to Rapsley, he insisted on defraying the expenses of the passage home. A further draft of £1,000 was added by the emancipated convict to the aforesaid £7,500, with many expressions of sincere sorrow for his crime.

By a curious chance Mr. Warrington got both his old shop and his old house again; and in a short time the former presented the same appearance which it had done a dozen years before. The marriage—postponed for so many years by reason of the robbery—took place immediately, and in a few years more the elder Warrington retired from business, being enabled by the restoration of his property, and subsequent successful business, to enjoy ease and tranquillity.

CHAPTER XIX.

TREASURE TROVE.

"WHEN any gold or silver, in coin, plate, bullyon hath been of ancient time hidden, wheresoever it be found, whereof no person can prove any property, it doth belong to the King, or some Lord or other of the King's grant, or prescription. The reason wherefor it belongeth to the King is a rule of the common law; that such goods whereof no person can claim property belong to the King, as wrecks, strays, etc."—Such is Treasure Trove as defined by an old writer, and in ancient times the punishment for concealing it was death; it is now fine or imprisonment

If after the Crown has taken possession of any treasure the rightful owner can be traced, the treasure belongs to the owner and not to the Crown. In the olden time, when money was found in a church-yard, the silver went to the priest, the gold to the King.

The right of the Crown to Treasure Trove is deemed by many people to be a somewhat arbitrary one, and finders of long-hidden treasures occasionally try to dispose of them without notifying the "find" to the proper authorities.

Some time since a laborer at Devizes, when moving the thatch from a barn, found thirteen old guineas and other curiosities, which had evidently been stowed away for many years. The finder in this case was honest, and handed over the money to the Lord of the Manor.

The right of a Lord of the Manor to Treasure Trove found on his estate is strikingly exemplified by the following anecdote which appeared in *Vanity Fair*:—

"A West-End jeweler endeavored to tempt a gentleman to purchase a piece of old-fashioned silver, by declaring that it had been found in a particular field near a certain town. "Will you certify that in writing?" asked the gentleman. "Certainly, sir," replied the tradesman. "Do so, and I will take the flagon," returned the gentleman. The tradesman wrote out and handed to him the required certificate, whereupon the customer pocketed certificate and flagon together, remarking, "I am the Lord of that Manor. I am glad to receive my dues."

In France, when money or valuables deemed Treasure Trove are discovered, one half of the value goes to the finder and the other half to the proprietor of the ground on which the "find" was made, as will be seen by the following case. The facts were these:—

"In 1867 some repairs were going on at the Lycee Henri IV., behind the Pantheon, and a workman discovered a large number of Roman coins in a sewer. The contractor in whose employ the workman was, claimed his share; but he was non-suited, and the Municipality paid the finder the handsome sum of 18,292 francs for his half of the treasure."

There was a discussion in Parliament, in 1877, as to whether some very valuable securities, found in the Begum Motee during the Indian Mutiny by our soldiers, were to be treated as Prize Money or Treasure Trove. The captors claimed the same as Prize Money, but the Government decided that these securities must be treated as Treasure Trove, and 25 per cent only of the value of the treasure was distributed among the finders. This seems to be the general rule in such cases, as far as can be gathered from the Parliamentary Returns on the subject.

In the year 1818 a curious Treasure Trove case was decided. The following is the short history of it:—The plaintiffs were the executors of a Mr. Noakes, deceased, and the defendant was a shopkeeper residing at Deal. It was an action of trover to recover certain property from the defendant, under circumstances very peculiar. A sale took place of the property of the plaintiff's at which the defendant attended. A chest of antique drawers was put up by the auctioneer and bought by the defendant for the sum of 4s. 3d. In the evening of the day of the sale the goods were removed, amongst them these old drawers. While the person employed by the defendant to remove his purchase from the premises was taking away the drawers, a secret drawer fell out containing a bag full of guineas. The defendant was present at the time, and upon seeing what had occurred he asked the porter what he should do. The porter advised the defendant to say nothing about it, but required five guineas as hush-money. This the defendant positively refused, and observed that he would rather go to law about it than give the hush-money. The porter immediately made a disclosure, and a law-suit resulted. It was proven by the auctioneer that the drawers were sold, and that the defendant had confessed the guineas were there. It was also proven by a person at whose house the guineas were counted by the defendant, that the number of guineas amounted to between 100 and 130 in the whole. The defendant's counsel contended that the plaintiff could not succeed, as it could not be proven that the guineas were actually his property; on the contrary, he contended that the jury must consider the property not to have belonged to the deceased, but to his ancestors, or to some one unknown. The guineas might have been placed there by some one wholly unconnected with the deceased. The Judge, however, held that the property being found in the house was sufficient to prove that it was the property of the deceased, and the jury immediately found for the plaintiff—damages one hundred and ten guineas.

In 1882 no less than 307,000 francs in gold were discovered by a carpenter rolled up in wrappers of the *Moniteur* newspaper of the time of the Revolution in the wall of a house at Dijon. The owner of the house claimed the money, but an adverse claim was set up by the descendants of the former owner. The Dijon tribunal decided in favor of the descendants, as memoranda on the wrappers proved the genuineness of their claim.

Persons lucky enough to find valuables likely to be claimed as Treasure Trove would do well to consult a solicitor before disposing of them.—*Preston's Unclaimed Money.*

CHAPTER XX.

ESCHEATS.

UNDER the law of England, no lapse of time will bar the claim of Next of Kin to a personal estate not specially bequeathed. This is a fact very important to be known in this country, inasmuch as an almost universal impression prevails amongst the people (not lawyers) that after the lapse of a certain time its recovery is forever barred, either by escheat or limitation. This is only true as to Real Estate, and the law of limitations as to that is pretty fully set out in our first chapter. It would seem a "sin of omission" however, were we to close this work without something on the subject of escheats.

This word is derived from the Norman-French *eschete* from eschoeoir, to fall to (in the sense of a "wind-fall"), Latin, *cadere*. Brett 28a.; Litt §682, Littre s. v. The first definition given to the word by our law writers is; "lands falling by accident to the lord of whom they are holden (Co. Litt. 13a 92b) or to the Crown." It is derived from the Feudal Rule. "that when an estate in fee simple comes to an end, the land reverts to the lord by whose ancestors, or predecessors the estate was originally created. (Wms. Real prop. 126), except in case of high treason, when the land always escheated to the Crown." (Co Litt. 13a). At the present day in England, seignories in freehold land are of no practical value, and the evidence of them has generally been lost, so that where an escheat takes place, the land in almost all cases goes to the Crown, as the ultimate lord of all lands in England. (Wms Real property 128, Co. Litt. 1a).

In the United States, the State is vested with the rights of the feudal lord, and the land reverts to it, where there is no one competent to inherit after office found, but the subject is, in almost all of the States, regulated by Statute, of which more anon.

An escheat may happen in two ways under English law. (1) *aut per defectum sanguinis*, (for default of heirs), or (2) *aut per delictum tenentis*, (for felony). The latter takes place where a person is outlawed for felony, upon which his blood is corrupted; that is to say, he becomes incapable of holding land, or of inheriting it, and at common law, it therefore escheats to the lord. Formerly in England judgment of death for felony caused an escheat in the same manner as out-lawry, but this has been recently abolished, (Stat 33 and 34 Vict. C. 23, see Attainder) as has also the rule that a person could not trace descent to land through an ancestor who has been attainted of treason or felony, so that the land escheated to the lord. (Stat. 3 and 4 Will. IV. C. 106 §10. 1 Steph Com. 445.)

Escheat is not properly a purchase in the technical sense of the word, for the land thus acquired by the lord descends as the seignory would have descended, into the place of which it comes. (Burt Comp. 325 Hargravis note to Co. Litt. 18 b).

Escheat is minutely defined in 2 Bl Com. 244. As to how it arises see 9 Mass.364, 368. As to title thereby see 1 Chit. Gen. Pr. 279

It seems the universal rule of civilized society, that when a disceased owner has left no heirs, his property should vest in the public, and be at the disposal of the Government. Code 10.10.1-10., Vin.Abr 139 ; 1 Brown Com. Law 250 ; 1 Swift Digest 156 ; 5 Binn 375 ; 3 Dane Abr. 140, §24 Jones Land Off. Letters in Penn'a. 5, 6, 93 ; 27 Barb 376 ; 9 Rich Eq. 440 ; 27 Penn'a, 36 ; 5 Cal. 373 ; 1 Smull 355 ; 4 Zab. 566, 2 Swan 46 ; 4 Md. Ch. 167 ; 16 Ga. 31 ; 9 Heisk 85 ; 48 Tex. 567 ; 28 Gratt. 62 ; 47 Md. 103 ; 86 Penn. 284 ; 63 Ind 33.

An action of ejectment commenced by writ of summons has taken the place of the ancient *writ* of *escheat,* against the person in possession, on the death of the tenant without heirs.

Land of a copyhold tenure could not escheat to the Crown, but to the lord of the manor of which it was holden, (1 Chit. Gen. Prac. 280,) and the lord could only seize for want of an heir *quousque*, that is until one appears.

The law of Escheats in the United States is different in the different States, mainly on the length of time required to bar an action for recovery by claimants after the property has passed by judgment to the State ; the longest time allowed in any of them is thirty years after the removal of disability. The State Laws are uniform in their application of the law to personal as well as real property ; and herein they differ wholly from the English law ; and not only so, but it is an entire departure from the reason of the law, and in its practical working is often as great a departure from justice ; if not in direct violation of that provision in the Constitution of the United States which says "nor shall private property be taken for public use without just compensation" I apprehend much of the law is yet to be made in this country on this subject. The Legislatures have had their say on it, but the courts are not yet done with it. Take, for example, the law of Connecticut, which is probably as liberal to the rights of Next of Kin as any of the States, if not the most so. Their Statute provides that :

"When no owner of any estate can be found, it shall escheat to the State ; and Judges of Probate, in their respective districts shall appoint an administrator therein, and give notice to the State treasurer, who shall receive it from the administrator The treasurer may manage or sell the property, and make a conveyance thereof If subsequently the owner appears, he shall be entitled to the property, or avails if it has been sold

When any personal estate of a deceased person shall remain unclaimed for five years after the settlement of his estate, in the hands of the administrator or executor, and the person entitled to the same is unknown or cannot be found, the Court of Probate, after a hearing, may order the same sold and avails paid to State treasurer, who shall refund it to the person entitled thereto if demanded within thirty years"

Now as liberal as this law is, yet what right has a State to take private property, and fix a limit beyond which a rightful heir may not recover it? The law may be applied to real estate, perhaps, with some show of reason, where a remnant of the old feudal system is still recognized as existing, but the reason for it wholly fails in regard to personal property It is not a reversion, because the State never had any interest in it. We hope no rightful heir will be deterred from seeking his remedy, notwithstanding the Statute of Limitations has barred it. The probabilities are he will not be forced to test the constitutionality of the law, for unless he has been guilty of some neglect in prosecuting his claim, the State will in almost every meritorious case pass a Special Act in his favor, which to our certain knowledge has been frequently done.

UNCLAIMED ESTATES IN THE COURT OF CHANCERY.

The following two extracts will give some idea of the enormous amount of money lying unclaimed in the Court of Chancery, in England:—

(From *The Times* of 8th October, 1873.)

"THE CHANCERY DIVIDENDS.—Yesterday, the Chancery Pay Office, which last year was called 'the Accountant-General's Office,' was opened, and will continue open for the payment of the October dividends. The payment in cash to a certain amount, about £50, was continued to the benefit of the recipients who had before the Chancery Funds Act of 1872 was passed, after getting their cheques, to proceed to the Bank of England for the money. Now they are accommodated with cash in Chancery Lane. In the year ended the 31st of October last there was paid into Court at the Chancery Pay Office £19,574,422, and £18,456,976 paid out. There were 51,623 cheques signed, and there were as many as 30,527 accounts. On the various accounts the stock amounted to £60,422,116, cash £3,535,670, and the balance of cash at the Bank £1,111,729. The Consolidated Fund owed the suitors of the Court on 1st of October last £2,428,340."

(From *The Times* of 7th October, 1874.)

"IN CHANCERY.—The first account of the Paymaster General under the Court of Chancery Funds Act of 1872 has been issued as a Parliamentary paper. It shows that on the 31st of August, 1873, the securities and money in the Court of Chancery belonging to suitors reached the value of £66,239,818, or perhaps we should say the nominal value, for the 'securities' are not put at their actual cash value, but are the amount of stock which has been brought into Court or purchased. There are also some few other securities expressed in foreign currencies. It is not stated why these are not included in the statement of amount, for they are as much a part of the Paymaster General's balance as any others. The 'cash' is not quite £4,000,000 sterling. Of this amount nearly £2,500,000 are due from the Consolidated Fund, being the 'book debt' due in cash from the Court of Chancery to the suitors. Nearly £600,000 had been placed 'upon deposit' under the 14th section of the Act. The item of "securities" amounts to above £62,000,000 sterling, and is constituted chiefly of Government or Indian stock, but includes a multitude of other investments, such as railway stock or shares, dock and assurance companies' stock, colonial bonds, Brazilian and various South American bonds, Spanish bonds, St Pancras Skinner's estate bonds, &c., all brought into Court for safe keeping during some strife or suit. There are also a large number of boxes and miscellaneous effects in the Bank of England, deposited there on behalf of the Court of Chancery—boxes containing securities, jewelry, title-deeds, a will, personal ornaments, plate, a portrait, diamond necklace, coronet, and earrings, and many other articles, each box being marked with the title of the cause or matter in which the contents are in dispute or under discussion. The account is made up to the 31st of August, as being a more convenient time than the last day of September, which has been heretofore the closing day of the Chancery year. The Comptroller and Auditor General has had to report on the account, and he observes that the audit hitherto has, since the abandonment of the system of check before payment, been confined to an examination (with reference to the accounts of the suitors) of the certificates and draughts of the Assistant Paymaster General, after they have been acted upon, and to the daily entry of all the transactions in the duplicate books (formerly kept at the Bank of England) *pari passu* with the entry of the same transactions in the books of the Paymaster-General. It is manifest that this limited audit does not fulfil the object contemplated by the Treasury in 1871—viz., the establishment of 'a complete check on Chancery expenditure,' for that would involve the examination not only of the documents prepared in the office of the Assistant Paymaster General, but also of the orders of the Court, and of all the subsidiary authorizing documents, with the view of ascertaining that the intentions of the Court have been duly and faithfully carried into effect. It may serve to give some idea of the amount of work involved in keeping a check upon the Chancery books if we state that the number of causes and matters on the 31st of August, 1873, was 31,146, and 43,477 draughts were paid in the eleven months ending on that day. It may here be added that the amount of dormant and unclaimed money in official custody is very large. Unclaimed dividends on the public 'Funds' have accumulated until the amount reached £991,711, in April, 1873, but at the beginning of the present year the amount had been reduced to £904,891. There is also a very large amount of unclaimed Army prize money, from which upwards of £600,000 has been expended on Chelsea Hospital pensions. The usual annual account of naval prize money has not yet, we believe, been issued this year. From these sources thousands of small sums are due to old soldiers and sailors, or their next of kin, and it should be known that these moneys are easily recoverable by the proper parties."

CONCLUSION.

FOR information concerning the following lists, we refer the reader to pages 6, 7, and 8 of this MANUAL. Additional lists will be inserted in each successive issue of the MANUAL, which will be revised and published once a year, and in the interim, supplemental lists will be issued; so that names sent us for insertion will be promptly and extensively advertised. We repeat that no charge whatever is made for insertion of names of persons wanted, and we again urge all our correspondents, clients, and friends to send in any names they wish advertised.

Any one, or more, entitled as Next of Kin to an unclaimed estate, can proceed to recover his or her share, or shares, independently of other claimants; but it is always preferable that all, or as many as possible, unite in the claim, as it greatly reduces the *pro rata* expenses.

In regard to the amount of wealth represented by the names in the following lists, we can only repeat what we say on page 6 of this MANUAL, but may add that many of them do represent very large estates. We might enumerate by the hundred, but will only mention as samples of a large class, that of Helen Sheridan, in "List 13," where there is *a million and a half pounds sterling* awaiting Next of Kin, and Leonard H Smith, in "List 17," who, amongst other property, left $10,000 in U. S. Government Bonds, all of which is in the hands of the Public Administrator, awaiting Next of Kin.

It will be observed that the information respecting identity of persons wanted, as published in the following lists, is often very meagre. In some instances this is intentionally done, so that Heirs will be forced to seek further information through this BUREAU. Otherwise they might ignore us in their investigation, and we would have no remuneration for our advertisement. It will be further noticed that the words, "Heirs Wanted," appear to some names, and not to others. This has no special significance, as Heirs are wanted in all of them.

Our business in the investigation of Old Estates, Unclaimed Money, etc., is not at all confined to the cases in which we publish names of persons wanted, but we will undertake any case that presents reasonable grounds for hope of its recovery. In this connection we would remind our readers that many ninety-nine-year leases are now expiring, and occasionally one falls on lands covered by a large city or town. Any one having a suspicion that his ancestors may have left such reversionary interests, may, with little expense, have the facts ascertained through this BUREAU.

The undersigned Manager, in his sixteen years' experience as Manager of the Martindale Law Association, has made the acquaintance of the leading lawyers in every county in the United States and Canada; and will be happy to give, as a reference to anyone desiring it, the name of some prominent man in his own neighborhood, to whom he can refer.

Very respectfully,

J. B. Martindale
Gen'l Manager.

UNCLAIMED MONEY, LANDS AND ESTATES BUREAU.
142 La Salle Street, Chicago.

SPECIAL LIST No. 1.

UNCLAIMED MONEY, LANDS AND ESTATES.

The following persons, if alive, or if dead, their representatives, are entitled to property. All letters must be addressed to **J. B. MARTINDALE, 142 La Salle Street, Chicago, Illinois**, and must contain a statement of all facts on which the writer bases his or her claim [See pages 6, 7 and 8 of this Manual.]

ALLEN, THOMAS, formerly of Tilehurst and Wallingford, in the County of Berks, England, who in 1793 emigrated to Springfield, in the County of Delaware, Pa., U.S.A., where he died about 1794, leaving five children, ABIZAH ALLEN, DANIEL ALLEN, ELIZABETH PENTYCROSS ALLEN, SARAH ALLEN, and AARON ALLEN
ANDERSON, JOHAN ADOLF (alias WIGHT), Mariner, of Tolo, in Sweden
ANDREWS, JOHN, formerly of Diss, County Norfolk, England, Draper, then residing at No 34 Marshall-street, London road, in the County of Surrey, afterwards of No. 1, Beulah Cottage, Clifton-street, Wandsworth-road, in the County of Surrey, who died at New York, U S A., 1847
ANDREWS, WILLIAM, left England for America about 1830.
ANSELL, SARAH (formerly SARAH FENN, Spinster), Widow of James Ansell, formerly of London, and afterwards of Hamilton, Ontario, Canada.
ASPDEN, MATTHIAS, of Pennsylvania, in the United States of America.
ASTON, JAMES, of Yorkshire, England, who went to America
ATKINSON, JAMES, and MARGARET his Wife, who went to America about 1825 or 1830.
ATKINSON,—Children of WILLIAM and KATE ATKINSON, now or formerly of Illinois, U.S.A., but previously of Douglas, Isle of Man, England
AULT, MISS JANE (See Roberts or Robinson)
AVERY, SAINT JOHN, formerly of Reading, Berks, Eng., Trunkmaker, who was residing in N Y in or about the year 1823.
BAGGS, LEVINE, formerly of Dublin, Ireland, supposed to be residing in Canada
BARTON, ALFRED, formerly of Ossett, near Wakefield, Eng, afterwards of the City of N Y who in 1869 was residing at Chicago, State of Illinois, U S A, Medical Practitioner, supposed to have died at Chicago aforesaid, about 1869
BATES, or HOPKINS, ANNE. (See Anne Hopkins)
BAUMAN, CHARLES, a German Swiss, late a Builder in London, at present in America.
BAYLY, THOMAS, formerly of Co Somerset, Eng, residing in 1858 at Bushville, L I, or elsewhere in America.
BENNETT, JOHN who left London in 1841, and sailed in the "Jolly Tar," for Galveston, Texas, U S A
BERRIDGE, THOMAS, of Lincoln, Eng, who emigrated to America in March, 1861, and is supposed to have gone to Cal
BEST,—. (See Dr Hall.)
BINNS, JAMES, who in 1883 lived at Toxteth-park, Liverpool, England, and was supposed to have emigrated to America
BIRCHALL, THOMAS and WILLIAM, left Liverpool in 1845 for America
BIRKETT (or BIRKET,) JOHN, Brother of James, who emigrated with his family to America about 1818.
BLEAKEY, ROBERT, a native of England, who went to America
BODKIN, FRANCIS, left England for America about 1842.
BOOTH, MARK, a Joiner and Carpenter, who married a servant of the Earl of Lonsdale, and afterwards went to Whitehaven, where his wife is supposed to have died, after which he emigrated to Canada
BOWN, JOHN, formerly of Notts, Eng, residing in 1882-3, at Petaluma, Chilano Valley, Sonoma Co., California.
BRADSHAW, JOSEPH, of Ballinacargy, Co Westmeath, Ireland, died in 1870. Next of kin are in America
BRADY, MARY ANN, Daughter of Dennis Brady, formerly of Louchbrickland, County Down Ireland, Blacksmith
BRAMWELL, GEO & THOS., of Derbysh, Eng, when last heard of, were living at Muckwonago, Waukesha, Co Wis., U S A
BRETT, BERNARD BALLARD residing in New York, U S A.
BREWER, HASTINGS and WILLIAM, of New York City, U S A.
BRIDGES, WILLIAM, late of Wiltshire, England, who left England in May, 1841, and was last heard of in 1851, when his address was, "Care of Mr Stewart, North Beach, San Francisco, California."
BROOKE, WILLIAM, a gentleman of property, in the County of Antrim, Ireland, and of Exeter, England, who emigrated to America in 1858, and has not since been heard of
BROUGH, WILLIAM PARKINSON, a native of Lincolnshire, who left England for the U S A about 1843.
BROWN, or COPLEY, or THOMPSON, MARY GRIEVE, who lived in Grub-street and Gutter lane London England, and it is supposed went to North America about 1765.
BROWN, GEORGE, who went to America in 1862
BURDON, WILLIAM, Mercer, who in 1755 went from Great Torrington, in the County of Devon, England, to New York, U S A., as a factor, and lived there for some time with a Mrs. Johnscourt, in the Meal-market.
BURROUGH, ROBERT, Son of Richard, who was a Carver, and lived in the Parish of St. Mary's, Rotherhithe, Surrey, England, and in 1731 went to Cheynes, Buckinghamshire, and thence, it is supposed, to some part of America.
CAMERON, ALEXANDER, eldest Son of the deceased Duncan Cameron, Wine and Spirit Merchant, Paisley, Scotland, he was a Sailor, and was last heard from about 1860, when he was at New Orleans, U S A.
CARDY, MARY, otherwise ELLICOT, who went to America in 1830
CARR, GEORGE, who left H M's Ship "Basilisk," at Picton, Nova Scotia, in June, 1853
CASSIDY, GEORGE HENRY, formerly of the County of Wexford, Ireland, afterwards of New Orleans, U S A.
CATER, ABRAHAM, Miller, and THOMAS CATER, Butcher, of the County of Suffolk, England, who left England for America in September, 1833. Thomas Cater was in New Orleans in May, 1839
CATER, CHAS., Miller, of Co Suffolk, who left Eng for America in Jan, 1833 He afterwards wrote from Detroit
CAWSTON, SEDGELY HENRY, who in 1865 was in the Canadian (Windsor) Volunteers, afterwards Travelling Agent for a Toronto Bookseller, subsequently employed at a Bookstall on the Vermont Central Railroad, and was last heard of from Boston, U S A.
CAYTON, JAMES, who left Manchester, England, about 1828, for Philadelphia, Pa., U S.A.
CHADWICK, JAMES, of Frankford, in Philadelphia, U S A.
CHALMERS, ROBERT KEMP, a native of Scotland, who left Liverpool for New York under the name of Wilson, was afterwards heard of at Baltimore, Manchester, Miss., and finally at New Orleans, where he was known under the name of Thomas Wilson, otherwise Alexander Paul.
CLAY, REGINALD GRAHAM MUSGRAVE (otherwise REGINALD GRAHAM), who was residing in 1848 and 1849 in Boardstown, Cass Co., Illinois, U S A., and thence proceeded to California.
COLHOUN, HUGH, who died in Pennsylvania, he had a brother, Fitzsimons Colhoun.
COLLENS, ELIZA. (See Eliza Pearce.)
COLLYER, JOSEPH, Linendraper, of London, 1892-3
COMBER, W G, who left the Isle of Wight, England, in 1869, and is supposed to be in America.
COOPER, GEORGE, formerly of Preston, Lancashire, England, last heard of in San Francisco, California, in 1856.
COPLEY, otherwise THOMPSON, otherwise BROWN, MARY GRIEVE (See Brown, Mary.)
COSTELLO, KATE, born about 1838, who was brought up by John Quane, of Townland Clautrian, Parish of Artlachy, County Limerick, Ireland, and when last heard of, was going to America.
COUPLAND, WALTER, born in 1818, at Seedley, near Manchester, England, when last heard from, in 1844, was on board the "Tarquin," an American ship, trading between the United States and France.
CRAMPTON, SARAH. (See Sarah Turner)
CRICHTON, ANDREW, a native of Glasgow, Scotland, residing in America.
CRONE, MARY, Wife of Joseph Crone, of New London, Henry Co, Iowa, U S A.
CROSSLEY, CHARLES, of New Jersey, America, Executor to the Will of John Crossley, of Hargreaves, Co. Lan., Eng.
CUNNING, SUSAN, formerly of Ballysteckard, County Down, Ireland, who went to America in 1823

DALE, WILLIAM DUNCAN, who sailed from Liverpool, England, in the barque, "Perthshire," in 1849, and was last heard of about 1843, to Boston, U S A
DANDO, JOSEPH, who in 1830 or 1831 married Ellen Sterling, or Sheriff, and was divorced from her in New York; afterwards married in Philadelphia, one Jane Clark, and after her death, one Sarah Clark, thereafter, in Philadelphia, he married one Harriet Catherine Williams
DAVIDSON, WILLIAM, of Lanarkshire, Scotland, lately residing at Heber City, Wasatch Co., Utah, U.S.A.
DAVIS, JOSIAH, Merchant, of London, 1892-3.
DAWSON, RICHARD, formerly of Yorkshire, England, last heard of in 1862 or 1863, in the employ of Pratt, Ropes, and Co., the Meriden Cutlery Company, West Meriden, Conn., U.S.A.
DEATH, JOHN, Son of Thomas, who is supposed to have left England for America, with his children, about the year 1790, and to have died on his passage out.
DEBNAM, MARY ANN, and JOHN DEBNAM, her Husband, formerly of Warminster, Wilts, Eng Address of the former, in 1868, was 4, King street, Staten Island, N Y   Address of the latter, in 1857, was Newburg, P O., N Y.
DELANNOY, PETER, Gentleman, of London, 1692-3
DERINZY, WM. RICHARDS, formerly of Clobernon Hall, Co Wexford, Ireland, then of Fredericksburgh, Va., U S A., and lastly supposed to have resided about the years 1840 and 1847 in Brooklyn, New York, U S A.
DOBSON, HANNAH   (See Hannah Kebly)
DOBSON, WM, Son of Robert, who married Margaret Leefe, of Thornton-le-Clay, and emigrated to America.
DONOVAN, DENIS and JAMES, Sons of Margaret Donovan, or Tobin, who are stated to have gone to Wales in the years 1824 and 1832 respectively, and to have subsequently gone to America
DOOLEY, PATRICK, late of Gorey, in the County of Wexford, Ireland, who left Ireland about the year 1846 for Shelkil County, United States, America, and has not since been heard of.
DOUGLAS, GEORGE, of Lancashire, England, who was residing in New York, U S A., in 1846.
DOWLAND, JOHN, formerly a Captain in the 67th Regiment, who died in 1866.
DUFRENE, THOMAS W, formerly of Brussels, lately residing corner of Tenth and Chesnut Streets, Phila., Pa., U.S.A.
ELDER, JAMES, a native of Scotland, who left England for America about the year 1851
ELLICOT, MARY   (See Mary Cardy)
ELLIS, THOMAS, a native of the United States, and belonging to the schooner "Albion;" who was drowned at the wreck of the "Coll-Castle," at the Feejee Islands.
FAIRBAIRN, ROBERT KINNEBURGH, of Edinburgh, Scotland, who was for some time resident in Canada West.
FENN, SARAH (See Sarah Ansell)
FERRIS, CHARLES, formerly of Kent, Eng , sailed for New York, U S A , about 1835, with his brother, James.
FETHERSTON, THOMAS and MARY, residing in New York, U S A., in 1854
FINLEY, ARCHER, of London, England, who went to America.
FLINT, LEONARD, formerly of Yorkshire, who left England by the ship "Silas Richards," for New York, U S A., in 1840 , he intended to proceed to Newark, in the State of Ohio, U S A
FOOT, FREDERICK DOLIER, and his Brother, BERKLEY FOOT, who left Ireland in 1859, viâ Galway, for the U S A.
FOWKS PETER, Gentleman, of London, 1692-3.
FRAMPTON, SARAH   (See Sarah Turner)
FREEMAN, JOHN, who was engaged, about 1844, as a Journeyman Baker in the employ of the Nantyglo Iron Company, and then at Sirhowey Blaenavon, Ebbw vale, Tredegar, and is supposed soon afterwards to have gone to America
FYFE, or FYFFE, ROBERT, Sister of (married), who went from Scotland to North America, many years ago
GARLAND, JOSEPH, Mariner, formerly of Dundee, Scotland, left Liverpool in 1803, on board of the "Earl Wycomb," for Picton, North America. In 1804 he shipped as Seaman, at Portsmouth, N H , on board an American vessel trading with the West Indies, and has not since been heard of.
GASKARTH, JAMES, of New Orleans, U S A.
GIBBONS, WILLIAM, Mariner, joined the ship "Free Trader," at Glasgow, in 1852, whence he sailed for Singapore and Penang in February of that year   He left said vessel at Singapore, and sailed for New Orleans or San Francisco
GIBSON, JOHN, of Llanelly, Co Carmarthen, Welsh, left England many years since, and proceeded to California, and has not been heard of since 1860, when he was residing at Angel's Camp, Calaveras County, Alta, California
GIDDINGS, JAMES, formerly of Cambridgeshire, England, who emigrated to America some years ago
GIFFORD, NATHANIEL, Gentleman, of London, 1692-3.
GILLART, FELIX, Son of Felix Gillart, who was last heard of in October, 1778, when he was engaged as a Seaman on board the merchant ship, "Union Horse," then lying in New York, U S A.
GOOD, ROBERT CHARLES HARRY, formerly of the City of Bristol, England, his last address was Post-office, Cornhill, Williamson County, Texas, U S A
GOUGH, SOPHIA HENRIETTA, residing in the United States of America.
GRAUNIS, WHITE, & CO., doing business in New York to 1833.
GREENE, ALFRED SMITHSON, of the City of New York, U S A.
GREENHILL, JOSEPH, PASCHALL, and DAVID, born in Virginia, U S A , between 1720 and 1730.   Father's name, Paschall Greenhill, who died in Virginia about 1730
GUY, MARY, born in London, England, in or about the year 1760, her representatives are supposed to be in America
HABERMEYER, JACOB FRIEDRICH, of Stralsund, Goldsmith, who was born in 1782, went to sea in 1790, and was last heard of in 1803, when he was in Philadelphia, Pa.
HACHING, ROBERT, formerly of Manchester, in the County of Lancaster, England, Warehouseman, who sailed from England for the Cape of Good Hope in the year 1836, and afterwards sailed for, and arrived at, Salem, in the United States, in March or April, 1837, whence he sailed to the East and West Indies , about the end of 1838 he left Salem for some place unknown, and has not since been heard of
HALL, DR., and his Wife, who was a daughter of Rev Dr Best, an Irish Clergyman   Dr and Mrs. Hall went to Charleston, South Carolina, his children by his first wife are supposed to be somewhere in Canada.
HALL, ROBERT (Brother of Joseph Hall, late of Carlisle, Cumberland, England), who emigrated from Arkengarthdale, in the County of York, England, to Canada, about the year 1838
HALPIN, or HALPINE (formerly ORD), Mrs. MARY , or, if dead, her Children.
HARGREAVES, WILLIAM, formerly of Galgate, near Lancaster, England, who was last heard from at Waynesville, Ohio, U S A , in September, 1850
HARRIS, THOMAS, formerly a Clerk in the General Post Office, London, England, one of the children of William Harris, of Hackney, County of Middlesex, and Elizabeth Mary Harris, his Wife, sailed from Portsmouth, England, for New York, per the "Philadelphia," in December, 1836
HARRISON, JOHN, residing in 1773 in Monmouth County, New Jersey, U S A.
HARRISON, JOHN, late of Hurstonfield, Co Cumberland, England, Farmer, Heirs-at-Law supposed to be in America.
HARTUNG, OTTO LOUIS, of Schellingstett, by Coslada, Prussia, arrived in America in 1850, left New York in 1854.
HAUKNALL, CHARLES, Bookbinder, of Phila , U S A., was in London, England, in the beginning of the century
HAY, or RATCLIFFE, or PHILLIPS, ELIZABETH, who went from Glasgow to New York, U S A., in 1835, said be to of unsound mind , she is said to have been the Wife of James Hay, of 133, William-street.
HAYWARD, JAMES, of Poole, County of Dorset, England, Mariner, sailed from Cork for Newfoundland in 1832
HEATH, GEORGE (Son of Robert and Letitia Heath), who emigrated to Jamaica, in or about 1812 and was in 1822 in South Carolina, engaged as Sailor in the Packet trade between Charleston and Beltimore, U S A
HENTIE, JOHN, who lived many years in South Carolina, U S A., and died in that province about 1770.
HERR, CHRISTIAN, formerly of Lancaster Co , Pa, U S A
HILL, DAVID, Mariner, a native of Edinburgh, Scotland, deceased, who was married in Boston, U S A., some considerable time prior to May, 1853   His Children wanted.
HILL, ESTHER.   (See Mrs. Esther Paskett)
HINDENBURG, FRIEDERICH JOHANN WILHELM, a native of Prussia, who went to America about the year 1846.

HOLLAND, JOHN, or JOSEPH, formerly of Yorkshire, England, who went to America
HOPKINS, or BATES, ANNE, was born in 1786, was married to John Bates, who was an Innkeeper near London; her Representatives are supposed to be in America.
HOPPS, WILLIAM, RALPH, and ROBERT (See Nicholson, Thomas, William, and Elizabeth)
HUDSON, EDWARD, a native of Dublin, Ireland. In the year 1861 he had an office at 66, Cedar street, New York.
HUDSON, GEORGE, formerly of Acklam, now supposed to be in America, or, if dead, his Children
HUNT, JOHN, of Lincoln, England, emigrated to America in 1850, last heard of in California in 1864
INGRAM, ADAM, formerly a Labourer at Roxburgh, in Scotland, and afterwards a Soldier in H B M's 21st Regiment of Royal Scotch Fusiliers, supposed to have been taken prisoner at New Orleans, in the year 1814.
JAMIESON ROBERT, who left Port Glasgow, Scotland, for New York, in or about the year 1818, he was a Rope-spinner by trade, his father's name was Joseph
JEFFRIES, or JEFFERY, JOSEPH BODKIN, who went to America, date unknown
JENKINS, WM, Schoolmaster, who left Eng for U S A., May, 1863, supposed to be in the English or American Navy
JOHNS, ROBERT, Cornwall, England, in July, 1848, was a Miner at the Bristol Copper Mines, Connecticut, U S A
JOHNSTONE, CHARLES JOHN COSENS, M D, who left England for America in 1844.
JONES, CHARLES, of Cheshire, England, who left England for America in 1858
JONES, JOSHUA, Son of John Jones, of London, England, went to America about the year 1805; was at New Brunswick, New Jersey, in the year 1827, when last heard from.
JONES, ROBERT, a Dyer, Son of Robert Jones, of Bradford, Whtshire, England, who went to America in 1811
JONES, THOMAS, now or late of New Orleans, U.S.A.
JOSERIN, CHRISTIAN, a Sailor, native of Finland; supposed to be on a vessel trading to and from some American port.
KEBLY, HANNAH, Daughter of Roger Dobson, and Wife of George Kebly, residing in North America about 1842.
KERSHAW, THOMAS, a native of Marsden, County York, England, went to America about the year 1806, he had two Sons, Thomas and Simeon. In 1836 he was residing at Forks, Pa., where he is said to have died.
KETTLEWELL, THOMAS, emigrated to America. He settled first in Salem, and went afterwards to Baltimore.
KEW, WILLIAM, who went to America in 1837.
KING, GEORGE, of Vancouver's Island. WALTER KING, of Guelph, Canada.
KRINITZ, ROLLINS, and AHLBORN, formerly Merchants in New York City, or any one of them.
LAW, CHARLES ROBERT, formerly of the City of Bristol, England, but late of New York City, U S A.
LAWRENCE, JOHN, formerly of Stone, in the County of Worcester, England, and at the time of his death resident in Norfolk, in the State of Virginia, U S A., Merchant, where he died in 1814
LEARMOND, ALEXANDER and ROBERT, formerly of the City of Hamilton, Canada.
LEES THOMAS, formerly of the City of Bristol, England, Merchant Seaman, who sailed from Liverpool in the ship "Columbia," for Philadelphia, U S A., in July 1834, he arrived safely at Philadelphia, and is believed to have sailed shortly afterwards for New Orleans, but no tidings have since been heard of him
LENNOX, GEORGE, born in Scotland, 1811, and became a Sailor; he sailed from Swansea, Wales, for America, 1856.
LEVY, BENJAMIN, Merchant, of London, 1892 3.
LEWIS, WILLIAM. (See William Lewis Pinfold.)
LINDSAY, GEORGE, of the City of New York, or Brooklyn, U.S.A.; ELIZABETH LINDSAY, or STIVINS, of N.Y. City, WILLIAM LINDSAY STIVINS, of Geneva, N Y, U S A., JOSIAH and DAVID LINDSAY, of N Y.
LINDSEY, JOHN, formerly of Lincolnshire, England, who emigrated to America in 1858, was in Carson City, Nevada Ter., U.S.A., in 1862, and was last heard of from Sacramento Valley, California, in March, 1863
LISTER, JAMES, of Wakefield, Yorkshire, who went to America.
LISTON, ROBERT, Baker, of Edinburgh, who left Scotland about 1836, and was last heard of at New Orleans, U.S.A.
LISTON, THOMAS, House-painter, of Edinburgh, left Scotland 1846, last heard of at Buffalo, New York, U.S.A.
LLOYD, ANNA M. (See Daniel McSheffrey)
LOCKWOOD, EDWARD, a native of Yorkshire, England; was residing in Philadelphia, Pa, from 1806 to 1810
LOIRE, JEAN JOSEPH, otherwise JOHN, a native of Geneva, who resided in 1852, at St Martinsville, Louisiana, U.S.A.
McCARTHY, DANIEL, residing in the United States of America, he was the Son of Charles McCarthy, of Ireland.
McGAW, PETER, of Scotland, a Sailor, who sailed from Liverpool to New York, U.S.A., about 1860
McKENZIE, JOSEPH, of Montreal, in Canada.
McKENZIE, RODERICK, of Danumsville, San Francisco, California, U S A
MACKNESS, WILLIAM COOPER, Carpenter, formerly of Bedford, England, who emigrated to America about 1852, and was at a Sailors' Home, Boston, U.S.A. in 1863
McLUNE, WILLIAM, Saddler, in Ohio, U S A.
McSHEFFREY, DANIEL, jun., and ANNA M McSHEFFREY, or LLOYD, who, with their father John and their mother Mary, left Ireland in or about 1829, and went to St. John's, New Brunswick, and afterwards to New Orleans, U S A., and were subsequently living in Philadelphia, Daniel was in Texas in 1840, Anna McSheffrey married Dr. Lloyd, of Baltimore, in 1833, who died before 1849, leaving the said Anna M Lloyd him surviving
MALLORY, WILLIAM and FRANCES, in or about the year 1766, residing on or near the James River, Virginia.
MARSHALL, JOHN, Executor of the Will of the late Joseph Smith, of Yorkshire, England who died in 1842
MALTMAN, GAVIN, a native of Fifeshire, Scotland, born in 1792, emigrated in early life to the West Indies In 1830 he left Jamaica for Halifax, Nova Scotia; in 1842 he was in Prince Edward Island, thereafter he was in New Brunswick, and the last letter from him is dated from Pugwash, Nova Scotia, 21st January, 1848 It is understood that he was afterwards seen in Shediac, New Brunswick, in or about the year 1854
MATTERN, MORITZ OSCAR THEODOR LUDWIG JULIUS, who left Sprottau for America in 1853, and was last heard of in St. Louis, Missouri, U S A., in 1854
MICKETHWAITE, JOSEPH, Merchant, of London, 1892 3
MIDDLEDITCH, LOWE, residing in America.
MILLER, THOMAS, Merchant of London, 1592-3.
MILLHOUSE, or MILLES, JOSEPH, ELIZA, ANN, THOMAS, and MARY, residing in America.
MORRIS, JANE, residing in 1864, in the State of Illinois, U.S.A.
MORRIS, THOMAS, Merchant, of London, 1692-3
MURPHY, MICHAEL, of Valentia, Co Kerry, Ireland, and his three Sisters, BRIDGET, KATE, and MARY, in America.
MURPHY, ROBERT, born in Ireland and went with his parents to America about 1780, he returned about 1785
NICHOLS, GEORGE WASHINGTON, born in Rhinebeck, N Y, in 1822.
NICHOLSON, ROBERT, of Newcastle-on-Tyne, England, residing in the United States of America
NICHOLSON, THOMAS, WILLIAM, and ELIZABETH, and WILLIAM HOPPS, RALPH HOPPS, and ROBERT HOPPS, Nephews and Niece of Robert Atkinson, late of Pontefract, York, England, and supposed to be residing in Cook County, in the United States of America.
NIEMANN, WILLIAM MATTHEW, who was residing in Boston, U.S.A., in 1843, and was last heard of in 1849
NIXON, RICHARD, of Skelton, Cumberland, England, who in 1823 was working in a ship-yard, in New York, U.S.A.
O'CONOR, MARIA, of Dublin, Ireland, went to America in 1846, in 1849 was living in Orange Co, N Y, U S A.
ODELL, WILLIAM THOMAS, only Son of William Odell, formerly of Bushfield Avenue, Donnybrook, Ireland, Barrister
ODIE, DOROTHY, Wife of William Odie, residing in the U.S.A.
ORD, MARY (See Halpine, Mrs. Mary)
PARCELL, JOHN and GEORGE, Brothers, who left England for America between the years 1830 and 1836
PARKER, CHARLES, late of Wickham Skeith, County Suffolk, England, Farmer, his Nephews and Nieces are supposed to be in America.
PASKETT, or HILL, Mrs. ESTHER, Widow of William Paskett, who resided for some time at St. John's, New Brunswick, and afterwards removed to New York, U S A., where they kept an inn or hotel, about the year 1836.
PASTOR, FRIEDRICH, a native of Germany, residing in America.

PAUL, MOSES, alias JOHN, alias MONTGOMERY, who left Coleraine, Ireland, in 1854, and was residing in June, 1884, in Hoopa Valley, Humboldt County, California, U.S.A.
PEACOCK, ELIZA ANN, who left England for America in 1844, with her father, Charles Peacock, and who resided for some time at Rhode Island, near New York, U S.A.
PEAR, SIR JAMES, or Heirs, in Newfoundland
PEARCE, ELIZA (formerly ELIZA COLLENS), of Maidstone, England, supposed to be in America
PHILLIPS, ELIZABETH. (See Elizabeth Hay)
PIERCY, WHYLEY, of Leicestershire, England, who was last heard of at West Troy, Albany County, New York, U S A., some years ago. If dead, his Child or Children
PINFOLD, WILLIAM LEWIS (otherwise WILLIAM LEWIS), who left England about the year 1820 for America, and carried on business until 1838 as Looking glass Maker, at Philadelphia, Pa., U S A
POUNDS, JAMES, ROBERT WALKER, and JOHN, Sons of James Pounds, formerly of 6, Parker st., Phila, U.S.A.
PRESTLAND, DANIEL, a native of Biggleswade, County Bedford, England, a Carpenter by trade, who left London, England, in 1854, and was last heard of from Chicago and New Orleans, in March, 1856.
PRICE, EDWARD THORETON GOULD, and ELIZABETH, his Wife, who sailed from Antwerp for Baltimore, U S A., in the brig "Emily," in April, 1830
PULLAR, ANDREW, of Dundee, Scotland, landed in New York, May, 1847. Three months thereafter, he sailed for Norfolk, and has not been heard of since. He was then about 35 years of age, and both deaf and dumb
PULTENEY, CHARLES SPEKE, formerly of the County of Dorset, England, Surgeon, who left England for America about 1780. Children of, wanted.
RATCLIFFE, or HAY, or PHILLIPS, ELIZABETH (See Elizabeth Hay)
READING, HENRY HUCKER, of Somersetshire, Eng., when last heard from, he was living in Oakland County, U S A.
REINHARD, EBERHARD, formerly of Handschuchsheim and then of Heidelberg, in Germany, who in 1849 came to London with the intention of proceeding to America.
RELFE, CHARLES OSBORNE, of London, England. In 1857 he was employed by T S. Wiswall, Nassau-street, N Y
REMINGTON, THOMAS, who sailed from London in the brig "Ocean," in October, 1846, and was last heard of at Charleston, U S A., in 1847, when he was on board the schooner "Medium," bound for Keywest.
RENTON, THOMAS LAIDLAW, a native of Scotland, who has not been heard of since 1843, in which year he left New Orleans for Texas, U S A
ROBERTS, BENJAMIN, now or late of New York City, U S.A.
ROBERTS, or ROBINSON, married a Miss Jane Ault, with whom he emigrated from England to Canada, in 1819, is said to have had the fitting up of the Huron Hotel, Gooderich, C W. He had two Sons, George and Reuben.
ROBERTSON, JOHN STARK, residing in Virginia, U S A., in 1779
ROBINSON, WILLIAM, formerly of Hertfordshire, who left England about 1855, and when last heard of, was holding an appointment on the Grand Trunk Railway of Canada, at Toronto
ROWTE, JOHN His representatives are in America; he was born in London, about the year 1760.
RUDDICK, MARY MARGARET, residing, in 1865, in Montreal, Canada.
RUSSELL, MARY, Spinster, who died in Ireland, intestate. Next of kin are in America.
RUSSELL, ROBERT, a native of Glasgow, Scotland, who emigrated to America in 1832
SARGEANT, GEORGE WILKINSON, of London, England, Chemist who left England for America, many years ago, supposed to reside in Ohio or California, U S A
SCARTH, HENRY, deceased. His Heir-at-Law and Next of Kin are supposed to be in America
SCHICKLER, JOHN, Farmer, formerly of Pushnch, Canada, who left Canada about 1862, and was last heard from near the Niagara Falls Suspension-bridge.
SEABY, RICHARD, Son of Nathaniel Seaby, of Ashwell, Co Bedford, England, now residing in America
SHAKESHAFT, CHARLES, Representatives of, wanted
SHARP, ROBERT CLUBLEY, and ELIZA ANNIE, his Wife, residing, about 1871, at Harrietsville, Ontario, Canada.
SHEPHERD, MARY, Widow, late of the County of Lincoln, England, but now living in the State of Ohio, U S A.
SHEPPARD, WILLIAM, Goldsmith, of London, 1692 3
SHEPPARD, ELIZABETH, Representatives of, wanted. She had a sister named Dorothy, who married John Hatfield, about the year 1756.
SHIPPORE, ELIZABETH; Representatives of, wanted. She had a sister named Dorothy, who married John Hatfield, about the year 1756
SIMS, otherwise DAVIES or DAVIS, JULIANA ELIZA, supposed to be residing at Utah, Salt Lake City, in America.
SINCLAIR, ALEXANDER (Son of Wood Sinclair, Cooper in Leith, Scotland), resided in St Louis, Mo, U S A.
SMITH, ELIZA (Maiden name, ELLIS), of Leicestershire, England, her next of kin in Phila or New Orleans, U.S.A.
SMITH, GEORGE, Hotel-keeper, London, who died 1843, at the age of 82 years
SPEECHLEY, JOHN, formerly of Woodston, Huntingdonshire, England, whose address in 1859 was P O, N Y
SPOFFORD and TILLOTTSON, doing business in New York in 1833.
SPRAKE, STEPHEN BAKER, formerly of Dorset, Eng., who was at the Star Hotel, N Y City, U S.A., in Sept, 1866.
STANBRIDGE, FREDERICK, formerly of London, who left England for New York, in May, 1832.
STIVINS, or LINDSAY, ELIZABETH, and WILLIAM LINDSAY STIVINS. (See George Lindsay)
STONE, ELIZABETH, Sister of Joseph Syms.
STONE, JOHN, residing in Long Island, New York, previous to 1790.
SWENSON, NILS, a native of Sweden, supposed to be living in New York, U S A.
TAYLOR, JOSEPH, formerly of Edinburgh, Scotland, last heard of in New Zealand, in 1862, he was then about to proceed to the diggings in British Columbia
THOMAS, DANIEL, residing in 1864, in Philadelphia, Pa., U S A
THOMPSON, or COPLEY, or BROWN, MARY GRIEVE. (See Brown, Mary)
TOBIAS, MARIA, of 114, Walnut-street, Cincinnati U S A.
TORIN, MARGARET (See Denis and James Donovan)
TOPHAM, THOMAS, late of No 7, Albert-square, Commercial-road East, London, England, who sailed from London as an Able Seaman in the "Mary Bradford," Captain Thompson, in November, 1858, and wrote to say he had arrived at New York, but has not since been heard of
TURLEY, BRIDGET, Daughter of Hugh Turley, of Ireland, formerly a Soap and Candle Maker. In 1852 she was living with a Mr Ayers, Jeweller, Madison-street, N Y
TURNER, SARAH (or FRAMPTON, or CRAMPTON), of New Romney, Kent, England, afterwards of America.
VAN DER HEYDEN, HENRIK, who lived at Luneberg in Nova Scotia, and died there in 1761
VEVERS, WILLIAM, of Yorkshire, Eng., a Painter and Grainer, was residing in 1862, 1863, at New Rochelle, N.Y
WALEY, HENRY and JOHN, of Co Sussex, England but now residing in America
WAITE, JAMES, late of Everton, near Liverpool, England, Builder, now residing in America.
WARD WILLIAM, Son of Mary Ward, who was in April, 1777, impressed into H M's Navy and sailed for New York, in North America, on board a transport called the "Jenny," and is supposed to have entered into a regiment called the Queen's Wood Rangers, and to have died in the course of the year 1777
WEBB, RICHARD, who left Woolwich, England, in 1856 or 1851, for America, and was last heard of from California, U S.A.
WESSONS and FIRASK, doing business in N Y in 1833.
WEST, EDWARD, Gentleman, of London 1692-3.
WHITEHOUSE, HENRY, of New York, in the U.S.A.
WIGHT, — (See Johan Adolf Anderson)
WILLIAMS, HENRY, or WILLELMS, HENDRICK, of Amsterdam, Holland; supposed to be in America.
WILLIAMS THOMAS, formerly of the County of Oxford, England, who left England in the year 1828, and went to reside at Parkman, or some other place near Painswell, Geauga County Ohio, U S A., and has not since been heard of
WILLOUGHBY, EDWIN, of Hull, Eng., sailed for America in the "Albion," in June, 1855. In 1856 he was in N O and St. Louis, and up to 1858 was at Council Bluffs, Iowa, U S A. He was last heard of in San Francisco, in 1860

SPECIAL LIST No. 2.

UNCLAIMED MONEY, LANDS AND ESTATES.

The following persons, if alive, or if dead, their representatives, are entitled to property All letters must be addressed to **J. B. MARTINDALE**, 142 La Salle Street, Chicago, Illinois, and must contain a statement of all facts on which the writer's claim is based [See pages 6, 7 and 8 of this Manual.]

ACONG, HENRY, who died in the United States
ALLEN, JOHN, of Bromsgrove, Worcestershire, England, went to America with his son John, about 1770; he resided sometime at Mr. Wells', Painter, New York, and was afterwards a Preacher in the Eastern part of Massachusetts Bay
ANDREWS, WILLIAM, died in America in 1850.
ANNING, WILLIAM, Son of James, formerly of Axminster, Devon, England, who has been many years in the United States.
APTHORP, Mrs., the Wife of Colonel Apthorp, of Boston, U S., who was travelling in England in Aug, 1869.
ARCHOE, CHARLES, who died in the United States.
ARMITAGE, JAMES, Son of John, and now or late of Philadelphia, Pennsylvania, North America.
ATKINSON, THOMAS, who left Liverpool for New York in 1829, and was last heard of in Toronto, 1830.
ATKINSON, THOMAS, a Gardener; native of Newcastle-on-Tyne, is supposed to have gone to the United States in the early part of this century
ATRILL, EDWARD, who emigrated to Canada about 1851.
BAIRD, MARY, who lived in Philadelphia, Pennsylvania, in 1842, and who had a sister named Ann Brison, living in New Jersey
BALLENY, WILLIAM, now or lately in Philadelphia, USA.
BALMONT, WILLIAM, formerly a Solicitor, in County Somerset, England; supposed to have left England for America in 1843
BARWISE, JOHN, Son of William Barwise, formerly of Tarnriggmoor, Wigton, Cumberland, England, who sailed in 1831, from Liverpool as mate in the Terra Nova to Newfoundland, and in 1832 embarked at St. John's, Newfoundland, in the schooner Osprey, for Cape Sydney, Breton.
BASAN, SARAH, and Three Children, living in America 1820–30
BECKER, CHARLES, late of No. 33A, Princes-street, Leicester square, in the County of Middlesex, London, England, Bootmaker, and supposed in 1869 to be residing in America.
BELIN, PETER, who resided at Charlestown and elsewhere in North America, and was afterwards of Knightsbridge, Middlesex, England, subsequently of Birmingham, Warwickshire, England, he died at sea, on his passage to South Carolina in North America.
BETHUNE, N and J, and Co, Montreal
BOLUS, MARY ANN, Daughter of Elizabeth Bolus, and Niece of James Turner, formerly of New York, Gunsmith
BORRETT, BALEY, formerly of Stradbrook, County of Suffolk, England, and residing in Hancock County, in America, in the year 1801.
BREAKWELL, ISRAEL, who left London for the United States about the year 1816.
BRIDGES, DAVID, son of John Bridges, who left England for North America some years since.
CAMERON, NEIL, sometime residing in Hunt County, Texas, USA.
CARMAN, WILLIAM L., deceased, Heirs of.
CHADWICK, ELIZABETH, formerly of Gildart's gardens, Liverpool, afterwards of Manchester, England, but now in America.
CHAFFERS, JAMES, late of Liverpool, in the county of Lancaster, England, Master Mariner, who resided for some time in the City of New York, USA., and is said to have married a person who kept a tavern there; it is believed he died in New York about 1800
CHARLWOOD, JOHN, formerly of Staines, Middlesex, England, Engineer, and Ann his Wife (formerly Ann Evans), late of Fleet-street, London, England, who emigrated to the United States of America in 1818, and resided in Philadelphia, Penn., US.
CHURTON, WILLIAM, Sisters of, who were married to William Thompson, and ———— Beddington. William Churton died in North Carolina, about 1780.
CLARK GEORGE OURRY, a Captain in H M 47th Regiment, in 1802 stationed at Montreal, in Canada, and NORMAN LEITH HAY CLARK, in 1882 a Midshipman in H.M S. Nile, on the North American Station.
CLARK, WILLIAM, a Subject of the Government of the United States of America, deceased in the East Indies in 1845
CLARKE, EDWARD AUGUSTUS, Son of Edward Goodman Clarke, of London, England, supposed to have died in America about the year 1815.
CLAYTON, THOMAS, who died in the United States.
CLEVELAND, MATTHEW, who left America for London many years ago.
CONNOR, JOHN, a native of Moyad, in the County of Down, Ireland, who left that country in 1857, with the intention of going to California, and has not since been heard of.
COOPER, ROSE, who resided in New York City, about 1855
COUNCELLOR, THOMAS, Son of William Councellor, of Pixley Hall, in the County of Durham, England, who went to America about 1765.
CRAIG, JOHN (Husband of the late Mrs. Helen Jamieson or Craig) formerly Ironmonger, in Forfar, latterly residing in Cupar, Fife, who is supposed to have left the country about 1850 for America
CRIDDLE, THOMAS, a Baker by trade, formerly of Richmond, Surrey, England, and residing in America in 1870
CROFTS, THOMAS, of Barking, County of Essex, England, who went to North America, probably to Philadelphia, about the year 1770.
DAY, or WOOD, MARY, Daughter of Dr. Wood, of Annapolis, and wife of Mr. Day, of Halifax, Nova Scotia.
DEAN, JOHN, late of Hognaston, in the County of Derby, England, Joiner, who in May, 1770, left his family with the intention, it is supposed, of going to America.

DE COUTY, ESTHER. See Elizabeth Harrison.
DE TURK, Abraham, U.S A.
DE WITT, JAN, who in 1764 went from Amsterdam to New York
DIAMOND, ELIZABETH, Daughter of Thomas Diamond, of Falmouth, England, who went to New York, about 1775.
DILLY, ANN, formerly of Fovant, Wilts, England, who was last heard of about 1830, when she was leaving Liverpool as companion or servant to a lady going to the United States of America. She had previously made several voyages to and from America as Stewardess to a ship
DONOVAN, DENNIS and JAMES, who went to America after 1832 They were Sons of Margaret Donovan, otherwise Tobin
DOOL, WILLAM, formerly of the 43rd British Regiment, born at Thorpe, County of Essex, England, and who was a prisoner at Winchester, in America, about the year 1783
DOWDELL, JOHN, supposed to be a native of Belfast, Ireland, died in a British Colony in 1850. He left a Niece in the United States
DUDDING, JOHN HICKS, who in 1794 left the house of his Father, John Dudding, at East Cottingwirth, in the County of York, England, for America, and afterwards resided at No 28, Liberty street, New York, U S
DUNKINSON, FERDINAND HENRY, who formerly resided at Islington, London, England, and was in the employ of Messrs Smith, stationers, of Queen street, Cheapside; he some time since occupied a house at Niagara.
EDMONDS, EDGAR BARNWELL, last heard of in Canada.
ELLANDER, DANIEL, native of Sweden, left England for some of the British Colonies in America, about the year 1768
EPHRAIM, PAUL, otherwise called WILLIAM WOOD, an American, formerly of Calcutta, which place he left in an American Ship previous to 1849.
ERMATINGER, F W, Montreal.
EVANS, ANN See John and Ann Charlwood.
EVES, WILLIAM, who died in Philadelphia, U S.A, in 1827. He was the Son of James Eves, Builder, London, England.
FARNHAM, B MORRIS, Notary, late of No 7, Warren street, New York City
FERGUSON, JOHN, House Painter, formerly of Downpatrick, County Down, Ireland, and residing in America in 1870.
FISHER, S W., Philadelphia.
FITZHARRIS, ANDREW, of Whitewater Valley, Ohio, U S, Drayman.
FITZHARRIS, PATRICK, of Whitewater Valley, Ohio, U S, Gardener
FRANKS, JOHN, formerly of Quebec, and afterwards of Montreal, in Canada, where he carried on business as a Merchant, and died at Quebec in 1794.
FROUD, CHARLES, of London went to America about the year 1770.
GANEST, HERMAN, who died in the United States
GARRETT, GEORGE, in 1748, being then 13 years of age, left Gravesend, England, for Charlestown, in South Carolina.
GILBERT, ANN, who married Watson Atkinson, an American, in the early part of the present century.
GODFREY, MARY See Thomas and Mary Taylor
GOUGH, HENRY THOMAS, Sister of, supposed to be residing in New York, U S.A.
GRAVE, ——, of Quebec, in the early part of the present century, a legatee under the will of Gabriel Clarmont.
GREGORY, or McGREGOR, JOHN, went to America, and was last heard of in 1764, when he was at Montreal, or elsewhere, in Canada.
GRIEVE, JAMES, formerly of Dundee, Scotland, supposed to be residing in the United States of America.
GRIFFITHS, MARY See Mary Turner
GRUSSY, BARBARA, who died in the United States.
HALL, CAPTAIN STEPHEN, and ELIZABETH his Wife, and NICHOLAS SALISBURY and MARTHA his Wife, all of Boston, New England, in 1747
HANCOCK, ROBERT, a native of Box, Wiltshire, England was in 1810 residing in Fue street, Portland, Maine, with a person named John Christie It was reported that he afterwards became a Corn and Cattle Dealer. He left England in 1805, being then 10 years of age.
HARRINGTON, WILLIAM, who died in the United States.
HARRISON, ELIZABETH, and DENISE HARRISON, Widows, residing in New York City, in the early part of present century, Sisters of Esther de Couty, Widow of Peter de Couty, late of New York City
HARRISON, JOHN, late of Hurstanfield, in the County of Cumberland, England, Farmer, his Heir-at-Law is supposed to be in America.
HEARNE, CHARLES HENRY, Seaman, or Henry Robinson, supposed to have been trading from Boston, U.S., about the year 1855.
HEATH, THOMAS, a Baker by trade, went to America about the year 1775.
HELDER, MRS. EMMA, who was married to — Helder, Harness and Saddle Maker, in Reading, Pa., in or about the year 1868
HENLEY, MARY, Daughter of William Hanley, late of Hailsham, Sussex, England, Bricklayer; she is supposed to have gone to America about the year 1793, with a family of the name of JOHNSON, and to have lived afterwards at Montreal
HERMAN, GEORGE, FREDERICK, and ADILIA, living in America.
HILL, MARGARET, JANE, CATHERINE, DELIA, Daughters of Michael Hill and Mary Burke, from Ballenbar, County Sligo, Ireland.
HOGAN, JOHN, late of Ballyhamlet, County Waterford, Ireland, deceased.
HOLMES, THOMAS, Montreal.
HOPTON, SIDNEY, a native of Newport, Monmouth County, England, who has been travelling in the United States of America since about 1850.
HOWELL, J. WILLIAM, an American Citizen, deceased in Australia.
HUGHES, RICE, of the County of Anglesea, England, a Carpenter by trade, went to Philadelphia about the year 1770.
HUTCHISON, JOHN, a native of the County of Lanark, in Scotland, was a Sergeant in the 28th Regiment, which left Ireland for America, in May, 1757
HUTH, or HERTZ, RICHARD, a native of Prussia.
INNES, or INNIS James Innes, Attorney-General of Virginia in 1771. Dr. Robert Innes, of Gloucester, Virginia. Judge Harris Innes, of Frankfort, Kentucky
JAMES, BENJAMIN, Son of John James, of St. Austell, County of Cornwall, England, emigrated with his Wife, whose maiden name was Ursula Newman, in 1796, to America, where he carried on the trade of Woolcomber, in Frankfort, in the County of Philadelphia.
JEFFREYS, REUBEN and ELIZABETH, late of Leicester, England, and residing in the United States of America, in 1870.

KENNY, or SANDERS, MARY, Wife of Thomas Sanders, late of Stone, Staffordshire, England, who emigrated to America about 1844, and resided in Toronto
KING, RICHARD, who went to America in 1832
KNOWLER, RICHARD FREDERICK, who was last seen in England in 1851; and is supposed to have emigrated to America.
LAWES, MARIA, Sister of Charlotte Wilby, and supposed to be residing in the United States of America.
LEAFE, WILLIAM, in 1799 carried on the business of a Shoemaker in New York City. He was a native of London, England, where his name was Labiffe.
LEAR, JEMIMA ELENORA, living in February, 1807, in Leonard street, New York City.
LEEKE, FRANK, of Maryland, in America, about the year 1820.
LENAN, or LEMAN, GEORGE, who died in the United States of America.
LIDDIARD and STORY, Halifax, Nova Scotia.
LINTON, MURDOCK D., whose family resided in Toronto, Upper Canada; he died on a voyage from New York to Melbourne.
LITHGOW, HUGH, who was brought up to the Sea, and resided at Halifax and Philadelphia, and other parts of North America.
McBEATH, DAVID, Son of Elizabeth McBeath, Limerick, Ireland.
McCARTY, CALLAGHAN, who died in the United States.
McDONOUGH, PATRICK, formerly of Mountjoy, in the County of Tyrone, Ireland, who went to reside in Charleston, in America, in or about the year 1840.
McGREGOR, or GREGORY, JOHN   See John Gregory.
McLAY, or SPEIRS, MRS HELEN, Wife of James McLay, supposed to be in the United States.
MACCOLLA, JOHN, formerly of Nova Scotia.
MACOUAT, or MACOWAT, WALTER and AGNES, went to America in 1818
MANSELL, SARAH, maiden name JONES, married William Mansell, and was supposed to be in North America in the early part of this century
MANVELL, JESSE, a native of the County of Surrey, England, who went to America about, or previous to, the year 1860.
MARSHALL, THOMAS, a native of England, who went to New York in 1791, carried on a cotton manufactory there in 1792, and resided in Philadelphia in 1796.
MASON, JOHN, a Surgeon, went to the United States in 1806
MAWSON, PERCIVAL, who left Liverpool, England, for the United States of America some years ago
MEDDOWCROFT, EDMUND, formerly of No 6, South-square, Gray's-inn, Middlesex, England, afterwards residing at Long Island, in the State of New York, U S, and at Niagara, in Upper Canada; and in 1843 residing at Liscard, in the parish of Wallasey, Cheshire, England.
MESSENGER, MARY, who went to the United States in 1840
MILLS, JAMES, Statuary and Mason, formerly of London, was, about 1800 1802, at Captain Willis's, corner of Greenwich and Cortland-streets, New York City.
MOORE, DAVID, Son of James and Agnes, who was born in Edinburgh, became a Sailor, and originally sailed from Greenock, Scotland, it is understood he is now, or was lately in California, U S.
MORGAN, CHANDOIS, who died at St. Nicholas, in Philadelphia, about 1760, and his Son CHANDOIS MORGAN, who died at Jamaica, near New York, about 1768
NASH, WILLIAM, of the County of Kent, England, who went to America about the year 1820.
NEWBY, SUSANNAH, was the Wife of a Builder in Philadelphia, about the year 1800. She was the Widow of John Newby, of London, England, who died about the year 1780.
OLDHAM, WILLIAM, who left England in October, 1829
PADGETT, JOHN, and the CHILDREN of HENRY PADGETT (supposed to be in America), of South Cave, East Yorkshire, England.
PEDDER, GEORGE, now or late of the United States of North America.
PHILIPPS, MARY, formerly of Halifax, Nova Scotia, afterwards of Rivers street, Bath, England, then of Great Russell-street, Bloomsbury, Middlesex, but late of Boulonge-sur-Mer, France. She was the Daughter of John Philipps, Chemist, at Halifax, aforesaid.
PHILLIPSON, JAMES, went to New York in 1836, he being then 40 years of age. He has not been heard of since 1830.
PLATT, GEORGE, of Mossley, near Ashton, Lancashire, England, who went to America about 1840.
POOLEY, EDWARD, the Younger, formerly of Cratfield, in the County of Sussex, England, resided at Palmyra, Wayne County, New York, in 1829.
PUTNAM, JAMES, formerly of Halifax, Nova Scotia, but afterwards of John-street, Portland-place, Middlesex, England, Esq
QUINN, MISS ROSE, was residing in Philadelphia, Pennsylvania, in 1860. She is supposed to have been since married.
RANKAN, HERMAN, who died in the United States.
RENWICK, THOMAS, a native of Scotland, by trade a Tailor, supposed to have gone to America about the year 1836
ROBINSON, HENRY See Charles Henry Hearne
ROBINSON, THOMAS (Steam Thrashing Machine Owner), who about the beginning of 1863 left Wetherby, England, for the United States of America, and sometime resided in Buffalo, United States.
RORKE, ELLEN, Spinster, a native of England, residing in the United States of America in 1870.
ROWE, JOHN, WILLIAM SNYTALL, and JACOB, who emigrated from Devonshire, England, to Boston, in America, about 1760
RYLAND, WILLIAM HERMAN, Quebec.
SALMON, JOHN BARKER, of the County of Norfolk, England, who resided at Baltimore, in America, with Elizabeth his Wife, in the early part of the present century
SANDERS, MARY See Mary Kenny
SATCHWELL, WILLIAM, residing at Philadelphia, in America, about the year 1785.
SAUL, JOHN, of Quebec, about the year 1793, sailed from Portsmouth to the West Indies, in the "Intrepid" Transport.
SCHMIDT, HENRY, who died in the United States.
SCOTT, DAVID, Son of Heugh Scott, of Cupar, Fifeshire, in Scotland, went to Charlestown, South Carolina, America, 1790.
SCRAGGS, WILLIAM, in 1754 supposed to be residing in Nova Scotia.
SEARCH, RICHARD LEWIS, of Cirencester, England
SEYMOUR, JAMES, who (in 1843) was connected with Star Printing Office, Toronto, Canada.
SHAKESHAFT, CHARLES and GEORGE, went to America about 1800,
SIMPSON, ROBERT, of Shepherfield, near Cockermouth, in the County of Cumberland, England, who went to America about 1703
SIMSON, JAMES, Accountant, 43, Exchange Place, New York, United States.

SINCLAIR, ALEXANDER, formerly resident at St Louis, Missouri, United States of America. He was the Son of Wood Sinclair, of Leith, Scotland.

SMITH, JOSEPH, ROBERT, and WILLIAM, Sons of Jonah Smith, formerly of Stroud, Gloucestershire, England; they left England many years ago, and are supposed to have gone to North America. A letter was received from William, date Quitivity, November 9, 1789.

SMITH, WILLIAM, formerly of Shadwell, County of Middlesex, England, went to Boston, in America, in 1775.

SPEIRS, MRS HELEN. See Mrs. Helen McLay.

SPENCE or STEPHENS, ELIZABETH (Wife of Jacob Spence), of the Post-office, Muskoko Falls, Ontario, Canada.

STARR, JOSEPH, and REBECCA his Wife, formerly of Papplewick, near Nottingham, England, who now or lately resided in the United States of America.

STEPHENS, ELIZABETH See Elizabeth Spence

STEVENS, JAMES DAY, born at Hindon, County of Wilts, England, late of Crab Orchard Springs, Lincoln County, Kentucky, United States of America.

STEVENS, JEROME, or his Heirs

STEVENS, WILLIAM NEIGHBOUR, born about 1808, who was a Silk Throwster at Congleton, near Wolverhampton, England, and a Draper at Hackney; about 1840 he arrived in New York, United States, with three children, Esther, Eliza, and Ebenezer

STOCKWELL, JAMES, formerly of Boston, U S, and late of Madras, and an Officer in the Service of the late Naboh of Arcot. He is supposed to have been born in Ireland, married Jane Crossley, of Boston, and died about 1790.

SYMONDS, JOHN, formerly of Penzance, Cornwall, England, Millwright, who sailed from Liverpool, in 1835, for New York, U S

TAYLOR, THOMAS, formerly of Brookland, in the County of Kent, England, Baker, and afterwards of 242, Adam-street, Brooklyn, New York, U.S.A., and MARY his Wife, whose maiden name was Godfrey, with their Children, Thomas, Godfrey, and Frances

TAYLOR, WILLIAM, Son of James Taylor, believed to reside in Nova Scotia, or some other part of North America

THOMAS, JENKIN, GEORGE THOMAS, and ROBERT THOMAS, Brothers of the late Arthur Thomas; supposed to be in Canada.

THOMPSON, WILLIAM, of California, in North America.

TOWERS, JOHN, who visited America in 1839

TOWNSEND, JOSHUA, of Oyster Bay, Long Island, who was pressed in London, England, in 1775, and put on board the "Conquestadore."

TURNER, JAMES. See Thomas Tyas.

TURNER, JONAS, who in 1783 lived in the family of Joshua Fisher and Sons, in Philadelphia, America.

TURNER, MARY, maiden name Griffithe, who went to America in the early part of this century She was a native of the County of Shropshire Her Husband's name was George Turner

TYAS, THOMAS, about the commencement of the present century left England for the United States of America, where he assumed the name of James Turner

WALKER, GERVASE, of Wakefield, Yorkshire, England, who went to Canada in 1862. When last heard of was at or near Toronto

WATSON, WILLIAM MICHEL, who landed at New York in 1868.

WATTS, JOHN, born at Upton-on-Severn, Gloucestershire, England, who died in New York, U S.A., in 1841.

WEBB, HENRY, at the age of 15, sailed from England in the year 1776, as an apprentice, in the ship "Artemissa," for some part of North America, he ran away, and entered the "Reveoge" or "Vengeance" privateer In March, 1780, he was at Savannah, but has not since been heard of

WELLS, DANIEL JAMES, HARRIET ELLEN, and CECILIA, formerly of Wisborough green, Petworth, Sussex, England, who went to Maryland, U S., about 1850.

WEST, FRANCIS ARCHER, who is believed to have emigrated to America in 1859, and was last heard of in July in the same year as the battle of Richmond.

WEST, WILLIAM ARTHUR, who is believed to be employed as a Ship Surgeon in vessels trading between England and America

WHITE, ROBERT, Commissary of H.M Stores at Pensacola, U S A.

WHITESMITH, WILLIAM WATSON, who left England for New York about the year 1852.

WILLIAMS, MARY, Wife of Benjamin Williams, who, in the year 1811 resided at Mount Jolie, near Frankford, Philadelphia, North America, the Daughter of James Pierrepont, of Boston, in the County of Lincoln, England.

WILSON, BENJAMIN, Philadelphia.

WOOD, MARY See Mary Day

WOOD, WILLIAM. See Paul Ephraim

WOODS, RICHARD, JOHN RICHARD, JAMES, THOMAS, and MARY ANN, Children of Richard Woods, formerly of Newton Moor, near Hyde, Cheshire, England; they left England about 1840, and went to reside at Louisville, Kentucky, in North America.

WOOTTON, HERBERT, left Liverpool, for Baltimore, in America, above the year 1783.

SPECIAL LIST No. 3.

UNCLAIMED MONEY, LANDS AND ESTATES.

The following persons, if living, or if dead, their representatives, are entitled to property. All letters must be addressed to **J. B. MARTINDALE, 142 La Salle Street, Chicago, Illinois**, and must contain all facts on which the writer's claim is based. [See pages 6, 7 and 8 of this Manual.]

AGGE, JOHN JAMES BAILEY, left England for America, is supposed to have enlisted there under an assumed name, and subsequently became a Sergeant in the 20th United States Infantry
ADAMSON, JAMES, formerly of Montreal, and of Edinburgh, Scotland, when last heard of, he was in Chicago
ALVAREZ SILVER SMELTING COMPANY, Creditors of
ANDERSON, SAMUEL BEGSON MELLOR, HENRY WILLIAM GODERICH, and JOHN GODERICH sons of Mrs. Elizabeth Hunter Robertson), residing in America.
ANDREWS, THOMAS WILLS, Widow and three Children of, residing in North Carolina, U S.A.
AULICKE, THEODORE, deceased in America.
BADCOCK, WILLIAM KINGSLEY, formerly of England, went to Australia, in or about the year 1858, whence, it is reported, he went to America
BARTON, GEORGE, formerly of Manchester, England, was at the Thames Gold Fields, near Auckland, New Zealand, in April, 1870, and is supposed to have gone from there to San Francisco.
BATES, WILLIAM JAMES, formerly of London, England, now residing in Canada
BAYNTUM, Sir ANDREW, Baronet, Sheriff for Wiltshire, England, in 1802. His daughter, Mary, is married (husband's name unknown), has sons, and in 1867-8 was residing in the United States.
BELLONI, JOHANNUS MATHIAS, and MARIA, natives of Holland.
BERGER, PIETER, a native of Holland
BETTONEY, ELIZABETH (See Elizabeth Mathews)
BLASDELL, or BLAISDELL, —, who left Scotland for America about 1770
ELEASE, JOHN, now or formerly of 63, Newark Avenue, Jersey City, N J, U S.A.
BOEIJE, PETRONELLA, a native of Holland
BOND, Sir ALLANSON, deceased. Representatives supposed to be in America
BONE, ROBERT, a native of England, residing at Claremont, New Hampshire
BRAKEFIELD, ALEXANDER, formerly of Headcorn, Co Kent, dealer, who left England for America in October, 1868
BRAND, EDMUND CAMERON, supposed to be in America
BROWN, MARIA MANGIN, Widow, deceased. Her next of Kin are supposed to be in America
BRYAN or BRIEN, JOHN, and PETER LINGUEST, of Poplar, Co Middlesex, England, residing at St. Raphael, California, in 1865
BRYANT, JOHN JOSEPH, formerly of Whitesboro, Oneida Co, N.Y, Surveyor
BYRNE, JAMES of Ardinary, Co Wicklow, Ireland. His children emigrated between the years 1830 and 1835.
CAFFREY, Mrs JANE, now or formerly residing in Albany, America.
CAMERON, JANE, and her issue, supposed to be in America
CAMPBELL, JAMES and CHESTER, Children or relatives of, supposed to be in California, or elsewhere in America.
CAMROUX, JACQUEZ, a native of Holland
CARLEY, WILLIAM JOHN, who left England for Canada in the year 1857
CASTILLO, DAVID, a native of Holland.
CHAMBERLAIN, JAMES CHARLES GEORGE, formerly of Chelsea, Co Middlesex, Grocer, left England about the year 1833, and in 1834 was residing in New York, in the name, it is believed, of FREDERICK STOKES.
CHATFIELD, RICHARD EDWIN, now or late of Virginia City, Nevada, U S A.
CLAPHAM, SAMUEL, a native of England, supposed to be in America.
CLARKE, JANE, formerly HOOPS, Widow of DANIEL CLARKE, of New Orleans, residing in Philadelphia in 1820.
CONNELL, BRIDGET, MARY, or MARGARET, Daughters of Patrick Connell, Co Limerick, Ireland.
COOPER, JOHN or JONAS, formerly of Hampshire, England, went to America about the year 1840, with his wife Ann and four children—viz., William, Charles, Edmund, and Hannah Cooper
CORR, HENRY, of Durham, Roscommon, Ireland
CUMMINGS, Miss MARY ANN, residing in America.
CYPRIAN, JOSEPH and FRANCIS, natives of Bavaria, supposed to be residing in America
DALLAS, ALEXANDER, WILLIAM, and ISABELLA. The latter married Duncan McKerroll. All natives of Scotland. Their descendants now reside in North Carolina, U S A.
DAVIDSON, Mrs MARION (See Mrs. Marion Stalker)
DAVIS, MARY ANN, Daughter of James Davis, a native of Scotland.
DAY, MARY ANN, formerly of London, left England for Boston, Mass, in or about the year 1855. Is supposed to reside in New York City
DEAN, SAMUEL, of London, England, two Sons of, supposed to be in America.
De BUISSONET, CHARLES, a native of Holland
De CALATRAVA, ANTOINE, or his Heirs, supposed to be in America.
De GROOT, MARIA, a native of Holland.
De HARDIN, JACOBUS, a native of Holland.
De PAANU, JOOST, a native of Holland
De RAPPERT, ESAJAS a native of Holland
DERMER, CHARLES, residing at Halifax in 1857
De WYN, ANNA CHRISTINA, a native of Holland.
DINGNUS, PHILLIPPUS, a native of Holland.
DOLIN, MICHAEL, formerly of Killeter, Co. Tyrone, Ireland, went to America in 1857, and resided in Cincinnati, Ohio, in 1860. He was born about the year 1830.
DONNELLY, PATRICK and FRANCIS, brothers, natives of Ireland.
DONOHOE, CORNELIUS, formerly of Nenagh, Ireland, who went to America in the year 1846, and afterwards resided at or near the City of St. Louis
DONOHOE, MARY ANN, formerly of Nenagh, Ireland, who went to America in the year 1854, and afterwards resided at or near the City of Jersey. She has not been heard of since 1861.
DREW, JOHN, who sailed from Cork, Ireland, on August 5th, 1867, for Boston, U S.A., thence 24 miles to see a friend named "Cogan"
DUNLOP, ROBERT, of Mayfield, Co Norfolk, Ont, Canada, Doctor of Medicine
ECCLES, DAVID, of Yorkshire, England, last heard of at Monterey, California.
EDGAR, ROBERT, formerly of Newfoundland
EMTINCK, CATHERINE THERESA, DOWAGER, &c., residing at Antwerp, Belgium, about the year 1750. Her Representatives supposed to be in America
EYRE, or EYRES, ELIZABETH, daughter of SAMUEL EYRE, or EYRES, formerly of Stockport, England, is believed to have been married about 1847 to some person whose name is unknown. The said husband left England in 1847, for the U S A., whither his wife followed him in the same year
FAIRBAIRN, Mrs. HELLEN (maiden name, MILNE), wife of ROBERT FAIRBAIRN, formerly of Edinburgh, Scotland, who with her husband emigrated to America about the year 1835.
FINLAY, Mrs. ANN, formerly of Dublin, Ireland, at present residing in America.

FOSTER, Mrs HARRIET P, formerly of Birmingham, England, supposed to be living in Chicago
FOX, JONATHAN, formerly of Yorkshire, left England for New York in 1862, per "Great Eastern" Steamship, and afterwards enlisted in the 5th U S Artillery
FREAR, PHILIP, a native of Ireland, late of Duchess Co, N S, U S A.
FRENCH, PATRICK, HENRY, ARTHUR, WILLIAM, JOSEPH, and THOMAS, formerly of Co Roscommon, Ireland, afterwards of New York
FRYE, DARBY, who in or about the year 1750 owned property on or near to Boston Bay, Mass, U S.A., called "Darby Castle," and afterwards changed to "Castle Huntley"
GALLOWAY, ROBERT, formerly of the U S. Navy, afterwards an Apothecary in N Y City
GAWLEY, JOSIAS, late of Templepatrick, Co. Antrim, Ireland, Farmer His next of Kin are in America.
GILCHRIST, WILLIAM WEIR, next of Kin, supposed to be in America.
GODERICH, HENRY, WILLIAM, and JOHN (See B M. Anderson.)
GRACIE, GEORGE, late of Shelburne, Nova Scotia.
GRIFFIN, EMILY, formerly of Baltimore, Maryland, U S A., which city she left about the year 1852
GROMETT, THOMAS, late of Denver, Co Norfolk, England, who left Southampton for New York in October, 1868, in the Steamship "Siberia," and is supposed to have resided for some time in Suffolk Co, and Brooklyn, L.L, and afterwards to have gone up the country
HAACK, MARIA, a native of Holland, supposed to be in America
HAMILTON, EDWARD DEAN FREEMAN, who left Adelaide, Australia, in the year 1850, for San Francisco, U S.A.
HAMMOND, ANDREW, formerly of Co Donegal, Ireland, at present in America
HAROCASTLE, JOSEPH, and ELIZABETH, his wife, residing many years ago near Charleston, S Co., U S.A.
HARKNESS, Miss ELLEN, a native of Belfast Ireland, residing in America
HARRINGTON, HENRY, a native of Aberdeenshire, Scotland, now in America.
HAZLEWOOD, WILLIAM, Carpenter, formerly of Howick, Ont, Canada
HOBBES, ALFRED (son of Mrs. ROSALIE BERANGER, widow of THOMAS HOBBES), last heard of in the year 1852, when he was in California, with wife and children.
HODGES, MARY ANN, of Co, Hereford, England, who went to the United States in or about the year 1860.
HOOPS, JANE. (See Jane Clarke)
HOWES, ROBERT CHARLES (Cook), residing in America
HOWES, W T, late of Hillsborough, Ireland who was last seen in Toronto, Canada, in October, 1872
HUNTER, FREDERICK, formerly a Master in the British Navy, who left the Port of Cardiff, in Wales, in the year 1866, with the intention of entering the American Navy.
HUNTER, JOHN, residing in or near Schenectady, New York; also MARY HUNTER, wife of John Millard, supposed to reside in Genesee Co New York.
HURLEY, WILLIAM, who left London, England, in 1856, and is supposed to be in America.
IRVIN, WILLIAM, who patented 5,000 acres of land in Virginia, U S A., in 1797
JACKSON, JOHN, formerly of Kersley, Warwickshire, England, who in the year 1858 was at Toronto, Canada.
JEAKINS, or JENKSON, BURFORD, left Battle, Co Sussex, England, in July, 1840, and arrived at No 27, Prince-street, New York, in September, 1840 His Children wanted
JELFS, GEORGE WATKINS, formerly of Birmingham, England; when last heard of, in March, 1870, he was in Patterson, N J, U S A.
JENKSON, BURFORD (See Jeakins)
JONES, MARY ANN, daughter of William and Maria Jones, formerly of Bath, England, now residing in America.
JONES, Mrs ANN, formerly of Scotland, but now residing in America.
KELLY, THOMAS, son of John and Harriet Kelly, formerly of Johnstown, Co. Kilkenny, Ireland.
KERMS, MICHAEL, a native of Dunarim, Co Monaghan, Ireland, went to the U S A. in or about the year 1863.
LAMBRECHTS, SARA ALIDA, a native of Holland, residing in America.
LANE, ROBERT CRISPIN, relations of, on the side of his mother, Elizabeth, daughter of James Strong, of Co Devon, England, and Elizabeth, his wife, formerly Elizabeth Luscombe, daughter of John Luscombe, and Sarah Prideaux, both of Co Devon, England.
LINGUEST, PETER. (See John Bryan, or Brien)
LIVESEY, THOMAS, who left London, England, for America, 5th April, 1851
LIVINGS ALFRED, born at Windsor, England, about 1840, in the year 1844 resided at Chicago, U S.A.
LLOYD, Mrs. ANNA. (See McSheffrey)
LLOYD, JOSEPH, in the year 1853 sailed in the ship "Northumberland" for Australia He is supposed to have gone to America afterwards.
LLOYD, THOMAS, formerly of Fincastle, Botetourt, Co. Virginia, U S A, afterwards of Versailles, Woodford, Co. Kentucky, previous to the year 1812
LONDON, ROBERT, son of William and Ann London, who went to America. He was born in London, England, about the year 1770.
LONGHURST, CORNELIA. (See Cornelia Morgan)
LUSCOMBE, Family of. (See Robert Crispin Lane)
McGOVERN, FELIX, deceased in America
McKERROLL, DUNCAN (See "Dallas")
McKETTRICK, PETER, born in Scotland, 1803, last heard of in New York in 1830
McMILLAM, MALCOLM CAMERON, Builder and Contractor, in 1864, residing in Toronto, Canada
McSHEFFREY, Dr DANIEL, and his Sister, Mrs Anna Lloyd Widow of Dr Lloyd, formerly of Londonderry, Ireland.
MAGEE, Miss ISABELL, formerly of Drumkirk, Co. Tyrone, Ireland, who left for America in 1846 or 1847
MAGUIRE, GEORGE, of Philadelphia, owning property in Texas, and who was lately at Memphis, and at Hot Springs, Arkansas
MAHOOD, SARAH, daughter of James Mahood, of Lisdonan, Co Cavan, Ireland.
MATFIELD, ERICK Representatives supposed to be in America
MATHEWS, ELIZABETH, otherwise Elizabeth Bettoney, of Oadby, near Leicester, England. Living in 1859, at 17, Washington-street, New York City, or, if dead, her Husband, Joseph Mathews, or their Children.
MERCER, ANDREW, who went to Canada with the late Chief Justice Scott, about the year 1801. Heirs wanted.
MILLARD, MARY (See John Hunter)
MILLER, —, a native of Scotland, residing in Patterson, N J, in 1870
MILLER, JAMES (son of George Miller, of Dundee, Scotland), now residing in America.
MILNE, Mrs HELEN (See Mrs Helen Fairbairn)
MITCHELL, WILLIAM, son of Thomas Mitchell, of Stone Call, Co Sligo, Ireland
MORGAN, CORNELIA (maiden name, LONGHURST), wife of David Morgan, formerly of Bristol, England, now residing in America.
MORGAN, WILLIAM ROBERT, formerly of Ravensdale, Co Kildare, Ireland, afterwards of Windsor, Canada West.
MUSGRAVE, BENJAMIN, formerly of Leeds, England, at present in America.
NESBITT, WILLIAM, late of the U S. Navy Steamship "Piscataqua"
ORMSBY, HANNAH (widow of Edward Ormsby, formerly of Castledargan, Co Sligo, Ireland, and afterwards of California), supposed to be in New York City
OWEN, TOMMY, or THOMAS CONRAD OWEN, son of Thomas Frederick Owen, who died at New Orleans, U.S.A., in June, 1858
PACKER HENRY JOHN, formerly of Ramsgate, Co. Kent, England who was in New York in January, 1871.
PALMER, JAMES, and MARIA, his sister, natives of England, residing in America.
PAXMAN, ROSETTA and REBECCA, residing in Illinois in the year 1865
PHILLIPS, ISAAC, born at Easton, Mass, in 1760 Said to have died at Mobille, Ala., in 1832
PONNAZ, WILHELM, of Brunschweig, who served in the Union Army in 1864

SPECIAL LIST No. 3.

POOLE, THOMAS, formerly of Co. Kildare, Ireland ; his next of Kin are in America.
PRIDEAUX, Family of. (See Robert Crispin Lane.)
PYLE, ELI, of Delaware, Co Pa., U S A.
PYNCHON, HENRY G, residing in California in 1868
RALPH, HENRY I, Master of the barque "Lenercoat," who sailed in said ship from Baltimore, U.S.A, Feb. 13, 1872.
RAMSKRAMER, DANIEL, a native of Holland
REILLY, EDWARD B, who served in C B of 2rd Division U S Infantry, Army of the Potomac, in 1803 and 1884, and who resided at Benson Mills, Virginia, and in December, 1883, at Greenville, Washington Co., Miss., U.S.A.
REILLY, MARGARET, last heard of in January 1883, at Gloucester, N J, U S A.
RENNER, CARL (See Max Sternberg)
REYNOLDS, THOMAS SMART, and JOSHUA, who left Wellington, Shropshire, England, for America in 1850
RICHOER, GUILLEAME, a native of Holland.
RIDGWAY, WILLIAM, Glass-blower, formerly of Fenton, Staffordshire, England, who went to America about the year 1823, and resided in Jersey City
RUBRENS, BONDEWIJN, a native of Holland.
RUBRIDGE, JOHN, who emigrated to America before 1760
SHAW, JOHN COX, formerly of Bristol, England, now residing in America
SHEPHERD, WILLIAM, formerly of No. 9, Liverpool street, City, London, a Glover by trade, who left England for America in or about the year 1847.
SHEPPARD, WILLIAM EDWARD, left England for America in 1836, was living in New Orleans in September of that year, at which time his son, William Henry Sheppard, was an Import Clerk in the N O Custom House.
SHERRARD, EDWARD, son of Edward Sherrard, mother's maiden name, Elizabeth Stone.
SLATER, GEORGE, a Morocco Dresser, a native of England, in 1830 residing in New York, and afterwards in Ohio.
SMIT, DERK, a native of Holland.
SMITH, WILLIAM, formerly of Balleysaygart, Co Waterford, Ireland, now in America.
STALKER, MRS MARION (maiden name, DAVIDSON), formerly of Scotland, afterwards residing at North Argyle, Washington Co., N Y, and Rev Duncan Stalker, her husband.
STARREMAN, PIETRO, a native of Holland.
STERNBERG, MAX, also called Carl Renner, formerly of Breslau, Prussia, now in America.
STOKES, FREDERICK. (See J C G Chamberlain.)
STOKES, JOHN (husband of Eliza Stokes), residing in America.
STRONG, Family of. (See Robert Crispin Lane.)
STROOF, HENRICH, from Cologne, on the Rhine, residing in America.
STUYS, MARIA and CORNELIA, natives of Holland
SUAVE, ANDRIES, a native of Holland.
SUTHERLAND, ROSETTA (maiden name, PAXMAN), residing in Illinois in or about the year 1865.
SYM, ELIZABETH, of Drumboy, in the parish of Glassford, Lanarkshire, Scotland, is supposed to have emigrated to America about the year 1847
SYMS, JOSEPH, who died in England about the year 1760 His Representatives are supposed to be in America
TARHETT, ROBERT, a Farmer near New York City, a native of Kirkcolm Parish, in Wigtonshire, Scotland
TAYLOR, M. E., who in May, 1882, or 1883, left England with her husband, and son Albert. When last heard of was in San Francisco, California.
TAYLOR, THOMAS, deceased, whose heirs are interested in lands in Georgia.
TEEKMAN, WILLEM and WILHELMINA, natives of Holland
TEPPER, SAMUEL, a native of England, went to America many years ago, and was last heard of at Camden, Wilcox Co., Alabama, U S A.
THOMSON, ANDREW, formerly of Selkirk, Scotland, a Baker by trade, went to America about 1850, and was last heard of at Delaware, Canada, in 1861.
TOWLE, ALLAN, of Lincolnshire, England Nephews and Nieces residing in America.
TYLEY, CHARLES, of Shropshire, England, a Joiner by trade, residing, 28th January, 1870, at 188, Second-street, Detroit, Mich, U S A.
VAN, BEEM, CORNELIS, a native of Holland.
VAN, HEYDE, JACOB, a native of Holland.
VON, HAENLEIN, CARL FRIEDRICH, a native of Prussia, who was in Lower Canada in the year 1850, when last heard of, in the year 1853, he was in hospital in Baltimore.
VYBE, RICHARD, late of Luton, Co Bedford, England, Straw Hat Manufacturer *Creditors* wanted.
WAKEFIELD, JOHN DAVIES, left England in the ship "Charles Richard," in 1849, deserted her at New York, 31st May, 1850, and afterwards resided in Mulberry-street, New York
WARN, JOHN WILLIAM, formerly of Poplar, Co Middlesex, England, now in America
WEBSTER, JOSHUA DALMER, formerly of Anglesea, Wales When last heard of he was in the vicinity of Chicago.
WEIR, JAMES, of Glasgow, Scotland. His children are supposed to be in America
WELHAM, JOSEPH, Carpenter by trade, formerly of Co Suffolk, England, when last heard of, in 1864, was at Pembroke, Canada West, and he then intended going to Gold Mines 70 miles below Quebec.
WESTLEY, ROBERT, who left Liverpool for New York about the year 1861
WHITE, EDWARD, formerly of Weymouth, Dorsetshire, England, left Swansea, Wales, for New York in or about 1862.
WHITEHEAD, JOHN, a native of Aberdeenshire, Scotland, supposed to be in America.
WHITTLE, JOHN, left England for Quebec in April, 1865, was in Boston, Mass, from October, 1865, until March, 1867, and his last letter was dated New York, 29th April, 1870, when he stated that he was ill
WRYTE, JOHN, born at Greenloaning, Scotland, about the year 1811, some time a Farm Servant at Muthill, and Strathearn, Scotland, thereafter in Delaware, U.S.A., and when last heard of was a Sailor on a steamboat trading between New Orleans and Cincinnati.
WILKIE, JAMES, formerly Ordnance Store-keeper, Kingston, Canada
WILKINSON, JOHN, and JANET, his wife (whose maiden name was JANET DALLAS), natives of Scotland. Their descendants are now residing in Canada.
WILLIAMS, GEORGE BANGLEY, of the Chief Engineer's Office, Alleghany Valley Railroad, at Pittsburg, Pa., U S.A.
WILSON, ARCHIBALD, of Co Armagh, Ireland, now residing in America.
WOODS, JOSEPH SHARRAD, left London, England, for New York, U S A., 1840.
WOODWARD, ROXEN, Relatives of, supposed to be in California, or elsewhere in America.
WRIGHT, SAMUEL, Shoemaker, Philadelphia, who removed from Walnut-street to Vine-street, in 1838 ; his wife's maiden name was Mary Park.
YOUNG, PETER, a native of Scotland, who went to Pennsylvania, U S A., in 1784
YULE, or YOOL, MOSES, who left Greenock, Scotland, for America, about the year 1820; was residing in Philadelphia, Pa., in or about the year 1840.

SPECIAL LIST No. 4.

UNCLAIMED MONEY, LANDS AND ESTATES.

The following persons, if living, or if dead, their representatives, are entitled to property. All letters must be addressed to **J. B. MARTINDALE, 142 La Salle Street, Chicago, Illinois**, and must contain a statement of all facts on which the writer's claim is based. [See pages 6, 7 and 8 of this Manual.]

ABBOTT, ALFRED, JAMES, and EDWARD, all of New York.
ABBOTT, CLARA HODGES, of Auburn, New York.
ADAMS, ANN, late of Lexington, Middlesex County, Mass., U S A.
ADAMS, JOSEPH, Son of Captain Joseph Adams, late of New York City, born September 18, 1836. He left New York in June, 1856, and was last heard from by letter written by him, dated Cora Mora Islands, Dec. 25, 1858.
ADAMS, JOSEPH, late of Roxbury, Norfolk, Massachusetts, U S A.
ADIE, JAMES MITCHELL, of Enola, Canada West
AFFOURTIT, PETER L, late of Company A, 17th Regiment New York Volunteers.
AITCHESON, JOHN, residing in Orange, County of Essex, New Jersey, U S A
AITKEN, WILLIAM KERR, Carpenter, from Berwick-on-Tweed, Scotland. When last heard of, was lodging in St Philip-street, New Orleans, U S A
AKERS, JAMES, formerly of London, England, died in the West Indies, 1821
ALLEN, BELLE, who left home in 1844, was married in 1849 to Jacob Van Dusen in Troy, and shortly afterwards came to New York City
ALLEN, HENRY, lately a soldier in Company K, 47th Regiment Illinois Volunteers.
ALLEN, THOMAS, died in America, 1794
ALLEYNE, HENRY, born 1800, who was married in Bristol, England, and went to America.
ANDERSON, ALFRED, of New York, U S A , 1832
ANDERSON, JAMES, Invernessshire, Scotland, he is supposed to have gone to London, England, New York, or Montreal, he wants the left arm from the shoulder, wears a dark wig, and has a halt
ANDREWS, GEORGE ERRICKER, Son of William Anderson, formerly of Esher, Surrey, and now of Cheltenham, England, he was last heard of at San Francisco
ANGELO, JOHN N , late of Boston, Suffolk County, Mass., U S A
ANTHOINE, PIERRE, born in Chateauroux, Hautes Alpes, France, supposed to have died in New Jersey, U S., about 1846.
APPLETON, THOMAS, formerly of Northallerton, York, England, went to America.
ASTILL, FRANK, formerly of Leicester, England, went to America in 1846
ASTOR, JOHN JACOB, formerly of New York. Heirs of.
ATKINS, CHARLES, who, about 1835, left England for America, and about 1838 was heard of at Quebec, in America
ATKINS, MAJOR RICHARD, who died in California.
ATKINSON, ANN, Wife of Watson Atkinson, an American, and Sister of Mrs Royston.
ATKINSON, JAMES, Son of Robert and Margaret Atkinson, of Lincolnshire, England , went to America.
AUSTIN, WILLIAM CORNELIUS, of Canada, Farmer
AVERILL, THOMAS, late of Burlington, Middlesex, Massachusetts, U S.A., now residing in New Boston, New Hampshire, insane
AYRES, GEORGE, Son of Sarah Ayres, formerly of Peekskill, New York
BACON, RICHARD, who was Clerk on the Great Western Railway, Birmingham, England, and who left that place in May, 1857
BAKER, JAMES, formerly of Lymington, Hants, England, went to America.
BAKER, SAMUEL, a Seaman on board the barque "Glen," in 1851
BALDWIN, JAMES F , late of Boston, Suffolk County, Massachusetts, U S.A.
BALL, AUGUST
BARKER, THOMAS, late of Ledyard, in the State of New York, America, who, in or about 1838, left Whitby, Yorkshire, England, for New York
BATES, FANNY, late of Cohasset, Norfolk, Massachusetts, U S A.
BATES, JAMES, late of Ulcombe, Kent, England, went to U S A. about 1847
BATES, JOSEPH, of Canada West
BAUM, HARRIET, formerly of Chester, Delaware County, Pa., U S A , supposed to have left New York for the South in 1861 or 1862
BRANLAND, WILLIAM, Son of Jonas Beanland, of Bowling, near Bradford, Yorkshire, England.
BEATTIE, GEORGE, the Younger, formerly of Southwark, in the County of Surrey, England, but late of New York, U S A , it is believed that he died in New York in 1830
BELCHER, WILLIAM S , late of Stoughton, Norfolk County, Massachusetts, U S.A.
BELIN, PETER, of London and America, died 1786
BELLEW, FRANK TEMPLE, of New York, in America.
BENNETT, MARTIN, went to Montreal in 1844
BENSHAW, ANN, who left England with Mrs John A Weir, March 14, 1848.
BENSON, MR., of Falmouth, Cornwall, England, and afterwards of Glasgow, Scotland
BENTLEY, EDWARD, Son of Edward, of Runwell, Essex, England went to Philadelphia, America.
BENTLEY, THOMAS, of America, 1783
BERNARD, HEWITT, one of the Godchildren of Henry Parker, late of Jamaica, West Indies
BERNEY, THOMAS, Victualler, formerly of No 1, Black Hall row, Dublin
BETHUNE, HUGH, formerly of London, England, Merchant, supposed to have died in America.
BETHUNE, N and F and Co , of Montreal, Canada
BICKELL, THOMAS and JANE NEWCOMBE, residing in Depeyster, St Lawrence County, New York, U S.A , and other Children of Mary Bickell (otherwise Williams, otherwise Rockey)
BISHOP, JOHN CROOK, formerly of Bushey, Herts, England , went to New York in 1831
BISHOP, ROBERT (sometimes called Stephen Robert, or Robert Stephen Bishop), formerly of Salperton, or Safperton, Gloucestershire, England, Shoemaker, who left England about 1846, for America, and was last heard of (in 1846) at Hamilton, Canada West.
BLACK, SAMUEL, resided at or near to Columbia river, Canada, and died therein 1841
BLACKALL, CHARLES, formerly of Wallingford, Berks, England , went to America in 1836.

SPECIAL LIST No. 4.

BLACKBURN, ROBERT, formerly of Glasgow, Scotland, Son of William Blackburn, who is supposed to have sailed from Liverpool on the 13th of March, 1828, for Newfoundland.
BLACKHALL, JAMES, formerly of Hampstead, near London, England, enlisted, and went to America.
BLATFORD, MR. and MRS. WILLIAM, came to U S A about 1840, from Dee County, Ireland
BLAZEBY, WILLIAM, formerly of Norwich, England, who emigrated to America about 1830, resided in New Orleans in 1835, and was killed at San Antonia, a Volunteer in the Texan Army
BLOOD, ADAH, late of Dunstable, Middlesex County, Mass., U S A
BLOOD, EDWARD W, late of Holliston, Middlesex County, Mass., U S A
BLOOMFIELD, ROBERT, of New York, 1833
BOGLE, ROGER, late of Boston, Suffolk County, Mass., U S A
BOLNEY, ANN, supposed to be in United States, Daughter of John and Mary Bolney.
BOLUS, MARY ANN, Niece of James Turner, of New York, Gunsmith
BONNELL, MRS, supposed to be in America
BOOTH, SAMUEL, died in America.
BOOTH, WILLIAM HENRY, late of Leeds, England, Clothdresser, went to America in 1852.
BORMAN, AMBROSE, formerly of Ockham, Surrey, England, went to America in 1830
BOTCHERBY, ESTHER, of Canada, in British North America, Widow of Morton Botcherby.
BOURKE, JOHN, formerly of Liverpool, went to America about 1853
BOWIE, WASHINGTON, George Town, U S, 1816
BRADBROOK, MR, formerly of 4, Bowery, New York
BRADFORD, LOUISA, Daughter of Sarah Cooper, she is supposed to have left England with the Mormons for Salt Lake, some years since
BRADLEY (otherwise HALLIDAY), CHARLOTTE, late of New York, Daughter of Henry Bradley, of Birmingham, England
BRADLEY, THOMAS H, died in America, 1826.
BRAMMER, EDWARD, formerly of Croydon, Saddler, who went to America, 1845
BRAY, PHILIP, born at Winchelsea, Sussex, England, went to New York and Buffalo in 1841.
BREIDING, HENRY, born in Ermschwerd, Witzenhausen, Kuhrhessen, who came to U S A in 1851.
BREMAR, HENRY, died in America.
BREWSTER, WILLIAM, of the firm of Brewster, Tildersley, and Co, of Chicago, Ill, or Virginia Brewster.
BRISSINGTON, JOHN, lately died at Newhern, North Carolina, U S A
BROMHEAD, BENJAMIN, in Virginia, 1771
BROOKE, EDWARD GOULD, left England for America about the end of October, 1857, and supposed to have died there.
BROOKS, JAMES, late of Oxford, supposed that his grandchildren are in America.
BROWN, ALEXANDER, late of Twenty fourth, U S, C T
BROWN, GEORGE THOMAS, Son of Christopher and Ann Brown, went to Boston, U.S.A.
BROWN, JAMES, late of New Orleans, U S A
BROWN, MARGARET, late of New York City
BROWN, MARY ANN, Wife of Stewart Brown, of New York.
BROWN, RICHARD, Woolcomber, who left Harberton, Devon, England, in April, 1836, was in Albany in May, 1836, and last heard from in Rapid, Louisiana, in July, 1841
BROWN, SIMON, late of Dorchester, Norfolk, Massachusetts, U S A.
BROWN, WILLIAM, late of Richmond, Virginia, Merchant, died 1811
BROWNE, THOMAS, formerly of Roscommon, Ireland, last heard of in 1856, in Cherry-street, New York. He is a sailor, and sometimes sails under the name of Thomas Blake
BRYANT, CHARLES, late of Skowhegan, Somerset County, Maine, U S A.
BUCHAN, WILLIAM F B, Doctor of Medicine, went to Canada in 1834
BUCKLEY, JAMES, Son of Abraham, deceased, of Whitfield, Lancashire, England, supposed to be abroad.
BUDD, CHARLES, of Cherry-street, New York, U S A, Shoemaker, who went to America in 1836
BUNN, THOMAS, of Rupert's Land, North America
BUNTING, MARY, Wife of Edward Bunting, and Daughter of Elizabeth Steward, of Wereham, Norfolk, England, who emigrated to America some time since
BURDELL, EMMA, died in New York, 1802
BURKE, THOMAS and PATRICK, Sons of Elizabeth Burke, of Dublin, Ireland
BURNAP, LYDIA, late of Holliston, Middlesex County, Mass., U S A
BURNS, ROBERT, of Belfast, Ireland, then in the employ of the British Consul in New York.
BURNS, ROBERT, Son of Robert Burns, of Newtownards, Down, Ireland He went to New York in 1836, and soon afterwards went on a whale-fishing voyage to the Northern Seas, and has not been heard of since 1843.
BURRELL, WILLIAM, of North Lopham, Norfolk, England, Heir at Law of, supposed to be a descendant of Stephen Burrell, who went to America many years ago
BYRNE, MARY (formerly CONNOLLY), Widow of Edmund Byrne. She had three Daughters living in New York, U S A named Anne, Margaret, and Elizabeth
BYRNES, CHRISTOPHER, late of Framingham, Middlesex County, Mass., U.S.A.
CAHILL, JOHN, of Dumfries-shire, Scotland, who landed in New York, U S A, in the year 1838
CAIN, MARY, last heard from in Yorkville
CAMERON, JOHN GEORGE, a Mulatto, who sailed from Liverpool for America about 1809 or 1819.
CAMMEYER, WILLIAM, in 1818 a Merchant at Chili, South America
CAMPBELL, JAMES, late of the City of New York, a native of Ireland, Dealer in Photographic Albums, deceased
CAMPBELL, MARY, late of Montserratt, West Indies.
CAMPBELL, MR, of New York U S A.
CANNING, WILLIAM, Son of Athaliah Canning, went to New Orleans in 1841.
CANOCHAN, MARGARET, of Baltimore
CAREY, ALICE, of Roscommon, Ireland, lived in Walker street, New York City, U S A, about 1847
CARPENTER, CORYNDON, WILLIAM FOUNTLEROY, NATHANIEL, and BUSHROD
CARPENTER, DR NATHANIEL, late of Virginia, U S, died in 1778
CARLTON, ENOCH, late of Boston, Suffolk County, Mass., U S A
CARSON, JOHN H, born in Washington County, New York, died in Liverpool, England, in 1858, Daughter of, supposed to be married and living in Virginia, U S A.
CARTWRIGHT, MATTHEW, of Philadelphia
CHADWICK, ELIZABETH, formerly of Gildart's gardens, Liverpool, England, afterwards of Manchester, but now residing in America.
CHAMBERS, CATHARINE, late of Bedford, England, relatives in America wanted (Maiden Name, PEPPIN).
CHAMPION, ALEXANDER, London, England, said to have lived some time in Baltimore, U S
CHARLES, RICHARD, ROBERT, and WILLIAM, all now in America, Sons of Richard Charles, of Dublin, Ireland.

CHESSO (or CHASE) EUGENE J., who, when last heard from, about 1853, was living at Spring Garden, Philadelphia, USA
CHIENNE, MARGARET, living in Philadelphia about 1830
CLAPP, BENJAMIN, late of Dorchester, Norfolk County, Mass., USA.
CLARK, ANNA. (See Winton, Anna.)
CLARK, JULIA, died in New York
CLARK, MARY, died in America
CLARK, THOMAS, formerly of Mosevale, Warwick, England, enlisted and sent to America about 1770
CLAUSSADEHOFF, MRS., a native of Keel, Propstei, Pretz, Germany, who arrived in New York in 1840, and afterwards removed to Philadelphia
CLIFFORD, MARGARET, of County Limerick, who left Ireland in August, 1860, for New York, U.S.A.
CLOUGH, JOHN, of Runcorn, Cheshire, England, Son of Thomas and Margaret Clough, went to Boston in 1848
CLOWERS, JOHN M., and JOHANNA, his Wife, who sailed from Rotterdam, 14th June, 1855, for New York, in the "Leila."
CLYNE, WILLIAM, Son of the late James Clyne, Leather Merchant, Aberdeen, Scotland.
COBSON, GEORGE, of California.
COCK, GEORGE, formerly of Plymouth, England, Grocer, went to New York about 1859 or 1860
COLEMAN, SARAH, Widow (formerly SARAH STICKNEY), of Newbury, Mass., USA.
COLLINGTON, NATHANIEL, who was formerly a Butcher at Mobile, and married in New York a Miss Combs, or Tombs, of Exeter, England, in 1845
COLLINS, J W, who formerly worked for H. Seymour & Co
COLSON, GEORGE, late of California.
COLT, SARAH (formerly LYMAN), who died either in the U S. or New Brunswick.
CONANT, PETER, late of Charlestown, Middlesex County, Mass., USA.
CONNOR, JAMES H., died in America.
COOKE, or COOK, SAMUEL, late of New York, a Builder, who owned property in East Chester in 1826.
COOPER, GEORGE, of California, 1856.
COOPER, JOHN, formerly of Misterton, Notts, England, went to America in 1820
COOPER, MRS JOHN, Widow of the late Dr John Cooper, late of Washtenaw County, Michigan, U.S.A.
COOPER, LOUISA. (See Bradford, Louisa.)
CORNELIA, JOHN B., JAMES CORNELIA, and MARY, Wife of Henry Thomas, the Heirs-at-Law of Peter Cornelia, formerly of New York
CORNER, JAMES, born at Wick, Scotland, went to America
CORNWALL, ANNE, Daughter of Mrs Julia Cornwall, formerly of Sackville-street, Dublin
CORRI, PHILIP ANTONY, Musical Composer and Teacher, who left this country for America.
COURTER, JOHN'S, a Mason by trade, was known in 1857 to be in Chicago, Illinois, USA.
COWELL, SARAH, Wife of Edward (Maiden Name, SARAH WILSON, who emigrated to America about 1700.
COWLING, EDWARD, who formerly resided at or near Holywell mount, Shoreditch, England, and left this country for America in or about the year 1839.
COX, MRS. ANN (formerly ANN WHITECHURCH, Spinster), left England in 1842 in the "Britannia" steamer from Liverpool, for Boston or Halifax, North America (under assumed name of Mrs Clarke)
COX, FREDERIC, late of Tiverton, Devon, England.
CRABTREE, JAMES, Son of John and Grace Crabtree, of Huddersfield, England, went to America in 1830.
CRAIG, JOHN B., died in America
CRANE, PEYTON, and NATHANIEL, who removed from Virginia many years ago
CRAWFORD, CHARLES, a Seaman, sailed to West Indies in 1616.
CREW, ROBERT, Son of John Crew, a Quaker, who died in America.
CRISP, WILLIAM, of North America.
CRISS, WALTER, died in America.
CROOK, ROBERT, was in U S.A in 1342.
CROSS, HORATIO, formerly a Customs Guard in the West Indies
CROWLEY, JAMES, late of Templemore, County Tipperary, Ireland, who emigrated to America about 1860.
CROXTON, PRISCILLA, who removed from Virginia many years ago
CRUICKSHANK, WILLIAM, formerly of East Smithfield, London, England, went to America.
CRUMBLEHOLME, GEORGE, formerly of Slaidburn, Yorkshire, England, late of New York, U S A.
CUDLIP, THEODOSIA HODGSON, Wife of Otty Cudlip, of St John's, New Brunswick
CUMMING, JAMES, lived at or near Brompton in 1838, and subsequently removed to Montreal, Canada.
CURRAN, JOHN, who is supposed to have emigrated to Canada about 1822, and to have died there about 1850
CURREN, MICHAEL, formerly of Belfast, Ireland, who went to America.
CURRIE, JOHN, was in Newport, Rhode Island, U S, in 1843
CUTTER, RUTH, late of Cambridge, Middlesex County, Mass., USA.
DAILEY, WILLIAM, died in America, 1812
DAILY, R H, was in Europe in 1855, and now understood to be in business in Virginia, U S A.
DANFORD, JACOB, of Quebec, 1800
DARLING, HANNAH. (See Robinson, Hannah)
DAVIDSON, ALEXANDER and JOHN, Sons of Mungo Davidson, who died in America, 1774.
DAVIDSON, MUNGO, Master of a Trading Vessel, died about 1774, leaving a Widow, who is believed to have kept a store in Philadelphia, after his decease
DAVIES, THOMAS (otherwise JOHN THOMAS), formerly of Wrexham, England, Omnibus Proprietor, subsequently of the 18th Regiment of Missouri Volunteers, North America
DAVIES, or DAVIS, THOMAS, Son of Mary Davies, or Davis, formerly of Reading, Berks, England, emigrated to America, a few years ago, and was employed in a Cotton Mill at North Attleboro Falls, Massachusetts
DAVIS, MARGARET, a native of Leitrim, Ireland, who sailed from Dublin in August, 1854, for New York
DAVIS, SARAH SUSANNAH (afterwards GRAHAM), died in America in 1822
DAWSON, ROBINSON JAMES, a native of Norfolk, Virginia, USA., went to the East Indies.
DEACON, ISABELLA, Wife of Thomas Deacon, of Kingston, Canada, Storekeeper, about 1830.
DE BONNE, PIERRE AMABLE, formerly one of the Judges of the Court of King's Bench at Quebec, Lower Canada, died at Quebec in 1816.
DE LA VALETTE, JOHN BAPTISTE DU VERDIER, New York, 1798
DE COURCY, HENRY LOUIS ARMAND POTIER, late of New York, native of France, Merchant, deceased.
DEE, CATHARINE, late of New York City, native of Ireland, Domestic
DEERY, JOHN, supposed to reside on Long Island.
DE LANCEY, SUSAN, late of the Plough Hotel, Cheltenham, in the County of Gloucester, England, who died in 1866.
DELATER (or DELATRE), ERNEST, late of New York, went to Sandwich Islands.
DENT, JOHN, born at Richmond, York, England, went to America about 1805

DERREVAN, PATRICK, a native of County Galway, Portumna, Ireland, supposed to be living in the City of New York
DEVINNY, JOHN, a follower of the United States Army, in the Mexican War, British subject.
DEYELL, THOMAS, died in America
DIMBLEBY, SARAH (afterwards MRS SARAH WORSDELL), of Hull, England, sailed for U S A. a few years ago
DIXON, GEORGE, a Seafaring man, in the employ of the Hudson s Bay Company, believed to have a brother, a Tailor, in Liverpool, England.
DOANE, BENJAMIN F, who was born at Springfield, Massachusetts, about 1818, he left New Bedford as Carpenter, in the Whaling ship "Eagle," in 1840, and was discharged in Chili, he had a half-brother named Strang, also of Springfield, who is supposed to have died about 1858.
DOBBS, WILLIAM LEMON, Currier, went to America in 1844
DOHERTY, BRIDGET (now MRS THOMPSON), when last heard from, about 1853, was in New York, U S A
DOHERTY, JOHN, late of Boston, Suffolk County, Mass., U.S.A.
DOLBEARE, THOMAS, of Boston, America.
DORMER, REV JAMES, resided in South Carolina, U S A
DOWLING, JOHN, born in Ireland, died in Philadelphia, 1859
DOWNHAM, JOSEPH, Farmer, formerly of Basingstoke, Hants, England, went to Canada, 1829
DOYLE, ANN, Widow, of America.
DRAPER, JAMES, formerly of Manchester.
DUCKETT, WILLIAM, and SARAH, his Wife, formerly of Tatcham, Berks, England, late of Baltimore, U S.A
DUFF, JAMES, of New York, America, 1790
DUFFY, MARGARET (supposed to have married a man named Doherty), a native of Ireland; when last heard from she was living in Brooklyn, New York, U S.A.
DUGAS, JOSEPH ANTON, of Russia, who is reported to reside somewhere in America.
DUKE, CAPTAIN CHARLES, of Quebec, 1800
DUKE, ROBERT, formerly of Colchester, England, then of America.
DUNN, JAMES, went to Montreal, Canada, in or about the year 1812; died there about 1837, leaving children— Thomas, Priscilla, John, Dorothy, Ann.
DUNN, JOHN, Seaman, some time residing at Charleston, North America
DUNN, JOHN, Miller, formerly of Etal Mills, Northumberland, England, went to Montreal, Canada, in or about the year 1812, died previously to 1834
DUNN, OWEN, of King's County, Ireland, who went to America about 1847
DURSTON, GEORGE, of Artichoke-row, Mile-end, London, England, who left England for New Orleans about 1843, and was living there in 1847
DUVAL, DAVID, of London and America
EAMES, AARON E, late of Hopkinton, Middlesex County, Mass., U S.A
EATON, WILLIAM, and his Sister, ALICE, of Waterford, Ireland, which they left about 1844, and when last heard from, in 1850, were in Boston, Mass., U.S.A.
ECCLES, THOMAS and ANN, of New York.
EDGE, GEORGE J, who, when last heard of, was in the United States of America.
EDMESTON, MARGARET (Maiden Name, JONES) (See Prevost, William.)
EDMONDS, EDGAR BARNWELL, last heard of in Canada.
EGAN, ELLEN, who, in 1861, lived in Orange-lane, Boston, U S.A.
ELGER, THOMAS, late of 99, White Lion street, Islington, England; supposed afterwards of America.
ELKIN, FRANCIS, born at Hanbury, Stafford, England, Engineer, went to Canada.
EMERSON, CAROLINE L, late of North Reading, Middlesex County, Mass, U S.A.
ENDRES, ERNST, of Oberndorf, Wurtemburg, Germany
ERHORN, LOUISA, Daughter of Mr ANDREW MACFARLANE, supposed to have gone to California a few years ago
ERMATINGER, F W, of Montreal, Canada
ERSKINE, SAMUEL McMICHAN, Seaman, formerly of Kirkcudbright, Scotland, went to South America.
EVANS, JAMES died in America.
EVERETT, JOSEPH C, late of Newton, Middlesex County, Massachusetts, U S A
FAYLE, WILLIAM formerly of Mount Mellick, Queen's County, Ireland, who arrived in America in 1851, when last heard from in 1853, he resided near Hudson City, New York
FEENY, MICHAEL, formerly Shopkeeper in Shrule, County Mayo, Ireland.
FENTON, JOHN, formerly of Williamsburgh, Virginia, U.S
FENTON, JOHN, died in America, 1799
FERDINAND, MADAME, late of Havana.
FERGUSON, HENRY, a native of America, found dead near the Tower London, England, about 1840.
FERRIS, BENJAMIN C, formerly of No 20, Chambers street, New York, Counsellor-at-Law, who left New York about the 20th June, 1856.
FIANDER, JOHN, late of the City of New York
FICKELL, JOSEPH (otherwise JOSEPH LLOYD), who left Liverpool, England, in 1849, bound to New York, thence to New Orleans, U S A.
FIELD, GEORGE C, who died, on his return to New York, of wounds received in the Riot of Panama
FILES, STEPHEN, Assignee of William Thompson, Savannah, Georgia, U S A.
FILZINGER, HEINRICH JOSEPH, from Dieburg, Hesse-Darmstadt, Germany, who was last heard of at Sacramento, California, June 11, 1854
FINLAY, WILLIAM, born in Yorkshire, England, went to America in 1820
FINLEY, JANE, MARGARET or ANN, formerly of M'Caskey Parish, County Londonderry, Ireland.
FINN, DANIEL, Teamster, U.S., Quartermaster's Department, War with Mexico.
FISHER, JAMES C, of Philadelphia, U S A
FISHER, S W, of Philadelphia, U S.A.
FITZGERALD, MRS PATRICK, from Recsail, County Limerick, Ireland
FLAGG, CHARLES A., late of Winthrop, Suffolk County, Mass., U S A
FLANAGAN, MICHAEL, Victualler, formerly of No 1, Black Hall row, Dublin.
FLEMING, JANE, Wife of Laurence Cunningham Fleming, of Ottawa, Canada.
FLETCHER, BETSEY, who removed from Virginia many years ago
FLETCHER, LINCOLN, who was left with a nurse about 1856
FONTAINE, CHARLES, died in America
FOORD, JOHN, native of Scotland, who lived in New York in 1835
FORMAN, WILLIAM, Brother of John Forman of Stepney, was at Boston, U S A, in 1848.
FORRESTER, JOSEPH JAMESON YOUNG (See Young, Joseph Jameson)
FOSGATE, EMMA MARGARET, Wife of William Fosgate, of Auburn, New York.
FOSGATE, MARA REBECCA, Wife of Blanchard Fosgate, of Auburn, New York.

FOWKE, PETER, late of Tygwyn, Wales, which he is supposed to have left for Pennsylvania or New Jersey, about 1650.
FOWLER, JOSEPH, died in America.
FOWLKES, JAMES (otherwise SEYMOUR), formerly of Canada.
FOYLE, JAMES, went to America.
FRANCOIS, JEAN, Seaman
FRANKLIN, HENRY, of Canada, 1851
FRASER, JOHN, Schoolmaster, of Bruce County, Canada West.
FRENCH, ANN BRAYNE, Wife of George French, M D , of Fredericksburg, Virginia, U S., living about 1787.
FRENCH, JAMES, formerly of Limehouse, England, then of Nova Scotia.
FROMENT, WILLIAM JACOB, JOHN CHARLES, DOROTHEA MARY, ELIZA, THEODORE, ANDRE, MARIE THERESE, and CHARLOTTE (married to — Peny), all living in New York in 1835
FURLONG, PATRICK, a native of St. John's. New Brunswick, Seaman on board brig "Alice Franklin."
GAHAGAN, JAMES, of the West Indies in 1708
GALE, JAMES, a Sailmaker and Seaman, a native of Scotland, who was seen in Charleston, S.C , in 1858
GALLIGAN, EDWARD, CATHARINE ELEANOR, MARGARET ELIZA, and ISABELLA (Children of Catharine Galligan, late of Lissogarton, County Monaghan, Ireland), who emigrated to New York, U S A., in 1846
GANCE, MRS. ANN ELIZA, who about 1839 resided in the City of New York, U S.A.
GARDENER, THOMAS, formerly of Tadmorton, Oxford, England, enlisted in Her Majesty's service, supposed to be in America
GARMES (otherwise HARNES), JOHN, native of Hanover, died at New York lately
GARTSIDE, JAMES, Son of Jonah, of Oldham, Lancashire, England, Hatter, deceased, a few years ago went to America.
GARTSIDE, SARAH, who was married in America to William Yeaton
GARVEY, LUCAS, late of the West Indies, died in 1814
GASH, MARY and JANE, Daughters of John and Ellen Gash, of Cork, Ireland.
GATES, ELIZABETH, late of Brighton, England, Daughter of Henry Gates, late of Charleston, U.S.A.
GEARY, WILLIAM, formerly of Nuneaton, Warwick, England, went to Boston, U S.A.
GEER, GEORGE W, late of New York, deceased
GIBSON, —, related to Richard Twede.
GIBSON, NICHOLAS, of North America
GILBODY, PETER, a Soldier of the 52nd Regiment, supposed to have gone to America.
GILL, FREDERICK JAMES, late of Axminster, Devon, England, supposed to be in America.
GILL, JAMES HENRY of Barbadoes, West Indies
GILLETT, THOMAS W, formerly of New Haven
GILLIGAN, or GALLAGAN, JOHN, a native of Ireland, Citizen of New York City, U S A.; supposed to have died in New Orleans.
GILLOOLY, THOMAS, who lived in Liverpool and came over to America about 1830 or 1834.
GIRAUD, CHARLES, Cook. went to New York in 1844
GLANHAM, CHARLES JONES, from London, England, last heard of, in 1850, at Brian Island, near Yarmouth, Nova Scotia.
GLASGOW, MAJOR GEORGE, of Quebec, 1800.
GLASIER, JOHN, late of Barlings, Lincolnshire, England, who went to America in 1834.
GLEADOW, ROBERT, formerly of Hull, England, afterwards of New York City, last heard of in July, 1853
GODDEN, WILLIAM (otherwise LEGGETT), Master Mariner, formerly of Dover, Kent, many years ago emigrated to Rochester, Massachusetts, U S , and died there about 1808
GOLDBOROUGH, ROBERT and SARAH, of America, 1770—1800.
GOOD, MRS JANE (Maiden Name RIORDAN), a native of Macroom, County Cork, Ireland, whose address in 1857 was Cosumnes River, Sacramento, California.
GOODALL, SUSAN, residing in some part of North America, Daughter of Alexander Goodall, Dairyman, late of Wright's Houses, Edinburgh, Scotland
GOODEVE, WILLIAM GODBOLD, born at Waltham, Essex, England, a Cooper, married Ann Leafe, went to America
GORDON, ALEXANDER, late of Tobago and Barbadoes, died in 1811
GORDON, ELEANOR ELIZA, formerly of the West Indies, then of Scotland.
GORDON, JAMES, of N Y, America, 1790
GORDON, JOHN and ANN, Children of Mrs Ann Gordon, or Battams, formerly lived at Earl's Barton, Northamptonshire, England.
GOUGH, HENRY THOMAS, late of 15, Cowley street, Westminster, Gentleman, deceased. His sister lived at New York.
GOURLAY, EMILY (See Whyte.)
GOWANS, HENRY, now or lately in America.
GRADDON, ANGELICA, Wife of John Graddon, of Quebec, Merchant
GRAHAM, SARAH SUSANNAH, Wife of John Graham, formerly of London, England, late of America.
GRANT, ROBERT, of New York, 1790
GRATE, CHARLES, supposed from Pennsylvania, died in Toronto General Hospital, Toronto, Canada.
GRAY, DAVID FINLY, Son of Thomas Gray, of St. Croix, West Indies
GRAY, PATRICK, of Natick, Middlesex County, Massachusetts, U S A
GREEN, DAVID JOHN, and JOHN HARRISON, Children of Robert Green, who died in America, prior to 1811.
GREENWOOD, ANN ELIZABETH, Daughter of William and Elizabeth Platten, born in County of Norfolk, England, in 1793 Married — Greenwood, a Silk Weaver, and went to America about 1842
GREER, THOMAS, Seaman, a native of Scotland, died in New York, 1862.
GREGORY, THOMAS, in 1824 kept an Academy at Hanwell, Middlesex, England, and, it is believed, left this country for America.
GRENFEL, LIEUTENANT-COLONEL GEORGE ST. LEGER, supposed to have been in the service of the Confederate States of America.
GREY, MRS, formerly Miss Cocks
GRIFFITHS, HENRY C , of America, 1854
GROAT, or GROTH, JAMES PELHAM, late of New York, native of England, Post Captain, R.N , deceased.
GRUBB, THOMAS, formerly of Porchester, Hants, England , went to America.
GUEST, ROBERT, formerly of Madeley, in the County of Salop, England, but since then of Charles County, Maryland, U S A.
GUIRY, JEROME W , who sailed from Queenstown in 1868, by steamship "City of Antwerp."
GUNNIS, ELIZABETH, formerly of Spilsby, Lincolnshire, England, but late of New York, U.S.
GUYER, JAMES, of St Bartholomew, W I
GWINNETT, BUTTON, formerly of Staffordshire, England, Grocer, but lately of North America. Children of

SPECIAL LIST No. 4.

HACKETT, CHARLES, of Philadelphia.
HAGUE, THOMAS, JOHN, and LUCY, Children of Elizabeth Hague, late of St Thomas-by Launceston, Cornwall, England, last heard of as residing in the State of Ohio, America.
HALE, WILLIAM, Civil Engineer, who, it is supposed, left England for America about 1863
HALFORD, JOSEPH (Son of Joseph Halford, late of Coombe-hill, near Tewkesbury, Gloucestershire, England), born at Utah, California
HALPIN, DENNIS, and WIFE; information wanted of.
HAMBRIDGE, RICHARD STEPHEN, Professor of Music, formerly of London, England, now in America.
HAMILTON, ELLEN, of Coalrain, County Derry, Ireland, who, when last heard of, resided in New York, U S A.
HAMILTON, MRS MATHEW WILLIAM, late of St Nevis, West Indies
HAMMAND, MISS OTTORIAHA, Daughter of Margaret and Edward Hammond, she is a native of Elton, Wales, and came to New York at the age of five years, and was adopted by a family named Garthwright in Craneville, N J , U S A.
HAMMOND, JOHN, died in America.
HAMMOND, ROBERT, formerly resident at Mr Greaves', Green Dragon-court, St. Andrew's-hill, London, England, left for Montreal, Canada, about 1856.
HANSON, MARY JANE, who lived in New York about 1849 or 1850.
HARDESTY, THOMAS and ELLEN, who left England in 1854 for America, when last heard from, were in Canada West
HARDMAN, JOHN, who went to America; Son of John Hardman, of London and Manchester, England.
HARE, BARZILLAI (otherwise ROBBARTS), born at Ipswich, Suffolk, England, late of Pennsylvania, U.S.A.
HARMS, MRS MARY, who left Ireland for America about 1828.
HARRINGTON, TIMOTHY, who was last heard from, in 1853, when residing in Berks County, Pennsylvania. Also JOHN and MARIA HARRINGTON, who, when last heard from, resided in Philadelphia, Pa., U S A, all Children of John Harrington, of Evansville, Indiana.
HARRIOTT, JOHN EDWARD, of Red River, in the Hudson's Bay Company's Territories, North America.
HARRIS, FORBES, of Blairlogie, Stirling, Scotland, went to the West Indies in 1818
HARRIS THOMAS, who went to New York in 1836, Son of William and Mary Elizabeth Harris, of London.
HARRISON, ALFRED W, from Wolverhampton, England, heard from last in 1848, from Cincinnati, Ohio, U S A.
HARRISON, JANE, Philadelphia.
HARRISON, JOHN, formerly of Kingston-on-Thames, England, late of Long Island, America.
HARRISON, MARY JANE, who lived in New York, U S., about 1849 or 1850
HARRISON, THOMAS FISHER, formerly of Lynn, Norfolk, England, went to America.
HART, CHARLES, formerly of Stafford, England, went to the U S., and resided at Baltimore.
HART, FREDERICK WILLARD, formerly of London, was married at Liverpool, England, and went to New Orleans, U S
HARTLEY, AQUILA, who was, when last heard of, in New York, U.S.A.
HARTWELL, CHARLES, was a Carpenter, last heard of at Brooklyn, near New York.
HARVEY, JOHN, Baker, who was born in England about 1755, moved to Detroit, Michigan, about 1796, and to Jeffersonville, Indiana, U S A., in 1816, where he died in 1825. He married a Miss Wilson, who died in 1822.
HARVEY, MARIA YORK, Daughter of John Harvey; she came from England to Jeffersonville, Indiana, U S A., in 1823, and died there in 1826 or 1827 She was married to Edwin Reeder in 1826
HATCHING, ROBERT, formerly of Manchester, England , was at Salem, U S A , in 1838
HAWKINS, ANNE, Spinster, afterwards DAME ANNE PEARL, of Newfoundland.
HAY, HUGH, of Belleville, Now Jersey, North America, and SUSANNA, his Wife (formerly SUSANNA NELSON, Spinster), a Husbandman.
HEALY, MARY, of Cheragh, Cork, Ireland ; when last heard from she was living with Mr Gold, Paterson, New Jersey, U S A
HEARNE, FRANCIS, who died in some part of America before 1850.
HEDGE, CAPTAIN, of New York
HEIS, CHARLES, who came to America from Amsterdam, Holland, about 1854.
HELM, —, went from Germany to America in 1806
HELM, WILLIAM, died in America.
HEMMING, GEORGE, formerly of Newbury, Berks, England, left for U S. in 1841
HENDERSON, FRANCES ELEANOR, Daughter of Lieut Colonel Laurens, of South Carolina, U.S.A.
HENDERSON, ROBERT, born in Louisiana , he died in the City of New Orleans
HENLEY, EDWARD, of America, 1760 80
HENNESY, JOHN, who was last heard of as working at the Union Mills, Fluvanna County, Virginia, U.S A.
HENNEY, JOHN and WILLIAM, last heard of at the Sailors' Home, New York, June, 1857, Seamen in the Merchant Service.
HENSHAW, ANN, went to America.
HENWOOD, SAMUEL, of Charleston, America, the Niece of, wanted.
HERBERT, JOHN RICHARDSON, late of St. Nevis, West Indies
HERBERT, JOSEPH, who, in 1789, emigrated from Nantes, France, to St Bartholomew's, West Indies, where he died about 1837, leaving a son, William Herbert, in the United States of America.
HERMAN, LEOPOLD, late of Boston, Suffolk County, Massachusetts, U S A.
HEYWARD, FRANCIS, formerly of Manchester, England, late of New Orleans, U.S.A.
HIEGLO, LOUISE VICTORINE (See Roger, Louise Victorine.)
HILL, ELI, late of Boston, Suffolk County, Massachusetts, U S A
HILL, ELIZA, Widow of Hon. Thomas Hill, of Montserratt, West Indies
HIRST, THOMAS, supposed to have resided in the United States of America since 1821, and to have died in 1831 in the State of Pennsylvania
HITCHCOCK, WILLIAM GEORGE, in 1820 was a Waterman at Woolwich, Kent, England, but shortly afterwards left this country to settle in the United States, and is supposed to have died there
HODGEMAN, ELIZABETH , having relatives in New York
HOFFMAN, FERDINAND, from Brunswick, Germany, when last heard from, in 1854, he lived in 114½, Ninth Avenue, N Y
HOLCOMBE, MARY ELIZABETH, late of Jamaica, she married Edward Pearson.
HOLLAND, ELIZABETH, Daughter of William Holland, of James River, Virginia
HOLLIHAN, WILLIAM, late of Boston, Suffolk, Massachusetts, U S A.
HOLLOWAY, SAMUEL, went to America in 1773, entered the United States Army.
HOLMAN, JOHN, formerly of South Carolina, U S , Brother of Samuel Holman.
HOLMES, ELIZABETH. (See Murphy, Elizabeth.)
HOLMES, THOMAS, of Montreal, Canada.
HOMER, HANNAH MARIA, formerly of Dudley, Worcestershire, England.
HORLDON, GEORGE, of Canada.
HORN, WILLIAM, late of Watertown, Middlesex County, Mass., U S A.

HORNBY, JOHN, died in America.
HORTON, CARLTON S, who resided some years ago at Madeira, and is reported to have died in the United States after his return there
HOUGHTON, THOMAS WATKINSON, Seaman, last heard of at Baltimore, U.S.A.
HOUNSHAM, A., died in America, 1853.
HOUSTON, ROBERT, late of Buenos Ayres.
HOWARD, ISAAC, went to America from Essex, England.
HOWELL, THOMAS, formerly Fish Factor at Billingsgate Market, London, England, supposed to be in America.
HOWISON, ARCHIBALD, born at Falkirk, Scotland, went to America in 1827
HOXSEY, THOMAS D, some time of Patterson, County of Passaic, New Jersey, U.S.A.
HUDSWELL, JOHN, Brother to Joshua Hudswell, of Wakefield, England, went to America.
HUFFMASTER, SUSAN, late of Medford, Middlesex County, Mass., U.S.A.
HUGHES, JONATHAN, of Castleblaney, County Monaghan, Ireland
HUMPHREYS, ISAAC, an American citizen, who died intestate in one of the British Colonies.
HUNTER, CAPTAIN JOHN, of Virginia, Sisters of
HURST, GEORGE, formerly of Kingston-upon-Hull, England, went to New York in 1850.
HUTCHINSON, EDWARD, late of Leith, Scotland, went to America in 1833.
HUTCHINSON, SARAH (formerly SARAH PENROSE), who in 1814, at Kingston-upon-Hull, England, intermarried with James Ferreman Hutchinson, and afterwards went to America, where she is supposed to have died in 1839
HUTTON, MRS MARGERET, late of Montreal, North America.
ILETT, WILLIAM, eldest Son of William Ilett, of West Meon, Southampton, England, Excise Officer, born in 1767, in the parish of Taunton Dean, Somerset, England, he afterwards lived with his father at West Meon. When a lad, he left home and went to sea, and rose to be a Captain in the U S N, last heard of in 1802 or 1803
INFIELD, JOHN, formerly of England, then of Montreal, Canada.
INGRAHAM, SARAH, Wife of Timothy (Maiden Name, SARAH COWELL)
INNES, ROBERT D, of Canada.
IRONMONGER, DAVID, formerly of Barton, Stafford, England, last heard of at Pittsburgh, U.S.A., in 1845.
JACKSON, JAMES (otherwise BAKER), formerly of Poplar, Middlesex, England, Mariner, last heard of in New York.
JACKSON, JOHN, died in America.
JACKSON, THOMAS (otherwise WILLIAM), late of New York City, Seaman, native of Nova Scotia.
JACOBS, JAMES MADISON, of Greenville, South Carolina, who, when last heard of, was in Selma, Alabama, U.S.A.
JAMES, ESTHER. (See Jones, Esther)
JAMES, HERBERT JARRETT, a Master in Chancery, of Jamaica, West Indies, late of Clifton, Bristol, England.
JAMES, MARY, died in America, 1793
JAMES, RICHARD, died in America.
JAMES, THOMAS. (See Prevost, William.)
JAMIESON, JAMES, died in America.
JAMIESON, JOHN, died in America.
JARRETT, JOHN, formerly of Abergavenny, Monmouth, Wales, went to West Indies.
JENKINS, SUSANNAH, late of Cowbridge Glamorgan, Wales, Widow, Grandchildren in America wanted.
JENKINS, THOMAS, of America, 1861
JENNENS, ROBERT, Certificate of Baptism of.
JOHNSON, ADAM, died in America.
JOHNSON, JOHN, an Englishman, late Surgeon on board the U S. ship "Itasca."
JOHNSON, PETER, late of New York, a native of Finland, Seaman, deceased.
JOHNSON, WILLIAM, of Canada, British North America.
JONES, BENJAMIN, of Philadelphia, America.
JONES, CHARLES, late of Williamsburg, Virginia, but last of Guildford, Surrey, England.
JONES, ESTHER, Daughter of Mary Jones, of Penlan Farm, Carmarthen, England, she is believed to have married a Mr James, a Blacksmith of Tyllwydd, Carmarthenshire, and to have left England many years ago for America.
JONES, JOHN, a Mariner, who was at St. John's, New Brunswick, in 1836
JONES, JOHN (otherwise JOHN S JONES), Gardener, formerly of Denbigh, Wales, afterwards supposed to be residing at Wilmington, Delaware, America.
JONES, LEWIS BRISSINGTON, late of North Carolina, U.S.A.
JONES, MARGARET. (See Prevost, William.)
JONES, PAUL, CHEVALIER, Admiral and Commodore in the American Navy; died 1792
JONES, SOPHIA, now or lately of Castleton, Rutland County, Vermont, U.S.A, Widow of Lewis Parry Jones, formerly of Bangor, in the County of Carnarvon, Wales, but afterwards of Castleton aforesaid.
JONES, THOMAS CLIFFE, formerly of London, Merchant, went to America in 1847
JONES, WILLIAM ROBERT, who left Bradford, Wilts, England, for America, about 1811.
JOSLIN, MRS. CAROLINE, late of Salt Fleet, Stoney-creek, Canada.
JOYNT, HENRY ROBERT, who in 1857 and 1858 was a Cotton-Planter in Barnwell District, South Carolina, U.S.A., he left Liverpool in April, 1858, for New York, and has not since been heard of in England.
KAHLER, EMIL, from Ahrensboek, Holstein, who left Neustadt in May, 1859, was in Washington in August, 1859.
KANE, HANNAH, who lived with a family in Fourteenth-street about 1858
KAY, JAMES, Son of David, went to America in 1853, supposed to be in the West.
KEEGAN, WILLIAM, of Killagown, County Wexford, who left Ireland about 1853, and wrote to his family from New York
KEITH, JAMES, late of Banff, Scotland, Merchant His relatives were of South Carolina.
KELLY, HORACE, who was in the Southern States of America just before the War, supposed to have been from Massachusetts.
KENDALL, FRANCIS, died in America, 1820
KENEDY, PATRICK, from Kilglass, Mayo, Ireland He was last heard of as residing in Washington, U.S.
KENNEDY, MARGARET, late of the City of New York.
KENNELY (or CANEELY), MAURICE, JAMES, and ELLEN, Children of Michael and Mary, who formerly resided in Halifax, Nova Scotia.
KENNY, THOMAS, Son of Bryan Kenny, of Keel, Ardagh, County Longford, Ireland. He went to America in 1842 or 1843, and was last heard from in Illinois, U S A, about 1852.
KENYON, CHARLES, Son of Esther Kenyon, of Manchester, England. It is supposed he went to America.
KERTON, JOHN and SARAH, went to America, 1848

SPECIAL LIST No. 4.

KEW, WILLIAM, formerly in the employ of Cubitt's, Builders, London, England, went to America in 1887.
KEYS, ALEXANDER, died in America
KEYS, WILLIAM DAVID, native of Canada, late Private in 10th Regiment New York Volunteers, deceased.
KING, JOHN, formerly of Virginia, late of Liverpool, England, Mariner
KINGSLEY, JOHN, formerly of Heulon, Beds, England, went to U S A. in 1831.
KINGSLEY, JULIA H
KINLOCK, ADINE and GEORGINA, Children of John Kinlock, who left England about 1829 for America.
KIRBY, JOHN, late of Sudbury, Middlesex County, Mass, U.S.A.
KIRBY, MR., who, with his family, left Yorkshire about 1830, to settle at or near Savannah, in America.
KIRBY, WILLIAM, went to Jamaica in 1814, a Servant in the 6th West India Regiment
KNOWLES, THOMAS, Seaman, formerly of Liverpool, England, late of Charleston, U S.A.
KOLME and MAXWELL, of Charleston, America, 1815
KOPPEL, MATTHIAS, late of the City of New York, a native of Hungary, Cabinet Maker, deceased.
KUNDIG, EDWARD, from Basle, Switzerland, who is supposed to have joined Walker's expedition to Nicaragua in 1856, and has not been heard of since.
KUNZ, RUDOLF, born in Basle, Switzerland, September 1, 1806.
KYZER, SAMUEL, left Amsterdam (Netherlands) for U S A about 1830 or 1832, last heard of at Little Rock in 1845.
LAHIFFE, CATHARINE, Wife of William Lahiffe, formerly of London, England, Shoemaker, then of New York.
LAMA, JOHN, late of Sudbury, Middlesex County, Mass, U S A.
LAMB, MRS AMELIA, formerly of Montreal, late of Edinburgh, Scotland.
LAMB, W D, from South Shields, England.
LAUGHLIN, ELIZA A., died in America
LAW, SAMUEL, late of Philadelphia, U S.
LAWRENCE, JOHN, formerly of Buckland, Gloster, England, late of Norfolk, Virginia, U S., where he died in 1814
LAWRENCE, THOMAS, late of Philadelphia, Schoolmaster, died at Mount Holly, New Jersey.
LEACH, CHARLES, Tailor, Son of Mrs. Mary Leach, formerly of the Old Kent-road, London, England; went to America.
LEADAM, JOHN WILLIAM, formerly of Loughborough, Leicestershire, England, Surgeon, sailed in 1853 from Liverpool, New York, in the ship "George Washington."
LEAHY, MR. JAMES.
LEAKE, JOHN G, formerly of Durham, England, late of New York, U S
LEE, EDWARD C, late of City of New York, Mariner, a native of Portland, Maine, deceased.
LEE, ELLEN, when last heard from she resided in Williamsburg U S A.
LEE, THOMAS, died in America.
LEGGETT, WILLIAM (otherwise GODDEN), Master Mariner, formerly of Dover, Kent, many years ago emigrated to Rochester, Massachusetts, U.S, and died there about 1808
LEIGH, WILLIAM, Mariner, who went to South America in 1849, and was last heard of in 1854.
LEMAN, ABRAHAM, of America.
LEVEE, DAVID, Son of the late Alexander and Clarissa Levy, of London, England.
LEWIS, JOHN, born in Shropshire, England, went to the Brazils, a Sailor.
LIDDIARD and STORY, of Halifax, Nova Scotia
LITCHFIELD, ELIZA, Daughter of John Litchfield, Esq, of Mansfield, Notts, England; both living in New York in 1807
LIVICK, J, left San Francisco, California, U S, in 1858, to visit some relations in Norwich, England.
LIVINGSTON, CHARLES
LIVINGSTON, JAMES (otherwise JOHN OSMUND), born at Livingston, Hants, England, now in America.
LLOYD, WILLIAM, went from Stafford, England, to Salt Lake City, America, in 1850
LOCKEY, GEORGE, formerly of London, England, afterwards of South Carolina, Merchant.
LONG, MICHAEL, who left Cork, Ireland, for Quebec in the year 1816
LOWTH, PRISCILLA, Daughter of Nathan and Sophia Lowth, formerly of Lincolnshire, England; now living in America.
LUCAS, MRS. ARMANDA.
LUCAS, F J, who left England in 1859 or 1860, on board the "Arizona," for New Orleans, America.
LYMAN, DANIEL, a Major in the Army, formerly of New Brunswick, late of London, England.
LYMON, CAPTAIN, Assistant-Quartermaster at Memphis, Tennessee, U S A, in 1863.
LYNCH, PATRICK, GEORGE, JOHN, MARY and CATHARINE, from Roceail, County Limerick, Ireland.
LYONS, MICHAEL, who arrived in New York, from Town, County Roscommon, Ireland, about 1857
McADAM, MARION, Daughter of Agnes McAdam (formerly McMURTRIE), who died at Chatham, Lower Canada, North America, in 1839
McAFEE, ANN, who died at the Bellevue Hospital in 1859
McANNALLY, FRANCIS (otherwise FRANCIS IRWINE) and JOHN, formerly of Dungannon, County of Tyrone, Ireland, Sons of Francis McAnnally
McAUGHTRY, THOMAS, of Belleville, New Jersey, North America, Farmer, and ELIZABETH HANNAH, his Wife (formerly ELIZABETH HANNAH NELSON, Spinster)
McCANN, ROSE (otherwise ROSE EVANS), and CATHERINE McCANN otherwise CATHERINE CHAMBERS), resident in some part of America, and THOMAS McCANN, resident in Vancouver's Island.
McCARDLE, CATHARINE J. J
McCARTY, MRS., of Billin Temple, Black Rock, Cork, Ireland.
McCLURE, MARTHA. (See Reed, Martha.)
McCONNELL, MARGARET, Daughter of the late James McConnell, John-street, Belfast, Ireland, who sailed from that country for Quebec in May, 1838
McCUE, MARY, of Coa, County Fermanagh, Ireland, when last heard from she was living in Brooklyn or New York, U.S.A.
McCURDY, JOHN, late of San Francisco, California, Gentleman.
McDERMOTT, JAMES, Son of Francis, of Edgworthetown, County Longford, Ireland, later of Coventry, England; was in Brooklyn, New York, U.S.A, in 1853
McDERMOTT, MARY, Wife of — McDermott, of Fernandiana, in the Southern States of America (formerly MARY O'CONNELL)
McDONALD, MARIA, formerly of Ireland, late of New York, a Servant.
McELDERRY, ROBERT, last heard of in the Southern States of America.
McELMAIL, PETER, formerly Surgeon in Glasgow, Scotland.
MACFARLANE, LOUISA, Daughter of Mr. Andrew Macfarlane, Wife of Mr Erhorn, supposed to have gone to California, some years ago.

MAGUIRE, RICHARD, of Killeagh, County Cork, Ireland.
McGHAW, JOHN, late of Brooklyn, deceased.
McGLEN, MISS MARTHA, of London
McGONNELL, PATRICK, late of the City of New York, a native of Ireland, deceased.
MACGRUDER, GEORGE, Columbia, 1816
McHALLEE, JOHN C, late of the City of New York, Tailor, and late of the 10th Regiment National Zouaves, N Y S V, deceased.
MACINTOSH, JOHN, formerly of Inverness, Scotland, went to America with a Mr Anderson, as a Millwright.
McINTYRE, ISABELLA, Daughter of Daniel McIntyre, Dumbartonshire, Scotland, supposed to have gone to America in 1829
McIVER, ALEXANDER, Son of Alexander McIver, of Georgia, U S
McIVER, ANN, Daughter of Donald McIver, of North Carolina, U S.
McIVER, JOHN, formerly of Stornaway, Scotland, who died at New York, U S.
McKAY, WILLIAM P, late of South Reading, County Middlesex, Massachusetts, United States. He died in 1861
McKEDDY, MAJOR, formerly of London, England, now in New York, U.S.A.
McKENZIE, ANGUS, died in America, 1867
MACKIN, MARY ELIZABETH, Daughter of Michael Mackin, of St Croix, W I, when last heard of, she was living in the family of Hugh Smith of New York.
McKINNEY, MRS MARY, who kept a Store at 228, Hudson-street, New York, U S A., in 1842 and 1844.
McLANAHAN, WILLIAM D.
McMULLEN, THOMAS, formerly of Ludlow, Salop, Shropshire, England, went to Newfoundland
McMURTRIE, DAVID, formerly of Ayrshire, in Scotland, and who died in New York, U S A., in 1860.
MACNAIR, JAMES, Hatter, left Glasgow for America about the year 1828.
McSWEENEY, TIMOTHY, of Ardnageehy, Banty, County Cork, Ireland, who landed in New York in 1865 when last heard of, was in Amsterdam, Montgomery County, New York
McWILLIAMS DOROTHEA BRAYNE, Wife of William McWilliams, of Fredericksburg, Virginia, U S.; living about 1787
MAHAN, JAMES, late of Boston, Suffolk County, Mass., U S A
MALLOUGH, JEREMIAH, late of New York, U.S.A., he died in 1823.
MANKS, WILLIAM, died in America.
MANN, COLONEL G, of Quebec, 1800.
MANNING, MISS HELENAH
MANWARING, JACOB, formerly of Baltimore, U S A, Sugar Baker
MARSH, JOHN F, died in New York, 1823
MARSHALL, JOSEPH, who left Nottingham, England, for America about 1852, he was residing for some years at Cincinnati, as a Butcher, but in January, 1859, was Engine-Driver in O and M R Railroad, Indiana, U S.
MARTIN, JOSEPH, Mariner, of Liverpool, England, sailed to America in 1848.
MARTIN, ROBERT ANTHONY, formerly of Ireland, was in Louisiana, U S.A., in 1837
MARTIN, THOMAS, JOHN, MARY ELIZABETH, and ROBERT, who emigrated to the United States of America. Thomas, in 1864, was in the employment of Messrs Campbell and Jones, Denver City, Colorado Territory, U S A.
MARTIN, WILLIAM WALLACE, of Belfast, who came to America in 1836.
MASON, WILLIAM, in 1868 about fifty years of age, who left England for America, when a young man; his parents resided at Friskney, Lincolnshire, England.
MATHER, THOMAS, supposed to be in Louisiana, U S A.
MATHIESON, JAMES L, formerly of Thornhill, Dumfries, Scotland, went to America in 1850
MATTHEWS, ROBERT, Son of Edward and Ann Matthews, of Cheltenham, Gloucestershire, England, now of Johnson's County, Cedar River, Iowa Territory, U S A
MAXWELL, JOHN, a native of Scotland, late of the City of New York, Bookbinder, and Private in 79th Regiment N Y S V, deceased
MAYO (or MAYHO), JANE, late of Canada; married James Robinson about 1830 to 1835; died about 1850.
MAZE, THOMAS, and his Children, HENRY, JOHN, and MATILDA, formerly of Lisburn, Ireland, emigrated to U S A about 1834, last heard of as residing near the Black Lake, Ohio, U S A.
MEANLEY, BENJAMIN and RICHARD Benjamin left this country about 1838, and information was received of his being in America. Richard went to sea about 1817, and about 1839 information was received of his being a Hawker in America
MESSITER, THOMAS, late of Rio Grande, Brazil, Merchant.
MIDDLETON, MRS, late of Blackheath park, Kent, England; supposed to be in the United States.
MILL, NICHOLAS P, Son of William Mill, formerly of London-wall, in the City of London, Silversmith; last heard of August, 1858, from on board the U S. frigate "Roanoke"
MILL, NICHOLAS PHENE, who left Oberlahnstein, Germany, in 1853, for America, and afterwards sailed in the ship "Roanoke" for Boston, U S A., as a Sergeant of Marines, and left that service in June, 1860
MILL, WILLIAM, Son of William Mill, formerly of London wall, England, Silversmith; who sailed from Portsmouth about December, 1851, in the ship "Victoria" for New York
MILLER, NATHAN, Son of James Miller, of Edinburgh, Scotland, Glover, resided in Michigan, U.S A.
MILLER, WILLIAM and PHILIP, went from Edinburgh, Scotland, to Philadelphia in 1841
MILLETT, JAMES, THOMAS, and MATHEW, Sons of James Millett, of St. Johnstown, County Tipperary, Ireland.
MILLETT, JOHN, died in America.
MILLIKEN, JOHN, Son of James Milliken, Farmer at Shortley, Crawfordjohn, Scotland, who, it is understood, went to America many years ago
MILLS, GEORGE, Nephew of Elizabeth Lewis, of Richmond, England, went to America.
MILLS, THOMAS K
MITCHELL, MRS ELIZABETH (Born Setor), of Edinburgh, Scotland; who lived in Boston, U S., about 1848, or her Son JOHN MITCHELL, who lived for some time in Watertown, Mass., U S A.
MITCHELL, FRANCIS, of Lewes, England, at one time in the employment of Mr John B Johnson, of Northford, Connecticut, last heard of in 1853, as Blacksmith, at Kinderhook, Columbia Co, State of New York.
MITCHELL, JOHN, of Newfoundland
MOFFATT, THOMAS, late of New York, U S., Gentleman, and formerly of Goswell-street, Old street-road, Middlesex, England, died 1819.
MOLLOY, CATHERINE, now MRS RILEY, of Dublin. She went to New York about 1857
MONROE, MRS. ELIZABETH L, late of Cayuga County, New York, U S A
MOONEY, WILLIAM, formerly of Ireland, last heard of at Newark, N J, supposed to have gone to Pennsylvania.
MOORE, NANCY, late of Holliston, Middlesex County, Mass, U.S.A.
MORAN, JOHN, a Private in the 69th Regiment New York Volunteers, late of the City of New York.

SPECIAL LIST No. 4.   145

MORAN, SAMUEL, born at Weybridge, Surrey, England, went to America, and died in Jamaica
MORGAN, EDWARD, born in Ludlow, Shropshire, England, went to Boston, U S A
MORGAN, JAMES, Son of John Morgan, London, England, and Mary, his Wife, married in 1834, at Ebensbury, Cambria County, U.S.A., to Matilda C Seely; last heard of in Detroit, Michigan, U.S.A., in 1848 or 1849
MORGAN, MARY (See Polon, Mary)
MORGAN, WILLIAM SHIELDS late of Kingston, Jamaica.
MORGAN, WILLIAM, of Philadelphia, U S A
MORRIS, CHARLOTTE, formerly of London, England, late of New York
MORRIS, ELIZABETH, Wife of Oliver Morris, formerly of England, late of Philadelphia, U.S.
MORRISON, HOWARD, in California.
MORSE, IRA, late of Roxbury, County of Middlesex, Massachusetts, America, deceased.
MOYLE, WILLIAM, WALTER, and HENRY, Brothers, born at Wendron, Cornwall, England, supposed to have gone to America.
MULLER, GEORGE, a native of Germany, who arrived in New York from Bremen, in January, 1853.
MULLINS, MARY ANN, otherwise SILLERY, who formerly resided at Thornton, near Finglas, County Dublin, Ireland, and who left Dublin for America in 1855
MULLIS, WILLIAM, who was formerly in service at Eisenham-hall, Essex, England, and in 1859 left for the United States, in 1860 he was in service in New York, and subsequently in the service of Lieutenact Kane, of Newport, Rhode Island, U S A., and is reported to have died from the effects of a railway accident in 1883.
MURPHY, ELIZABETH, formerly ELIZABETH HOLMES, who sailed from Glasgow to Boston, on board the "Claybourne," about 1855, and is supposed to be now in America.
MURPHY, HANNAH L late of Boston, Suffolk County, Mass, U S A.
MURPHY, JOHN, late of Quebec, Canada East, and native of Fermoy County Cork, Ireland
MURPHY, MARY, of Kilkenny Ireland, when last heard of (about 1858) she lived with a family named Robison, at 166, Walker-street, New York.
MURPHY, PATRICK, born in Ireland, came to London, England, and died in America.
MURPHY, THOMAS, Shoemaker, late of Hamilton, Canada West, who emigrated to America from County Cork, Ireland, about 1832
MURPHY, WILLIAM STACK, of U S
MURRAY, ROBERT ARTHUR (alias ROSE), deceased, formerly of Halifax, Nova Scotia, he sailed from London in October, 1857, in the ship "Tamar," for Auckland, New Zealand, where he died in 1858
MUSSELL, MARIA (alias McDOUALD), formerly of Ireland, late of New York.
MYERS, ARTHUR, formerly of Rotherhithe, London, England, went to America
MYERS, JOHN, of Liverpool, England, sailed for New York in the ship "Toronto," in 1839, resided afterwards in New York and New Orleans
MYLARD, MILLERD, or MILLAR, JOHN, supposed to have been in California in 1860. It is understood that he has a Brother in New York.
NEAL, JOSHUA, of North America, 1815
NEILL, JOHN JAMES and MARGARET ANN
NELSON, JANE ISABELLA, SARAH, and ELEANOR, all of Belleville, New Jersey, North America, Spinsters.
NELSON, J THOMAS, late of the City of New York, Sailor, a native of Virginia.
NELSON, SAMUEL, of Belleville, New Jersey, North America, Joiner
NEVILLE, WILLIAM, formerly of York, England, then of West New Jersey, America, Grandchildren of, wanted.
NEWSHAM, ISABELLA, formerly of Bishops Cam, in North America.
NICHOLSON, THOMAS, formerly of Walthamstow, Essex, England, went to Canada.
NILMAN, WILLIAM M, of America, 1843.
NOBLE, JOHN, Housewright, late of Malden, Middlesex County, Mass., U S A.
NOBLE, NOAH, who went to America some years ago
OAKLAND FURNACE ESTATE, Greenup County, Kentucky, U S A., Owners of, wanted.
OAKLEY, JANE, Daughter of John and Margaret Oakley, formerly of Hoxton, England; left Plymouth with her Mother in 1834, for Halifax, Nova Scotia.
O'BRIEN, FRANCIS, died in America.
O'CONNELL, JAMES, House Carpenter, late of Galloway-road, Waterford, Ireland, who resided, about 1855, in Halifax, Nova Scotia.
O'CONNELL, MARY, Wife of — McDermott of Fernandiana in the Southern States of America.
O'DYER, WILLIAM, GEORGE, and RICHARD, born in France, went to America in 1818.
O'KEEFFE, THOMAS, now or lately residing in the United States of North America.
O'LAWLEE, MAJOR JOHN, formerly of London, England, died in South America.
OLIVER, A. G
OLNEY, HARVEY ALLEN.
OLSEN, O CHRISTIAN, late of Boston, Suffolk County, Mass U S A.
OMMANNY, JOHN, Son of William Ommanny, of Portsea, England, went abroad in 1788
O'NEIL, PATRICK, who in April, 1856, lived at 131, Chrystie-street, New York, and died from wounds received in the Riot of Panama, in that year.
O'NEILL, JOHN, of Bandon, Cork, Ireland, last heard of in September, 1856, at Paw Paw Tunnel, Bloomberry Furnace, Hampshire County, Virginia, U S.A.
ORD, DENNIS (See Shea, Dennis.)
O'SULLIVAN, or CLARK JULIA, late of New York, native of Ireland, Lodging house Keeper
OWEN, JOHN, Son of Samuel; born in London in 1682, was in America in 1738.
PAGE, ALFRED, who left England for America in 1837
PARK, WILLIAM ENGLISH formerly of Carlisle, in the County of Cumberland, Labourer, but now supposed to be residing in America.
PARKHURST, LEONARD, late of Hopkinton, Middlesex County, Mass, U S A.
PARKINSON, GEORGE, born in 1827, went to U S.A. in 1854
PARRY, WILLIAM, formerly of Anglesea, Wales, supposed to have gone to America.
PATCHETT, HENRY, and SARAH, his Wife, left England for America.
PATERSON, NATHANIEL H, Son of George Paterson, of Edinburgh, Scotland, some time Seaman in American Navy.
PATTEN, MATILDA, Nurse, late of the City of New York.
PATTERSON, JOHN, formerly Storekeeper at the Dockyard, Jamaica.
PATTERSON, WALTER
PAUL, ANDREW, Son of James Paul, of Linlithgow, Scotland.
PAUL, EPHRAM (otherwise WILLIAM WOOD), an American, formerly of Calcutta : was in London, England, in 1849.

PAWSON, WILLIAM JOHN, Mariner, supposed to be now in South America.
PEACE, ALFRED, formerly of Toronto, Canada
PEACOCK, ELIZABETH ROSE (otherwise ELIZABETH ROSE), in U S A about 1848.
PEARL, DAME ANNE, formerly of Newfoundland, late of London, England, Widow.
PEARSON, MARY ELIZABETH, married Edward Pearson in 1822, in Jamaica.
PECK, THOMAS, JOHN, ANN, Sons and Daughter of J Peck, late of Boston, U.S.A.
PEEK, MARTHA and KATE, had a Brother, Frederick, of New York
PEMBERTON, BENJAMIN, born at Walsall, Staffordshire, England, in 1806, who left England for Waynesboro', Georgia, U S A in 1840.
PENROSE, WILLIAM, who is supposed to have sailed from Kingston upon-Hull, England, for America in 1818; and to have died at New York in 1827
PEPPIN, JOSEPH, formerly of Clipstone, Northamptonshire, England, who is believed to have removed to Charleston, South Carolina, America
PERCIVAL, CHARLES PIERRE LOUIS, and RACHEL, his Wife, he was born near Paris, France, in 1784, and is believed to have died at No 39, Market-street, Providence, State of Rhode Island, in 1830
PERNELL, JOB, formerly of Trowbridge, Wilts, England, went to the U S in 1842.
PEROT ELLISTON and JOHN, of Philadelphia, U S A
PERRY MRS AMELIA formerly of Montreal, late of Edinburgh, Scotland
PETERKIN, ALEXANDER, Baker, formerly of Edinburgh, Scotland, of New York in 1851
PHILLIPS, MARY, formerly of Nova Scotia, late of London, England, Daughter of John Phillips, of Nova Scotia.
PICKBOURN, JAMES died in America.
PINDER, GEORGE, Son of George Henry Pinder, late of Shanghae.
PITCAIRN, ROBERT and MARTHA, formerly or now of Poughkeepsie, U S.A.
PLACE, DANIEL, late a Private in the 67th Foot
POLON, MARY (Maiden Name, MARY MORGAN), Widow of John Polon.
POND, MOSES, late of Holliston, Middlesex County, Mass., U S A
POSTLE, HENRY, formerly of St Bride's London, England, Carpenter, he went to America shortly after his marriage in 1835, and was in the Timber trade at St. Louis, in America, in 1842.
POTTERTON, THOMAS, of America
POWELL, DELIA, late of the City of New York.
POWELL, JOHN, Son of Thomas Powell, formerly of Peter-street, Dublin who went to America in 1833, and was working as a Saddler at Newark, and other places in the State of York, in 1838
POWERS, WILLIAM who left Montreal, in Canada, 1832; and his Sisters, CATHARINE and ELLEN, who are in New York, U S A, natives of County Waterford, Ireland.
PREDIGER, J RUDOLPH, Batavia, U S A, 1810
PRENDERGAST, JAMES LAWRENCE, of Enniscorthy, County Wexford, Ireland, who went to New York, and lived in Brooklyn, U S, in 1842.
PRESSLAND, DANIEL, Carpenter, late of Biggleswade, Bedfordshire, England, who was in New Orleans, March, 1855.
PRESTON, SARAH, died in America, 1806.
PREVOST, WILLIAM, Son of William Prevost of London, England, who left London, England, for Cincinnati, U S, where in November, 1825, he married Margaret Jones He died in March, 1826, leaving Thomas James of Cincinnati, as his executor His Widow married Robert Edmeston.
PRICE, WILLIAM ANDREW, born about 1724 or 1726
PRIDE, ROBERT The Party or Parties who advertised, about 1857 for papers supposed to have been lost at the time of the death of Robert Pride, of Pleasantville, at Stanford, Connecticut, U S, on the 27th November, 1846
PUTMAN JAMES, formerly of Halifax, Nova Scotia, at the time of his death residing at 9, John-street, Portland-place, Middlesex, England.
QUANCE, ROGER NOYES formerly of Landulph, Cornwall, England; last seen in New York.
QUIN, THOMAS, formerly a Merchant Tailor, of Dublin, Ireland who went to America about 1820.
QUINN BARNEY, Carpenter, residing in New York, U S A, in 1851
QUINN, ISABELLA, who formerly lived with Mr Charles Goodyear in Newhaven, Conn.; supposed to be now living in New York, U S
RADCLIFFE, JOHN, was in business in New York about the year 1808
RADFORD, JOHN, formerly of Belper, Derbyshire, England, which he left about 1818, he was last heard of in 1824, as living at Beaver Creek, near St. Francisville, near New Orleans, U S.A.
RAMSEY, COLONEL ALBERT C.
RAMSEY, GEORGE, late of Buenos Ayres.
RASIMI, JOSEPH, born in London, in 1813, left that city, in 1831 or 1832, for New York, he was a Dancer at a Theatre in New York
RAWLINS, JOSEPH, died in America, 1784.
RAY, SAMUEL, late of Newton, Middlesex, Mass., U S.A.
READ, EZEKIEL, who went to America.
READE, JOSEPH He was a native of Spalding, Lincolnshire, England, and, when upwards of forty years old, went to America.
REDHEAD, JOHN, of London, Canada West.
REECE (or RACE), ANN (formerly SCORAH), Daughter of William Scorah, of Ardsley, Yorkshire, England; went to Canada about 1800.
REED MRS. MARTHA (formerly MARTHA McCLURE), and her Son, JAMES McCLURE REED.
REED, STEPHEN late of Cambridge, Middlesex County, Mass., U S A.
REEKS, SARAH, late of the City of New York, Widow, deceased.
REEVE, ISAAC, late of Ellington, Hants, England, supposed to have gone to America.
REEVES MRS ELIZABETH, of America.
REID MARGARET (formerly MILLER), Wife of John Reid, of Freehold, New Jersey, America.
RICHARDSON, JOHN THOMAS (Son of John Richardson, formerly of 14, Great George-street, Bermondsey, England Gentleman), formerly Schoolmaster at Demerara, West Indies.
RICHARDSON, PHILIP, late of the State of Kentucky, U S A.
RICHARDSON, WILLIAM, died in America 1824.
RICKARD, HENRY, Seaman, was on board an American Ship; formerly of Doncaster England.
RICKWOOD, ELI (commonly called JOHN RICKWOOD or ELI JOHN RICKWOOD), late of Faversham, Kent, he was last heard of in California, whence he intended to go to Australia.
RIDLEY, MATTHEW, died in America. 1805
RIELY, PATRICK, Contractor on the Delaware and Hudson Canal; Daughter of, who resided in Sixth Avenue about 1840.
RIGGS, JOHN, of Newry, when last heard of, in 1856, he was in San Francisco, California.

RILEY, MRS. (Maiden Name, CATHERINE MOLLOY), a native of Dublin, she went to New York about 1857.
RIORDAN MRS JANE (See Good Mrs Jane)
ROBBARTS, JOHN, late of New Britain, Pennsylvania, U S A, born at Ipswich, Suffolk, England
ROBERT, CHRISTOPHER, of New York U S A
ROBERTS EDMOND, Son of Wolston Roberts, of Derby, England, went to America in 1858
ROBERTS JOHN, formerly of Scot Willoughby, then of Stamford, Lincolnshire England, and afterwards of Pike Town, Alleghany County State of New York, North America, he sailed from Liverpool, England, in June, 1842, and wrote home in April, 1843
ROBERTS JOSEPH R. who left Liverpool, England in the "City of Baltimore," in August, 1861, and whose last address was Post-office, New York City, America.
ROBERTSON, JAMES and JOHN, died in America
ROBERTSON, WILLIAM, formerly of Annapolis Nova Scotia.
ROBINSON, HANNAH, Daughter of John Darling, Ecclesfield, York England; she left England about 1827, and married a Storekeeper, named Robinson, in New York
ROBINSON, JANE (See Mayo, Jane)
ROBINSON, WILLIAM, of East Ayton, Yorkshire, England, who emigrated to Canada about 1830, was apprenticed to a Joiner in Montreal, and afterwards removed to Toronto.
ROBINSON, WILLIAM, late of Liverpool, Lancaster, England (Son of Richard Robinson, of Carlisle England, Weaver), who left Liverpool about 1850, and went to reside at New York, when last heard of, he was trading in coals on the Pennsylvania Canal
ROCKEY, THOMAS, supposed to reside in Plymouth, Illinois, U S A; and PHILIP ROCKEY, residing, when last heard of, in New York, U S A
ROGER, LOUISE VICTORINE (Maiden Name, HIEGLO)
ROGERS, ANN now or late of Council Bluffs, in the U S A, Widow.
ROGERS, WILLIAM, Mariner, who left England for South America in 1839
ROGERSON, MARY ANN who left Manchester, England, for America in 1842.
RONNEBERG, GABRIEL HEIBERG, born in Norway, in 1831.
ROONEY, MARY ANN, a resident of New York
ROOT, THOMAS, formerly of Leytonstone, Essex England, who emigrated to California about 1856.
ROSE, ELIZABETH (otherwise ELIZABETH ROSE PEACOCK), in U S A, about 1818
ROSE, JOHN ROBERT, formerly of Inverness, Scotland, late of Guadaloupe, West Indies.
ROSS CHARLES WILLIAM Merchant, of Quebec
ROSS, JAMES M, who left San Francisco California in June 1863, for Noyo Mills.
ROSS, RODERICK, of Aithabasca, in the Hudson's Bay Company's Territories, North America.
ROSS, WILLIAM C, of Quebec
ROTHVOSS, ADOLPH, Farmer, late of Konigsberg, East Prussia, Europe, when last heard of, in 1857, he was in Troy, Madison County Illinois, U S A.
ROWLEY, WILLIAM (Irishman)
ROWLEY, WILLIAM, left England for India in 1790, with his brother John, but settled in Washington County, Pa, U S A.
ROYLE WILLIAM, of Williamsburgh, Virginia, U S A.
RUFF, MR who married a Miss Burton supposed to be in America.
RUSSELL, JAMES BACKHOUSE, of Utah and California, Son of Hannah Russell, late of Wistow, near Selby, Yorkshire England.
RUSSELL, REBECCA, late of West Cambridge Middlesex County, Mass., U.S.A.
RYLAND WILLIAM HERMAN, of Quebec, Canada.
RYNO JOSEPH
SANDIESON, WILLIAM, JAMES, HELEN and JANE, supposed to be in America.
SANSFIELD, GEORGE, late of Newbury, Lancashire, England; went to America about 1835
SARGEANT, AMELIA, Daughter of George Wilkinson Sargeant, who, many years ago, left England for America.
SAVAGE HENRY, Painter. who in 1853 resided in 197, Buffalo-street, Rochester, New York.
SCARDEOLI, PIETRO a native of Leghorn, Tuscany, Italy
SCHLESINGER ALBERT HENRY Short-hand Writer. left England for New York in 1850
SCHOFIELD, THOMAS, late of Ashton-under-Lyne, Lancaster England, Pork Butcher, who left England for U S in January, 1848.
SCHOVELL, NOAL, of New York.
SCORAH, ANN (or REECE or RACE), Daughter of William Scorah, of Ardsley, Yorkshire, England, went to Canada about 1800
SCOTT JAMES, went to America about 1838
SCOVELL, NOAH formerly of New York late of London, England; Ship Agent.
SCRIVEN, GARDNER RUSSELL, of Philadelphia.
SEWELL GEORGE Mariner, sailed for Philadelphia in 1822
SEYMOUR, FREDERICK Z., late of Newton, Middlesex, Massachusetts, U S A.
SEYMOUR, JAMES otherwise FOWLKES; in 1843 he was connected with the Star Printing Office, Toronto.
SEYMOUR, THOMAS, Seaman, formerly of Tilbury, Gloucester, England, went to America.
SHAW, EZRA, late of New York, U S A
SHAW, THOMAS, who in 1783 was of Virginia, U S.; afterwards of London.
SHAW, WILLIAM, who left New York in October, 1828, and held property at Lake George
SHAW, WILLIAM and ANDREW, Sons of Andrew Shaw, of Montreal, Canada. Andrew was last heard of in London, on board the ship "Wagoola," from Calcutta.
SHEA, DENNIS (late ORD), Seaman, on the United States steamer "Kennebec," U.S.N.
SHIELD, BENEDICT, formerly of London, England, went to Baltimore, U S A
SHIR HENRY and DANIEL, last heard of in Jersey Shore, Pennsylvania, U S A.
SHUBBRICK RICHARD, formerly of Charleston, South Carolina, in North America.
SIDERBOTHAM, JOHN, died at Havana, 1854.
SILLERY, MARY ANNE (See Mullins, Mary Anne.)
SIMMONS, THOMAS, formerly of Covenham, Lincoln, England, late of Burtonville, U S.A.
SIMPSON, HANNAH, Wife of James Simpson, formerly of England, but afterwards of Fairfield County, Ohio, U S.A., who died in 1832 (Maiden Name, HOGARTH)
SIMPSON, ROBERT, formerly of West Auckland, Durham England, Butcher
SIMPSON, WILLIAM, formerly of Crail, Scotland, went to West Indies in 1788.
SIMPSON, WILLIAM G, died in America.
SINGLETON ELIZABETH, Daughter of William and Ann Singleton, formerly of Lincolnshire, England; living in America.
SKYRME AMOS JONES, who left the City of Hereford, England, in 1830, for America; age then about 47.
SMIT, HENRY EDWARD, from Stockholm.

SMITH, DOROTHY and NELSON, of Newark, in America.
SMITH, EDGAR P., or GILBERT H., formerly residing at Tarrytown New York, U S A.
SMITH, ED, Farrier, Bath England, Son of late John Smith, also of Bath, England.
SMITH, GEORGE formerly of London, Linendraper, went to America in 1823.
SMITH, JAMES, formerly of Leith and London, went to New Orleans, U S.A.
SMITH, JAMES, WILLIAM, and MATTHEW, natives of Paisley, Scotland, last heard from in the fall of 1860
SMITH, JOSEPH, ROBERT, and WILLIAM, Sons of Jonah Smith, of Stroud, Gloucester, England, they went to America many years ago.
SMITH LEWIS G, late of Boston, Suffolk County Mass., U S A
SMITH SAMUEL, formerly of Bedford England, he went to America, and passed by the name of Lyon.
SMITH, MRS. SARAH, Wife of Rev Robert Smith formerly of Charleston, South Carolina, U S.A.
SNOW, SARAH S S, late of Brighton, County of Middlesex State of Massachusetts, America, deceased.
SOUTHERN, WILLIAM, Cabinet-maker, who left Liverpool for the United States in 1849, and went to reside at New Jersey, and was last heard of in 1856 at Cohoes, Albany County, U S A.
SOWARD, EDMUND, of Kentucky America 1810.
SPEIR, ELIZABETH M, late of Honesdale, Penn, U S A.
SPENCE, ABRAHAM, who left Albany, N Y, about 1864, for New Orleans, it is supposed he died in New Orleans or vicinity
SPENCER, ELIZABETH, formerly of London, late of America.
SPENCER, JOHN, Master Mariner who died in Jamaica in 1828.
SPOKESFIELD, FERNALD D late of Reading, Middlesex County, Mass, U S A.
SPROULE, ANN, about 30 years of age, of Clover hill, Tecumseth America.
STACHWELL, WILLIAM, of Philadelphia, Nephew of William Stachwell, of London, England.
STANBRIDGE, FREDERICK, of Cambridge-street, Hackney-road, Middlesex, England, proceeded to New York in 1832, where he was last heard of
STANES, RICHARD, who left England for Canada in April 1860, a Saddler
STARLING, MATTHEW, born in Norfolk, England, settled in America.
STEDWELL, CHARLES, a Tailor, who in 1865 resided at 263, Court street, South Brooklyn, New York, U S.A.
STEFFENBURG BERNHARD, born in 1833, near Fahlun Sweden who went to California in 1851
STEINBERG, HEINRICH GUSTAV, who landed at New York in April, 1858, a native of Riga, Russia.
STENTON, HARRIETT United States.
STEPHENS, SUSANNA late of Boston Suffolk County Mass., U S A.
STEPHENS, WILLIAM and JOHN, born in Lothbury, London, England; Sons of John Stephens, of Jamaica.
STETSON, LEMUEL, late of Newton, County Middlesex, Massachusetts, U S.
STEVENS, EDMUND PIPER, formerly of London, was born in 1793, was heard of in New York in 1841, supposed to have gone to California in 1848
STEVENS, MARTHA Widow, of Boston who died in 1766
STEVENSON WILLIAM, of Philadelphia, U S A.
STEWARD, MARY, Daughter of Elizabeth, and Wife of Edward Bunting late of Wereham, Norfolk, England, emigrated to America some time since.
STEWART, JOHN left Scotland as a Seaman in 1856; supposed to be in America.
STEWART, ROBERT, Baker, formerly of Scotland, went to America in 1855
STEWART, THOMAS, formerly of Kirkwall, Orkney Scotland, he went to U S about 1800
STICKNEY, ENOCH, Master Mariner formerly of Newbury Port, Mass, U S A., late of London, England.
STINSON, HARRIET, Widow, in the U S
STIRRIDGE, JANE, supposed to have gone to America about 1812.
STOCK, WILLIAM HENRY, formerly of Bristol, England, went to Canada in 1845
STONE, ABIGAIL, late of Cambridge, Middlesex County, Mass., U S A.
STRATHDEE, GEORGE, who left Irvine, Ayrshire, Scotland, in November, 1854, for Canada, by steamer "New York," or a sailing vessel.
STREETER, BARZILIA, who kept a Finding Store in 1828, at 109 Chatham-street, and afterwards was of the Firm, Streeter and Co, Shoe Dealers, 82, Pearl-street, New York.
STUART, JAMES P, native of Ireland, late of New York, Cotton Factor.
STUART, PRICILLA, Widow of James P, late of New York, deceased.
SUMNER, MISS who in 1860-61 was residing in Quebec, Canada East.
SWAN, BONNER, who was born in Northumberland, England about 1796, and served in the Navy for a time, but afterwards joined the Merchant Service, and is supposed to have gone to North America.
SWAN, TIMOTHY, late of West Cambridge, Middlesex County, Mass, U S A.
SWEENEY, EDWARD, and his Daughter MARY, from Boyle, County Roscommon, Ireland, some years ago they lived in Greenwich-street, New York City
SYMONDS, JOHN, formerly of Penzance, Cornwall, England, he went to New York in 1835
TALLY, ELLEN and MARY, natives of Emmely, Canada West, when last heard from they were living in Rochester, New York. U S A., about 1856.
TANDY, CHARLES, Son of Thomas Frederick and Sarah, born in Greek-street, Dublin, about 1801, was educated as an Architect, and enlisted in the Grenadier Guards, from which he purchased his discharge about 1819, last heard of at 17, Summerville-street, Birkenhead, in the house of a person named Hubgood, in latter end of 1849, supposed to have emigrated to Australia or America
TANNER, THOMAS and MARY, who left Newbury, Berkshire, England for America in 1851
TATE, GEORGE, whose Parents went from Weston, in England, about 1847, and at one time lived at 19 Avenue, New York.
TAYLOR, JOHN, formerly of Bromwich, Stafford, England, went to America with family in 1843.
TEDCASTLE, JOHN, formerly of Langholm, Scotland.
THATCHER, CHARLES, late of the City of New York, a native of New Hampshire, Seaman deceased.
THOMAS, THOMAS CHARLES, a Carpenter, aged about 33, he left England in May, 1857
THOMPSON, WILLIAM, Savannah, Georgia.
THOMSON, ALEXANDER GREIG, Son of Major James Thomson, of Stonehaven, Kincardine, Scotland; resided in Philadelphia, U S, where it is supposed he died.
THOMSON, JOSEPH and JAMES, left the vicinity of London, England, about 1802, and up to 1840 carried on the business of Bakers in New York, U S A.
THOMSON, ROBERT, Brassfounder, Son of the late Robert Thomson, of Stockwell-street, Glasgow, Scotland, who sailed in the "Tuisco," from the Clyde to San Francisco, in 1853, and was last heard of in San Francisco, in 1865 or 1868
THORNTON, THOMAS, who left England about 1662, and died in New England, U S A., in 1700-1.
THORPE, WILLIAM, Son of John Thorpe, of Eltham, Kent, England, Farmer, went to America.
TINDALL, MRS (Christian Name probably ANN, and an Englishwoman), she kept school in New York in 1823.
TINKLER, JOHN, formerly of Grantham Lincoln, England, went to New York in 1834.
TIRRILL, MIRIAM, late of Boston, Suffolk County, Mass., U S A.

TINDALE, JOHN, died in America, 1805.
TOINTON, JOHN, formerly of Kirton, Lincoln, England, went to America
TOMLINS, ELEANOR HENWOOD, late of Charleston, America.
TONEY, JAMES, who, about 1850, was Travelling Agent for some House in the Northern States, U S A.
TORR, JOHN, Surgeon, formerly of Lancashire and Dorset, England, went to America many years ago.
TORRENTE, GIACOMO native of Italy, late of New York
TOWNLEY REV WILLIAM Vicar of Orpington, Essex England
TOWNSEND, WILLIAM, Son of Joseph, formerly of Charleston, South Carolina, U S A.
TRACEY, JOHN, Seaman, late of Boston Suffolk County, Mass., U S A.
TRAPP, FRANZ, of Oggersheim, Germany
TRENHOLME, GEORGE ALFRED, of Charleston, South Carolina U S A
TRULL, THOMAS D M, late of Watertown, Middlesex County, Mass , U.S.A.
TUFTS EUNICE, late of Newton, Middlesex County, Mass U S A
TUOHY, THOMAS PATRICK, late of Limerick, he was in Middleboro', Mass., in 1855 and in 1859 in Geneva, Ontario County, New York U S.A
TURNER, CHARLES HARTLEY of Kedliston, Derbyshire, England, in the American Navy about 1851
TURNER, ROBERT, formerly of Sunderland, England, went to America in 1809
TURNER, THOMAS, of Epping, Essex, England, a Leather-dresser, went to America in 1800, and was in Philadelphia in 1807
TUTE, HENRY, Son of Sarah Tute, who left England many years ago, and went to Mexico, or elsewhere abroad
TWISS, LYDIA ANN, late of Chelsea, Suffolk County, Mass , U S.A.
VAN DUSEN, BELLE (Maiden Name, ALLEN), married in 1849 to Jacob Van Dusen, in Troy, she had left home in 1844, and soon after her marriage came to New York City
VAN WART, ABRAHAM, and JULIA ANN, his Wife, resident in New York about 1825
VECTOR, CHARLES, left England for America in 1804
VERREN or WARREN, GENERAL JOHN GABRIEL, born in Switzerland, went to America many years ago
VILLARS, ALPHONSE, of Evillard, Canton Berne, Switzerland.
VOSMUS ORIN D, formerly Engineer of Boston, Massachusetts, U S
WADDUP, ANN, Daughter of William and Hannah Turner, went to America.
WADE, JOHN, late of Boston, Suffolk County, Mass , U S A.
WAITE, JOHN, late of Antigua, then of America.
WALCOTT, ELISHA, late Firm of Northropp, Abbe and Co , Montreal, Canada, 1811.
WALES, FREEBORN G, late of Hopkinton, Middlesex County, Mass , U S A
WALKER, FRANK, of North Carolina, U S A
WALLACE, JAMES, formerly of London, England, now in New York, U S A
WALLACE, THOMAS, who was apprenticed to a Copper in Forfar, Scotland, in 1784, afterwards was Purser's Steward on board H M S. "L'Oiseau" in 1794, he subsequently left the Navy, and went, as is believed, to the U S A.
WALLEY, HENRY and MARY, Children of Ann Walley, went to Maryland, America.
WALSH, RICHARD, Son of the late Andrew Walsh, of Dublin, Ireland, Tanner, about 1839 he was working at the Docks, or as a Journeyman Tanner, in Liverpool, supposed to have gone to New York, and subsequently to Savannah Georgia U S A.
WALSH, RODDY, formerly of Boyle County Roscommon, Ireland.
WARWICK, JOHN, who came to New York, about 1834, from near Redford. Notts, England, and resided in Sixth Avenue
WATERS, CHARLES, a native of Ireland and citizen of New York City, U S A
WATKINS, ELIJAH, formerly of Monmouth, Wales, went to America in 1854
WATKINS, JOHN GEORGE ROBSON Musician in the 8th or King's Regiment of Foot, who died at Quebec in or about October
WATSON, DUDLEY, of Newmarket, America, 1815
WATSON, WILLIAM, CAPTAIN, died in America.
WEBB, WILLIAM, formerly of Compton Martin, Somerset, England, went to North America some years ago
WEBSTER, GEORGE, late of Cayuga, in the County of Haldimand, Ontario, Canada, who died in 1865
WECKLEY, THOMAS, born at Malling, Kent, England, went to South Carolina or some other part of America.
WELCH, JAMES, formerly of Dublin, Ireland, Cabinet maker, went to the United States
WELLINGTON, JEDUTHAN, late of West Cambridge, Middlesex County, Mass , U S.A.
WESTLAKE, MRS. ANNA.
WESTMORELAND JAMES, formerly Head Waiter at Bath Hotel, Long Island, U S
WETHERILL, GEORGE, formerly of Yorkshire, England, went to America in 1841, late of Cincinnati, Ohio, U S.A.
WETHERILL, RICHARD, formerly of Yorkshire, England, late of Geatersvill, Rock Port, Connecticut, U S A
WHALEY, MARY, formerly of Bruton, Williamsburg, Virginia, afterwards of London, England, Widow
WHITAKER, GEORGE, of Neuse River, North Carolina, Nephew of Charles Whitaker, of Durham, England.
WHITBROOK, ANN, and CHARLES, Engineer, went to America.
WHITE, DAVID, supposed to be in America.
WHITE, HENRY, late of New street, Shadwell, England, he was at Fayette, Jefferson County, Mississippi, in 1852, and in Texas, Anderson County, in the commencement of 1853
WHITE, JOHN, Attorney-General for Canada in 1796
WHITE, MRS. MARY THOMPSON, formerly of Australia, late of Huntington, Long Island, supposed to be in Brooklyn, U S.A.
WHITE, WILLIAM, born at Windsor, England, about 1839, formerly employed in W H Smith and Son's Dublin Newspaper Agency.
WHITECHURCH, ANN, Spinster, afterwards MRS. ANN COX, left England in 1842 in the "Britannia" steamer, from Liverpool, for Boston or Halifax, North America, under assumed name of Mrs. Clarke
WHITELAW, DAVID, of Musselburgh, Scotland, Sailor, last seen at New Orleans in 1850, intended to go to California.
WHITROW, RICHARD, or MARY ANNE Richard was a Farmer at Ely, England, in 1837 he was at Poughkeepsie, New York, as Shoeing Smith, supposed to have proceeded to Baltimore, then up the country
WHITTENBURY, MRS ELIZABETH, formerly of Spilsby, Lincoln, England, late of New York, U S
WHYTE, — of Barton Lodge, Hamilton, Toronto, Canada West, Widow of John Whyte, and EMILY GOURLAY, Wife of — Gourlay, Esq , a Colonel in H.M.'s Army, hereto EMILY WHYTE, daughter of John Whyte
WHYTE, JOHN, of Toronto.
WIGAN, FREDERICK, formerly of Melbourne.
WILDEY, THOMAS, died in America
WILKIE, —, married Janet Lothian in 1796.
WILKINSON, HERBERT, of America

WILKS, REBECCA, Wife of George Wilks; in U S A in 1848
WILLIAMS, JOHN HITCHCOCK, late of Manchester, England, and at present supposed to be in Indianapolis, Indiana, U S A ; Fancy Box Manufacturer
WILLIAMS, JOSEPH, who left England in 1828, and went to reside at Parkman, near Painswell, Geauga County, State of Ohio, North America, he is believed to be still residing in some part of America.
WILLIAMS, VINE, formerly of London, England, went to Canada in 1808
WILLSTEED, WILLIAM H H., of Southsea, England, who left Liverpool for America in 1857
WILSON, BENJAMIN, of Philadelphia, U S A
WILSON, CHARLES JOHN, formerly of Charles street, Hatton garden, London, England, who went over to the United States about 1858 or 1859, with Elizabeth, his Wife (formerly Elizabeth Woodward), and who is supposed to have resided some time at New York, U S A.
WILSON, JOHN, formerly of Leeds, York, England, late of Philadelphia, U S A
WILSON, JOHN, formerly of Little York, now called Toronto, in Canada
WILSON, JOHN, and MARY, his Wife, formerly of South Cave, Yorkshire England; went to America
WILSON, THOMAS, Stone cutter, or his Wife SUSAN, who came to America from Ireland, about 1850, and lived in Avenue A near Twelfth street, New York Also JOHN MATHEWS or MRS MITCHELL
WINN ELIZABETH, born at Warwick, went to America.
WINTER, SAMUEL, left England in 1780, and carried on business as a Shipwright in Virginia, U S
WINTON, ANNA (otherwise CLARK), late of the City of New York, Seamstress, a native of Albany, New York, USA.
WITTINGHAM, RICHARD, left London, England, in 1847, for America
WOLLEY, CHARLES S., late of Charlestown, County of Middlesex, State of Massachusetts, America, Cook; deceased
WOOD, CLEMENT, Son of Margaret and Carey Wood, left England for Florida, U S, in 1785.
WOOD, GEORGE, who left England about the year 1800, and was last heard of by a letter from Demerara.
WOOD, JUDITH, Daughter of Dr Wood, of Annapolis, she married John Phillips, of Nova Scotia.
WOOD, MARY ANN, who went from London to America in March, 1881
WOOD, SAMUEL and BENJAMIN, of Long Island, U S A
WOODROW, PHILIP, who sailed from Southampton, Dec 3, 1851, in the ship "Hermon," for New York ; then 14 years old
WOODWARD, GEORGE ROBERT, Grandchildren of, late of Leather-lane, Holborn, England, Turner, died 1849
WOOLWARD, — formerly of West Indies
WORSDELL, MRS SARAH (formerly MISS DIMBLEBY, of Hull, England, and afterwards Wife of Mr William Worsdell) who with her husband sailed for the U S A a few years ago
WORTH, JAMES, formerly of Reading, Berks, England, went to New York in 1841
WOUNDY, JAMES, formerly of Newburyport, England late of New York
WRIGHT, DAVID SCOTT, Son of Hugh Scott Wright, in Cupar, Fife, went to Charleston, South Carolina, about 1840.
WRIGHT JAMES Seaman, formerly of Paisley, Scotland, then of America.
WYBURN, DR. ROBERT, formerly of Dublin, who practised in New York about 1857
WYCKOFF, P R, of Mobile, Alabama, U S A
WYNDHAM, J C, formerly of Bristol England, Bookseller, but who has since resided in New Orleans, and Texas U S
YEATON SARAH, Wife of William Yeaton, Mate of an American Ship (formerly SARAH GARTSIDE)
YOUNG, JAMES, Mariner, Son of Archibald Young, Watch maker, Dundee, Scotland, he was last heard of in California about 1849
YOUNG, JOSEPH, late of 24th U S C T
YOUNG, JOSEPH JAMESON (otherwise JOSEPH JAMESON YOUNG FORRESTER), of Easter Culmore, Stirling, Scotland, presently residing at Indiana, Indiana County, Pennsylvania, U S A
YOUNG, THOMAS T, of North America
YUILL, JOHN a native of Glasgow, Scotland, supposed to be in the United States

SPECIAL LIST No. 5.

UNCLAIMED MONEY, LANDS AND ESTATES.

The following persons, or heirs are entitled to property. All letters must be addressed to **J. B. MARTINDALE, 142 LaSalle Street, Chicago, Illinois**, and must give all facts on which the writer bases his claim. [See pages 6, 7 and 8 of this Manual.]

ADAM, WILLIAM, of Montrose, Scotland, who went to America previous to 1871
BAIN, WILLIAM, a native of Scotland, who went to America previous to 1869
BANNISTER, BENJAMIN, of Co Essex, England, who went to America about 1838
BIRCH, WILLIAM EDMUND, of Bristol, England, who went to America previous to 1856.
BISHOP, JOHN, of Bath, England, who went to America previous to 1862
BLOOMFIELD, JOHN, who left England for America about the year 1836.
BOOKLASS, JAMES and GEORGE, of Edinburgh, Scotland, who went to America previous to 1851.
BOWDLER, FREDERICK WATKINS, who left Liverpool, England, for America, in 1839
BOWNES, otherwise JOHN RADCLIFF, who left England for America about 1828
BRADY, OWEN, of Trim, Co Meath, Ireland, who went to America previous to 1852.
BROOKE, LETITIA, of Margate, England, who went to America previous to 1859
BURROUGHS, Mrs JUDITH, of Ireland, who went to America previous to 1857.
CAFFRAY, JAMES, who left England for America previous to 1856
CLARK, ANDREW, a native of Scotland, who went to America previous to 1849
CLEGHORN, Miss MARY of Perthshire, Scotland, who went to America previous to 1869
COLLINS, BURY, of Blankney, Lincolnshire, England, who went to America previous to 1867
COONEY, JOHN and MARY, of Navan, Co Meath, Ireland, who went to America previous to 1865.
DALTON, WILLIAM, who left Ireland for America previous to 1670
DENHAM, THOMAS, a native of Scotland, who went to America previous to 1867
DIXON, JOHN and MARY, of Westmoreland, England, who went to America previous to 1856.
DOBSON, Mrs. FRANCIS, of Ireland, who went to America previous to 1857
DODGSON, JOHN, who left England previous to 1854.
DOYLE, THOMAS, of Dublin, Ireland, who went to America previous to 1857
EDGE, THOMAS HALL, of Edinburgh, Scotland, who went to America previous to 1864.
EVANS, THOMAS, of London, England, who went to America previous to 1851
FETHERSTON, JOSEPH and ANNE, otherwise ADAMS, of Westmeath, Ireland, who went to America previous to 1865.
FLAVELL, HENRY a native of England, who went to America previous to 1850
FORBES, ALEXANDER, a native of Scotland, residing in Vermont previous to 1838
GEDDES, ALEXANDER CATHCART, of Perthshire, Scotland, who went to America previous to 1859.
GEY, THOMAS, a native of England, who went to America previous to 1853
GRAVES, WILLIAM VALENTINE, who went to America previous to 1852
HAWLEY, Mrs. MARY A., whose husband was a Broker in New York in 1844.
HAYES, DENIS, of Cork, Ireland, who went to America previous to 1868
HELY, MARY ANN, of England, whose relatives resided in America previous to 1858.
HILL, MARY ANN, residing in Philadelphia, U S A , previous to 1865
HORNBY, JANE, who left England for America previous to 1876
HUGHES, MARIA, of Drayton, England, who went to America previous to 1865
JOHNSON, JOHN, residing in Georgetown, D C , U S A., previous to 1853
JONES, THOMAS LOTER, who left New York for New Orleans in 1852
KAY, JAMES, a native of Scotland, who went to America previous to 1859
KEMP, WILLIAM, of Crieff, Perthshire, Scotland, who went to America previous to 1847.
KEOGH, or KEHOE, Mrs FRANCES, of Ireland, who went to America previous to 1852.
KNOWING, WILLIAM, of Co Surrey, England, who went to America previous to 1855.
LOWE, WILLIAM, who left England for America previous to 1869
LUDLAM, GEORGE of Leicester, England, who went to America previous to 1855.
LUDWIG, or DAVIES, LETITIA, residing in America previous to 1876.
McCALL, JAMES, residing in New York City previous to 1859
McNAIR, JAMES, of Glasgow, Scotland, who went to America in 1828
McNAIR, THOMAS, of Glasgow, Scotland, who went to America previous to 1864
MADRALL, HANNAH ELIZABETH, of Douglas, Isle of Man, England, who went to America previous to 1865.
MANN, THOMAS, of Stokely, Yorkshire, England, who went to America previous to 1859
MARCH, formerly HALL, MARTHA, of Carlisle, England, residing in America previous to 1834.
MATHERS, GEORGE, who went to America in 1849
MORTON, WILLIAM ALEXANDER, of Edinburgh, Scotland, who went to America previous to 1852.
MOYLE, or MILES, JOHN, of Wondron, England, who went to America previous to 1849.
MUNNINGS, GEORGE GARNET HUSKE, Ship Captain, was in New York in 1834.
NASH, JOHN, of Ireland, residing in America previous to 1859
O'CONNELL, ELLEN, a native of Ireland, residing in America previous to 1889.
O'CONNOR, JULIA, residing in America previous to 1853
OLIPHANT, JAMES BLAIR, a native of Scotland, residing in America previous to 1850.
PARTRIDGE, JOHN, or DAVID, who left England for America previous to 1853.
PATTON, MARY, a native of Scotland, who went to America previous to 1876
ROBERTS, EDWIN and SARAH, of Yorkshire, England, who went to America previous to 1855
SHEPARD, THOMAS, EDWARD, and SAMUEL, of Penrith, England, who went to America previous to 1844.
SKINNER, JOHN, a Cabinet-maker, residing near Albany, N Y , U S A , in 1843
SLOANE, CHARLES and CATHERINE, of Kilkenny, Ireland, who went to America previous to 1863
SMITH, GEORGE and WILLIAM, of Glasgow, Scotland, who went to America previous to 1851
SOMMERVILLE JOHN, of Glasgow, Scotland, who went to America previous to 1855
SOUTHERN, JOHN, who left Liverpool, England, for America in 1836
STEPHENS, JAMES ASTLEY, of Manchester, England, who went to America previous to 1862.
STERLING, ROBERT WRIGHT, of Sheffield, England, who went to America previous to 1851.
STEVENS WILLIAM GEORGE, a native of England, residing in America previous to 1858
STOCKS, BENJAMIN, a native of England, who went to America previous to 1859
STOKES, EDWARD of Dublin, Ireland, who went to America previous to 1863
TAIT, ANDREW BURNETT, a native of Scotland, who went to America in 1853.
TAYLOR, LAMBERT, or STAYDOLF, ANNA, of Belfast, Ireland, who went to America in 1834.
TAYLOR, RALPH and JOHN, of Darlington, England, who went to America previous to 1865.
TRIVETT, SAMUEL, of Nottinghamshire, England, who went to America previous to 1857
WALKER, W W , jun , who left England for America previous to 1856
WARRENDER, MARY ANN, of St Helen's, England, who went to America previous to 1864.
WATSON, JAMES, who left England for America about the year 1845
WATSON, JOHN, of Lincolnshire, England, who went to America previous to 1858
WAUGH, JOHN FRITH, of Limerick, Ireland, who went to America previous to 1854
WHITWORTH, JAMES, a Stone Mason, of Rochdale, England, who went to America previous to 1864
WIGGLESWORTH, JOHN, of Yorkshire, England, afterwards of Ellicott's Mills, Maryland, previous to 1865.
WING, WILLIAM, of Denton, Lincolnshire, England, who went to America previous to 1865
WOOLLEY, JOSEPH, of Salford, England, who went to America previous to 1853
WOOD, RICHARD, a native of England, who went to America previous to 1866.

SPECIAL LIST No. 6.

UNCLAIMED MONEY, LANDS AND ESTATES.

The following persons (or heirs) are entitled to property All letters must be addressed to **J. B. MARTINDALE, 142 La Salle Street, Chicago, Illinois,** and must contain all facts on which writer's claim is based [See pages 6, 7 and 8 of this Manual]

ABBOTTS, MARY (See Mrs. Mary McKewan.)
ADAMS, EDWARD, nephew of Captain George Adams, at present in Canada.
AINSLEY, HARRIET, and JOHN, her son, who left England for America in 1858, and resided at Cherry Street, New York.
AITKEN, JOHN and WILLIAM, of Scotland, supposed to be in America.
AKED, THOMAS LORD, native of Halifax, England, recently residing in Washington, U S.A.
AKERLAY, MRS. (See James Peacock)
ALBRECHT, GEORGE, a Farmer, native of Saxony, last heard of in New York in 1849
ALEXANDER, CAPTAIN JOHN RICHARD, formerly a Commander in the British Navy
ALLAN, DAVID, formerly of South Fredericksburg, Ont., Canada
ALLWRIGHT, JAMES WILLIAM, otherwise J W BENTLEY, left Liverpool for America in 1863.
ANDERSON, MARGARET (Maiden name, BEAM), residing in Canada West in 1843
ANDERSON, PETER, son of James Anderson, of Glasgow, Scotland, was taken while an infant by his mother to America, about the year 1842
ANDERSON, ROBERT, of Killymore, Co. Down, Ireland, last heard of at 204, Magnolia Street, N O., U S.A.
ANDERSON, WILLIAM, formerly of Elgin, Scotland, who went to America many years ago.
ANDERSON, WILLIAM, formerly of Virginia, living in 1792
ARCHER, WILLIAM (See James Bruce Street.)
ARMSTRONG, ROBERT Plumber, Edinburgh, Scotland, in or about the year 1795.
ARNOLD, SARAH, Co. Kent, England Her daughter went to America about 1845
ARTHURS, ——, a native of England, became a Mormon, and was last heard of in Utah, U S.A.
ASKEW, MICHAEL, of Derbyshire, England, in 1867 residing at Drummondville, Ont , Canada.
ATKINSON, JOHN, formerly of Mullertown, Co. Down, Ireland, supposed to be in America.
AYRES, MISS EMILY, formerly of Co Somerset, England, now residing in America.
BACON, MATHEW DOWLING, formerly of Ireland. His Next of Kin are residing in America.
BAILEY, JAMES, formerly a Jeweller in Sacramento City, Cal., who left there in 1860 for Troy, N Y.
BAILEY, NATHANIEL ANDREW, now or lately residing at Stratford, Canada.
BAILEY, JACOB R., in 1837, a Clothier, at 197, Cherry Street, New York.
BAILY, DANIEL, of Golcar, near Huddersfield, England, residing in Canada.
BAKER, RICHARD BELL, formerly of London, England, now residing in America, or elsewhere abroad
BAKER, WILLIAM, and BENJAMIN FERRAND FERRAND, Merchants, Philadelphia, U S A , in 1814.
BALDERSTON, MARY (See Mary Mackenzie)
BALLANTYNE, WILLIAM, whose mother was Elizabeth, daughter of John Forrest, of St. Mungo's, Dumfriesshire, Scotland, and who went to America many years ago.
BANKS, DANIEL, of Bootle, near Liverpool, England, residing in America.
BARBER, HOLT, a Seaman, in 1858, on board American ship, " Queen of the East," at Callao
BARKER, WILLIAM, son of Edward Barker, residing, in 1861, at Carlisle, U S A.
BARNES, ELIZABETH (Maiden name, BRESCHARD), wife of Gilbert Barnes, Butcher, now in America.
BATEMAN, MARY and PATRICK, formerly of Co Cork, Ireland, who went to the USA about 1840
BAUER, JOHANN, a Shoemaker, left Bavaria about 1845. Supposed to be residing in America.
BAXTER, COSLETT, formerly of Lurgan, Ireland, who went to America in 1867
BAXTER, JOHN, formerly of Forres, Scotland, now residing in Canada.
BEAM, MARY, who, about 1779, married, in New Jersey, a McGee, or McKee, and removed to So. Carolina.
BEARD, JOHN, of Boughton, Monchelsea, Kent, who left England for America to 1867
BEDDOWS, WILLIAM, of Co Stafford, England, and afterwards of Dawson Station, Fayette Co., Pa , U S A.
BENTLEY, J W (See James William Allwright)
BENTLEY, SARAH (Maiden name, BEAM), residing in Canada West in 1866.
BERGH, JOHANNES ANDRIES, who left Amsterdam for New York, and entered the U S. Military Service in 1861 Last heard from in New York, 21st April, 1865
BERGIN, WILLIAM, who left Manchester, England, about 1845, was living in Ohio about 1860.
BEVERIDGE, Family of, or Representatives, residing in America.
BEWSHER, JOHN OLIVANT and WILLIAM, residing in America
BIGGAM, HUGH, Seaman, born about 1625, left Drumore, Wigtonshire, Scotland, in 1858, for New York.
BINDER Miss LORANE, residing in Toronto, or Hamilton, Ontario, Canada.
BINNY, JOHN, a native of Forfar, Scotland, now residing in America
BIRKETT, JOHN, a Hatter, formerly of Co Westmoreland, England, who went to the U S A in 1818, supposed to have settled in Philadelphia, and afterwards to have lived at Martinsberg, Mich., U S.A , and to have died there in November, 1833
BLACK, JOHN, a Painter, formerly of Glasgow, Scotland, now residing in America
BLAKE, MRS. HELEN, (Maiden name, SHERIDAN) married, in 1819, to General Robert Dudley Blake.
BLATCH, WILLIAM, and CHRISTOPHER, residing in America.
BLIMLINE, JOSEPH, of Reckendorf, Bavaria, went to America in 1837, and lived at Portsmouth, Va., U S.A.
BODWELL, HERBERT JAMES LOVELL, now or lately residing at Framingham, Mass , U S A
BOLD, JOHN, formerly of Edinburgh, Scotland, of BOLD and FARNWORTH, Paperhangers, 1084, Fulton Avenue, or of 1045, Atlantic Avenue, both in Brooklyn, N Y , U S A , his last known address
BOLKEN, WILLIAM, of Oldenburg, Germany, residing in America.
BORJESSON, CARL FREDRIK, of Akers, Sodermanland, Sweden, now residing in America.
BOYD, HUGH, JAMES, JOHN, and THOMAS, residing in America
BOYLE EDWARD, born in Ireland in 1830, who went to America many years ago
BOYLE, Family of, formerly of Co Donegal, Ireland, residing in America
BRADBURNE, SAMUEL T, Children of, last heard of at Springfield, Mass., U S A
BRADFORD, ALEXANDER, formerly of Deptford, England, now residing in America.
BRADY, Miss MARY Her mother married Mr Fleming, Grocer, New York City
BRAMMER, EDWARD, formerly of Croydon, Co Surrey, who left England for America.

SPECIAL LIST No 6

BREMAR, Dr HENRY, previous to 1838 in business in Charleston, U S.A.
BRENNAN, THOMAS, who left Hackensack, New Jersey, in May, 1876, for California.
BRESCHARD, AGLAE ROSE, ELIZABETH, JEANNE LOUISE, and JOHN LEWIS, residing in America.
BRIESE FAMILY, originally from Germany, who emigrated to America.
BRIGGS, EDWARD, of Bourn, Co Lincoln, England, who went to America several years ago
BRIMBLE, CHARLES, born at Dunkerton, Co Somerset, England, now residing in America
BROUARD, THOMAS W., a native of the Island of Guernsey, England, was at St. Louis, in November, 1873; afterwards at Lebanon, Laclede Co., and Pacific City, Franklin Co., Mo., and in June, 1876, at Hard Times Landing, Tensas Parish, La , J S.A.
BROWN, HENRY (or FREDERICK PLEWS), a Coachman, residing in Canada.
BROWN, LOUISA JAN b., daughter of Thomas Boak Brown, of London, England, residing in America.
BROWNE, or CODY, CATHERINE, formerly of Co. Kilkenny, Ireland, now residing in America
BROWNE, ROBERT W., left Dublin, Ireland, about 1854, was on board the U S gunboat "Wasp" about 1861.
BROWNE, THOMAS BLAKENEY, formerly of Dublin, Ireland, now residing in America.
BRUCE, JAMES, a native of Scotland, now residing in America.
BUCKLEY, PATRICK COADY, otherwise PATRICK COADY, relatives residing in America
BURBERICK, THOMAS, of Co. Surrey or Co. Middlesex, England, formerly in the Rifle Brigade, last heard of in Upper Canada about the year 1850.
BURBRIDGE, JAMES, a native of England, residing in America
BURDGE, FREDERICK, late of New Kent Road, London, England, now residing in America.
BURK, MARY, of Co Clare, Ireland, residing in America.
BURKITT, GEORGE, JAMES, and JOHN, of Hazel Green, Grant Co., Wisconsin, U S.A.
BURNHAM, JOHN BURTON, in 1859 a Steward or Purser of a steamer plying between Quebec and Montreal.
BURTON, SAMUEL ROWSTON (otherwi PLUMTREE), formerly of Great Grimsby, Co Lincoln, who left England for America many years ago.
BUTTERFIELD, CAPTAIN JOHN, of Bermuda, in 1784.
BYERS, JAMES, formerly of Mannah Cross, Co Fermanagh, Ireland, now residing in America.
BYRNE, CHARLES, from Co. Wicklow, Ireland, in 1826, a Tailor in N Y City
BYRNE, Mrs. CATHARINE (Maiden name, HOGAN), late of Ireland Children supposed to be in America.
CADDY, JOHANNA LANE, formerly of Appledore, Devonshire, England
CAFFALL, CHARLES JOHN, and SARAH, his wife, who left England for Dubuque, Iowa, U S.A., in 1854
CAFFREY, JOHN, formerly of the City of Dublin, Ireland.
CALLAHAN, MARY (Maiden name, BATEMAN), of Co. Cork, Ireland, who went to the U S.A. about 1840
CAMERON, JOHN, of Finch, County Stormont, Canada
CAMPBELL, ARCHIBALD, a Ship's Steward, who sailed from Liverpool for New York in 1842.
CARMICHAEL, W., Furrier, who emigrated to New York in August, 1871.
CARRIGAN, THOMAS, late of New Brunswick, who went to Philadelphia in May, 1876.
CARRY, THOMAS, GEORGE, JOHN, brothers, who went from Ireland to America between 1840 and 1850.
CARSON, ELIZA MARIA, born about 1814, who married —— Oakey, of New York.
CASS, LEVERETT HENRY, who left England for America about 1870
CHALMERS, WILLIAM, and his Wife, (Maiden name, ANN MUNRO,) residing in Massachusetts, U S.A.
CHAMBERS, MARY, otherwise JULIA RILEY, otherwise Mrs. DEXTER, residing in America
CHAPMAN, or SMITH, ANN HINDS, Representatives of, residing in America.
CHATTERTON, JONATHAN, a Hat Shaper, supposed to be in America.
CHEFFERY, JANE, wife of Patrick Cheffery (Maiden name, WOOLLEY), about the year 1864, residing at Whitehaven, Luzerne Co., Pa., U S A
CHESHIRE, HARRY, a native of Lancashire, England, now residing in Canada.
CHICK, FRANCIS, Carpenter, who left England for Canada in 1857 In 1859 he was in Tennessee, U S A
CHURCH, SAMUEL, formerly of Godlington, Co Bedford, England, and RACHEL (Maiden name, WOOLEY), Widow of William Church, of same place, residing in America.
CLAPPERTON, ALEXANDER, formerly of Goreoridge, Scotland, now residing in Canada.
CLARE, Mrs. ELIZABETH (Maiden name, LEWES), Children of, supposed to be in America.
CLARK, or WARNER AMY, or her Representatives.
CLEARY, JOHN CHARLES, a native of Sligo, who left Ireland in the year 1845 Supposed to be in America.
CLEMENCE, HENRY A., formerly of Co Cornwall, who, at three years of age, left England with his father about the year 1830, and afterwards lived at Albany, N Y, U S A.
CODY, Family of, formerly of Co Kilkenny, Ireland, now residing in America
COLE, JOHN DAVID, an American, deceased. Next of Kin wanted.
COLE, THOMAS GOODING, formerly of Ipswich, England, who went to New York or New Jersey in 1823,
COLLINGER, THOMAS, and LAURA ANN (Maiden name, SUGDEN), late of Leeds, Yorkshire, England, now residing in Canada.
COLLYER, JANE (See Jane Harper)
CONKLIN, GEORGE, formerly of Mount Vernon, Westchester Co., N Y , U S.A.
CONNOR, MARY and ALICIA, who left Ireland for America about 1855, and WALTER CONNOR, who was at San Francisco, U S.A., about 1864
CONWAY, SUSANNAH, formerly of London, Eng , widow of W T Conway, M D, who died at Boston, U S., in 1832.
COOMBS, WILLIAM HENRY, of Shropshire, England, last heard of at Cedar Falls, America.
COOPER, JAMES, a Stonemason, late of Ireland, afterwards of Toronto, Canada.
COPINGER, THOMAS BARTRAM, late of the Township of Trafalger, Ontario, Canada, Teacher
CORBETT, WILLIAM, a Tailor, in 1846, resided at 353, Greenwich Street, New York.
CORRIE, WILLIAM, of Cumberland, England, who went to Canada about 1856
CORVES, HEINRICH, of Holtzminden, Germany, was at Alton, Illinois, and St. Louis, Mo, in 1872.
CORWINE, ANNIE (Maiden name, BEAM), formerly residing in Co Lincoln, Ont , Canada.
COUTTS, JOHN, a native of Yorkshire, England, who went to America in 1842.
COWEN, ELIZABETH, recently residing in Cincinnati, U S.A.
COX, JOHN, Pianoforte Tuner, in 1863, of Brighton, England, now residing in America.
COX, WILLIAM HAWKINS, formerly of Bath, Co Somerset, England, now residing in America
COX, WILLIAM, who left England about 1837, and is supposed to have gone to Philadelphia, U S.A.
COYLE, THOMAS FRANKFORT, a native of Ireland, relatives residing in America.
CRAFT, HART, and PITCHER, formerly of Troy, U S.A , Merchants.
CRAIG, DAVID C., about 1828, United States' Consul to Panama
CRAIG, DONALD, of Glasgow, Scotland, was at Silver Mines, Las Casitas, Lower California, in Jan , 1870.
CRAIG, ROBERT, who left Bonhill, Dumbartonshire, Scotland, for America, about 1845.
CRANE, ALFRED, who arrived at San Francisco in 1852, was at Eureka, and Lancha Plana, California, in 1864.
CRARY, PETER, and JOHN S , Merchants, New York, U S.A , 1826.
CRAWLEY, THOMAS, formerly of Manchester, England, last heard of at Chicago.
CROGDON, JOHN LANG, who left England for Canada in the spring of 1870
CROUCH, GEORGE, formerly of Crouchville, St John, N B., Canada.
CROWE, EDMOND, formerly of Co Limerick, who went to the U S A about the year 1867
CUMMINS, ESTHER, formerly of Newent, Co. Gloucester, England, now residing in Michigan, U S A.
CUNNINGHAM, JOHN RAMSAY, native of Fifeshire, Scotland, went to America about 1852. When last heard of was a Foundry Worker in Ogdensburg, N Y , U S A.
CUTHBERT, ALFRED, formerly of Newark, New Jersey, U.S.A.
DALLAS, Family of, residing in America
DALEY, CHARLES, formerly of Magherafelt, Ireland, residing in New Orleans between 1843 and 1853.
DALZELL, WILLIAM, SAMUEL, MARTHA, ISABELLA, JANE, AGNES, Children of residing in America.
DARGIE, DAVID, Mason, from near Dundee, Scotland ; supposed to reside in America.
DAVIS, GEORGE, late of Yorkville, Canada, Hotel-keeper
DAVIS, MARGARET ANNA and WILLIAM, who left New York about 1860, and went West.

DAY, HARRIET, formerly of Leeds, Yorkshire, who left England for America in September, 1874.
DEXTER, Mrs (See Mary Chambers)
D BBLE, CHARLES, formerly of Miner's Fork, California, U S A
DICKSON, FLORY, a native of Scotland, formerly residing at White Cottage, Ohio U S.A.
DOMETT, CAPTAIN GEORGE, R N , who left England for Boston America, in 1827
DONCOURT, M JO-EPH, the Sons of, residing in Long Island, near N Y , U S A
DONE, Family of, residing in America
DONNELLY, PATRICK, son of MARTHA and EDWARD, late of Co. Kildare, Ireland, Carpenter
DORIAN, HUGH, JAMES, and DAVID, residing in America
DORMAN, MATTHEW, of Co Rutland, left England for America in 1852, and lived in Erie Co., N Y , U S A.
DOUGLAS, BRYCE KERR (Currier), who left Scotland for America about the year 1855.
DOUGLAS, ROBERT, a native of Perthshire, Scotland, afterwards of the Navy Yard, Brooklyn, N Y , U S A.
DOYLE Mrs MARIA CATHERINE, formerly of the city of Dublin, Ireland
DUFFIELD, WILLIAM MUNRO, formerly of Bury Saint Edmunds, Suffolk, and of Torquay, Devon, who left England for Canada between 1868 and 1869
DUFFY, ANTHONY, formerly of Dublin, Ireland, who emigrated to Canada in 1882
DUNN, ROBERT WORLEY, at present residing in Canada.
DUNNING, GEORGE, of County Hertford, England, went to Canada in 1850, and was employed by Mr Beaty, Farmer, Eglinton, near Toronto
DWYER, ELIZABETH (formerly MOONEY, Maiden name LAWLOR), residing in Canada.
DYER, ELIZABETH, JANE, and WILLIAM, supposed to be in the U S A
EDEN, or EDENSON, of Dover, England. His son supposed to be in California, U S A.
EDWARDS, ALEXANDER, of Nassau, in the Bahamas, the Daughter of, residing in the Southern States, U S A.
EDWARDS, ALICE BUXTON (See Alice Buxton Robinson)
EDWARDS, GEORGE, a native of Woodstock, England, who landed at Quebec, Canada, about 1828 or 1830.
ELLIOTT, or WARNER, MARY ANN or her Representatives
ELLISON, MARGARET, wife of John Ellison, of Wigan, Lancashire, England; went to America, 1855
FARRAR, RICHARD, supposed to be a Lieutenant in the American Navy
FERRAND, BENJAMIN FERRAND, and WILLIAM BAKER, of Philadelphia, U.S.A., Merchants, in 1814
FINCH, HENRY, in 1838 ? residing in New York.
FINN, MARY. (See John Kinnully)
FISHER, DANIEL PARKER, of Tealby, Lincolnshire, England, now residing in America.
FITZGERALD, JAMES, of Co Dublin, Ireland, born in 1832, residing in New York in 1860.
FITZGERALD, WILLIAM, formerly of Glin, Co Limerick, who left Ireland for New York in 1854.
FLANNIGAN, Miss MARY (See Mrs Mary Mehern.)
FLETCHER, R HENRY, who was in the employ of Budlong Bros., 88, W Lake St., Chicago, Ills, U S A , in 1874.
FORD, ARTHUR BEEVOR, Surgeon, who left England in 1854 for America, and resided at Buffalo; St. Paul, Minnesota , and New York city, where he was last heard of in 1859
FOWLER, WILLIAM, Plumber, formerly of Edinburgh, Scotland, now residing in America.
FRASER, THOMAS, a native of Scotland, in the year 1835 residing in Florida, U S A.
FREEAR, WILLIAM, formerly on the Commissariat Corps, who left England for Canada in 1861.
FRENCH, JOHN, formerly of Liverpool, England
FREYMARK FAMILY, originally of Germany, who emigrated to America.
FEUER, R P , late of 210, Ontario Street, Toronto, Canada.
GAHAGAN, MICHAEL and JAMES, residing at New Orleans, U S A , about the year 1859.
GAMMON, LOUISA. (See Louisa Hyde.)
GARDINER. (See Peter Young)
GARDNER, GEORGE, formerly of London, left England for America in 1885
GARNER, JAMES G , residing in New York City in 1675
GATH, WILLIAM, formerly of Bradford, Yorkshire, supposed to have gone to America.
GAVAGAN, MARY JANE, late of Kingstown, Ireland, now residing in America
GAY, FREDERICK A , in 1840, in business at 316, Broadway, New York City
GAYLAY, JOSEPH and ABRAHAM, residing in New York about the year 1837
GIBBONS, JOHN, formerly of Ireland, now residing in the United States of America
GILL, THOMAS FRANCIS, residing in New York, U S A.
GORTLIN, MARGARET, who left Ireland in 1852, with James Lawrence, and settled in Canada.
GOULARD, PROFESSOR, (a Painter) of New York City
GRAFTON, Mrs GEORGE (See Mrs. Mary McKewan)
GRASSEN, BERNARD, formerly of Glasgow, Scotland, who went to America about 1870.
GRAY JOHN, of Co Donegal, Ireland, went to America in 1838 His nephew supposed to reside in Canada.
GREEN, JAMES, of Wilmington, North Carolina, U S A , Farmer, 1803
GREENHAM, CHARLOTTE, who went to America in 1845, again in 1859, and remained there.
GREWANDER, AMELIA, WILHELMINA, ELIZABETH, LOUISA, formerly living in Newark, N J , U S A
GRIEVE, CHARLES and NINIAN, formerly of Hexham, Northumberland, England, now residing in Canada.
GRIFFIN, CHRISTINE (Maiden name, BEAM), residing in Canada previously to the year 1858
GRIFFITH, FREDERICK, formerly of London, England, supposed to be now in Canada
GRIFFITHS, JANE, married, 1792 William Williams , or their Children, Mary Ann and Jane, born 1796-1800.
GUNN, FRANCIS and ANTHONY, formerly of Castlemartyr, Co Cork, who left Ireland for America some years ago, and were last heard of keeping store in San Francisco, California, U S A.
GUY, CHARLES, formerly of Birmingham, England, residing in Boston, U S A , in 1873.
HAEFFELY, EDWARD, a native of Alsace, heretofore of Briton, Mulhausen and Lowell
HALE, ROBERT DAVID, an Englishman, residing in America
HALL, ROBERT, born 1817, left England on board the South Sea Whaler, "Brixton," was in Chili 1840.
HAMMOND, ANDREW, formerly of Co Donegal, Ireland, now residing in America
HAND, MATHEW, who left Dublin, Ireland, for America about the year 1845
HANDLEY, JOHN and DANIEL, who left Ireland for America in the years 1857 and 1859
HANLON, Mrs. WILHELMINA THOMASON (formerly HOYSTED), late of Ireland, now in America.
HANNA, FRANCIS, Stone Cutter, formerly of Belfast, Ireland , went to America about 1864.
HARE, JANE, daughter of Charles Hare, who died at St. John's, New Brunswick, Canada, about 1857
HARPER, JANE, sometime LEVEKING, then married to Robert Hanham Collyer, in Philadelphia, in 1836
HARRISON, MARY G , formerly of Newark, New Jersey, U S A
HARRISON, Miss LUCY ANN, who graduated in the Convent in Montreal, Canada, in 1846-7
HARRISON, HENRY, son of William and Frances Harrison, who went to sea in 1830
HARTLEY, JAMES C. L , formerly of Belfast, Ireland, now residing in America.
HAVLIN, DANIEL, late of "Gourock Rope Work Company," Scotland, now residing in America
HAWKINS, JOHN, WILLIAM, MARY, ELIZABETH, HANNAH, JANE, ANN, SARAH, JAMES, HENRY, ELIZA, RICHARD, and CHARLOTTE, who, about the year 1828, left England for Ohio, U S A
HAWORTH, JOHN, born about 1813, left Blackburn, Lancashire, about 1834 , supposed to have gone to America.
HAWTHORNTHWAITE, JOHN, formerly of Lancashire, who sailed from England for New York in 1841
HAY, JOHN RADCLIFF, believed to be residing in Canada
HAYES, T W , who left Plympton Devonshire, England, in July, 1874 supposed to be in America.
HAZZARD, NANCY and ROBERT, children of George and Cynthia Hazzard, who were sold as slaves in Virginia many years ago , also, HENRY WILLIAMS, formerly of Cincinnati, Ohio U S A
HEDGES, THOMAS CRESSALL, late of the "Quarries," Gornal, England, now residing in America.
HEIRONS, CHARLES, Sailor, who left London in 1866, in a merchant vessel, for New Orleans, U S A.
HEIRONS, JOHN, who left London for New York in 1868, and thence to San Francisco
HENNESSEY, JOHN, Copper plate Printer, who left London for New York in 1870,
HENNESSY, JAMES, of Co Cork, Ireland, in 1806 had a Fancy Goods business at 169, Spring St , N Y. City.
HENRY, Miss MARIAH (See Mrs Mariah Love.)

HEWETSON, JAMES, BRIDGET MARIA, HONORA, and MARGARET, formerly of Brooklyn, N Y, U S.A.
HICKLING, SAMUEL, a Chairmaker, and his sister, MARY ANN HICKLING, left England for New York about the year 1832, and afterwards lived at Warren, Pa., U S A. In 1835, Samuel went to Pittsburg In 1836, Mary Ann went to Clair, Mich, in 1837, she was Chambermaid at an Hotel in Detroit, in 1838 and 1839, she was Stewardess on board the steamer "Columbus," on Lake Huron
HITCHCOCK, THOMAS TANNER, formerly of London, England, now residing in America
HOBSON, JOHN, formerly of Stockport, England, afterwards in 40th Regiment N.Y. Volunteers.
HOCKLEY, RICHARD, left London in 1832 for Canada, was at Norwich, Conn., U S A, in 1848.
HOFMANN, FERDINAND, born at Mohren, Police, Bohemia, by trade a Locksmith, now in America.
HOGAN, CATHARINE (See Mrs Catharine Byrne.)
HOLME, THOMAS CROSS, residing in America.
HOPKINS, ROBERT, Junior, formerly of Threadneedle Street, London, England, now residing in Canada.
HORNE, JAMES, native of Scotland, a Sailor supposed to have left London for New Orleans in 1857.
HORTON, JERRY, who was in Ireland in 1861 2, now residing in America.
HOWICK, FRANCES, who, in 1871, lived in Hamilton, Ont., Canada.
HOYSTED (See Mrs. Wilhelmina Thomason Hanlon)
HUDSON, WILLIAM PRIDDEN, in 1874 residing at 51, New Street, New York City
HUGHES, Miss JANE, formerly of Glyncoirog, North Wales, now residing in America
HULL, Miss (See Mrs Schofield)
HUTCHINSON, JOSEPH, native of Corby, Lincolnshire, England, now residing in America
HUME, WILLIAM, Engineer, a native of Scotland, residing in Philadelphia, U S A, about 1859
HYDE, LOUISA (Maiden name, GAMMON), widow of John Hyde, formerly of Co Kent, England, recently residing in the Township of Hindon, Co Victoria, Canada.
HYNES, JOSEPH, who left Ireland for America about the year 1850.
IRVING, GEORGE, of Dumfriesshire, Scotland, residing in Gilpin Co, Colorado Ter, U S A., in 1870.
IRVINE, WILLIAM, a Seaman now or recently living in Canada
JACKSON, ROBERT WILLIAM, of Armagh, Ireland, residing in Alabama, U S A, in 1859
JACKSON, JOHN STAMER, went to Australia in 1854, now residing in America
JACKSON JOHN, born in London, England, in 1808, residing in Arizona Territory, U S.A, in 1870
JAMIESON, JOHN, a native of Glasgow, Scotland, born in 1793, who went to Canada early this century
JARDINE, JAMES, formerly of Beatock, Dumfriesshire, who left Scotland for Canada in 1853
JESSOP, TOM, who left Lincolnshire, England, for America in 1850
JOHNSON, Mrs. ELIZABETH, (wife of Lysle W Johnson), recently living on Staten Island, N Y U S.A.
JOHNSTON, JAMES, of Cork, or Bandon, Ireland, formerly in the employ of Hudson's Bay Company
JOHNSTON, WILLIAM, of County Dublin, Ireland, Nephews and Nieces of, residing in America.
JONES, THOMAS LONG, formerly of Llanelly, Wales, now residing in America.
JONES, (See Peter Young)
JONES, JOHN, a native of Bunbury, Co Chester, England, went to America in 1816, was last heard of at Lowell, Mass., U S.A., in 1829
JONES, WILLIAM, formerly of Nantyglo, Wales, afterwards, in 1858-9, in London and Shrewsbury
JONES, RICHARD, Esq, late of England, now residing in Canada
JONES, RICHARD, late of Ballarat, Australia, his widow supposed to be in America.
JONES, JOHN, of Tynllwyn, Parish of Llannor, near Pwllheli, Wales, residing in New Orleans in 1848.
JOHNSTON, or McWILLIAMS, AGNES, a native of Paisley, Scotland, residing in America.
KAY, JOSEPH, a native of Lancashire, England, lately residing in New York State
KAY, ALEXANDER RUSSELL, residing at Glencoe, Elfrid, Middlesex, Ont, Canada.
KEEN, WILLIAM, formerly of Devonshire, England, now residing in America
KELLY, THOMAS WORVALLO, formerly of London, England
KEMP, HENRY R., who was a Banker in Pit Hole City, Pa., U S.A., in 1865
KENNEDY, ROBERT V; in 1858, residing in Minnesota, U S A
KENNY, ANN, formerly ANN NOLAN, who left Carrickfergus, Ireland, for Philadelphia, U S.A., in 1856
KERR, JAMES, a Painter, formerly of Glasgow, who left Scotland for America about 1855
KERR, WILLIAM, JAMES, JOHN, and DANIEL, sons of William Kerr, of London, England, who died in 1802.
KERNAHEN, WILLIAM, who left Belfast, Ireland, in 1831, for New York, supposed to have gone to Canada.
KEYS, WILLIAM SAMUEL, JOHN CHARLES, and LESLIE, residing in Ohio in 1850
KILLEN, JAMES, of Belfast, Ireland. In 1858, he was in Providence, Rhode Island, U S.A.
KILLORN, ANNE, residing in the United States of America
KING, HENRY, twelve years in the U S Marine Service, who died in the year 1873, aged about 35.
KING, JOSEPH HENRY THOMAS, late of England, now residing in America
KING, HENRY, an Englishman, in 1856, residing in Minnesota, U S A
RINGROSS, WILLIAM, a native of Stirling, Scotland, a member of a Musical Company in America
KINNILLY, or KILLEALLY, JOHN, enlisted into 68th Regiment, at Castlebar, Ireland, in 1817, married, in Tipperary, Mary Finn. In 1828 they were at Quebec, Canada, with the Regiment
KITCHEN, ALICE (Maiden name, BEAM), residing in Canada West in 1848
KNIGHT WILLIAM and JOHN, of Co. Sussex, England, who went to America many years ago
KNOWLES, THOMAS, formerly of Co Lincoln, England, who went to the U.S A about the year 1868.
LAWLOR, ELIZABETH (See Elizabeth Dwyer)
LAWRENCE, CHARLES (otherwise GEORGE C LUCAS), who left England for New York in 1853
LEADBETTER, JEAN, married —— Wilson, and died at Richmond, Ont, Canada, about the year 1843.
LEAR, THOMAS, eldest Son of, residing in America.
LEWES, ELIZABETH (See Mrs. Elizabeth Clare.)
LEWIS, J D, late of New York City, Merchant, deceased Representatives wanted
LEWIS, GRIFFITH, who went to California in 1859, was at Elko, Nevada, U S A, in 1869
LEWIS, JOSEPH L, born in Jamaica, W I, in 1791, son of Lemuel Lewis, of Portland, Conn, U S.A.
LEVERING, JANE (See Jane Harper)
LINFOTT, JOHN, of Co Sussex, England, who went to America many years ago
LIPPMAN, or HENRICHSON, SAMUEL, a native of Germany, afterwards of New Jersey, U S A.
LITTLEWOOD, JANE, wife of George Littlewood, residing in America
LONDRIGON, DANIEL and JOHN, supposed to be in America
LONEGRAN, WILLIAM, formerly of Clonmel, who left Ireland for America about the year 1844
LONG, JOHN, of Kingstown, Ireland, last heard of in San Francisco, Cal, U S A
LOVE, Mrs. MARIAH, formerly HENRY, was in Philadelphia in 1856, and went to New York in 1858 or 1859.
LOW, THOMAS HOOD, and HENRY, brothers residing in America
LOW, JAMES, and WILLIAM D, residing in Canada
LUCAS, GEORGE C. (See Charles Lawrence.)
LUCAS, JOHN, of Somerset, England, in 1834, was trading between New York and New Orleans.
LUNDIE, GEORGE, formerly of Scotland. In 1837, a Plumber and Painter in New York, C S A
LUTWYCHE, JANE (See Mrs. Jane Taylor.)
LYONS, Mrs. ELIZABETH, now or lately residing in Toronto, Canada.
LYON, W W, Owner of 1,600 acres of land in Lavacca Co, Texas, U S.A.
McCAW, ALEXANDER, a native of Scotland, who went to Canada in March, 1876
McCORMACK, ARTHUR, formerly of Bailieborough, Co Cavan, left Ireland for Canada about the year 1818.
McCORMICK, ANDREW, of Wigtonshire, Scotland, went to America about 1846, and resided in Cleveland, Ohio.
McCOMBE, ROSE ANN, formerly of Ireland, who went to Toronto Canada, about 1850
McCONVILLE, HUGH, who died in the U S. of America, in December, 1873 He left Ireland about 1804.
McGEE, or McKEE, MARY. (See Mary Beam)
McINTYRE, JOHN, from the North of Ireland, who emigrated to America about 1851.
McISAAC, JOHN, of Paisley, Scotland, or his two daughters, residing in America.

McINNES, DUNCAN, a native of Scotland, in 1888 residing at Cambridgeport, Mass., U.S.A.
McKAYE, ELIZA, Spinster, deceased in America. Representatives wanted
MACKENZIE, MARY (Maiden name, BALDERSTON), widow of William Mackenzie, formerly a Blacksmith, in Glasgow, Scotland. She left Scotland many years ago for America.
McKENZIE, JOHN, formerly of Ross-shire, Scotland, late of Kingston, Canada.
McKEWAN, Mrs. MARY (formerly ABBOTT), some time since residing at Watertown, Jefferson Co., New York, U S A., under the name of Mrs. GEORGE GRAFTON
MACKINNON, DONALD, recently residing at Kansas City, Mo., U.S.A.
McLEAN, THOMAS, a native of Scotland, residing in New Brunswick about 1835.
McMARTIN, PETER, formerly of Milwaukee, U.S.A.
McPHERSON, or WHITEHEAD, Mrs ELIZABETH, wife of Dr. Nathan or Nathaniel C. Whitehead, formerly of Norfolk, Va., U S A
McWILLIAMS, or JOHNSTON, AGNES, a native of Paisley, Scotland, residing in America.
MAGEE, CHARLES, formerly of Co. Cavan, Ireland, Mariner, residing in Boston, U S.A., in 1854.
MALCOLM, H. F., formerly a Clerk in Toronto, Canada.
MALLIBAND, WILLIAM, of Leicestershire, England, now residing in America
MALONE, PATRICK, in June, 1865, he was a Sergeant in Company H, Indiana Volunteer Regiment, 2nd Brigade, 1st Division, 23rd Army Corps, U S A.
MALONEY, ELLEN and MARGARET, late of London, England, went to the U S.A. about the year 1855.
MANN, ROBERT J., a Dealer in Woollens, residing in New York City, in 1866
MANSON, CHARLES LEWIS, residing in New Orleans, La., U S.A., in the year 1834.
MARTIN, GEORGE, who left England for New York about the year 1851, with his brother, Lewis Martin.
MARTIN, JOHN, formerly of Forfarshire, Scotland, last heard of in Florida, U S.A., in 1842.
MARSHALL, ISAAC, of Berkshire, England, who went to America about 1856.
MARSHALL, Mrs. MARGARET, in 1873, living at Mr McArthur's, Grocer, Market St., Philadelphia.
MASON, JOSEPH, formerly of Manchester, England, in 1871, residing at Galveston, U S A.
MASON, JAMES, formerly of London, England, a Painter, now residing in the U.S.A.
MATTHEWS, Miss N E., in 1862, residing in 14th Street, New York City.
MAUGHAN, JOHN, of Newcastle, England, now residing in America.
MEAD, WILKINSON, who left England for America about 1851.
MEAR, SAMUEL, of Co Somerset, England, Carpenter, at present in America.
MEHERN, Mrs MARY, formerly Miss MARY FLANNIGAN, now residing in America.
MERCER, ANDREW, a native of Co. Sussex, England, residing in Toronto, Canada, previously to 1871.
MERSON, PHILIP, who left Toronto, Canada, for the United States in 1871
MERRILL, CATHERINE (Maiden name, BEAM), formerly of Co Lincoln, Canada West.
METZGER, THIEBAUD, former v Governor of Breda, and Lieutenant-General of the Dutch Cavalry
MILLIKEN, JOHN, formerly of Glasgow, Scotland, now residing in America.
MILLER, THOMAS, left Belfast, Ireland, for America, about 1825.
MILLER, JUSTUS D, in 1847 at 327, East Broadway, New York City, in Dry Goods and Lime business
MITCHELL, JOHN, born in Edinburgh, Scotland, in 1827, was employed by Luther Bent, Cabinet Maker, Watertown, Mass., U S, until October, 1847
MOLLOY, JOHN, formerly of Derrinboy, King's Co., Ireland.
MOONEY, ELIZABETH (See Elizabeth Dwyer)
MOORE, WILLIAM, formerly of Co. Dublin, Ireland, now residing in America.
MOORHEAD, JAMES ANDREW, of Co Monaghan, left Ireland for America in 1845, settled in Cincinnati, Ohio, which place he left in 1850 for California.
MORGAN, PHILIP JOHN, formerly of Newport, England, went to America in 1854. Lived in Rochester, N Y.
MORRISON, ANDREW, House Carpenter, a native of Tillicoultry who left Scotland for Canada in 1827
MORTON, WILLIAM ALEXANDER, residing at 171, Thompson Street (Dessau Place), New York.
MUGGERIDGE, EDWARD JAMES, who left England for America about 1866.
MUIR, THOMAS, formerly of Cumberland England, served in 56th Regiment, N Y V., up to Oct, 1866.
MULDOON, JAMES, now or lately of Quindaro, Wyandotte Co., Kansas, U S A.
MUNRO, ANN (See William Chalmers.)
MURNEY, JOHN and HENRY, brothers, natives of Ireland, went to America about 1843
MURPHY, or CODY, BRIDGET, formerly of Co Kilkenny, Ireland, now residing in America.
MURRAY, JOHN, son of James Murray, who left Co. Huron, Canada, for the U S.A. about 1845.
NADIN, THOMAS, formerly of Nottingham England, now residing in America.
NAGLE FAMILY, late of Limerick, who left Ireland for America about the year 1851 or 1852.
NEEDHAM, CHARLES BRITTAIN, who left England for America in 1861
NOLAN, ANN (See Ann Kenny)
NOLAN, MARY, of Bagenalstown, Co Carlow, Ireland. Her married niece went to America years ago
NOLAN, MICHAEL, of Co. Wexford, Ireland, who emigrated to New York in 1852
NOLAN, JAMES, of Dublin, Ireland, in 1861 resided at Rocky Mount, and De Kalb, Miss., U S A.
OAKEY, —— (See Eliza Marie Carson)
O'BRIEN, MICHAEL, of Co Clare, who left Ireland for America about the year 1816
O'DELL, CONSTANCE, or SCANLAN, and son, WILLIAM THOMAS O'DELL, residing in America.
O'DWYER, SAMUEL WILLIAM, RICHARD, and GEORGE FIRMIN, who left England about the year 1825.
O'FARRELL, JOSEPH, a native of Tralee, Ireland, now residing in America.
OLIVANT, THOMAS CATTERALL, residing in America in 1800
OPPENHEIMER, MORITZ, formerly of Germany, now residing in America.
ORMISTON, JOHN ANDREW, a native of Roxburghshire, Scotland, in 1860, Second Mate of the "Kent"
O'SULLIVAN, JOHN FRANCIS, born at Cork, Ireland, then of Liverpool, Eng, afterwards of New York
OWEN, DAVID, of Glasgow, Scotland, born 1826, a Sailor, was in New York in 1855.
PARRY, EMMA, her Parents, THOMAS and MARY ANNE PARRY, left England for America in 1832
PARSONS, Mrs ELIZA, late of Toronto, Canada
PATRICK, GEORGE, of Stepney, Middlesex, England, who settled in New York in or about the year 1840.
PEACOCK, JAMES, a native of Scotland, killed by explosion on board steamship "Black Warrior," at New York, in 1858. His widow is said to have married a Mr Akerlay
PEACOP, WILLIAM, formerly of Liverpool, England, Fruiterer
PELISSIER, Mlle MARIE ROSE CLARISSE, of Point St. Esprit (Gard), supposed to be residing in America.
PENTON, AUGUSTUS, formerly Lieut. in H.M 63rd Regiment, who left India for the U S A. or Canada in 1851.
PERRY, FREDERICK, late a Seaman in H.M S "Bellerophon," supposed to be in America.
PIETZKER, CHRISTIAN LUDWIG RUDOLPH, in 1858, went as a Seaman in a merchant ship to America Last heard of in New York City, in the year 1862
PIKE, HENRY, formerly of Chesterfield, England, now residing in America.
PIM, JAMES, otherwise PATRICK MALONE (See Patrick Malone)
PLASKETT, WILLIAM, in 1860 resided in Toronto, Canada, and last heard of in Pennsylvania.
PLEWS, FREDERICK (or HENRY BROWN), a Coachman, residing in Canada.
PLUMER, Family of, formerly of Co. Dorset, England, now residing in America.
PLUMTREE, SAMUEL ROWSTON (See Samuel Rowston Burton.)
PLUNKETT, HENRY EDWARD, of Ireland, was in Wisconsin, U S A., in 1875.
POOLE, ALICE BUXTON (See Alice Buxton Robinson)
POWELL, JOHN, a native of Scotland, now residing in America.
POYNTON, JAMES, and sister, JANE ELIZABETH, of Co Lincoln, England, now in America.
PROTHEROE FAMILY, late of South Wales, at present in America
RAYSON, CHARLES, ANNE, ELIZABETH, and MERCY BOYNE, now residing in America.
REID, ROBERT NISH, of Ontario, Canada.
REILLY, or O'REILLY, JAMES, late of Co Meath, Ireland, residing in New York City
RIGBY, JOHN PETER, of West Smethwick, near Birmingham, England, now in America.

SPECIAL LIST No 6.

RILEY, JULIA (See Mary Chambers)
RITCHIE, WILLIAM A, formerly residing at Holly, Mich., U.S.A.
ROBERTSON, WILLIAM, of London, England, went to America in 1845. Last address, Cooper and Holt's, Merchants, Hamilton, Canada.
ROBINSON, JAMES, born in 1812, at Lifford, Ireland, went to Philadelphia, Pa., U S.A., in 1832.
ROBINSON, HENRY, late of Co Antrim, Ireland, deceased. His Next of Kin are residing in America.
ROBINSON, ABRAHAM, late of Burnley, Lancashire, England, now residing in America.
ROBINSON, ALICE BUXTON, afterward EDWARDS, afterward POOLE, last address, 333, 6th Avenue, N.Y
ROBERTS, JAMES, formerly of Holloway. Co Middlesex, England, now residing in America.
BOLJER, CORNELIS GERARDUS, a native of Amsterdam, Holland, who left the Island of Curacoa for California in 1849, last heard of at Chagres, 24th October, 1849.
ROMANS, ISABEL (See Isabel Stewart.)
ROPER, HENRY, born in America about the year 1788
ROSS, WILLIAM and Miss ELIZA, residing in America.
ROWE, Dr J L, residing in America
RYAN, MICHAEL and PATRICK, of County Cork, left Ireland for America about 1820.
SALTERS, NICHOLAS, SOLOMON, and FRANCIS, New York, U S A, Merchants, in 1817
SARGEANT, ROBERT ALEXANDER, a Sailor, born 1848, landed at New York about December, 1861.
SAWYER, MARY (See Mrs. Mary Watson)
SAWYER, WILLIAM, formerly of Ireland Children supposed to be residing in America.
SCANLAN, CONSTANCE. (See Constance O'Dell)
SCHAAF, LEWIS, enlisted in Brooklyn, N Y, 1862, re-enlisted in regular (U S) Army, 1866, discharged, 1870.
SCHOFIELD, Mrs (Maiden name, HULL), formerly of Loughborough, England, now residing in America.
SCHOFIELD, TIMOTHY, late of Hampshire, England, Platelayer, now residing in Canada.
SCHRADER, CHARLES FRANCIS DAVID, formerly of Westphalia, now residing in America.
SCLATER, JAMES, now or lately of South Brooklyn, U S A.
SCOTT, JOHN, of Co. Kent, who left England for New York, U S A, in May, 1878
SEATH, or SEAD, JAMES, formerly of Stirlingshire, Scotland, last heard of in Upper Canada.
SELMES, JOHN, late of England, at present living in America.
SEWELL, HENRY, formerly of Bradford, Yorkshire, England, now residing in America.
SHARP, EDWARD P, formerly of Woodstock, Ont, Canada
SHEEHY, THOMAS, MARIA, and ELLEN, residing in America.
SHERIDAN, HELEN, born about 1800. (See Mrs Helen Blake)
SHERLOCK, Family of, residing in America
SINCLAIR, JOHN, Sailmaker, formerly of Glasgow, Scotland, now residing in America.
SKIFFINGTON, Family of, residing in America
SKILLMAN, WILLIAM, supposed to reside in St. Louis, Missouri, or San Francisco, California, U S.A.
SLATER, PYTHIAS, of Oldham, Lancashire, England, living in Troy, N Y, U S A., in November, 1875.
SMITH, SUSAN (Maiden name, BEAM), residing in Canada West in 1819
SMITH, JOHN, a Miller, a native of Yorkshire, England, residing at Three Rivers, Canada, about 1860.
SMITH, GEORGE W, lately Section-Man on Whitby and Port Perry Railway, Canada
SPEECHLEY, JOHN, formerly of Co. Huntingdon, England, residing in New York in 1859
SPEIGHT, CHARLES S, of Ireland, afterwards of Liverpool, England, children now residing in America.
STAFFORD, MOSES, formerly of County Wexford, who left Ireland for America about 1858.
STEARN, ARTHUR, formerly of London, England, lately residing in Toronto, Canada.
STEELS, PETER, formerly of London, Ontario, Canada
STEVENSON, HUGH, who left Glasgow, Scotland, for Canada, about the year 1842
STEVENSON, JAMES, of Co Down, Ireland, now residing in America.
STEWART, PATRICK, formerly of Aberdeen, Scotland, went to America in 1880, served in the 79th N.Y.V, and afterwards in the 67th N Y V, from which he deserted in 1882
STEWART, ISABEL, formerly of Scotland, and who married Archibald Romans
STEWART, PATRICK, formerly Tea Grocer and Spirit Dealer in Aberdeen, Scotland, now residing in America.
STILES, Miss ANN, residing in New York City about 1835
STIRTON, Family of, formerly of London, England, now residing in America.
STOPFORTH, WILLIAM, of Lancashire, England, in 1847; worked for a Farmer named Simon Condliff, near Albany City, U S A and afterwards went to Michigan
STRATTON, JOHN, Machinist, of Perthshire, Scotland, in February 1877, residing in Elizabeth, N J, U S.A.
STREET, JAMES BRUCE, native of St. John, New Brunswick, enlisted as William Archer in Northern Army, served in the U S. Cavalry, last heard of in 1865 at Washington.
STRONG (See Peter Young)
STUBBS, ROBERT BAYNES, who left England for America about the year 1832.
SUGDEN, LAURA ANN (See Collinger)
SWALE, JOHN LAMBERT, formerly of Yorkshire, England, and Captain in a British Cavalry Regiment.
SWARBRECK, AMELIA MARTHA, who was residing in Chicago, U.S.A., about 1858
SWORNE, LYDIA, native of England, last heard of at Spring Valley, Rockland Co., New York.
TAAFFE, ANNE (See Walsh)
TAYLOR, Mrs JANE (Maiden name, LUTWYCHE), of Birmingham, England; went to America in 1809 with her husband, who was a Methodist Minister
TAYLOR, JOHN, formerly of Yorkshire, England.
TEVINI, JOSEPH, (Giuseppe,) a native of Trieste, now residing in America.
THOMAS, Mrs FRANCES MARY, wife of Philip Thomas, in the year 1820, of Ibberville Parish, La., U S.A.
THOMPSON, SAMUEL COULTHARD, last heard of at Philadelphia, U S.A.
THOMPSON, WILLIAM ABRAHAM, left England in March, 1871, supposed to be residing in Canada.
TINDALL, HENRY formerly of Scarboro', England, afterwards of Road Eau Harbour, Ont, Canada.
TOBICIS, WILLIAM, formerly of Buffalo, N Y, U S A.
TRENCH, JOHN, formerly of Liverpool, Co Lancaster, and also of Liscard, Co Chester England, Porter
TROJAHN FAMILY, originally from Germany, who emigrated to America.
TUCKER, HENRY, formerly of Co. Somerset, England, now residing in America.
TUCKER, JOHN W; in 1875, residing in Newry, Ont, Canada.
TUCKFIELD, JOSEPH, formerly of Cornwall, England, now of California, Miner.
TUPPER, JAMES, of Nova Scotia, Merchant, about the year 1830.
TURLEY, BRIDGET, otherwise MARGARET, daughter of Hugh Turley, a native of Ireland. In 1852, she lived as Nursemaid with Mr Ayres, Jeweller, Madison Street, New York
TURNBULL, DALRYMPLE, a native of Scotland, residing at Oliver Gulf, Cal., U.S.A.
UPTON, JAMES THORLEY, formerly of County Chester, England, supposed to be in America.
VAN DE VELDE, DON PEDRO CLEMENTE, a native of Holland, now residing in America
VAN WEZEL, JACOB, in 1852 with Charles C. Elliott, 23, Harrison Street N.Y. City
VIDEON, CHARLES, formerly of Faversham, Co. Kent, Eng and, now residing in America
WACHTMAN, JOHN DIEDRICH, who deserted his ship, "Johann Gottfried Leume," in England, in 1866
WALKINSHAW, ANDREW CROMBIE, left Scotland in 1880 for Toronto, Canada
WALSH, FRANCIS, JOHN, and VALENTINE, sons of Anne Walsh (Maiden name, TAAFFE), who with her husband, Dr. John Walsh, resided in Brooklyn, N Y, in 1842.
WALLACE, WILLIAM, who left Linlithgowshire, Scotland, about 1838; last heard of at New Orleans about 1845
WARDROP, WILLIAM, formerly of Glasgow, Scotland, afterwards of Kingston, Jamaica, which he left in 1848 for California, U S
WARNER, AMY, MARIA, MARY ANN, THOMAS, and WILLIAM
WATSON, Mrs. MARY, otherwise SAWYER, formerly of Ireland. Her children are now in America.
WATSON, JAMES F, in 1839, residing in New York City
WEBB, THOMAS, late of Hessle, Co York, England, went to Chicago, Ills., U.S., in 1854.

WEBER, JOHANN KARL EDWARD, a native of Silesia, was in Milwaukee, U S A., in April, 1862.
WEGNER FAMILY, who emigrated from Germany to America.
WELDRICK, JOSEPH, late of Wolton, now residing in America.
WEST, GEORGE, who left England for America in 1885
WHEELER, THOMAS, JOSEPH, and **WILLIAM**, formerly of County Oxford, England, now in America.
WHITE DAVID, in 1872 residing in Queen Street West, Toronto, Canada.
WHITEHEAD, Mrs ELIZABETH (See Mrs Elizabeth McPherson.)
WIESE FAMILY, late of Germany, now residing in America
WIGHTMAN, Family of, residing in America.
WILKIE A Family of this name emigrated from Germany to America.
WILKIE, GEORGE, formerly of Edinburgh, Scotland, who went to the United States of America.
WILLIAMS, JAMES, of Portsmouth, England, last heard of at 55, Allen Street New York
WILLIAMS, HENRY and **THOMAS**, of London, England, brothers, who went to America many years ago
WILLIAMS, JOHN and **THOMAS**, formerly of Brecon, Wales, sons of John Williams, Turner, who died in New York in 1854   John went to California, and Thomas to New Orleans.
WILLIAMS, JANE (See Jane Griffiths.)
WILLIAMS, HENRY (See Nancy and Robert Hazzard.)
WILSON, EDWARD, formerly of Yorkshire, who left England for America in 1865.
WILSON, WILLIAM, a native of England, and late of No 25, Vine Street, Boston, U S.A.
WILSON, JOHN, of Ardrossan and Glasgow, Scotland, now residing in America.
WILSON, JEAN (See Jean Leadbetter.)
WILSON, GEORGE PORTER, of Croydon, County Surrey, who left England for America in 1868
WINTER, AUGUST WILHELM, a native of Prussia, who went to America in 1560, and entered the U S Army.
WINTER, JOHN FRANCIS; was in New York in 1836, and in Hartford, Conn., in 1851
WITCHLEY, WILLIAM HENRY, who left Ireland in June, 1872, and was afterwards employed by a Scotch gentleman in America   Has lost the thumb off his left hand
WOOD, ANN, WILLIAM, and **ROBERT**, who left Canada for the United States about 1849. William and Robert supposed to have enlisted in U S Army
WOOD, MARY ANN, formerly of Westcote, Co Oxford, England, now residing in America.
WOLCOTT, NORTHROP, and **ABBE**, Merchants, of Montreal, Canada, in 1810
WOOLEY, RACHEL (See Samuel Church.)
WOOLLEY, JANE (See Jane Cheffery.)
WRIGGLESWORTH, JAMES, formerly of Ipswich, England, supposed to be at present in America.
YOUNG, JAMES, an Engineer, formerly of Glasgow, Scotland, now in America.
YOUNG, MARY, recently residing in Ont., Canada, or her Representatives
YOUNG, PETER, went to America about 1770, and died in 1784   By his wife (Maiden name, ELEANOR BEST) he had several children. Of the daughters, Eleanor married WILLIAM JONES, and Rebecca married, first, JOSEPH STRONG, and, secondly, PETER GARDINER.   Representatives wanted.
YULE, JOHN, a Seaman, native of Scotland, supposed to be in America

SPECIAL LIST No. 7.

UNCLAIMED MONEY, LANDS AND ESTATES.

The following persons, if living, or if dead, their representatives, are entitled to property. All letters must be addressed to **J. B. MARTINDALE, 142 La Salle Street, Chicago, Illinois**, and must contain a statement of all facts on which the writer bases his or her claim. [See pages 6, 7 and 8 of this Manual.]

ADIE, JOHN, of Aberdeenshire, Scotland, went first to Canada, afterwards to the U S A. about 1840.
APLIN, JOHN ORLEBAR, who left England for America in 1865
ARCHER, GEORGE CHARLES supposed to be residing in Canada.
ARENDS, FREDERICK, who in 1880 resided in Huntsville, Randolph Co., Mo., U S.A.
ARPP, SAMUEL, otherwise EARP, who left England for America about the year 1830.
ASHLEY, FAMILY of, residing in America.
AULD, JOHN MURRAY, Junior, residing in America
AVERY ROBERT, late of No 95, Liberty Street, New York City In 1861 Captain of Co A 102nd Regt N Y V
BAILEY, LEWIS, formerly of Northamptonshire who left England for America about 1864
BAILLY, CHARLES FRANCIS, Representatives of, supposed to be in Canada
BAKER, JAMES, son of Thomas and Ann, a Sailor, who left Cardiff, England, in 1880, in a sailing vessel.
BAKEWELL CAROLINE ANNIE (See Mrs. C. A Jordan)
BARNETT, DRUMMOND TOWNSEND, last heard of in the North west Territory, British America
BARTON, ANNA, now or recently residing in Canada
BAYLOR, REBECCA, who left Ireland for New York in or about the year 1840
BEMISH, WILLIAM, formerly of Co Surrey, Eng., last heard of in Brooklyn, N Y, in 1872
BENJAMINE, ABRAHAM (See Abraham Michael)
BENSON, P M, born early in the present century, formerly of Co. Cork, Ireland, afterwards of the Province of Quebec, and last heard of in Kingston, Ont., Canada
BEST, JOHN, whose descendants reside in Red River, or Province of Manitoba, Canada.
BIRCH, ARTHUR WILLIAM SWINBURN, Mariner, now residing in America.
BLAKE, PATRICK, formerly of County Waterford, Ireland, now residing in America.
BOGARDUS, ANEKA JANS, Heirs of, residing in America
BOLD, JOHN, of St Helen's, Lancashire, who left England for America in 1854
BONTHRON, Mrs CHRISTINA ANN (See Mrs Christina Ann Jolly)
BOYLE, WILLIAM HENRY, formerly of Dublin, Ireland, now residing in America.
BRADBURY ELIZA (Maiden name, PLATT), who left Staleybridge, Lancashire, for America in 1854.
BRADLEY, JOHN (See John Wilbrough)
BRISKE, LOUIS, a native of Posen, Prussia, now residing in America.
BROOKE, JOSEPH, who left Eng about the year 1858, and was afterwards heard of in Ontario Co., N Y, U.S.A.
BROOKS, EDWARD, late of Detroit, Mich, U S A.
BROWNJOHN, MARY, widow, residing in New York, U S.A., about 1784
BRYAN, or CRAWFORD, MARGARET, of Ayr, Scotland, afterwards at Saint Ousten, Montreal, Canada.
BUCKLY, KATE, who lived with Mrs. Flora Bedell, in Custom House Street, New Orleans, La, in 1862.
BUGGY, THOMAS PRICE (otherwise THOMAS PRICE), who left England for America in 1870, and in 1873 was at Fulton, Callaway Co, Mo, U S A.
BURKE, WALTER, son of Sarah or Sally Burke (Maiden name, HEALY), residing in America.
BUSH, or BUSCH, FRANK, a Conductor and Mail Agent, formerly of Washington City, U S.A
BUSH GEORGE, Engineer, of London, England, who emigrated to America.
BUTTLER, FAMILY of, residing in Canada.
BYLES, SARAH, Spinster, of St. John, New Brunswick, Canada, about 1806
CAIN, or KAIN, PETER, PATRICK, OWEN, and BRIDGET, formerly of Co Roscommon, Ireland, afterwards of Brooklyn, N Y., U S A. Peter Cain afterwards kept an hotel in St. Paul, Minnesota, U.S.A
CALDWELL, NATHAN, a Carpenter, of Columbus, Ohio, about the year 1830.
CAMERON, BELLA (See Bella McLellan)
CAMERON, CHARLES, born about the year 1810, supposed to be residing in Canada.
CAMPBELL, CHARLES, son of George, last heard of at San Francisco, Cal, U S A.
CARPENTER, CORYNDON, WILLIAM FAUNTLEROY, NATHANIEL, and BUSHROD, sons of Dr. NATHANIEL CARPENTER, who died in Virginia, U S A., in 1778
CARROLL PATRICK and ANN, who left Oldcastle, Co Meath, Ireland, for New York in 1842.
CARTER, WILLIAM, Judge of the Vice-Admiralty Court, Newfoundland, about 1819
CARUTHERS, ELIZABETH, or her son, FINICE, from 1820 to 1840, residing either in Tenn., Ky., Inda, Ills, or Mo., U S A.
CARY, JOHANNA. (See Johanna Lynch.)
CARY, MARY. (See Mary Murphy)
CHALDER, GEORGE (JAMES SMITH), late of Manchester, England, now residing in America.
CHALMERS, ALEXANDER, formerly a Merchant in New York City
CHEESMAN, EDWARD, formerly of Margate, England, who sailed for Boston, U S.A., in 1860.
CHRISTISON, Mr, formerly of Toronto, Canada, Boot and Shoe Maker
CHRISTY, THOMAS, formerly of County Mayo, Ireland, now residing in Canada.
CHURCH, WILLIAM, born at St Catherine's, Ont., Canada, in 1839
CHURCHILL, HENRY, an Attorney-at Law, who left England for America Was at Omaha, Neb., in 1870.
CLARK, Mrs ISABELLA last heard of in Elizabeth, N J, U S A.
CLEMENTSON, ZACHARIAH, who, when last heard of, was living in New York City, U S A
COBB, EDWARD, of Co. Kent, Labourer who left England, in 1830, for America, and resided in Second Street, near Fourth Avenue, in New York, in 1847
COLLINS, LEONARD, a native of England, now residing in America.
CONKLIN, JAMES, residing in New York City in 1858.
CONWAY, ELIZA, who lived at 225, West 40th Street, New York City, until May, 1877.
CONWELL, EUGENE A., supposed to be in America.
COOK, ANN, born in Bristol, England, in 1820, now residing in America.
COPE, JOHN, left Liverpool, England, for New York in 1870, was an inmate of Ward's Island Hospital; also lived for a time at No, 154, William Street, N Y City
CORBETT, ALEXANDER, who left Glasgow, Scotland, for America in 1881.
COWLEY FAMILY, of England, residing in America.
CRAWFORD, or BRYAN, MARGARET, of Ayr, Scotland, afterwards at Saint Ousten, Montreal, Canada.
CROAKE, JOHN, LAWRENCE, BRIDGET, and MARGARET, formerly of Co. Kilkenny, Ireland, went to Lower Canada about 1840
CROFT, JOSEPH, formerly of England; last heard of in Cincinnati, Ohio, U S.A.

CROPLEY, EDWARD, a native of England, last heard of in Canada in 1858
CROTEAUX, MARTHA ROSALIE, and her brother, CHARLES LOUIS BERNARD CROTEAUX, in U.S.A.
CULHANE, FAMILY of, residing in America.
CUNNINGHAM, JOHN, a native of Fifeshire, Scotland, went to America about 1862, and when last heard of was a Foundry worker in Ogdensburg. N Y, U S A.
CUYLER, JANE, widow, of Montreal, Que, Canada, about 1818
DA COSTA, SARAH MENDES, born 1744, Representatives in America
DALEY, EDWARD, a native of Portland, Conn, was in Columbus, Ohio, in 1877
DANIELL, JENKIN Family now resident in the Province of Manitoba, Canada.
DARDS, EMMA, a native of England, now residing in America
DARROW, CHARLES W, residing in America
DAWSON, HENRY WHITEHEAD, who left England in 1868, and resided in Toronto, Canada.
DAWSON, JAMES DANIEL and WILLIAM, residing in America
DEAN, JOHN NEWBERRY, of Leicestershire, who left England for America in 1868
DECAEN, ADOLPHE, who left New York for Mobile in the year 1831
DERRIVAN, THOMAS, of Co Galway, Ireland, and in 1851 of West Roxburgh, Mass, U.S.A.
DETTMER, MARIA CATHERINA LISETTE. (See Leiding)
DEVANEY, MICHAEL, of Sligo, Ireland, left Brooklyn for Ohio in 1869
DILLON, JAMES, a native of Ireland, last heard of in San Francisco, Cal., U S A
DINGLE, JAMES, formerly of Devonshire, England, now residing in Canada.
DONALD, Mrs. ALICE, formerly residing at New Rochelle, N Y, U S A
DONNELLY, SOPHIA. (See Mrs Francis Hogan)
DOOLEY, JAMES, who in 1838 was residing in the State of Ohio, U S A.
DOWNING, PATRICK, of County Waterford, Ireland, now residing in America.
DOYLE, ELLEN and MICHAEL Michael was in America in 1862, Ellen married Bernard Loughrey, of New York, their daughter, Ellen Loughrey, when last heard from, was in Galveston, Texas, U S A.
DOYLE, JOHN, formerly of Ireland, afterwards of Toronto, Canada.
DOYLE, MARTIN L, late of Co Wexford, Ireland, in 1867, was in Kilbourne, Van Buren Co, Iowa, U S A.
DRAYTON, Mrs. HENRI, residing in America.
DURANT, FREDERICK, a native of England, now or lately of Empire City, Nevada, U S A.
DUTILH, FAMILY of, residing in America.
DWYER, JOHN, of Co Tipperary, left Ireland for America about 1867 In 1874 was at St Louis, Cal, U S A.
EAGLE, ALEXANDER, who lived in New Orleans, La, U S A., about 1832
EARP, SAMUEL, otherwise ARPP, who left England for America about 1830
EBENHOECH, CHARLES and FRANZ NICOLAUS of Würzburg, since 1867 in America
EBERT, JOHN T, LOUISA H, and GEORGE W, residing in St Paul, Minn, in 1867
EBSWORTH, RICHARD NATHANIEL, formerly of London, Eng, last heard of in Salt Lake City, U S A.
EDWARDS, DAVID BUSH, formerly of Cambridge, England, now residing in America.
ELDER, Captain CHARLES, late of the Royal Navy, Representatives of, in America.
ELLIOTT, JEREMIAH, last heard of at King, County York. Canada
ELLIS, ALFRED, Wine Merchant, late of Co Dorset, left England for Canada, and thence to New York, U S A.
ELSWORTH, THOMAS, Jun, in 1851 of Ohio, or State of New York.
EMMOTT, CHRISTOPHER, residing in New York City in 1869.
EVERETT, HARRY, late of Guelph, Ont, Canada.
FAHEY, or FAHEE, PATRICK, two Sisters of, residing in Massachusetts, U S A.
FARR, Representatives of, now residing in America.
FENNELL, JAMES, a Comedian, residing in New York, U S A., about 1810
FENTON, WILLIAM, formerly of Co. Stafford, England, was at Jefferson, Iowa, U S, in 1857.
FINDLAY, WILLIAM, of Morayshire, Scotland, now residing in America
FINLEY, CHARLES ALDEN, formerly of Almira or Coushant, Lake Erie, U S A
FISCHER, KATHARINA, afterwards FLEISCHBACH, residing in New York
FITZGERALD, ROSANNAH. (See Rosannah Murphy)
FLEISCHBACH, KATHARINA (Maiden name, FISCHER), now residing in New York.
FLITCROFT, FAMILY, residing in America.
FLOWERS, HENRY, a native of Co. Somerset, England, now residing in America.
FOLD, MARY ANN, formerly of Longford, Ireland, afterwards of New York.
FOSTER, JOHN, formerly of Pontefract, England, who went to the United States in the year 1852
FOXWELL, EDWARD CHARLES, who sailed for New York in 1871, and was at Cleveland, Ohio, in 1876.
FRAZER, CATHERINE (See Catherine Paterson)
FREEMAN, MARY (Maiden name, NEWLAN), residing in America in 1860
FRY, JAMES, formerly of Southampton, England. Mariner, who sailed for America in 1848.
GAGE, ALFRED, a native of England, supposed to be in Canada.
GARDENER, J, formerly of Birmingham, who left England for America in 1849
GASKIN, GEORGE, residing in America.
GILES, EDWARD, who died in 1842, his Heirs, or Next of Kin, residing in America.
GILMORE, SMITH, residing in Montreal, Que, Canada, about 1833
GILTNER, JOHN FRANCIS, formerly of Northumberland Co, Pa., U S A.
GLENNON, MARY, formerly of Co Roscommon, Ireland, was at Keyport, N J, U S A, in 1866
GOBLE, MARY (Maiden name, PENFOLD), who left England for Salt Lake City, U S A., many years ago.
GOODMAN, WILLIAM, a native of New York, U S A.
GOODRICH, EDWARD, a native of England, last heard of in Yorkville, Ont., Canada
GORDON, Mrs., formerly of Bromley, Kent, England, afterwards, in 1877, of Chicago, U S A.
GORDON, WILLIAM, formerly of Upper Canada, afterwards of Montana, U.S.A.
GRAHAM, Miss CECILIA, in 1868 acting under the name of FLORENCE, at the Arch Street Theatre, Philadelphia, U S A.
GRAHAM, LOUISE, who lived in New Orleans in the winter of 1860-1
GRANT, JAMES FORBES, formerly of England, now residing in Canada
GRANT, MARGARET, widow, of County Kerry, Ireland, in 1860.
GREATHEAD, FRANCIS TIDDY, and MARY, his wife, residing in America
GREEN, JAMES, formerly of Liverpool, who left England for America in 1810
GREY, IDA (otherwise IDA SCHAER), residing in America.
GRIEVE, ROBERT, who left Scotland for New York in the year 1881
GRIFFIN, MICHAEL, PATRICK, FRANK, THOMAS, and MARY, who eft Co. Clare, Ireland, about the year 1860, and afterwards resided in Cattaraugus Co, N Y, U S A
GRIFFITHS, GEORGE, left England for America in 1870, and was in California, U S.A., in 1873.
GROVENBERRY, FAMILY of, residing in America.
GRUNDY, ELIZABETH. (See Elizabeth Houghey)
GUNTER, FANNY, afterwards HAASE, residing in Baltimore, U.S.A.
HAASE, FANNY (Maiden name, GUNTER), residing in Baltimore, U S A.
HADDOX, Mrs. JANE, residing in Canada.
HALPIN, JAMES, formerly of County Dublin, Ireland, now residing in America
HAMMERS, BERNARD, a native of Germany, residing in St. Louis, Mo, U S A., in 1875.
HAMMOCK, CHARLES DAVID, who left England for America, in 1851
HAMMOND, WILLIAM DAVID, late of Wardsville, Ont, Canada
HANLON, THOMAS A., residing in Pittsburg, U S A, in December, 1874
HARDCASTLE, PEARSON, late of Brighouse, Co York, England, Plumber and Glazier, residing in America.
HARDING, JAMES HENRY, in 1842 of Ipswich, Co Suffolk, England, afterwards of America
HARMS, CARL JACOB HERMAN, a native of Germany, now residing in the U S A

HARRISON, THOMAS, recently residing in Boston, Mass., U S A.
HARROP, FAMILY of, residing in America
HARVEY, WILLIAM, formerly of Glasgow, Scotland; supposed to reside in America.
HATT, RICHARD, of Montreal, Canada, about 1814
HAWKER, CHARLES, formerly of Co Stafford, England, now residing in Canada.
HAYES, FREDERICK, formerly of Co Dorset, England, last heard of in 1867, when he was residing at 102, Public Square, Cleveland, Ohio, U S A.
HEALY, SARAH or SALLY (See Walter Burke)
HEATH, HENRY, Sen, formerly of County Essex, England, who emigrated to Canada many years ago, and resided in or near Guelph, Ont
HEATH, HENRY JORDAN, son of Robert Heath, now residing in America.
HEATH, THOMAS, formerly of Birmingham, England, now residing in America.
HENDERSON, or STEWART, JAM S, of Glasgow, Scotland, was at Kingston, Canada, in 1876
HENTSCHEL, MATHILDA ULRIKA (Maiden name, LINDQVIST), residing in America.
HERRING, JAMES, a native of Wales, left England in the 90th Regiment for St. John, N.B.; last heard of at Portland, Maine, U S A.
HOGAN, Mrs. FRANCES, widow of MICHAEL, and her Children, WILLIAM, HARRIET (or STYLES), and SOPHIA (or DONNELLY), residing in America
HOLLINGS, JOSEPH, supposed to be residing in Canada.
HOLMES, WILLIAM COURT, formerly of Croydon, England, now residing in America
HOPE, THOMAS, formerly of Co Durham, England, Shoemaker, and JANE, his wife, now residing in America
HOPKINS, BRIDGET (See Dominick Lynch)
HOPKINS, RICHARD, and ANN, his wife (Maiden name, ANN LOYAL), Representatives of, in America.
HOPKINS, RICHARD, of Whitechapel, London, England, in 1779 Representatives of, in America
HOSENBURG, ANDREW, formerly a Seaman on board the South Sea Whaling Ship "Kent," and afterwards of New Orleans, La., U S A.
HOUGHEY, ELIZABETH (Maiden name, GRUNDY), formerly of Gloucestershire, Eng, now residing in America.
HOUGHTON, WILLIAM, a native of England, born about 1844, now residing in America.
HUDSON, JAMES, residing at Red River, Canada
HUGER, BENJAMIN and ISAAC, of South Carolina, U S A, about 1767
HUGHES, ANN (Maiden name, OWEN), wife of Richard Hughes, Collier, residing in the U S A
HUGHES, EDWARD, of Halifax, Nova Scotia, Canada, about 1806
HUNTER, JOHN, an Iron moulder, formerly of Kilmarnock, Scotland, who went to New York in 1860, was afterwards an Engineer in the "Kearsage."
HYDE, Mrs LOUISA, a widow, formerly of Maidstone, England, afterwards of Peterson, and Gull River Canada West, she was last heard of in the backwoods of America, 1865 66
ISAAC, ISAAC, of Quirpoon, Newfoundland, Planter, about 1811
JACKSON, ROBERT WILLIAM, formerly of Alabama, then of New Jersey, and afterwards of South Walpole Norfolk Co, Mass, U S A
JACKSON, Mrs. SAMUEL, formerly of Centreville, Passaic Co, N J, U S A.
JACKSON, WILLIAM, a native of Sheffield, England, served as a Soldier in the U S Army, last heard of at Atlanta, in 1869
JEANS, JAMES MEAD, born in Caledonia, Ont, Canada, in 1859
JOLLY, Mrs CHRISTINA ANN (Maiden name, BONTHRON), married at Tampico, Mexico, in 1846.
JONES, JOHN, a native of Llanor, Wales, was at Rochester, Ky, in 1845, and at New Orleans in 1847
JORDAN, CAROLINE ANNIE, formerly of London, England, afterwards of Staten Island, N Y, U S A.
KAIN, FAMILY of (See Cain Family)
KEANE, JAMES, and ELIZABETH ALICE KEANE, his wife, formerly of Ireland, now residing in America.
KEEFE, ALICE   (See Alice Lane)
KEEFE, MARY   (See Mary Power)
KEEGAN, JULIA, formerly of Wexford, Ireland, now residing in America.
KELLY, HONORA, who, when last heard from, was in San Francisco, Cal., U S A.
KELLY, LAWRENCE, formerly of Dublin, Ireland, afterwards of America
KENT, ELIZABETH (See Elizabeth Newnham)
KIDDELL, CHARLES, of South Carolina, U S A., about 1815
KILPATRICK, JOHN, and ROSE, his wife (Maiden name, MAGRATH), who left Ireland for New York in 1871.
LACY, JAMES, formerly of 1028, Chestnut Street, Philadelphia, Pa., U S A.
LAMBERT, HENRY, lately residing at No 76, Broadway, New York City
LAMONT, NORMAN, Royal Engineers, residing in Montreal and Quebec, from 1848 to 1849.
LANE, ALICE, otherwise KEEFE, of Co. Waterford, Ireland, now residing in America.
LANGTON, ANNIE   (See Annie Pix)
LANHAM, GEORGE and HENRY, Brothers, who left England for America in 1836 and 1837, respectively
LEFEBURE, or LEFEBVRE, MARY SUSANNE, residing in America
LEHNEN, WENDEL, a native of Germany, residing in America
LEIDING, Mrs MARIA CATHARINA LISETTE, born DETTMER, and her daughter, HENRIETTE LOUISE EMMA, residing in America.
LEIGHTON, JANE, who left Northampton, England, for America about 1858
LENNOX, JOHN, son of ALEXANDER and MARY LENNOX, who went to America many years ago.
LEONARD, JAMES, in 1864 residing in the township of King, Co York, Ont, Canada
LEONARD, JOHN, residing in Canada   Was in Edinburgh, Scotland, in 1808
LEVY, ELLA, formerly of Savannah, Ga., U S A
LEWIS, Miss CORDELIA, who was in Savannah, Ga., during the War, and left there for California.
LEWIS, EZRA, ABNER, and FLORA, Children of, residing in America.
LINDQVIST, MATHILDA ULRIKA   (See Hentschel)
LITHERLAND, JAMES, Seaman, who left Liverpool for Quebec, Canada, in 1863.
LOUGHREY, ELLEN   (See Doyle Family)
LOYAL, FAMILY of, residing in America.
LUMLEY, MATTHEW, a native of Yorkshire England, residing in Brooklyn, or Jersey City, U S A
LYNCH, or LYNSKI, DOMINICK, and BRIDGET, his wife (Maiden name, HOPKINS), residing in America.
LYNCH, JOHANNA (Maiden name, CARY), formerly of Upper Street, Boston, Mass, U S A.
McAFEE, HENRY, formerly of Co. Antrim, Ireland, now residing in America.
McARDLE, FAMILY of, formerly of Ireland, now residing in America
M'BEATH, JAMES, a Saddler, who left Scotland for America about the year 1838.
M'CARRON, HUGH, a native of County Donegal, Ireland, now residing in America.
McCANN, ROBERT, Boot-closer, who left Edinburgh, Scotland, for New York in 1851
MACEWAN, GEORGE WILLIAM, formerly of Edinburgh, Scotland, now residing in Canada.
McDONALD, EDWARD, last heard of in Beverley, Mass, supposed to have left there for Portland, Me., U.S.A.
McDONALD, or McDONOUGH, GEORGE, formerly of Manchester, England, now residing in America.
MACDONOUGH, FELICIA, HARRIET, and RACHEL, Spinsters, of Boston, Mass., U S A, about 1817.
McDONOUGH, GEORGE   (See George McDonald)
McDOWELL, WALTER, from Pennsylvania, who purchased land in Missouri in 1856.
McGLINN, ELIZABETH, who left Ireland for Providence, R I, U S A, about 1858
McGREEVY, PETER, who left Ireland for New York, U S A, in the year 1845
McINTYRE, SUSAN, formerly of County Tyrone, Ireland, afterwards of Brooklyn, N.Y., U.S.A.
McKENNA, Mrs JOHN, formerly of Boston, Mass, U S A.
McLAUGHLIN, MICHAEL, formerly of Mayo, Ireland, afterwards residing in Canada
McLELLAN, BELLA, afterwards CAMERON, who left Ross-shire, Scotland, in 1832, for Cape Breton, America.
McLELLAN, JESSIE, afterwards ROBERTSON, who left Ross-shire, Scotland, in 1832, for Cape Breton, America.

McLEOD, NORMAN, Tree Agent, residing in Ontario Canada.
McNEICE, JOHN and JAMES, formerly of Co Louth, Ireland; now residing in America.
MACONOCHIE, DUGALD, formerly of Argyleshire, Scotland, now residing in America
McWILLIAMS, MARGARET, late of Wylie Street, Pittsburg, Pa U S A
MACARTY, JOSEPH OSCAR, a native of Santiago de Cuba, supposed to be residing in the USA.
MACHIN, FAMILY of ISAAC and WILLIAM MACHIN resided in Indianapolis, U.S.A., in 1868, and JOSEPH MACHIN, in Jersey City, U.S.A., in 1888
MAGRATH, ROSE. (See John Kilpatrick)
MARONEY, or SETWRIGHT, Mrs., when last heard of was in Brooklyn, N Y, U.S.A.
MARTIN, JAMES, formerly of Worcestershire, England, residing in New York in 1859.
MATHER, JOHN, late Captain of the 14th Hussars, British Army, now residing in America.
MATTHEW, JAMES, Ironmonger, late of London, England, then of Brockville, Ont, Canada.
MAXEY, Rev MICHAEL, formerly of Co Waterford, Ireland.
MEECH, Miss HELEN A, now residing in America.
MEIKLE FAMILY, of Scotland now residing in America.
MICHAEL, ABRAHAM, otherwise ABRAHAM BENJAMINE, who left England about the year 1848, and in 1872 was at La Paz, Mexico.
MIDGLEY, AMOS, formerly of New York, and Cleveland, Ohio.
MINAHAN, ANN, left England for America about 1850, resided in Water Street, New York, in 1858, afterwards in Illinois, U S A.
MINCHIN, Mrs., and her Son, who left Ireland for New York in 1852.
MITCHELL, JOHN, late of Co Westmeath, Ireland, went to America, 1827, and was in Penn., U S., n 1852
MONAHAN, Mrs, of County Mayo, Ireland, Children of, residing in America.
MONIGHAN, JOHN, formerly of Newcastle-on-Tyne, England, now residing in America
MOORE, ADAM, and ANN, his wife (Maiden name, WOOLISCROFT), formerly of Co. Stafford, Eng, residing at Cleveland, U S A, in 1859
MOORE, JAMES, formerly of Athenry, Co Dublin, Ireland, now residing in America.
MOORE, Mrs MARY MAWMAN, residing in London, Ontario, Canada, in 1853.
MOOREHOUSE, Mrs CORNELIUS H (Maiden name, QUICK), now residing in America.
MORONY FAMILY, of Co. Clare, Ireland, last heard of in Salem, Ind, U S A.
MORRISON, MALCOLM, a native of Scotland, afterwards residing in Chicago, U S A.
MORTON, CATHARINE CECILIA, formerly of Boston, Mass., U S A
MULLENS, MARGARET, of Carrick on Sour, Ireland, was living at Shoemakers' Hotel, New York City, in 1867
MULQUEEN, FAMILY of, residing in America
MURPHY, JOHN C, and his wife, SARAH B MURPHY, who lived in New York in 1836.
MURPHY, MARY (Maiden name, CARY) formerly of Upper Street, Boston, Mass., U S A.
MURPHY, PETER, late of Wylie Street, Pittsburg, Pa., U S A
MURPHY, ROSANNAH, formerly FITZGERALD, married in Ireland, 1858, last heard of in Chicago Ills, U S A.
MURRAY, ANDREW, formerly of Coupar Angus, Scotland, now residing in America
MURRAY, ANN ELIZA, widow (Maiden name, WETHERELL), late of England afterwards of Hamilton, and Guelph, Ont, Canada, then of Grand Rapids, Mich., U S A., and last heard of in St. Joseph Co., Mich
MURRY, JOHN, formerly of Co. Kildare, Ireland, now residing in America
MYLIUS, JOHANN GOTTLIEB AUGUST, a Miller, born in Germany, 1832, now residing in America.
NAYLOR, JOSEPH, a native of England, in 1855, was a Machine Tool Maker in New York City, U S A.
NEED, EDGAR, now resident in North America.
NEILSON, FAMILY of, residing in Ontario, Canada.
NEWLAN, MARY (See Mary Freeman)
NEWMAN, FRANK A, residing in New York in the year 1843.
NEWNHAM, RICHARD, and ELIZABETH, his wife, supposed to reside in America.
NEWTON, JANET, last seen at Montreal, Canada, about 1837, when three years old.
NEY, JOHN, residing in America.
NUSSEY, JOHN EDWARD VARLEY, residing in America.
O'BRIEN, MARGARET and PHILIP, who left Kenmare, Ireland, for Canada in 1856.
OCKER, JOHANN GEORG, who left Hechingen, Germany, for America in 1849.
OLIVEY, WILLIAM, who left England for New York in 1852, and resided at Elmira.
ORCHARD, JOSEPH (Baker), and ANN, his wife, residing in New York City in 1790.
O'TOOLE, RICHARD (otherwise DICK), a Carpenter by trade, now residing in America.
OTT, LUDWIG, son of Katharine, formerly of England, now residing in America.
OWEN, ANN, who married Richard Hughes, a Collier, now residing in America.
OWEN, JOHN, THOMAS and WILLIAM, Masons by trade formerly residing in Pittsburgh, Pa., U S A.
PALMER, H W, who owned some Californian Securities in the year 1884.
PARDEW, WILLIAM HENRY HEAD, who left Plymouth, England, for America about the year 1849.
PARR, JOHN, of Nova Scotia, Canada, about 1890.
PATERSON, CATHERINE (or FRAZER), a native of Inverness, who left Scotland for America about 1858, and was last heard of in Philadelphia, U S A.
PATTISON, ROBERT, of Ireland, late of the 3rd Regiment of Foot, British Army, now residing in America.
PENFOLD, MARY (See Mary Goble.)
PERCY, GEORGE WASHINGTON, a native of County Kilkenny, Ireland, now residing in America.
PERKINS, JOSEPHINE, of Philadelphia, widow of JAMES ROBERT SULLIVAN, who died in Italy in 1872
PICKMAN, HENRY, a native of England, now residing in America
PIX, Mrs. ANNIE (Maiden name, LANGTON), who left England for America in 1853
PLATT, ELIZA (See Eliza Bradbury)
POWER, MARY, otherwise KEEFFE, formerly of Co Waterford, Ireland, now residing in America.
PRENTICE, JOHN TABOR, who left England for America previous to the year 1841
PRICE, THOMAS. (See Thomas Price Buggy)
QUICK, Miss. (See Mrs C H Moorehouse.)
QUIN, FAMILY of. DENNIS, PATRICK, CATHERINE, and ELLEN, the latter married to JOHN SMITH, Marble Cutter, all residing in New York City in 1859
QUINN, ANDREW, who sailed from Londonderry, Ireland, for New York in 1873
REDDISH, SAMUEL STEINGER, formerly of Cheshire, who left England for Queenstown, U S A., in 1867
REDFIELD, SIDNEY, who left New York in the winter of 1871
REES, WILLIAM, late of Aberdwr, Tregaron, Wales, who left England for America a few years ago
REID, or ELLIOTT, JEREMIAH, last heard of at King, County York, Canada.
REYNOLDS, JOHN WILLIAM, Gold Miner, between 1858 and 1861 resided on Yuba River, San Francisco.
RICH, OBADIAH, who is supposed to be living in the U S A.
RICHARDS, JOHN F, who purchased lands in Missouri in 1859.
RINK, CHARLES, alias HAVERLE, residing in America.
ROACH, Mr, formerly residing in Newark, U S A.
ROBERTSON, JESSIE. (See Jessie McLellan.)
ROBERTSON, PETER, an Engineer, of Glasgow, Scotland, worked in some N.Y. Machine Shop about 1875.
ROBINSON, MARGARET (See Margaret Taylersen.)
ROBINSON, THOMAS LITTLE, formerly of Sligo, Ireland, afterwards of Brock Street, Toronto, Canada.
RUSCHHAUPT, FRIEDRICH MORITZ, of Moravia, last heard of at 762, Eighth Avenue, New York City
RUSSELL, JOHN, married in Scotland in 1873, and afterwards went to New York.
RYAN, FRANK A, recently residing in New York City
SALTERIO, or SALTERO, ALBINO, formerly of London, England, residing in Ohio, U.S.A., in 1880.
SAUNDERS, HORACE, in 1880 residing in Ills, Inda, or Ohio, U S A.
SCHARR, IDA (formerly IDA GREY) residing in America.

SCHMIDT, GEORGE CARL CHRISTIAN, a native of Bavaria, now residing in America.
SCHWAB CASPPER, of New York USA, Sugar Baker, about 1812
SCOTT, WILLIAM, a Farmer, of Wigtonshire, Scotland, last heard of at Greenville, Washington Co, Miss, USA
SETWRIGHT, Mrs (Maiden name, MARONEY), when last heard of was in Brooklyn, NY, USA.
SHERIDAN, Miss HELEN, born about 1790-1800 Representatives of, in America
SISBALD, JOHN, residing in Canada.
SKIFFINGTON, FAMILY of, now residing in America.
SMALLEY, RICHARD and ANNIE, his wife, of Girard, Erie Co, Pa., USA.
SMITH, CHARLES, last heard of at New Orleans, La, USA, in 1845.
SMITH, or QUIN, ELLEN (See Quin Family)
SMITH, JAMES (See George Chalder)
SMITH, JOHN, formerly of Timdergarth, Scotland; supposed to be residing in Canada.
SMITH, ROBERT, Gasfitter, late of Liverpool, England, now residing in America
SMITH, THOMAS, formerly of Kennington, London, England, now residing in America
SMITH, THOMAS, who left England for America on the 8th of June, 1869
SMYTH, JOHN, son of Patrick, formerly of County Donegal, Ireland, now residing in America.
STEAD, JOHN, Architect and Engineer, now residing in America.
STEWART, ALEXANDER, a Jeweller, late of Richmond, Que, Canada.
STEWART, or HENDERSON, JAMES, of Glasgow, Scotland, who was at Kingston, Canada, in 1876.
STRATEN, SARAH, wife of Charles Straten, of New York, USA., Merchant, about 1799
STRONG, WILLIAM, of New York, USA, Merchant, about 1790.
STYLES, HARRIET (See Mrs. Frances Hogan)
SULLIVAN, JAMES ROBERT (See Josephine Perkins.)
SWEENEY, EDMOND, formerly of Dublin, Ireland, now residing in America.
TAYLERSON, MARGARET, who left England for America in the year 1784 with Robert Robinson.
TAYLOR, ELIHU, in 1842 of Detroit, or vicinity of New York.
TAYLOR, JOHN GABRIEL, of Halifax, North America, about 1800.
TAYLOR, JOSEPH, a native of Co. Surrey, England, supposed to be residing in America.
THEVENIN, MICHAEL, Wax Bleacher, of Hammersmith, England, 1800, Representatives of, in America.
THOMAS, CAROLINE R., who is supposed to be residing in the USA.
THURSTON, ADA CLARA, living in Philadelphia, USA., in the year 1856
TIBBETTS, WILLIAM, MD, who left Edinburgh, Scotland, in 1845, for America.
TODD FAMILY, of England, now residing in America.
TRIPP, BENNET L, in 1836 supposed to have been residing in New York State, USA.
TURNER, GEORGE, a Labourer, who left Yorkshire, England, for Canada, in 1873
TURPIN, JOHN, formerly of Cork, Ireland, now residing in America.
UPTON, JAMES T, formerly of England, now residing in America.
VALENTIN, STIEGLITZ, who landed in New York, per steamer "Wisconsin," in November, 1873.
VON KŒNIG, OSWALD EDUARD TRAUGOTT, who, up to the year 1836, was an Officer in the 30th Roya. Prussian Regiment of Infantry, at Luxemburg; afterwards Professor of Languages at the Midway Female Academy in Virginia, USA., whence he disappeared in the year 1852.
WALKER, Mrs DAVID, formerly of Brechin, Scotland, residing in 1867 at No. 284, Grand Street, NY City.
WALKER, WILLIAM, a Butcher, who left Edinburgh, Scotland, in 1833, for Toronto, Canada.
WALLS, HUGH, a native of Canada West, now residing in the United States.
WALSH, MICHAEL, formerly of Attyflinn, County Limerick, Ireland, now residing in America.
WARD, WILLIAM, residing at 130, Cherry Street, New York City, USA.
WEBB, Miss CLARISSA JULIA, born about 1827, now residing in America.
WEBBER, KATE, formerly of Northumberland Co, Pa., USA.
WELLS, Mrs AFFRA, residing at St. Joseph, Michigan, USA.
WEST, WILLIAM, formerly of Sheffield, Co Lennox, Ont, Canada.
WETHERELL, ANN ELIZA. (See Ann Eliza Murray)
WHITE, PATRICK, son of JOHN, born in 1830, in Dundalk, Co. Louth, Ireland, last heard of at Newark, NJ.
WHITSITT, RICHARD, formerly of Dublin, Ireland, now residing in America
WILBROUGH, JOHN (alias JOHN BRADLEY), left England for America about 1834, and resided at Greensboro', Ala., USA., same year, then went to Demopolis, and next to Mobile, where he was employed in the building of the Cathedral He left Mobile, Ala., in 1852, for California.
WILKES, Miss MARY, residing in New York City, in 1876
WILSON FAMILY, formerly of Yorkshire, England, now residing in America
WILSON, WILLIAM, of Co Fife, afterwards of Edinburgh, Stocking Maker, left Scotland for America about 1849 His daughter, Margaret, married a Shoemaker, and went to reside in New York.
WISEMAN, ROBERT and DORA, of Co Cork, Ireland In 1860 resided in Piermont, Rockland Co., NY, USA.
WOODS, GEORGE, last heard of in Philadelphia, Pa., USA.
WOOLLCROFT, ANN (See Adam Moore.)
WRIGHT, JOSEPH, in 1857 Captain of a vessel trading between the West Indies and New York.
WRIGHT, THOMAS BLOXSOM, formerly of England, now residing in America.
YOUELL, FAMILY of, formerly of England now residing in America.
YOUNG, SARAH, supposed to be the sister or daughter of William or John Young, who in 1861 were in the Marble business in Second Avenue, and later in Houston Street, New York City, USA.
YOUNGER, ALEXANDER, recently residing in London, Ont., Canada.

SPECIAL LIST No. 8.

UNCLAIMED MONEY, LANDS AND ESTATES.

The following persons, if living, or if dead, their representatives, are entitled to property All letters must be addressed to **J. B. MARTINDALE, 142 LaSalle Street, Chicago, Illinois.** The writer must give all facts on which his claim is based. [See pages 6, 7 and 8 of this Manual]

ABBOTT, MARY, last heard of at Danbury, Conn., U S A.
ADAM, CHARLES, a native of Scotland, now residing in America
ADAMS, EMMA, formerly of St Thomas, Ont., Canada, residing in New York City in 1852.
ADAMS, JAMES, Iron Moulder, a native of England, now residing in America
ADAMS, THOMAS and ROBERT, late of 34, South Park Street, Toronto, Canada.
AHLERS, ERNST, a native of Domitz, in Germany, now residing in America.
ALEORN, JAMES FRANTZ, now or recently residing in the U S A.
ALLINGHAM, ANN, left Dublin, Ireland, for America in 1854, and was last heard of at New Orleans, La.
AMERICAN FRIENDS' SOCIETY, *Legacy for*
ANDERSON, GEORGE, ALEXANDER, and MARGARET, afterwards STUART, brothers and sister, now residing in America.
ANTRAM, CHARLES WILLIAM WOODROW, residing in New York City, U S A., in 1872
ARMSTRONG, Mrs JANE, Widow, last heard of in California, U S A.
ARNIES, SHELSY L, now residing in America.
ATKINSON, GEORGE, was in Canada in 1788, afterwards married and settled in East Maine, U S A.
BAILEY, ASHER or ASHAL who left England for the U S A some years ago
BAILEY, LEWIN, late of Watford, Hertfordshire, England, now residing in America
BALLANCE, ISAAC, who left England for America in 1871.
BANNAN, Mrs. ELIZA, now or formerly residing in Toronto, Canada.
BARKE, ARTHUR, emigrated to the U S A, and last heard of in 1809
BARNES, Mrs. MARY, formerly of Kingston, Ont., last heard of in Toronto, Canada, in 1875.
BARNES, WALTER G, last heard of in the U S A, in June, 1879
BARNUM, JAMES K, last heard of in Steward Co, Ga, U S A.
BARNUM, NOAH K, and CYNTHIA, last heard of in Brooklyn, N Y, U S A.
BARTON, CASPER W, residing in Albany, or Troy N Y, U S A., in 1842
BAVIN, JOHN, formerly of Co. Cambridge, England, residing in New York City U S A., in 1876.
BAXTER, THOMAS, late of Lincolnshire, Farmer, who left England for America about 1852.
BEACH, HENRY in 1859 residing in the State of Michigan, U S A.
BEARD, or PEARD, Mrs. H (Maiden name, McDONALD), now residing in Canada.
BEEBEE, or BEEBE, LUTHER, residing in the State of Michigan, U S A, in 1842
BENTON, SIMON ENOCH, and his sister, ELIZABETH HANNAH, wife of PETER MARTIN, in America
BERRY, OSWALD PHILIP, left England for America in 1859, last heard of at Helena, Montana, U S A.
BEZINE, WILLIAM S., now or recently residing at Amsterdam, N Y, U.S.A.
BINGHAM, DELIA ANN. Maiden name, EARL), residing in America.
BLAIR, AGNES (Maiden name, McKENNELL); formerly of Scotland, now residing in America.
BOCKELMAN, LOUISA P, a native of Co. Limerick, Ireland, now residing in America.
BOLD, JOHN, formerly of Lancashire, who left England for America about 1856.
BOLEN, ANN (See John and Ann McCauley, or McCulla.)
BOON, GEORGE, who, in 1849, resided in Ontario, Canada.
BOURNE, or BYRNE, MARY, who, in 1835, married —— Kaye, in New York, U S A.
BOUVERAT, CLAIRE CELESTINE LOUISE, now or late of Fort Wayne, Inds., U S A.
BRAHAM, JOSEPHINE (See Josephine Wilson.)
BREMAR, FRANCIS, who died at Charleston, S C, U S A., in 1808
BRENNAN, JOHN, THOMAS, or NICHOLAS, brothers, left Co. Kildare, Ireland for America, about 1830.
BRIDGEMAN, HENRY ST JOHN, and FRANCES, his wife (Maiden name, DEWAR), now in America.
BRITTAIN, SARAH formerly HAWKER, now or late of Peshtigo, Oconto Co., Wis, U S A.
BROWN, DAVID (See David Brown Huggins.)
BULLINGER, ANN (See John and Ann McCauley, or McCulla)
BURDICK, SARAH, a native of England, supposed to be residing in America
BURGIS, ROBERT GREGORY, last heard of as a Captain on a voyage from America to Australia
BURKE, ANDREW, last heard of in Washington, D C., U S A.
BURR, Mrs JANE (formerly Mrs JOHN STOREY), now or recently of West Hartford, Conn, U S A.
BURRELL, FRANCES J, residing in New York City about the year 1889
BUTCHER, PHILIP, formerly of Co Essex, England, now residing in America.
BUTCHER, WILLIAM, of Norfolk, England, now residing in Canada.
BUTLER, Mrs ELIZABETH (Maiden name, WALL), now or late of 593, Ash Av, San Francisco, Cal, U S A.
BUTLER, KATE (See Kate Donnelly)
BYRNE, JAMES, formerly of County Cork, left Ireland for America about 1854, and served in the Southern Army during the late War
BYRNE, MARY (See Mary Bourne)
CADLEY ROSE ABIGAL and MARY ANN, sisters, who left England for America about 1850
CALLAHAN PATRICK, formerly of Lynn, Mass, U S A
CAMP, THOMAS HENRY, who left England for America about the year 1851
CAMPBELL, HUGH JOHN, now or late of New York U S A
CAMPBELL, JOHN, Joiner, left Scotland for Montreal, Canada, in 1869, then went to Lorimore, Minn., last heard of in Iowa, U S A.
CAMPBELL, PATRICK, who resided in Schoharie Co., N Y, in 1870, afterwards of Ashland, Mass, U S A.
CAMPBELL, ROBERT JAMES CAULFIELD, late of Charlotteville, Va, U S A. *Creditors wanted*
CAMPBELL, THOMAS, formerly of Yorkshire, Eng, afterwards of Yellows Spring College, Iowa, U.S.A.
CARLISLE, Mrs., who lived at 146, East 27th Street, N Y City, in the winter of 1877-78.
CARPENTER, JOHN MORGAN, who left South Wales in 1868, now residing in America.
CARR FAMILY, formerly of Ireland, now residing in America
CARSON, Miss ELIZA MARIA, otherwise ELLIOTT, of Charleston, S.C., U S A, in 1836
CARTER, TIFFIN, or TURTON, ELIZABETH, who left England for America about 1830.
CASE, SARAH, last heard of at Bridgeport, Conn., U S A.
CASSIOY, HUGH, who left Co. Donegal, Ireland, for New York, U S A., about 1850.
CEBALLOS, Dr DOMINGO, residing in New York City in 1870
CHAMBERS, Dr E M, who was in Oak Harbor, Ohio, U S A, in 1874 or 1875
CHAMBERS, GEORGE, Liquor Dealer, formerly of New York, U S A *Creditors wanted.*
CHAMBERS THOMAS W, formerly residing in Barnwell Co, So Ca., U S A
CHEVERS, THOMAS BERTRAND, supposed to be residing in America

SPECIAL LIST No. 8.

CHIPMAN, Dr J H H, now or late of Bridgetown, Annapolis, Nova Scotia, Canada.
CLARK, Mrs, late of Dollor, on the third concession of Markham, Ontario, Canada.
CLARKE TERENCE, ALBERT, in 1871 residing at Clarke's Row, Fifth Avenue, Pittsburgh, Pa, U S A.
CLEMENTS, WILLIAM, formerly of Co Essex, who left England for America in or about the year 183?
CLOUSTON, EDWARD, of Hudson Bay, in 1788.
COEN, Miss WINIFRED. (See Mrs Glynn.)
COLE, THOMAS GOODING, a native of Ipswich, England, who went to N J, or N Y, U S A., in 1823
COLLINGS, RICHARD, formerly of Co Somerset, England, now residing in America.
COLLINS, MELISSA JANE (Maiden name, LEVI), when last heard of was residing in Brooklyn, N Y, U S A.
COLLINS, OWEN, THOMAS, and RICHARD, who left Co Mayo, Ireland, for Boston, Mass, U S A., in 1857.
COMYNS, MARGARET, a native of Ireland, now residing in America.
CONKLIN, JAMES, left N Y about 1854 on a Whaling voyage, from New London, or New Bedford. U S A
CONWAY, DAVID, a native of Co. Limerick, Ireland, in July, 1870, residing at Riverside, Chaffe Co., Colo, U S A.
COOK, JUSTIN E, formerly Recorder at Hot Creek, Nev, U S A   *Brother of, wanted*
COOPER, SARAH, MARY, and MARIA, sisters, supposed to reside in Canada.
CORBISHLEY, HENRY, a native of England, last heard of in New York City, U S A.
CORNWELL, MARY ANN L F (See Mary L Lee)
COSMAN, THOMAS, of Co Cork, Ireland, now residing in America.
COTTLE, Miss (See Robert Law)
COULSON, JOHN, and MARY, his wife, residing in Toronto, or elsewhere in Canada, about 1844.
COWAN, EDWIN R, formerly of Brookline, Mass, U S A.
COWIE, Mrs. M F, formerly of West 21st Street, New York City, U S A.
CRANE, STEPHEN, who entered land in Minnesota U.S.A., in 1858
CRAWFORD, HANNAH, now or lately residing in Ontario, Canada.
CREAN, DANIEL (See Daniel Curran)
CROESE, EDUARD FELIX GERARD, a native of Holland, now residing in America.
CULLINY, or MORRISON, Mrs ANNE, formerly of Co Clare, Ireland; now residing in America.
CUMMINGS, FRANKLIN, residing in New York, U S A., in 1842.
CUMMINGS, THOMAS F, who left Co Carlow, Ireland, for America, 1845 to 1850.
CURRAN, DANIEL, was living in Jekalet, Fort Gamble, California, U S A., in 1863.
CURTIS, GEORGE, last heard of at Walsingham Centre, Pleasant Hill Post, Co Norfolk, Ont, Canada.
DALTON, PATRICK, and his sister ELIZABETH, of Co Kilkenny, Ireland, last heard of in St Louis, U S A.
DALY, MARY, formerly MARY KEENAN, residing in America
DAVIS, ABAGAIL F, and her daughter, MARTHA L DAVIS, of New York, or Brooklyn, U S A , in 1867
DAVIS, Mrs EMMA (Maiden name, DRAPER); left England for America in 1852, and resided at Dr Robinson's, Bidford, near Cleveland, Ohio, U S A
DAVIS, PHILIP JOHN, and BENJAMIN LEE DAVIS, brothers, left England for America in 1871 and 1874.
DAWSON, ROBERT, of Scotland, went to America about 1855, afterwards heard of in Pa and Ohio
DAWSON, ROBERT, who left Scotland about 185o, and afterwards resided in Pennsylvania and Ohio, U S A.
DEAL, WILLIAM and FREDERICK, now residing in Canada.
DEAN, JOHN NEWBERRY, of Leicestershire, who left England for America in 1888.
DEDEKAM, CARSTEN, how residing in America.
DERUCHE, JAMES, last heard of in Thomaston, Conn, U S A.
DEWAR, Mrs. FRANCES. (See Henry St John Bridgeman)
DEWAR, Mrs. MARGARET   (See Hugh Dickson)
DICKSON, HUGH, and MARGARET, his wife (Maiden name, DEWAR), of Standon, Que, Canada.
DILLON, MICHAEL, who served as Engineer in the U S Navy, 1883-4
DOLAN, JOHN, Stonemason, of England, who went to N Y, U S A, and was last heard of there about 1866.
DONAHUE, JOHN, of New York, or Pennsylvania, U S A, in 1854, and was employed about Railways
DONNELLY, ARTHUR, residing in New York about the year 1858
DONNELLY, KATE, who left New York in 1865, and afterwards resided in Nevada City, Cal, U S A.
DONNELLY, MARY, supposed to be residing in either Brooklyn, or New York, U.S.A.
DONOVAN, MARGARET, now or lately residing in Ontario, Canada.
DOWDELL, FAMILY of, natives of Ireland, now residing in America.
DOWNING, DAVID and ROGER, formerly of Castletown, Berehaven, Ireland, now residing in America.
DRAKE, JEREMIAH J, residing in New York City, U S A, in 1815.
DRAPER, EMMA. (See Mrs. Emma Davis.)
DRAPER, RUFUS, now or formerly of New York, U S A.
DUNCAN, MARY, afterwards SYMINGTON, last heard of in Canada, in 1888.
DUNLOP, MARY JANE, supposed to reside in or near Toronto, Canada
DUNNE, THOMAS, formerly Lieutenant and Adjutant 55th Regiment, now residing in America.
DWYER, JOHN and MATTHEW, natives of Lattin, Co Tipperary   John left Ireland for America about 1865, and when last heard of was at St. Louis, U.S.A.   Matthew enlisted in the British Army, served in India, and now residing in America
DWYER, JOHN and MICHAEL, of Co. Tipperary, Ireland; last heard of in Brockville, Ont., Canada
EARL, CHARLES, formerly of Brooklyn, U S A., and his sister, DELIA ANN EARL, afterwards BINGHAM.
ELSWORTH, RICHARD NATHANIEL, formerly of London, Eng, last heard of in Salt Lake City, U S.A.
EDEN, WALTER REUBEN, a native of Co. Sussex, England, supposed to be in America.
EDWARDS, JOHN, by trade a Wire-drawer, formerly of Co. Monmouth, England, now residing in America.
EGAN, EDMOND, formerly of Co Clare, Ireland, now residing in America.
EISENBERG, FAMILY of, residing in America
ELKINTON, SUSANNAH, formerly of Co Lincoln, Eng, now residing in America.
ELLIOTT, ELIZA MARIA   (See Miss Eliza Maria Carson)
ELMES, THOMAS   (See Galbreath and Elmes)
ELSOM, GEORGE FREDERICK, residing in New York, U.S.A, or Montreal, Canada, in 1870.
ENNOS, CHARLES JAMES, who left England in 1850.
EVANS, JAMES, ELIZABETH, and ANNE, brother and sisters, formerly of Wales, now residing in America
EVANTURELLE, FRANCOIS, of Quebec, Canada, in 1841
FARRELL, GASPAR   M EMILY, late of Dublin, Ireland, now residing in America.
FAVELL, or FAVIELL, WILLIAM, who left England for America in 1860, and afterwards resided at Clarksburg Mich ; Toledo, Ohio, Rome, N Y, U S A.   Moncton, N B , Lake Superior, Toronto, and Montreal
FENDT, HEINRICH and RUDOLPH, natives of Bavaria, now residing in America.
FENNER, AUGUSTA GOODWIN, who left England for America about 1850
FINLEY, ARCHER THOMAS, of Alexandria, Va., Norfolk, Va., Buffalo, N Y, and elsewhere in America.
FITZPATRICK, PATRICK B, who in 1870 resided at White Pine, Nevada, U S A.
FONTANNES, Mrs. JULES, now residing in America
FOOT, FAMILY of, residing in America
FOOTE, JOHN, Grocer, at 264, Front Street, New York City, U S A, from 1841 to 1849
FORREST, FRANCIS, a Shoemaker, and ELLEN, his wife, who lived in Troy, N.Y., U.S.A, about 1840.
FORSYTH, WILLIAM, of Halifax, N S , Canada, Merchant, in 1792
FORT, JAMES GILL, formerly of London, England, now residing in America.
FOSTER, GEORGE PEARCE, now or late of Ellenville, U S A
FOSTER, MARY, formerly of Co Lincoln, Eng, Heirs of, now residing in America.
FOWLER, ABBOTT, EPHRAIM, and MARTHA, residing in America.
FRY, ALEXANDER, supposed to be residing in Ontario, Canada
FULLEN, HENRY A., formerly Justice of Westchester Co., U S A.
GABOURIE, FAMILY of, residing in Ontario, Canada.
GAIR, JOHN, Brass Worker, now residing in America
GALBREATH, DAVID (See Galbreath and Elmes)
GALBREATH and ELMES, in business at 234, Pearl Street, New York City, U S A., in or about the year 1809.
GAMARRA, JOSE MIO, when last heard of was residing in Chicago, Ills., U S A.

GARCIA, WILLIAM R., residing in New York, U S A., in 1837.
GARDINER, M., formerly of the Rhode Island Braiding Machine Co., Providence, R I., U S A.
GARRICK, PERCIVAL EGERTON, in 1859 residing in Scott Township, Inda., U S A.
GERMAN, JOHN H., who left Leavenworth, Kansas, U.S.A., in 1877, for Salt Lake City.
GESERICK, H., who formerly lived at 115, Ludlow Street, New York City, U.S.A.
GIANNI, JOSEPH, formerly of Newcastle-on-Tyne, England, now residing in America.
GIBBONS, THOMAS, Builder, residing in New York, U S A., in 1865.
GILBERT, THOMAS, who left England for New York, U S A., about the year 1860.
GILES, FAMILY of, formerly of England, now residing in America.
GIRIG, FRANCIS, a native of France, last heard of in Iowa, U S A., in October, 1879
GLOVER, THOMAS and WILLIAM, formerly of Co Leicester, Eng. now residing in America.
GLYNN, Mrs. WINIFRED, (Maiden name, COEN), formerly of Co Galway, Ireland, now residing in America,
GOLDSCHMIDT, SOLOMON, and JOSEPH, his brother, both residing in America.
GOODALL, ANN (See Ann Allingham.)
GOODFELLOW, JAMES HENRY, emigrated to America, last heard of from Quebec, Canada, in 1854.
GOOLD, SARAH. (See Sarah Staites.)
GRAHAM, JOHN, of Perthshire, who left Scotland for the U S A. about 1838.
GRANT, WILLIAM PETER. Relatives of, residing in America.
GRANGER, PRESTON, residing in America.
GREAVES, EDWARD, who left Manchester, England, in 1808, now supposed to be in America.
GEELENN, or HAGAN, BRIDGET, a native of Ireland, residing in Albany, N Y, U S A, in 1865
GRIEGSON, MARY ANN, late of Manchester, or Bolton, Lancashire, Eng., afterwards residing in America.
GRIFFIN, ORAMEL, residing, in 1837, in Albany Co, N Y, U.S.A.
GROVE, SARAH, who left Stourbridge, Worcestershire, England, for America about 1840.
GROZART, or TAYLOR, JANET, a native of Scotland, who went to America in or about 1830
GUYOT, BARTOLOME, who left France for America, many years ago
HACKETT, Mrs MARY, who formerly lived at the British Legation, Washington, D.C., U S A.
HAGAN, BRIDGET. (See Bridget Geelenn.)
HAMBURGER, WILHELM, formerly of Frankfort on the Maine, Germany, now residing in America.
HAMILTON, JAMES, now or lately residing in Wallaceburg, Ont., Canada.
HAMILTON, JOHN JAMES, who left Hamilton, Ont., Canada, for the U S A. in 1873.
HANSDOTTER, BENGLA, wife of the Carpenter HOLMSTROM. Relations of, in America.
HANSON, AMOS, formerly of Maine, U.S.A.
HARPER, JOHN C., formerly of England, now residing in America.
HARPER, MARY, formerly of Selkirk, Scotland, at present residing in America.
HARRIS, JAMES M., who served as Engineer in the U S Navy, 1863 4
HART, JAMES, residing in New York, U S A., in 1841
HASSELMANN, LOUIS, a native of Prussia, residing in America in 1850.
HAWKER, SARAH (See Sarah Brittain.)
HAYS, Mr, now or recently residing in Harlem, N Y, U.S.A.
HAZZARD, NANCY and ROBERT, who were sold as Slaves in Virginia many years ago
HEALY, HYLARO, formerly of Johnstown, Ireland, who went to Cannda many years ago.
HEDGE, or HEDGES, THOMAS, of Birmingham, England, last heard of in 1866, from Newark, N.J., U S A.
HENCHEY, JOHN WILLIAM, residing in America.
HERBERT, THOMAS, formerly of Co Clare, Ireland, now residing in America
HEWITT, PHILIP, formerly of Gosfield, Co Essex, Ont., Canada, Blacksmith, and afterwards of Toronto.
HILBERG, MARIA JOSEPHINA, a native of Amsterdam, Holland, who went to Philadelphia, U S A., in 1854.
HILL, JOSIAH, of Georgia, U S A., who formerly travelled with a gentleman n Europe
HILL, SAMUEL, residing in 1837 in Orleans Co, N Y, U S A
HOGAN, RICHARD J, Sail maker, late residence, 249, Johnson Avenue, Brooklyn, N Y, U S A.
HOGG, ALEXANDER, now or late of Baltimore, U S A.
HOLBROOK, GRIFFIN, now or lately residing in America.
HOLEHAN, JAMES, formerly of Co Kilkenny, Ireland, now residing in America.
HOLMES, JAMES, Tailor, left London, Eng, for Boston, in 1780, afterwards of Richfield, N Y, U S A.
HOLMSTROM, BENGLA. (See Bengla Hansdotter.)
HORTON, ARTHUR TROBRIDGE, in November, 1878, Watchman at Pier 22, N Y City, U.S.A.
HOUGH, JOHN, formerly of Liverpool, England, now residing in America.
HOWARD, Mrs. JANE (Maiden name, McLAUGHLIN), late of Washington, D.C., U S A.
HUBENER, CARL RITTER VON, a native of Bohemia now residing in America.
HUFF, JOHN, who served as Engineer in the U S Navy, 1863 4
HUGGINS, DAVID BROWN (otherwise DAVID BROWN), of Warwickshire, Eng, now residing in U S A
HUGHES, MARY, formerly MARY UPTON, of Camberwell, Co. Surrey, Eng., in 1854 *Children of, in America.*
HUNT, CYRUS and LINCOLN, residing in New York, or elsewhere in America.
HUNT, JOHN FARR, a Sailor, a native of England, last heard of in 1868
HYDE, JOHN, formerly of England, residing at Oyster Bay, or Cold Spring, L I, N Y, U S A., about 1874
INSTITUTION FOR CHILDREN OF DECEASED OR DISABLED U.S. SOLDIERS, *Legacy for*
JAMESON FAMILY, formerly of Liverpool, England, now residing in America.
JANSEN, EDWARD, formerly of Hamburgh, Germany, now residing in America.
JOHNSON, ANTHONY, who left England for the U S A about 1847, EDWARD JOHNSON, for Canada in 1844 HENRY JOHNSON, for the U S A in 1854, JAMES JOHNSON, for Canada in 1839; and WILLIAM JOHNSON, for the U.S.A. in 1849
JOHNSON, or WARREN, MARIA, residing in Canada in 1830
JOHNSTONE, ROBERT, who left Ireland for America about 1778.
KAHN, JULIUS, now or lately Clerk in a Fur Store, New York City, U.S.A.
KAYE, MARY (See Mary Bourne.)
KEARNS, JOHN STEELE, Druggist, in 1848, of No. 1, Mott St, then 8th Av and 34th St, N Y City, U S A.
KEATINGE, Mrs JULIA, (Maiden name, WALL), now or late of 38th St, and 6th Av, Brooklyn N Y, U S A.
KEENAN, MARY (See Mary Daly.)
KELLY, Mr P O'CONNOR, formerly of Co Roscommon, who left Ireland for America about 1860.
KELSO, FAMILY of, residing in America.
KENNEDY, JAMES, left Scotland for Canada, 1873, supposed to have gone to Michigan, U S A, about 1876.
KENNY, JOHN, a native of Ireland, now residing in America
KERR, JAMES, formerly with Arnold, Constable, and Co., New York City, U S A
KING, SARAH ELIZABETH and GEORGE FREDERICK, who left England for New York, U.S.A, in 1848.
KNAPP, FAMILY of, residing in America
KNIGHTS, JOHN, formerly of Bungay, Co Suffolk, who left England in 1829 for parts abroad
KOEHNEN, BARBARA, formerly of Dayton, Ohio, U S A.
KRAUSEN, MARIA JOSEPHINA (See Hilberg.)
KRUEGER, THEODORE AUGUSTUS, a native of Hanover, Prussia, now residing in America
LAMOND, PATRICK, who left Aberdeen, Scotland, for America about 1830
LAMONT, NORMAN, of R E. Department, Montreal, Canada, in 1849, and in 1853 of the 5th Infy, U S A.
LARGY, JAMES, when last heard of, was residing in New York City, U.S.A
LARKIN, WILLIAM HENRY, now residing in America.
LARROW, ARCHILLES L., in 1837 residing in the State of Michigan, U S A
LAW, ROBERT (who married Miss Cottle), formerly of Dublin, Ireland, now residing in America.
LEACH, DAVID, a native of England, last heard of in Jersey City, N J, U S A
LEE, MARY, formerly of London, England, afterwards residing in New York U S A
LEE, MARY L, formerly of New York City, afterwards of San Francisco, Cal, U S A.
LEFEVRE, or MARTIN, EUGENIE, last heard of in Cincinnati, Ohio, U S A
LEGETTE, Mrs E——— C., now or late of Franklin Co., Miss, U S A.
LEGO, or LETTIGO, WILLIAM MARK and JANE, now residing in America.

SPECIAL LIST No 8

LEONARD, WILLIAM, Printer, residing in Ontario, Canada.
LEVI, MELISSA JANE (See Melissa Jane Collins)
LESHLEY, or LASHLEY, FAMILY, formerly of England, now residing in America.
LESUER, E. C., formerly of Broadway, near 29th Street, New York City, U S A.
LETTIGO, WILLIAM MARK and JANE (See Lego)
LEVEQUE, or LEVIQUE, ISRAEL MYRLETTO, formerly of Hull, Yorkshire, England, afterwards of New York City, U.S.A., and last heard of in Toronto, Canada, in 1876
LINDER, FRANZ, a native of Würzburg, Germany, now residing in America.
LITTLE FAMILY, formerly of Co Dumfries, Scotland, now residing in America.
LITTLE, JOSEPH, when last heard of, he was a Seaman on board the ship "Morning Light."
LITTELL, SARAH, now or late of Delaware, Ohio, U S A
LOEWENFELD, VICTOR, from Prague, Bohemia, now residing in America.
LOGHLEN, JOHN O, who was in 1856 Amanuensis for the late General Walbridge.
LOWE, SAMUEL, now or lately residing at Cleveland, U S A
LUBY, Mrs. KATE, last heard of at York Avenue, New Brighton, Staten Island, N.Y., U S A, in 1872.
LUCEY, JOHANNA, residing in New Hampshire, or Massachusetts, U.S.A.
LUNDHOLM, Mrs ANNE (Maiden name, O'BRIEN), a native of Ireland, now residing in America.
LUPTON, RICHARD, a Butcher, formerly of Lancaster, Eng, now residing in America.
LYNSKA, PHILLIP, who left Youngstown, Ohio, in 1874, for Cheyenne, Wyo. Ter., U.S.A.
McARDLE, FAMILY of, residing in America.
McAULIFFE, HANORA. (See Hanora Mooney.)
McBRIDE, HUGH, son of Daniel and Bridget, of Co Tyrone, Ireland, was in Albany, N Y, in 1845.
McCANN, LUCY, supposed to be residing in Ontario Canada
McCAULEY, ANN, who left Philadelphia, Pa., for Ohio, U S A, about 1854, and is reported to have married a German, named Bolen, or Bullinger
McCAULEY, JOHN, formerly of Co Tyrone, Ireland, who left Philadelphia for Ohio, about the year 1840.
McCORMIC, Mrs. M——V, of Franklin Co., Miss., U.S.A.
McCORMICK, JAMES STEELE, now or late of Nevada Co, America.
McCOY and HERWIG, formerly Produce Dealers, of New York, U S A.
McCULLA, ANN and JOHN. (See Ann and John McCauley)
McDONALD, Miss MARY. (See Mrs. H Beard or Peard)
McDOUGAL, Lady, of England Representatives in America.
McDOUGAL, MARY ANN, now or late of Boston, Mass, U S A.
McEACHRAN, ARCHIBALD, killed in the U S Civil War, *Widow of, wanted*
McEACHRAN, JESSIE, COLLIN, and ARCHIBALD, residing at Buffalo, N Y, in 1834.
McECHRAN, COLIN, last heard of from California, U S A, about 1870
McENTYRE, ANN, a native of Co Louth, Ireland, afterwards residing in America.
McGARY, ROBERT or JAMES, who lived, in 1847, at No 96, Maiden Lane, New York, U.S.A.
McGOWN, KATE, who formerly lived with Mrs Morse, West 22nd Street, New York City, U.S.A.
McINTIRE, WILLIAM, Carpenter, residing in New York City about 1850
McKENNELL, AGNES and JANET, natives of Scotland, now residing in America.
McKENZIE, ELIZABETH, in 1879 residing in Stamford Township, Ont, Canada.
McKEY FAMILY, formerly of Co Down, Ireland, now residing in America
McLAUGHLAN, JEAN and MARY, sisters, residing in America.
McLAUGHLIN, MICHAEL, formerly of Mayo, Ireland, afterwards residing in Canada.
McLENNAN, BELLA and JESSIE, who left Scotland in 1832 for Cape Breton, America
McMAHON, LOUIS EDWARD, now or late of Toronto, Canada.
McMILLAN, JOHN and JAMES, natives of Wigtooshire, Scotland, now residing in America
McNAB, or McNAL, CHARLES EDWARD, in 1873 Chief Officer of the "Eureka," of New York, U S A.
McNAMARA, PATRICK, of Cork, Ireland, in 1833, afterwards went to America.
McNEAL, ISAAC, Children of, residing in America.
MACUEN, CHARLES, who left Renfewshire, Scotland, for America about 1840.
MAIRIN, FERNAND, formerly of Angers, France, now residing in America
MANSER, DANIEL, when last heard of, was residing in Baker Co, Oregon, U.S.A.
MARQUIS, HUGH and ERNEST, now residing in America.
MARSH, ROBERT, formerly of Yorkshire, Eng, last heard of at Sacramento, Cal, U S A.
MARSH, WILLIAM formerly of Yorkshire, Eng, last heard of at Keysville, Kero River, Tulare Co, Cal, U S.A.
MARSZALE, FREDERICK BEAULERC, a native of England, now residing in Canada.
MARTIN, ANTOINE, when last heard of was residing in Cincinnati, Ohio, U S A.
MARTIN, CHARLES STEPHEN, from 1851 to 1861 in the "Black Cross" Line of American Clipper Ships
MARTIN, ELIZABETH HANNAH (See Simon Enoch Benton)
MARTIN, Mrs JOHN, widow, who resided in New York, U S A, in 1876
MARTIN, MICHAEL, a native of Co Mayo, Ireland, when last heard of, in 1858, was working on the Balt. and Ohio R R, at Mount Savage, or Wheeling, Va., U S A.
MATHESON, CAMPBELL, formerly of London, England, now residing in America
MAUGHAN, FAMILY of, now or lately residing at No 74, Wellington Place, Toronto, Canada.
MEGRAU, BERNARD, of Co Down, left Ireland for New York many years ago
MERRIAM, WILLIAM C, in 1867 residing in the U S A.
MEURS, ANTONIE or TONY, who left Holland for America in 1848
MEYER, FRIEDRICH LOUIS, a native of Saxony, who went to America in 1848.
MILLER, CAPTAIN THOMAS, of New England in 1723
MILLETT, MICHAEL, who left Afton, Iowa, in 1878, for Ottumwa, afterwards of St Louis, Mo, U S A.
MINAHAN, ANNE, who left Ireland for New York, U.S.A., about 1848, with her Mother, Margaret Driscol.
MOCKLAR, JOHN, who left Boston, Mass, U.S.A., in 1878, and when last heard of was in Nevada
MONAHAN, Mrs, formerly of Co. Mayo, Ireland, or Children, supposed to be residing in America.
MONNET, CHARLES, a native of Switzerland, last heard of at Detroit, Mich, U.S.A.
MOONEY, HANORA (Maiden name, McAULIFFE), of Co Cork, who left Ireland for America in 1852.
MORAN, JOHN C, formerly of Co Wicklow, Ireland, last heard of in America in 1878
MORGENSTERN, GUS, born about 1850, when last heard of, was residing in Greenville, Miss., U S A.
MORIN, or MOIRIN, FERNAND, formerly of Angers, France, last heard of in America, about 1876.
MORRIN, ELIZABETH and MARY ANN, residing in Ontario, Canada
MORRIS, Mrs JOHN or JANE, formerly of St Asaph, Wales, who left England for America about 1876.
MORRISON, ANNE. (See Mrs Anne Cullity)
MORRISSY, MICHAEL, formerly of Co Waterford, Ireland, now residing in America.
MOSLEY, ——, when last heard of he was a Seaman on board the ship "Morning Light."
MOYER, ELIZABETH, who resided at Preston, Ontario, Canada, about 1870.
MULLIGAN, MARY, formerly of County Monaghan, left Ireland for America in 1862.
MULVIHILL, PATRICK, son of Thomas, of Co Kerry, Ireland, last heard of in America about 1858.
MULLIN, MICHAEL, who left Baldensville, N Y, about 1870, supposed for Memphis, Tenn., U.S.A.
MULROONEY, SARAH, SIMON, and THOMAS, residing in Ontario, Canada, or Wisconsin, U S A.
MURDOCH, EDWARD, now or lately with Dun, Barlow, and Co, America.
MURE, Mr C. S., now or formerly of 83, Water Street, New York City, U S A
MURGATROYD, JOHN, formerly of Manchester, or Bolton, Lancashire, Eng, afterwards of America.
MURNAN, JAMES, of Ireland, left Fayette Co., Pa., about 1864, was last heard from at St Paul, Minn., U.S.A.
MURPHY, JOHN, Blacksmith, last heard of in Poughkeepsie, N Y, U.S.A.
MUSGRAVE, FAMILY of, residing in America.
NEIL, or O'NEIL, CHARLES, coloured, a Seaman, formerly of Nova Scotia; was in Newfoundland in 1876.
NURSE, HENRY, a native of England, last heard of in New York in 1867
O'BRIEN, ANNE (See Mrs Anne Lundholm)
O'BRIEN, TIMOTHY, CORNELIUS, and BRIEN, brothers, residing in America
O'BRIEN, WILLIAM, of Co. Cork, left Ireland for America in 1862, and was in 1879 in Mono Co, Cal, U S.A.

O'CONNER, HANNAH, formerly of Co. Kerry, Ireland; last heard of in New York City, U S A., in 1875
O'CONNER, PATRICK, now or late of the U S Army
ODDY, THOMAS, a native of England, residing in America in 188?.
O'DONNELL, EMILY, JAMES, JOHN, MICHAEL, and PATRICK, residing in America
O DONOHUE, THERESE, now or lately residing in Ontario, Canada.
OELERICH, JOHANN CHRISTIAN, of Mecklenburg Schwerin, was residing in New York City in 1843
OLIVER, JAMES FALKLAND, Mariner, serving as Carpenter's Mate in the U S Steamer "Saco," 1857—1858.
O'LOGHLEN, JOHN (See John O Loghlen)
O'MARA, MICHAEL (otherwise MICHAEL POWER), who left Ireland for Galveston, Texas, U.S.A., in 1870.
O'NEIL, CHARLES (See Charles Neil)
O'NEIL, JAMES H , formerly of Oswego, N.Y , served on board the "Winckoski,' U S. Navy, and was discharged at Portsmouth, N H , 8th February, 1868
O'NEILL, SARAH ANN, now or late of Ontario, Canada.
O'NEILL, THOMAS and MARGARET, formerly of Portarlingtop, Ireland , now residing in America.
O'NEILL, TIMOTHY, now or late of Lexington, Mass., U.S.A.
OSBORNE, EDWIN a native of Dublin, by trade a Carpenter , at one time an Hotel Keeper in N Y , U.S.A.
O'SHANAHAN, JOHN, now or formerly of Penotanguishene, Ont Canada.
PACK, STEPHEN OLIVE, formerly of Carbonear, Newfoundland, afterwards residing in the U S A.
PARKE, JOHN STOREY, formerly of Co Leitrim, Ireland, afterwards of Newbliss, Ont., Canada.
PATERSON, THOMAS V , residing in New York, or elsewhere in America.
PAUL, THOMAS HAIG, last heard of at Frostburgh, Maryland, U S.A.
PEARD, Mrs H. (See Mrs H Beard)
PEARSON, MARVIN B , in 1837 residing in Erie Co , N Y , U.S.A.
PEIGER, Monsieur Dz, an Engineer, now residing in America
PEIRCE, Miss JOSEPHINE, daughter of the late Mr Joseph H Peirce, now residing in America.
PENFOLD, JOHN CULLEN, late of the R H Artillery, England , last heard of in America in 1852
PERRIER, VICTOR, Hotel or Restaurant Waiter, residing in America
PERRIN, ALFRED, formerly of Co Surrey, who left England for America in 1855.
PETERKIN, JOHN, a native of Scotland, residing in Poughkeepsie, N Y , U S A. , in 1865
PETERSON, JOHN, a Seaman, last heard of on board an American Merchant Ship.
PFEIFFER, OTTAMAR, formerly of Albany, N Y , afterwards of 23rd St., near 10th Ave , N Y City, U.S.A.
PHELPS, Mrs ROZETTE HENRIQUES, now or late of Toronto, Canada
PHILLIPS, ALFRED, a Frenchman, in 1871 residing at 108, Waverley Place, New York City, U S A.
PHILLIPS, BRIDGET, now or lately residing in Ontario, Canada
PIERCE, Mrs N E , when last heard of was residing in Chicago, U S A.
PILE, HENRY THOMAS, of Big Stream, Yates Co , N Y , U S A
PINNIGER, LYDIA, formerly of Wiltshire, England , now residing in America.
PLACE, REUBEN, in 1837 residing in the State of Michigan, U S A
PORTER, JAMES, a Tailor, left Aberdeenshire, Scotland, for Canada, in 1852 , was at Guelph, Ont , in 1864.
PORTER, JAMES W , now or late of Faribault, Minn U S A.
POTTER, DANIEL, a native of England was residing in New York, U S A., in 1873.
POUZETTE, MARY, now or late of Ontario, Canada
POWELL, JOHN, was working as a Saddler in Newark and elsewhere in N Y State, U.S.A., in 1836.
POWER, MICHAEL (See Michael O'Mara)
POWER, WILLIAM, son of Michael, who emigrated from Ireland to America in 1859
POWER, WILLIAM, formerly of Co Waterford, Ireland, who left Bombay for Boston, U.S.A., in 1879.
PROCTER FAMILY, formerly of England, now residing in America.
PUTNAM, AMOS P , formerly of Salem, Mass , U S A
RAMBO, CHRISTIAN, who left Altona, Germany, for America in 1864.
RANNIE, SOPHIA, Spinster, of Halifax, N S., Canada, in 179?
REARDON, JAMES, in 1849 at Mount Holly. Vermont, and afterwards resided in the State of Maine, U S.A.
REID, ROBERT NISH, supposed to be residing in Ontario, Canada.
REILLY, EDWARD, left Co. Meath, Ireland, about 1840, when last heard of, was near Milwaukee, Wis., U S A.
REILLY, EDWARD was in Co. B, 2nd Division. U S Infantry, in 1884, in 1869 at Greenville, Miss , U S A.
REILLY, MARGARET, who was residing, in 1863, at Gloucester, N J , U S A.
REYNOLDS, JAMES, who left Co Longford, Ireland, for America, about 1835, last heard of in Ontario, Canada.
RHODES, EMMA, formerly of Wakefield, England , last heard of at 150, Nassau Street, New York City, U S A
RICARD, Mr , formerly of Tottenham, Co Middlesex, Eng , now residing in America
RICE, ANDREW, who left Liverpool, England, for America in 1852
RICE, BERNARD, of Co Armagh, left Ireland for America in 1857, and resided in Albany, N Y , U S A.
RICHARDSON, JOHN PIRIE, formerly of Co Glamorgan, England, afterwards of San Francisco, Cal, U S A.
RIDGWAY, JAMES formerly of London, England, in 1851 Cook in the ship "Eudee "
RILEY, CORNELIUS, formerly of Herefordshire, Eng , now residing in America.
ROBERTS, Mrs BESSIE, who resided in Hamilton and Toronto, Canada, in 1857 8.
ROBERTS, GEORGE H , now residing in America.
ROBERTS, JANE. (See Mrs John or Jane Morris.)
ROBSON, EDWARD, now residing in the U S A , whose brother formerly lived in Uruguay, South America
ROBSON EDWARD, a native of Dumfries, Scotland, was a Draper's Assistant in New York about 1843, afterwards of Quebec and Moutreal, then of Montevideo , now residing in the U S A
ROCHFORT, PHILIP, of Melksham, England, last heard of in 1855, supposed to have gone to America.
RODRIGUEZ, JACINTO, formerly of Puerto Principe, Cuba , now residing in America.
ROGERS, HARRY, a native of England , was in Stockton, Cal , U S A , in 1854.
ROGERS, JOHN, formerly of Co Pembroke, Wales , afterwards emigrated to America.
ROGERS, WILLIAM, Stevedore , when last heard of was residing in America
ROONEY, BRIDGET, formerly of Co Roscommon, who left Ireland for America in 1808
ROSSI, GEORGIO (See Moriz Schönerer)
ROTTEN, BENJAMIN, formerly of Co Gloucester, Eng , last heard of in Philadelphia, Pa , U S.A., in 1797.
ROTTEN, BENJAMIN, left Woodchester about 1794, last heard of from Philadelphia, U S A
RUSSELL, FRANK and MARY, formerly of Co Cork, Ireland , Children of, residing in America.
RUSSELL, Miss MARION, formerly of Glasgow, Scotland , now residing in America
RYAN, MICHAEL, formerly of Galway, Ireland , residing in Minnesota, U.S.A. about 1858
ST LUKE'S HOME FOR INDIGENT FEMALE CHILDREN (in America), Legacy for
SAFE, JAMES, formerly of Texas, U S A. Creditors of wanted
SANDS, or SANDYS, JAMES, who left Liverpool, England, for New York, U S A , in 1872
SCHEURICH, ANN C , last heard of in New York City in 1837
SCHMIDT, CATHARINE DORATHEA, when last heard of, about 1865, was residing in Cleveland, Ohio, U S A
SCHÖNERER, MORIZ (alias Georgio Rossi), Mariner , and ADOLF SCHÖNERER, both natives of Austria.
SCHWARZ, EDWARD ROBERT, a native of Prussia, who emigrated to America in or about the year 1851.
SCOTT, ANNIE, formerly of Newry, who left Ireland for America about 1803.
SCOTT FAMILY, formerly of Co Dumfries, Scotland , now residing in America.
SCOTT, WILLIAM, formerly of Annan, Scotland , now residing in America.
SCUDAMORE FAMILY, formerly of England, now residing in America.
SEILER, CAROLINE, now residing in America.
SELBY, WILLIAM, a native of Norfolk, England , now residing in America.
SHAREMAN, JOHN, a native of England , last heard of in the U S A , in 1856.
SHARP, MARGARET, now or late of St. Louis, Mo , U S A
SHELTON, GEORGE, formerly of Buckinghamshire, Eng , now residing in America.
SHERIDAN, Miss HELEN, born about 1790—1800. Representatives of in America
SHIPMAN, RICHARD EGGLESTON, formerly of Yorkshire, Eng , now residing in America
SHUNK, JEREMIAH, and Family, killed by American Indians about the year 1836.
SILY, EDWARD, Albany Factory, Canada in 1878.

SPECIAL LIST No. 8.

SIM, JOHN, a Baker; was in Hamilton, Ont, Canada, in 1852, afterwards of Dakota, U S A, whence it is supposed he went to California.
SIMEON JOHN EDWARD, residing in New York City U S.A., in 1874.
SIMONDS, HENRY CARBOURN, formerly of Boston, Eng ; now residing in America.
SKINNER, TIMOTHY P , residing, in 1842, in Herkimer Co , N Y , U S A.
SKIPPER, JOHN, formerly of London, Eng , now residing in America.
SMITH, DANIEL D , Law Clerk, residing in New York City, U S A , in 1888.
SMITH, ROBERT, a Farmer, supposed to be living at St. Peter's Creek, Troy, or Empire, Kansas. U.S.A
SMITH, UZZIEL P , formerly of Chicago, Ills , afterwards of New York U S A.
SMITHWICK, GEORGE PERCEVAL, last heard of at 42, Front Street, Upper Wharf, Nashville, Tenn , U S A.
SNYDER, WILLIAM H , now residing in America.
SPAULDING, JOHN B., Merchant or Agent, residing in Brooklyn, N Y , U S.A., in 1888.
SPINK, EDWARD, a native of Yorkshire, who left England for America in 1857
SPRAGUE, ISAAC, in 1836 residing in Steuben Co , N Y , U S A
STAITES, SARAH (Maiden name, GOOLD), about 1880 residing at 4, High Street, Washington, U.S.A.
STANTON, EDWARD, who left Co Roscommon, Ireland, for America about 1840.
STEBBINS, MARY L. F (See Mary L Lee.)
STEIN, GEORGE, now or late of Texas, U S A
STEIN, JAMES, now or late of Peoria, or of McDonough Co., Ills.. U S A.
STERN, BERNHART, Merchant , residing in New York, U S.A., in 1869
STEVENS, Miss, the daughter of James H Stevens, late of Houston, Texas, U S A.
STEWART, ALEXANDER, formerly of Co Antrim, Ireland , Next of Kin in America.
STEWART, WILLIAM and ELIZABETH (or BESSIE), of Co Armagh, left Ireland for N Y some years since.
STILLMAN, FRANCES, now or late of Bridgeport, Conn , U S A
STILLWELL, Dr , supposed to reside in America
STONER, PHILIP, Relatives of, residing in America.
STOREY, Mrs JOHN (See Mrs Jane Burr)
STORM, FAMILY of, residing in America.
STUART, MARGARET (See Margaret Anderson.)
STURTEVANT, EMMA, now or late of Bridgeport, Conn.. U S A.
SULLIVAN, DENNIS, son of TIMOTHY, in 1855 living in Kentucky, and was afterwards in Hinsdale, N.Y , U S A.
SULLIVAN, GILES and WILLIAM, brothers, formerly of Co Kerry Ireland , now residing in America
SULLIVAN, RICHARD, left Arlington, for St Louis, Mo., about 1873, last heard of was in Chicago, Ills , U S.A.
SUNSHINE, Dr , living at 315, South Fifth Street, St. Louis, Mo. , U S A , in 1875
SYMINGTON, MARY (See Mary Duncan.)
TAPNER, ELIZABETH, who left England for Canada in or about the year 1854.
TARRANT, HENRY FREDERICK, who left England for San Francisco in 1855
TAYLOR, JANET (See Janet Grozart)
TAYLOR, JOSEPH, a native of England , now residing in America.
TAYLOR, WILLIAM Tailor, residing in Burlington, Ont , Canada, in July, 1879.
TEETER Reverend Mr , last heard of in Cannington, Ont , Canada
TREBBY, JOHN, in 1871 residing in Bradford Township, McKean Co , Pa , U S A.
THOMPSON, EDWARD, House Carpenter, formerly of Edinburgh, Scotland. His last address, in 1855, was Mr Harper, Stapleton, Staten Island , N Y , U S A.
TIFFIN, or TURTON, ELIZABETH. (See Elizabeth Carter)
TINKHAM, FRANK J , formerly of Boston, Mass, U S.A.
TOMKINS, JAMES N , residing in America
TOWER, G B N , in 1865, an Engineer in the U S s.s. "Canandaigua."
TREADWELL, Mis MARY, residing in New York in 1877.
TUNBRIDGE, JOHN, who left England about 1850, and was last heard of in Mexico.
TURNBULL FAMILY, formerly of Glasgow, Scotland , now residing in America
TURNER, WILLIAM, a native of Scotland, sailed from Glasgow, in the ship "Iona," in 1841.
TURTON, or TIFFIN, ELIZABETH (See Elizabeth Carter.)
TYTLER, WILLIAM, residing in the State of New York, U S A., in 1831.
UPTON, MARY (See Mary Hughes.)
VON HUBENER CARL RITTER (See Hubener, C R. von)
VOWLES, HENRY, a native of Somersetshire, England , now residing in America.
WALDING, FAMILY of formerly of Co. Northampton, England, now residing in America.
WALKER, AMOS and HENRY, brothers, formerly of England, now residing in America.
WALL, ELIZABETH (See Mrs Elizabeth Butler)
WALL, JULIA. (See Mrs Julia Keatingo)
WALLIS, SARAH ANNE Next of Kin of, residing in America
WALSH, PATRICK, of Connecticut, U S A , Carpenter , or his children
WALSH, PETER, of Dublin, Tanner, who left Ireland for the U S A about 1835
WALSH, RICHARD, formerly of Dublin, who left Ireland for America in or about the year 1835
WALTON, SARAH, now or formerly residing in East 65th Street, near Madison Avenue, N Y, City, U S.A.
WARD, DIXON, formerly of Manchester, England , now residing in Ontario, Canada.
WARNOCK, WILLIAM and HUGH, left Ireland for America in 1840, and when last heard of were in Montreal and Buffalo, respectively
WARREN, MARIA. (See Maria Johnson)
WATERBURY, DAVID, formerly a Clerk in Philadelphia Navy Yard, U S A.
WEEKS, BENJAMIN F , formerly of Boston, Mass , U S A
WELSH, Mrs. CATHERINE, Widow, formerly of Co. Clare, Ireland , now residing in America.
WENKE, GEORGE. Cabinet maker, a native of Prussia, resided in Philadelphia, Pa , U S.A , about 1870.
WHELAN, Mrs. ALICE, who left Boston, Mass , in 1861, for California, U S.A.
WHITE, WILLIAM G , late of Windsor, England , last heard of in Brooklyn, N Y , U S A.
WHITEHOUSE, JAMES, Engineer, formerly of England , now residing in America.
WHITFIELD, JOHN, formerly of Newry, Ireland , now residing in America.
WHYTE, JOHN, now or late of Hamilton, Ont., Canada
WILKE FAMILY, formerly of Germany , now residing in America.
WILSON ,CHARLES FRANCIS, or FRANCIS CHARLES, of England , last heard of in N Y City. U.S.A
WILSON, JOHN, Plasterer, formerly of Wemyss Bay, Scotland , now residing in America
WILSON, JOSEPHINE, formerly JOSEPHINE BRAHAM, of London , last heard of at Boston, Mass U S A
WILSON, Rev THOMAS, a native of Lancashire, England, when last heard of, he had joined the Federal Army, it is believed the 14th Infantry, then quartered at Fort Trumbull, New London, Conn , U S.A.
WILSON, WILLIAM HENRY, Actor or Minstrel, formerly of Pennsylvania, U S A.
WILSON, WILLIAM and HENRY, late of Yorkshire, who left England for America about 1854
WINTER, THOMAS BASSALL, last heard of in Halifax, Nova Scotia, Canada.
WISEMAN, ROBERT and DORA, of Co Cork, Ireland , in 1860, of Piermont, Rockland Co , N Y , U S.A.
WOODCOCK, AGNES, now or lately residing in Ontario, Canada.
WRIGHT, ISAAC, a Shipper during 1812 Representatives in America.
WYATT, J HARRY, late of the U S. Navy , was Secretary to the late Commodore W D Porter
YEARNSHAW, THOMAS, of Manchester, or Bolton, Lancashire, Eng , afterwards residing in America
YOUNG, ROBERT, of Manchester, or Bolton, Lancashire, Eng , afterwards residing in America.

SPECIAL LIST No. 9.

UNCLAIMED MONEY, LANDS AND ESTATES.

The following persons, if living, or if dead, their representatives, are entitled to property Address J. B. MARTINDALE, 142 La Salle Street, Chicago. [See pages 6, 7 and 8 of this Manual.]

ALLEN FAMILY, supposed late of Scotland, now residing in America.
ANDREWS, ALFRED GAMAGE, who left England for America in 1876
APPLEGARTH, WILLIAM, and REBECCA (maiden name McPHERSON), last heard of at Plainsberg Merced Co., Cal., U S A.
ARMSTRONG, SAMUEL T, formerly in business at No. 181, Broadway, New York City, U S A.
BACKHOUSE FAMILY, now residing in America.
BALDWIN, MATILDA, afterwards DIMMOCK, last heard of in San Francisco, U S A
BALDWIN, THOMAS and WILLIAM, brothers, last heard of at St. John's, Newfoundland.
BARRETT, DANIEL, lately residing in N Y , U S A.
BARTLETT, JANE (maiden name DREW), a native of Wiltshire England, who went to America in 1858
BECKLEY, WILLIAM, and SARAH, formerly of Co. Middlesex, who left England for N Y., many years ago.
BELL, JOHN, ANNE and MARY ANNE, formerly of England, now residing in America.
BERESFORD, Captain (see Robert Gregory Burgis)
BERTRAM, JANET (maiden name McLARDY), and JOSEPH THOMAS, last heard of at Ottawa, Canada.
BEST, NANCY and JOSEPH, now residing in America
BOYD, JOHN, a Baker, formerly of Belfast, Ireland, now residing in America.
BRIDLE, LOUISA, who went to Chicago, U S A., in 1889, and there married one Alfred George.
BROWN, MARY (maiden name McLARDY), and HORACE T, last heard of in Ottawa, Canada.
BRYAN, HENRY, formerly of La Hogue, supposed to be residing in America
BRYAN, JOHN and WILLIAM, residing in Somerset Co , N J , U S A., about 1810
BULLEN, THOMAS, who left Co Lancaster, Eng, for New York, U S A , about 1880.
BURGIS, ROBERT GREGORY (otherwise CAPTAIN BERESFORD), last heard of in America about 1856.
BURRITT, HENRY OSGOODE, late of Ottawa, Canada Creditors wanted
BURSLEM, JANE (maiden name Doust), married ——Carter, in Philad., Pa , U S A., previous to the year 1821
CAMPBELL, Dr CHARLES JAMES, of Co York, Eng , and Co Ayr, Scotland. Heirs of, in America.
CANTIN, LOUIS (see Louis Marcuet de Cugy)
CARLIN, JAMES R., formerly employed on Central Park, New York City, U.S.A.
CARMICHAEL, BETSY, now or late of Bronks, Co Lambton, Ont., Canada.
CARTER, JANE (see Jane Burslem).
CASEY, JERRY, or MICHAEL, formerly of Co. Cork, Ireland, now residing in America
COCK FAMILY, residing in America.
COLMAN, JOHN JEANE (otherwise THOMAS ROWLANDS) and his wife JANE (Maiden name, TROOD), formerly of Co Somerset, Eng , now residing in America.
CONKLING, JAMES, residing in New York City, about the year 1800.
CONNEL, MARY, BRIDGET, CATHERINE, and DAN, who left Utica, N Y , for New York City in or about 1853, and afterwards went to California, U S A.
CONWAY, JAMES, Saddler, formerly of Co Mayo, Ireland ; now residing in America
COTTON, EDWARD W , born in England about 1820, and who afterwards went to America.
COULSON, MARY, and JOHN formerly of Yorkshire, England , and who afterwards went to America
CULGAN, Mrs. ANN or NANCY (Maiden name, ROONEY), of Co. Leitrim, Ireland, now residing in America.
DARK, ANN (See Mrs. Ann McCagie.)
DAWSON, Mrs. ISABELLA (Maiden name, DOHERTY), formerly of Co Londonderry, Ireland , and her husband, JAMES DAWSON, now residing in America.
DAY, EDWARD, who left England for America about 1847.
DE CUGY, LOUIS MARCUET, formerly of the Canton of Friebourg, Switzerland, and who lived at Thorn, Prussia, in 1874, under the name of Louis Cantin.
DEDEKAM, CARSTEN HENRICK, a native of Norway, and who in 1877, was serving under the name of Robert Stewart, on board the U S S "Trenton."
DELEVAN, JAMES, last heard of in Canada
DENHAM, or McLARDY, Mrs. CHARLOTTE, lately residing at 205, Union St., St. John's, N B , Canada.
DE PEIGER, Monsieur, an Engineer, now residing in America.
DICKINSON FAMILY, formerly of England, now residing in America.
DIMMOCK, MATILDA (see Matilda Baldwin).
DOHERTY, ISABELLA (See Mrs. Isabella Dawson)
DONAHUE, Mrs. MARGARET (See Walsh Family)
DONOGHUE, JOHN, who left Edinburgh, Scotland, for New York or Pennsylvania, U S A., about year 1854.
DOUST, JANE (see Jane Burslem)
DRAYTON, Mrs. HANNAH (Maiden name, OMANS); now residing in America.
DREW, JANE (See Jane Bartlett)
DUFFY, ANN (See Mrs. Joe Paro)
DUNCH FAMILY, residing in America.
EARLE, EDWARD O, residing in New York, or elsewhere, in America.
EBSWORTH, RICHARD NATHANIEL, a Printer, a native of London, England. Family of, in America.
EDE, GEORGE formerly of Co Surrey, who left England for America about 1850
ENNETT FAMILY, formerly of Ireland, residing in America
EDWARDS FAMILY, residing in America.
FELLOWS, CHARLES WILLIAM, residing in Staten Island, N Y , U S A., in 1854
FERGUSON, ALFRED, (otherwise GEORGE WEST), who left England for America about 1865.
FILLINGHAM, ROBERT, Saddler, formerly of Co. Middlesex, England Creditors of in America
FITCHETT FAMILY, residing in America.
FLEMING, GEORGE, formerly of Co. Dublin, Ireland, now residing in America
GENT FAMILY, residing in America.
GEORGE, LOUISA (see Louisa Bridle).
GOODSON, WILLIAM, who in 1888 resided with J Cooper, South Bergen, Bergen Av , N J., U S A.
GRANT, BARBARA, a native of Scotland, last heard of in San Francisco, U S A., in 1879.
GRANT FAMILY, formerly of Scotland, now residing in America.
GRANT, Mrs ROBERT, (Maiden name SINCLAIR), residing in America.
GREEN JAMES, who left England for America in or about the year 1810
GREENWOOD, BRIAN, late of Yorkshire England, last heard of in London, Ont , Canada.
HADDOW, or WRIGHT, Mrs DOROTHEA, who left England for New York, U S A , in 1848
HAILE, CHARLES AUSTIN, who left England for America in 1873
HALL, HENRY TAYLOR, who left England for America in 1873
HAMMOND, ALEXANDER, formerly of Ireland, supposed to have gone to the United States, and died there.
HARTY or MASON, MARY ANN, residing in Montgomery, Ala, U S A , in or about the year 1851
HEEL, ESTHER (See Mrs. Esther Stanton.)
HENDERSON, Mr H., formerly of New York, last heard of in Montreal, Canada
HOCHHEIMER, Professor JOSEPH MICHAEL, now residing in America
HOUGH, MICHAEL, formerly of Co Clare, who left Ireland for America in 1853.
HUNT, CYRUS and LINCOLN, residing in New York or elsewhere in America.
HUNT, FITCH K., now or late of Texas, U.S.A.
HUNT, JOHN FARR, Seaman, a native of England, last heard of in September, 1868 Now in America

SPECIAL LIST No. 9.

JENKINS, MARY W., daughter of Francis John Jenkins, who left England for America many years ago
JOHNSON, ANTHONY, EDWARD, HENRY, JAMES, MARIA, RICHARD, and WILLIAM, formerly King's Co., Ireland, who went to America many years ago
KENNEALLY, EDWARD, residing in Canada, 1820 to 1830
KING, JOHN, residing in Lowville, N.Y., U.S.A., in or about the year 1863.
KNAPP FAMILY, formerly of England, now residing in America.
LAWTON FAMILY, residing in America.
LEDERER, GEORGE, who left Germany for America in or previous to 1870.
LEDGER, JOHN, SARAH, and HENRY, formerly of England, now residing in America.
LEIGHTON, ROBERT, a Blacksmith residing in New York City, about 1832
LEONARD, WILLIAM, ormerly of Dublin, Ireland, now residing in America
LEVI, ANTONIO, formerly of Castel S. Pietro, Ticino; supposed to be residing in California, U S A
LITTLE, JOSEPH, MARGARET, and JANE, formerly of Ireland, then of Moriah, Essex Co., N Y, U S A.
LOYD, SAMUEL P., residing in New York City, in or about the year 1810
McCAGIE, Mrs. ANN (Maiden name, DARK), a native of Scotland, now residing in America.
McCANNA, PATRICK, formerly of Co Longford, who left Ireland for America in 1869
McCARGOW, WILLIAM, M.D, now or late of Caledonia, Ont., Canada
MACFARLANE, ANDREW, Joiner, formerly of Scotland, when last heard of was at Allentown, Pa., U S.A.
MoKENTY, or RILEY, JANET, formerly of Cork, who left Ireland for America some years ago
McLAROY, ADAM, a native of Scotland, last heard of in Oregon, U S A.
McLARDY, Miss ANNE, a Teacher, now or late of Ottawa, Ont., Canada.
McLARDY, Mrs. CHARLOTTE (see Mrs. Charlotte Denham)
McLARDY, ELIZABETH (see Elizabeth Stirling).
McLARDY, HENRY RANKINE, now or late of Greenback, near Woodstock, N B., Canada.
McLARDY, JANET (see Janet Bertram)
McLARDY, JOHN, a Baker, now or late of Delanco, Burlington Co, N J, U S A.
McLARDY, MARY (see Mrs Mary Brown).
McLARDY, THOMAS, now or late of Victoria, British Columbia
McPHERSON, GEORGE, now or recently with Messrs H B Claflin and Co., New York City
McPHERSON, REBECCA (see Mrs. Rebecca Applegarth)
McPHERSON, ROBERT M., now or late of Collingwood, Co. Simcoe, Ont., Canada.
MANDALL, NICHOLAS, formerly of Lancashire, who left England for America in December, 1879.
MARSHALL, HENRY A., who married Alice Jones, in Albany, N Y U S A., about 1875
MASON, MARY ANN (see Mary Ann Harty)
MAXWELL, JOHN M., residing in New York City, U S A., about 1832
MAYNARD, Mrs. MARY, now residing in America.
MILLER, THOMAS MASON REED, formerly of Newcastle-on-Tyne, who left England for America in 1858.
MONCK, CHARLES STEPHENS, last heard of in 1872, at Pittsburg, Pa., U S A.
MORRIS, MACK, now or recently residing in California, U S A.
MUNDEN, HENRY, now or late of Brigus, Newfoundland.
MURPHY, ANNA, last heard of at Indianapolis, Ind., U.S.A., about 1871.
MURPHY, EDWARD, formerly of Co Kilkenny, Ireland, and afterwards of Cincinnati, Ohio, U S.A.
MURRAY, ALEXANDER, and Co., of No 81, New Street, New York City, in 1842
NORTON, Mrs JULIA V, residing in America.
NURSE, HENRY, formerly of Co Suffolk, England, now residing in America.
O'BRIEN, JAMES, and ROBERT WILLIAM, who left England in 1889 for Newark, U S A
O'CONNELL, PETER, of Co Limerick, Ireland, when last heard of in 1878, was at Milwaukee, Wis., U.S.A.
ODDY, THOMAS, formerly of Yorkshire, who left England for America about 1865.
OMANS, HANNAH (See Mrs Hannah Drayton.)
O'NEILL, PATRICK E., formerly of Co Donegal, Ireland, now residing in America.
PARKER, CHARLES T., residing in America.
PARO, Mrs. JOE, formerly of Montreal, Que, Canada, afterwards of N Y, U S.A.
PARSLOW, WILLIAM FRANK, or LOU, now or recently residing in America.
PAYNE, CORNELIUS W., residing in America.
PEIGER, DE (see Monsieur De Peiger).
PICKELMANN, ULRICH, formerly of Eschenbach, Germany, who went to America in or previous to 1870.
PIRNER, JOH. HEINR., formerly of Wether, Germany, who went to America in or previous to 1870
POETTICHER, HERMAN, now or late of 117, North 6th Street, Williamsburgh, N Y, U S A.
POSEY, JAMES, last heard of in New Orleans, La. U S A
RAMMELSBERG, CHARLES, late Agent in the U S.A. for the Stettin line
RAPER, FELIX VINCENT, who left England for America in or about the year 1871.
REYNOLDS, ROBERT, a native of Ireland, afterwards of East Flamboro', Ont., Canada
RIELY, FRANCIS, of Co. Meath, Ireland. In 1873, was a Partner in brickmaking, near Terrell, Texas, U S.A.
RILEY, JANET (see Janet McKenty).
RILEY, WILLIAM, Gunsmith, now or late of 58, New Block Street, ———, Connecticut, U S A.
ROGERS, HARRY, formerly of Co. Pembroke, Wales, England, was at Stockton, Cal., U S.A., in 1854.
ROONEY, ANN or NANCY (See Mrs. Ann or Nancy Culgan.)
ROW, ANNA and JOHN, formerly of Co. Herts, Eng., now residing in America.
ROWLANDS, THOMAS. (See John Jeane Colman.)
RYAN, ELLEN, formerly of Co Sligo, Ireland, now residing in America
SACKETT, SAMUEL, residing in New York City, in or about the year 1810
SARGENT, THOMAS BLENNERHASSET, Surgeon, residing in New York City, U S A., in 1873
SAUTER, CHRISTIAN ALBRECHT, of Hersbruck, Germany, who went to America in or previous to 1870
SCANLAN, DANIEL, residing at Brandon, Vermont, U S A., in or about 1869
SHEEHAN, MARIA, who left Liverpool, England, about the year 1880, for Montreal, or Toronto Canada
SHORTT, Family of, formerly of Co. Tyrone, Ireland, now residing in America.
SINCLAIR, BARBARA. (See Mrs Robert Grant.)
SINCLAIR FAMILY, formerly of Scotland, now residing in America.
SMITH, Mrs ELLEN (See Walsh Family)
SMITH, JOHN and MARGARET, formerly of Glasgow, Scotland, last heard of in New York, U S.A., in 1872
SMITH, WHITFIELD, Veterinary Surgeon, who left Liverpool, England for America about 1855.
SOUTER, JOSEPH, a native of Forfarshire, Scotland, residing near Cookstown, Ontario, Canada, about 1858.
STANTON, Mrs. ESTHER, formerly of England; last heard of at St. George's, Co. Brant, Ont., Canada
STEWART, CHARLES, a native of Scotland, now residing in America.
STEWART, ROBERT (see Carsten Henrick Dedekam)
STIRLING, ELIZABETH, formerly McLardy, and ROLAND MORION STIRLING, now or late Watch maker, of Windsor, N S., Canada
SUOCH, JOSEPH, a native of Italy, now residing in America
SUSS, CHRISTIAN, formerly of Guntersreith, Germany, who went to America in or previous to 1870.
SUTCLIFFE, JAMES, residing in Canada, or the U S A
TOLWORTHY, GEORGE WILLIAM, who left England for New York, U S A., 1885.
TROOD, JANE. (See John Jeane Colman.)
UEBERROTH, AMANDA, residing in Philadelphia, Pa., or elsewhere in America.
WALKER, Mrs. ANNA. (See Anna and John Row)
WALSH FAMILY, formerly of Ballyneague, Co Cork, who left Ireland for America about 1847
WARD, JAMES, formerly of England, now residing in America
WARING, CAULFIELD B., formerly of Co. Galway, Ireland, now residing in America.
WARREN, MARIA (maiden name Johnson), formerly of King's Co., Ireland, now residing in America.
WEST, GEORGE (See Alfred Ferguson.)
WRIGHT, DOROTHEA and her husband, JOHN WRIGHT of Newcastle-on-Tyne, Eng., now in America

SPECIAL LIST No. 10.

UNCLAIMED MONEY, LANDS AND ESTATES.

The following persons (or their heirs) are entitled to property. Address J. B. MARTIN DALE, 142 La Salle Street, Chicago, Illinois, stating all facts on which claim is based [See pages 6, 7 and 8 of this Manual]

ACFORD, ROBERT OWEN, formerly of London, England; now residing in America.
ACKERMAN, DAVID R., last heard of in Philadelphia, U S A
AHERN, JOHN, a native of Killorgen, Co Kerry, Ireland, last heard of at Poughkeepsie, N Y, U.S.A.
ALCORN JAMES FRANK, now residing in America.
ALLCOCK, SAMUEL, supposed to have gone in 1861, to Salt Lake City, Utah, U.S.A., along with his mother
ALSON, WILLIAM, in the U S Navy, 1865.
ANDREAE, FRANCISCA VON (Maiden name, SEWIGH); next of kin of, in America
ARCHIBALD, Mrs. ALICE (Maiden name, TAYLOR), recently residing at Egmond Villa, Ont., Canada.
ATKINSON, MILTON B, residing in America.
AUTRAM, CHARLES WILLIAM WOODROW, in 1872, Clerk in Small-Pox Hospital, N Y. City, U.S.A.
BAILHACHE, CLEMENT NICOLLE last heard of at Salem, Mass., U S A., in 1864.
BAKER, HARRY, Boatswain's Mate, U S Navy, 1865
BALDWIN, FRANKLIN, formerly of Co Cork, Ireland, now residing in America.
BALL, GUILDFORD, a Seaman in the U S Navy, 1863-5.
BALL, L C., formerly of Ohio, in 1864 Assistant Master's Mate, U.S. Navy
BALLANCE, ISAAC, formerly of Co Antrim, Ireland Went to America about 1875.
BALMAIN, JAMES H., last heard of at 86, Gouraze Street, New York City, U S A
BAMBER, MARGARET (Maiden name, WILKINSON), who left England for America previous to the year 1830.
BARBER, WILLIAM, formerly of Liverpool, England, residing in America in 1865.
BARBOUR, JAMES, Landsmen, U S. Navy, 1862
BARLOW, JAMES ALFRED, who was living with Mr Grundy, or Mr Spinks, of Paterson, N J, U.S.A.
BARNES, ROBERT JOHN, last heard of at Kingston, Ont., Canada.
BARNES, SAMUEL WILLIAM, last heard of at Stamford, Ont., Canada.
BATES, N D., First Assistant Engineer, U S Navy, 1863
BAUTISTA, JUAN, a native of Cuba, now residing in America.
BEAUFORT, FRANCIS, a Gunner in the U S Navy, 1862 3
BEEM FAMILY, residing in Houghton, Canada, about 1855.
BENSON FAMILY, formerly of Co Cork, Ireland, now residing in America.
BILLBROW, ROBERT, Qr Gr, U S Navy, 1865.
BLACKWELL, JOHN, Seaman, U S Navy, 1861
BLAIN, or BLAINE, WILLIAM, Coal-heaver, U S. Navy, 1863-4.
BLAIR, ROBERT BROWNE, formerly of Berwickshire, Scotland, now residing in America.
BODINE, ELLA, now or lately residing in Brooklyn, N Y, U.S.A.
BOOTLE and JOHNSON, of New Providence, 1830.
BORLAND, DAVID, in 1873, residing in the Co. of Bruce, Ont, Canada.
BOYD, JOHN J, residing in America
BRADRAKE, WILLIAM, Ordinary Seaman, U S. Navy, 1863
BRADSHAW, EMILY (See Mrs Emily Copelan)
BRAINARD, PHILIP, last heard of at Holyoke, Mass, U S A.
BRASCAMP, Mrs MARY (Maiden name, SHERIDAN) married in New Jersey, U S, in 1868.
BRISKE, LOUIS, who left Prussia for America, in or about the year 1870.
BRISTOL, MILES A., who resided in Miss, U S.A., from 1845 to 1865.
BROCKENBERGER, H, a seaman in the U.S. Navy, 1863-5.
BRODRICK FAMILY, residing in America
BROWN, MARY ANN (See Mary Ann Wilson.)
BROWN, PETER, Ordinary Seaman, U S. Navy, 1863.
BRUNT, WILLIAM, left Franklin Co., N Y, about 1827 for N.J, U S A. His parents were from Ireland.
BRYSON, HUGH, in 1878 was at Samish, Whatcom Co, Wash Terr, and afterwards went to California, U S.A
BUCKLEY, JOHN, Landsman, U S. Navy, 1863.
BURKE, ANNE, BRIDGET, and MARGARET, formerly of Co Galway, Ireland, now residing in America.
BURKE, ARTHUR, emigrated to the United States, and last heard of in 1869
BURKE, MARY, daughter of John, who left Ireland for America about 1840.
BURNS, MICHAEL, in the U S Navy, 1865.
BURROUGHS, JOHN HEGEMAN, now or formerly of Queen's Co., N Y, U.S.A.
BURTON, CHARLOTTE (Maiden name, ELLIS), now or formerly of Palmyra, Wis., U S A.
CADDICK, RICHARD, was in Cincinnati in 1832, afterwards joined the Wesleyans, and went South.
CAMBRIDGE, S.D., Officer's Steward, U S Navy, 1863.
CAMERON, CHRISTINA C, now or recently residing at Sarnia, Ont, Canada.
CAMPBELL, LEWIS, last heard of on the frontier of Texas, U S A.
CAPPS, Mrs. EMMA (Maiden name, GOODWIN), Representatives of, residing in America.
CARROLL, PATRICK and ANN, born near Oldcastle, Ireland, went to New York, U S A., in 1818.
CARTER, OSCAR, formerly with Mr Fayer, in Buffalo, N Y, and said to have served in the U S Army.
CARTER, WILLIAM, born in Philadelphia, U S A, about 1820 His mother's given name was Jane.
CARTWRIGHT FAMILY, Representatives of, residing in America.
CARTWRIGHT, W. and BENJAMIN, now residing in America.
CASSIDY, ROSANNA. (See Mrs. Rosanna McCallum, or McCullum)
CATHCART FAMILY, formerly of Ireland, now residing in America
CAVIE, EDWARD F, formerly of England, now residing in America
CHALMERS, ALISON, in 1851, of Edinburgh, Scotland, now residing in America.
CHAMBERLAIN, NATHAN, late of Co Leeds, Ont, Canada.
CHAPPEL, DEODOTUS, a Seaman in the U S Navy, 1863 5.
CHARLES, JOHN JARVIS, who left Liverpool, Eng, for America in 1831
CHAUVERT, JUAN LUIS, supposed to have resided in Texas, U S A.
CHISHOLM, JANE, formerly GEDDES, who left Dumfricsshire, Scotland, for Canada, about 1852.
CLARK, S. B., Third Assistant Engineer in the U S Navy, in 1863
CLARKE, GEORGE BOOTH, who left Mr Duckett, with a farmer going to Owen Sound, Canada.
CLEMENTS, THOMAS, who left England for California about the year 1830.
COADY FAMILY, formerly of Co Kilkenny, Ireland, now residing in America
COLCLOUGH FAMILY, residing in America.
COLE, ISAAC, now or formerly of Philadelphia, Pa, U S A
COLE, LEONARD. (See Leonard Stanley)
COLLINS, ISABELLA, formerly of Scotland, lately living in Houston and White Streets, N Y City, U.S.A.
COLLINS, LEMUEL, Seaman, U S Navy, 1861
CONLON, or DICK, JAMES, a Sailor, who went to America about 1870
CONWAY, PATRICK, formerly of Australia, now supposed to reside in America.
COOK, EDWARD H, a Saddler, residing in New York City, U S.A., about 1864.
COOK HENRY, Boatswain's Mate, U S. Navy, 1864

COPELAN, Mrs. EMILY (Maiden name, BRADSHAW); now residing in America.
CORCORAN, PAT, a Seaman in the U S Navy, 1863 5.
COYLE, BRIDGET, a native of Co Longford, Ireland, now residing in America.
CRAIG, JOSHUA JOHN, formerly of Dublin, Ireland, Children of, residing in America.
CROOK FAMILY, formerly of England; now residing in America.
CROWELIEN, ROWLAND, who in 1859 was a Merchant in New York City, U S A
CROWELL, A. F, Third Assistant Engineer, in the U S Navy, 1862-3
CUMBERLAND, HENRY JAMES, formerly of England, now residing in America.
CUMMINS, JAMES, a native of England, now residing in Michigan, U S A
CUNNINGHAM, WILLIAM ALLAN, recently residing in Toronto, Canada.
CURRELL, WILLIAM, formerly of Belfast, Ireland; lately residing in West 16th Street, N Y City, U S A.
DALE, DANIEL, formerly of Hampshire, England, afterwards a Farmer, near Louisville, Kans., U.S.A.
DALTON, THOMAS, Seaman, U S Navy, 1861
DARGAN, MICHAEL C., who left Dublin, Ireland, for America in 1862.
DART, THOMAS, formerly of Devonshire, who left England for America about 1664
DAVIDSON, J R, Third Assistant Engineer in the U S Navy, 1864
DAVIES, or DAVIS, JULIANA ELIZA (otherwise SIMS), last heard of at Salt La City, Utah, U.S.A.
DAVIS, JOHN, formerly of Co. Donegal, Ireland; now residing in America
DECKER, E. A., a Pilot, U S, Navy, in 1863
DELVERT, HANNAH, who formerly resided at No 393, Second Street, South Boston, U S.A.
DICK, or CONLON, JAMES, a Sailor, who went to America about 1870
DILLON, JOSEPH K., who in 1865 was in business in Washington Street Market, N Y, U S A
DILLON, NICHOLAS, formerly of New York, Third Assistant Engineer, U S Navy, 1863-4.
DINSMAN, DANIEL, Seaman, U S Navy, 1862
DONNELL, JOHN O, Landsman, U S Navy, 1862.
DONOVAN, JOHN, Seaman, U.S Navy, 1863.
DONOVAN, ROBERT, born about 1847, was residing in Arizona Terr, U.S.A., in 1879.
DORAN, ALEXANDER, supposed to be residing in Canada.
DOWDALL, or MURRAY, ALICE, residing in Leavenworth City, Kas, U S A., about 1870.
DOWDALL, or LEE, MARY, residing in Leavenworth City, Kas., U S A, about 1870
DOWNES FAMILY, formerly of England, now residing in America.
DOWNES, HENRY, Landsman, U S. Navy, 1862
DOWNING FAMILY, formerly of Co. Cork, Ireland; now residing in America.
DOYLE, JOHN, Ordinary Seaman, U S Navy, 1862.
DRISCOLL, PAT, Coal-heaver, U.S. Navy, 1861
DROUGHAN, ROSA, formerly of Co. Fermanagh, Ireland, now residing in America.
DRUMMOND, TERRANCE, who left Glasgow, Scotland, for America, about 186.
DUNKHASE, HEINRICH EDWARD, a Sailor on the "Rhine," sailed from Havre, France, for N Y, 1858.
DUNLOP, JAMES, Merchant, of Montreal, Canada
DUVERDIER DE LA VALETTE, JEAN B, of New York, U S A, in 1810.
DWYER, JOHN, formerly of Co. Tipperary, Ireland, afterwards of New York, or St Louis, U.S.A
EAGER, PAT, Seaman, U S Navy, 1863
EDWARDS, JAMES MOLYNEUX, an Engineer; formerly of New Jersey, U.S.A.
ELLIS, CHARLOTTE. (See Charlotte Burton)
ELLIS, SARAH, formerly of Co Kent, who left England for America some years ago.
ELLVERTON, CATHERINE (See James, William, and Catherine Fitzgerald)
ELVERT, CATHERINE (Maiden name, FITZGERALD), formerly of Co. Wexford, now residing in America.
ENGLISH, CHARLES ALFRED, formerly of the 5th U S infantry
EREXSOL or ERRICSON, MARY JANE, now or formerly of Palmyra, Wis., U S A
FALLON FAMILY, formerly of Co Galway, Ireland, residing in New York City about 1857.
FARRELL, Mrs HANNAH, who resided at 316, East 27th Street, and in 31st St., New York, U.S.A., in 1877
FATHOM, JAMES, last heard of in Philadelphia, Pa., U S A, in 1805.
FEARENSIDE, WILLIAM, formerly of Yorkshire and Hampshire, Eng; afterwards of Philadelphia, U S A.
FELIX, SEBASTIEN, Landsman, U S Navy, 1861 6
FERGUSON, CATHERINE (or KATE), ISABELLA (or BELL), who left Scotland for Canada with their father, between 1820 and 1830.
FINDLAY, MARGARET and WILLIAM, last heard of at Cohoes, N Y, U S A.
FINNIE, JOHN and DAVID, brothers, formerly of Scotland, now residing in America
FITZGERALD, JAMES, WILLIAM, and CATHERINE, natives of Co Wexford, Ireland, now residing in America. James emigrated about 1847, and when last heard of, was in Cleveland, U S A. Catherine married Patrick Ellverton, a Blacksmith
FLEMING, SAMUEL, of Peebles, Scotland, and recently working as a Stone-cutter in New York, U.S.A.
FLEMMING, GEORGE, in 1873 was employed in the Daily Times Office, Brooklyn, N Y., U.S.A.
FLETCHER, HENRY, Landsman, U S. Navy, 1862.
FLING, MARTIN, a Fisherman, of Newfoundland, in 1818
FLOWERS, GEORGE THOMAS, now residing in America.
FOLEY, KATE, formerly of Co Leitrim, Ireland, now residing in America.
FORREST, JOHN, Seaman, U S Navy, 1863.
FORSEY, SAMUEL, a Fisherman, of Fortune Bay, Newfoundland, in 1814.
FRAMPTON, ROBERT, Ordinary Seaman, U S. Navy, 1862
FRANCIS, FREDERICK WILLIAM, who left Sydney, N S W, for London, 1868; now residing in America.
FRANKLIN, JANE. (See Jane Robinson)
FREY, MARY, residing in New Jersey, or elsewhere in America.
GARLAND, FRANK, a Seaman in the U S Navy, 1862-5
GEDDES, JANE (See Jane Chisholm)
GIFFORD, WILLIAM, a Seaman in the U.S. Navy, 1863 5.
GILDERSLEEVE, Mrs. HETTY (Maiden name, WARD), now residing in America.
GILLESPIE, GEORGE, a native of Scotland, supposed to be residing in America.
GILLILAND, ELLEN, who with her husband left Ireland for America in 1832
GOODWIN, EMMA. (See Mrs. Emma Capps.)
GORDON, WILLIAM, C.A.G, U S Navy, 1865.
GOTTEL, RICHARD, formerly of London, England, now residing in America.
GRAHAM, JAMES, who left Edinburgh, Scotland, for America, about 1840, with his wife and children.
GRAHAM, JOHN PILOT, formerly of England, now residing in America.
GRANT, MICHAEL, formerly of Co Kerry, Ireland, afterwards of Boston Highlands, Mass., U S.A.
GRAPER, FRED, Ordinary Seaman, U S. Navy, 1861-5.
GRAY, GIBSON, last heard of at Fonthill, Co. Welland, Ont, Canada.
GREEN, JAMES, in 1839 residing in New York, U S A., and who married Anne McLellan, of that city.
GREEN, THOMAS, of Green's Pond, Newfoundland, Planter
GUSTAVE, CONRAD, a Seaman in the U S Navy, 1863-5
HAGAN, JAMES, Assistant Master's Mate, U S Navy, 1865.
HALE, GEORGE, or JOHN B, Seaman, U S Navy, 1862.
HANSON, HENRY, Ordinary Seaman, U S Navy, 1863
HARE, ARTHUR, last heard of in 1864, near the line of the Indian Territory, Texas, U S A.
HARRIS, JAMES M., formerly of New York, in 1863 a Second Assistant Engineer in the U S Navy
HARRIS, STIRLING CARTER, formerly of Liverpool, Eng, residing in New York City, U.S.A., about 1867
HARROLDSON. or PEASE, MOLLIE, residing in America.

HAWTHORNE, JOHN BRADFORD, now residing in America.
HAYDEN, WILLIAM H, First Class Boy, U S Navy, 1863.
HAYES, GEORGE, Seaman, U S Navy, 1863.
HAYES, JOHN, residing in Henry Street, New York, U.S.A., in the summer of 1880.
HEALY, AUSTIN and SARAH, children of James, who left Co Mayo, Ireland, for America about 1862
HEALY, PATRICK, who left Co Kerry Ireland, about 1862, for Xenia, Ohio, U.S.A.
HEATH, JULIA W (formerly DOWNES), now residing in America
HEBBLETHWAITE, MARK, last heard of at Cleveland, Ohio, U S.A.
HENRY, MARY (See Mary Parker)
HERNANDEZ, ANDRES V, a native of Cuba, now residing in America.
HERRON, JOHN, last heard of at March, Ont., Canada
HIGHETT, Mrs (Maiden name MOORE), formerly of Co. Warwick, England; now residing in America.
HILL, ELIZABETH (otherwise JAQUES), formerly of Co Rutland, England, now residing in America.
HILLIARD, JOHN who left Ireland for America, with his aunt, in 1850
HITCHCOCK, PHŒBE (Maiden name, OAKLEY), last heard of at Yonkers, N Y, U.S.A.
HODGSON FAMILY, formerly of Co. Cumberland, England, now residing in America.
HOLME, THOMAS CROSS, formerly of England, now residing in America.
HORNFIELD, SAMUEL, a Seaman in the U S Navy, 1863-5.
HOWARD, CORNELIUS, a native of Co Cork, Ireland, was in St. Paul, Minn., U S A., in 1880.
HOWELL, EDWARD C, Quartermaster in the U S Navy, 1862
HUFF, JOHN, Second Assistant Engineer in the U S Navy, 1863.
HUGHES, RACHEL and HANNAH, sisters, natives of England, now residing in America.
HYDE, EMMA and ANNE, daughters of John Hyde, who, in 1855, kept the Tontine Coffee House, N.Y., U S A.
HYNES, Miss MARIA, who left Ireland for America about 1862
JACKSON, THOMAS, formerly of Lincolnshire, England, now residing in America.
JACOBS, JOHN, C F C, U S Navy, 1863.
JAQUES ELIZABETH (See Elizabeth Hill.)
JONES, GRIFFITH (or GRIFFITH LEWIS), of Elko, Nevada, U S A, in 1869
KANE, JOHANNA, formerly of Mayeville, Ky., residing in Keokuk, Iowa, U S A, about 1858.
KEATING, WILLIAM J, a Seaman in the U S Navy, 1864-5
KEITH, JULIA W (formerly DOWNES), now residing in America
KELLY, THOMAS, of Co. Waterford, Ireland, now residing in America.
KELLY, WILLIAM, a Tinsmith, a native of Manchester, England, afterwards of Boston, U S A.
KENAH, GEORGE and ANNE, residing in America.
KENEALY, JOHN, formerly of New York, Third Assistant Engineer, U S Navy, 1861 1865.
KENEHAN, JOHN, and his sister, ROSE, formerly of King's Co., Ireland, now residing in America.
KENNEALEY MICHAEL, last heard of in Boston, Mass., U S A.
KENNEALY, JOHN, who was at Quebec, Canada, in 1828, with his Regiment, the 68th British Infantry.
KERFOOT FAMILY, formerly of Ireland, now residing in America.
KINNEY, JAMES, in 1850 residing in Rye, Westchester Co, N Y, U S A.
KLEIN, PETER, formerly of Arnsburg, Prussia, now residing in America.
KNOX, MARY, formerly of Co Londonderry, Ireland; now residing in America.
KOOP FAMILY, formerly of Germany, now residing in America.
KOVESSY, JOHN, a native of Hungary, now residing in America.
KUHL, HUGH, formerly of England, was Acting Ensign in the U S. Navy, 1863-4.
LACKNER, GEORGE, a native of Austria, who went to America some years ago
LAFOY, or LAFARGE, PERICHA A., Relatives of, residing in America.
LAKE, GERHARD ANTON JACOB, and JOHANN BERNARD LAKE, now residing in America.
LAWDEY, CHARLES ALEXANDER, formerly of Halifax, N S., Canada.
LEARY, JOHN, of Philadelphia, Pa., U.S.A., in 1837
LECOMPTE, JULIUS, residing in Houston, Texas, U.S.A., between 1855 and 1860.
LEE, MARY (See Mary Dowdall)
LEIGH, JOHN E, formerly of Lancashire, who left England for America about 1871.
LEVER, JOHN, Seaman, U S. Navy, 1862
LEVERMORE FAMILY, Representatives of, supposed to be residing in America.
LEVERTON, WILLIAM, formerly of Nottinghamshire, who left England for America some years ago.
LILLEY, ELIZABETH and JOSHUA, last heard of at Toronto, Clinton Co, Iowa, U S A.
LING, JOHN A., Landsman, U S Navy, 1862
LITTLEWOOD, JANE, formerly of England, now residing in America.
LOMBARD, GASTON LOUIS, a native of Angers, France, now residing in America.
LOWE, WILLIAM and CHARLES, natives of Wisbech, Cambridgeshire, England, now residing in America.
LYNCH, MARY, born about 1852, was in Cincinnati Hospital in 1872
LYNSKEY, BRIDGET, wife of Dominick, who left Ireland for America about 1810.
McADAMS, S H, formerly of New York, Assistant Master's Mate, U S. Navy, 1861-1865.
McANOREW, HANNA, formerly of Co Sligo, now residing in Boston, Mass., or elsewhere in America.
MACAULEY, JOHN, MICHAEL, and PATRICK, natives of Co Leitrim, Ireland, now residing in America
McBAIN, Reverend JAMES AFFLECK FRASER, and his wife, MARY M (Maiden name, QUIN), now or recently residing at Chatham, N B, Canada.
McCABE, JOHN, Coal heaver, U S Navy, 1862
McCALLUM, or McCULLUM, Mrs ROSANNA (Maiden name, CASSIDY), with her three children, residing in New York City, U S.A., in 1865.
McCARTHY, ANN (Maiden name, TWIGG) It is believed that her husband, George McCarthy, with several of their children, emigrated to America
McCARTHY FAMILY, formerly of London, England, now residing in America.
McCONNELL, JAMES, Ordinary Seaman, U S Navy, 1862
McCULLUM, ROSANNA. (See Mrs Rosanna McCallum)
McDONALD, HUGH, Second Class Fireman in the U S. Navy, 1862-4.
McDONOGH, Miss HARRIETT, of Boston, Mass, in 1816
McDOWELL, ROBERT, who owned land in Texas, U.S A., about 1850.
McHUGH, PATRICK, who left Dublin, Ireland, for America in 1837
McINTYRE, JOHN, formerly of Co Londonderry, Ireland, last heard of in Illinois, U S.A.
McLELLAN, ANNE. (See James Green)
McLEOD, FRANCIS, formerly of New York, in 1861, a Boatswain in the U S Navy
McLOUGHLIN, ELEANOR, who left Springhill, Ireland, for America about the year 1865.
McMALLEN, NEWTON, last heard of in 1845, in Texas, U.S.A.
McNAMARA, Miss ELLIE, formerly of Co. Limerick, Ireland; now residing in America.
McNAMARA, MICHAEL, Second Class Fireman, U S. Navy, 1863.
McNELLY, JOHN, a Seaman in the U S Navy, 1863 5.
MADDISON, BRIDGET (otherwise WRENCH), Children of, residing in America.
MAGINNESS, ALEXANDER, and NOBLE, formerly of Co Armagh, Ireland, now residing in America.
MAISEY, JOB, who left England in 1856 Was at Cass River, Watrousville, Tuscola Co., Mich., U.S.A., in 1868.
MARCKWALD, ALEXANDER, who left Prussia for the U S.A. in 1868.
MAULE, THOMAS, residing in Pearl Street, New York, U S A., in 1805.
MAY, CHARLES, Seaman, U S Navy, 1863
MAY, JOHN, formerly of England, now residing in America.
MENDORGA, EMANUEL, Gunner's Mate, U S Navy, 1864.
MILLER, J. H., Seaman, U S. Navy, 1861

MILLER, THOMAS McL., formerly of Massachusetts, in 1885, an Ensign in the U S. Navy.
MINOT, LOUISA, formerly of Jamaica, drowned off the coast of Texas, U S A, in 1862.
MOLLNAN, LADISLAUS, a native of Hungary, supposed to reside in America.
MONTAGUE, JOHN, in 1863, a Pilot (probably River) in the U S Navy
MONYHAN, HENRY, a native of Co. Limerick, Ireland; in 1868 was at Beaver Springs, Snyder Co., Pa., U S.A.
MOORE, Miss. (See Mrs Highett.)
MOORS, RUFUS, last heard of at Groton, Mass., U S A
MORGAN, THOMAS, of Shoe Cove, Newfoundland, in 1811
MORRIS, THOMAS, a Bricklayer, who left Liverpool, England, for America about 1876.
MORTON, WILLIAM, and MARY, his wife (Maiden name, ROCHELLE), left N C., for Texas, U.S.A., in 1830.
MULLEN, JOS., Private, Marines, U S. Navy, 1863
MURPHY, CORNELIUS, a Seaman in the U S. Navy, 1863-5.
MURRAY, ALICE. (See Alice Dowdall.)
NEILD, JOSEPH, now or recently residing at Dresden, Ohio, U.S.A.
NETHERSOLE, GEORGE F, formerly of Dover, England, now residing in America.
NICHOLAS, GEORGE, Seaman, U S Navy, 1883.
NICHOLSON, MICHAEL, Landsman, U S Navy, 1862
NORRIS, Mrs. PHALON, formerly of San Francisco, afterwards of Fulton Avenue, Brooklyn, N Y, U S A.
NORTON, MARY, formerly of Co Galway, Ireland, residing in Brooklyn and New York, U S.A., in 1884.
NUTTER, RUFUS, a Seaman in the U S. Navy, 1882 6
OAKES, SARAH, JAMES, and WILLIAM, last heard of in Toronto, Canada.
OAKLEY, ISAAC, residing in Westchester Co., N Y., U S A. about 1797, and his daughter PHŒBE.
O'BRIEN, AGNES, who resided in 1879 in the City of Albany, N Y, U S A.
O'BRIEN, JAMES, a Contractor on the Erie R.R., U S A., in 1841
O'BRIEN, JULIA, formerly residing at 393, Second Street, South Boston, U S.A.
O'BRIEN, MICHAEL, Second Class Fireman, U S Navy, 1882
O'CONNOR, J. K., who in 1876 was in a Law Office, at No. 126, Broadway, New York City, U S A.
O'DONNELL, JOHN, Landsman, U S. Navy, 1862
OHLSEN, CHARLES, a Seaman in the U S. Navy, 1862-5.
O'MEALEY, JOHN, Landsman, U S Navy, 1863.
O'NEAL, PAT, Landsman, U S. Navy, 1862
O'NEIL, BRIDGET and DANIEL, when last of, were residing in the State of New York, U S.A.
O'NEIL or O'NEILL, ROSA, who came from Canada to New York City, U S.A., a few years ago.
OVATT, JAMES, a Seaman in the U S Navy, 1883 5.
OWENSON, JOHN, Ordinary Seaman, U S Navy, 1863.
PACLY, JOSEPH, who left England for America in or about the year 1885
PARKER, MARY (Maiden name, HENRY), formerly of Albany, N Y, last heard of in N Y City, U S.A.
PARSONS, GEORGE, a native of England, was at Sodorus, Champaign Co., Ills, U S.A., in 1876
PARSONS, JOHN H., a native of England, was at Silver Star Hotel, Corrine, Utah, U S.A., in 1871.
PARSONS, NICHOLAS, a native of England, now residing in America.
PATTISON, JOHN, last heard of at Houston, Texas U S.A.
PEARSE, HENRY, now or lately residing at White Water, Wis, U S.A.
PEASE, or HARROLDSON, MOLLIE, residing in America.
PERKIN, THOMAS, formerly of Leeds, Yorkshire, England, now residing in America.
PETERKIN, DAVID, now or lately of Poughkeepsie, N Y, U S A.
PETERS, JOHN, a Seaman in the U S. Navy, 1863-5
PHELAN, LEILA TATEM, residing in the U S A. in 1888
PIERCE, FRANKLIN, Gunner's Mate, U S. Navy, 1863
PLUMMER, EDWARD, formerly of London, Eng.; residing in New York City, U S A. about 1862
PODMORE, RICHARD LATHAM, formerly of Co. Stafford, England. When last heard of, in 1852, was at New Orleans, La., U S.A.
POST, DANIEL, Seaman, U S. Navy, 1861
PRICE, EDMUND ARTHUR, late of Co Surrey, England, now residing in America.
QUIN, ANDREW, who sailed for America in September, 1873
QUIN, CHARLES WILLIS, and the Rev JOHN CHAS. QUIN, last heard of at Port Dover, Ont., Canada.
QUIN MARY M (See Reverend J. A. F McBain.)
QUINN, EDWARD and BRIDGET, now residing in America.
RANSON, MARY, of London, Eng., in or about the year 1790. Representatives of, in America
READY, THOMAS A., Seaman, U S. Navy, 1861.
REED, JOHN, Ordinary Seaman, U S. Navy, 1883.
REID, Captain LEWIS, formerly Mate on the ship "Preston;" and left for New Orleans, U S.A., in 1871.
REID, THOMAS SMITH, formerly of London, Eng. In 1882, a Reporter or Sketcher for a New York Paper.
RENTON, ROBERT PENN, who left Dublin, Ireland, for New York, U S A., in 1869
REYNOLDS, ANNIE, of Ireland, born about 1856, and lived in 1888, in Albany, N.Y., or Newark, N.J., U S A.
RIACH FAMILY, now or formerly residing in New Orleans, La., U S A.
RIGBY, ROBERT EDWIN, formerly of the Bahamas, now residing in America.
RILEY, SYLVESTER, Second Class Fireman, U S Navy, 1862-4
RILEY, THOMAS F., a Printer, residing in New York City, U S A, in 1852.
ROBINSON, or FRANKLIN, JANE (coloured), now residing in America.
ROCHELLE, MARY (See William and Mary Morton.)
RODER, FRANCIS, a native of Hungary, now supposed to reside in America.
ROURKE, JAMES, Second Class Fireman, U S. Navy, 1864.
ROWLAND, HENRY, formerly of Holland, supposed to be residing in Brooklyn, or New York, U S.A.
RUNNALLS, HENRY, formerly of Penzance, Cornwall, England, now residing in America.
RUSSELL, GEORGE and THOMAS, natives of Co Durham, who left England for Canada about the year 1815.
RYAN, WILLIAM, a native of Ireland, who went to Texas, U S.A., 1830-1840.
SANDERS, FANNY. (See Fanny and Henry Wright)
SAYERS, HENRY, a native of Dublin, Ireland, afterwards of London, England, and now residing in America.
SCHRAN, CHARLES, Second Class Fireman, U S Navy, 1862-4.
SCHULTZ, HENRY, formerly of Leith, Scotland; now residing in America.
SCOTT, HENRY M., formerly of Ohio, Assistant Master's Mate, U.S Navy, in 1863.
SEAMAN, WILLIAM H., formerly residing at No 463, Broadway, N.Y. City, U S.A.
SEWIGH, FRANCISCA. (See Francisca von Andreae)
SHAFER, JOHN H., in 1859 residing in Lancaster, Pa., U S.A.
SHEPARD, JAMES, Seaman, U S Navy, 1862
SHERIDAN, HELEN, born about 1800 Family supposed to reside in America
SHERIDAN, MARY (See Mrs. Mary Brascamp)
SHERWOOD, NANCY ANN, now or lately residing in Bangor, Maine, U S.A.
SHEVLLIN, BERNARD, a native of Co. Down, Ireland, now residing in America.
SHIRSTON, WILLIAM, Coxswain, U S. Navy, 1861
SILIMAN, or SILINORE, J S, a Mate in the U S Navy, 1862-3.
SIM, WILLIAM NEILSON, who left Glasgow, Scotland, for America, in 1831.
SIMESS, JOS., O Sergt. Marines, U S. Navy, 1863
SIMOND FAMILY, formerly of Lyons, France, who emigrated to America many years ago.
SIMS, JULIANA ELIZA. (See Juliana Eliza Davies, or Davis.)
SINCLAIR, H., Seaman, U S Navy, 1881.
SMALL, ANDREW or JAMES, who left Scotland for Canada about the year 1815.

SMITH, CHARLES HERBERT, late of Cambridgeshire, England; last heard of in Toronto, Canada.
SMITH, DANIEL, First Class Boy, U S Navy 1863
SMITH, DAVID, JONATHAN, and JOSEPH, who left London, England, for America about the year 1834.
SMITH, JAMES, Boatswain in the US Navy, in 1862
SMITH, JAMES (otherwise *Irish Jim* Smith), last heard of in Texas, U S A.
SMITH, JOHN, a Miller, formerly of Girvan, Ayrshire, Scotland, now residing in Canada.
SMITH, JOHN, a native of Scotland, lately residing in Sullivan Street, Toronto, Canada.
SMITH, JOHN (*Jack* Smith), formerly residing in Oswego, N Y, U S A
SMITH, THOMAS, who left England for America about 1838, and was living at Mill River, Berkshire Co, Mass., U S A., about 1866
SMITHER, FRED. N., in 1863, Assistant Master's Mate in the U S Navy
SOMERS, SOMERSGILL, or SUMMERSGILL, GEORGE, who left England for America about 1842
SOMERS, SOMERSGILL, or SUMMERSGILL, SARAH, who left Eng for Cincinatti, U S A., about 1830.
SOMMEL, PH R., Upholsterer, formerly of Wuerzburg, Germany, now residing in America.
SPINNEY, C W, Seaman, U S Navy, 1861
SPOFFORD, LYDIA P, now or recently residing at Manchester, N H, U S A.
STANLEY, LEONARD (otherwise COLE), formerly of Texas, and in the Western States of America in 1876.
STEECE, GEORGE, a Midshipman in the U S Navy, 1861
STEEL, GEORGE, son of Daniel, who left England for Canada, in 1873.
STEPHENS, EDWIN, Seaman, U S Navy, 1863.
STRATHMORE, AGNES M D. (afterwards THOMSON), last heard of in Toronto, Canada.
STRUBE, FRITZ, Landsman, U S Navy, 1861 5
STULTZ, ROBERT C, supposed to be residing in the U S A.
STYLES, WILLIAM HALL, and EMILY, his wife, now residing in America.
SULLIVAN, ELLEN, and JAMES, her brother, he was formerly in the Navy, and was last heard of at Waterbury, Conn., U S A, in August, 1880
SUMMERSGILL, SARAH and GEORGE. (See Sarah and George Somers, or Somersgill.)
TANNER, JAMES, a Seaman in the U S Navy, 1864-5.
TAYLOR, ALICE (See Mrs. Alice Archibald.)
TAYLOR, HANNAH, MARY, and THOMAS, recently residing at No. 26, West Market Sq, Toronto, Canada
TAYLOR, JOHN Second Class Fireman, U S Navy, 1863.
TAYLOR, WILLIAM, residing in Hamilton, Ont., Canada, in November 1880.
TAYLOR, WILLIAM, recently residing at No 15, Mutter Street, Toronto, Canada.
TEMPLE, GEORGE, who left England for America, about 1860, was at Cheyenne, Wyo. Ter, in 1870, and in 1874, resided in or near Baltimore, U.S.A.
THOMPSON, JOHN, who left Glasgow, Scotland, for Toronto, Canada, in 1845
THOMPSON, SUSAN, residing in New Jersey, or elsewhere in America.
THOMPSON, WILLIAM H, ship's Cook, U.S. Navy, 1862
THOMSON, AGNES M D (See Agnes M D Strathmore.)
TOMLINSON, SAMUEL, formerly of New York, in 1863 Third Assistant Engineer, U S Navy.
TOWNSEND, Mr, a Baker, formerly of London, England, now residing in America.
TRENCH FAMILY, now residing in America.
TREUTLER, FRIEDRICH W A, formerly of Breslau, Germany, now residing in America.
TURNER, THOMAS, C F C, U S. Navy, 1862
TWIGG, ANN. (See Ann McCarthy.)
VANPELL, C. L., now residing in America
VAUGHAN, ANN, formerly of Co Monmouth, England, now residing in America.
VENNELL, THOMAS, late of Co Kent, Eng.; residing at Pittsburgh, or Pittston, Pa., U S A., about 1825.
VON ANDREAE, FRANCISCA (Maiden name, SEWIGH), next of kin of, in America.
WADE, ROBERT, late of Co. Waterford, Ireland, now residing in America
WALGARMUTH, ROBERT, a Seaman in the U S. Navy, 1863-5.
WALLEY, CHARLES HENRY, who left Yorkshire, England, for New York, U.S.A., about 1865.
WARD, Mrs. or Miss FANNY, now residing in America.
WAREHAM, JOS, Seaman, U S Navy, 1861
WARREN, MICHAEL, formerly of Culmore, Ireland, now residing in America.
WASHINGTON, BENJ F, Officer's Steward, U S Navy, 1862.
WATSON, GUY, Landsman, U S. Navy, 1862
WEBB, THOMAS, now or late of Chicago, Illa, U S A.
WEBSTER, H C, Acting Master, U S. Navy, 1861
WEBSTER, H C. C., of Massachusetts, a Mate in the U S. Navy, in 186L
WEST, JAMES and MARY ANN, residing in America
WHEATON, D H, an Officer in the U S Navy 1861 1865.
WHITE, WILLIAM ALEXANDER, residing in East Broadway, N Y., U.S.A, in 1877.
WHITEHILL FAMILY, formerly of England, now residing in America.
WHITING, CATHERINE R, now residing in America.
WHITTLESEY, WILLIAM, who left Co. Cambridge, England, for America about 1868.
WILCOXEN, JOHN S, Third Assistant Engineer, U S. Navy, 1861 1865
WILKINSON, MARGARET (See Margaret Bamber)
WILLIAMS, HENRY H. and JOSEPHINE, now or formerly of Petersburgh, N Y, U.S.A.
WILLIAMS, Mrs EMMA (Maiden name, WARD), now residing in America
WILLSON, MARGERY, supposed to be residing in Canada
WILSON, CHARLES, Master-at Arms in the U S. Navy, 1862
WILSON, CHARLES, Ordinary Seaman, U S Navy, 1862
WILSON, Mrs MARY ANN, formerly widow of ELISHA V BROWN The latter left Virginia in 1855, and married in Missouri or Kansas, started for California, U S A., and died on the way, leaving his wife and one child. His widow afterwards married a person named Wilson.
WOOD, HENRY, in 1864, Third Assistant Engineer in the U S. Navy
WOODWORTH, ALFRED, Seaman, U S Navy, 1862.
WRAGG, WILLIAM, of Charleston, S C., U.S A, about 1810
WRENCH (otherwise MADDISON), BRIDGET, Children of, now residing in America.
WRIGHT, FANNY (Maiden name, SANDERS), and HENRY, her son, who left N O for Texas about 1830.
YOUNG, F J, Surgeon's Steward in the U S Navy, 1862-4.
YOUNG, GEORGE, Second Class Fireman, U S Navy, 1862

SPECIAL LIST No. 11.

UNCLAIMED MONEY, LANDS AND ESTATES.

The following persons (or their heirs) are entitled to property. Address **J. B. MARTINDALE, 142 La Salle Street, Chicago,** stating all facts on which claim is based. [See pages 6, 7 and 8 of this Manual.]

ABBOTT, OLIVER, otherwise OLIVER GOLDSMITH ABBOTT, a native of Ireland, who enlisted in the British Army about 1840, and afterwards went to America.
ALEXANDER, MATTHEW and ANN (afterwards SMITH), residing in America
ALUME, JOSÉ MARIA, supposed to be living in the U S A.
ANDERSON, ROBERT J, when last heard of, resided at 109, West 38th Street, New York City, U.S.A.
ANDERSON, WILLIAM, a Bootmaker, who left Co Sligo, Ireland, for America, about 1868
ARMSTRONG, MARY (See Mary F Horn)
ARMSTRONG, ROBERT, a native of Scotland, last heard of at Kingston, Canada, about 1845
ARNOLD, Mrs. MARIA, FAMILY of, now or formerly of Coburg, Ont., Canada
ARNOTT, DAVID, a Sailor, who left Scotland for abroad in the year 1562
ATKINSON, CATHERINE (Maiden name, WILLIAMS), who left London for New York, about 1830, and when last heard of was in Pennsylvania, U S A.
BALDERSTONE, THOMAS, residing at Chatham, Ont., Canada in 1849
BARASFORD, ROSALIE (See Rosalie Osler)
BARKER, WENDELL R., Seaman, a native of Boston, Mass., U S A.
BARNES, SAMUEL WILLIAM, last heard of in Buffalo, N Y, U S A., in 1878
BEAMONT, JAMES, in 1869, of Westminster Bridge Road, London, Eng, now residing in America
BEARDSLEY, WILLIAM, late of Derbyshire, Eng, a Cooper, then a Soldier, now in the U S A.
BEATTY, Mr W R., formerly of Elizabethport, N J, who left New York for Toronto, in November, 1881
BEIRNE, ROGER and JOSEPH, formerly of Ireland, now residing in America.
BELLEW, PETER, a Labourer, last heard of at Washington, D C, U S A
BENNETT, JANE (See Jane Martin)
BENNETT, Mrs. J, who was at Monaco and Paris in 1878, and returned to N Y in November of that year.
BERESFORD, ROSALIE (See Rosalie Osler)
BIRCH, JAMES, who left England for New York, U S A. about the year 1883.
BIRCH, MARY ANN TARNEY VALLOE, who left England for Canada in or about the year 1861
BLOOMFIELD FAMILY, formerly of Co Essex, England, now residing in America.
BOND, ELIZA HARVEY, afterwards RICKARBY, now or formerly residing in New Orleans, La, U S A.
BOND, HENRY, formerly of Liverpool, England, afterwards residing in the U S A.
BONNELL, ANN, wife of William Bonnell, Merchant, in Nova Scotia in 1819
BOUTON, or BOUTEN, REBECCA (formerly Mrs DIMON), now residing in America.
BRADLEY, JAMES, formerly of London, who left England many years ago for St John, N B, Canada.
BRADLEY, THOMAS, formerly of London, who many years ago left England for St. John, N B., Canada.
BRENNAN, PATRICK, JOHN, and THOMAS, formerly of Co. Roscommon, left Ireland about 1850, for America, and were afterwards at Chapel Hill, Perry Co., Ohio, U S A.
BRIEN FAMILY, residing in America
BRITTON, SAMUEL C, now or recently residing in Jersey City, U S A
BROWN, DAVID, a native of Scotland, who emigrated to America about the year 1845
BROWN, Mrs. MAGGIE, (Maiden name, HELPIN), now or formerly residing in Washington, D.C., U.S.A.
BROWN, Captain THOMAS MITCHEL, Widow and Children supposed to reside in America.
BUCHAN, ALEXANDER, a Blacksmith, who left Scotland for New Providence, W I, about the year 1840.
BULGER, KATIE, who formerly worked in East 70th Street, New York City, U S A.
BURGESS, ANNE (See Mrs John T Davis.)
BURKE, THOMAS, formerly of New York City, who was afterwards in California, U.S.A., about the year 1858.
BURLE, THEODORE, a native of France, now residing in America.
BURNS, OWEN, formerly of East 11th Street, New York City, U S A.
BURNS, Mrs. ROSE, last heard of in New York City, U S A., in 1885.
BURT, RICHARD, a native of Staffordshire, who left Eng for America in 1810
BYRNES, JOSEPH, a Zinc-worker, was in Virginia City, Nevada, U S A, in 1878.
CAIRNS, or CEARINS, FAMILY, formerly of Ireland, now residing in America.
CAMPBELL, GEORGE, formerly of Richmond, Va., U S A, Tobacco Merchant   *Creditors wanted.*
CAMPBELL, JAMES, a native of Scotland, now or lately residing in New York, U S.A.
CARR, MARY, Relatives of, supposed to be residing in America
CARR, Rev Mr, a Clergyman in Toronto, Canada, in or previous to the year 1850
CARRAHER, or CARAHER, FRANCIS, owning real estate in 18th Ward, N Y City, in 1859
CARRINGTON, MICHAEL, and ANN, Powerloom Weavers, who left England for America about 1850.
CARROLL, DANIEL WILLIAM, in 1874 was in a French Merchant's house in Bogota, Columbia, S A.
CARTER, JOHN, was at Decatur, Ill., in 1889, and last heard of at Heyworth, Ill., U S A.
CASKEY, JOHN, formerly of Co. Antrim, Ireland, now residing in America.
CEARINS. (See Cairns Family)
CHARPENTIER, ANTHONY LE, who left the Island of Jersey, for Illinois, U S A., in or about the year 1869.
CHEVALIER, P. F, now or formerly residing in the U S A
CLARK, THOMAS, son of John and Sarah, who left England for America about 1825
CLARKE, WILLIAM, a native of Co. Monaghan, Ireland, in 1863 he was at Thunder Bay, and afterwards at Bruce Mines, Canada.
CLIFTON, THOMAS, who left Halifax, England, for America in or about the year 1831.
COCKMAN, THOMAS, formerly of Co Surrey, England, last heard of in Brooklyn, N.Y., U.S.A.
COGSWELL FAMILY, formerly of England, now residing in America.
COLLERAN, MARTIN, formerly of Co. Clare, Ireland, now residing in America
CONDELL, or OUSLEY, EMILIA, Children of, now residing in America.
CONGREVE, FREDERICK WILLIAM, supposed to have left Liverpool, England, for Halifax, N S., in 1862.
COOPER, ELIZABETH (See Elizabeth Smith)
COREAN, J E. DE, who left Havre, France, for Havannah, in 1875, supposed to be residing in America,
CORK, MARY (See Mary Hickey)
COUSIN, JEAN, who left France for America about the close of last century
COVINGTON, JOHN T, last heard of at No 107, West 24th Street, New York City, U S A., in 1855.
COVINGTON, WILLIAM B., last heard of at Louisiana, U S A, about the year 1858.
COWARD, DAVID WILLIAM, formerly of Ottawa, afterwards of St. John, N B, Canada.
CRAIG, ROBERT, formerly of Glasgow, Scotland, afterwards residing in New York, U S A.
CRAIG, THOMAS GEORGE, now or recently residing at Sherman, Grayson Co., Texas, U.S.A.
CROFT, ESTHER FRANCES, formerly of Co Kent, England, now residing in America.
CROSSLAND, JAMES, who left England for Nova Scotia in December, 1881.
CUMMINS FAMILY, formerly of Gloucestershire, England, now residing in America.
DAVENPORT, THOMAS, late of Co Londonderry, Ireland, about 1850, residing in Lexington, Ala, U S.A.
DAVIS, CHARLES A, now or recently residing in New York City, U S A
DAVIS, Mrs JOHN T., (Maiden name, ANNE BURGESS), when last heard of, was in New York City, U.S.A.
DAVIS, MARY, daughter of CAROLINE and CHARLES DAVIS, residing in New York, or elsewhere in America.
DEARLOVE, JOHN, now or formerly of K Co, 10th Regiment, U S Infantry
DE COREAN, J E (See Corean, J E. De.)
DE HAERNE, EMILE, Banker, of Brussels, Belgium, now residing in America
DE LABESSE, LEON JUGE, a native of France, supposed to be residing in Dakota, Wyo Ter, U.S.A.
DE MORA FAMILY, when last heard of, were residing in America

177

DICKERSON, or DICKINSON, ESTHER. (See Esther Hand)
DIMON, Mrs. (See Mrs. Rebecca Bouton)
DINGWALL, ALEXANDER and JANET, who left Scotland for America about 1852, and when last heard of were at Detroit, Mich. U S A
DOLAN FAMILY, residing in America.
DONOHOO, or OUSLEY, ANNE, Children of, residing in America.
DONOR, JOHN, late of Co. Limerick, who left Ireland for New York, U S A., in 1869
DRUGAN, JOHN, formerly of Dublin, Ireland, now residing in America
DUESBERY, WILLIAM, of Lancashire, who left England in 1877, supposed to be in America.
DUNANT FAMILY, formerly of Switzerland, now residing in America.
DUNN, Mr M A, supposed to be residing in America
DURAN, DON JOSE JUAN and DON JOSE JOAQUIN, residing in America
DUXFIELD, JOSEPH J, formerly of Sunderland, who left England for New York in or about the year 1870
DWYER, FRANCES GRACE HELEN, and SUSANNAH KATHLEEN, formerly of Ireland, now in America.
DWYER, JOHN MATTHEW, Heirs of, residing in America
DYKES, ANDREW, formerly of Yorkshire, England, now residing in America.
EAGER, MARIA, now or formerly of Springfield, Mass., U S A.
EBBERN, THOMAS, who left England for America about 1867
EDWARDS, WILLIAM JAMES, formerly of Co. Donegall, who left Ireland for Canada some years ago.
ELPHINSTONE FAMILY, formerly of Scotland, now residing in America
EMERSON, THOMAS R., formerly of Co. Down, Ireland, now residing in America.
FANCOURT, HENRY ROBERT AUSTIN, in 1867 a Ward room Steward on the U S.S. "Winooski."
FARNES, JOSEPH, formerly of Co Middlesex, England, now residing in America.
FARRELL, PHILIP HORLOCK, a Carpenter, formerly of Co. Dorset, Eng., residing in the U S A. about 1874.
FASHOWITZ, FARENZBACH, a native of Russia, residing in the U S A. about the year 1848
FERGUSON, JAMES, now or formerly residing in the U S A.
FIRBANK, RALPH, a native of Newport, Mon, Eng., was at Chicago, Ills., U S A., in June, 1880.
FISCHER, JULIUS, a native of Wurtemberg, was at Hays City, Kansas, U S A, in 1874
FISHER, CHRISTOPHER, who left London, England, for America about the year 1850
FITZHARRIS, DENIS, Coachmaker, a native of Ireland, in 1875, residing in New York City, U S A.
FONTANA, GIOVANNI B, supposed to have left Birmingham, England, for America in 1861.
FORBES, JOHN C, who was in Washington, D.C., U S A., in 1865.
FRASER, JAMES THOMAS, supposed to be residing in America
GARREAD, JOHN, who in 1858 was a Seaman on board the whaling barque "C Coming"
GAY, ROBERT and ELIZA (Maiden name, STEWART), of Co. Tyrone, Ireland, Children of, in America.
GILBERT, THOMAS, who left England for New York, U S A, in or about the year 1810
GILL, FELIX, now or formerly of Philadelphia, Pa., U S A
GILLETT, WILLIAM, who went to America about 1840, and was last heard of in California.
GLOYN, WILLIAM, who, it is supposed, left England for America about the year 1855.
GOEPPERLE, Mrs MARY, residing in New York City, U S A, in 1888
GOGGIN, MICHAEL, formerly of Co Limerick, Ireland, now residing in America
GOMAUX, VICTORINE, (Maiden name, MAHIAS), Children of, residing in America,
GOODE, EMILY and SARAH ANN, residing in America.
GOURLAY, WILLIAM K, a native of England, in 1870, residing at Columbus, Inda U S A.
GRANT, JOSEPH, formerly of Co Kerry, Ireland, afterwards of Boston Highlands, Mass., U.S.A.
GREEN, HENRY, formerly of Co Lincoln, who left England for America in the year 1864.
GREENE, CHARLES A, a Seaman, and formerly Mate of the ship "Gamecock"
GRIFFITHS, DAVID, who was last heard of at Pittsburgh, Pa., U S.A., in 1872
GRIFFITHS, JOSEPH, who in 1832 was residing in Mexico
GRIMES, JOHN, now or formerly of 335, East 77th Street, New York City, U S A.
HAERNE, EMILE DE. (See De Baerne, Emile)
HAND, ESTHER, (afterwards DICKERSON or DICKINSON); supposed to be residing in New Jersey, U S A
HAND, FAMILY of, residing in America.
HAND, JOSEPH W, supposed to be residing in the U S A.
HANSEN, GUSTAV and ELISE, formerly of the province of Dusseldorf, now residing in America.
HARKIN, MICHAEL, in 1872 was trading between Chicago, Ill., and Grand Rapids, Mich, U S A.
HARRIS, JANE, (Maiden name, JEAVONS), formerly of England, now residing in America.
HARRIS, Mrs. (Maiden name, MAMNICE WALLACE), now or recently residing at Washington, D C., U S.A.
HARTINGER FAMILY, who left Europe for America in or about the year 1855
HARTMAN FAMILY, formerly of England, now residing in America
HARWOOD, RACHEL, residing in Baltimore, Md, in or previous to 1852
HAWKINS, RICHARD W M, was at Mineral Ridge, Ohio, in 1877, and afterwards at Jackson, Mich., U S.A.
HELPIN, MAGGIE (See Mrs Maggie Brown)
HENDRIX, MRS. I J, supposed to be residing in the United States
HERBERT, Miss EMMA, (whose father was a Sergeant in the British Army), now residing in America.
HEUVELDOP FAMILY, supposed to be residing in New Orleans, La, or elsewhere in the U.S.A.
HICKEY, MARY, (Maiden name, CORK), formerly of England, now residing in America.
HICKS, JOHN H, now or late of Laramie, Wyoming Ter, U S A.
HILLS, GEORGE WILLIAM, formerly of Banff, Scotland, now residing in America.
HOARE, THOMAS, who left England for America in 1881
HOGEBOOM, HENRY JAMES, now or formerly of Albany, N Y, U S A.
HOLGATE, JOHN, now or recently residing in Hamilton, Ont., Canada.
HOLLINS, WILLIAM, formerly of Nottinghamshire, England, afterwards of Canada
HOLT, JANE. (See Jane Upton.)
HONE, JAMES, formerly of Co Oxford, Blacksmith, who left England for America in 1852
HORN, MARY PATERSON, (Maiden name, ARMSTRONG), now or formerly residing in Ontario, Canada.
HORSFALL, JOHN TOMLIN, who left England for the U S A in 1858.
HORSLEY, GEORGE, when last heard of was residing at Princeville, Peoria Co, Illa, U S A.
HOWELL, WILLIAM, late of So. Brooklyn, N Y, last heard of at Big Springs, Howard Co, Texas, U S A
HUMBERT, LIZZIE, now or recently residing at Far Rockaway, N Y, U S A.
HUTTON, WILLIAM, a Seaman, a native of Scotland, sailed from Shields, Eng., for the Brazils, about 1848
HYDE, ARTHUR LEMAN, a native of England, supposed to have enlisted in the U S Army, previous to 1865.
HYDE, JOSEPH, formerly of England, now residing in America
HYDE, LOUISA, late of Peterson, Gull River, County Victoria, Ont., Canada.
IBBOTSON, MARY, formerly of Yorkshire, who left England for America in 1848.
IMPLETON, THOMAS, supposed to be residing in America
JACKSON, ALEXANDER H, now or late of Division Avenue, Brooklyn, E.D., N Y, U S A.
JACKSON, JAMES, formerly of Broad Street, London, Children of, residing in America
JACKSON, WM WATSON, of Eng, last heard of, keeping a Bar-room, at San Antonio, Texas, U S A.
JANSEN, JOHANNES, a native of Holland, afterwards residing at 14, Hamilton Avenue, Brooklyn, N Y., U.S.A.
JARDINE, JAMES, a native of Scotland, who emigrated to Canada in 1853.
JEAVONS, JANE (See Jane Harris.)
JEPSON, SARAH A, and LOUISA A., residing in America in 1856.
JESSOP, TOM, formerly of Lincolnshire, England, who emigrated to America in 1850.
JOHNSTON, ANN, (formerly McINTIRE), late of Londonderry, Ireland, now residing in America.
JOHNSTON, ROBERT, Seaman, of Lerwick, Shetland, who left London for Quebec about June, 1867
JONES, ABNER W, supposed to be residing in America.
JONES, ELIZABETH ANN, HONOR, and ROBERT S, who left Cornwall, Eng, for America in 1851.
JONES, EVAN and ELIZABETH (Maiden name, LANIGAN), formerly of Wales, in 1823, living at Valley Town, Cherokee Co., N C, U S A

SPECIAL LIST No 11.

JONES, HANNAH, formerly of America, who, when last heard of, was in Rome, Italy
JONES, HENRY, formerly of Cornwall, England, now residing in America
JONES, THEOPHILUS JOHN, of Cornwall, formerly a Master in the Royal Navy, residing in America.
JOUANNE, VICTOR ARMAND, of France, when last heard of was residing at Deversath, Colo, U S A.
KEANE, JOHN and MATHEW, formerly of Co Cork, Ireland, now residing in America.
KEANE, THOMAS C L, when last heard of was residing in Ohio, U S A
KEOGH, FRANCIS, formerly of Dublin, Ireland, now residing in America.
KEYES, HEMAN, residing in Ontario Co, N Y U S A, in 1856
KING, FIFE ELLETSON, FAMILY of, supposed to be residing in America.
KING, HUGO WALTON, formerly of Co Cumberland, Eng, supposed to reside in America.
KIRKBRIDE, FRANK H, last heard of in Philadelphia, Pa, U S A, in 1865
LA BESSE (See Leon Juge De La Besse)
LAKEMAN, RICHARD, residing in Brooklyn, or elsewhere in America.
LAMONT, NORMAN, a native of Scotland, formerly of the Royal Engineers, was in Quebec in 1848, in Montreal in 1849, and by letter dated "New York, 20th October, 1849," he resigned his commission
LANE, JOHN, a Tailor, who left London for America about the year 1854
LANIGAN, ELIZABETH (See Evan and Elizabeth Jones)
LEARY, JOHN and PATRICK, sons of James Leary, now residing in America
LE CHARPENTIER, ANTHONY (See Charpentier, Anthony Le)
LE MOULT, E P, formerly of Hamburg, was in Buffalo, N Y, U S A, in the fall of 1872
LEONARD, JOHN, or his son, EDWARD, formerly residing in Hester Street, New York City, U.S.A.
LEWIS, ROBERT WAGSTAFF, supposed to be residing in America
LIDDELL, JOHN W, a Joiner, a native of Durham, England, supposed to have gone to America in 1876.
LOGAN, PATRICK and MAGGIE, residing in Pennsylvania, or elsewhere in America
LORY, ELIZABETH L, formerly of Co Cornwall, England supposed to be residing in the U S.A.
LOWDON, JOSEPHINE WILSON, Heirs of, residing in America.
LOWNDES, SELBY, formerly of England, now residing in America.
LYMAN, EDWARD, residing in America.
MACARTNEY FAMILY, formerly of Great Britain, now residing in America.
MACAULEY, JAMES BENJAMIN, Relatives of, residing in America.
McBEATH, MARY. (See John and Mary Scott)
McBETH, FINLAY and DONALD, formerly of Scotland, when last heard of, in 1867. Finlay was in San Francisco, Cal, and Donald in Portland, Oregon, U S A.
McCARTNEY, THOMAS, of Ireland, a Bootmaker, who when last heard of was in Pennsylvania, U.S.A.
McCLELLAND, ROBERT, a native of Scotland, afterwards of Philadelphia and New Jersey. U S A
McCREADY, THOMAS STUART, formerly of Co Londonderry, Ireland, now residing in America
MACDONALD, JAMES, a native of Aberdeen, Scotland, residing in America about 1845
McEACHRAN, ARCHIBALD, when last heard of in 1868, was going to Peace River, Canada.
McENANCY, ROBERT, WILLIAM, and MARGARET, formerly of Ireland, now residing in America.
MACFARLANE, ANDREW, Joiner, a native of Scotland, was residing at Allentown, Pa., U S.A., in 1862.
McFARLANE, SARAH, who left Scotland for America about 1870
McGIVEN, DONALD, now or recently residing at St Augustine, Fla., U S A.
McGLONE, BARTHOLOMEW, residing in Toronto, Canada, or elsewhere in America.
McGOWAN, HUGH, formerly of Ireland, now residing in America.
McINTIRE, ANN (See Ann Johnston)
McKENNA, JAMES, now or formerly residing in East 11th Street, New York City, U.S.A.
MACKLIN, or MURPHY, SUSAN (Maiden name, OUSLEY), Children of, residing in America.
McMILLAN FAMILY, formerly of Glasgow, Scotland, now residing in America
McQUAID, CATHARINE and JOHN, now or recently residing in Brooklyn, U S A.
McTURK, JOHN, a native of Scotland, who went to America in or about the year 1862
MAGEE, CHARLES ROBERT, formerly of Co Armagh, Ireland, now residing in America.
MAHIAS, VICTORINE (See Victorine Gomaux)
MARTIN, JAMES, Blacksmith, formerly of Greenock, left Scotland for New York or Boston, U S A, in 1878.
MARTIN, JANE, (Maiden name, BENNETT), formerly of Co. Tyrone, Ireland, now residing in America
MARTIN, MARY ANN (Maiden name, WALKER), formerly of Co Lincoln, England, now residing in America
MARTIN, SUSANNAH (afterwards ELKINGTON), of Co Lincoln, Eng, now residing in America.
MATTRAS, SAMUEL, a native of Holland, residing in New Orleans, La, U S A., about the year 1865
MAXWELL, WILLIAM B, formerly of Nassau, N P, Bahamas, afterwards residing in America.
MAY, NATHANIEL, supposed to have left England for America in the year 1869
MELVIN, JAMES, a native of Scotland, last heard of at St Fergus, Ont., Canada
MENDENS, JOSEPH, formerly of Philadelphia, now residing in New York, or San Francisco, U.S.A.
MESTER, ERNST LOUIS A., formerly of Hamburg, who left Germany for America in 1880
MICKLEWOOD, PHILIP H, a native of England, now residing in America
MITCHELL, JOSEPH, of Co. Monaghan, Ireland, residing at Fall River, Mass, U.S.A. about 1874.
MOODY, RUTHERFORD, formerly in the Steam Saw Mill business in America.
MOORE, HENRY, in 1861, of Co. C, 11th Regiment New Jersey Volunteers, U S A
MORA. (See De Mora Family)
MORGAN, FRANCIS H, formerly of Co Somerset, Eng, now residing in America
MORGAN, Dr J. T, formerly of Wales, now residing in America.
MORRISON, JAMES, a Sailor, of Scotland, son of Charles Morrison, supposed to be residing in America.
MORTON, Dr, and ANN, (Maiden name, WILLIAMS), of Cheshire, who left England for America in 1860.
MOULT, E P LE. (See Le Moult, E P)
MURPHY, Miss CATHERINE, residing at Richland Station, N Y., U S.A, in 1878.
MURPHY, SUSAN (See Susan Macklin.)
NEILSON, JAMES and MICHAEL, who left Scotland for America about 1840.
NICOLAN, JOSEPH, residing in the U S A, or Canada.
NOLAN, ROGER, a native of Longford, Ireland, afterwards residing in America.
OBERLEY FAMILY, residing in America.
O'DWYER, JANE, when last heard of, was residing in Louisville, Ky., U S A
O'DWYER, WILLIAM, GEORGE, and RICHARD, born in France, and who went to America in 1818.
OLWANT, THOMAS CATTERALL, who, in or about the year 1800, left England for America.
ONDERBEEK, JEAN BAPTISTE, residing in New York City, U S A, in 1873
O'SHEA, MARY, a native of Co. Kerry, Ireland, last heard of in Boston, Mass, U S A.
OSLER, ROSALIE, who married a Mr BARASFORD, or BERESFORD, was in New York, U S A., in 1859.
OUSLEY FAMILY, residing in America.
PASSAPAE, MARY, residing in Baltimore, Md, U S A, in or previous to 1862.
PATCHETT, HENRY, who left England for New York about 1848
PATCHING, or PATCHIN, GEORGE, formerly of Co Sussex, England, supposed to be residing in America
PEARL, FRANK, a native of Onondaga County, N Y, afterwards of Kentucky, U S A
PELLATT, ALFRED HOPE, formerly of England, now or late of San Francisco, Cal, U.S.A.
PEMBROKE, STEPHEN, (coloured), in 1850 was interested in land in Essex Co, N Y, U S A
PERTON FAMILY, formerly of England, now residing in America
PFEIL, JOHANN and CAROLINE WILHELMINE, who left Germany for Baltimore, U S A., in 1858.
PHILLIPS, JOHN, who is supposed to have left London, England, for America, in November, 1876.
PITCHER, ROBERT, formerly of Co. Norfolk, who left England for America about 1870.
PORTEOUS FAMILY, formerly of Scotland, now residing in America.
PORTER, THOMAS, Second Mate of the Schooner "Agneda," who sailed from London, Eng, for America in 1845.
POSS, Mrs PAULINE, residing in St. Louis, Mo, U S A, in 1864
PRINGLE, WILLIAM and THOMAS, who left Scotland for America about 1842.
PRISEMAN, ROBERT, formerly of London, England, was in Sacramento City, Cal, U S A, in 1889

REDMOND FAMILY, of Co. Tipperary, Ireland, now residing in America.
REEVES, FRANCIS formerly of Co Kent, England, last heard of at Chicago, Ills, U.S.A, in 1858,
REILLY, THOMAS T, now or formerly residing in New York City, U S A.
RICHARDSON, EDWIN, last heard of at Chatham, Chester Co, Pa., U S A, in 1870
RICHARDSON, Mrs ELIZABETH, formerly of Old Street, London, Eng, now residing in America.
RICKARBY, ELIZA H. (See Eliza H. Bond.)
RISHTON, JOHN, now or late of Dougherty's Station, Cal, U S A.
ROACH, JOHN, formerly of Limerick, Ireland, now residing in America.
ROBB FAMILY, formerly of Scotland, now residing in America
ROGAN, PATRICK and ANNIE, formerly of Co Down Ireland, afterwards of New York, U S A
ROPER, WILLIAM F, residing in San Francisco, U S A, in 1853
ROSENFELDER, LUDWIG, Cabinet Maker, living in San Francisco, Cal, U S A, between 1863 and 1870.
ROUND, JOHN (See John Round Slyfield.)
ROUQUIER, JULES, last heard of at Indianapolis, Inda, U S A.
RUBY FAMILY, formerly of Ireland, afterwards settled in America
RULE, JAMES, a native of Scotland, in or about 1800, a Seaman on the Peruvian Frigate, "*Amazones*."
RUSH, JOHN, now or formerly residing in East 11th Street, New York City, U S A
RUSSELL, ADAM, formerly of Edinburgh, who left Scotland for America in or about 1850
RUSSELL, SELINA GRACE, supposed to be residing in the U S A.
SALTMARSH, NATHANIEL R, who left England for New York in January, 1891
SAMPSON, WILLIAM, Provision Merchant, who left Glasgow, Scotland, for Canada, in 1879.
SARSON, FREDERICK, formerly of Leicestershire, Eng, now residing in America.
SAUNTER, MICHAEL and PAUL, last heard of in New Durham, Co Bergen, N J, U S A.
SCOTT, JOHN and MARY, (Maiden name, McBEATH), left Scotland for Boston, Mass, U.S.A., in 1841
SCULLEN, JAMES or PATRICK, who was in the N Y City Police about 1866
SEEGEN, SALOMON, formerly of London, Eng, supposed to be residing in New York, or elsewhere in America.
SEERY, BRIDGET, late of Westmeath, Ireland, then of 592, Pacific Street, Brooklyn, N Y, U S A.
SHAW, HECTOR, a native of Scotland, residing, in 1876, in Jersey City, N J, U S A.
SHELDON, M L, now or formerly residing in the U S A.
SHERIDAN FAMILY, formerly of Queen's Co, Ireland, now residing in America.
SHERIDAN, HELEN, born about 1800, family supposed to be residing in America.
SHINTON, THOMAS, last heard of at Paterson, N J, U.S.A., in October, 1873
SIMEON, JOHN EDWARD, who left England for New York, U S A, in 1874
SIMPSON, LEVI, an Engineer or Joiner, who left England for America about 1871
SKINNER, PATRICK, a Mariner, a native of Scotland, supposed to be residing in America
SLATER, ROBERT, of Glasgow, Scotland, when last heard of was engaged as Mate on a Steamer
SLYFIELD, JOHN ROUND, (otherwise JOHN ROUND), of Peterboro', Ont., Canada, about 1876.
SMITH, ANN (See Matthew and Ann Alexander.)
SMITH, ELIZA, wife of John Smith, who left Eng, for Salt Lake City, U.S.A., in 1858
SMITH, ELIZABETH, (Maiden name, COOPER), last heard of at New Orleans, La, U.S.A.
SMITH, GERALD, formerly of Co Louth, Ireland, who emigrated to America in 1880.
SMITH, HAZIEL, supposed to be residing in America
SMITH, THOMAS JAMES, formerly of Co. Kent, who left England for British Columbia, in the year 1864.
SPARKS, ROBERT ADAMS, formerly of Co Somerset, Eng, now residing in America
SPREULL FAMILY, formerly of Scotland, now residing in America.
STACKHOUSE, THOMAS, who left New Orleans for California, between 1850 and 1855
STANGER, FREDERICK, last heard of in America, in January, 1881
STEVENS, JOHN WILLIAM, who left London, Eng., for America in 1840.
STEWART, ELIZA. (See Robert and Eliza Gay.)
SULLIVAN, JOHN T, now or formerly residing in the U S A.
SUTLIFF, Mrs ELIZA, residing in New York, U S A, in 1853
SWEENEY, JOHN, formerly of Co Cork, Ireland; now or lately residing in Co. Perth, Ont, Canada.
TACON, RICHARD E, formerly of Wiltshire, Eng, now residing in America
TAYLOR, JANET, a native of Co Stirling, Scotland, who went to America about 1830
TAYLOR, JOSEPH and WILLIAM, of Queen's Co, Ireland, who arrived at New York, U.S.A., in 1848.
THOMPSON, ALEXR, a Sailor, of Scotland, in 1862, when on a voyage from Hong Kong to New York.
THOMPSON, MARY ANN, now or late of Locust Street, Philadelphia, Pa, U.S.A.
THOMSON, EDWARD, Carpenter, a native of Scotland, was at Stapleton, Richmond Co, N Y, in 1855.
THORNTON, DAVID, a Carpenter, who left Scotland for America about 1872.
TONGE, Mrs ANN, now or formerly residing at Patiscaster Falls, Md, U S A.
UPTON, JANE (otherwise HOLT), who left Dublin, Ireland, for America about the year 1862
VALLIS, JOHN, formerly of London, Eng, now residing in America
VANDEVYVER, JOSEPH and JEANNE, Children of Joseph Vandevyver; now residing in America.
WALKER, HORATIO, who deserted from the 15th British Regiment of Foot, at Halifax, N S, Canada, in 1818.
WALKER, MARY ANN. (See Mary Ann Martin.)
WALLACE, MAMNICE. (See Mrs Harris.)
WATT, JANE, formerly of Co Tyrone, Ireland Representatives of, residing in America
WEBSTER, JOHN, of England, now or recently residing at Bowmanville, Ont, or elsewhere in Canada.
WEHLI, BENEDICT and JACOB, formerly of Bohemia, now residing in America.
WEISS, FRIEDRICH, who left Germany for Baltimore, U S A., in 1838
WELTER FAMILY, supposed to be residing in America
WHEATLEY, JOSEPH, formerly of Co Gloucester, Eng, last heard of in New York, U.S.A., in December, 1826.
WHELAN, THOMAS, who emigrated to America about 1861, and was last heard of at Concord.
WHITFIELD, WILLIAM, late of Co Dublin, Ireland, now residing in America.
WILD, WILLIAM, formerly of Yorkshire, Eng, now residing in America.
WILKINS, CALDWELL R., formerly employed by Hamilton and Easter, in Baltimore, Md., U S A.
WILLEY, KATE MARGARET, formerly of Lambeth, County Surrey, Eng; now residing in America.
WILLIAMS, ANN. (See Dr and Ann Morton.)
WILLIAMS, CATHERINE (See Catherine Atkinson.)
WILLIAMS, EDWARD, whose Mother was born at Flushing, LI, N Y, U S A.
WILLIAMS, PHILIP, formerly of Glamorgan, Wales, Children of, residing in America
WILLIAMS, SAMUEL and LEVI, supposed to be residing in the U S A
WILSON, WILLIAM, late a Seaman on the "*Clyde*," of Glasgow, Scotland, now supposed to be in America.
WINGERTZ, SENOR SORUBABEL, supposed to be residing in America
WISE, HENRY, formerly of Eng, last heard of at Albany, Delaware Co., Inda., U S A.
WOLF, LIZZIE, supposed to be residing in America
WOOD, JAMES, Relatives of, residing in America
WRIGHT, HENRY, (right Name, ADAM RIACH), residing in America under the former name.
ZAUGER, MATTHIAS, of Wurtemburg, now or lately working on a Railroad at Paterson, N J., U.S A.
ZIMLICH, Mrs. HEINRICH, residing in Memphis, Tenn., U S A, in 1864

SPECIAL LIST No. 12.

UNCLAIMED MONEY, LANDS AND ESTATES.

The following persons (or heirs) are entitled to property Address **J. B. MARTINDALE, 142 La Salle Street, Chicago, Illinois.** [See pages 6, 7 and 8 of this Manual.]

Brig "*General Armstrong*," at Fayal, in 1814 Captain, Owners, Officers, and Crew of.
ABERDEEN, Miss ELIZABETH, deceased abroad in or about the year 1828.
ADAM, ELIZABETH, deceased abroad in or about the year 1868
ADAMS, CATHERINE (maiden name SLOANE), deceased in or about the year 1849.
AMERY, ALFRED, who in 1873 was at Van Dyke's Hotel, Catherine Slip, New York City, U S.A.
ANDREW, Miss JANE, deceased abroad in or about the year 1841
ANDREW, Miss JANE (daughter of PETER ANDREW), deceased in or about the year 1859
ANN, Mrs MARY, deceased abroad in or about the year 1808
APPLETON, CHARLES E , when last heard of was at Hyde Park, or Lobo. near London Ont , Canada.
ASSINDER, CHARLES, a native of Eng., Architect and Surveyor, supposed to reside in America.
BABER, HENRY EDWARD, deceased abroad in or about the year 1834
BAILEY, ESTHER, afterwards HEYFRON when last heard of was residing in California, U S A.
BARLOW, A , deceased abroad in or about the year 1834
BARNES, WILLIAM HUDSON, who died in 1864 Widow of, supposed to be in America.
BARTLEY FAMILY, formerly of England , now residing in America
BARTLEY, WILLIAM T , when last heard of was residing in Louisville, Ky , U S A
BARTON, WILLIAM, a native of Lancashire, Eng , who went to America about 1821.
BEATTIE, ISABELLA, formerly of Belfast, Ireland , now residing in America
BENN FAMILY, formerly of England, now residing in America, or elsewhere abroad.
BERGIN, PATRICK, now or recently residing in New York City, U S A
BEST, FREDERICK JAMES, who left England in the year 1866 supposed for America.
BIGGS, ELIZA, Relatives supposed to reside in the U S A., or Canada.
BIRD, MARTHA, Representatives of, supposed to reside in America, or elsewhere abroad.
BONEL, LUCY, deceased abroad in or about the year 1808
BREEN, JAMES, deceased abroad in or about the year 1839.
BREEN, JOHN, a Merchant, deceased abroad in or about the year 1843.
BREMAR, ANNA, deceased in or about the year 1800 Representatives of, supposed to be in America.
BROWN, Miss ELLEN, deceased abroad in or about the year 1855
BROWN, Miss HENRIETTA, deceased abroad in or about the year 1838
BROWN, JAMES. (See James Cahill.)
BROWN, THOMAS, late of Co York, England, next of kin believed to be living in America, or Canada.
BROWN, WILLIAM H , and FRANCIS S , brothers, now or late of New York City, U S A.
BUCKINGHAM, J , deceased abroad in or about the year 1823
BUCKLEY, CHARLES A , residing in New York City, U S A , in 1859
BUNNING, JOSEPH, a Carpenter and Builder, residing in Boston, U S.A., previous to the year 1877.
BURRELL, ANN (daughter of WILLIAM BURRELL, who died abroad in or about the year 1841.)
BUXTON, EDWARD, who left England for Prince Edward Island, Canada, in 1849
BYAR, WILLIAM THOMAS, who died abroad in or about the year 1854.
CAHILL, BERNARD or BRYAN, when last heard of was residing in New York City, U S A.
CAHILL, JAMES, otherwise BROWN, who left Ireland for America in or about the year 1867
CAHILL, MARY (See Mary Sillery.)
CAIN, MICHAEL , Representatives of, supposed to be in the U S A , or Canada
CALDWELL, Major-General ALEXANDER, deceased abroad in or about the year 1853
CAMERON, ANN (Maiden name LONDON), widow of ALEX. CAMERON, deceased about the year 1829.
CAMPBELL, JAMES, deceased abroad in or about the year 1851
CARPAU, BAZIL, deceased in or about the year 1813
CARTER, JOHN, a native of Scotland, now residing in America
CASTELLAN, CECILE MARIE, who died in or about the year 1835.
CAVAYE, WILLIAM, a native of Scotland, supposed to be residing in America.
CHAMBERS, AURIOL THOMAS, deceased abroad in or about the year 1823.
CHAMBERS, CHRISTOPHER and REUBEN, deceased abroad
CHAMBERS, ELIZABETH, deceased abroad in or about the year 1870
CHAMBERS, SARAH J , now or recently residing in New York City, or elsewhere in the U S A.
CHEMIER FAMILY, natives of France, now residing in America
CHIENE, JOHN, deceased abroad in or about the year 1837
CHRISTOPHER, Mrs ELIZABETH, now or recently residing in Philadelphia, Pa , U S A
CHURCHILL, JAMES, when last heard of was residing in North 7th Street, Philadelphia, Pa., U S A.
CLARE FAMILY, formerly of Co Carlow, Ireland , now residing in America.
CLARK, HENRY F , now or recently residing in Charleston, S.C., U S A.
CLARK, RALPH, a Merchant, in 1873, of 44, East 9th Street, New York City, U S A.
COLLINS, Sergeant DENNIS, deceased abroad in or about the year 1842
CONNOR, or O'CONNOR, PATRICK, of Co Tyrone, Ireland , who left for New York, U S A., about 1867.
CONWAY, SUSANNA, widow of W T Conway, of Boston Relatives of, in America
CORSIE, JAMES, who left Scarboro', Ont., Canada, for Michigan, U S.A., in September, 1861.
COUPLAND, AGNES (See Charles and Agnes Whitbreok)
CRANAGE FAMILY, supposed to reside in America.
CROFTS, CHARLES FREDERICK, now, or recently residing in New York City, U S A
CROKER, ROBERT, formerly of Co Down, Ireland, who emigrated to America about 1860
CROOK, MARIA, late of Co Surrey, England , Relatives of, supposed to reside in the United States.
CUMMINGS, MARGARET, deceased abroad in or about the year 1815.
CURELL, WILLIAM, now or late of New York, U S A
DA COSTA, ANTONIO, deceased abroad in or about the year 1861
DALLAS, Lieut.-Colonel PETER, deceased abroad in or about the year 1806
DALY, JOHN, late of Co Middlesex, England , next of kin of, supposed to be in America.
DAVIES, ELIZA, deceased abroad in or about the year 1865.
DAVIES, GEORGE, formerly of London, deceased in or about the year 1841
DAWSON, JOSHUA, of Otley, Yorkshire, Seaman, now residing in America
DAWSON, JUSTIS, formerly of Yorkshire, Eng , now residing in America
DAY, Miss, formerly with ARNOLD, CONSTABLE & CO , and A. T STEWART & CO , of N.Y City, U S A.
DEANE, DUKE, deceased abroad in or about the year 1866
DEARDEN FAMILY, residing in America, or elsewhere abroad.
DE MONTMORENCY, Miss. (See Montmorency, Miss De)
DE SOUZA, Surgeon FRANCIS, deceased abroad in or about the year 1829.
DICKSON, Captain JOSEPH, deceased abroad in or about the year 1805
DIXON, JOHN, when last heard of in 1845, was in the Bermuda Islands W I
DODDS, MARY, daughter of James, formerly of Eng , now residing in America.
DODSWORTH, HENRY THOMAS deceased abroad in or about the year 1862
DONNELY, Captain FRANCIS SQUIRE, deceased abroad in or about the year 1854.
DONOHOE, PATRICK, formerly of Kingstown, Ireland , now residing in America
DONOHUE, JUDY (See Judy Linnane)
DOOLEY, JAMES, JOSEPH, and THERESA, brothers and sister, residing in New York, U S A , in 1867
DOUGLAS, RALPH, a native of Co. Cumberland, who left Eng for America in or about the year 1821
DOUGLAS, THOMAS, a native of Eng., who, about the year 1817, went as a Sailor to the West Indies

DOYLE, ANNE, formerly of Ireland, and who is supposed to have emigrated to America.
DOYLE, DENNIS, residing in New York City, U S A , in or about the year 1825.
DOYLE, MARGARET and SUSANNAH, sisters, residing in New York, U S A in or about the year 1821.
DUMONT, Mrs WILLIAM, now or formerly of New York City, U S A.
DUNBAR, Mrs MARGARET, formerly of London, who died in or about the year 1844.
DUNDAS, JAMES OWEN, late Dealer in Dry Goods, New York City *Creditors of*
DUNLOP, Captain JOHN, deceased abroad in or about the year 1860
EALES, THOMAS ELLIOT, deceased abroad in or about the year 1858.
EAMONSON, ELIZABETH MARY, of Co Middlesex, England, next of kin, supposed to be in America.
ELLIOTT, OLIVER O G , formerly of Philadelphia, and Pittsburgh, Pa., U S A.
ELLIS, Mrs LOUISA, now, or late of No. 100, East 39th Street New York City, U.S.A.
ENNIS, JOHN CHARLES deceased abroad in or about the year 1822
EVANS, JOHN, a native of Abergele, Wales, last heard of in Brooklyn, N Y., U S.A., in May, 1871.
EVANS, MARY, deceased abroad in or about the year 1841
EVANS, Lieutenant WILLIAM, deceased abroad in or about the year 1807
EWBANK, THOMAS, late Commissioner of Patents, U S A.
FAWCETT, JOHN and JONATHAN, who left England for America previous to 1852
FAY, JULIA (See Julia and Patrick Muldoon)
FEENEY, JOHN, formerly of Co. Sligo, Ireland, a Sailor, residing in New Orleans, U S A., in 1871.
FELL, Mrs SARAH, deceased in or about the year 1813.
FENN, Captain CHARLES, deceased abroad in or about the year 1817
FERNANDES, Mrs ANN, deceased abroad in or about the year 1819
FERRIERRA, FRANCIS, deceased abroad in or about the year 1874
FLATHER, JOHN E , who left England in 1807, he was in Angel Island, Cal., in September, 1870 and in Salem, Oregon, U S A., in December, 1871
FOGARTY, ANDREW, deceased abroad in or about the year 1832
FOGARTY, JOHN, formerly of Co Waterford, Ireland, now residing in America.
FORD ARTHUR BEEVOR, formerly of Staffordshire, Eng , now residing in America.
FORREST, Captain JAMES, deceased abroad in or about the year 1836.
FOSTER, WILLIAM H , residing in New York City, U S A , in 1870.
FRANCIS, CHRISTINA, deceased abroad in or about the year 1861.
FRANKLIN, ARTHUR, deceased in or about the year 1839
FRASER, SIMEON, deceased abroad in or about the year 1830
FUSSELL FAMILY, residing in America.
GEED, CHARLES, a Mariner, deceased abroad in or about the year 1855
GIBSON, Mrs ANN, deceased abroad in or about the year 1828
GIBSON, WILLIAM, deceased abroad in or about the year 1808
GITTENS, ELIZABETH, deceased abroad in or about the year 1860
GOARD, JAMES, deceased abroad in or about the year 1835
GOOUCH, RICHARD and JOHN, left Ireland for America in 1862, and were engaged in the late Civil War
GRAHAM, THOMAS, formerly of Fifeshire, Scotland, enlisted in the 79th Highlanders, was then in the Royal Canadian Rifles, and afterwards Keeper of the Masonic Hall, Toronto, Canada.
GRAVE HENRICUS WILHELMUS now residing in America
GRAY, SINLEY, deceased abroad in or about the year 1875.
GREGORY, WILLIAM HENRY, formerly of Co Chester, England , now residing in America
GRIFFIN, Miss SOPHIA, deceased in or about the year 1843.
HACKETT, BESSIE, afterwards McLOUGHLIN, residing in New York City, U S A , in or previous to 1862
HAILEY, or HAYLEY Sergeant THOMAS JORDAN, deceased abroad in or about the year 1809
HALL, MARGARET, afterwards MITCHELL, of Scotland , when last heard of was in Philadelphia, U S A
HARRIS, SELINA, formerly of Co Surrey, England; next of kin of, supposed to be in America
HART, JULIUS, now or recently residing in New York City, U S A.
HARTSHORN, RICHARD H , who in 1843 resided in Brooklyn, or New York, U S A.
HAYLEY, or HAILEY, Sergeant THOMAS JORDAN, deceased abroad in or about the year 18 9.
HELLYER, ALBERT G , formerly of Co. Middlesex England, now residing in America.
HERNAGE, JAMES W , a native of England, who in August, 1881 was at the Rocky Mountains, U S.A.
HEYFRON FAMILY, supposed to reside in California, or elsewhere in the U S.A
HOLT, JULIA, wife of E. W HOLT, residing in New York City, or elsewhere in America.
HOPKINSON, ELIZABETH, deceased abroad in or about the year 1868
HOWES, CATHERINE (See Mrs Catherine Yarnold)
HOWARD, or ONGLEY, SARAH, residing in New York or elsewhere in America
HUBBARD, CHARLES J , who left London, Eng, for New York in or about May, 1880
HUGHES, JOHN, formerly of London, England, now residing in America.
HULSE FAMILY, of England, who emigrated to America.
HUTTON, JOHN, of Scotland, a Mariner, who left the "Laboramus," at Boston, U S A , in December, 1868.
HYLAND, Mrs EMILY, formerly of Ireland , now residing in America
INCE, GEORGE BARTON, formerly of Lancashire, Eng , who went to America about the year 1800
JENKINSON, WILLIAM, formerly of Yorkshire, Eng , afterwards residing in the U S A
JOHNSTON, Captain JOHN McMAHON, deceased abroad in or about the year 1847
JONES, ANTHONY O , Wig maker, residing in Rivington-street, New York City, in 1868.
JONES, Lieutenant GEORGE, deceased abroad in or about the year 1807
KAIN, or KANE, MICHAEL (See Michael Cain.)
KAUNTZE, JULIA, deceased abroad in or about the year 1849
KAVANAH, RUDOLPH, who left England in 1863, and is now supposed to be in America.
KELLOGG, Rev R J , now or formerly residing at New Milford, Pa , U - S A
KENNEALLY, JOHN, born in Co Tipperary, Ireland, about 1775 , married 1810 , enlisted in the British Army in 1817, and was in Canada between 1825 and 1835.
KENNEDY, JAMES BEATTIE, who left Ireland for America about 1871
KENNEDY, SARAH, deceased abroad in or about the year 1872
KERR, JAMES, a native of Co Forfar, Scotland, supposed to be in the Western States of America.
KEYSER, MICHAEL , Representatives of, residing in America.
KILGOUR, P , deceased abroad in or about the year 1829
KIRTLAND, FREDERIC S , now or late of New York U S.A.
KLUG FAMILY, residing in New York City, or elsewhere in America
KNOWLES, Lieutenant JOHN JAMES deceased abroad in or about the year 1850.
KNOX, GEORGE McLEOD, deceased abroad in or about the year 1827
KUREZYN, GEORGE L residing in New York City, or elsewhere in America
LACON, Dr HENRY R., Representatives of, believed to reside in America.
LAMB, Dr JAMES, deceased abroad in or about the year 1832
LANGLEY FAMILY, formerly of England, now residing in America
LASTOR, C. EDWARDS, residing in America.
LAW, JAMES SYLVIUS, at present presumed to be in the West Indies, or America
LEACH, WILLIAM, deceased abroad in or about the year 1805
LEAHY, DAVID, who, in 1866, resided in Mott Street New York City, U S A
LEFEVRE, JEAN BAPTISTE NICOLAS, a native of France , now residing in America.
LEGRAND, JOHN, deceased abroad in or about the year 1869
LEVIN, COLIN, deceased abroad in or about the year 1870.
LEWIS, Lieutenant Colonel CHARLES, deceased abroad in or about the year 1853.
LINDSAY, CATHERINE, deceased abroad in or about the year 1854
LINDSAY, CATHERINE JEMIMA, deceased abroad in or about the year 1853

SPECIAL LIST No 12.

LINNANE, PATRICK, MICHAEL and JUDY, formerly of Co Galway, Ireland, now residing in America
LINNEY, Mrs. ELIZABETH, widow of JOSHUA, recently residing in Toronto, Clinton Co, Iowa, U S.A.
LLEWELLYN, THOMAS, a native of Co Pembroke, Wales, a Sailor supposed to be residing in America.
LOCKINGTON, Mrs. CHRISTIANA, deceased abroad in or about the year 1852
LONDON, ANN (See Ann Cameron)
LOWINE, ARCHIBALD, deceased abroad Representatives wanted.
LOYD. THOMAS KIRKMAN, deceased abroad in or about the year 1858
LUDLOW, JANE MARIA, late of Co Middlesex, England, next of kin supposed to be in the West Indies.
LYNCH, Mrs. ROSE, deceased abroad in or about the year 1849
McCARTNEY, WILLIAM, a native of Liverpool, who left England for New York, U S A., about 1842
McCLUER, JOHN, deceased abroad in or about the year 1831
McCULLUM, BERNARD, Junior, deceased abroad in or about the year 1859.
McDONALD, ALEXANDER, who left Aberdeen, Scotland, in 1858, for America, or elsewhere abroad.
McDOUGALL, MURDOCH, a Seaman, late of Orange County, America.
M'ENNIENY, DAVID, a native of Co Tipperary, Ireland, residing at Montreal, Canada, in 1860
McGOUGH, SAMUEL, deceased abroad in or about the year 1842
McGRATH, STEPHEN, a native of Ireland, residing in New York City, or elsewhere in America
McGREGOR, ALEXANDER, lately residing at Mr William Callan's, Clark Street, Waterbury, Conn., U.S.A.
McGUIRE, WILLIAM, deceased abroad in or about the year 1822
MACKENZIE, HENRY, deceased abroad in or about the year 1842
McKERNON FAMILY, formerly of Ireland, now residing in America.
MACKEY, ELIAS O, residing at Oil City, Pa., U S A, about 1870
McKINNON, LEAH, deceased abroad in or about the year 1851
McLEOD, CRAWFORD, deceased abroad in or about the year 1841.
McLOUGHLIN, BESSIE. (See Bessie Hackett.)
McQUEEN, KENNETH, deceased abroad in or about the year 1811.
MACE, JAMES, deceased abroad Representatives wanted
MAGNESS, RICHARD, deceased abroad in or about the year 1857
MAINWARING, BOLTON, deceased abroad in or about the year 1817
MARTIN, FRANCES, of Co. Middlesex, Eng, Representatives of, residing in Canada or elsewhere in America.
MARTIN, PETER J, formerly employed as a Book-keeper, in New York City, U S,A
MARTIN, Sergeant THOMAS, deceased abroad in or about the year 1808
MASSEY, Mrs, formerly of Dublin, Ireland, supposed, at present, to be in America
MATHER, JAMES, deceased abroad in or about the year 1844
MAXWELL, CHARLOTTE, deceased abroad in or about the year 1825.
MECHAM, Captain C H, deceased abroad in or about the year 1885
MEIKLEJOHN, EDWARD, Master Mariner, deceased abroad in or about the year 1811
MENGE FAMILY, formerly of the Kingdom of Hanover, and who emigrated to America.
MEULH, Major THOMAS, deceased abroad in or about the year 1805
MEYERS, JOHN LEYDEN, now or late of McKillop, Huron County, America
MILLER, ROBERT, a native of Glasgow, who left Scotland in 1850, and is supposed to reside in America
MITCHELL, MARGARET (See Margaret Hall)
MONTMORENCY, Miss DE, formerly of Dublin, Ireland, at present in New York City, or elsewhere in America.
MOODIE, A, deceased abroad in or about the year 1871
MOORE, Captain THOMAS PALMER, deceased abroad in or about the year 1849.
MOUAT, NANCY, deceased abroad in or about the year 1819
MULDOON, PATRICK, and his sister, JULIA (afterwards FAY), now residing in America.
MUNRO, NICOL, deceased abroad in or about the year 1889
MURRAY, JOHN, deceased abroad in or about the year 1874
MYERS Mrs. ROSE MARY, deceased abroad in or about the year 1828
MYLES, SAMUEL, deceased abroad in or about the year 1818
NEAL, GEORGE WILLIAM, deceased abroad in or about the year 1856
NEAL, JAMES, formerly of Leicestershire, who left England for America in or about the year 1840
NELSON, or NEILSON, Captain CHARLES, late of the "Jane M Brainard," of New London, U.S A.
NEVIL, ROBERT, late of Belfast, Ireland, and, in 1870, residing at 10, Suffolk Street, New York City, U.S.A.
NEWALL, G B, residing in New York City, or elsewhere in America
NICHOLS, or NICOLS, EDMUND, residing in the United States of America, or Canada
NICOLL, JAMES, deceased abroad in or about the year 1857
NISBET, JOHN, deceased abroad in or about the year 1838
NOLAN THOMAS, late of Co Galway, Ireland, deceased Relatives of, residing in America.
O'BRIEN, JOHN, deceased abroad in or about the year 1859
O'BRIEN, PATRICK, formerly of Co Sligo, Ireland, now residing in America.
O'CALLAGHAN, MARY, last heard of in Toronto, Canada
O'CLARE, MICHAEL, formerly of Wicklow, Ireland. Representatives of, residing in America.
O'CONNOR, PATRICK (See Patrick Connor)
O'DWYER, MICHEL, formerly of Co. Limerick, Ireland, now residing in America.
ONGLEY FAMILY, Representatives of, residing in America
ORD, WILLIAM CHRISTOPHER, deceased abroad in or about the year 1815
O'REILLY, HUGH, deceased abroad in or about the year 1828
ORR, ROBERT, deceased abroad in or about the year 1858
OSGOOD, J. W, who was in business in New York City, U S A., in or about the year 1859.
PAXTON, ANNE, deceased abroad in or about the year 1825
PASSOS, F.A., deceased abroad in or about the year 1845
PATTON, ROBERT, deceased abroad in or about the year 1816
PAUL, EUGENE (See Eugene Von Poll)
PENROSE, JAMES, deceased abroad in or about the year 1824
PICKERING, Dr WILLIAM, in 1832 residing in Boston, Mass U S A.
POLL, EUGENE (See Eugene Von Poll)
POLLARD, JOHN HENRY, deceased abroad in or about the year 1855
POPE, ALFRED, a native of Co Sussex, Eng, supposed to be residing in America.
PORTER, GEORGE DAVIS, formerly of Strabane, Ireland, now residing in America
PROSSER, JOHN, deceased abroad in or about the year 1851
PUTTOCK, Mrs MARIAN, supposed to be residing in New York City, or elsewhere in America.
QUIN, JAMES STANLEY, deceased abroad in or about the year 1827
REYMOND, FRANCES, deceased abroad in or about the year 1828
RICKETTS, WILLIAM HAMILTON, deceased abroad in or about the year 1852
RIORDON, THOMAS, deceased abroad in or about the year 1846
RITCHIE, JOHN, who left Fifeshire, Scotland, about 1872, and served on the "Red Sea," about a year
ROBERTSON, ROBERT, deceased abroad in or about the year 1840
ROBINSON, THOMAS, a Private Soldier, deceased abroad in or about the year 1827
ROBINSON, WILLIAM, a Mariner, deceased abroad in or about the year 1808
RODRIQUES, JOHN, deceased abroad in or about the year 1863
RODRIGUES, ROQUE, deceased abroad in or about the year 1868
ROGERS, Lieutenant HENRY, deceased abroad Representatives wanted
ROWLES, MICHAEL THOMAS T, a native of Ireland, now residing in America
ROWLINGSTOFF, Captain deceased abroad
RUSSELL, THOMAS, deceased abroad in or about the year 1804
RYLAND, CHARLOTTE HARRIET CROFT, residing in New York City, or elsewhere in America.
ST. GEORGE, Commander WILLIAM, deceased abroad in or about the year 1812
SABINE FAMILY, residing in New York City, or elsewhere in America

SCHOPP, EDWARD, formerly of Newburg, now residing in Brooklyn, N Y, U S A.
SCOTT, Mrs. HANNAH, deceased abroad in or about the year 1842
SCOTT, TITUS, deceased abroad. Representatives wanted
SCRIBA, AUGUSTUS M, who in 1858 resided in New York City, U S A.
SEATON, ROBERT H, formerly of England, now supposed to reside in Canada
SEMPLE, ALEXANDER, a native of Scotland, last heard of at Mobile, U S A., in or about the year 1853.
SHANLEY, Mrs. ELIZA, in 1878 resided and taught School at 80s, De Kalb Ave, Brooklyn, N Y, U S A
SHEPPARD, ANN, (Maiden name, WARD), a native of England Next of kin of, presumed to be in Canada
SHERIDAN, HELEN, born about 1800, family supposed to be residing in America
SHUEL, Mrs MARGARET (Maiden name, McENANCY), formerly of Ireland, now residing in America.
SIBLEY, JAMES, an Engineer, deceased abroad in or about the year 1860
SILLERY, MARY, otherwise CAHILL, last heard of in Philadelphia, Pa., U S A.
SIZMUR, WILLIAM, formerly an Apprentice on board the ship "*British Empire*"
SLATTER, Captain JOSEPH, deceased abroad in or about the year 1808.
SLEVIN, FAMILY of, formerly of Ireland, now residing in America.
SLOAN, HORATIO, formerly of Co Antrim Ireland, now residing in New York City, U S.A
SLOANE CATHERINE (See Catherine Adams)
SMITH, GEORGE, formerly of Limehouse, Co Middlesex, England
SMITHWICK, GEORGE F, formerly of Co. Tyrone, Ireland, now residing in America.
SOMERS, JAMES and RICHARD, who left London, Eng, for America in 1862.
SOUTH, CECILE MARIE, deceased in or about the year 1835
SOUZA, Surgeon FRANCIS DE. (See De Souza, Surgeon Francis.)
SPENCER, Major ROBERT, deceased abroad in or about the year 1858
STACKPOLE, Lieutenant THOMAS, deceased abroad in or about the year 1832.
STAFFORD, Mrs HARRIET, deceased abroad in or about the year 1853.
STANTON, BENJAMIN S, who in 1857 resided in Minnesota, U S A.
STEELE, Dr GODFREY, who left London, Eng, for America in 1878
STEVENS, ROBERT, deceased abroad Representatives wanted
STEWART, CHARLES, deceased abroad in or about the year 1835
STEWART, CHARLOTTE, deceased abroad Representatives of wanted.
STEWART, GEORGE N, now or formerly of New York City, U S A
STOCKWELL, CATHERINE, residing in New York City, or elsewhere in America
STROHSCHEIN, CHRISTOPH HERMANN, a native of Germany, now residing in America.
STUNT, THOMAS WILLIAM, a Mariner, deceased abroad in or about the year 1824
SULLIVAN, TIMOTHY, formerly of South Wales deceased in or about the year 1873
SWARRIS Mrs AUGUSTINE, deceased abroad in or about the year 1808.
SWEENEY, CHARLES WARD, formerly of London, deceased in or about the year 1875
SWEENEY, Miss MARIA, deceased in or about the year 1812. Representatives of wanted.
SYNE, WILLIAM, deceased abroad in or about the year 1842
TALLEMACH, Captain WILLIAM, deceased abroad in or about the year 1818
TART FAMILY, residing in the United States of America, or the West Indies.
TAYLOR, WILLIAM, of Leeds and Manchester, Eng., was at San Francisco, Cal, U S A., in March, 1889
THOMPSON, CHARLES ALEXANDER, deceased abroad in or about the year 1875
THOMPSON, Mrs. VIRGINIA WILKINSON FOSTER, residing in New York City, or elsewhere in America.
TOMLINSON. Mrs JANE, deceased abroad in or about the year 1843
TOUSEY, GEORGE, deceased abroad Representatives of, supposed to be in America.
TRUFITT, JOHN, a Seaman, who left London for America in 1856.
TURNER, DAVID, who, when last heard of, was residing at La Paz, Lower California
VALLE, BARTHOLOMEW deceased abroad in or about the year 1830
VANZETTE, Captain GEORGE LEWIS, deceased abroad in or about the year 1834.
VARLEY FAMILY, formerly of Worcestershire, England, supposed to have emigrated to Canada
VAUGHAN, JOHN and ARTHUR, now or recently residing in New York City, or elsewhere in America
VICKERS, THOMAS AUGUSTUS, deceased abroad in or about the year 1828
VON POLL, or PAUL, EUGENE, was in San Francisco in 1868, and in Yankton and Chicago in 1875.
VOSS, ANNA, who left Bremen, Germany, for America, about 1854
WADDELL, GEORGE, deceased abroad in or about the year 1840
WALKER, or ONGLEY, CHRISTINA residing in New York or elsewhere in America.
WALLER, Mrs. SOPHIA MARGARET, deceased abroad in or about the year 1850
WARD, ANN (See Ann Sheppard.)
WARD HETTY, (afterwards Mrs GILDERSLEEVE), now residing in America.
WATERS, JAMES A. In 1876, at No 134 Bowery, and in 1877 with Holyoke Bone Co, N Y City, U S A
WATKINS, Mrs ANN, late of Co Brecon, Wales Representatives of, residing in America
WEAR, Major DANIEL, deceased abroad Representatives wanted
WEBB, JOHN, a Solicitor, deceased abroad in or about the year 1802
WELTON, JOHN, late of Co Middlesex, England His next of kin supposed to reside in the U S A., or Canada
WHEATALL, JOHN, deceased abroad in or about the year 1807
WHITALL, JAMES D W, who in 1835 resided in New York City, U S A
WHITBROOK, CHARLES and AGNES (Maiden name, COUPLAND), the former late an Engineer in Dunkirk, N Y, and Susquehanna, Pa, U S A, and the latter at one time resided in Windsor, Ont., Canada, afterwards in Detroit, Mich, and Buffalo, N Y, U S A.
WHITE, JOHN, a Mariner, deceased abroad in or about the year 1807
WHITE, THOMAS ROWAT, deceased abroad in or about the year 1883
WIGGINS, Lieutenant CHARLES HENRY, deceased abroad in or about the year 1828
WILKINSON, JOHN, deceased abroad in or about the year 1831
WILLIAMS, Captain JAMES HENRY, deceased abroad in or about the year 1833
WILLIAMSON, Lieutenant J, deceased abroad Representatives wanted
WOODWARD, HERBERT, deceased abroad. Representatives of wanted
WRIGHT, CHARLES, FRANK, FREDERICK, HENRY, RICHARD, and WILLIAM, brothers, who went to America many years ago.
WYNNE, NATHANIEL, formerly of Co Cork Ireland, now residing in America.
YARNOLD, Mrs. Catherine, (Maiden name, HOWES), deceased in or about the year 1859
YATES, HENRY, formerly of Yorkshire, deceased in or about the year 1878
YEOMANS, JOSEPH PROUD, deceased in or about the year 1818
YOUNG, Mrs ANN, deceased in or about the year 1841
YOUNG, Captain JAMES, deceased abroad in or about the year 1806.
YULE, ANDREW, deceased abroad in or about the year 1851

SPECIAL LIST No. 13.

UNCLAIMED MONEY, LANDS AND ESTATES.

The following persons (or heirs) are entitled to property   Address **J. B. MARTINDALE, 142 La Salle Street, Chicago, Illinois**, stating all facts on which claim is based. [See pages 6, 7 and 8 of this Manual.]

ABBEY, SARAH, born about 1820, daughter of Thomas Abbey, supposed to be connected with the Law The family resided in or near Exeter, England
ALDERMAN, LOUISA, (formerly MAYHEW), who left England for America about the year 1837
ALLAN, WILLIAM K, born about 1815   Supposed to have gone to America
ALLEN, ANDREW, a Tinsmith, who died abroad in the year 1834.   Relatives of, supposed to be in Canada
ANTON, GEORGE J, a native of Scotland, residing in New York or elsewhere in America
ASKIN FAMILY, formerly of England, supposed to reside in America.
ARNOLD, Mrs. ELIZABETH   (See Sarah Gray)
ASTE FAMILY, supposed to be residing in America
BAKER, WILLIAM, of Hoxton, Co Middlesex, Eng, in 1780   Representatives of, supposed to be in America.
BARLOW, ANN, in 1731 residing at Turnham Green, County Middlesex, England
BARNES, CATHERINE (afterwards PARDUE or PERDUE) who went to America in 1840.
BARNES, Mrs MARY, formerly of Co Middlesex, England, deceased in or about the year 1842.   Next of kin supposed to be in Canada.
BARNSLEY, Miss ELIZABETH, deceased abroad in or about the year 1832
BARRACLOUGH, W P, formerly of London, who is supposed to have left England for America in 1885
BARTH, GEORGE, formerly a Landowner, in Islip, L I, N Y, U S A
BASTIEN, MARCELIN, a native of France, a Baker by trade, supposed to be in America since 1881.
BATTEN, J, deceased abroad.   Representatives of, supposed to be in America
BATTEN, WILLIAM, in 1780 residing in Hoxton, Co Middlesex, England
BAYLEY, WILLIAM T, a Painter, living in New York City, U S A, previous to 1863
BEARD, PRUDENCE, deceased in or about the year 1878
BEATON, HAGGAR, deceased abroad in or about the year 1863
BEATSON, GEORGE, deceased abroad in or about the year 1884
BEAUCHAMP, PHILIP, last heard of from Rio de Janeiro about 1830
BEDFORD, EDWARD, deceased in or about the year 1860   Next of kin supposed to be in America.
BEEBY, SARAH, of London, Eng, about 1870   Representatives of, residing in America
BELL, WILLIAM, whose wife was last heard of as a Dressmaker in Philadelphia, Pa, U S A.
BELLINGHAM, JOHN, deceased abroad in or about the year 1845
BENNET, CAPTAIN WILLIAM, deceased abroad in or about the year 1813
BENNETT, SARAH of London, Eng., about 1877.   Representatives of, supposed to be in America.
BENYON, WILLIAM, deceased abroad in or about the year 1877
BERG, BERNHARD, formerly of Bavaria, now residing in America
BERMINGHAM, WALTER, of London, Eng, in or about the year 1740
BETHAM, Miss MARY, deceased abroad in or about the year 1809
BEZINE, WILLIAM S, now or recently residing at Amsterdam, N Y, U S A.
BEZZENBERGER, WILHELM, supposed to be residing in the United States, or Canada.
BIDWELL, JOHN of Yelverton, Co Northampton, Eng, in 1855   Representatives of, in America
BIGGS, ELIZABETH, or her brother, ALFRED SAWYER, supposed to have emigrated about 1844.
BIRD, JAMES, residing in New York, U S A, in 1863   He was the son of Thomas Rawlins Bird.
BIRD, WILLIAM, JAMES, or JOHN, sons of Joseph Bird, left England about 1838
BIRDSALL FAMILY, now or recently residing in America
BLUNDELL, Mrs. A J M, deceased in or about the year 1826
BOLDERO, CAPTAIN CHARLES, deceased abroad in or about the year 1843
BOLTON, MARY, when last heard of, about 1840, was residing in Co Kent, England.
BRADSHAW, JOHN, in 1775 of Greenwich, Co Kent, England
BRADY, WILLIAM, of London, Eng., in or about the year 1770.
BRAIN, JOHN C, now or recently of Chicago, Ills, U S A.
BRAME (or BRAHAM) FAMILY, formerly of England, supposed to be in America
BRAZIER, ELLEN, deceased abroad.   Relatives of, supposed to be in America
BREISACHER, ANNA MARIA, residing in New York, or elsewhere in America.
BRIDGE, THOMAS, late of Wigan, England, was in 1868 at Salt Lake, Utah, U S A.
BROOKS, SALLY (afterwards wife of HUGH WILLIAMSON), living in or about the year 1780.
BROOMAN FAMILY, supposed to be residing in America.
BROWN, MARY ANN, deceased in or about the year 1878
BROWN, THOMAS, late of Hull, Yorkshire, England
BURLAND, JAMES A, formerly of Bristol, England, who went abroad about the year 1853
BURKE, ALEXANDER, son of Richard Burke, formerly of Co Cork, Ireland, now residing in America
BURKE, PATRICK, deceased abroad in or about the year 1870
BURTON, ELIZABETH JANE, deceased abroad   Next of kin supposed to be in America.
BUTLER, MARY ANN, deceased in or about the year 1880
BYRNE, Mrs ELIZABETH   (See Cromein Cromeen)
CAESAR, CHARLES, who in 1714 was Treasurer to the British Navy.
CAMPBELL, WILLIAM THOMSON, formerly of Aberdeen, Scotland, was in Van Dieman's Land, in 1852
CARROLL, MARGARET   (See Dugidos, Alphonse.)
CARTER FAMILY, formerly of England, now residing in America
CARY, THOMAS, formerly of London, England, now supposed to be residing in America.
CAYGILL, WILLIAM H, last heard of in Memphis, Tenn, U S A, in 1879.
CHAMBERLAYNE, FRANCES, alive about 1720.   Next of kin of supposed to be residing in America.
CHEW, JAMES, formerly of Swindon, England, now residing in New York, or elsewhere in America.
CILIERS FAMILY, supposed to be residing in America
CLARK, AMY, (Maiden name, WARNER), last heard of in Iowa, U S A.
CLARK, THOMAS, son of John and Sarah Clark, who left Eng for America about 1825
CLARKE, SAMUEL, of London, Eng, in 1720   Next of kin supposed to be in America.
CLAUWERS FAMILY, formerly of Noord-Brabant, Holland, last heard of in New York, U S A.
COLLINS, GEORGE, deceased abroad in or about the year 1823
CONGER Mr, a Fresco painter, now or recently residing in East 5th Street, New York City, U S A
CONNELL, JOHN, deceased abroad in or about the year 1807
CONNOR, HENRY, deceased abroad in or about the year 1828.
CONYERS, Miss ELIZABETH, deceased in or about the year 1871
COOPER, EDWARD, deceased abroad in or about the year 1830
COOPER, ELIZABETH   (See Elizabeth Smith)
COPE, DANIEL RICHARDS, of Battersea, Co Surrey, England, in 1882
CORNISH, F, deceased abroad.   Relatives of, supposed to be in America.
CORF, FREDERIC, deceased abroad in or about the year 1835.
COTTELL, Mrs ANN, deceased in or about the year 1873
COTTRELL, THOMAS, deceased abroad in or about the year 1838
COTTRELL, THOMAS, deceased abroad in or about the year 1823
COXALL, WALTER, of Hertfordshire, Eng, who emigrated in 1894.
CRAIG, THOMAS GEORGE, who in 1880 resided at Sherman, Texas, U S A.

CRICHLOW, HENRY, deceased abroad in or about the year 1887
CRICHTON, JAMES, deceased abroad in or about the year 1838
CROFT, JOHN JAMES, a native of England, supposed to be residing in America
CROMEEN CROMEEN The Children who are supposed to be in America, of Joseph Cromein, who married early in this century; and whose brother Lawrence had, it is believed, the following children, viz Mrs. Elizabeth Byrne, Mrs. Ann Smith, John and Joseph Cromein.
CROMPTON FAMILY, formerly of Yorkshire, Eng now residing in the U S A., or Canada
CROMPTON, WILLIAM, of London, Eng, about 1722 Next of kin supposed to be in America
CROSWELLER FAMILY, formerly of England, now residing in America
CUMMINGS, MARY, who when last heard of was residing at Elizabeth, N J, U S A.
CURLE, NATHANIEL, alive about 1730 Representatives of, residing in America.
CURTIS, Mrs. FRANCES, deceased about 1722 She had a son GEORGE, who went to America.
CUSSENS ANN, afterwards wife of William Woods
DALY FAMILY, formerly of London, Eng, now residing in America
DA SILVA, EVE, born in Batavia about 1826 Representatives of, supposed to be in America.
DAVIES, HENRY JOHN, formerly of London, Eng, now residing in America.
DAVIES, JOSIAH, Merchant, London, Eng, 1892. Descendants of, supposed to be in America.
DAVIES, WILLIAM, a Labourer, in 1889 residing near Abergavenny, Wales Representatives of, supposed to be residing in America.
DEAL, WILLIAM and HENRY, residing in New York, or elsewhere in America
DEARDEN FAMILY, formerly of England, supposed to be in America
DE BRETTON, LUDWICK, and his wife ELIZA, formerly residing in St. Kitts, W I, which island they left in 1873 for America.
DE LA PENHA, LOUIS, a native of Holland, deceased 1881 Representatives of, residing in America
DEMING, LORENZO, late a Seaman on the U S Naval Vessel "Vermont"
DESTANDEAU, PETER, of London, Eng, about 1730 Descendants of, supposed to be in America.
DESVAUX, STEPHEN, of London, Eng, about 1730 Descendants of, supposed to be in America
DEVON, CAPTAIN RICHARD, living about 1722 Representatives of, supposed to be in America
DICK, JAMES WILLIAM, a Marine Engineer, formerly of Birkenhead, England, now residing in America.
DILLON, JAMES, formerly of Manchester, Eng, was at Salt Lake City U S A., in 1872
DIX, THOMAS, living in 1723 Descendants of, supposed to be in America.
DOLAN, THOMAS, whose parents now or formerly resided in Dutchess Co, N Y, U S A
DONALD, SAMUEL, who left Perthshire, Scotland, for America, in or about the year 1866.
DOUGLAS, JAMES, (son of George Douglas) a native of Scotland, who went abroad previous to 1883
DOWLAND, CAPTAIN JOHN, formerly a Captain in the 67th British Regiment He was alive in 1859
DUNCAN, JOHN, a native of London, who left England to go abroad in the year 1843.
DUNKHASE, HEINRICK EDWARD, a Sailor supposed to be residing in America
DURHAM, JOHN, of London, Eng, in 1780. Representatives of, supposed to be in America
DWYER FRANCES GRACE H, and SUSANNAH K, formerly of Ireland, now residing in America
EATON, PETER, living in Co Chester, England, in 1860 Nephews and nieces of, supposed to be in Ameri
EBBERN, THOMAS, who left England for America about the year 1857
ELDRIDGE, THOMAS, of London, Eng, in 1767 Descendants of, supposed to be in America.
ELMS, JULIA EMMA, daughter of John Elms, born about 1818
ESCHAUZIER, JAMES JOHN VAN DER TUNK, a native of Holland, supposed to reside in America
EVANCE, REBECCA, of London, Eng, in 1780. Representatives of, supposed to be in America.
EVERINGTON, JAMES, a Sailor, formerly of London, who left England for America in 1873.
FALK, JOHN, who in 1856 was residing in California, U S A
FANSHAW, LETITIA, residing in New York, or elsewhere in America.
FAWCETT, JOHN and JONATHAN, (sons of Betty Fawcett) who went to America previous to 1852
FLAHERTY, BERNEY, a Mariner in 1780 Representatives of, supposed to be in America.
FLEMING, MARIA, formerly of Co Fermanagh, Ireland, was in 1879 residing at Tremont, N Y, U S A
FOGLEWAIT, FRANCIS, a Gardener, residing in or near New York, U S A., about 1830.
FORD FAMILY, formerly of England, now residing in America.
FORTUNE, JOHN, late Quartermaster 61st Regiment, British Army, who died in 1813
GALLAGHER, BRIDGET, left Co. Sligo, Ireland, for America in 1872, last heard of in Orange, N Y, U S A.
GAUNT, CATHERINE, of London in 1733 Representatives of, supposed to be in America
GAVIN JOHN, a native of Scotland, last heard of in 1879 at Poughkeepsie, N Y, U S A.
GEELENN, or HAGAN, BRIDGET, a native of Ireland, residing at Albany, N Y, U S A, in 1885.
GENT, FREDERICK WILLIAM, Ship Captain, in 1874 of Stepney, Co Middlesex, England.
GEORGE, DANIEL G, late a Seaman on the U S Naval Vessel, "Chickopee"
GIBBINS, GEORGE, deceased abroad. Representatives of, supposed to be in America
GILCHRIST FAMILY of, formerly of England, now residing in America.
GLEASON, JULIA. (See Mrs Julia Vine)
GOLDIE, PETER, a native of Scotland, who left Glasgow for New York in 1874, and was in Brooklyn, New York, in January, 1877
GOOD, ELIZABETH, formerly of London, now residing in America.
GORHAM, JOHN, of London, Eng, in 1780 Descendants of, supposed to be in America.
GRAY, JOHN, of London, Eng, in 1881 His representatives supposed to be in America
GRAY, SARAH, widow of Samuel Gray The latter died in Clerkenwell, London, Eng, in 1791, and had a brother, Francis Abercromby Gray, and a sister, Mrs Elizabeth Arnold Descendants of, supposed to be in America
GREEN FAMILY, residing in Georgia, or elsewhere in America.
GREEVES, PETER, a Surgeon, living in 1770. Representatives of, supposed to be residing in America.
GRUBE FAMILY, formerly of Hamburg, now residing in America
GUINET, BRIDGET, left Co Sligo, Ireland, for America in 1872, last heard of in Orange, N J., U S A.
GUTHRIE FAMILY, formerly of Scotland, now supposed to be in America
HAINES, MARY, now or recently residing in New York, U S A
HALEY, ISAAC, son of Thomas and Betty Haley, who went to America in 1839
HALFPENNY FAMILY, formerly of England, now residing in America
HAMILTON, WILLIAM, late of Maryhill, Glasgow, Scotland, now residing in America.
HAMMOND, MARTIN, deceased abroad in or about the year 1808
HANDASYDE, GEORGE, deceased abroad in or about the year 1841
HARDING, MAJOR RICHARD, deceased abroad in or about the year 1821
HARDING, WILLIAM, formerly of Canada, afterwards of New South Wales, Australia.
HARRISON, LIEUTENANT G L, deceased abroad in or about the year 1820
HART, WILLIAM, late of Maryhill, Glasgow, Scotland, now residing in America
HARTLEY FAMILY, formerly of Lancashire, England, now supposed to be in America.
HAWKINS, CHARLES, deceased abroad in or about the year 1843
HAY, Miss HELEN, deceased abroad in or about the year 1828.
HEFTY, HELEN and EDWARD, residing in New York City, or elsewhere in America
HENCHMAN, ROBERT, deceased abroad in or about the year 1844.
HENEY, Miss MARY, deceased in or about the year 1848
HEWETT, GEORGE, deceased abroad in or about the year 1857
HICKEY, DANIEL, who emigrated to America in 1885, and was residing in New York City in 1881
HICKS, HENRY, a Carpenter, who left England for New York City, U S A, in or about the year 1877
HIGGINS, MICHAEL REGAN, a native of the West Indies, now supposed to reside in America
HIGGINS SAMUEL, late Fireman on U S S. "Princeton"
HILBERS, THOMAS HERMANN, last heard of in Brooklyn, New York, U.S.A., about 1858

SPECIAL LIST No 13.

HINDE, SUSANNA and **ELEANOR**, alive in 1734   Representatives of, supposed to reside in America.
HINSON FAMILY, formerly of England, now supposed to be in America
HINTON FAMILY, formerly of England, now residing in America.
HISCOX, CAPTAIN JOSEPH, living in 1722   Representatives of, supposed to be in America.
HOCKLY, GEORGE, who left Calcutta, E I , for New York, U S A , in 1868
HOLLINS, WILLIAM, formerly of Co Nottingham, Eng , and afterwards of Canada.
HOLME, Miss **MARGARET**, deceased in or about the year 1873
HOOD, JAMES A, a Jeweller, now or recently of Providence, U S A
HOPLEY, ANN, of Hoxton, Co. Middlesex, Eng., in 1780   Representatives of, supposed to be in America
HOUGHTON, EDWARD J, late Seaman on U S Naval Vessel, ' Chickopee '
HUGHES, WILLIAM (Mother's name SUSANNAH) of Herefordshire, Eng , supposed to be in America
IMPLETON, THOMAS, son of Sarah Impleton, supposed to be in America
INVERARITY, DAVID, formerly of Forfarshire, Scotland, now residing in America
IRELAND, JOHN, of Mile End, Co Middlesex, Eng , in 1741   Representatives of, supposed to be in America.
IRWIN FAMILY, formerly of London, Eng , now residing in America
JACK FAMILY, formerly of Scotland , now residing in America
JAMES, WILLIAM, deceased abroad   Next of kin of, supposed to be in America
JENKINS, EDWARD B, and C C B , living in Texas, U S A , in 1860.
JENKINS, THOMAS, son of Thomas Jenkins, of Golden Square, London, Coal Merchant, and who in the year 1788 was apprenticed to Archibald Hamilton, Printer and Stationer, of London, Eng
JEPSON, SARAH A, and **LOUISE ABBOTT JEPSON**, wife of Titus Jepson, in America in 1855
JOHNSON, PRUDENCE, living in or about the year 1878   Next of kin of, supposed to be in America.
JOHNSON, SAMUEL, of Bristol, Eng , about 1720   Representatives of, supposed to be in America.
JOHNSON, WILLIAM W, in 1841, a Clothier, at 86 Cedar Street New York City, U S A
JONES, H S W, late of Cardenas, Cuba, W I   now residing in America.
JONES, MARTHA, formerly of Co Hereford, Eng , living in 1880.
KEARNS, WILLIAM, a Farmer, who emigrated from Ireland, and died abroad in 1855
KEMP, THOMAS, of London, Eng , in 1733   Representatives of, supposed to be in America.
KING, ROBERT H, late Seaman on U S Naval Vessel, "Vermont"
KIRK, Mrs. C L , now or formerly of Boston, Mass, U S A
KNOWLES, WILLIAM, deceased abroad   Next of kin of, supposed to be in America
LAMB, PETER, of London, Eng , in 1723.   Representatives of, supposed to be in America.
LANDER FAMILY, formerly of England, supposed to be in America.
LANO, CATHERINE, residing in Wolverton, Co Durham, England, in 1881
LANGLEY, JANE, daughter of William Langley, of Liverpool, Eng , who married and went to America 1840.
LA PENHA, LOUIS DE, a native of Holland, deceased in 1881   Representatives of, supposed to be in America
LEVERT FAMILY, now or recently residing in Mobile, U S A
LEWIS, JANE, formerly of the City of Chester, England
LICHIGARAY FAMILY, formerly of England, supposed to be now in America
LOANE, GEORGE W, now or late of Baltimore, U S A
LORY FAMILY, formerly of England, supposed to be residing in America
M'CLELLAND, Mrs **MARIA**, now or formerly residing in East 104th Street, New York City, U S A.
McDOUGALL, AUGUSTUS, formerly of Co Surrey, Eng , livi g in 1878
McELWEE FAMILY, formerly of Ireland, now residing in Orleans Co , New York U S A
McGUIRE, CAPTAIN JOHN, now or formerly of Butler Co , Pa., U S A
MacKENZIE, DUNCAN, formerly of Islington, Co Middlesex, Eng , living in 1877
M KIMM, JAMES EDWARD, formerly of the Royal Engineers, British Army, now residing in America.
M'LAREN, MATTHEW TURNBULL, a native of Scotland, who emigrated in 1859
M'LEAN, DUNCAN, formerly of Glasgow, Scotland, now residing in America.
McMAHON, MICHAEL, formerly of Co Kildare, Ireland, now residing in America
MADDOX, GEORGE, formerly of Worcestershire, who left England in 1878, it is supposed for America.
MANNINGS FAMILY formerly of London, Eng , now residing in America.
MARNEWICK FAMILY, supposed to be residing in America
MATTRASS, SAMUEL, who, in or about the year 1885 was in business at New Orleans, La , U S A.
MAY, JAMES, born in Dublin, Ireland, about 1820   Representatives of, supposed to be in America
MAY, WILLIAM and **GEORGE**, of London, Eng , in 1730   Representatives of, supposed to be in America.
MAYHEW, LOUISA   (See Louisa Alderman)
MEARES, GASTON, who in 1851 was in the Cotton business in New York City, U S A.
MELVIL, Mr **W E**, who in January, 1882, lived in East 110th Street, New York City, U S A.
METCALFE, EDWARD, of London, Eng , a Merchant in 1722.   Representatives of, supposed to be in America
MILLER, PAUL, of Whitechapel, London, Eng , in 1760   Representatives of, supposed to be in America
MITCHELL, EDWARD, formerly of Co Galway, Ireland, now residing in America
MONAHAN, THOMAS LEWIS, a Midshipman, who left Ireland to go abroad in 1866
MOORE, CARLOTA ELIZABETH, deceased   Heir-at law and next of kin supposed to reside in America.
MOORE, CHARLES CHRISTOPHER, JAMES, and **BRIDGET**, brothers and sister, residing in Canada
MOUNTJOY, GEORGE and **JAMES**, who left England many years ago, it is supposed for America
MOUSSERONE, JOHN, supposed to reside in the New England States, U S A.
MUNDY, MARIA, formerly of Oxfordshire, England, now residing in New York or elsewhere in America.
MUREAY, WILLIAM, who left Co Cork, Ireland, about Avril, 1872, for Portland, Maine, U S A.
MURRELL, DINAH, living in 1840   Representatives of, supposed to be in America.
NAUGHTON, MARY, of Co Galway, Ireland, residing in Brooklyn and New York, U S A., in 1868.
NEATE, S, of Wiltshire, Eng , in 1860   Next of kin of, supposed to be in America
NEEDHAM FAMILY, formerly of England, now residing in America
NOAD FAMILY, formerly of England, now residing in America.
NORTJE, J P, and **J S**, deceased abroad   Representatives of, supposed to be in America.
OWEN, GRACE, alive in 1775   Representatives of, supposed to be in America
PAGE, HENRY, son of Margaret and Henry, who left the West Indies in 1871, in barque "*Conllow*," to England, and who is believed to be now in America
PARDUE, or **PERDUE, CATHERINE** (See Catherine Barnes)
PARLEY, JOHN S, deceased abroad.   Representative of, supposed to be in America.
PARROT, WILLIAM S.   *Creditors of*, residing in America
PARRY, THOMAS, formerly of Lancashire, who left England for Canada in or about the year 1830
PATTERSON, Mr **D W** , residing in New York, or elsewhere in America
PEARCE, WILLIAM PIKE, of Co Devon, England   Next of kin in America
PENHA, LOUIS DE LA, a native of Holland, deceased in 1881   Representatives of in America.
PHILLIPS, BENJAMIN, and **SARAH** his wife, formerly of Pembrokeshire   Next of-kin in America.
PIGOTT FAMILY, formerly of England, now residing in America
PITKIN FAMILY, formerly of England, now residing in America
POND, Mr **W H** , residing in New York City, or elsewhere in America
PREVOST, WILLIAM PETER, and **THOMAS**, sons of William Prevost, of St John's, Southwark, County Surrey, Eng., in 1764.
RADCLYFFE, WILLIAM, of London, England, 1828   Next of kin in America
RAND FAMILY, formerly of England, now residing in America
RAVENEL EDWARD, supposed to have emigrated to America in or after the year 1744
REED FAMILY, formerly of England, now residing in America
REEVES, JOHN PASSMORE, and **PETER PASSMORE**, formerly of England, now residing in America
RISELY, MARY, widow of Henry John Risely, of Isleworth, Middlesex, Eng , in 1758.
ROBINSON, ANN, born about 1796, sister of Dorinda Robinson
ROBINSON, FANNY, of St John's, Wapping, Co. Middlesex, Eng , born about 1793.

ROGERS, HENRY, son of Jane Rogers, of Wales. He was last heard from in Stockton, Cal., U S A., in 1858
ROGERS, PATRICK, who left Ireland many years ago, and settled in Upper Canada
ROHFRITSCH, CHARLES FRANCIS, a native of France, born about 1848. Supposed to have gone to America.
ROSSELL FAMILY, formerly of Liverpool, England, now residing in America.
ROWLLS FAMILY, formerly of England, now residing in America.
SADLER, ELIZA, alive in 1875. Her next of kin supposed to be in America.
SAVERY, THOMAS, serving in the British Navy in or about the year 1715.
SAWYER, ALFRED, or his sister, ELIZABETH BIGGS, supposed to have emigrated about 1844.
SCOTT, Mrs AGNES, formerly residing corner of Marcy and Flushing Avenues, Brooklyn, N Y, U S A.
SCOTT, FRANCIS, deceased abroad in or about the year 1878. Next of kin residing in America.
SCOTT, JOHN, of Glasgow, Scotland, was in Hawesville, Ky, 1880, and afterwards went to New Orleans.
SCOTT, JOHN BRODIE, a Sailor, a native of Glasgow, who left Scotland on a foreign voyage in August, 1882.
SCRIVENER, JOHN, of London, Eng, in 1780. Representatives of, supposed to be in America.
SEATON, ANNIE. (See Annie Tellefsen.)
SHELLEY FAMILY, formerly of England, now residing in America
SHERIDAN, HELEN, born about 1800. Representatives of, supposed to be in America.
SHERIDAN, MARY and MARGARET, who left Ireland for America in the year 1848
SHERMAN, EZEKIEL, living in 1722. Representatives of, residing in America
SHORE, Miss. (See Mrs Alexander Thomson.)
SHOWER, BARTHOLOMEW, Barrister-at-law, in 1730. Descendants of, supposed to be in America
SHUTTLEWORTH, THOMAS, alive in 1724. He afterwards left England for America.
SILVA, EVE DA. (See Eve Da Silva.)
SIMMONS FAMILY, formerly of England, now residing in America.
SIMMONS, GEORGE, Surgeon's Steward on board the "Winipec," at Annapolis, in March, 1866.
SLEATH, CAROLINE L, deceased abroad. Next of kin of, supposed to be in America
SMITH, ANN, widow of John Smith, of New Orleans, La., U S A., in 1880.
SMITH, Mrs. ANN. (See Cromein-Cromeen.)
SMITH, ELIZA, wife of John Smith, who left England for Salt Lake City, U S A., in 1858.
SMITH, ELIZABETH, of New Orleans La, U S A., a sister of JONATHAN COOPER
SMITH, JAMES, now or late of 274, Grand Street, New Haven, Conn, U S A.
SMITH, WILLIAM, formerly of Wivenhoe, Co. Essex, who left England in 1863, it is supposed for America.
SMYTHE, GEORGE, an Engineer, now or late of No 2,420, Braddock Street, Philadelphia, Pa, U S A.
SPENCER, WILLIAM ROBERT, who left Eng. for the U S A. in or about the year 1871
SPITT FAMILY, formerly of Hamburg, now residing in America.
STARK, ARCHIBALD, a Liquor Dealer, residing in New York City, U S A., previous to 1863.
STEM, or STERN, Mr O H P, formerly of Richmond, Va, then of New York City, U S A.
STEWART, DAVID, MARY, and HANNAH, natives of Co Donegal, residing in New York, U S A., in 1873.
STRONG, PELEG, or PEREAN, now or formerly of Northampton, Mass, U S A
SYMONS, CAROLINE, in 1880 residing in Co Devon, Eng. Relatives of, supposed to be in America.
TALLMAN, FRANK, now or recently residing in New York City, U S A.
TATE, JOHN, of Bristol, Eng, in 1722. Representatives of, residing in America.
TAYLOR, ALFRED P., a native of Eng, at one time in the British Army, now supposed to reside in America.
TAYLOR, GEORGE, of Co Monmouth, Wales, living in 1879. Next of kin of, residing in America.
TAYLOR, MARGARET, formerly of Co Bruce, Ont., Canada, afterwards of Ann Arbor, Michigan, U S A.
TEDD, EDWARD, living in 1754. Descendants of, supposed to be in America.
TELLEFSEN, ANNIE, (born SEATON or WILSON,) of Co. Surrey, Eng., married in 1861, and now supposed to reside in America.
THIENE, COUNTESS of, deceased. Heir-at-law and next of kin of, supposed to reside in America.
THOMPSON, ANN, of Islington, Co Middlesex, Eng, in 1722. Representatives supposed to reside in America
THOMSON, Mrs ALEXANDER, (Maiden name, SHORE), who left London, England, for New York in 1864
THORNTON, PETER, a Stonemason, formerly of Yorkshire, England, residing in the U S A in 1835.
THOROWGOOD FAMILY, formerly of London, Eng., now residing in America.
TOLWORTHY, GEORGE W, a Bricklayer, who left England for New York in March, 1885.
TUNECLIFF, RICHARD, a Tailor, of Hammersmith, Co Middlesex, Eng, in 1816
TUNNY FAMILY, formerly of Ireland, now residing in America
UNGIDOS, ALPHONSE, or his wife MARGARET, formerly CARROLL, who in 1870 were of London, Eng.
UPTON, WILLIAM, a Tailor, of 35, Dean Street, Oxford Street, London, Eng, in 1870
VANHIZEN, Mrs., residing in New York, or elsewhere in America.
VEINRICH, SAMPSON, now or recently residing in N Y City, or elsewhere in America
VINE, Mrs. JULIA, (Maiden name, GLEASON,) residing in or near Albany, N Y, U S A, in 1840
WALTERS, R., deceased abroad. Next of kin of, supposed to be in America.
WARNER, AMY. (See Amy Clark.)
WASTFELD, SARAH, living in 1788. Descendants of, supposed to be in America.
WATSON, GEORGE, a Blacksmith, a native of Scotland, residing at Cincinnati, Ohio, U S A, in 1858
WATSON, WILLIAM, formerly of Edinburgh, who left Scotland for America in 1867
WELLS FAMILY, formerly of England, now residing in America.
WELSH, EDWARD GEORGE, of London, Eng, living in 1878. Next of kin supposed to be in America.
WELTON, PEGGY, widow of John Welton, of Chatham Row, Bath, Eng in 1812
WHITE, JOHN, a Gardener, formerly of Co Dublin, Ireland, now residing in America
WILKS, HENRY, formerly a Seaman on the U S Naval Vessel, "Vermont."
WILLIAMSON, HUGH, of London, Eng., in 1780. Descendants of, supposed to be in America.
WILLIAMSON, SALLY. (See Sally Brooks.)
WILLS, THOMAS and SARAH, deceased abroad. Next of kin of, supposed to be in America.
WILSON, ANNIE. (See Annie Tellefsen.)
WILSON, RICHARD, formerly of Co Norfolk, who left England for Canada many years ago
WINDMUELLER, MORRIS, a Furrier formerly of Berlin, now residing in America.
WIRE, WILLIAM HENRY, formerly of England, now residing in New York, or elsewhere in America.
WOODCOCK, EDWARD and BETTY, residing in London, Eng, about 1702
WOODS, ANN. (See Ann Cussens.)
WRIGHT, LEONORA B, who left England many years ago, it is supposed, for America
WROTH, HENRY, of Guildford, Co. Surrey, Eng, in 1720. Representatives of, living in America
YEO, THOMAS, formerly of London, Eng, afterwards of Barbadoes, W I, Attorney at-Law, 1771
YOUNG, CHARLES WILLIAM, late of Ringwood, Hampshire, Eng, now residing in America.
YOUNG, WILLIAM, a native of England, who in 1849 was trading in skins at New Orleans, La., U S A.

SPECIAL LIST No. 14.

UNCLAIMED MONEY, LANDS AND ESTATES.

The following persons if living, or if dead, their representatives, are entitled to property Address J. B. MARTINDALE, 142 La Salle Street, Chicago, Illinois, giving all facts on which claim is based. [See pages 6, 7 and 8 of this Manual.]

AITON, SINCLAIR, who left Scotland for America about the year 1839
ASHFORD FAMILY, formerly of England, now residing in America.
ATTO FAMILY, formerly of England, supposed to have emigrated to America.
BAILEY, WILLIAM T, a Painter by trade, now or recently residing in New York City, U S A
BARRY, GEORGE R., formerly of Liverpool, England, now residing in America
BIRD, MARTHA, living in 1876   Representatives of, supposed to be in America
BIRKS, WILLIAM, formerly of Co. Lincoln, England, but at present in the U S A or Canada
BRENNAN, MICHAEL J, a native of Ireland   Representatives of, residing in America
BURKE, HENRY, formerly of Co Dublin, Ireland, supposed to have emigrated to America
CARROLL, CATHERINE, formerly of Dublin, Ireland   Her next of kin supposed to be in America
CHURCHILL, CATHERINE, HENRY, and JAMES, supposed to be residing in America
COWLEY, HENRY, formerly of Co Kent, England, went abroad some years ago
DOUGLAS, JAMES (son of George Douglas), a native of Scotland, who went abroad previous to 1863.
DOUGLAS, DR. ROBERT (otherwise R MIDDLEMORE), was at Baltimore and Reading, U S A, in 1880.
EDGAR, Miss HENRIETTA MoD   (See Mrs Daniel H Wright.)
EVANS, THOMAS, who left Scotland for America in 1862.
FARRELL, CAPTAIN THOMAS, who left Co Galway, Ireland, for America, in 1846.
FERGUSON, ROBERT, a native of Scotland, last heard of in New York, in 1848
FERGUSON, WILLIAM, who left Scotland for America in or previous to the year 1828
FLANAGAN, ANN, formerly of Lancashire, England, now residing in America.
FOX, CHARLES, residing in New York, Philadelphia, or elsewhere in America.
GILCHRIST, JAMES A, now or formerly Seaman in the ship "Horatio Harris," of Boston, U S A
GODDARD, SAMUEL, of Birmingham and London, England, in 1862, and who afterwards went to America.
GORMAN, GEORGE and THOMAS, formerly of Co Kildare, who left Ireland for America about 1849.
GROVER FAMILY, supposed to be residing in New York or Baltimore, U S A
HALEY, TIMOTHY, Boot-tree Finisher, residing in Philadelphia, U S A, in 1872
HALLIGAN, EDWARD J, employed on Elevated Railroad, New York City, in 1879
HAMILTON, GEORGE, late of Co Essex, Canada, next-of-kin wanted
HATHERLEY FAMILY, formerly of Co Norfolk, England, supposed to be residing in America.
HOOME, Mr T F, Organ Builder, now or formerly of Toronto, Canada
JAMES, CATHERINE, HENRY, and JAMES, supposed to be residing in America
JOHNSON, JOHN, formerly of Yorkshire, England, now residing in America   He had a sister, Eleanor.
KENDRICK FAMILY, formerly of England, now residing in America.
KRAUSE CARL, Cigar-maker, a native of Dresden Saxony, supposed to be in America.
LASKEY FAMILY, formerly of England, now residing in America
LYNDWART, FAMILY of, residing in the United States or Canada
MACKIE, J GOULDEN, formerly of Co Kent, England. now residing in America
McLACHLAN, WILLIAM.   (See W H W Reed)
M'LAREN, JANET, of Stirlingshire, Scotland, two of whose children went to Cincinnati, U.S.A., years ago.
McLEAN, JOHN, who emigrated from Nairn, Scotland, to Canada, in or about the year 1843
McLELLAN, WILLIAM, supposed to be residing in America.
McREYNOLDS, JOHN W, who, when last heard of, about 1859, was in Philadelphia, U S A.
MANLIK, JOHN and ANNA, supposed to be residing in America.
MATTHEWS, JAMES, formerly of Falmouth, England, who went to Canada about 1843
MIDDLEMORE, R.   (See Dr Robert Douglas)
MILLER, JOHN, Tinsmith and Horse Dealer, a native of Ross-shire, who left Scotland for Canada about 1836.
MONAHAN, PETER, THOMAS, and WILLIAM, formerly of Ireland, residing in America
MUNNS FAMILY, formerly of England, now residing in America.
MURRAY, THOMAS, Bricklayer, a native of Scotland, residing in Texas, U S A, in 1849
NEWBERRY, SARAH, residing in New York or elsewhere in America.
NORTH FAMILY, now or formerly of Massachusetts or Connecticut, U S A.
NUTT FAMILY, formerly of England, now residing in America.
O'FLYNN, Mr. J T ; left Birmingham, England, in 1857, and was afterwards employed in the N Y Exhibition.
O'GORMAN, GEORGE and THOMAS, of Co Kildare, who left Ireland for America about 1849
O'GRADY, CATHERINE, formerly of Dublin, Ireland.   Her next-of-kin supposed to be in America
PHILLIPS, THOMAS, a Butcher, formerly of Ruabon, Wales, who went abroad in 1853
PORTEOUS FAMILY, formerly of Scotland, now residing in America.
RAMSHAY, JOHN, and ELIZABETH, his Wife, living in 1851.   Next-of kin supposed to be in America
REED, W. H W, who, in December, 1870, engaged in the name of WILLIAM McLACHLAN as Cook on the "Agnes," which then left London for China, and arrived at Singapore in April, 1871
RELAY, GEORGE W., residing in New York, Philadelphia, or elsewhere in America
RIPPLEE, GEORGE, formerly of Liverpool, England, who went to New Brunswick, Canada, about 1825.
ROBERTSON, JAMES and ANN S, formerly of Scotland, now residing in the United States or Canada.
ROSE, BARNABAS, residing in 1859, at Otter, Fulton, Co Ills., U S A.
RUSSELL, JOHN, a Compositor, who left England for New York about 1853.
SANGSTER, JOHN, a native of Scotland, who was supposed to have gone abroad about 1870.
SHERIDAN, HELEN, born about 1800.   Representatives of, supposed to be in America.
SILK, WILLIAM THOMAS, living in 1879   Next-of kin supposed to be in America
SMITH, WILLIAM, late a Seaman on the U S Naval Vessel, "Chickopee."
STANTON, ROBERT and ALEXANDER, formerly of Ireland, went abroad many years ago
STEVENS, GEORGE, who left England for America about 1879
STEVENSON, JOHN, a native of Scotland, now or recently of the Grand Hotel, Indianpolis, Inda., U S A.
THIES, A WILLIAM, who, in 1874, kept a Shop at 416, Seventh Street, Leavenworth, Kansas, U S A
THOMAS, SARAH (afterwards Wife of BENJAMIN PHILLIPS), of Pembrokeshire, who went abroad.
TROTTER, MARGARET, now or recently residing in New York City, U.S A.
UMPHELBY FAMILY, formerly of England, now residing in America.
WADDELL, or WADDEL, FAMILY, formerly of Scotland, now residing in America
WAKEFIELD, JAMES A., of London, England ; when last heard of, was at No 3, W Third St., N.Y. City, U S A.
WALLACE, HARRY, last heard of at Coney Island, U S A.
WAUGH, GEORGE, a Seaman, native of England, last heard of in San Francisco, Cal., U.S.A., in 1863.
WELCH, ANN, formerly of Lancashire, England, now residing in America
WILSON, Mrs. ELIZABETH (Maiden name, WOODWARD), formerly of England, went to America in 1805, and was last heard of at 43, Coles Street, Newark Avenue, Jersey City, U S A
WOODWARD, ELIZABETH   (See Mrs Elizabeth Wilson)
WRIGHT, Mrs DANIEL H. (late EDGAR), residing in New York, Philadelphia, or elsewhere in America.
WRIGHTSON, JOHN, now or late at Delamater Iron Works, U S A.
ZUBER, FAMILY of, formerly of England, now residing in America

SPECIAL LIST No. 15.

UNCLAIMED MONEY, LANDS AND ESTATES.

The following persons, if alive, or if dead, their representatives, are entitled to property All letters must be addressed to **J B MARTINDALE, 142 La Salle Street, Chicago, Illinois**, and must contain a statement of all facts on which the writer's claim is based [See pages 6, 7 and 8 of this Manual]

ADAMS, HARRIET, (maiden name, MOORE), wife of HENRY V. ADAMS, who went to America after 1836

AMES, MRS E , who, when last heard of, was residing in 402, Fourth Avenue, N Y , U S A

ANDERSON, ELIZA (See ELIZA DIXON)

ANDERSON, JOHN and MARY, late in the employ of MARY V CAMPBELL, late of Bucks County, Pa , U S A

ANSCHUTZ, LEOPOLD, formerly of Budapest, who arrived in N Y , from Hamburg, in August, 1883.

AYMAR, GEORGE W , and ELIZA, married about 1830, in or near Boston, Mass , U S A

BARCLAY, DACRE BRUCE, supposed to be residing in America or elsewhere abroad

BARRET, or BARRETT, CLAUDE, (mother's maiden name, ISABEL CLARK), supposed to have gone abroad

BEAKBANE, THOMAS WILLIAM, of Lancashire, England, now residing in America or elsewhere abroad

BEAN, JOHN W , born at York, about 1813, and who landed in Jamaica, W I , January 15, 1828

BENNETT, BENJAMIN T , formerly of Haggerston, London, England , living in 1848

BENWELL FAMILY, formerly of England, now residing in America

BERRY, ANNE, formerly of Oxfordshire, deceased in 1818 Next of Kin wanted

BLYTH, THOMAS H , born in or about the year 1828, and who afterwards went abroad

BREWER, JOHN GEORGE, formerly of Hampshire, saddler. His representatives are supposed to be abroad

BRIDGE, ROBERT E , formerly of Essex, who left England for abroad in 1853

BROADBENT, THOMAS, a carpenter, born at Bradford, Yorkshire, 1850, and who left England about 1875.

BRUCE, WILLIAM HENRY, supposed to be residing in America or elsewhere abroad

BUCHANAN, JOHN A , who, when last heard of, was in Savannah, Ga , U S A

BUCKLAND, ROBERT, late of Co , Surrey, who is supposed to have left England for America

BURLAND, JAMES ANTHONY formerly of England, who emigrated to America or elsewhere

BUTLER, JOHN HENRY, late of Lincolnshire, England, last heard of from Caldera, Chili, in March, 1871

CAMPBELL, ARCHIBALD, (M D.), of Bedale, Yorkshire, who died in 1837 Representatives of in America

CAPPER, MABEL, formerly of England, who is supposed to have gone abroad

CARDEN, WILLIAM, formerly of Armagh and Dublin, Ireland Descendants wanted

CASTLE, SUSAN, (maiden name, DICKINSON), who left England many years ago for some foreign country

CASTLE, WILLIAM, (See WILLIAM MARTIN)

CLARET, ELEANOR, (maiden name, MATIGNON), who, in 1800, resided in London, England Next of Kin wanted

CLARK, MISS CHARLOTTE, in 1876 living at No 64, George Street, Euston Square, London, England

CLARK, EDWARD, formerly in the 7th Hussars, and who is supposed to have left England for America

COLLINS, ELIZABETH, of Shropshire, England, living in 1878 Next of Kin wanted

COLLYER, O HENRY, a jeweler, formerly of Co , Somerset, supposed to have left England for America

COMPTON, SUSANNA, late of Co , Sussex, England Next of Kin wanted

CONKEY, JAMES, a shoemaker, supposed to be residing in Canada, or elsewhere in America

COOK, GRACE (maiden name, PAYNE OR PAINE) Grandchildren of wanted

COOMBE FAMILY, formerly of Co Somerset, supposed to have left England for America, or elsewhere abroad

CORBETT, PATRICK, in 1835 of Marylebone, London, and who is supposed to have gone abroad

CORK, ELEANOR, of London, who married CHRISTOPHER WINKLER, about 1790 Representatives wanted

COURTLAND, NORA, who, about the year 1865, was engaged in business in New York

CREAMER, GEORGE H , now or formerly of Queen's County, N Y , U S A.

CROMELIEN, MRS SARAH, residing in N Y , or elsewhere in America.

CULLEN, MR , a compositor, formerly of London, England, now residing in N Y., or elsewhere in America

DAVIES, HENRY, formerly of Camberwell, England, living in 1872. Representatives of residing abroad

DAWE, THOMAS and JOHN, formerly of Co Louth, Ireland, now residing in America

DICKINSON, MARY, of Huddersfield, Yorkshire, England, living in 1870. Representatives residing abroad.

SPECIAL LIST No. 15.

DICKINSON, SUSAN. (See SUSAN CASTLE)
DIXON, ELIZA, (maiden name, ANDERSON), now or formerly of Blackheath, near Hamilton, Ontario, Canada
DOLLING, SARAH, (maiden name, PAYNE or PAINE) Grandchildren of wanted
EDEN FAMILY, formerly of Co Sussex, England, now residing in America or elsewhere abroad
EGGLESTON, J B., a carpenter, now or formerly residing at 145, West Houston Street N Y, U S A.
FORSTER, MARY (See MARY JANNISON)
FURLONG, CAPTAIN GEORGE H , living in 1845 Representatives of, residing in America, or elsewhere abroad
GAMLEN FAMILY, supposed to reside in America, or elsewhere abroad
GIBBS, JOHN, late of Co Dorset, supposed to have left England for America, or elsewhere abroad
GIBSON, ROBERT, of Yorkshire, England, living in 1838 Representatives supposed to be residing abroad
GOTT, JOHN and WILLIAM, deceased Children of, supposed to reside in Canada or elsewhere in America
GOURLAY, SAMUEL, sailor, a native of Scotland, last heard of at Honolulu and San Francisco.
GRIFFIN, WILLIAM and GEORGE, formerly of England, supposed to have gone to America.
GROWCOTT, MARY (See MARY PEARSON)
GUY, CHARLES, formerly of Birmingham, who left England for Boston, U S A , May 1, 1872
HARRIS, JANE, (maiden name, MATIGNON), wife of JOHN HARRIS, residing in London, England, about 1880 She had a sister named ELEANOR Representatives of both wanted
HATHORN, VANS, late of Scotland, deceased Representatives of, are supposed to reside abroad
HAYTER, HENRY, JAMES S, and THOMAS S, supposed to have left England for abroad
HAYWARD, RICHARD WILLIAM, in 1878 a private in the 36th Company, Royal Marines, H. M. S. *Flora*
HEATLEY, JAMES EDWARD, who when last heard of was residing in Ontario, Canada
HENDERSON, Mrs EMILY, or JULIA, now or formerly residing in Brooklyn, N Y , U S A
HISSINK, or HESSINK, HENRY, of Holland, last heard of in 1879, at 171, East 79th Street, N Y, U S A
HODGES, CLIFFORDIER ELIZABETH, residing, in 1875, near Boston, Mass, U S A Next of Kin wanted
HOLLIER, SYDNEY, late of Co Surrey, England Representatives of wanted
HOLT, THOMAS, a master mariner, born at Chatham, Kent, England, about 1807. His Next of Kin wanted.
HOWKINSON, JAMES, living in 1846. Representatives of supposed to be residing in America or elsewhere abroad
HUNT, HARVEY, formerly of Hampshire, Miller His representatives are supposed to be residing in America
JANNISON, MARY (maiden name, FORSTER), formerly of England, who emigrated to America, and is supposed to have died there.
JOHNSON, MARIA L, a nurse in the employment of MARY V CAMPBELL; late of Bucks County, Pa , U S A
KEARNON, MARY, ELIZA, and PETER, (children of ANNE KEARNON,) residing in America.
KINDER, JOHN, living in 1838 His Next of Kin are supposed to have gone abroad
KNIGHT, GEORGE B , formerly of Islington, Co , Middlesex, England His Next of Kin wanted
LANE, ANN, of Yorkshire, England, living in 1876 Her representatives are supposed to be living abroad
LATOUR, General PETER AUGUSTUS, living in 1841, or, if dead, his representatives wanted.
LENGILINEY, ALCIDE URBAIN, who, in 1868, left France for Pa , U S A
LIEBERT, JOHN F , formerly of Co , Kent, supposed to have gone to America, or elsewhere abroad.
LITTLE FAMILY, formerly of Scotland, supposed to have gone to America or elsewhere abroad
LIVESAY, Mrs ANNIE (maiden name, READE,) formerly of Ireland, supposed to have gone to America
LOWE, FAMILY of, formerly of England, now residing abroad
LYNS, Mrs MATILDA L , formerly of Bethnal Green, London, England, living in 1865 Representatives wanted
LYONS, ELIZABETH, in 1835, of Marylebone, London, and who is supposed to have gone abroad.
M'LAUGHLIN, WILLIAM, a carriage blacksmith by trade, years ago, a resident of Bridgeport, Conn , U S A
McNEEL, or TURNER, Mrs MATILDA, living in 1876, widow of HENRY TURNER. Representatives wanted
MARSHALL, ANNE ELIZA, and JOHN, (children of JANE MARSHALL), residing in America or elsewhere abroad
MARTIN, WILLIAM, (otherwise CASTLE), of Guildford, Co. Surrey, England Representatives wanted
MATHER, JAMES, of Berwickshire, Scotland, living in 1867 His representatives are residing abroad,
MATIGNON, ELEANOR and JANE, who, between 1790 and 1810, resided at Woolwich, Co Kent, and London, England Next of Kin wanted,
MAXWELL, JOHN and WILLIAM, natives of Scotland, who went abroad and have not been heard of since 1863
MILES, LUCY, formerly of Co , Surrey, England, living in 1880 Representatives of are supposed to reside abroad
MOORE, GEORGE HENRY, son of GEORGE MOORE, of Plymouth, England, who went to America after 1836
MOORE, HARRIET (See HARRIET ADAMS)
MORE, EDMUND M , of London, England, living in 1872. His Next of Kin are supposed to reside abroad
NEWDICK, MARY (maiden name, FORSTER), who married JOHN JANNISON and went to America
NEWMAN, DINAH JANE, of London, England, 1877. Next of Kin wanted
PARKER, Mrs MARY ANN, formerly of Oxfordshire, England Her legal personal representatives wanted
PAVELIN, GEORGE, of Co Essex, but who is supposed to have left England for America or elsewhere abroad

PAYNE or PAINE, JAMES, THOMAS, GRACE, MARY, and SARAH Representatives of wanted
PEARSON, MARY, (maiden name, GROWCOTT), last heard of at East Brady, Clarion County, Pa., U S A
PEIRCE, ALBERT, who left England for America or elsewhere abroad about 1866
PINN, A., sailor, who, about 1857, married Kate Savage, a barmaid at Liverpool, and had two children
PONSFORD, MARY, (maiden name, PAYNE or PAINE) Grandchildren wanted
RABE, CHARLOTTE W F (See CHARLOTTE W F RETTSCHLAY)
READE, ANNE (See Mrs ANNE LIVESAY)
RETTSCHLAY, Mrs CHARLOTTE W F, (maiden name, RABE), supposed to have gone to America.
RICE, JOHN, formerly of Belfast, Ireland, last heard of in Pa, about 1867
RINSKY, VINCENT, formerly a student in St Petersburg, Russia Supposed to have gone to America
RITCHIE FAMILY, formerly of Scotland, supposed to have gone to America or elsewhere abroad
RODGERS, JOHN, formerly of Barnsley, Yorkshire, England, at present residing in America
ROEBUCK, JOHN HENRY, formerly of Leeds, England, and who was in Ark, U S A, in 1871
ROSS, ALEXANDER, late of Dumfries, who left Scotland for New York in 1869, and in February, 1871, was residing at South Colton Street, Lawrence County, N Y, U S A
RUDDICK FAMILY, formerly of Ireland, supposed to have gone to America or elsewhere abroad
RYDER, Mrs., who in 1877 resided at 332, West Twenty-third Street, New York City, U S A
ST. AUBYN, GRENVILLE, (otherwise SULLIVAN), living in 1872 Next of Kin supposed to be residing abroad
SAVAGE, KATE (See A PINN)
SHARP FAMILY, formerly of Scotland, supposed to have gone to America or elsewhere abroad
SHARP, ROBERT (Son of ROBERT SHARP) Children of are supposed to have gone abroad
SHAY, MARGARET, formerly of Ireland, at present residing in America or elsewhere abroad
SINCLAIR, WILLIAM formerly of Caithness-shire, Scotland Representatives of residing in America.
SKIPP, ARTHUR HENRY, formerly of Gloucestershire, England, now residing abroad
SLATER, JOHN, of Northamptonshire, 1867, supposed to have gone to America or elsewhere abroad
SMAUL HAROLD, supposed to reside in the United States of America or Canada
SMITH, JOHN, son of JOHN ROBERT SMITH, formerly of Hampshire, supposed to have gone abroad
STEVENS, HUGH, formerly of New York City, afterwards of Danbury, or Bridgeport, Conn, U S. A
SULLIVAN, GRENVILLE (See ST AUBYN, GRENVILLE)
SUYDAM, ANNA and PHEBE, now or formerly residing in New York City, U S A
TAIT, ELIZABETH, formerly, of Midlothian, who left Scotland for New York about June, 1858
TAYLOR, CHARLES, formerly of Bradford, Yorkshire, afterwards of Poplar, London, England who went abroad in or previous to the year 1865
TAYLOR, WILLIAM E (M D), formerly of Co Sussex, England, living in 1874
THOROWGOOD, ALICIA, JAMES, and MARIA JEMIMA, of London, England, 1836, or Next of Kin
TRACEY, THOMAS (colored), formerly in the employ of MARY V. CAMPBELL, late of Bucks County, Pa, U S A
TURNER, Mrs MATILDA (See Mrs MATILDA McNEEL)
WALTERS, JAMES (colored), formerly in the employ of MARY V CAMPBELL, late of Bucks County, Pa, U S A
WALTERS, THOMAS, ship-captain, living in 1878 Next of Kin wanted
WARREN, JOSEPH and JAMES, of Tredegar, Co Monmouth, supposed to have left England for America
WATSON, BROOK, (son of JOHN WATSON), who is believed to have left England for America or elsewhere
WAUGH, Miss ALISON, a native of Scotland, who, it is believed, is residing in America or elsewhere abroad
WEIGHT, ELLEN or ELEANOR (See WILLIAM and ELEANOR WOOLGAR)
WELLSTED, THOMAS P, formerly of London, supposed to have left England for America in 1881
WILKINSON, ANDREW, formerly of Boston, afterwards of Providence, U S A, or representatives wanted
WILLIAMS, JOSHUA, surgeon, late of Hampshire, England Next of Kin wanted
WILLIAMS, WILLIAM, chemist, of Reading, England Next of Kin residing abroad
WINKLER, CHRISTOPHER (See ELEANOR CORK)
WOOD, CHARLEY and BETSY, supposed to be residing in Toronto, Ontario, Canada
WOODWARD ELIZABETH (See Mrs ELIZABETH WILSON)
WOOLGAR, WILLIAM and ELEANOR or ELLEN WEIGHT, his wife, who, about 1790, resided in the East end of London, England
WORME FAMILY, formerly of England, now residing abroad
WRIGHT, Mrs DANIEL H, (late EDGAR), residing in New York, Philadelphia, or elsewhere in America
WRIGHT, FREDERICK, born in 1841, formerly of Detroit, Mich., U S A, a tailor
WRIGHT, MARY, residing in London, England, about 1850 Representatives of supposed to be in America
WRIGHT, WILLIAM, son of THOMAS WRIGHT, left England for America in 1858, and was a wheelwright in Chicago, Ill, U S A
WRIGHTSON, JOHN, now or late at Delamater Iron Works, U S A
ZILLARD, WILLIAM, deceased His representatives are supposed to be residing in Canada.
ZUBER, FAMILY of, formerly of England, now residing in America.

SPECIAL LIST No. 16.

UNCLAIMED MONEY, LANDS AND ESTATES.

The following persons, if living, or if dead, their representatives are entitled to property. All letters must be addressed to **J B. MARTINDALE, 142 La Salle Street, Chicago, Illinois.** and must state all facts on which the writer's claim is based [See pages 6, 7, and 8 of this Manual]

ABBOTT, OLIVER, otherwise OLIVER GOLDSMITH ABBOTT, enlisted in British Army about 1840
ADAMS, HARRIET, wife of HENRY V ADAMS, formerly MOORE, Spinster.
ALDER, ALFRED, supposed to have left England for New York about 1873
ALDER, WILLIAM, supposed to have gone to New York in 1873
ALEXANDER, ——, resided in Hunter Street, Brunswick Square, London, in 1871 He is supposed to have gone to America
ALTON, SINCLAIR, of Edinburgh, left Scotland for America 1838
ALLEN, WILLIAM K , born about 1815, supposed to have gone to America
ALLCOCK, SAMUEL, supposed to have gone, in 1861, with his mother to Salt Lake City, Utah, and is supposed to be now residing in Nevada Territory.
ARCHIBALD, ALICE, sometime resident at Egmond Villa, Ontario, Canada
ARNOLD, ALBERT HASTINGS, St Louis, Missouri
ASSINDER, CHARLES, formerly of Birmingham, architect and surveyor, supposed to be in America
BAKER and FERRAND, Philadelphia, 1815
BALDERSTONE, THOMAS, Chatham, West Canada, 1849
BALLANCE, ISAAC, emigrated from Ireland in 1875, and supposed to be in North America.
BAMBER, MARGARET, married in America, 1830, RICHARD BAMBER.
BARCLAY, JAMES, son of the REV. GEORGE BARCLAY, a sailor in merchant service, sailed for New Orleans, on board the "Herald," 1878
BARKER, WENDELL R , a native of Boston, mariner.
BARTON, WILLIAM, went to America in 1821
BEARDSLEY, WILLIAM, a cooper, who enlisted some years ago in the 82nd Foot, and is now supposed to be living in America
BEATTIE, ISABELLA, spr , formerly of Belfast, Ireland, but supposed to be now in the United States of America
BECKLEY, WILLIAM, a whitesmith, and SARAH his sister, left England many years ago for New York.
BEIRNE, ROGER and JOSEPH, residing in the United States of America
BELLEW, PETER, Washington, Penn , laborer
BEST, JOHN, descendants now supposed to be residing in Red River, or Province of Manitoba, Canada
BEWICK, SPARK, formerly of Newcastle-on-Tyne, chemist, last heard of at Thorold, Ontario, as employed on a farm
BIRCH, JAMES, son of THOMAS RAWLINS BIRCH, left England for New York about 1863.
BIRD, EDWARD, brother of JOSEPH BIRD, of Bethnal Green, London, went to Canada 1831.
BLOOMFIELD DANIEL, of Colchester children of in America
BOLENA, OWEN, son of PATRICK and WINIFRED BOLENA, emigrated from Ireland, in 1847, for Canada, which country he left in 1860 for the United States of America
BONNELL, ANN, wife of WM BONNELL, Nova Scotia, merchant, 1819
BRADLEY THOMAS (or JAMES), emigrated many years since to St. John's, New Brunswick. His sister married a Mr Hone
BREALEY, HENRY JOHN, brother of THOMAS STORER BREALEY, Toronto, Canada, 1841
BREMAR —Information wanted respecting the parentage of HENRY BREMAR, formerly a dentist in Charleston, S C . where he died in 1835 He had two brothers, JOHN and FRANK, who predeceased him and died without issue, and an uncle who is stated to have been married three times His Next of Kin will hear of considerable property
BRIDLE, LOUISA, married, Chicago, believed, ALFRED GEORGE
BRISKE, LOUIS, born 1832, formerly a merchant at Posen, Prussia , left that city, 1868, for America
BRODRICK, BRIDGET MARY, MORRIS, THOMAS, JOHN, NELLY
BROWN, DAVID, grandson of DAVID BROWN, of Linlithgow, left Great Britain in 1845
BROWN, THOMAS MITCHELL, captain, a native of Scotland, his widow and children are supposed to be in America
BUCHANAN, JOHN AMBROSE, last heard of in Savannah, Ga
BULGER, KATIE, recently worked at No 22 East 70th-street, New York
BURKE, ANN, BRIDGET and MARGARET, formerly of Lickles. Co Galway, but now in America
BURLE, THEODORE, born in France, and now residing in America
BURROWS, JOHN HEGEMAN, son of JAMES.
BURT, RICHARD, of Smethwick, Staffordshire, left England in 1810 Descendants of
CADDICK, RICHARD, he was in Cincinnati in 1832, and is supposed to have joined the Wesleyans and to have settled in the Southern States
CARBACK, CHARLES A , son of DAVID S and MARTHA ANN CARBACK, 1851
CARPENTER, WILLIAM, CORYNDON, FAUNTLEROY, NATHANIEL, or BUSHROD, sons of DR NATHANIEL CARPENTER, late of King and Queen's County Va.

CARR, ——, a clergyman in Toronto, Canada, descendants of——. The Rev —— CARR had a brother named ROBERT CARR, a surgeon in Australia

CARRINGTON, MICHAEL and ANN, power-loom weavers, left England for America about 1850

CARROLL, DANIEL WILLIAM, was in a French merchant's house in Bogota, Columbia, in 1874.

CARROLL, MICHAEL, left Pawtucket, R I , 1878, last heard of in New Orleans, La.

CARTER, WILLIAM, son of JANE CARTER, formerly DOUST, spinster, who, it is supposed, married, in Philadelphia, Mr CARTER The said WILLIAM CARTER was in England about the year 1824, and is stated to have returned to America shortly afterwards

CATHCART, JAMES, MARY ELEANOR, or WILLIAM W

CAVAYE, WILLIAM, plumber and gas-fitter, left Edinburgh about 1863

CEARINS, or CAIRNS, JOHN, born in Ireland, son of JOHN CEARINS, or Cairns Nephews and nieces of

CHAPELLE, PIERRE-JEROME, or LOUIS, born in France about 1810, was formerly cook on board American vessels, and left New York about 1858 for Connecticut

CHURCHILL, HENRY and CATHARINE, left England for America 1841, and died at or near Key West, Monroe, Fla , 1857

CHURCHILL, JAMES, last known address is 2nd Frame House, North 7th-street, Philadelphia

CLARK, ROSNY ROBERT, residing in America

CLARK, THOMAS, son of JOHN and SARAH CLARK, who emigrated from England, and is supposed to have gone to America about 1825

CLEMENTS, THOMAS, supposed to have left England for California about 1830

CRAIG, ROBERT, sometime divinity student in Scotland, and afterwards in New York, but whose present address is unknown

CRAIG, THOMAS GEORGE, Sherman, Greyson Co , Texas, 1880

CRAMPTON, SARAH, wife of WILLIAM CRAMPTON, of New Romney, emigrated to America

CRISPIN, GEORGE WILLIAM, died at New Orleans 1866

CROFT, ESTHER FRANCES, supposed to be residing in America

CROKER, ROBERT, sometime of County Down, went to America with his family about 1852

CUMBERLAND, HENRY JAMES, or JOHN PILOT GRAHAM, or JOHN MAY

CURELL, WILLIAM, formerly of Belfast, and lately of New York

DAVENPORT, THOMAS, believed to have settled at Lexington, County Lauderdale, Ala , and to have died there about 1853

DAVIS, MARY, daughter of CHARLES DAVIS and C B DAVIS (nee SWAIM)

DAWSON, JOSHUA, Otley, Yorkshire, seaman, supposed to be in America

DAWSON, ROBERT, son of THOMAS, left Scotland about 1855, and resided for some time in Pennsylvania and Ohio

DINGWALL, ALEXANDER, and JANET his wife, left Perthshire, Scotland, about 1853, when last heard of they were residing in Detroit, Mich

DIXON, THOMAS, born in 1781, and died 1822 He was son of Captain —— DIXON and SARAH DIXON, of New York.

DODDS, MARY, daughter of JAMES and JANE DODDS, formerly of England, and afterwards of Australia

DOLAN, ELIZABETH, children of, who emigrated to America many years since

DOMETT, GEORGE, captain H M Royal Navy, left England for Boston, 1827

DONALD, SAMUEL, born at Perth, left Scotland about 1866

DONOR, JOHN, left Co Limerick, and last heard of from New York, 1869,

DORY, CHARLOTTE, who, with her husband, JOSEPH DORY, left England for Canada, 1829

DOUGLAS, JAMES, son of GEORGE DOUGLAS, born 1809, left Scotland in 1863

DOUGLAS, RALPH, left England about 1821 for America He had a brother THOMAS, who was a sailor

DOUST, JANE, supposed to have married in Philadelphia, prior to 1821, —— CARTER, and to have had a son, WILLIAM CARTER

DUESBURY, WILLIAM, Bulimba, Queensland, architect, 1877, and supposed to be now in America

DUMFORA, D , born in Canada, and who afterwards resided in the U S A

DUNANT, MAURICE-EMILE, AIME-MARIE, and ADRIANNE-JULIE, in America

DUNKHASE, HEINRICK EDWARD, a sailor, supposed to be in America

DUVERDIER DE LA VALETTE, JEAN-BAPTISTE, New York, 1810.

DUXFIELD, JOSEPH JAMES, sailed from Liverpool to New York about 1869

DWYER, FRANCES, GRACE ELLEN, and SUSANNAH K , daughters of ROBERT DWYER, formerly of Dublin

DWYER, JOHN, formerly of Ireland, and lately of New York or St Louis

EBBERN, THOMAS, went to America about 1856

EDE, GEORGE, who about 1850 resided at Ewell, in Surrey, where he carried on business as a maltster and brewer, and then, it is supposed, emigrated to America.

EDEN, WALTER REUBEN, Santiago, Cuba, 1879

ELLIOTT, MARY ANN, daughter of Mrs MARIA WARNER

ELLIS, SARAH, spr , sometime of St Paul's Cray, Co Kent, who left England some years since for America

EMERSON, THOMAS R , a native of Ireland, supposed to be residing in America

EVERINGTON, JAMES, supposed to have sailed from Hull as a seaman about 1873

FANCOURT, HENRY ROBERT AUSTIN, a steward on U S steamer *Winooski*, 1867

FARNES, JOSEPH, born about 1848, and supposed to be in America

FAWCETT, JOHN and JONATHAN, sons of BETTY FAWCETT, deceased, went to America prior to 1852

FENNER, AUGUSTINE GOODWIN, went to America, 1850

FERGUSSON, SARAH, Lower Baggott Street, Dublin, deceased Relations in America

FERRAND and BAKER, Chestnut-street, Philadelphia, 1815

FIELD, JOHN, mother's maiden name SARAH JEFFCOAT, born in London, and emigrated to America about 1843

FLANAGAN, or WELCH, ANN, formerly of the County of Lancaster, but now in the United States of America

FLEMING, SAMUEL, who a few years ago was working as a stonecutter in New York

FLING, MARTIN New Foundland, Fisherman, 1818

FONTANA, GIOVANNI BATTISTA In 1861 he was residing at Birmingham Supposed to have gone to America

FORSEY, SAMUEL, Fortune Bay, Newfoundland, fisherman, 1814
FRAMPTON, SARAH, wife of WILLIAM FRAMPTON New Romney. Went to America
FURGERSON, ALFRED, went to America in 1865 When last heard of he was residing at Ionia, Mich.
GEE, GEORGE, and his children, ANN, SARAH, JOHN, and CHARLES, last heard of from Milwaukee, Wis , 1849
GEORGE, LOUISA, nee BRIDLE, married in Chicago, it is believed, ALFRED GEORGE
GILBERT, THOMAS, son of JOHN GILBERT, went to New York about 1810
GODDARD, SAMUEL, married in 1854, and resided in Birmingham until 1862, from whence he is supposed to have removed to London, where he was in the employment of stable-keepers
GOEPPERLE, MARY, wife of CHRISTOPHER GOEPPERLE, New York, 1868
GOODALL, MARIAN, Detroit, Co Wayne, Mich
GOTT, JOHN and WILLIAM, children of JANE GOTT
GOURLAY, SAMUEL, a sailor, son of Mr, GOURLAY of Scotland, last heard of in San Francisco
GRANT, BARBARA, who is stated to have resided in San Francisco previous to 1879
GRANT, JOSEPH, formerly of Co Kerry, Ireland, and afterwards of Boston Highlands, Mass , 1863
GREEN, HENRY, left England in 1862 for America
GREEN, JAMES, Wilmington, Carolina, farmer, 1802
GREEN, THOMAS, Green's Pond, Newfoundland, planter
GRIFFITHS, DAVID, Pittsburg, Ohio, 1872
GRIFFITHS, JOSEPH, Mexico, 1832
GRIMES, JOHN, formerly of 835 East 77th St , New York
GURR, GEORGE, formerly of Bradshaw St , Old Kent Road, London, Coke Contractor Left England in 1869, and is supposed to have gone to America
HALEY, ISAAC, son of THOMAS and BETTY HALEY, went to America in 1839
HALL, HENRY TAYLOR, left England, 1873, for America
HAMPTON, WILLIAM, in 1872 residing at Colesberg, Kopje Diamond Fields, South Africa, supposed to be now in America
HANSEN, GUSTAV and ELISE of Dusseldorf, supposed to be in America
HARRIS, JANE, daughter of JOSHUA JEAVONS, residing in America
HARTY, MARY ANN, who was known by the name of MARY ANN MASON, late of the city of Montgomery, Ala , where she died in 1851
HASTINGS, BETSEY ANN, a native of Ireland, went to U S A
HAWKINS, RICHARD WYNDHAM MONTONNIER, who, in 1877, resided at Mineral Ridge, Trumbull, Ohio, and afterwards at Jackson, Mich
HEAP, GEORGE W , son of BENJAMIN HEAP, 1852
HEAP, MARY, EMMA, and LAVINIA, daughters of SAMUEL HEAP, 1861
HELLYER, ALBERT GEORGE, left England for South America, and is supposed to have died at Laguna de los Padres, near Buenos Ayres, about 1875
HELLYER, HENRY NEALE formerly of London, went to South America, and is supposed to have died in Buenos Ayres, 1871
HENNESSEY, DANIEL, left Ballyraget, Co Kilkenny, Ireland, 1852, when last heard of, in 1863, he had a farm of his own, four miles from Louisville, Ky
HERRON, JOHN, March, Canada, Gentleman, deceased
HEUVELDOP, JOHANNES GERARDUS IGNATIUS, New Orleans, La
HEYFRON, MATTHEW, who, with his wife and children, emigrated, in 1840, from Dublin to Australia, and afterwards to California
HICKS, JOHN H , late of Laramie City, Albany, Wyoming
HILBERS, THOMAS HERMANN, Brooklyn, N Y , 1858
HOARE, THOMAS, left England in 1861
HOCKLY, GEORGE CLEGHORN, born at Calcutta, 1845, went to New York 1858
HODGES, CLIFFORDIER ELIZABETH, Weston, near Boston, Mass , widow, deceased Next of Kin supposed to be in U S A
HOLLINS, WILLIAM, formerly of Co Notts, England, and afterwards of Canada Children of
HOLME, THOS CROSS, and JANE his sister, left England some years ago for America
HONE, JAMES, a blacksmith, left Hampton-in-Arden, Co , Warwick, about 1857, for America
HORSFALL, JOHN TOMLIN, emigrated to the United States, America, in 1858
HORSLEY, FRANCIS, the younger, of Tulare County, Cal
HORSLEY, GEORGE, of Princeville, Peoria County, Ill
HORSLEY, JOHN, of Franklin County, Ind , United States, America.
HOWARD, SARAH, nee ONGLEY, N Y
HUDSON, JAMES, Red River, Canada
HUGHES, WILLIAM, formerly of Kent, England, and afterwards of Tuscola, Mich
HUTTON, JOHN, mate on the Lamboramus of Yarmouth, Nova Scotia, left his ship in Boston 1866
HUTTON, WILLIAM, born at Leith, Scotland, 9th November, 1816, a seaman, sailed from Shields in 1847 on a voyage to the Brazils, South America
HYDE, ARTHUR LEMAN, emigrated in 1852 Sailed from Talcahuano, Chili in 1863, in the whaling-ship Atkins Adams, to New Bedford, Mass , and he is believed to have enlisted from that place in the American Army of the North, and to have died in that service before 1865
HYDE, LOUISA, late of Peterson, Gull River, Co , Victoria, Ontario
IMPLETON, THOMAS, son of MRS SARAH IMPLETON, supposed to be now in America
INCE, GEORGE B , supposed to have gone to America in 1880
ISAAC, ISAAC, Quirpoon, Newfoundland, planter, 1811
JACKSON, BRYCE DOWNIE, sometime of Scotland, emigrated about 1856
JACKSON, JAMES, Broad-street, London, children of in America
JACKSON, WILLIAM, left England in 1856, and in 1862 was known as "Corporal WM WATSON JACKSON, of Company B, 7th Infantry, Madison Barracks, Sackett's Harbor, Jefferson Co , N Y " In 1863 he was a wardmaster in the United States General Hospital, Pa , and had been wounded in battle When last heard from, in 1866, he was keeping a bar-room, at San Antonio, Bexar County, Texas, and letters were addressed to him care of Mr Lockwoods, Forage Master, San Antonio It is supposed that he was in Chicago in 1881
JAMES, HENRY and CATHERINE, left England for America in 1841, and died at or near Key West, Monroe County, Fla , 1857
JANNISON, JOHN, and MARY, his wife, formerly MARY NEUDICK.

JARDINE, JAMES, formerly a farmer at Beattock, near Moffatt, left Scotland for Canada in December, 1853
JEAVONS, JANE, spr , afterwards wife of———HARRIS, residing in America
JENKINS, MARY W , daughter of FRANCIS JOHN JENKINS, who assumed the name of CHARLES WILLIAM FELLOWS, and died at Staten Island, N Y , in 1854
JEPSON, SARAH A., and LOUISA ABBOTT JEPSON, wife of TITUS JEPSON, residing in America 1855
JOHNSON, JAMES, ANTHONY, WILLIAM, EDWARD, RICHARD, HENRY, and MARIA, who left Ireland many years since for North America and Canada
JOHNSON, GEORGE, son of GEORGE JAMES JOHNSON, left England in 1873
JOHNSON, JOHN, brother of MRS ELEANOR BURRELL, of the Co . Yorks, went to America
JOHNSTON, ROBERT, of Lerwick, Scotland, seaman, left London for Quebec 1867
JONES, ABNER W , or his heirs
JORDAN, FREDERICK, residing in 1874 with his brother, WALTER JORDAN, at Toronto, Canada, which city he left in the same year for the U S A
JOUANNA VICTOR-ARMAND, Deverseh, Col
KEANE, JOHN and MATTHEW, natives of Ireland, and in 1873 residing in America
KEANE, THOMAS C L Ohio
KERFOOT, THOMAS, formerly of Dublin, Ireland, died 1809, descendants of a brother or sister, supposed to be in America
KERNAGHAN, KERNOCHAN, or CUNNINGHAM, BRIDGET, born in 1839, went to New Orleans, in 1858
KIDDELL, CHARLES, South Carolina, gentleman, 1815
KING, FYFE ELLETSON, Next of Kin supposed to be in America
KNOX, MARY, daughter of FRANK KNOX, residing in America
LACKNER, GEORGE, formerly of Austria, emigrated to America
LAMONT, NORMAN, left Scotland for Canada in 1846 , he held an appointment in Royal Engineers in Montreal in 1849, which appointment he resigned , when last heard of, in that year, he was at N. Y
LANE, JOHN, London, tailor, left England about 1854
LANGLEY, JANE, daughter of WILLIAM, married and emigrated to America about 1840
LAWDER, EMMA or LOUISA, left England for Toronto
LEARY, JOHN, Philadelphia, 1837.
LEARY, JOHN and PATRICK, children of JAMES LEARY, otherwise McDONNELL
LE CHARPENTIER, ANTOINE, left Jersey in 1869 with his family, for Illinois
LEIGH, JOHN EDWARD, left England for America about 1861
LEONARD, JOHN, or his son EDWARD formerly residing in Hester-street, N Y
LEVERTON. WILLIAM son of JOHN LEVERTON, of Lincoln, went to America several years ago
LEWIS, ROBERT WAGSTAFF, supposed to have left Cape Town for America
LIDDELL, JOHN WENTWORTH, a joiner by trade, but latterly a building clerk of works, last heard of from Dover, in 1872
LITTLEWOOD, JANE. wife of GEORGE LITTLEWOOD, formerly HOLME, spr., sometime of Flint, left England for America some years ago
LLEWELLYN, THOMAS formerly of Ambleston, Co. Pembroke, sailor, supposed to be in America
LODGE. MATTHEW. of Dorchester, Mass.
LOMBARD, GASTON-LOUIS, born in France 1855, emigrated from Spain to America
LORY, ELIZABETH LYNE, spr , emigrated to North America in 1849, and supposed to have died in Cincinnati
LYMAN, EDWARD, of the United States
MACAULEY, JAMES BENJAMIN relations of in America,
McBRIDE, MARIA, wife of ROBERT McBRIDE, Hamilton, Canada
McCALLUM, ROSANNA, wife of JAMES McCALLUM, N Y , 1863
McCARTHY, GEORGE. a coachmaker and ANN his wife, children of in America
McLAWS, WILLIAM, born in 1832, went in 1850 to Salt Lake City Utah He sailed about 1855 from San Francisco for Los Angelos, Cal , on board the " Sea Serpent," which was wrecked on her passage
McCREADY, THOMAS STUART, a native of Ireland
MACDONALD, JAMES, son of WILLIAM MUIRHEAD MACDONALD, supposed to have died in America about 1846
MACDONOGH, HARRIET, Boston, spr , 1818.
MACDOWAT, WALTER, of Glasgow, merchant, went to America 1808.
McGLONE, BARTHOLOMEW, last heard of from Toronto, Canada
McGOWAN, HUGH, born in Ireland
McINTYRE, JOHN, late of Illinois America, formerly of Co Londonderry, book-keeper
McIVER, ANN, daughter of DONALD McIVER, of North Carolina, 1824
McLACHLAN, WILLIAM, whose real name is Reed, left London, 1870, as a cook on the *Agnes*
McLEAN, DONALD. born in Nova Scotia, and died recently in Montana Territory Heirs of———
McTURK JOHN left Great Britain in 1862, and supposed to be now in America
MADDOX -GEORGE, formerly of Park Farm, Bewdley, afterwards employed at Walker's Brewery, Warrington, left home 1878, supposed to be in America
MAGEE, CHARLES ROBERT, formerly of Blackwatertown,' Ireland, went to America some years since
MARCKWALD, ALEXANDER, formerly of Berlin, emigrated to the United States in 1868
MARTIN, JANE widow, daughter of late Rev ———BENNETT, of Dungannon, Ireland, supposed to be residing in America
MAY, NATHANIEL, late of Bristol, left England in 1869 for America, it is supposed
MAY, WILLIAM and FREDERICK nephews of Mrs HOMER, supposed to be in America
MEYER, GUSTAV THEOPHIL, born in North Germany, relatives now in America
MILLIGAN, PETER, last heard of about 1840, when he was a hawker with a two-horse wagon in the U S A He was often about Mobile, Ala , and Charleston, S C
MINAHAN, ANN, daughter of DANIEL and MARGARET, left Ireland 1850 with her mother and stepfather, JOSEPH DRISCOLL, for America, and last heard of in 1858, when she was residing in Water-street, New York
MINOT, LOUISA. formerly residing in Jamaica, but who was drowned off the coast of Texas in 1852
MITCHELL, JOSEPH, Monaghan, Ireland, but late of Fail River, Bristol, Mass , gent

SPECIAL LIST No. 16

MITCHELL, EVE, JOHN and THOMAS supposed to have gone to America
MONCK, CHARLES STEPHENS, formerly of Pittsburgh, Pa , but has not been heard of since 1872
MOORE, GEORGE HENRY, son of GEORGE MOORE of Plymouth, went to America
MOORE, HARRIET or ADAMS, daughter of GEORGE MOORE, living in America
MORGAN, FRANCIS HENRY, formerly of Co Somerset, who some years ago went to America
MORGAN, THOMAS, Shoe Cove, Newfoundland, gent., 1811
MORRIS, THOMAS, bricklayer, left Waterloo, Liverpool, in 1870, for the United States
MURPHY, ANNA, left Indianapolis about 1871 for the East Her mother married, after the death of her father, one James McNeilis
MURPHY, CATHERINE, Richland Station New York, spr , 1876
NEILD, JOSEPH, formerly of Dresden, Ohio Children of——
NEILSON, JAMES and MICHAEL, left Scotland about 1814, and went, it is believed, to America
ODDY, THOMAS, left England about 1865, and is supposed to have gone to America
O'DWYER, JANE, Louisville, Ky.
O'NEIL, DANIEL and BRIDGET, son and daughter of DANIEL O'NEIL, last heard of from New York
PACEY, JOSEPH, left England for the United States about 1863 If dead, a reward for evidence of his death
PARRY, THOMAS, son of JOSEPH PARRY, of Liverpool, emigrated to Canada about 1830
PATCHING, GEORGE, son of GEORGE and MARY ANN PATCHING, supposed to be in America.
PAYNE, JOHN, who married SARAH CHOAT BURLEIGH, and went abroad.
PAGDEN, HENRY, born 1825, emigrated to America in 1853
PATERKIN, ALEXANDER, a baker in New York, 1851.
PFEILL, JOHANN, left Stuttgart, Germany, with his wife, CAROLINE WILHELMINE PFEILL, for Baltimore, Md , 1838
PLUMMER, EDWARD, left London many years ago for the United States In 1862, he is supposed to have kept an eating-house in New York.
PODMORE, RICHARD LATHAM, New Orleans, La , 1852
POINTIN, THOMAS, HINKLEY, sailed from Liverpool to America in ship Barreda Brothers 1862
PORTEOUS JANE, spr , representatives of in America
POTTER, DANIEL, son of REBECCA POTTER, was in New York in March, 1873, and intended proceeding to the Far West
POWELL, JOHN, born about 1809, went to America in 1803, and was working as a saddler at Newark and other places in the State of New York in 1836
PRATT, JAMES and ROBERT, sons of JAMES PRATT, of Oxford, deceased, now resident in America Children of.
PRINGLE, THOMAS and WILLIAM, sons of GEORGE PRINGLE, left Scotland about 1840 for the gold diggings in California
PRISEMAN ROBERT, left England in 1860, and was last heard of from Sacramento, California, in 1869
QUIN, ANDREW, who arrived in Quebec by the steamship Caspian in 1873
RAMSHAY, JOHN and ELIZABETH his wife, and HENRY WILLIAM and JOHN JAMES RAMSHAY, all residing in North America 1861
REED, HENRY WILLIAM WEBBER, otherwise WILLIAM McLACHLAN, left London 1870 as a cook on the "Agnes"
REEVES FRANCIS, formerly of Hawkhurst, Kent, England, last heard of at Chicago in 1858
REID, THOMAS SMITH. formerly of Camden Town, London, but in February, 1862, a reporter or sketcher for New York Illustrated News
REILLY, EDWARD, or EDWARD B , served in Company B, 2nd Division, U S Infantry, Army of the Potomac, 1863-64, and who resided at Benson Mills, State of Virginia, and afterwards at Greenville, Washington Co , State of Mississippi
REILLY, MARGARET, spr , in 1863 resided at Gloucester, State of New Jersey
REYNOLDS, ANNIE, born about 1851, supposed to have removed to Boston from Albany or Newark
RIACH, ADAM, alias HENRY WRIGHT, supposed to be in United States
RICHARDSON, EDWIN, left England about 1870, last heard of at Chatham Chester County, Pennsylvania
RICHARDSON MRS ELIZABETH, formerly of London, now in America.
RISHTON, JOHN, Dougherty's Station, Alameda, California
RITCHIE, JOHN, left Cupar, Scotland, about 1872. and who served on board the Red Sea
ROBINS, WILLIAM brother of GEORGE FRANK ROBINS, formerly of Lye, parish of Oldswinford County Worcester, supposed to be now in America
RODGERS, JOHN, born at Barnsley Yorks Went to America
ROCHFORT, PHILIP, son of GUSTAVIS ROCHFORD, Commander R N., supposed to be in North America
ROGAN, ANNIE, wife of PATRICK ROGAN, formerly of Ireland, late of New York
ROGERS, HARRY, son of JOHN and JANE ROGERS, who, about 1850, went to California, and in 1854 was living at Stockton, in California
ROHFRITSCH, CHARLES FRANCOIS, born in France about 1848, supposed to be now in America He was formerly a hair-dresser
ROSE BARNABAS, of Otto, Fulton County, Illinois, 1859
ROTTEN, BENJAMIN, Gloucester, clothworker, last heard of about 1797 from Philadelphia
ROUGHAN, BRIDGET, daughter of John Ronghan, left Loughrea, County Galway, Ireland, about 1854
ROUQUIER, JULES, formerly of Indianapolis, Ind
RULE, JAMES, born in 1837, a seaman in H M S Indefatigable, 1857, and afterwards in Peruvian frigate Amazones but has not been heard of since 1863
RUSSELL, ADAM, brother of JAMES BROWN JOHNSTON RUSSELL, left Scotland for America, 1850
SALTMARSH, NATHANIAL RICHARD, left Liverpool for New York in ship *Garnholm*, 1881.
SANGSTER, JOHN, formerly employed at Stanley Railway Station, Perth, Scotland, which place he left in 1870
SCHEIDT, CORNELIA AGATHA, wife of WILLIAM SCHEIDT, Helena, Ark , 1878
SCHWAB CASPER, New York, sugar-baker, 1811
SCOTT, JOHN BRODIE, left Scotland in 1862, and supposed to be now in America

SCOTT, MARGARET, born MCINTOSH, wife of A SCOTT, formerly a bread and biscuit maker in Edinburg supposed to be residing in America

SCOTT, MARY, formerly McBEATH, wife of JOHN SCOTT, a blacksmith, who both emigrated to Boston, 1841

SCULLEN, JAMES or PATRICK, between 1855 and 1857 was in New York Police Force

SEEGEN, SOLOMON, London, merchant, but who, in 1855, was in New York

SEMPLE, ALEXANDER, emigrated to Nova Scotia in 1848, and last heard of at Mobile, Ala, 1852

SHAW, HECTOR, born in Scotland about 1826, last heard of in 1876, when he directed his letters to be addressed care of EDWD BARRY, Newark-avenue, Jersey City

SHERIDAN, HELEN born about 1800 Her Next of Kin are entitled to considerable property

SHERIDAN, MARGARET, of Stradbally, Queen's County, Ireland, now deceased. Next of Kin supposed to be in America

SHERIDAN, MARY and MARGARET, left Ireland for America 1848

SHERWOOD, NANCY ANN, Bangor, County Penobecot, Maine, widow

SILK, EDWARD Albany Factory, Hudson Bay, 1830

SIM, JOHN, left Hamilton, Canada, in 1858, with GEORGE WRIGHT, a baker, and afterwards heard of in Dakota It was rumored that he was seen in California

SIM, WILLIAM NEILSON, born in 1810, left Glasgow for America in 1831

SIMPSON, LEVI, formerly of Lincoln, England Believed to have emigrated to America about 1871

SINCLAIR, WILLIAM, Fishcurer, Willowbankwich, Scotland His Next of Kin supposed to be in America.

SKINNER, PATRICK, mariner, son of PATRICK ALEXANDER SKINNER, of Aberdeen

SLATER ROBERT, born in 1843, son of R SLATER, shipsmith, Glasgow, when last heard of, in 1866, he was engaged as a mate on a steamer

SMITH, ANN, widow of JOHN SMITH, New Orleans, La, 1860

SMITH, DAVID and JONATHAN, brothers of THOMAS SMITH, who left London for America about 1836

SMITH, ELIZA, wife of JOHN SMITH, left England for Salt Lake City, Utah, in 1858

SMITH, ELIZABETH, formerly COOPER, widow of NATHANIAL SMITH, New Orleans, La, 1860.

SMITH, JOHN, of Edinburg, and MARGARET, of Glasgow, son and daughter of JOHN SMITH, they were in New York in 1872

SMITH, THOMAS JAMES, formerly a clerk in the Bank of England, and who, about 1864, left England for British Columbia

SMITHWICK, GEORGE PERCEVAL, left Nashville, Tenn, and when last heard from in 1863, he was in the State of Kentucky.

SOMERS, or SOMERSGILL, or SUMMERSGILL, SARAH, went to Cincinnati about 1830 Children of

SOMERSGILL, or SUMMERSGILL, or SOMERS, GEORGE, left England for America about 1842

SPENCER, WILLIAM ROBERT, went to U S A about 1871

STACKHOUSE, THOMAS left New Orleans for California between 1850 and 1855,

STEEL, GEORGE, son of DANIEL and CATHERINE STEEL, left England for Canada in 1873

STRATEN, SARAH, wife of CHARLES STRATEN, New York, merchant, 1800

STRONG, WILLIAM, New York, merchant, 1783

SYLVESTOR, ELIAS JOSEPH, son of ABRAHAM SYLVESTOR, died in America 1850

TAYLOR, HANNAH, MARY and THOMAS children of HANNAH TAYLOR, sometime resident at 26 West Market-square, Toronto, Canada

THAIN, JOHN, a sailor on board the "Othello" bound for St Johns, Newfoundland, in 1859 He was in the hospital at St Johns and afterwards shipped on a Colonial vessel

THISS, ANTON WILLIAM, 415, 7th-street, Leavenworth, Kan, 1874

THOMPSON, ALEXANDER, a native of Lochgilphead, Argyleshire, last heard of when on a voyage from Hong Kong to New York about 1862

THOMPSON, MARY ANN, formerly in Locust-street, Philadelphia, Penn, housekeeper

THORNTON, PATRICK, left Ireland for America 1845

THORNTON, PETER, stonemason, a native of Yorkshire, left England for the U. S. A, where he married about the year 1885

TIFFIN, ELIZABETH, wife of WILLIAM JABEZ TIFFIN, went to New Orleans, about 1832, with JOSEPH TURTON, of New York

TODD, SARAH, Northampton, Mass, widow, deceased. Children of living in 1853

TOLL, HENRY, a mariner, last heard of from New Bedford, near Boston, Mass, 1840.

TOWNSEND, KATE, otherwise KERNAGHAN or CUNNINGHAM, born 1839, went to New Orleans, La, in 1858

TRENCH, JOHN, late of Liverpool, died 1875 Next of Kin of

TUPPER, JAMES, Nova Scotia, timber merchant, 1830

TWELL, JOSEPH, brother of GEORGE ALEXANDER TWELL, Chicago, 1869

TYTLER, WILLIAM, gent New York. 1832

UNGIDOS, ALPHOUSE, supposed to be residing in South America

UPTON, JANE, formerly of Dublin, supposed to have gone to America in 1862, or her children

VAUGHAN, ARTHUR and JOHN, grand-nephews of ARTHUR VAUGHAN, of Ireland

WALKER, CHRISTINA, formerly ONGLEY, spr, New York

WALLEY, CHARLES HENRY, born 1853, sailed to New York in 1865 in ship *Mikado*

WARREN, MARIA, left Ireland many years since for North America or Canada

WARREN, MICHAEL, son of DENNIS WARREN, last heard of from Cold Spring, New York

WAUGH, GEORGE, sailed from England, 1855 in the *Nazarene* for South America He afterwards worked for Messrs Death & Star, of San Francisco and is believed to have died about 1863.

WEHLI, BENEDICT and JACOB, natives of Austria, supposed to be in America

WEISS, FREDERICK a native of Germany, emigrated to Baltimore, Maryland, 1838

WELCH, ANN, *alias* FLANAGAN, formerly of the county of Lancaster, but now in the United States of America

WESTON, REUBEN, son of CHARLES WESTON Residing, it is believed, in America.

WESTBURRY, THOMAS, formerly of Stratford-on-Avon Went to America about 1850

WETHERELL, NATHANIEL THOMAS, late of Easton, Pa, but who left England for Canada, 1877

WHELAN, THOMAS, son of DARBY WHELAN, emigrated about 1851, last heard of at Concord

WHEELER, JOSEPH, born 1811, son of JOHN and ELIZABETH WHEELER, left England for New York in 1830

WHITTLESEY, WILLIAM, left London about 1868 for America, last heard of from Brooklyn

WILD, WILLIAM, son of SARAH WILD, of Leeds, England

WILKINS, CALDWELL R., when last heard of was employed by Messrs Hamilton & Easter, Baltimore
WILLIAMS, EDWARD, whose mother was born at Flushing, Long Island, New York
WILLIAMS, MARY ANNE and JANE, daughters of WILLIAM and JANE WILLIAMS, born about 1800, children of, supposed to be in America
WILSON, Rev. THOMAS, left England in 1856 He joined the Federal Army, it is believed the 14th Infantry, then quartered at Fort Trumhill, New London, Con , and has not since been heard of
WILSON, WILLIAM, formerly a seaman on board the *Clyde*, of Glasgow, last heard of in 1829, or his brother JAMES, formerly a surgeon in the Hon East India Company's service, last heard of in 1823
WISE, HENRY, (from Somersetshire, England), Albany, Delaware, Ind
WRAGG, WILLIAM, Charleston, South Carolina, gent , deceased, 1810
WRIGHT, CHARLES, FRANK, HENRY, and RICHARD, sons of THOMAS WRIGHT. They all left England for America in 1858
WRIGHT, FREDERICK, born in 1841, formerly of Detroit, Mich., tailor
WRIGHT, HENRY, correct name ADAM RIACH, supposed to be in the United States
WRIGHT, WILLIAM, son of THOMAS WRIGHT, left England for America, 1858, when last heard of he was a wheelwright in Chicago, Ill.
ZAUGER, MATTHIA, a native of Wurtemburg, when last heard from he was working on a railroad at Paterson, N J.

SPECIAL LIST NO. 17.

UNCLAIMED MONEY, LANDS AND ESTATES.

The following persons if living, or if dead, their representatives are entitled to property. Address all communications to **J. B MARTINDALE, 142 La Salle St, Chicago, Ill.**, giving all facts on which claim is based (See pages 6, 7 and 8 of this Manual)

AHART, POLLY, deceased, died in Missouri Heirs wanted.
ALCOTT, ALIZA, last heard of at Taylorville, Ohio Supposed to have served in the Mexican war
ALDRIDGE, WILLIAM, deceased, died in a Western State Heirs wanted
ALLARD, JOHN B, deceased, died in Missouri Heirs wanted
ANDERSON, SAMUEL, last heard of at Jasper, Tenn Served in Mexican war
ANDERSON, CHRISTIAN L, late of Carroll County, Ind
ARCHER, WM, last heard of at Louisville, Ky Served in Mexican war
ARMOR, EDWARD, or SARAH, or RUTH, supposed to reside in Chicago, but letters addressed to them are returned to the writer Their address wanted in reference to interest they have in property
ARNSON, HODSA, (for Hersh Arnson) died in Missouri Heirs wanted
ATKINSON, MILTON B Supposed to be in America if living Heirs wanted
BACON, WILLIAM, deceased, died in Missouri Heirs wanted
BAKER, JAMES, died in Idaho Territory in 1877 Heirs wanted
BANCE, PETER, last heard of at St Louis, Mo Served in Mexican war
BARNARD, JOHN, deceased, died in Missouri Heirs wanted
BEARD, FRANCIS, late of Bedford County, Pa
BECKER, AUGUST, died in New York about 1881 Heirs wanted
BEHRENS, FRED, deceased, died in Missouri Heirs wanted
BELL, JAMES G, deceased, died in a Western State Heirs wanted
BENTLEY, THOMAS, deceased, died in Missouri. Heirs wanted
BERRY, ISAAC, died in the State of Maine about 1868 Heirs wanted
BETTS, (or BETZ), BARBARA, (nurse) died in New York Heirs wanted
BINDER, JOHN S, deceased, died in Missouri Heirs wanted.
BIXTON, ISAAC, late of Fairfield County, Conn.
BOENICK, JOSEPH, last heard of at St Louis, Mo Served in the U S Army.
BONDEY, JAMES I, deceased, died in Missouri Heirs wanted,
BOND, MARY F, deceased, died in a Western State Heirs wanted
BOROUGH, EBANEZER, late of Cambria County, Pa
BOTTOMLEY, THEOPHILUS, (book-keeper), died in New York, 1883 Heirs wanted
BOUGNOIR, NICHOLAS, deceased, died in a Western State Heirs wanted
BOYD, BEATRICE, (nurse) died in New York, 1882 Heirs wanted
BRADSHAW, WILLIAM, bachelor, came from England to America about 1850 Settled in Missouri, Heirs wanted
BROWN, ELISHA V See MARY ANN WILSON
BROWN, PHILANDER, last heard of at Santa Fe, N Mexico Belonged to the U S Army at one time
BUCKHOLLY, GEORGE, deceased, died in Missouri Heirs wanted
BUCKLEY, MICHAEL, deceased, (person No 16, lost on the steamer "Stonewall") Heirs wanted
BUCHER, CASPER, deceased, died in a Western State Heirs wanted
BURKE, JOHANNA, (dressmaker) died in New York 1882
BURGESS WM J, (manager) died in New York, 1883
BURR, THOS, J, last heard of at Chicago, Ill Served in U S Army
BUSH, G B, deceased, died in Missouri Heirs wanted.
BURNSIDE J D, was killed at Gaylesville, Ala, in March 1883 Address of his widow or children wanted
CALVERT, LEONARD, deceased, died in a Western State, Heirs wanted
CAMPBELL, JOHN, last heard of at St Louis, Mo, about 1860
CAMPBELL, LEWIS, died somewhere on the frontier of Texas Heirs wanted
CAMPBELL, RUSSELL, deceased, died in Missouri Heirs wanted
CARLISLE, WILLIAM, deceased, died in a Western State Heirs wanted.
CARPENTER, CALVIN, deceased, died in Missouri Heirs wanted
CARR, FRANCIS, deceased, died in a Western State. Heirs wanted.
CASEY, ANNIE, deceased, died in Missouri Heirs wanted
CASEY, HUGH (policeman) died in New York, 1883 Heirs wanted
CASTLE, HENRY, last heard of at Indianapolis, Ind Served in U S Army in War of 1812, or Mexican war
CHALFANT, P. G, deceased, died in a Western State Heirs wanted
CHAMBERS, ABIJAH A, left Blue Earth County, Minn, in 1856, and went off trapping, never returned Wife and children returned to Iowa Heirs wanted
CHAVERT, JUAN LUIS, supposed to be in America if living Heirs wanted.
CHAPMAN, DAVID, deceased, died in Missouri Heirs wanted
CHILDRESS, E, deceased, died in a Western State Heirs wanted
CHRISMAN, GABRIEL, deceased, died in Missouri. Heirs wanted

SPECIAL LIST No. 17

CHRISMAN, VINA, deceased, died in a Western State since 1870. Heirs wanted
CHRISTIAN, DAVID G W, last heard of at Cincinnati, Ohio. If dead, heirs wanted.
CLARK, REBECCA, (wife of EDWIN CLARK), daughter of WILLIAM HATCHER, who died in Illinois about 1860. He was from Ohio
COLLINS, GEORGE, deceased, died in a Western State. Heirs wanted
COLLINS, JOHN, last heard of at Louisville, Ky. Served in U S Army
COLSON, THOMAS W, late of Allegheny City, Pa. Went West about 1860. Heirs wanted
COOMBS, J I, was a volunteer in the U S Army in the War of 1812, or Mexican war. Heirs wanted
COUSLO, JERRY, deceased, (person No 86 lost on the Steamer "Stonewall") Heirs wanted,
CONWAY, (or WALSH) ELLEN, (newsdealer), died in New York, 1883. Heirs wanted
COOK, NATHANIEL, deceased, died in a Western State. Heirs wanted
CORCORAN, THOS. C., last heard of at St Louis, Mo
CORVING, JAMES, deceased, died in a Western State. Heirs wanted
CRANEY RICHARD, last heard of at St Louis, Mo.
CROOK, RICHARD, deceased, died in a Western State. Heirs wanted
DARDEN, or DURDEN, ROBERT J, a lawyer who formerly lived in Aberdeen, Miss. If living his address wanted. If dead, the place of his death
DAVIS, JAMES H, last heard of at St Louis, Mo, about 1860
DAVIS, LUCIUS H, came to Minnesota from Fall River, Mass, in 1857. Last heard of at Galveston, Tex. Heirs wanted
DAVIS, THOS J, was a soldier in 1812 or Mexican war.
DE HAM, C L, late of Kingston, Tenn, was a Civil Engineer on some R R, in Ky, lived a while in Louisville, Ky. His family were from Pittsburg, Pa
DELICHAUX, FRED A, supposed to have lived at St Louis, Mo, several years ago
DEVINE, RICHARD, died in Idaho, Ter, 1877. Heirs wanted.
DICK, AUGUST, deceased, died in Missouri. Heirs wanted
DICKERMAN, ALLEN, deceased, died in a Western State. Heirs wanted
DICKINSON, ADAM, deceased, died in Missouri. Heirs wanted
DIXON, ENNIS, deceased, died in a Western State. Heirs wanted
DOBSON, ROBERT, died in Iowa in 1859. Heirs wanted. He was from the South. His brothers and sisters were JAMES, CHARLES, JOSEPH, POLLY (married to —— SHOEMAKER), ANN (married to —— DEAM), and JEMIMA (married to —— WINN). The family is supposed to have got scattered during the late war
DOLAN, JOHN, died in Kansas between 1870 and 1880. Heirs wanted
DOLL, PETER, late of San Francisco, Cal
DONOVAN, MICHAEL deceased, died in Missouri. Heirs wanted
DOYLE, JOSIAH, late of Palmyra, Mo.
DUDLEY, WM, late of New Albany, Ind
DUNCAN, WILLIAM, deceased, died in Missouri. Heirs wanted.
DUNGAN, JOHN, deceased, died in a Western State. Heirs wanted
DURNS, MICHAEL, residence not known. Once owned land in Nebraska
ELLIOTT, CHARLES, (alias WILLIAM,) deceased, died in the West. Heirs wanted
ELLIOTT, W D, deceased, died in about 1875. Heirs wanted
ELMS, RICHARD, deceased, died about 1880. Heirs wanted
ENHNEST, EDWARD, deceased, died in Missouri. Heirs wanted
ERLS, JACOB, deceased, died in a Western State. Heirs wanted,
ESLINGER, CHRISTIAN, deceased, died in a Western State. Heirs wanted
EUELL, JOHN E, deceased, died in Missouri. Heirs wanted
FERRIS, ANTONIE, deceased, died in Missouri. Heirs wanted
FITCH, ARTHUR T, was in the banking business in New York City in 1876. Supposed to have gone to Europe
FITZSIMMONS, BERNARD, deceased, died in the West about 1870. Heirs wanted
FLEMING, RICHARD, St Louis, Mo
FLUNER, NICHOLAS, deceased, died in the West. Heirs wanted
FOGG, JAS B, late of Buffalo, N Y.
FOSTER, RUSSEL B (clerk) died in New York in 1883. Heirs wanted
FRIEZARD, PHILLIP, late of Jacksonville, Ohio.
FULTON, GEORGE, last heard of at Stockton, Cal, was once a soldier,
FURER, HARVIER, deceased, died in Missouri. Heirs wanted
GALLAHER, JAMES, deceased, died in a Western State. Heirs wanted
GALLIHAN, JAMES I, deceased, died in Missouri. Heirs wanted
GAZAWAY, PETER, about 1790 leased for 99 years certain real estate supposed to be in or near London, England, and he and his two sons (NICHOLAS and THOMAS) emigrated to America. The heirs in America can easily trace their heirship, if they can only find the record of the lease
GERHEART, ISAAC, late of Jasper County, Mo, died leaving six children. JOHN went to California, and died. Address of the others wanted
GIBSON, THOMAS, born in England. Owned land in Kansas some years ago. Has a brother in Chicago, Ill. Heirs wanted
GIFFORD, HENRY, last heard of at Brownsville, Tex. Was once a soldier
GILBERT, THEO, last heard of at Sante Fe, N Mexico. Was once a soldier
GITLEY, JAMES S, last heard of at St Louis, Mo. Was once a soldier
GLASSCOCK, SAMUEL W, deceased. Heirs wanted
GLEASON, DANIEL, deceased, died in the West. Heirs wanted
GOODYEAR, MARY, owned land in Missouri in 1847. Heirs wanted
GRANT, JOHN, deceased, died in a Western State. Heirs wanted.
GREBE, FRED, deceased, died in Missouri. Heirs wanted
GRIMSLEY, LIZZIE B, deceased, died in a Western State. Heirs wanted
GROVE, E R, deceased, died in Missouri. Heirs wanted
GUGENET, CELESTIE, deceased, died in a Western State. Heirs wanted
HAAGGE, JOHN, from Hamburg, Germany, died in Idaho Territory, 1877. Heirs wanted
HALE, WILLIAM, deceased, died in Missouri. Heirs wanted
HAMILTON, MARION N, residence not known. Once owned land in Nebraska
HAND, CHAS S, last known place of residence was San Francisco, Cal
HANKE, WILLIAM, (cabinet-maker), died in New York, 1882. Heirs wanted,
HARDEN, GEORGE, deceased, died in Missouri. Heirs wanted

HARDIN, SARAH, deceased, died in Missouri   Heirs wanted
HARE, ARTHUR, last heard of in 1864 in Texas, near the line of Indian Territory.
HARZERNDT, WILLIAM, (tanner), died in New York, 1882   Heirs wanted
HARPER, MARY, late of Taylorville, Ohio   Heirs wanted
HARTMAN, F K , deceased, died in Missouri   Heirs wanted
HARRIS, WM A , late of Columbia, S C   His heirs offer a liberal reward for information as to location of a large tract of land owned by him on the Brazos River in Texas
HATCHER, WILLIAM, died in Illinois about 1860   REBECCA CLARK, (wife of EDWIN CLARK), wanted as an heir
HAYS, SIMON, supposed to have served in War of 1812, or Mexican war   Heirs wanted
HASSE or HOPE, WM , last heard of at St Louis, Mo   Was U S volunteer in Mexican war, or in 1812.
HAYS, ELLEN, deceased, died in Missouri   Heirs wanted.
HEITEL, H , deceased, died in Missouri   Heirs wanted
HELT, JOHANN, HERMANN, (cigar-maker), died in New York, 1881   Heirs wanted
HENDERSON, THOMAS, emigrated from Ireland to America about 1838   Supposed to have settled at New Orleans, La   His children were JOHN, ROBERT, LAWRENCE, JANE and MARY
HENITZ, FRITZ, deceased, died in Missouri   Heirs wanted
HEINRICHS, CATHARINE, deceased, died in Missouri   Heirs wanted
HENRY, S H , late of Cincinnati, Ohio   Was once a soldier
HEPBURN, ARABELLA E , (from Nice, France), died in New York, 1883   Heirs wanted
HERBERT, WM , late of St Louis, Mo   Was once a soldier.
HERTZOY, PETER, late of Dayton, Ohio   Was once a soldier
HILLIARD, JOHN, (bachelor), came to America about 1850 from Ireland, with an aunt, had an uncle in Ireland   Heirs wanted
HILLIMAN, WILLIAM F   Heirs wanted
HOCK, JACOB F , late of Sacramento, Cal   Heirs wanted
HOOK, GEORGE B , place of residence not known   Once owned land in Nebraska
HOOPER, HENRY, owned land in Nebraska in 1877   Heirs wanted
HOUVET, DESIRE L , (cook), died in New York, 1883   Heirs wanted
HUGHES, OWEN, deceased, died in Missouri   Heirs wanted
HUGHES ANN (day laborer), died in New York, 1883   Heirs wanted
HUMPHREY, JAMES, deceased, (colored) died in Missouri   Heirs wanted.
JOHNSON, WM , deceased, died in Missouri   Heirs wanted
JOHNSTONE, JOHN A , (sea captain), died in New York in 1883
JONES, EDWIN B , served in Mexican war   Heirs wanted
JONES, FINLEY, late of (near) Aberdeen, Miss.   Supposed to have left land and money at his death, which his heirs would like to find
JUBLO, JOHN, late of New Orleans, La   Served in U S Army
KARNAGAN, KATE, (See KATE TOWNSEND)
KEANE, THOS J (student), died in New York, 1882.   Heirs wanted
KEIPHOLD, CHARLES, deceased died in Missouri   Heirs wanted
KELLEY, S H , deceased, died in Missouri.   Heirs wanted.
KENNEDY, A R , late of Sarpy County, Neb
KENT, C W , a painter who left Tennessee for Canada about 1859
KILBURN, ISAAC N , (watchman), died in New York, 1882   Heirs wanted
KIRKPATRICK, CHARLES, deceased, died in Missouri   Heirs wanted
KISKER, FRED , deceased died in Missouri   Heirs wanted
KOENIG, H A , deceased, died in Missouri   Heirs wanted
KOURDGR, AUGUSTUS, residence not known   Once owned land in Nebraska
KULL, WM , died in New York, 1883   Heirs wanted
KUNG, JOHN GEORGE late of Coloma, Cal   Heirs wanted
LANCEMENT, JEROME, deceased, died in Missouri   Heirs wanted.
LANGENBURG, KARL, late of Dusseldorf, Rhenish, Prussia   Supposed to be now living in America under an assumed name
LANHAM, SARAH M, deceased, died in Missouri   Heirs wanted
LANIE JOSEPH or CHARLES, (cook) died in New York in 1882   Heirs wanted
LANKENAU, HENRY, (bartender), died in New York 1883   Heirs wanted
LECOMPT, JULIUS, lived in the early days of the Republic of Texas at Houston, Texas.   Heirs wanted
LEDIGH, CHRISTIAN, late of Hamilton, Ohio   Was once a soldier
LEE, P H , deceased, died in Missouri   Heirs wanted
LEMON, JAMES, deceased, died in Missouri   Heirs wanted
LOCKWOOD, ISAAC, late of San Jose, Cal   Was once a soldier in U S A.
LOGAN, THEODORE, late of Philadelphia, Pa   Served in the U S A
LONDON, JOHN, deceased, died in Missouri   Heirs wanted
LOVELACE, BARTON D , deceased, died in Missouri   Heirs wanted
McCALEB, JOHN, deceased, died in Missouri   Heirs wanted
McCARDLE, BERNARD, late of Franklin, Texas   Served in the U. S A.
McCAIT, JOSEPH C , late of Douglas County, Neb
McCAREW, NATHAN, deceased, died in Missouri   Heirs wanted.
McCLARE, ELIZABETH, deceased, died, in Missouri   Heirs wanted
McCLOSKEY, HENRY, deceased, died in Missouri   Heirs wanted
McDONOUGH, ELIZABETH, deceased, died in Missouri.   Heirs wanted
McGALLIARD, WM , late of Logan County, Ill
McGLOTHLIN, PATRICK, late of Vancouver, Oregon.   Was once a U S soldier.
McHALE, M S , died in Idaho Territory, 1881   Heirs wanted
McKENNA, ELIZABETH, died in New York, 1883
McKENNA, FRANCIS, owned land in Nebraska in 1875   Heirs wanted
McMALLAN, NEWTON, last heard of in 1845 in Harrison County, Texas
McMILLEN, ELIZABETH, deceased, died in Missouri   Heirs wanted
McMULLEN, JOHN, late of St Louis, Mo   Served in U S A
McNALLEY, JOHN, deceased, died in Missouri   Heirs wanted
MAHER, JAMES, deceased, died about 1870   Heirs wanted
MAHOOD, ALLAN E (boatman) died in New York, 1881   Heirs wanted

SPECIAL LIST No. 17.

MALOWNEY, STEPHEN, deceased, died in Missouri Heirs wanted
MANN, HAMAN, late of Nash or Edgecombe County, N C , left there many years ago Wife's maiden name was TEMPY DEW Heirs wanted
MARCUS, ADAM, deceased, died in Missouri Heirs wanted
MARCHISE, CHARLES, (cook), from Switzerland, died in New York, 1883
MARKS, JOHN and EDWARD, left Ireland for America in 1856 When last heard of were residing in Brooklyn, N. Y
MARTIN, GEO W , deceased, died in Missouri Heirs wanted
MARTIN, HENRY H , place of residence not known Once owned land in Nebraska.
MAUS, CONRAD, deceased, died in Missouri Heirs wanted
MAUS, BARBARA, deceased, died in Missouri Heirs wanted
MAYBERRY, FRANK, deceased, died in Missouri Heirs wanted
MADDERS, CATHARINE, deceased, died in Missouri Heirs wanted
MELLON, JOHN, late of Savannah, Ga. Was once a soldier.
MELTON, PETER C , late of Camden, Ala
MALKER, JOHN, deceased, died in Missouri Heirs wanted
MEINECKE, FREDERICK, (tailor), died in New York, 1883
MERRICK, ARLINGTON, late of Brownsville, Texas Was once a U S soldier.
MEYMAL, MARRIAETTE, (dress-maker), died in New York, 1883
MEYERS, CHRISTINA, deceased, died in Missouri Heirs wanted
MILLER, JAMES H , died in the State of Maine about 1871. Heirs wanted
MILLER, P B , deceased, died in Missouri Heirs wanted
MILLER, WM H , late of Louisville, Ky Was once a soldier.
MOCK, JACOB H , deceased, died in Missouri Heirs wanted
MORGAN, JAMES, late of St Joseph, Mo Was once a soldier
MOLTER, GEORGE, deceased, died in Missouri Heirs wanted.
MORLEY, RICHARD, lived in Mason County, Michigan in 1865 Heirs wanted
MONTGOMERY, MARK D , late of San Antonio, Texas Served in Mexican war
MONTGOMERY, JOHN, late of Georgetown, Ky Served in U S A
MOONEY, ANNIE, died in New York in 1881 or 1882 Heirs wanted,
MOORE, JOHN, deceased, died in Missouri Heirs wanted
MOORE, SAMUEL, deceased, died in Missouri Heirs wanted
MORIATTO, ALEXANDER, deceased, died in Missouri Heirs wanted
MOYERS, ANNIE D , deceased, died in Missouri Heirs wanted
MUELLER, V , deceased, died in Missouri Heirs wanted
MULLEN, PATRICK, late of Houston, Texas Was once a soldier.
MULLINS, CHARLES, deceased, died in Missouri Heirs wanted
MURPHY, THOMAS, deceased. died in Missouri. Heirs wanted
MURTA, HENRY, deceased, died in Missouri Heirs wanted
MYERS, GEORGE, late of Warsaw, Mo Heirs wanted.
NEEDERHOFF, WILHELMINA, deceased, died in Missouri Heirs wanted.
NEELEY, THOMAS, deceased, died in Missouri Heirs wanted
NELSON, JOSEPH B , deceased, died in Missouri Heirs wanted.
NEWMAN, ALBERT, (teacher) died in New York in 1883
NICHOLL, FRANCIS, died in New York 1882. Heirs wanted
NOETZER, WM , deceased, died in Missouri Heirs wanted
NOWAK, J., deceased, died in Missouri. Heirs wanted
O'CONNOR, ELLEN, deceased, died in a Western State Heirs wanted
O'CONNOR, JOHANNA, (washerwoman) died in New York 1883
OLFSTAG, JACOB A , late of Caloma, Cal Heirs wanted
O'NEIL, JAMES H , late of Laramie, Wyoming Ter
O'TOOLE, MICHAEL, deceased, person No 50 lost Steamer "Stonewall" Heirs wanted.
OWENS, JOHN B , deceased, died in Missouri Heirs wanted
PAULING, JOHN R , late of Marion, Ala Heirs wanted
PEPPERMAN, JOHN, deceased, died in Missouri Heirs wanted.
PEARSON, ROBERT H , (from California,) died in New York 1882 Heirs wanted.
PEAQUESTE, GEORGE, died in the State of Maine about 1879 Heirs wanted
PECHET, LOUIS, (French) died in Idaho Ter , 1877 Heirs wanted
PHILLIPS, JAMES, late of Troy, Ohio.
PICON, BAPTISTE, deceased died in a Western State Heirs wanted
POWELL, LAZARUS J , removed from Pitt or Green Co , N C , many years ago, to one of the Northern cities, and died, leaving a large estate. His heirs would pay liberally for information leading to the finding of his estate
PRATHER, WALTER G , born in Clark Co , Ind , in 1820 Heirs wanted.
PRICE, CATHERINE, (cook) died in New York 1882 Heirs wanted
PRICE, WILLIAM, deceased, died in a Western State Heirs wanted
PROBOUGH, JOHN U , late of Howard Co , Ind
REID, ANNA, deceased, died in a Western State Heirs wanted
RENOX, RUFUS, deceased, died in Missouri Heirs wanted
REVETT, CHAS , late of Franklin, Mo
RITTERBUSCH, JOHANN F , (watchmaker, German,) died in New York 1882 Heirs wanted.
ROARK, JOHN, deceased, died in Missouri Heirs wanted
ROBERTS, JAMES, owned land in Minnesota in 1858 Heirs wanted
ROBEY, NICHOLAS, deceased, died in Missouri Heirs wanted
ROHR, WM., deceased, died in a Western State Heirs wanted
ROCKENBRODT, ELIZABETH, (day laborer) died in New York 1883 Heirs wanted.
ROGERS, MARY A , deceased. died in a Western State Heirs wanted.
ROY, SOPHIA, deceased. died in a Western State. Heirs wanted
RUSSEL, JOHN, (printer) died in New York 1883 Heirs wanted
ST ANGIE, MONSIEUR, deceased, (French) died in Missouri Heirs wanted
SAUBRIER, LORENTZ, deceased, died in Missouri Heirs wanted
SCHINDE, FRANCIS, deceased died in Missouri Heirs wanted
SCHNELL, JACOB, died in Minnesota about 1878 or 1879.
SECHLAR, W H , late of Cambria Co , Pa
SCHOROCK, LUDWICK, late of Somerset Co , Pa.

SCHULTZ, JOHN, deceased, died in a Western State. Heirs wanted
SCHWARTZ, JOHN, (German) died in Idaho Ter., 1884 Heirs wanted.
SCHWIGERT, NICHOLAS, late of Kane Co., Ill
SCHWEND, CATHERINE, late of Madison, Ind Heirs wanted
SCOTT, OLIVER, died in a Western State Heirs wanted.
SCOTT, THEODORE, late of Mobile, Ind Heirs wanted
SCOGGIN, WM., late of Tillabindi, Miss Heirs wanted
SCROYER, JACOB, deceased, died in a Western State Heirs wanted.
SEYMOUR, CHAS., late of Dona Ana Tex
SHALE, HENRY, deceased, died in a Western State. Heirs wanted
SHAFER, JOHN H., in 1859 was in Lancaster, Pa,
SHERIDAN, HELEN, born about 1800 Married in Scotland about 1818 No children Next of Kin supposed to be in America Estate very large Heirs wanted
SHERMAN, HENRY, deceased, died in a Western State Heirs wanted
SHOEMAKER, GEO., deceased, died in a Western State. Heirs wanted
SHOTT, LOUIS, late of St Louis, Mo Heirs wanted
SHRIEVE, JOHN N., late of San Antonio, Tex. Heirs wanted
SUHMAN, FREDRICK, deceased, died in a Western State Heirs wanted
SIKES, KATE (see KATE TOWNSEND)
SIMMS, ELISHA, deceased, died in Missouri Heirs wanted
SMITH, PETER, (baker) died in New York 1882 Heirs wanted
SMITH, WILLIAM, deceased, died in a Western State Heirs wanted
SMITH, JOHN (JACK), mother's maiden name McCARTHY, lived in Oswego, N Y Heirs wanted
SMITH, WILLIAM, owned land in Nebraska in 1870 Supposed to be dead Heirs wanted
SMITH, AGNES, married to one —— SMITH Maiden name THOMSON, resides somewhere in Scotland
SMITH, LEONARD H., died suddenly in a Western State in 1881 Supposed to have once lived in Canada, engaged in the potash business there Had relatives in Toronto—is supposed to have had a wife from whom he was separated Had a nephew on the Pacific Coast He was a miser, and left a large amount of money Heirs wanted
SMITH, GEORGE C., died in the State of Maine about 1879 Heirs wanted
SNYDER, MARGARET, late of Cincinnati, Ohio Heirs wanted
SPAULDING, ANDREW J., late of Plattsburg, Mo Heirs wanted
STANLEY or COLE, LEONARD formerly of Texas. Heirs wanted.
STECK, DORETHEA, died in a Western State Heirs wanted
STEPHENSON, THAD W., late of Circleville, Ohio. Heirs wanted.
STEINKEMPER, E., died in Missouri Heirs wanted
STOKES, CLAYTON, place of residence not known He was a soldier in the Mexican or War of 1812
STYLES, LEWIS, late of New York, N Y Was a soldier in some war of U S
SUNERRIET, (or SUMERSIET,) GEORGE I., a German, was in the army of the late Civil War from the State of Maine Died about 1869 Heirs wanted
THIES, ANTON WILLIAM, married Oct 19th 1857, at St Peters, Derby, England, to JANE STEVENS Last heard of April, 1874, at 415 Seventh st, Leavenworth, Kans
THOMPSON, HUGH, (restaurant keeper) died in New York 1882. Heirs wanted
THOMSON, ALEXANDER, died in Illinois lately—brothers and sisters in Scotland wanted as heirs Their names are ISABELLA (married to PETER WADDELL,) AGNES (married to —— Smith,) MARY, (married to PETER MARSHAL,) and JOHN THOMSON
THOMAS, PEYTON, died in Missouri Heirs wanted
TOWNSEND, KATE, alias KATE KARNAGAN, died in New Orleans, La., in 1883 Came from Liverpool, England, in August, 1858. Supposed to have relations in Liverpool Her whole estate which is very large, is claimed by one SYKES, who claims to have been married to her
TOUBY, THOS H., died in a Western State Heirs wanted
TURNER, ALLEN C., died in a Western State Heirs wanted
TIENAN, CHAS F., died in a Western State Heirs wanted
TRUELOVE, SAMUEL, died in a Western State Heirs wanted
TWELVETREE, JOSEPH, died in a Western State, Heirs wanted
UNKNOWN MAN, (No 9), lost on the Steamer "Stonewall"
USHER, JOSEPH, died in a Western State
VANDERVALLE, S H., died in a Western State Heirs wanted.
VAN BECHMAN, FRED., died in a Western State Heirs wanted
VERDANEL, WM., residence not known Once owned land in Nebraska
WADDELL, ISABELLA, (wife of PETER WADDELL), maiden name THOMSON Residence somewhere in Scotland
WALKER, H R., died in a Western State Heirs wanted
WALLACE, TYE, died in a Western State Heirs wanted
WALSH, (or CONWAY) ELLEN, (newsdealer), died in New York, 1883 Heirs wanted
WAVERS, ELIZABETH, died in a Western State
WELDO, WATSON, residence not known Once owned land in Nebraska
WENDORF, CHARLES, late of Madison County, New York Supposed to have gone West in 1859 or 1860 Heirs wanted
WHEATON, THEODORE D., died in a Western State Heirs wanted
WHITE, MILTON, publisher of a monthly paper in Chicago up to time of the great fire, went to California. Last heard from in New Mexico
WHITE, CASPER, late of Peoria, Ill Was once a soldier Heirs wanted
WHITEHOUSE, BENJ., late of Stockton, Cal
WHITLEY, WM. F., late of Jefferson City, Mo
WEIR, ——, (first name not known) died in Kansas, between 1870 and 1880
WILLIS, JAMES, died in a Western State Heirs wanted
WILSON, EDWARD, late of Covington, Ky
WILSON, MRS MARY ANN Wanted to find the heirs of ELISHA V BROWN, who left Virginia in 1858 or 1859, married either in Missouri or Kansas, went to California and died on the trip, leaving one child His widow afterwards married a man by the name of WILSON The last heard of MRS WILSON, she resided with her child either in Missouri or Kansas
WILDHABER, JACOB, (or JUSTICE), carpenter, died in New York, 1882 Heirs wanted
WILLIAMS, HENRY, late of Pensacola, Fla

SPECIAL LIST No. 17.

WILLIAMS, ROBERT, removed from Pitt County, N C, to Kentucky many years ago. His heirs would pay a liberal reward for information as to the whereabouts of the estate left by him
WILLIAMS, WM, died in a Western State. Heirs wanted.
WILLIAMSON, JARVIS, deceased, died in a Western State   Heirs wanted
WINCKELMAN, JOHN, died in the State of Maine about 1867   Heirs wanted
WOLF, JOHN, died in the State of Maine in 1864, leaving property. Heirs wanted.
WORSTER, PRESLEY, died in a Western State   Heirs wanted
YETTER, JOSEPH, died in a Western State   Heirs wanted

The following list, received too late to incorporate in one of our regular lists, represents persons who own land in a certain Western State, which has, since 1878, been sold for taxes. It could still be recovered if the place of residence of the owners could be found. We will undertake its recovery on very reasonable terms

Address, **J. B MARTINDALE**, 142 La Salle St, CHICAGO.

Burgham John A, Residence unknown
Carter, Alexander,   "   "
Charles, Martin M,   "   "
Charles, John D,   "   "
Corpeney, F J,   "   "
Donnell, James D, of Texas.
Edwards L B,   Residence unknown
Emery, Louis,   "   "
Farrar, D W,   "   "
Fee, O. P S,   "   "
Foye Christian,   "   "
Gray, Robert,
Gregory, Henry, of Illinois
Griswold, Cyrus,   Residence unknown
Hackney, James S,   "   "
Halpane, S. P,   "   "
Hamilton, Vincent,   "   "
Hamlin, J F,   "   "
Haoley, John M,   "   "
Harper, John, and
    Geo Johnson,
Howell, Sarah, of Illinois.
Jenkins, Geo W,   Residence unknown.
Johnson Geo., and
    John Harper,   "   "

Johnson, Jacob,   Residence unknown,
Kisler, C. B,   "   "
Klenhaus, Peter,   "   "
Lester, P Smith,   "   "
Manship, Henry,   "   "
Mathis, Fred,   "   "
Millican, O. W.,   "   "
Millican, Wesley,   "   "
McBride, John M.,   "   "
Read, Solomon,   "   "
Robbinson, James,   "   "
Smith, Eliza J,   "   "
Snyder, Abraham,   "   "
Stewart, James,   "   "
Stewart, Susanna,   "   "
Steel, Geo W,   "   "
Thompson, Jeff,   "   "
Vickery, Thomas,   "   "
Waite, John M,   "   "
Welch, Geo S, (heirs of) "   "
Weir, Phœbe,   "   "
Williams, Geo W.,   "   "
Wright, Wm. H.,   "   "

TABLE OF DISTRIBUTION OF INTESTATES' ESTATES.

Under 3 & 4 Wm. IV., c. 106, 22 & 23 Car. II , c 10, 29 Car II., c 30, and 1 Jac. II., o 17.

Customs of London and York and other places are now abolished so far as they affect *personal* property of persons dying after 31st Dec., 1856 (19 & 20 Vic., c 94); but the customs of Gavelkind and Borough English still affect *real* property in certain localities, the former principally in County Kent.

The following is a short Table showing how Property is distributed in cases where the owner dies entitled in his own right, without having made a will or settlement; the fourth column also shows what persons would be entitled to letters of administration entitling them to the right of receiving and distributing the personal estate.

N B —In each instance it is supposed there are no nearer relations than those named.

If a person die leaving	LAND —Real Property (except leaseholds) would descend	MONEY —Personal Property (including leaseholds) would be divided	Persons entitled to administration.
Wife and no relations	One third to wife for life, rest to the Crown if the deceased had the legal estate (copyholds to the Lord of the Manor) (*Note A.*)	Half to wife, rest to the Crown	Wife.
Wife and father	One-third to wife for life, rest to father if the deceased had acquired the fee by purchase and not by descent (*Note A.*)	Equally	Wife.
Wife and mother	One third to wife for life, rest to mother in default of any heirs on father's side (*Note A.*)	Equally (*Keilway v Keilway, 2 P Wms, 344.*)	Wife.
Wife, father, brothers, and sisters	One-third to wife for life, rest to father if the deceased had acquired the fee by purchase and not by descent (*Note A.*)	Equally between wife and father	Wife.
Wife, mother, brothers, and sisters, whether by whole or half blood	One-third to wife for life, rest to eldest brother (by whole blood) (*Note A.*)	Half to wife, rest equally divided between mother, brothers and sisters	Wife.
Wife mother, nephews, and nieces (children of deceased brother)	One-third to wife for life, rest to nephew (eldest son of brother) or niece (daughter of deceased brother if he left no son (*Note A*)	Half to wife, one fourth to mother, rest between nephews and nieces (*Stanley v Stanley, 1 Atk.*)	Wife.
Wife, brothers, and sisters	One-third to wife for life, rest to eldest brother (*Note A*)	Half to wife rest equally to brothers and sisters	Wife.
Wife, sons, and daughters (*Note C*)	One third to wife for life, rest to eldest son (*Note A*)	One-third to wife, rest equally amongst sons and daughters	Wife.
Wife and daughter (*Note C*)	One third to wife for life, rest to daughter (*Note A*)	One third to wife, rest to daughter	Wife
Wife and daughters (*Note C*)	One third to wife for life, rest equally between daughters (*Note A.*)	One third to wife, rest equally between daughters	Wife
Wife and grandchildren (sons of deceased son)	One-third to wife for life, rest to eldest grandchild (*Note A.*)	One-third to wife, rest equally between grandchildren	Wife
Husband (where there has been issue born alive capable of inheriting the realty)	All for life, afterwards to heir-at-law (*Note B*)	All (*Note E*)	Husband
Husband (where there has not been issue born alive capable of inheriting the realty)	To heir-at-law	All to husband (*Note E*)	Husband
Husband, sons, and daughters	All to husband for life afterwards to eldest son (*Note B*)	All to husband (*Note E*)	Husband.
Husband and child (son or daughter)	All to husband for life, afterwards to child (*Note B.*)	All to husband (*Note E*)	Husband
Husband and daughters	All to husband for life, afterwards to daughters equally (*Note B*)	All to husband (*Note E*)	Husband
Husband and grandchildren (daughters of deceased son or daughter)	All to husband for life, afterwards to grandchildren equally (*Note B*)	All to husband (*Note E*)	Husband.
Sons & daughters whether by one or more wife or wives, & whether or not posthumous	All to eldest son	Equally divided (*Wallis v Hodson, 2 Atk., 117.*)	Either son or daughter, or any number not exceeding three of either or both.
One child, either son or daughter	All	All	Child.
Daughters	Equally divided	Equally divided	Either or any number of them not exceeding three.

TABLE OF DISTRIBUTION.

If a person dies leaving	LAND.—Real Property (except leaseholds) would descend	MONEY—Personal Property (including leaseholds) would be divided	Persons entitled to administration
(Eldest) son and grandchild son or daughter of younger son)	All to eldest son	Equally divided	Eldest son
(Younger) son and grandchild son or daughter of eldest son	All to grandchild	Equally divided	Younger son
Eldest son, sons and daughters, and grandchildren	All to eldest son	Equally divided (but grandchildren only take deceased parent's share equally between them)	To any son or daughter or any number not exceeding three of either or both
Daughters and grandchild (son or daughter of deceased son	All to grandchild	Equally	To any daughter, or any number of them not exceeding three.
Daughters and granddaughters (children of deceased son.	All to granddaughters	Equally (but granddaughters only take their father's share between them)	To any daughter, or any number of them not exceeding three
Daughters and grandchildren sons and daughters of deceased daughter)	Equally between daughters and eldest son of deceased daughter	Equally (but grandchildren only take their parent's share equally between them)	To any daughter, or any number of them not exceeding three.
Grandchildren, sons and daughters of two sons and daughter	All to grandson, eldest son of eldest son	Equally (per capita, i.e. in their own right.) (*Walsh v Walsh*, 1 Eq Cas Abr, 249 pl. 7—S C Prec Chan 74.)	To any grandchild, or any number of them not exceeding three
Grandchildren (daughters of a son, and sons of a daughter)	All to granddaughters equally	Equally per capita	To any grandchild, or any number of them not exceeding three
Grandchildren (sons and daughters of a daughter, and daughters of another daughter)	Half to eldest son of one daughter, and half equally between daughters of other daughter	Equally per capita	To any grandchild, or any number of them not exceeding three.
Deceased son's widow, and child (*Bridge v Abbott*, 3 Bro C C 226)	All to child	All to child	Child.
Grandchild and great-grand child, elder branch	Great grandchild	Equally	Grandchild.
Father and mother and brothers and sister	All to father	All to father	Father
Mother and brothers and sisters	All to eldest brother	Equally	Mother
Mother and sister	All to sister	Equally	Mother
Mother only	All (in default of any heirs on father's side)	All	Mother
Sisters, and nephews, and nieces (children of deceased brother	All to nephew, eldest son of deceased brother	Equally, but nephews and nieces take *per stirpes* (i.e. their deceased parent's share)	To one or more of the sisters, not exceeding three
Sisters, and nieces (children of deceased brother)	All to nieces equally	Equally, but nieces take *per stirpes*	To one or more of the sisters, not exceeding three
Sisters, and nephews, and nieces (children of deceased sister)	Equally between sisters and nephew, eldest son of deceased sister	Equally, but nephews and nieces take *per stirpes*	To one or more of the sisters, not exceeding three
Sisters, and nieces (children of deceased sister	Equally but nieces take *per stirpes*	Equally, but nieces take *per stirpes*	To one or more of the sisters, not exceeding three
Brother or sister of whole blood, and brother or sister of half blood on father's side, and brother or sister of half-blood on mother's side	All to brother or sister of whole blood	Equally	Either or both
Brother or sister of the half-blood on father's side, & distant cousin on father's side	All to half-brother or sister	All to half-brother or sister	Brother or sister of half blood
Brother or sister of half blood on mother's side, and distant cousin on father's side	All to distant cousin on father's side	All to half-brother or sister	Brother or sister of half blood.
Brothers and sisters, and grandfather or grandmother	All to eldest brother	Equally between brothers and sisters (*Evelyn v Evelyn*, 3 Atk 762)	To one or more of brothers and sisters, not exceeding three
Nephews and nieces by deceased brother, and nephew and niece by deceased sister	All to eldest nephew (son of deceased brother)	Equally *per capita* (i.e shared equally without reference to the number of each family)	To either of the nephews or nieces, or any number of one or both, not exceeding three
Niece by deceased brother, and nephews and nieces by deceased sister	All to niece (daughter of deceased brother)	Equally *per capita*	To either of the nephews or nieces, or any number of one or both, not exceeding three.
Nieces by deceased brother, and nephews and nieces by deceased sister	All to nieces (daughters of deceased brother)	Equally *per capita*	To either of the nephews or nieces, or any number of one or both, not exceeding three.
Nephews and nieces by one deceased sister and nieces by another deceased sister	Half to eldest nephew by one deceased sister, and half equally between nieces by other deceased sister	Equally *per capita*	To either of the nephews or nieces, or any number of one or both, not exceeding three.

MARTINDALE'S UNCLAIMED MONEY MANUAL.

If a person die leaving	LAND.—Real Property (except leaseholds) would descend	MONEY.—Personal property (including leaseholds) would be divided	Persons entitled to administration.
Nephew (son of deceased sister) and great niece, granddaughter of deceased brother	Great niece	Nephew (Pett v Pett, 1 Salk 250)	Nephew
Niece (brother or sister's daughter) and great nephew (eldest brother's grandson)	All to great nephew, eldest brother's grandson	All to niece, brother's or sister's daughter	Niece
Father's father, or mother and mother's father or mother	All to father's father or mother	Equally (Moor v Badham, cited in Blackborough v Davis, P Wms 53)	To either or both
Grandfather, great grandfather, uncle and aunt on father's side, and grandfather, uncle, and aunt, on mother's side	All to grandfather, on father's side	Equally between two grandfathers	To either or both grandfathers
Grandfather on mother's side, and uncle or aunt on father's side	All to uncle or aunt	All to grandfather	Grandfather
Grandmother, uncle, or aunt (all on same side)	All to uncle or aunt	All to grandmother (Mentney v Petty, Prec Chan., 593)	Grandmother
Grandmother on father's side, and uncle or aunt on mother's side	All to grandmother	All to grandmother (Mentney v Petty Prec Chan 593)	Grandmother
Great grandfather, uncles and aunts on father's side	All to eldest uncle	Equally per capita (Lloyd v Tench, 2 Ves Sen., 215)	To either or any number not exceeding three of either or both,
Uncles and aunts on mother's side, and nephews (sons of deceased sister) and nieces (daughters of a deceased brother)	Equally between nieces, daughters of brother	Equally per capito	To either or any number not exceeding three of either or both
Uncles and aunts on father's side, and uncles and aunts on mother's side	All to eldest uncle on father's side	Equally among them	To either or any number not exceeding three of either or both
Aunts on father's side, and uncles or aunts on mother's side	All equally to aunts on father's side	Equally among them	To either or any number not exceeding three of either or both
Cousins	The eldest son of the deceased father's eldest brother (or according to heirship, as the case may be)	Equally per capita	To either or any number not exceeding three of either or both
Uncle on mother's side, and cousin (son of another uncle on father's side)	All to cousin	All to uncle	Uncle
No relations	All to the Crown (copyhold would go to the Lord of the Manor)	All to the Crown	To the Crown, or to a creditor, should he apply

Note A.—The wife is only entitled to the third of the gross rental of the real estate for life as her dower, but in most cases this is barred, rather as a matter of form by lawyers, than for any other reason, and she then takes no interest in the real estate

Note B—This only applies to real estate in possession, the husband would take no benefit from his wife's reversionary interests in real estate.

Note C—Children who have had advances from the *father* in the lifetime are to bring them into account

Note D.—The above table to succession to real property does not extend to the decease of any person dying before 1st January, 1834, nor to Gavelkind lands in Kent and other places, nor to land held subject to Borough English custom, nor to Copyholes, nor to Estates Tail

Note E—The husband is entitled by canon law right and not under the Statute of Distributions. He would, therefore, be excluded from taking any share of his wife's effects if given by any deed or will to "her next of kin" at her decease.—Milne v Gilbert, L. J vol 23, N S. Chy 628

CPSIA information can be obtained at www.ICGtesting.com
Printed in the USA
BVOW07s1015090414

350183BV00009B/329/P